ADVANCED AUTOGRAPH COLLECTING

Mark Allen Baker

Published by

krause
publications

700 E. State Street • Iola, WI 54990-0001
Telephone: 715/445-2214

www.krause.com

Please, call or write us for our free catalog of antiques and collectibles publications.
To place an order or receive our free catalog, call 800-258-0929. For editorial comment and further
information, use our regular business telephone at (715) 445-2214.

Library of Congress Catalog Number: 99-67810
ISBN: 0-87341-632-5

Printed in the United States of America

Dedication

To Jim Bird

My best friend in high school, and still a great friend decades later.

Acknowledgments

I would like to thank everyone at Krause Publications for their continued support of my work, especially Pat Klug, Don Gulbrandsen, Paul Kennedy, Seiche Sanders and Tracy Schubert.

Many organizations, corporations, dealers and collectors assisted either directly or indirectly in this book and I am extremely thankful for their contributions: Acco USA, Inc., Adobe Systems, Agfa-Gevaert, BATF, BIC Corporation, Cornell & Finkelmeier, Inc., DNA Technologies (Deborah Smith), Eastman Kodak Company, FBI, Fisher Company (Paul C. Fisher), Forensic Scientific Investigations, Fuji, General Electric, Hewlett Packard (Larry J. Farmer, Engle Systems Group), IACC/DA, IBM, Stephen Koschal, Lancaster County Historical Society, Mastro Fine Sports Auctions, PADA, Penalli PensPSA - Professional Sports Authenticator (Sharon Fong Picture Perfect Framing (Lancaster, PA)), Steven S. Raab, Remington, Sanford, Studio Fan Mail/Tamkin Color (Jack Tamkin), The Gillette Company, The Manuscript Society, The National Archives, The U.S. Postal Service, Time Incorporated, UACC, University Archives, and the Xerox Corporation.

Also the law offices of Thomas H. Reed, Esquire.

A special thanks to Mr. & Mrs. Ford W. Baker, Aaron Baker, Elizabeth Baker and Rebecca Baker and Alison Long for their continued support.

Table of Contents

Autograph Gallery

Introduction

This is my tenth book for Krause Publications, that's over 4000 published pages in book form since 1991. I have also published hundreds of pages of articles, in numerous periodicals, during this time. Most of what I have written about surrounds one topic, autographs. While I'm not certain who has sold the most books about autographs, it's my guess that I have given them a run for their money.

Having collected autograph since 1965, I have interacted with most of the major contributors in the industry. From Charles Hamilton and Paul Richards to John Reznikoff and Steven Raab, I believe I have also purchased items from some of the best autograph dealers of their time. While some people could challenge my claim, I can support it!

Always making sure that I keep the lowest possible profile, there are no photographs of me in this book. It's not because I don't have any or that I'm embarrassed, it's because my readers would rather see a facsimile autograph of a signature that's important to them, than a photograph of me with Bo Derek.

As you will soon realize, writing for the genuine love and appreciation of history and what this hobby brings to it is what I am all about. While detractors often trash the hobby every time another hoax surfaces, I have gone out of my way to show how mistakes can be made and how they can be corrected. We are part of a wonderful hobby and as long as we keep our priorities straight it will stay that way.

While I have been retained by numerous legal firms in cases involving autographs, I intend to be involved in a lot more following this project. After reading this book and understanding the material, from only a very surface oriented perspective, you can join me in proclaiming "the forgery era in autographs is over." It's a tough claim to make, but it is one that I am personally committed to and believe is true. Never have we ever been better equipped, through both technology and experience, to battle the forger than now. If someone is going to forge a signature he is writing his ticket to a jail cell.

I would be remiss not to mention something many of you already know, in recent years we have lost some key contributors to our hobby—Charles Hamilton, George Sanders and Mary Benjamin. I don't want to call them pioneers, because as you will see, many came before them, but they were indeed special. If this God's way to say the torch is being passed, then let's take it. Preserving the integrity of the hobby, is the best way we can show those who have gone before us that we care.

Through some of the studies I have underway—much of it for court purposes, I will do my best to continue to build around the material presented in this book. Following most of my books, I receive a substantial amount of mail, and I welcome it, just be patient with me. I already have numerous projects in progress, including some major updates to previously published material.

I have always wanted to give the hobby a book like this and if it wasn't for a publisher who cares, I would not have had that chance. After reading the book, if you are pleased with your purchase, drop Krause Publications a line. As you look through the numerous chapters feel free to drop me one also, not about what you liked, but about ways to improve various sections. Because I am a collector also, I care.

I take a lot of criticism for not being an autograph dealer. While this is likely to change, I still remain a collector. I prefer to spend my time researching, writing about and collecting autographs. While many take from the hobby, right now I choose to give. I give to the collector, who in a hobby filled with dealers and "so-called experts", often is forgotten.

I have the honor, and I truly mean it, of having Steven S. Raab as the author of the Foreword to this book. I know your asking yourself why does a self-proclaimed, dedicated collector, choose a dealer to write his Foreword? I believe once you get to know Steven you will understand. If you ever pick up a copy of a Steven S. Raab autograph catalog, you will find in it not only a plethora of exciting items, but within each page is a deep and pronounced appreciation of history.

While some dealers simply ignore artifacts that take too much time to present, can't meet the desired profit margin or perhaps are even controversial, Raab seems to welcome it. He brings to the hobby catalogs filled with the autographs of Medal of Honor winners, diaries from Civil War soldiers and artifacts of the holocaust. It's as if he says, "here is your history, but remember not a single item is more important than the next." If that were not enough, he then turns to the collector and offers some of his fine educational publications, such as *The Educated Collector's Guide to Buying Autographs*. I am proud to have Steven a part of this book.

Mark Allen Baker
May 24, 1999

Foreword

I think it's both important and useful for the advanced autograph collector to understand the market from a dealer's perspective, especially if it's from the view of a successful and established dealer. I am honored to have Steven S. Raab give his tips on successful autograph collecting here in this Forward. This article is reprinted with the permission of the author and is copyright Steven S. Raab. It is presented here with minimal editing.

The 9 Rules For Successfully Collecting Autographs Today
By: Steven S. Raab

It is the best of times, it is the worst of times, it is an age of opportunity, it is an age of opportunism, it is the epoch of honesty, it is the epoch of greed, it is the season of Light, it is the season of Darkness, it is the Spring of our hopes, it is the Winter of our Despair, we have everything ahead of us, we have nothing ahead of us.

For both the autograph collector and dealer, this is time like none before. There has been great expansion of interest in the hobby, and the Internet promises to make an ever growing number of people aware of it. The number of people joining the autograph community via the Internet has created undreamed of possibilities for buying and selling. Increased knowledge of the value of autographs by the general public has led to more material being available. These are all wonderful developments, laden with promise for a future full of opportunities.

Under the surface, all is not well in the world of autographs. The growth in the marketplace through the early and mid 1990s led to a large increase in the number of fraudulent dealers and auctions, and the increase from the Internet since then is much greater yet. Until 1995-6, someone who wanted to get into the autograph business had to have a shop, issue catalogs or attend shows. Most also had to advertise to develop a mailing list. All of these activities took time and money (sometimes lots of time and money), and exposed the new dealer to the open scrutiny of knowledgeable people in the autograph community. Phonies could usually be exposed or shoved to the periphery. Today, anyone with a computer, $150 scanner and access to the Internet can become a dealer on the spot, and have access to millions of potential customers. Crooks have swarmed out of the woodwork to take advantage of this golden opportunity, and the number of bad dealers and the amount of forged material on the marketplace have turned into an avalanche. It also appears that the huge profits to be reaped have caused some dealers and auctions previously considered reliable to offer forged or questionable material.

As long as people remember history and are inspired and moved by the great events of the past, as long as they want to feel close to the men and women they admire or who had an impact on their lives, so long will they collect autographs and manuscripts. We cannot escape their lure, and would not if we could. Yet with so many dangerous reefs in the autograph waters, how do we navigate safely? How do we know what is authentic, when so many bogus wears come with certificates of authenticity? How can we determine whom to trust, when sellers all have broad smile and smooth words? I here provide 9 rules to help answer these difficult questions. But I will tell you straight away that reaching a meaningful answer will require work on your part. The easy way is the fool's way out.

I started out in this hobby in 1986 as an excited new collector, and the first two things I bought were not authentic. A hotshot baseball dealer sold me forged signed photographs of Christy Mathewson and Walter Johnson for $300 (if real they would have been worth $5000). Later I discovered what an unbelievable rarity a signed picture of Mathewson would be. A major, well-known auction sold me a secretarial signed program of the Beatles (it cost me $2,000 and boy, did I have a hard time getting my money back, even after they acknowledged the truth about the piece and also discovered that I am an attorney)! I practiced law for 25 years before taking down by shingle to become a full time autograph dealer in 1997. As a lawyer, you learn to dig for facts, accept what the evidence shows (rather than what you hope to be true) and to be skeptical (and not just accept whatever you are told, even if you like the people doing the telling). I applied these lessons in the autograph field, and investigated the three autographs I mentioned above. I determined that they were not authentic, pursued the sellers until I got my money back, and did not become discouraged (but did become somewhat wiser). I searched for and found dealers I could trust, learned the telltale signs of the crooks, and remained a collector (I am still one today). The 9 rules I developed to make collecting fun and safe can work for you too.

1. **Recognize reputable dealers.** Yes, this really is possible. Most of them issue regular printed catalogs, so get samples from a variety and review them

critically and with care. The catalogs should be well done, the dealers should sound like they know (and care) about the subject matter, the descriptions should be accurate and not false, exaggerated or misleading, and there should be no bogus or spurious claims nor a hard sell. The condition of an item should be correct, not calling something torn and stained 'choice extra fine.' Never be fooled by sizzle or glitter. Avoid dealers who sell autographs as investments. I say this not because autographs cannot serve as investments, but because those who use this sales pitch appear to me to be invariably selling something for a great deal more than it is worth, if it is authentic at all. A reputable dealer or auction will guarantee authenticity without time limit in writing. After you have seen enough detailed catalogs, you will get a feel for 'who's who' in the autograph world. What about dealers who don't issue catalogs? Well, some of them are legitimate, and some of their wares are real, but they offer you a much smaller window in determining whether it is safe to deal with them, and therefore increase your risk. Galleries are an example. A few are excellent, but many are the arteries through which the very worst pieces flow into the marketplace. Also quite risky is buying from ads in autograph magazines, unless you know about the dealer outside the confines of the publication. An ad doth not a catalog make. Buying from dealers on the Internet is high stakes gambling, and nothing less. There is so much bad material being pumped through cyberspace that it boggles the imagination.

2. **Never buy because of certificates of authenticity.** Avoid people who 'sell' authenticity on the basis of appealing for your trust directly or through certificates of authenticity. Remember that a certificate of authenticity is just a piece of paper with fancy language, and, like money is worth no more than the issuer behind it. The reputation of a seller, and not the certificate, is the core of a valid guarantee. The public thinks that the certificates are somehow regulated by the government or some agency like Good Housekeeping, and actually guarantee authenticity, but this is not true. They are so often just a sales tool for the unscrupulous, the very sword of the criminal, who use them to lull the unsuspecting. It has been my experience that the harder a seller pushes certificates of authenticity, the more certain I am of the need to buy elsewhere. Certificates issued by so-called forensic examiners make me grasp my wallet tightly.

3. **Don't rely on membership credentials.** We are members of the Universal Autograph Collector's Club (UACC), the Manuscript Society, the International Autograph Dealers alliance (IADA) and the Professional Autograph Dealers Association (PADA).

Except for PADA, membership has nothing to do with a dealer's knowledge or honesty. All a dealer really needs to do to maintain membership in the other three is pay a small annual fee, so almost everyone takes out membership. Bad apples can be theoretically be ejected, but to our knowledge very few have been. PADA does screen applicants for the authenticity of their material, and dealers have been rejected membership. This is a giant leap in the right direction, though not a foolproof guarantee. Avoid dealers who want their association with an organization to be proof that they are knowledgeable and honest and to be wary of organizations who recommend that you deal only with their members or claim that they are reliable. Also, I have seen bad dealers try to establish credibility by claiming that their 'goods' are in museums or that they are consultants to institutions. Be slow to credit such claims, and even if they are true, that is no proof that the museum staff is qualified to determine a reputable autograph dealer or to authentic the things the dealer gave them.

4. **Avoid things that are too good to be true.** Beginners in the autograph field naturally want exciting things, and quickly gravitate toward the most spectacular looking pieces. They don't realize that what they want either doesn't exist in the real world or is so rare that its appearance would create quite a buzz of conversation. This spells opportunity for the crooks that pollute the waters. Some of today's best forgers specialize in group shots, such as those featuring an entire cast of a television program or show five American presidents together. They also love to choose "best case" photographs to sign, often those showing film stars in their greatest roles, as Judy Garland playing Dorothy in the classic "The Wizard of Oz". Many routinely produce signed photographs and signatures, which would be very rare if authentic (the Marx Brothers and John F. Kennedy come to mind right away). Although Garland did sign photographs, I have never seen an authentic one of her from any of her films, no less a s Dorothy. I recall seeing authentic real Marx Brothers signed photos in the last decade, and as for JFK, his signed photos are uncommon and those with Jacqueline too are non-existent. An enormous percentage of signed group shots are not real. Rare, best case pieces must be greeted with great skepticism, and if low priced should be avoided altogether. Learn what is rare and act accordingly. Forewarned is forearmed.

5. **Know where the greatest dangers lie.** The problem of forged and secretarially signed items is greatest in the fields of sports and entertainment. Autographs of current entertainment, rock music and sports figures are unsafe to buy from any but a handful of dealers, as

little is really known about their signing habits, and bad apples shine in this segment. The greatest possible caution must be exercised if you collect in these areas. However, other collectors must not be complaisant, as forgers are at work to some degree in all autograph fields. I have seen forged Einsteins, U.S. Presidents and Robert E. Lees, and bad Martin Luther King, Jr. signatures are everywhere. A disturbing new development is the appearances of bogus Washington signed discharges, as these are forms and were not known to be forged before.

6. **Be careful about what you buy.** Some items are simply safer than others. Official signed documents, correspondence on printed letterhead and lengthy, handwritten letters are hard to forge well. They are much less likely to be bogus than easier to concoct things like signed photographs. "Cuts" don't make the cut, as they are just two words on a piece of paper. Simple to forge, rare signatures on pieces of paper should be viewed skeptically; cuts should only be purchased from a dealer you know very well and have reason to trust. It used to be that forgers generally kept away from inscriptions, handwritten letters, forms like contracts and items on letterhead, nor did they lower themselves to forge autographs of minor people. In today's brave new world, documents created (as per Washington above), bogus contracts are typed out and signed, inscriptions and handwritten letters are produced, and letterhead is even printed up (last year I saw a pretty convincing Ty Cobb forgery on a reprinted copy of his real letterhead). The crowning indignity is that many worthless signatures are now being forged and placed in books and albums in proximity to the rarer ones, to make the valuable ones appear in a natural setting. All these strategies are designed to lull the unwary into thinking that these kinds of things just aren't forged, so they are safe. The words "in person" are magic to some people, but they mask a host of sins. A signature that looks nothing like the real McCoy is said to be "in person, rushed". I ignore claims that autographs are in person and check them out as if they were not, unless I am looking at a large collection and talking to the original people that obtained them.

7. **Develop a library.** Nobody should be buying autographs who has not at least begun to compile a library of authentic examples, and read some basic books on autographs and how to enjoyably collect them. The late Charles Hamilton wrote quite a number; some are still in print and the others are finable at used bookstores in the "books about books" category. We have written four, and other fine ones are on the market. Then you can begin looking at examples and judging autographs for yourself. That's

how I started! There's nothing like an educated consumer to outwit the crooked sellers.

8. **Know the basics in authenticating autographs.** It may be hard to believe, but you have the ability to determine for yourself whether most autographs are authentic. Here are some of the things you need to know:

a. *The look.* The first step in authenticating is simply; does it look right and natural? Sign your own name a few times and look at other things your friends or relatives have signed. The signatures might be illegible, but they will all have a flow to them. They will not be shaky, odd shaped or lumpy, nor will they look drawn with care. All of the autographs signed by the same person will basically be consistent, and the breaks between letters in the name will almost always be the same each time. Compare an autograph you have been offered to the known authentic examples in the books in your new and expanding library. Signatures that look shaky, drawn, inconsistent with examples or just unnatural should be avoided.

b. *Paper and ink.* The manufacture, physical makeup and sizes of paper have differed over the years. Letters of Washington, Franklin and others of their generation were almost never written on paper smaller than about 8 by 10 inches. You would often (but by no means always) see letters on slightly smaller sheets from Jefferson's administration on, and small notepaper size stationery was generally used from 1860 (it made its appearance earlier - about 1840) until about 1900 (when stationery assumed its present size). Parchment was reserved for documents and religious manuscripts. Paper made before around 1820 was "laid" paper and, held up to the light, will show parallel lines throughout, like ribbing. And much paper manufactured between about 1840 and 1890 had little embossed imprints of the manufacturer, or occasionally stationer, usually at the upper left. Another point to remember is that envelopes didn't come into general use until the late 1840s. Prior to that, letters were generally folded up to a size approximating today's small envelopes and addressed on the back. Inks varied too. Most before about 1850 were iron based, which over the years has literally rusted. This causes the older inks to eat into the paper to a greater or lesser extent, and often to take on a brownish tone. Blue ink was generally not used much before about 1850. Also, watch for blurring. Paper loses its "size" over the years, and the strands of cloth in older paper separate slightly, so modern ink applied to old paper will be absorbed slightly and will blur. Ballpoint pens were invented about 1940 and felt tips about 1960.

c. *Photographs.* The first photographs that are found signed are called "carte de visite", or CDVs. They were popular from the late 1840s until about 1865, though almost all authentic signed ones date from at least 1850. They were replaced by the larger "cabinet" photographs. Generally about 4 by 6 inches, they could on occasion be much larger, with various names such as Imperial Cabinet. Both the carte de visite and cabinet photographs had the actual photo mounted to a heavier board, usually with the photographer's imprint on the bottom front or back. The cabinet photograph remained in vogue until about the turn of the 20th century, when it was replaced by photographs with sizes pretty much as we know them today, ranging from postcard size to 8 by 10 inches, occasionally larger. The 11 by 14-inch photo didn't become popular until about 1920, and seldom seems to have been used except by movie stars. The earliest 8 by 10s tended to be sepia in tone (brownish) or black and white, about 50/50. Sepia started to be phased out in the 1930s, and was eventually virtually replaced by black and white altogether, which was supplemented by color about 1960. Beware the signed photograph that is out of this dating context.

d. *Autopens.* The autopen is a machine that uses a real pen and real ink to draw an exact replica of an autograph. Presidents, public officials and others who have just too much correspondence to handle have them. The owner makes templates from three or four different examples of his signature. His secretary inserts one of them into the machine, which signs his correspondence. The only saving grace is that each template signs each signature exactly the same way time after time, so a simple comparison is all that is needed. There are several books with facsimiles of most known autopen patterns from Eisenhower's time until 1988 when the last one was published. Telltale signs of an autopen are shakiness, extra drops of ink at the end of words and the entire signature has the ink uniformly applied.

e. *Secretaries and stamps.* Secretarial signatures have been around hundreds of years. A lot of documents supposedly signed by kings of France, up through at least Louis XVI, were signed by their secretaries. American presidents in the 19th century had secretaries sign land grants, and in the 20th century, other kinds of documents and letters. JFK had perhaps a dozen secretaries sign for him, and from then on each President seems to have had several secretaries who could forge his signature. Carter's was particularly adept. Movie stars often used secretaries, especially to sign photographs for them. With Hollywood signed photographs, remember that

postcard photographs generally have a printed or photographic signature on the front, 5 by 7 inch ones are 80% secretarial, 8 by 10 inch ones are 60% genuine, and 11 by 14 inch ones are 80% genuine. Fortunately, once they learn to sign the boss's name, secretaries almost invariably sign the same way each time. Some famous people preferred a stamp to a secretary if they could not sign themselves, like Woodrow Wilson, Rudolph Valentino and King Henry VIII. Modern stamps usually have a very pale, light ink, and don't have a natural ink flow.

f. *Facsimiles.* A facsimile is an exact copy of something (like the copies of the Declaration of Independence on fake parchment sold in souvenir shops). They were often published as souvenirs to honor a person or event, without ever intending to fool anybody into thinking they were real. Many facsimiles have been around for up to a hundred years, and consequently have that aged look. Some were bound in books and have come out over the years. By nature, facsimiles often copy important documents or letters, like the Gettysburg Address, Robert E. Lee's Farewell Address, the message of King George V thanking American troops for coming to Europe in World War I, and a letter of Lord Byron to his publisher denying that he wrote "The Vampire". Sometimes facsimile letters, always without salutations (such as "Dear Mr. Jones"), were made for bulk mailings, like the thanks for birthday wishes sent out by Winston Churchill and Harry Truman. So be extra careful of important documents and letters without salutations.

g. *Use common sense.* Think about the circumstances of an autograph. Here are some examples. Did you ever write to a President-elect congratulating him on his election and get a thank you letter back? Could he have signed all the letters his office sent out? Of course not. Did you ever write to a celebrity and get an immediate impersonal response? Could he have signed all such generic letters? Would Mark Twain have written a letter from New Orleans while he was in England? Don't laugh, I saw it. It was a super job of forgery as far as the writing was concerned. Would Lincoln have written a letter referring to the Battle of First Bull Run as such before the second battle had been fought there? Lincoln and Kennedy were very succinct in their letters, never using tow words where one would do. Any letter with either of their names which has extra verbiage or is gossipy in tone could not have been written by them, no matter what the autograph on it looks like. Not long ago, some supposed Kennedy material came onto the market related to Marilyn Monroe, which subsequently proved forged. A note of JFK's from this group, published in a national magazine, was rambling, utterly unlike the terse language he actually used in correspondence. You are not likely to see a letter of Washington which ends with anything much shorter than "I am very truly your most obedient servant" as closings were long in his time, nor a letter of Lincoln's which end much longer than "Truly yours", as they were short in his. A letter earlier than 1800 without a flowery closing, or after 1850 without a short closing, is suspect. All of these show how application of basic common sense can answer many questions.

9. **Understand the meaning of provenance.**
Provenance means, basically, proving where the autograph came from. In some cases this is desirable, in many today it is essential. It is of greatest benefit when trying to authenticate a signature that could be easily forged. The existence of a letter or notation claiming to describe the circumstances under which an autograph was obtained is not in itself sufficient provenance. Every forgery seems to come with a story, and forgers use the technique of providing cooked up "provenance" letters to deceive the unwary. There can also be innocent but very misleading errors. I once saw a situation where a girl at a concert gave a program to the Beatles road manager to have signed.

She observed him take it into the dressing room and return with it signed ten minutes later. Her long and honest letter about her attendance at the concert and getting the program signed left out what she never knew - that the manager himself had forged the Beatles'signatures behind the closed dressing room door. To establish valid provenance, you must look at the entire history of an item, where it originated, and determine which dealers sold it in the past. The story behind it should be provable and not just a mere claim. Only if an item can "prove" itself outside a claim does it have provenance.

"Never despair." So said Winston Churchill in his farewell speech in 1955, and so I urge today. It is easy to become discouraged or angry under the conditions we face, and some have even stopped collecting. Instead of throwing in the towel or handing victory to the immoral swindlers, if all who love this hobby will work to make autograph collecting work by educating themselves, and carry their interest forward with confidence, then we will in the coming century be able to look back and say, "We had everything ahead of us."

Copyright Steven S. Raab 1999

Chapter 1

Collecting Autographs

There are many important aspects to autograph collecting such as identifying items, detecting forgeries, and properly maintaining a collection. However, to truly understand the business it is important to look back historically and see its evolution to the current day. To help you I have created a brief history of the autograph collecting field's highlights spanning the years 1989-1999.

In this chapter you will also find some of the most obvious but often-overlooked resources for historical autographs. From old family bibles to hotel registers you just might come across something special if you take the time to look.

In additon to finding autographs, it is important to know how to preserve and handle the paper-based items in your collection. Handling these delicate collectible objects properly is imperative, because there are many environmental factors that can destroy them. Tips are included for both preservation and handling.

Autograph Collecting—A Look Back

As man slowly developed so did his form of writing, from pictures to the wedge-shaped characters of cuneiform writing. Unfortunately, we know little about this transition other than it took thousands of years. An advanced form of Sumerian cuneiform was in existence by the middle of the third millennium B.C. From this came the first detailed accounts of what had transpired before, both fact and fiction, cut into flat pieces of clay with a stylus, then baked for posterity. Needless to say, the cumbersome nature of clay tablets did little to promote the preservation of the written word.

The cuneiform of Mesopotamia preceeded the hieroglyphics of Egypt by about a hundred years. Since we know that many of the Egyptian rulers enjoyed private libraries, we assume inside these walls were vast amounts of knowledge in all forms. Papyrus was the desired medium and was a handy natural resource lining the banks of the Nile delta.

Collections were gathered by both leaders and scholars alike. When the supply of papyrus was cut off by the Egyptians, parchment and vellum became possible solutions to the shortage of writing materials. These materials also evolved and their shortfalls were finally overcome by the advent of paper.Complementing the acceptance of paper as a medium was printing. The preservation of letters and documents, both handwritten and printed, migrated from scholars and rulers to libraries and universities. Institutions, such as the Vatican, were also compiling and preserving the written word at a feverish pace. Adding to the collectibility of letters and correspondence was no doubt its expense and delivery both of which could challenge the purse of many of the era.

By the sixteenth and seventeenth century, large and comprehensive collections were beginning to form all across Europe. Numerous collectors were spending enormous amounts of time and money compiling some of the most impressive letters and documents of their day. Many of these collections would eventually find their way to the archives of major institutions, such as the British Library, and be the first testaments to the value of autograph and manuscript collectors.

The eighteenth century, would follow the same path as its predecessor, with many impressive individual collections amassed and then presented or sold to certain institutions. Notable autograph collectors were also emerging by the nineteenth century, as the hobby's intrigue attracted both Queen Victoria and Prince Albert. European autograph collecting was strong, and as it continued to attract new generations of collectors, its importance in history was clearly being established.

Collecting in the United States

The first autograph collector of note, but not the first collector in America, was Rev. William B. Sprague *, a tutor of the nephew and adopted daughter of George Washington. Sprague, through his contacts, built an enormous collection that was highlighted by the correspondence of George Washington. Some autograph historians have also attributed the quest of collecting a complete set of signers to Sprague. Whether or not the pursuit was the collector's idea, it would go on to be one of the most sought after quests in the hobby. Sprague was the first man to form an unbroken set of the immortal fifty-six, followed by Dr. Raffles of Liverpool.

Noted American Autograph Collectors

- William B. Sprague, 1795-1876.
- Israel K. Tefft, 1795-1862.
- The Morgan Family, Junius S. Morgan 18-13-1890, his son J. Pierpont Morgan 1837-1913 and his son J. Pierpont Morgan 1867-1943.
- Henry E. Huntington, 1850-1927.
- William Randolph Hearst, 1863-1951.

A peer of Sprague's was Israel K. Tefft * of Savannah, a bank clerk. Tefft has been labeled the first autograph collector in America. Both collectors struck up a rapport and even exchanged items. Autograph collecting was beginning to take shape in America and with it, some outstanding collectors were emerging such as Eliza Allen (Providence), Lewis J. Cist (Cincinnati), Mellen Chamberlain (Boston) and Robert Gilmor (Baltimore).

Also some key contributors to the early years of collecting include Louis Bamberger, Oliver R. Barrett, Estelle Betzold, W. H. Bexby, Chas. De F. Burns, G. W. Childs, William L. Clements, Joshua J. Cohen, Telamon Cuyler, Augustin Daly, Elliott Danforth, Dr. Frederick M. Dearborn, W. J. De Renne, Ferdinand J. Dreer *, Dr. Arthur Elliott, Thomas Addis Emmet, Frank Etting, Dr. Otto Fisher, Dr. John H. Fogg, Allyn K. Ford, John W. Garrett, Simon Gratz, Charles Gunther, Louis J. Haber, John M. Hale, Zachary T. Hollingsworth, Mrs. John Hubbard, Charles F. Jenkins, Charles C. Jones, Foreman M. Lebold, Richard M. Lederer, James Lenox, Josiah K. Lilly, James H. Manning, Brantz Mayer, Bailey Myers, George Cardinal Mundelin, Robert C. Norton, Frederick S. Peck, Dr. Frank L. Pleadwell, Herbert L. Pratt, Thomas R. Proctor, Philip D. Sang, David M. Stauffer, Rodderick Terry, John B. Thatcher, Charles Roberts, and Dr. George C.F. Williams.

Some early orators on the hobby include, Daniel M. Tredwell ("Privately Illustrated Books"), Adrian H. Joline ("Meditations"), Lyman C. Draper ("Autographic Collections of the Signers of the Declaration of Independence and the Constitution") and Benjamin B. Thatcher.

Many early dealers also emerged and contributed greatly to the hobby (see chart).

Noted American Autograph Dealers

- Charles De F. Burns, New York, 1864; published *The American Antiquarian*.
- William E. Benjamin and Walter R. Benjamin, New York; later Mary A. Benjamin Henderson, published *The Collector*.
- Patrick F. Madigan and Thomas F. Madigan, New York.
- C.E. Goodspeed, Boston; Gordon Banks—autograph department; published *The Month* until 1969.
- The Rosenbach Company, Philadelphia; A.S.W. Rosenbach and Philip Rosenbach; later the Rosenbach Foundation; a portion was purchased by John F. Fleming, New York.
- Forest G. Sweet and Forest H. Sweet, Battle Creek, Michigan; New York.
- Charles Hamilton, New York; noted author and historian.

Other notable dealers included, Benjamin Bloomfield, Guido Bruno, the Carnegie Book Shop, Emily Driscoll, King Hostick, and Julia Newman.

Auction Houses

Many auction houses also benefited from the boom in autograph collecting. Gradually increasing in value since WWII, autograph collecting exploded during the 1980s and with it the continued interest of the auction houses. Early auction houses of note include, American Art Association, Anderson Galleries, Bangs and Company, Christie's, C.F. Libbie, and Sotheby's.

Key Autograph Dates During The Last Fifty Years

January 3, 1948	Launch of the National Society of Autograph Collectors (NSAC)
Summer, 1952	The NSAC recommends a new name—The Manuscript Society
1954	The Lewis & Clark Case—The first instance in which the U.S. Government had sued to reclaim historical manuscripts from private hands.
January 23, 1958	An appeals court upheld a lower court's decision on The Lewis & Clark Case in favor of the papers remaining in private ownership. **
1960	Greer Allen becomes the first professional editor for *Manuscripts* published by The Manuscript Society
1961	Charles Hamilton publishes *Collecting Autographs and Manuscripts*
November, 1965	The Universal Autograph Collector Club (UACC) is founded
October, 1972	The twenty-fifth annual meeting of *The Manuscript Society*
October, 1973	A Bicentennial Exhibit opens and is the collaboration of The Manuscript Society and the Smithsonian Institution (SITES)
1978—1981	A large portion of the Sang Foundation Collection is sold through Sotheby's during five sales.
November, 1989	An International Conference on Forged Documents is held in Houston, TX *

Note:

*—Conference notes were published by Oak Knoll Books of New Castle, DE, 1990. **—The Manuscript Society had a monumental contribution to this case and one that every collector should be appreciative of. Numerous other key hobby events are mentioned throughout the book.

A Decade Of Autograph History, 1989-1999

For the last decade of this millennium, I thought it would be useful to provide a time line of events. While this list is far from comprehensive, it should establish a starting point. If I have overlooked a specific event, please feel free to contact me through the publisher of this book, with suggestions, corrections, additions, elaborations or deletions.

1989

- Noted autograph collector Wayne Bramble died at the young age of 50.

- First worldwide Autograph Computer Network was established in California.

- The library of H. Bradley Martin, consisting of over 7,000 volumes, was sold at Sotheby's in a series of nine auctions.

- A 1934 Hirohito document sold for $42,000 in a New York City auction held by Herman Darvick.

- Noted autograph sleuth Charles Hamilton claimed the signature found on the late singer/songwriter

Harry Chapin's will is a forgery. Despite the observation, a New York judge ruled it valid.

- A museum dedicated exclusively to autographs opened at 8349 68th St. SE, in Alto, Michigan.

- A letter from Maria Callas sells at Swann Galleries Autograph auction for $25,300—a record price for any letter by an opera singer.

1990

- On April 28th & 29th Guernsey's sold over 2,000 lots in New York City during the largest sale to date of sports collectibles.

- UACC celebrated its 25th Anniversary.

- A document signed by gangster Al Capone sold for $14,300 in a New York City auction held by Herman Darvick Autograph Auctions.

- On December 6, 1990, during an auction run by Herman Darvick, a signature of former Chicago White Sox player Joe Jackson sold for $23,100.

1991

- A complete set of signers of the Declaration of Independence sold for $396,000 at the 1991 Manuscript Society Sale.

- On March 14, 1991 Swann Galleries sold a 2-1/4 page signed document written in George Washington's hand for $35,200.

- The Attorney General of New York decided to regulate the sales of sports autographs and memorabilia by requiring dealers to provide certificates of authenticity to buyers of items selling for $50 or more.

- A battle ensues over the second half of the novel *The Adventures of Huck Finn,* as the Erie and Buffalo County Public Library sued Barbara and Pamela Gluck of Buffalo, NY for possession of the manuscript.

- Syracuse university acquires more than 1,300 letters from Nobel laureate Dr. Albert Schweitzer.

- A dispute continues over a 108-page manuscript by Gustav Mahler, offered for sale by Sotheby's of London.

- It was announced on June 4th that Sotheby's would offer for sale a printed copy *of The Declaration of Independence* pulled by John Dunlap. In January of 1990, another copy of the document sold for a record $1.59 million.

- Camden House of Los Angeles, CA sells an original portrait of James Dean, signed and inscribed by the actor, for $17,600.

- An article in the November 4th issue of *Newsweek* challenges the position of autograph collecting, business or hobby.

- On December 5th, a 2-1/4 page letter from President Abraham Lincoln shatters the former record of $440,000—set by a letter from signer Caesar Rodney, by commanding $748,000.

1992

- Despite a recession autograph auctions continue to set record prices. One example was Camden House that set new auction records at their June 7th sale. The sale was highlighted by the witch's hourglass from "The Wizard of Oz" that sold for $66,000. A love letter from Elvis Presley also fetched $8,800.

- Herman Darvick announced that a 1971 Academy Award won by Beatle John Lennon for scoring the film "Let It Be" would be offered for sale on October 5th.

- Odyssey Auctions sets an all-time record for the highest price paid at auction for space memorabilia in their November 22nd Beverly Hills sale. The space suit of Russian Vladimir Lyakonv brings $49,500.

- An Abraham Lincoln signed manuscript of the final paragraph of his 1865 second inaugural address sells at Christie's in November for a record $1.32 million. The document was sold to Profiles in History at the highest price ever paid for an autographed presidential manuscript.

1994

- Sanders Meanders column is featured in *Autograph Collector* magazine. Authored by the renowned collectors George and Helen Sanders this column will become enormously popular with readers of the hobby magazine.

- In an auction held by Nate's Autographs a letter written by *Gone With the Wind* author Margaret Mitchell sells for $2,475. Other items sold include a document signed by Joseph Stalin—$4,950, a George Washington document —$6,600 and a signed photograph of actress Jean Harlow—$1,760

- A new world record for a signed photo of a 20th century personality is set on February 27th during an Odyssey Auctions sale. The autographed photograph of baseball great "Shoeless" Joe Jackson sells for $28,750.

- Steven S. Raab publishes an excellant new reference book, *Movie Star Autographs of the Golden Era, 1930-1960.* Raab, a highly respected autograph dealer, continues his ongoing commitment to collector education.

- Late in the year, a Capitol Hill source steered author Seymour Hersh toward some documents that were found by a Lex Cusack, son of lawyer Lawrence X. Cusack— who reputedly had worked with President John Kennedy. The documents, thought to be original, linked John Kennedy to both the mob and Marilyn Monroe. Like all forgeries, the documents contained numerous clues that were found during forensic analysis.

- Superior's Hollywood and Rock 'n' Roll Memorabilia auction attracted considerable attention with the results of their Saturday, March 19th sale, highlighted by the sale of three autographed 8"x 10" photographs of Bruce Lee which sold for up to $6,300 each.

- Clement Moore's autographed manuscript of *A Visit From St. Nicholas* sold at a Christie's auction for $255,500.

- Bill Gates, of Microsoft fame, purchased Leonardo Da Vinci's Hammer Codex for $30 million.

1995

- The I.R.S. began to crackdown on celebrity signings at autograph shows. The organization contended that many could face tax evasion charges.

- Eric Clapton collaborated with Martin Guitars to create a signature model. Only 461 of the models (000-42EC) will be made and individually signed by Clapton and C.F. Martin IV. The cost of this slow hand special was—$8,100.

- Herman Darvick Autograph Auctions featured President Richard M. Nixon's resignation letter. The 15 typed word letter brought an impressive $82,000 at the group's February 23, 1995 sale.

- A recent auction saw a handwritten letter from Abraham Lincoln reach the $1,000,000 price level.

- R.M. Smythe held successful April 19, 1995 sale which includes a variety of material, including some exceptional financial documents. A highlight of the event was a sale of a collection of clipped signatures of George A. Custer and his contemporaries which brought $26,400.

- Autograph scholar Neale Lanigan and noted dealer Steven Raab publish *The Educated Collector's Guide To Buying Autographs.*

- *The Rail Splitter,* a publication specializing in the reporting of Abraham Lincoln memorabilia, published its first issue.

- Two men, including a former Secret Service officer assigned to President Reagan, were indicted by a federal grand jury on charges they sold counterfeit presidential memorabilia.

- The son of baseball legend Ted Williams claimed that three quarters of his father's autographs in the market are fake.

- According to a market source, the signature of Prince Charles is considered the most valuable autograph of any living person.

- A U.S. Marshal's document, signed by Robert Dalton, sold for $6,735 at the November 1995 auction conducted by American West Archives of Cedar City, Utah.

1996

- Civil War auction exceeded expectations at the American Historical Auctions' inaugural sale held in Boston on February 24th. Highlights included, a requisition from Confederate Brig. General James Johnston—$12,000, a Gen. Quincy Adams Gillmore 1863 ALS—$7, 250 and a Gen. Samuel K. Zook ALS—$7,250.

- PADA, The Professional Autograph Dealer Association was formed by founding president David Lowenherz of Lion Heart Autographs. Membership will require sponsorship by at least three PADA members who will follow a rigorous approval process.

- A poster that was being signed for actor Christopher Reeve, by his peers attending the Academy Awards at the Dorothy Chandler Pavilion, disappeared before it was presented to the actor.

- A copy of "From the President's Pen: An Illustrated Guide to Presidential Autographs", by Larry Vrzalik and Michael Minor, that was given to Jacqueline Kennedy Onassis in 1991, sold for $8,050 at a much publicized Sotheby's auction in New York.

- Highlights of the April, 1996 Jacqueline Kennedy Onassis auction included: fake pearls Jackie wore in the White House—$211,500, the Nuclear Test Ban Treaty signing desk—$1.43 million, JFK's cigar humidor—$574,500, a pair of obelisks—$85,000, a check—$46,000, a White House carpet—$51,750 and Jackie's silver tape measure—$48,875.

- Both the Boston Globe and the popular television show *60 Minutes* cast doubt on an autograph market they felt was filled with forgery and deception. According to the television show, 75% of all autographs in the market are not authentic.

- The Chicago Sun-Times reported that a suburban Chicago collectibles dealer pleaded guilty in federal court on July 11th to selling $2.4 million worth of forged autograph sports memorabilia.

- Former Governor George Wallace signed autographs to benefit the Wallace Center for the Study of Southern Politics.

- R&R Enterprises successfully auctioned 1422 lots presented during their July auction. The sales of over $340, 000 are highlighted by a candid snapshot signed by Marilyn Monroe—$2,040, a photograph signed by Monroe and Arthur Miller—$4,200 and a signed photograph of Ernest Hemingway—$3,087.

- Julian Lennon paid $39,030 for the recording notes of Paul McCartney pertaining to the classic Beatle composition "Hey Jude." Ironically, the song pertained to Lennon and was originally titled "Hey Jules." Also sold at the September Sotheby's auction was one and a half verse of the song "Being For the Benefit of Mr. Kite" written in the hand of John Lennon—$103,500.

- On December 11, 1996, one of the hobby's treasures passes away, Charles Hamilton. Hamilton, perhaps the most respected autograph authority of the century, leaves behind a legacy that will never be matched, as well as numerous unfinished manuscripts/studies.

1997

- Profiles in History, Spring 1997 Auction included furnishings from the last home of Marilyn Monroe.
- An autographed 8" x 10" signed and inscribed picture of actress Sharon Tate sold for $3, 600 in R&R Enterprises January auction.
- Officials at the Corcoran State Prison uncovered a suspected plot to sell Charles Manson autographed material.
- Bonnie & Clyde memorabilia goes on the auction block on April 14th in San Francisco during a sale conducted by Butterfield & Butterfield. A highlight of the sale was a one-page handwritten letter from Clyde Barrow which brought $5,175.
- Two Florida autograph dealers, Stephen Koschal Autographs and Lynn E. Keyes of Remains to be Seen, lobbied the U.S. Postal service to issue a stamp saluting the hobby of autograph collecting. To date the effort has been unsuccessful.
- Remember When Auctions Incorporated grossed more than $1.5 million in their two-day, March 15 and 16, sale. Highlights included an Abraham Lincoln ALS—$17,500 and a letter written by King Henry VIII—$15,500
- Former Beatle Paul McCartney sued Lily Evans, widow of Beatles' road manager Mal Evans, to return lyrics of "With a Little Help From My Friends." Evans was planning to auction the scrap of paper.
- Four men were arrested outside the gates of the Augusta National Golf Club—site of The Masters tournament, for selling material allegedly bearing the forged signatures of PGA golfers Arnold Palmer and Tiger Woods.
- A prominent Ohio autograph dealer was arrested on May 8th on suspicion of bilking nearly a dozen investors out of more than $250,000 in a scheme devoted to purchasing a copy of the Japanese surrender document that ended WWII.
- Thirteen love letters penned by *Gone With the Wind* author Margaret Mitchell brought $32,200 at Christie's April 20th auction.
- Sotheby's June 3rd auction in New York brought impressive biding. Highlights included: a two-page ALS from painter Peter Paul Rubens—$31,050, a rare one-page unpublished autograph poetical manuscript of Emily Dickinson—$24,150 and a William Faulkner autograph manuscript—$11,500.
- The FBI in Chicago, investigating the $750 million-a-year sports memorabilia market, estimated that 70% of all autographed balls, shoes and jerseys were fake. The investigation will continue for years.
- Esteemed autograph collectors, authors and researchers George and Helen Sanders decided to auction off their impressive collection of autographs and memorabilia.
- IACC/DA—The International Autograph Collectors Club & Dealer Alliance is formed.
- R.M. Smythe, an admired specialist in paper collectibles, witnessed impressive prices realized during their October 30th sale in New York. Items sold include a Winfield Scott ALS—$9,500, a Louisa May Alcott ALS—$4,500 and a John F. Kennedy ALS—$3,500
- R&R Enterprises continued to post impressive results following their now highly-anticipated monthly auctions. The company's October sale brought $355,000—its best results ever, only to be topped the following month when November set the bar at $433,000.

1998

- One of the largest and most impressive autograph shows ever was scheduled for December 20 and 21 at Bally's in Las Vegas. The Celebrity Fair and auction included over 40 guests, actors and actresses such as Jane Russell, Tony Randall and Eli Wallach.
- Noted autograph dealer Stephen Koschal severs his UACC ties and withdraws his nomination for another term as director of the organization.
- The first auction of material from the Sanders autograph collection generated $440,000 in a sale conducted by Pieces of the Past Auctions of West Palm Beach, FL. Another 800 lots will be offered in November.
- A Los Angeles Superior Court judge ruled that an autograph dealer from New York state—J.P. Productions (CPG Direct) must pay X-Files co-star David Duchovny $300,000 plus interest and attorney's fees for selling signed photographs of the actor without his permission.
- The original lyrics to "Candle in the Wind 1997"—a tribute to Diana, Princess of Wales, penned by Bernie Taupin for a recording by Elton John was sold at a special Christmas charity auction in Los Angeles, CA on February 11, 1998 for $442,500.
- Forgotten records were found in an Indiana state prison pertaining to notorious gangster John Dillinger, including some nice writing examples that would wet the appetite of many autograph collectors.
- British police arrested a woman, Anna Ferretti, in connection with an alleged theft of numerous letters written by Diana, Princess of Wales to her lover James Hewitt.
- R&R Enterprises *1998 Autograph Price Guide* is published detailing all the prices paid for autograph items during the company's twelve monthly mail, phone and fax auctions of 1997.

- Bob Eaton, owner of R&R Enterprises of Bedford, New Hampshire was praised by former U.S. President Jimmy Carter for returning a five-page 1974 ALS after learning that the document had apparently been stolen.

- A check written by Diana Spencer just prior to her engagement to Prince Charles sold for $3,100 at the June 4th, R.M. Smythe & Co. auction in New York.

- The autographed sports memorabilia market continued in a tailspin as accusations of forged Mark McGwire signatures are encountered as often as one of the slugger's home runs.

- The "Double Fantasy" record album that Beatle John Lennon signed for his assassin, Mark David Chapman, was offered for sale at an asking price of $1.8 million.

- Dealer Stephen Koschal advertised that he was willing to pay $1 million to anyone who can bring him an authentic signature of an extraterrestrial on a letter, photo, etc.

- The hobby loses another giant, George Sanders, who died suddenly on August 26th. A gifted radio and television personality, Sanders contributed immensely to the hobby of autograph collecting through his wonderful articles and respected price guides.

- Twenty experts, representing seven major collectibles markets assisted in compiling a new rarity rating system for collectibles. The study was commissioned by (PCGS) Professional Coin Grading Services of Newport Beach, CA.

- "The Eisenhower Files: An In-Depth Philographic Study" by Paul K. Carr was published by the UACC. The publication is part of an overall effort to continue educating collectors.

- Still mourning from the passing of Charles Hamilton and George Sanders, the hobby faced another loss with death of Mary A. Benjamin on November 30th in Hunter, NY. The Benjamin family's contribution and legacy to the hobby of autograph collecting has been nothing short of monumental.

- An anonymous telephone bidder paid $126,500 for the "First Home Run Hit at Yankee Stadium, April 18, 1923" by Babe Ruth. The baseball, signed and inscribed by "The Sultan of Swat" topped the previous price ($93,500) paid by actor Charlie Sheen for the now infamous "Mookie Ball."

- A diary disputing Davey Crockett's death at the Alamo sold for $387,500 during a November 18th auction conducted by Butterfield & Butterfield.

1999

- Auction house Butterfield & Butterfield placed the former belongings of O.J. Simpson under the gavel to raise money to help satisfy a $33.5 million judgment in the civil wrongful-death lawsuit brought by the families of Nicole Brown Simpson and her friend Ron Goldman. The highlight of the auction was Simpson's 1968 Heisman Trophy, which sold for $230,000.

- Monica Lewinsky attracted 1,500 at a book signing at Brentano's Bookstore in Century City, CA on March 22nd. The event prompted rumors that one of the signed books sold for $1,200.

- The UACC Annual Convention was slated for June 26th and 27th at The Beverly Garland Holiday Inn in North Hollywood, CA. The event featured the crew of Apollo 12 signing autographs.

- IACC/DA became first club to offer authentication services.

Where To Look

Good Sources For Finding Historical Autographs

The first step in becoming an advanced autograph collector is knowing where to look for signatures. There are numerous sources that have historical merit because man has always kept records. Listed here are some of the typical items where writing can be found.

Autograph Albums

Tracing back to the sixteenth and seventeenth centuries, autograph albums were popular during the

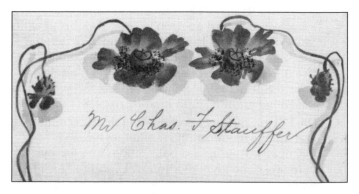

Example of an early calling card. These signed cards were left by visitors calling on a guest.

An example of an early calling card. Often these were enhanced with imagery or by the flourishing strokes of an ink pen.

Victorian era of sentimentality. Friends or acquaintances would jot down a few verses before signing their name. Many would add flourishes, such as hand-drawn calling cards or calligraphic figures. While the custom of keeping an album originated in Germany, it would spread throughout Europe by the eighteenth century. Like any format, it evolved from containing coats-of-arms to include silhouettes or even locks of hair. The albums also varied in size, color, and quality. As the custom migrated to young schoolgirls, the design of these albums was simplified to lower cost.

Most of the autograph albums you will find contain signatures of friends and relatives of the original owner and seldom a signature of a famous figure. However, you can never be sure, so spend a minute or two glancing through the pages. Most autographs of prominent celebrities of the era were obtained indirectly and by the nineteenth century were clipped from other sources such as letters or documents. Worth noting is that it was not uncommon for some of these "cut signatures" to be pasted inside an autograph album.

Bible

It was traditional, at one time, for families to keep important documents or papers relating to genealogy inside the family bible. Often one might even find the family history written inside on one of the end papers of the bible, or inserted on a separate piece of paper. The passing of generations also meant the bequeathing of this important family record, so it is not unusual to find numerous transformations of handwriting inside such a record.

Important family documents such as marriage, death, and baptismal certificates could also be found in the family bible. While such documents have a priceless sentimental value to family members, some can also be valuable to autograph collectors. For example, a famous officer could have signed military documents. As an advanced autograph collector, as

you search for signatures at estate auctions and garage sales, always take time to peer inside any family bibles you may run across, as you might be pleasantly surprised at what you may find.

Certificates

As a society we have often acknowledged accomplishments through the use of certificates. These come in all shapes and sizes, printed or handwritten and saluting just about everything imaginable from handwriting and attendance, to etiquette and spelling. If there is a worthy task, then a certificate probably exists to give a recipient proof of its completion. While most of these will not bear a signature of an historical figure, some have included signatures worth collecting. As an advanced autograph collector always thoroughly examine such documents.

Some certificates can also be a source for well-known local figures, and have regional collecting appeal. As an advanced autograph collector you should schedule regular visits to your local historical society. Not only will you find many valuable sources of information, but also by brushing up on your local history you may uncover facts about important figures. Familiarize yourself with the prominent individuals who may have visited or resided in your area. By retracing the paths they may have chosen you may unearth a document they have signed.

Documents

As an advanced autograph collector you will often spend time educating yourself on the documents of a particular era, occupation or event. Sample documents alone could fill many books twice this size, but as a collector you need only be familiar with those that pertain to your collection. If you are focusing your efforts on the era of temperance and prohibition in America you will need to familiarize yourself with not only the standard documents of the era, but those specific to it, such as a temperance pledge, alcohol prescriptions, etc. Or if you are looking at an occupation (such as that of a professional baseball player), you will need to recognize authentic contracts, licensing agreements, scorecards, line-up cards and all the other items associated with the sport.

Collecting the signatures of those patriots of the American Revolution, a key event in our history, will require you to learn to recognize the size, format and structure of documents such as arrest warrants, bills of sale, colonial currency, payroll authorizations, promissory notes and ship's papers. Colonial currency alone is a fascinating study, as such notes were actually signed by many important figures whose autographs are now very valuable.

Remember that some events, such as the Civil War, may have unique markings or additions to documents.

For example, from 1862 to 1867, documentary stamps were issued as a means of collecting federal government revenues and were attached directly to papers. These additions can prove very useful in authenticating and dating a document.

Family History Books

Chromolithographed registers titled "Family Record" have been around for over a century and can be found in all shapes and sizes. Most contain a family tree, baptismal information, information on awards, etc. While these books excite genealogists and many times photography collectors, few will have interest to an advanced autograph collector except for authentication purposes. Do be sure to glance inside those you find and always examine the front and backs of all photographs and documents that you may run across.

Journals & Diaries

Often overlooked, as they are seldom a source for key autographs, are journals and diaries. Many make fascinating reading and can be valuable, such as those kept during the Civil War. Over the years I have owned numerous fascinating journals, many of which highlight trips. Inside I have been delighted when coming across drawings or glued in photographs. I have also encountered calling cards, tickets, postcards and even programs from various events. As an advanced autograph collector always spends some extra time examining such items when they are found.

Registers

Hotels, rooming houses, ships, camps and retreats often had guests sign a register. Naturally, the caliber of guests can vary considerably depending upon the place and the era, but often registers can be a valuable source of autographs. Since registers are typically one-of-a-kind items, they are far from prevalent in the autograph market and can be difficult to value.

Stock Certificates

Stock certificates are a specialized area of collecting, but one well worth some time to an advanced autograph collector. It involves more than pricing the signatures that appear at the bottom of the document however in order to accurately determine value. A collector must understand the rarity, condition, and significance of a document to approximate an item's value. Because of the many important names that have graced stock certificates, autograph collectors can not afford to ignore this area of the hobby.

This journal was kept by a little girl who was traveling by ship overseas to Spain. Inside of it were some very early photographs and even some bullfighting programs.

This is a register kept by an area Inn. Inside of it guests sign their name, address and date. The register spans many years with guests from all over the United States.

Journals were often kept by soldiers and inside them are typically fascinating accounts of historical events.

Telegrams

The telegram began competing with the letter after 1844, following the installation of the first telegraphic line (Washington, D.C. - Baltimore). Often interesting to collectors because of content, few include valuable signatures. An occasional margin note from a prominent individual however can bring some value to an item sold in the autograph market.

Paper-based Preservation And Maintenance

Paper Preservation

Paper preservation is a paramount concern of most advanced autograph collectors because a majority of historic documents entering the market are paper-based. Not only does the significance of the document command the interest of most collectors, but in most cases so does the price. Ironically, how often have you witnessed collectors take more care of their cars than documents of equal value? Trust me when I tell you that the first time you witness an expensive document in your collection crumble in your hands because you have failed to preserve it properly your priorities will change.

Fortunately, as a society we have become more discriminating in our use of paper. We know that the paper must be suited for the purpose, but with every lesson in life there is a price. The price we paid was witnessing magazines, newspapers and inexpensive books deteriorate beyond use in a very small period of time. During the early 1980s, the federal government teamed with the paper industry to address this area of concern. A committee was formed to establish national standards for paper permanency. To be considered permanent, the paper must meet criteria established in the ANSIZ39 Permanent Paper Standard. Paper must have a pH level of 7.5 or greater, contain an alkaline buffer (often calcium carbonate), be free of chemical impurities, resistant to handling (tears, folding, etc.) and optimally contain cotton or other rag fibers.

Paper production has now gone full circle, as ancient paper making methods used acid-free and alum-free pulp made of the purest of fibers. Modern paper makers now use cotton and pure high-alpha cellulose in their production. Some fine, acid-free papers even compensate for external factors with methods such as the addition of alkali to neutralize any possible acid contamination from handling. While many of us understand that paper is fragile, not all of us know the reasons why, so let's take a look at both internal and external factors that contribute to deterioration.

Internal Paper Deterioration Factors

During paper production, stray fragments of various materials and defections from the process can contribute to deterioration, but the key components are typically the fibers used and the chemicals they come in contact with. Historically, both strength and longevity has been compensated during the process because of cost. Inferior fibers, bleaches and the addition of other chemicals such as alum, all but guaranteed destruction.

While the past was more circumstantial than choice, it did manage to prompt manufacturers to determine the definition of paper permanence. We now select paper fully aware of the shelf life of the final product. Artists can now choose all-rag papers to prolong the life of their work and when the work is ready for framing, we can choose all-rag mats, acid-free papers and safe adhesives. We now fully realize that everything visible and invisible that can come in contact with a piece of paper will have some type of effect on its chemical state.

The proper use of archival safe materials is paramount to the proper matting and framing of an image.

External Paper Deterioration —Environmental Factors

Air Pollutants

The air we breathe is filled with contaminants, many of which can harm both man and his environment. One of the most notorious pollutants is sulfur dioxide—a gas produced from the burning of fossil fuels (coal, oil, etc.). Paper absorbs this gas and converts it into sulfuric acid, which breaks down paper fibers and causes discoloration. Archivists commonly witness the phenomena in images framed with improper backing or in other words those images partially or entirely exposed to the air. Book collectors witness the same deterioration in leather bookbindings. The sulfur dioxide depletes the pliability and strength inherent in the binding.

Countless stories have been told over the years of the horrors sulfur dioxide created in libraries illuminated with gas. Prior to electricity what were the options? In those early years, little was known about air pollutants and what effect they could have on our archives.

Air pollutants are often commonly associated with large cities, areas where there is often a concentration of libraries and art galleries. Archivists, now aware of the hazards of air pollutants, make air conditioning a paramount concern. They also take into consideration all their options, such as deacidification of paper or reframing images to archival standards.

Fortunately for everyone, manufacturers such as those associated with the production of paper-based supplies are constantly reviewing ways to prolong their products and reduce deterioration. Paper manufacturers have introduced alkaline chemicals to neutralize some damaging effects. Bookbinders have also modified procedures and even offered to archivists ways to neutralize the acidic substances inherit in leather bookbindings. *

Heat

Paper burns, so don't expose it to heat. Obvious, right? Then why are paintings found over fireplace mantels? Not only is the heat harmful, but the soot and residue from the fireplace can be destructive. Pay careful attention to how heat or temperature is controlled in your environment and make the proper adjustments.

Humidity

Humidity, or the degree of wetness in the atmosphere, must be controlled to avoid the growth of mold. Advanced autograph collectors are advised to store items only in atmospheres where the humidity is less than seventy percent, since mold can not grow until it exceeds this point. Most, myself included, suggest fifty-percent humidity as the ideal.

In situations, such as airtight containers or exhibition cases, small bags of silica gel—a dehumidifying agent can be helpful. Colloidal silica resembles coarse white sand and has many fine pores that are extremely absorbent. Always be cognizant of sources of moisture, such as stone walls and be sure the storage area has adequate air circulation.

If your document or signed book has dull rusty patches that discolor it, you have mold growth, typically referred to as "foxing." Mold feeds on the sizing and paper fibers on the sheets of paper in your book. Left alone, it will weaken and destroy your item. To kill the mold, conservators remove it first to a dry environment. If it is a book, the pages are carefully spread open to allow the air to circulate. The book is then exposed to direct sunlight for a period of time determined by the conservator or, preferably placed in a special container with some crystals of thymol. Thymol is a crystalline phenol ($C_{10}H_{14}O$) of aromatic odor and antiseptic properties found especially in thyme oil. It can be made synthetically—the form you are likely to encounter, and is used chiefly as a fungicide and preservative. While I do not advocate placing any document or work of art in direct sunlight, this is a process that is used in certain instances, thus as an advanced autograph collector you should be made aware of the technique. The conservator will make the judgment as to the length of time that your book or document should be exposed to the thymol.

Some book collectors adapt or build special cabinets for using thymol—"thymol cabinets." Many designs exist all in attempt to maximize the spread of thymol fumes. Thymol crystals are volatilized through heating in a process not proper for an amateur bibliomaniac or advanced autograph collector. Like many preservation processes, adverse conditions can be encountered. Improper conditions can result in small oily droplets forming on your image. Thymol also acts adversely to oil paint and can destroy a work of art.

Some final reminders on humidity: Take advantage of air conditioning and always keep the humidity at about fifty percent. Be aware of your storage environment and the potential exposure to all environmental factors. Be sure your image is matted, framed, cleaned, and stored to archival standards. Remember that part of a proper storage environment is proper air circulation. Keep all storage areas clean and periodically monitored. Consult a professional conservator before undergoing any preservation process.

Insects

Silverfish, wood worms, cockroaches and termites all post a threat to paper based products. While I'm not suggesting that you transform yourself and overreact, I am letting you know about a potential danger, as it has faced me. Depending upon where you live and what you live in, you may already be familiar with all or some of these insects. Most of these critters favor warm, damp and dark places, areas where no serious autograph collectors would store their prized possessions in the first place. But if you're like myself, you are probably guilty more than once of storing reference books and old newspapers in some part of the basement or attic.

First and foremost, monitor all storage areas, from safe deposit boxes to the smallest confines of your basement. Take every affordable option from air conditioning to calling a professional exterminator for advice on how to prevent these insects. Silverfish, are small and often difficult to detect. They move quickly and avoid the light, but can and will eat their way through your paper-based product, especially wood-pulp paper, to feed on flour paste or glue sizing.

Termites and wood worms love to eat cellulose. This substance is a complex carbohydrate that forms the cell walls of plants and is the principal component of wood, paper, cotton, etc. Don't let them have access to such items.

Cockroaches, familiar to those of you in the deep south, come out at night and cause damage to many items, especially those that may contain sugar, such as certain glues and painting media.

Personally, I take every precaution possible, from controlling vegetation outside of my home, to the periodic inspection of hard-to-reach areas in the basement. As an advanced autograph collector, build into your routine certain inspections to prolong the preservation of your belongings.

Light

Light can be incredibly destructive to paper-based products. As an advanced autograph collector, you must familiarize yourself with all of the destructive elements of light. The incredible increase in both autograph and art collecting has led to an enhanced interest in the preservation of framed images. Many have paid significant sums of money for some of these paper-based images. As a result, collectors frequently find themselves asking conservators how to display these items without deteriorating their value. Often their first concern is light, as the last thing a collector wants is his Norman Rockwell porous tip pen drawing faded as a result of over exposure.

First and foremost, all light fades images on paper! Smaller amounts of light only mean smaller amounts of fading. The only way to stop the fading is to place the item in complete darkness, not a good viewing condition. A misnomer is that placing an item in the complete darkness will actually rejuvenate the image—it will not! Fading is NOT reversible, so as a collector you better take precautions with your paper-based images.

Another typical question of collectors is, "How much light should be used to view a document or work of art? Typically, the response is about reading level or five foot candles. A foot candle is a unit of luminance on a surface that is everywhere one foot from a uniform point source of light of one candle and equal to one lumen per square foot. Casual reading level, or the output of one 150-watt light bulb at a distance of three or four feet should be fine in most instances. NEVER hang an image in direct sunlight!

Light quantity can be very deceptive, because the human eye adjusts to it. Just ask a photographer! If you have a concern about the light levels you are using, use a light meter. Grab a piece of white copy paper, and place it where you are planning to hang your image. Then take a light reading to accurately determine the foot candles. Additionally, don't forget about reflected light!

To guard against light damage rotate your framed images and even consider storing some of them for a awhile. Where necessary, mask the light. By using louvered blinds, shades and curtains you can redirect the light. Sunlight is a source of ultraviolet light, and though invisible, can cause significant damage. Even fluorescent light can be a source of UV radiation, so mask the bulbs with protective sleeves that filter out this radiation.

Handling Factors

Everyone has rules for handling paper-based collectible objects, so here are a few of mine.

- Always wear gloves! Matting board stains extremely easy and the oils in your skin can leave marks on items.

- Only examine items in a properly lit condition and upon a clear, smooth and dry surface area free of open containers and extraneous objects.

- Always use both hands to support the item being examined.

- Don't stack unmatted objects on top of each other. If objects must be stacked, separate where appropriate with non-acid cover tissue.

- Valuable images, such as photographs should be matted to protect when handling.

- Do not allow other objects to come in contact with the image, don't drag the corner of a mat across a valuable image.

- Use archival approved or developed adhesives only!

- Since framed, matted or backed images give a false sense of security, handle them with equal care and concern.

- When not in use, matted pictures should be properly wrapped or protected with archival safe cover tissue.

- Never handle a matted image via the picture window, always fully open by the outer edge.

- When moving a fragile document or image do so only in a fully supported form.

- Store all images in archival safe boxes and envelopes, etc.

- Never fold or roll an image! Transport in a flat form only!

Matting & Framing

Matting

Most think of matting as an aesthetic process, which it indeed is; however mats also serve to protect an image. As an advanced autograph collector, any surface that is in close proximity to an image is a preservation concern. For years wood-pulp matting board was used for framing. This inexpensive board was acidic and contained large amounts of unrefined grounded pulp. In most cases the wood pulp disintegrated and the destructive chemicals in the board discolored the framed image. Some manufacturers faced the mat board with better quality paper, but when the board was cut, the inner core of low-grade material was exposed allowing it to migrate to the image. Collectors are advised to examine all matted and framed images for signs of inappropriate conservation material.

All-rag matting board, or museum quality matting board is safe and used by many framers. While the term is somewhat deceiving, as the board is created from cotton fibers and not actual rags, museum quality matting board is acid-free. While initially manufactured in white and off-white, this matting board now comes in a variety of colors. Three thicknesses of matting board are common, 2-ply (1/32"), 4—ply (1/16") and 8-ply (1/8"). The applications for all three differ, with 4-ply being the most common. If cost and storage space are a concern, 2-ply is an option, while 8-ply is useful for larger images—the thicker the board the harder it is to cut manually. Most framers purchase their matting board (30"-32" x 40") at bulk quantities, but for collectors these sheets can be purchased individually at commercial art stores.

If you didn't study art in school, then you maybe unfamiliar with the basic window mat. You begin with two pieces of mat board, one cut with a window opening and one used as a backing board, hinged together with gummed cloth tape. Contrary to what many might think, the window opening is not cut in the center of the mat, but instead cut with the lower margin slightly larger than the upper. This is done to compensate for how the eye would view the image directly set in a proportionally correct mat. Enough space in the window is allowed around the print, so that the subject is not damaged when the top mat board is opened or closed.

Cutting a mat manually takes practice before a level of proficiency is reached. To do so all you need for tools is a straightedge, like a ruler and a mat knife with a new or very sharp blade. This procedure is not recommended for children and even adults should exercise caution when using the mat knife. Never grip a mat knife with any of your fingers extended or with any part of your body in the knife's path. You should always watch someone familiar with the process demonstrate the proper technique before you attempt to cut a mat yourself. There are a wide-variety of mat cutters or devices, available at commercial art stores, so you may want to explore your options before deciding on the manual technique.

Even when using the proper technique you will encounter some initial problems ranging from not using a sharp enough blade to not keeping a consistent knife angle or even trying to cut directly through the mat with a single cut. Using scrap mat board pieces,

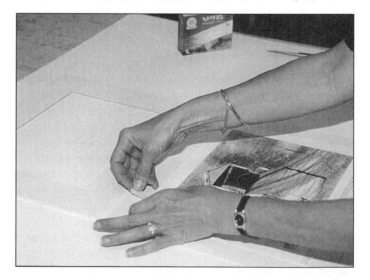

The proper hinging of an image is down with care and typically involves the use of Japanese Hinging Paper.

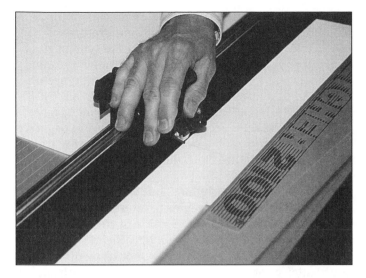

Professional framers use quality mat cutters such as this to create a consistent beveled edge to the inside of a mat.

practice holding the knife at a comfortable angle to get the proper beveled edge you desire. A beveled edge is more appealing than a ninety-degree cut. Practice completing each desired cut with two strokes, the first for proper tracking, and the second to finish the cut. Once a proper picture window is cut, you can use various grades of sandpaper to smooth out rough areas of the cut. Since the goal of your cut is to go directly through the entire thickness of the matting board, be sure a clean and protective surface resides underneath the board. I always had a 45" x 45" x 2" piece of clean softwood, such as pine, underneath the mat. The softer woods will absorb cuts better and damage the blade less. This is not a process that should be undertaken on top of an antique dining room table.

I always recommend using gloves to handle any artwork or document. Be sure they are gloves that do not contain any external chemicals. Some gloves are treated with various powders and are not for handling artwork. With the mat fully opened, hold the picture in the proper position, that you have already determined, and attach it to the backboard using two hinges affixed to the upper edge of the reverse side of the picture. Do not try to keep the mat open, while maneuvering the image, as inevitably the top will drop and could damage the piece. NEVER paste the corners of an image directly to the backboard. Hinging the image allows it to hang freely in the mat, allowing it to adapt to environmental conditions such as expansion and contraction. NEVER use pressure sensitive tapes of any kind, as items such as masking tape or Scotch tape contain adhesives, many of which could harm an image. Use gummed paper or the proper Japanese

paper applied with starch paste for your hinges. A list of suppliers is provided in this section.

Gummed paper offers sufficient flexibility, as length will be determined by the size of the picture it must support. The folded strips are applied first to the picture, then to the backing board. Gummed paper or cloth hinges are also easier to use and do not involve the potential mess that could be created with paste. Japanese paper is often used by archivists or curators, as they take greater patience and practice. Paper weights are selected to match the size of the desired image. A paste is applied smoothly so the picture won't buckle under the hinge. Once the hinges are attached, absorb the excess moisture with blotting paper. Some archivists weight down a portion of blotting paper and allow it to stand for a few hours until dry.

Starch is used as an adhesive for hinges, often wheat or rice. You can either make your own paste or buy it from a supplier. For starch recipes consult conservation books or your local archivist. You can purchase paste from some of the suppliers listed in this section.

Hinging is not an art, but may take some experimentation before you feel comfortable with the process. Making hinges of lengths too short to be effective, is a common occurrence. Most archivists would agree that an image is more likely to incur damage as a result of a weak hinge, rather than one that is too strong. Remember that hinges must be strong enough to withstand improper handling.

The color of a mat should complement the picture, not the surroundings. A surrounding may change, a picture will not! To achieve the best understanding of this relationship, visit some major museums and examine the selection of mat colors to the image they are in conjunction with and also to the frame. Believe me when I tell you that aesthetics can change with various color combinations. I have seen the same print framed many times, with few achieving the full aesthetic quality of the print. The goal of the mat, or mats, and frame is to complement the print, not detract from it!

Not all matted images are framed, so collectors should bear this in mind. Archival matted images should be kept in acid-free folders, which come in a variety of styles and sizes. If the matted images are stored in some other fashion, be sure to take in consideration all elements that may come in contact with the image.

Framing

Only your creativity and budget will limit the framing options you have available to you for your picture or document. Once again a visit to an area art gallery or museum may prove helpful in sparking your creativity. A document or picture can be damaged if improperly framed. For example, I have seen document stains as a result of placing it directly against a wooden backing. The staining in this incidence was due to resins excreted by the wood backing.

During the late 19th century, many images were framed with wooden backing and as a result, some became disfigured or stained. If you are not sure how an image is framed, it would probably be worthwhile to find out. The image should only be in contact with an all-rag matting board; anything else should be replaced. Since some frames can be tricky to open properly, don't be afraid to contact your local framer for assistance.

I know you have probably heard this a thousand times, but it is worth repeating—NEVER place an image in directly against the glass. Glass condenses moisture easily and the result can be catastrophic. Mold can quickly form and ruin a paper-based image. Framers insist upon having a "breathing space" inside the frame to react to adverse changes in the environment. If a mat is not desired, as is sometimes the case, a framer will be able to give you a list of options to protect the image.

Options to glass exist, as do different forms of glass. A popular alternative has been acrylic plastic. Although it condenses slower, is harder to break and can through additives filter out UV (Ultraviolet) rays, acrylic scratches easier and is very static. NEVER use acrylic to frame images created with charcoal, pastel, or other powdery pigmented media—even if the drawing is fixed.

Different forms of glass exist, from simple and inexpensive to even optically coated nonreflective glass. Your local framer can recommend various glass options for your frame. (See the light section here) Light is extremely destructive and must be controlled at all times. This is not an area of framing to cut expenses.

Documents and images should NEVER be framed between two pieces of glass, with or without a mat. Besides the obvious concerns previously mentioned, what would happen if an object hit the glass? Not only could it break both pieces of glass, but it could puncture the document. A quality framer can show you a variety of options using acrylic plastic, if both sides of the document must be visible.

The back of your framed document should be sealed firmly, using acid-free corrugated cardboard or styrofoam-filled board to protect from the environmental elements, including insects. The space between the frame and the backing should be sealed with gummed wrapping tape, which reacts to environmental conditions. The seal need not and should not be airtight. Paper and wood expand and contract at different rates due to environmental conditions, such as humidity and temperature.

For instructions on how to clean the type of glass used in your frame, consult a quality framer. Certain types of cleaners cannot be used on certain types of glass. Additionally, DO NOT EVER SPRAY A CLEANING SOLUTION ONTO THE GLASS! More than once I have witnessed moisture seep inside the frame and begin its destructive process. If a proper cleaner is being used, always apply it to the cloth directly and with moderation.

Another perhaps obvious, but worth repeating rule, is never allow the framer to alter your document to fit a stock frame. Make the frame fit the document, not vice versa. I have even seen letterhead trimmed; can you imagine the loss in value, not to mention the authenticity concerns that are now created with such a process?

On occasion labels or pertinent information to an image may be adhered or attached to the back of a frame. Opinions differ in this regard, but I prefer to store attachments or documents independently from the image and store them properly in acid-free folders. Hinged items on the back of frames have a tendency to fall off or get lost. As far as an adhered label, if the image is properly backed it probably won't be a preservation issue; however, periodically inspect it as you would the image. Obviously, never destroy or alter any relevant component to the image.

Permanently framed images should also be opened, albeit seldom—such as once every decade if properly framed, to inspect for damage or possibly just to have the inner glass cleaned. If possible, have the person who framed the image open it up, as they are

Framing has become an art and along with it suppliers have created more and more options for the customer including alternative to a simple wooden frame.

most familiar with their own techniques. Many images can be damaged during such a process, so having this done professionally may be a viable option.

Hanging a framed picture doesn't take the knowledge of a rocket scientist, but it does take some logic. Just because the framer included a free hanger, doesn't mean it's going to be strong enough to hold the picture in place. A quality professional framer no doubt included wiring of proper strength on the back of the frame. Picture wire exerts tension on the side of the frame, and if attached improperly can damage the frame. You may opt to attach the frame without wire from two separate wall hooks through the screw eyes. Consult your framer for his opinion. Be cautious when using gummed or self-adhesive hooks, as they are only for very lightweight and expendable or commodity items.

As an advanced autograph collector, you will have some documents or images framed. You must remember that even the best archival framers can make mistakes or not anticipate certain circumstances

and thus you should anticipate some problems with framed images. The most common problem encountered is buckling. This may be due to much pressure on the image—a problem easily fixed by a framer. Many problems are indications of a deteriorating factor, such as the presence of old tape, or the presence of an adhesive on the back of an image. All problems should be evaluated with your framer, as many freely advise cures to the problem since they want the business. If an item is buckling, do NOT have it mounted down—a common and often destructive process.

In some instances, such as an old movie poster, it may be necessary for conservation purposes to have a fragile item backed with handmade paper or other archival material. In these instances a professional conservator or restorer should be consulted and used. If you acquire an item that has been mounted down, consult a professional conservator for ways to detach the image.

Restoration & Art Conservation

Even documents and images at the brink of destruction can be rescued and preserved, but it is far from an effortless process. While many cases have similarities, most are unique. Allow the restorer to examine the document and advise you on treatment and the prevention of future deterioration. You may be pleasantly surprised at some of the things they can do,

such as removing water stains or foxing. As an advanced autograph collector, you will find the field of conservation and restoration fascinating. Take every opportunity to learn more about the preservation of paper-based documents and images. Worth repeating again, consult a professional conservator or framer before undergoing any preservation process.

Sources for Archival Material

Aiko's Art Materials Imports
714 North Wabash Avenue
Chicago, IL 60611
Supplies include Japanese papers.

Andrews/Nelson/Whitehead
31-10 48th Avenue
Long Island City, NY 11101
Supplies include acid-free matting board, Japanese papers, covers, tissue, acid-free papers (numerous applications).

Charles T. Bainbridge's Sons
50 Northfield Ave, P.O. Box 3028
Edison, NJ 08818
Supplies include acid-free matting board, Styrofoam-filled cardboard (backing board).

Materials, Ltd.
240 Freemont Blvd.
Box 2884

Sparks, NV 89431
Supplies include wheat starch for paste, silica gel, fungicide (thymol).

Conservation Resources
1111 N. Royal St.
Alexandria, VA 22314
Supplies include document cases and solander boxes.

Crestwood Paper Co., Inc.
315 Hudson Street
New York, NY 10013
Supplies include acid-free matting board.

Fisher Scientific Co.
711 Forbes Ave.
Pittsburgh, PA 15219
Supplies include wheat starch for paste, silica gel.

Gane Brothers and Lane, Inc.
1400 Greenleaf Street
Elk Grove Village, IL 60007

Supplies include gummed cloth tape, archival restoration supplies, library supplies, bookbinding supplies.

Gaylord Brothers, Inc.
P.O. Box 4901
Syracuse, NY 13221
Supplies include gummed cloth tape, archival restoration supplies, library supplies, bookbinding supplies.

The Hollinger Corporation
3810 South Four Mile Run Drive
Arlington, VA 22206
Supplies include acid-free matting board, document cases and solander boxes, acid-free papers (numerous applications).

Light Impressions
439 Monroe Ave., P.O. Box 940
Rochester, NY 14603
Supplies include acid-free matting board, document cases and solander boxes, acid-free papers (numerous applications), flexible plastic sheeting, paper quality testing material (acidity).

New York Central Art Supply
62 Third Avenue
New York, NY 10003
Supplies include Japanese papers.

Pohlig Brothers, Inc.
2419 E. Franklin St.
P.O. Box 8069
Richmond, VA 23223
Supplies include document cases and solander boxes, paper quality testing material (acidity).

Process Materials Corporation
301 Veterans Boulevard
Rutherford, NJ 07070
Supplies include acid-free matting board, cover tissue, acid-free corrugated board, acid-free papers (numerous applications).

Showcase Portfolios
115 S. Union St.
Alexandria, VA 22314
1-800-Frames/703-299-0100
Email: RBADWEY@mindspring.com
www.museumframing.com

Spink and Gaboruc, Inc.
11 Troast Court
Clifton, NJ 07011
Supplies include document cases and solander boxes.

Strathmore Paper Co.
South Broad Street
Westfield, MA 01085
Supplies include acid-free matting board, Japanese papers.

Talas
213 West 35th Street
New York, NY 10001
Supplies include gummed cloth tape, wheat starch for paste, cover tissue, Styrofoam-filled cardboard (backing board), document cases and solander boxes, acid-free papers (numerous applications), flexible plastic sheeting, archival restoration supplies, library supplies, bookbinding supplies, paper quality testing material (acidity), silica gel, fungicide (thymol).

University Products
P.O. Box 101
Holyoke, MA 01040
Supplies include acid-free matting board, Japanese papers, document cases and solander boxes, acid-free papers (numerous applications), flexible plastic sheeting.

U.S Programs in Art and Paper-Based Conservation
Art Conservation Department
S.U.N.Y. at Buffalo
P.O. Box 71
Cooperstown, NY 13326

Art Conservation Program
219 McDowell Hall
University of Delaware
Newark, DE 19711

Center for Conservation and Technical Studies
Fogg Art Museum
Harvard University
Cambridge, MA 02138

Conservation Center, Institute of Fine Arts
New York University
1 East 78th St.
New York, NY 10021

Conservation Programs, School of Library Science
Columbia University
516 Butler Library
New York, NY 10027

Notes:
* A solution of potassium lactate can be applied to leather book bindings to neutralize the acidic substances. You may want to consult an archivist or purchase books familiar with the process for further information.

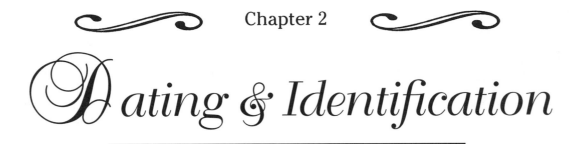

Chapter 2

Dating & Identification

Advanced collectors use many methods of dating autographs that go far beyond simply looking at a signature. Collectors use technologies that were available from different time periods to aid in determining whether a piece of autographed material is authentic. For example, you can compare when a certain writing instrument was created with the lifespan of the signer—George Washington obviously could not sign with a ballpoint pen. Also, certain watermarks can be dated back to papermakers, and different types of printers were used during different periods (Nixon didn't have a laser printer while he was in office), etc.

In this chapter I have included detailed information on writing instruments and ink, papermaking, printing, typewriters, and photography that will help you inspect your documents/items. Additionally, there is information about handlettering and numeral analysis, which is important because not all documents are handwritten. If you take the time to scrutinize potential additions to your collection, I can guarantee that it will be well worth the effort.

Writing Instruments

As writing systems evolved so did writing instruments. Civilizations such as the Chinese illustrated their ideograms with camel's hair brushes as far back as about 1000 BC. Other cultures used reeds, hollow pieces of bamboo and even metal styli to record their thoughts. But for western civilizations, it would be the quill that would become a dominant form.

The Quill

While goose feathers were perhaps the most sought after for quills, swans, turkeys, pelicans, peacocks and even crows also found preference. Delicate handwriting and fine line drawing was best accomplished with crow quills, while durability was often synonymous with goose feathers. Assorted quills, ink, inkwells, quill penknives, pencils, a chunk of rubber (for erasures), paste disks (used to seal letters) were incorporated into writing kits, which were marketed and sold.

The quill user assumed the task of shaping and sharpening his instrument. The era's writing style determined how the quills were to be cut. For example, round hand, fashionable during the Revolutionary War, required a pointed shape. Special knives (penknives), in a variety of styles, were used to accomplish this delicate task.

Quill-written script can be easily identified by its thin upstrokes and thicker downstrokes, the latter being produced by the points of the pen separating due to the increased pressure. As the point of the quill deteriorated, thicker, ragged writing would become increasing apparent. Occasional ink spattering was also common and similar to the ragged writing, could be corrected by a new point. In order to maintain the smooth flow of ink, quills had to be kept clean and never allowed to dry out. Ink stands and holders, used for this task, became common fixtures on writing desks. By the mid-nineteenth century however, the quill was displaced by the development of metal pens.

Durable Pens

The idea of a metallic pen, with metal pen points or nibs, can be traced back hundreds of years, but it wasn't until an efficient method manufacturing was founded that the concept came into fruition (See the

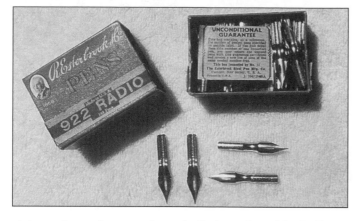

A box of popular pens (metal nibs) produced by R. Ester-brook & Company.

chart on the chronology of writing instruments). Most nibs were made of steel. Although machinery had added much to the process, many of the finer pen points had to be finished by hand.

The first steel-pen company in the United States was established in 1858 by Richard Estabrook, Jr. Working out of Camden, New Jersey, Estabrook began his business by selling English pens. He eventually managed to recruit a few English craftsmen who would assist him in setting up his own manufacturing process. Camden was eventually transformed into the "metal pen capitol", as Estabrook became the largest steel-pen producer in the world.

Writing from a steel pen can be distinguished from that of a quill, by the appearance of "nib tracks." The pressure of a downward stroke causes the metal nib to dig into the surface of the paper. These furrows fill in with extra ink and appear as if someone has outlined the stroke. Variable line quality was accomplished by the use of distinctive nibs. For example, the Estabrook sold a "Double-Line Ruling Pen" (nib) that created two thin lines simultaneously in place of a single stroke.

Dip pen writing is easily identified by the repetitive ink graduation from dark to light. This quality is often exhibited with other anomalies indicative of this style of writing. For example, ink failure, a result of the pen running out of ink, causes the appearance of separate nib marks to occur at the end of the last ink stroke. Upon exposure, the document authenticator will become increasingly familiar with such characteristics.

Both gold and glass pens were also manufactured and sold in the marketplace. Gold was a logical choice for its durability and resistance to corrosion left by acidic inks. In America these pens were popularized by watchmaker John Holland, who established a plant in Cincinnati in 1842. Glass was experimented with as early as 1850, but just the thought of material alone led to connotations of frailty. Glass pens, while often extremely attractive in design, were considered more of a novelty.

Reservoir Pens

Efficiency was the motivation behind the development of reservoir pens. The need to replenish the supply of ink in order to continue writing slowly became a burden to the user of the quill or other dip pens. While some modifications to the dip pen were helpful, the problem with ink supply was never solved until the introduction of reservoir pens.

The concept of reservoir pens, storing a supply of ink inside the penholder, was centuries old by the time of the first successful commercial introduction. In 1809, the first two English patents were granted, with a third issued a decade later to John Scheffer. Scheffer's "Penographic' Fountain Pen," which replenished ink with the use of a lever on the pen, was successful enough to entice numerous others to enter the market. By the 1870s, users had many varieties of reservoir pens to choose from.

Lewis Waterman marketed the first truly successful fountain pen in 1884. Ironically, the insurance salesman was motivated by his encounters with unsuccessful pens and was determined to improve upon previous designs. Waterman's design refined the ink flow from the barrel to the nib, resulting in sales of millions of fountain pens worldwide.

George S. Parker, an agent for the John Holland fountain pen, was so convinced he could build a better pen, that he formed his own company in 1888. His improved ink-feed designs led to numerous achievements and by the end of the 1930s he had become the premier American fountain pen manufacturer.

Unlike the graduated writing of dip pens, fountain-pen writing is more continuous in intensity. It can be recognized by the contrast between upstrokes and

Reservoir pens were a logical and popular solution to dipping pens. This advertisement highlights the Parker Duofold along with some new pencil offerings.

downstrokes and like other forms of writing will become easier to recognize through familiarity.

Fortunately for autograph enthusiasts, if you ever have a question about a previous style of reservoir pen, it won't be hard to find a fountain-pen collector to give you an answer. Pen collecting has grown significantly in its popularity over the past few decades, resulting in numerous publications. These excellent resources range from dedicated magazines to detailed collector price guides. As for the popularity of fountain pens, it often amazes many that the current annual production for such writing devices is about 11 million.

Ballpoint Pens

The concept of a reservoir pen with a rotatable ball can be traced back to the end of the 19th century. The modern type of ballpoint began in 1935 with the introduction of the Rolpen in Prague. A rotatable-ball pen followed this design in 1938, developed by Hungarians Ladislao and George Biro. Moving to Argentina to manufacture their pen, the Biro brothers quickly caught the eye of the Eberhard Faber Company who obtained rights to it.

Having seen the Biro pen in Buenos Aires in April of 1945, entrepreneur Milton Reynolds seized an opportunity to sell the pens through Gimbel's Department store in New York. Six months and 25,000 ball pens later, the Reynolds International Ball Point Pen became the first success of its kind.

Early pens had their troubles. The oily base of the ink—necessary for the smooth flow of ink, led to smudges due to slow drying. This, combined with the blotting and skipping of strokes, were key initial concerns of manufacturers.

Correcting some of the initial deficiencies, Parker introduced its first ballpoint, the now famous Jotter in 1954. Durable, both in the length of its writing and construction, the Jotter was even offered in a variety of point sizes. The "Parker Jotter Ball Pen/Liquid Lead Pencil" boxed combination was marketed after the introduction of the latter in 1955. The Liquid Lead Pencil was a ball-type pen using a liquefied form of graphite. Lacking acceptance this design was phased out during the 1960s.

Ballpoint pens use a precision-ground ball tip that is manufactured to the size of 0.7 to 1mm (0.028 - 0.04 inches) in diameter. The ball is then fitted into a socket that has several ink channels that feed the fluid from the main reservoir. The capillary action of the ink flow deposits itself onto the rotating ball.

In April of 1979, Paper Mate introduced an easily erasable ink ballpoint, the Eraser Mate pen. While it was accepted in the market, it too had initial flaws including ink buildup around the point. While the ink could be erased, some nearly always lingered and on unusual surfaces, such as a baseball, additional solvents needed to be added to remove the ink.

Many types of "roller ball" and "floating-ball" varieties have been introduced over the years with a far smoother line quality. As the bridge between ballpoint pens and porous-tip pens has diminished with each passing year, it will become increasingly difficult for autograph collectors to tell the difference between strokes generated by both technologies. Still enormously popular, about 2 billion ballpoint pens are produced annually in the United States alone.

Porous-Tip Pens

With a fibrous, or other porous material tip and a spongy material to absorb ink

porous-point pens, or "markers" as they were affectionately labeled, have competed successfully against ballpoint pens. Manufactured in the early 1940s

It wasn't long after their creation that ballpoint pens began to show up in all shapes and sizes.

The writing arsenal of current collectors often includes a variety of porous tip pens, along with the staple ballpoint pen.

and marketed as a "brush pen," these devices were initially a bit awkward in size. A decade later, using an improved design, the canister-type marker was introduced. These markers quickly gained acceptance, especially in the graphic and industrial arts.

Wanting a share of the writing market, manufacturers introduced a fiber-tip pen in 1964. Fine-pointed, easy to use, and sleek in its design, this pen became widely accepted. Using a variety of colored inks, these markers became classified into two distinct segments, "washable" (water-based) and "permanent" (petroleum-based).

With the boom in autograph sports memorabilia during the 1980s, Sanford's Sharpie ®, a fine point permanent marker, quickly became the ad hoc standard for collectors. Quick drying on a variety of surfaces, including color photographs and baseball bats, this marker was ideal for the needs of most autograph collectors.

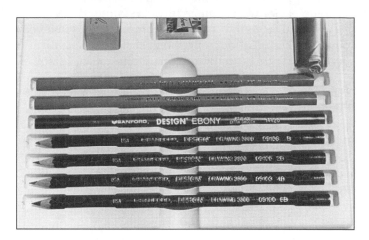

Similar to ink, pencil lead differs. Artists often uses a variety of pencils to accommodate their needs.

The Pencil

The wooden pencil has always been the keystone of writing instruments. The reasons are simple: cost, practicality and portability, ease of use, flexibility and self-containment. Marks are produced by means of abrasion. In ancient times, Romans lined their scrolls with a pencillus—hence the name, as did scribes. During the Renaissance artists used a rod of lead or lead alloy, as well as a silver point tool. In 1564 however, the birth of the true "lead" pencil came when a storm uprooted an oak tree in the town of Borrowdale, Cumberland, England. Inside the tree a large deposit of pure graphite was discovered, giving birth to the Borrowdale mine. Originally chunks of the graphite were used as "marking stones", but later sticks were cut and wrapped with string for both protection from breakage and for cleanliness while in use.

When the supply at Borrowdale began running low, attempts at binding graphite dust with various adhesives began to be undertaken. Finally a sufficient recipe was found for the newly formed sticks in 1662 in Nuremberg, Germany. Later, Frenchman Nicolas Jacques Conte and Viennese Joseph Hardtmuth, separately experimented with mixing graphite with clay and water. Hardtmuth even discovered that by varying the amount of clay, he could also regulate the hardness of the lead.

The first pencil dynasty was formed in 1761 in Stein, Germany by Kaspar Faber. He passed on the business to Anton Wilhelm (A. W. Faber Co.), who passed it to Georg Leonhard Faber. Georg then passed it to Johann Lothar von Faber, who would dynamically change the direction of the corporation by modernizing its facilities, expanding both products and production sites while acquiring key raw material sources. While the company eventually passed out of family control, it left behind a legacy that was enhanced even greater by John Eberhard Faber — Johann Lothar von Faber's younger brother who had immigrated to America and set up his own lead-pencil business in 1861. This first American large-scale pencil manufacturing business supplied the domestic market that had up to that point turned to John's brother's European business or to William Monroe of Massachusetts. The Eberhard Faber Pencil Company was finally incorporated in 1898 and would continue to embellish its legacy during the next century.

While the basic pencil-making process has changed little over the years, modifications to ingredients and design have. Drawing pencils have been modified with both "H" (hard) and "B" (soft) grades made available to artists. A wider range of writing pencils has also been marketed. Dominated for years by the no. 2 soft writing pencil, common users now had options for softer and harder leads. Application and occupation specific pencils were also marketed.

Other modifications that authenticators of pencil samples should acquaint themselves with include: indelible pencils (ink pencils) patented in 1866 (methyl-violet, graphite and binder), these created an ink-like line; copying pencils (which contained pigment and were first made in 1857) and paper-wrapped pencils (patented in 1895).

A Writing Instrument Chronology

1748	In France, steel nibs are first made by Johann Jansen.
1761	In Stein, Germany, Kaspar Faber founds pencil-making dynasty.
1780s	Pencils become common as a working writing instrument, but are still not acceptable for correspondence or legal documents.
c.1800-1805	Homemade steel pens are made and sold in London.
1809	A patent for a "Metallic writing pen" is issued in the U.S. to Peregrine Williamson. The first two English patents for reservoir pens are issued.
1818	Quill nibs are dipped in nitromuriate of gold by Charles Watt to make them more durable.
1819	The English Penograph reservoir pen is patented.
1820	The mass production of steel slip pens is done by Joseph Gillott in England. The modern version of the metal nib is invented.
1828	The manufacture of nibs with a central slit and an ink-hole is accomplished through improved manufacturing.
1830	A D. Hyde of Reading. PA receives the first American patent for a fountain pen.
1851	Through the combination of gold and an alloy called irium pen points are made more durable.
1857	"Copying" pencils are first manufactured.
1858	Richard Estabrook establishes the first steel-pen company in the U.S. The prototype of what would be the "penny pencil" is patented by Hyman L. Lipman.
1861	John Eberhard Faber establishes first large-scale manufacturing facility in the U.S. to make pencils. Richard Estabrook begins manufacturing his own nibs.
1866	"Indelible" pencils are patented.
1870s	Stylographic pen, an "ink pencil" patented in 1849, enjoys wide-spread popularity. Fountain pens are also widely publicized.
1884	Lewis Edson Waterman invents the fountain pen.
1888	A ballpoint pen patent was issued to John Loud, who can not produce the pen commercially due to the lack of ink development. George S. Parker establishes his fountain-pen company.
1895	A.W. Askew and G.A. Werner produce and sell a ballpoint pen. Blaisdell invents paper-wrapped pencils.
1903	A pump-type filler is invented by L.E. Waterman.
1908	The fountain pen is enhanced through a lever-fill principle developed by W.A. Sheaffer.
1913	The W.A. Sheaffer Pen Company is established.
1916	Another ballpoint pen is patented, this time by V.V. Riesbery, but still can not be sold commercially due to ink problems.
1922	Fountain pens are enhanced when the Sheaffer Pen Co. introduces a non-sediment ink.
1943	Ladislas Biro manufactures and sells a ballpoint pen he has invented. The pen, sold in South America, eventually migrates to the United States. Unfortunately, ink will continue to limit the success of the ballpoint pen for the next six years until a chemist, Fran Seec, invents a practical ink for the device.
1945	The ballpoint pen, adopted the year before by the U.S. Army, is sold and marketed in New York City.
1950	The Paper Mate retractable ballpoint pen is introduced by Patrick J. Frawley.
1951	Felt-tip markers are introduced.
1954	The Jotter, by Parker, is introduced as the company's first ballpoint pen.
1955	The Liquid Lead Pencil, a ballpoint with erasable graphite ink, is introduced by Parker.
c.1964	The porous tip pen is introduced and gains considerable acceptance. It will continue to be refined over the years that follow.
1968	The rolling ball marker is introduced in the U.S. by Uni-Pen and Pentel.
1969	Paul Fisher develops the "Space Pen" for the American Space Program.
1970s	The advent of erasable inks.
1975	ATF begins ink tagging program which leads to nemerous court convictions.
1979	Paper Mate markets Eraser Mate pen.

Pencil-related Developments	
1770	Solidified vegetable gum (caouthouc) used to remove pencil mistakes.
1822	Patent for "ever-pointed" pencil—mechanical pencil.
1839	Term "rubber" applied to above following discovery of vulcanizing process.
1858	Patent for placing a (India) rubber eraser at the end of a pencil.
1869	Patent for crank-style sharpener using a wheel and belt mechanism.

Collectors and authenticators should remember that during the days of our founding fathers, pencils were not used for legal documents or other permanent records. Additionally, etiquette precluded a pencil's use for correspondence.

Inks

As an advanced autograph collector you should have a solid understanding of inks and what they can reveal to the authenticator. Many documents have been easily unmasked as forgeries through the analysis of ink. This is because of two primary factors: first, the ink is commonly overlooked by the document forger and second, trace elements have now been added to inks for decades. The markers added to inks allow for precise dating. At the forensic level, the Bureau of Alcohol, Tobacco and Firearms (Department of the Treasury) has been responsible for many of the advances in ink analysis. Although it may take some time, I am certain that many of the techniques employed by the ATF will economically trickle down into the autograph market. When it does, the market is going to be able to identify forged documents faster, and with a greater degree of accuracy than ever before.

Carbon-based Inks

While time has obscured much about the origins of writing fluids, historians have been able to trace some roots as far back as the third millennium B.C. The Egyptians were using lampblack combined with gum or glue, while in China pine soot was combined with gum and powdered jade.

Today such mixtures are commonly termed India or Indian ink. Ironically, although these mixtures at first seem primitive, the carbon base employed is extremely stable and thus many early examples exhibit little degradation. Although fluid carbon-based inks are impervious to many elements that can typically destroy documents, such was not the case for the Chinese who dried and pressed their ink into sticks which when used deposited on the surface of the writing material only. Because the ink was not absorbed into the writing material, it could easily be removed by erasure, washing or abusive handling.

Iron-Gall Inks

A solution was needed to solve the abrasion problem associated with carbon and gum ink. A fluid mixture of iron and tannin may have existed as early as the second century, although the mention of such a recipe would not find its way into writings until the eleventh century.

Later it would be the female gall wasp that would contribute her small nut-like excrescencies to the recipe. Her eggs, deposited on certain species of oak, were referred to as galls, gall nuts, oak galls and even oak apples. Tannic and gallic acid was extracted from the galls by soaking them in water. An iron salt solution (hydrated ferrous sulfate) and gum arabic were then added to the clear gall extract to produce a purplish-black compound that gets darker with age. These ingredients formed the base for most of the ink recipes of the day. Other ingredients could also be added, such as sugar candy to make the ink glossy, indigo for color and even cloves to prevent molding.

Later Ink Development

As still nibs began to replace quill pens, special inks had to be formulated to replace iron-gall ink, which could no longer be used because of its corrosive properties. Dyes were added to iron-gall inks to reduce corrosive properties and prolong the life of the steel pen. Other solutions to the iron-gall problem included potassium chromate logwood ink, a synthetic indigo ink (1861), nigrosine ink (marketed first in 1867), aniline dye inks and vanadium ink.

As the fountain pen replaced the steel pen, new inks again had to be formulated, the most popular being Sheaffer's Skrip. There are two basic types of ink for this reservoir writing instrument, an iron-gallotannate solution or an aqueous type of synthetic dye. The iron-gallotannate recipe was similar to that of the past and included the combination of iron salts combined with gallotannic acid. This solution, when applied to paper, would appear colorless at first, then it would darken through oxidation. In contrast, modern inks for fountain pens now include a synthetic blue dye that first appears blue, then oxidizes to black—hence the term blue-black fountain pen ink. These stable blue-black inks absorb into the paper fibers and are insoluble in water. Synthetic dye solutions became popular with users because of the bright colors they produced. Since synthetic inks fade and are soluble in water, pigmented dyes have been added which add greater permanence to the ink.

John Loud invented and received a patent for what he deemed a ballpoint pen in 1888, but at the time there was little public interest. In fact, seventeen years later the patent reentered public domain. Then in 1895, A. Werner and A.W. Askew patented, produced and even sold a ballpoint commercially. The ink for their version was made from lampblack and castor oil. Numerous other attempts followed but all failed to garner much interest.

But in 1939, Ladislas Biro, and his brother George, succeeded in producing a working version of the ballpoint that utilized a unique ink-feed system. Instead of using ordinary ink, the pen used a gelatinous dye that had an oil base. As WWII was winding down, the U.S. Air Force exhibited a keen interest in the pen and contacted the three largest U.S. pen manufacturers—Parker, Eversharp and Sheaffer. Ironically, Eberhard Faber, the premier pencil manufacturer had rights to the pen. Eventually

Eversharp won out and began modifying the design for production. As luck would have it, a one Milton Reynolds saw an opportunity and took it.

The first pens produced suffered from numerous imperfections, one of which was ink drying speed. This problem was solved by the end of the decade with a new ink recipe that was nearly instant drying and nontransferable. This recipe, purchased by the Frawley Pen Company (Gillette Co.), was used in the successful introduction of the Paper Mate ball pen.

Solvents consisting of synthetic dyes make up ballpoint pen inks. This very viscous ink also includes other ingredients known only to the manufacturer. Often these secret components are acidic materials—used as a lubricant, resins—for cost and viscosity adjustments, and surface active agents—to control the inks wetness. Other additives may include material to prolong pen use or additional solvents.

Oil-based solvents common in ballpoint pens prior to 1950 include mineral oil, linseed oil, glycerin monoricinoleate, methyl and ethyl esters of recinoleic acid, along with many others. The dyes used were basic for colored inks, while black ink used nigrosine. On occasion carbon or graphite was added for permanence.

Those ballpoint pens made after 1950 commonly use ethylene glycol as a solvent for the dyes. The modern ballpoint pens contain chelated metalized dyes, the most popular of which are blue based (copper phthalocyanine). The newer dyes are far more soluble and less sensitive to light.

One of the most popular pens of the 1960s was the fiber tip pen, introduced in 1963 by Pentel. These porous tip markers competed aggressively against other writing instruments. The pen initially was marketed as an industrial marking device that could write on multiple surface by means of a wick-type felt tip. The inks used in these pens are typically water or xylene-based. The ink also contains dyes and additives similar to fluid inks, like those used in fountain pens. The first significant problem encountered by these pens was the tip drying out if the cap was left off. Numerous formulations were tested before it was

Parker's "Super chrome" blue-black ink. Collectors often don't realize that even today unopened bottles of this ink can be found in many antique stores.

A box and full container of Waterman's popular "Blue Black" permanent ink.

An Early Ink Recipe

Take a half pound of gall, a quarter pound of copperas, a quarter pound of gum Arabic, one half ounce of alum, and half an ounce ordinary salt. Grind these ingredients to a fine powder. Put it into a stoneware jar, and pour a pint (or as much as necessary to cover the powder) of the best cider vinegar over it. Close it tightly, and let it sit for a few days. Then add three pints of rainwater, and let it sit for several days more in a warm place. If it is winter, set it on a stove; in the summer, simply place in the sun. Shake it well several times each day. When it is needed or when it is dark enough, it may be poured into other vessels. Add some more gum to it, as much as you think needed, and do as before, then you will have a good ink.

For red ink, take three-pints of sour beer, which works better than vinegar, and add four ounces finely ground Guinea redwood; boil them together for one hour, then add four ounces alum. Simmer all three together gently for half an hour. Filter this through a cloth, put in a bottle, stopper it tightly and put it away for later use.

---

determined that formamide, glycol, or a combination of both, could enhance the moisture of the tip. Permanent or durable markers use xylene-based inks, rather than water.

Paul Fisher developed the pressurized cartridge that used nitrogen to move the very thick ink. When the ink is applied to a surface it liquefies into a smooth formula. The Anti-Gravity Pen, patented in 1965, was developed by Fisher for NASA so that the astronauts would have a pen that would continue to work well while writing upside down or in pressurized capsule flying conditions where there is no gravity.

Rolling ball markers, which used water based ink with organic liquids, were first produced in the late 1950s, but lacked the popularity to sustain themselves in the market. The strokes left by these devices resembled that of a fountain pen. Although people found them very easy to use, the ink was used up far faster than that of a ballpoint pen.

Inks for special applications were also becoming increasingly popular. These included formulas for use with rubber stamps and recipes for marking cloth (Indelible inks). Copying inks—used for making "letter press copies", synthetic dye inks—also used for letter press, packers' inks—used for crates and cartons, printing inks and even sympathetic ink—used for invisible writing were just some of the new challenging applications for ink manufacturers.

Understanding How Ink is Manufactured

Ink making as a trade can be dated back to the sixteenth century. Local shops made ink in quantity and bottled it for sale. These shops were gradually replaced by large ink manufacturing firms such as Carter's (Established 1858). Although carbon and iron-gall inks dominated other available inks it is worth noting that animal and mineral substances were employed as well as plant materials in ink making.

Understanding how ink is manufactured is very important to both the autograph authenticator and the forensic scientist. Formulas are developed by ink scientists who combine ingredients into a substance specific for a particular ink application. The percentages of each element are accurately determined to produce a standard ink formulation.*

These standard ink formulations are only altered for product and performance adjustments. Product adjustments include material availability, part or design alterations. Performance adjustments include flow properties, drying times and climate variations.

Ink manufacturers have faced numerous challenges forcing the alteration of many standard ink formulas. The availability and quality of dye/raw materials is one common example. In order to lower costs and improve quality, synthetics have now replaced most raw materials. Like all manufacturers, when raw materials arrive at an ink company they are tested. These tests include content and absorption measurements, parametric testing, such as pH tests and TLC (Thin-Layer Chromatography) examination. Since many writing instruments are shipped all over the world, climate adjustments, in the form of minor viscosity variations, are all concerns of quality control engineers.

Ink manufacturers are also concerned about the stability of the fluid in bulk state, while it is housed in a cartridge and finally its arrival on paper. Since products in their finished state may not be purchased right away, shelf life—or the amount of time before the ink dries out is also of paramount importance to a writing device manufacturer.

As an authenticator most of your concerns begin when the ink hits the paper. Its deterioration characteristics include ink composition, and its reaction to paper surface chemistry, the type of writing device used and the ambient conditions facing the document.

Dyes, which are included in inks have characteristics. One may be sublimation, or the transformation of a substance from a solid state directly to a vapor phase—which on a cooler surface can return again to a solid. Most of us remember the phenomena from high school chemistry when we used iodine for such an experiment. Sublimation has caused some inks to fade forever from the surface of a document. To reduce sublimation many manufacturers have added non-fading components such as carbon or nigrosine to their ink formulas.

Basic ballpoint ink manufacture includes two primary materials, coloring agents and solvents (carriers). Other ingredients include acidic materials, resinous materials, corrosion control elements and surface active agents. Solvents are heated before the introduction of the dye or coloring agents. Ballpoint ink is very thick and once filtered can be adjusted to the proper viscosity. The mixture is then strained and filtered again before cooling. Other elements can be added during the cooling process, with agitation provided if necessary. Finished products are also subjected to a variety of tests depending upon the manufacturer. These tests may include pH, viscosity and even a thin layer chromotogram. The latter will provide a visual representation of the proportions of the dyes used.

The manufacture of fluid inks for porous tip markers is far less complicated than ink manufacture for ballpoint pens. The ink is freer flowing and often less concentrated. The process for water-based inks is simple. We begin with water placed in a container that may be heated. Solvents and the various surfactants are added, followed by corrosion inhibitors and plasticizers. Other ingredients are also added, depending upon the ink's application, then finally the dyes. The liquid is then mixed, cooled and filtered.

The type of writing instrument being produced will determine the quality and quantity of ink to be manufactured. Raw materials vary depending upon the grades of ink, with the premium brands requiring significantly larger amounts of dyes. Typically a larger

ink manufacturer will also make pen parts, such as fountain pen cartridges.

Ink manufacturers produce batches of ink based on their standard ink formulas and the performance needs of the client. The client will also determine quantity of ink produced. Over-produced batches may be matched by components and used with other batches or stored and reformulated.

Just a reminder to you autograph authenticators: Oil-based (oleic acid) ballpoint inks were produced prior to 1951, after which glycol (with resins)-based recipes were used. Therefore, if a questioned document is dated 1946, but was written with a glycol (with resins) based ink, one could safely say that they are dealing with a post-dated document.

Permanent markers are solvent based (such as Xylene) and can be fine or broad tipped. Felt or fiber-tipped pens, fountain pens and rolling markers are water or glycol based. The two most common components found in modern ballpoint ink are Hexylene Glycol and A-1-3 Resin Solution. The most common in element in a fountain pen ink is water, which can vary from about 94 % to as high as 98%.

Comprehensive Standard Ink Libraries are now used to determine manufacturer, formula and the first date that a particular ink could have been used for writing purposes. Micro quantities of ink can be removed from a questioned document and then tested using a variety of techniques to match questioned and known samples. The testing techniques involve the ingredients in the ink and that is why this information becomes important to the advanced autograph collector. These tests have led to many convictions in forgery cases.

* Knowing this the ATF could develop a program of ink tagging that could determine the exact year of a specific ink since 1975.

Papermaking

If you're going to be a serious autograph collector you must acquaint yourself with the art of papermaking. Understanding the evolution of paper will help you in the authentication of many documents, as many of the finest forgeries have been unmasked as result of dating paper. Similar to understanding the evolution of ink, writing devices and print, your knowledge of paper will play an important role in your development as an autograph collector.

Writing Substances

Without getting into a myriad of details surrounding mans earliest developments, understanding that writing was pivotal in his evolution will help put paper into its proper perspective. From

An outstanding example of an early papermaking machine.

the ancient hieroglyphics on the walls of the Altamira caverns to the invention of the camel hair brush in 250 B.C. man experimented with a variety of writing devices and materials. It was the brush however that really altered the writing of Chinese characters, enhanced interest in fluid pigment development and sparked the cultivation of wove cloth as a new writing surface.

The birth of paper is attributed to T'sai Lun of the Chinese Empire in AD 105. Vegetable fiber was softened in liquid then formed on flat porous molds. These thin sheets, formed by fibers intermixing with water, were lifted from the liquid by the use of fine screens that allowed the water to drain away from the fiber that when dried became paper. This simple formation technique would last for hundreds of years.

Other substances, such as papyrus, tapas (mulberry), rice paper (papyrifera tree), along with genuine parchment and vellum were being experimented with, but due to their manufacture are not considered true paper. Prior to these substances man had used stone, bricks, metals (brass, copper, bronze, lead), wood, tree leaves, and even tree barks to convey his ideas.

Papyrus, of the genus Cyperus, was developed by the Egyptians and replaced many materials such as soapstone. Native to the marshy shores of the Middle East and Persian Gulf, papyrus was formed with thin crisscrossed strips that were formed into sheets. Two layers of the sheets were then pounded together and bound using the plant's own adhesives and applied pressure. If a roll or scroll of papyrus was needed, individual sheets would be glued together. Under magnification papyrus strands can be seen in non-symmetrical patterns and at various sizes.

The problem with papyrus was that it was brittle and lacked the flexibility needed for the applications of the times. A new material, made from animal hide, was far more durable and from it a codex, or book, could be formed. Realizing that this new form essentially antiquated the troublesome need winding or rewinding a scroll, it gradually displaced papyrus between the first and fourth centuries AD. The new material was called parchment.

Parchment & Vellum

The advent of parchment, split skin of a sheep, dates back to about 1500 BC, and was developed to compete with papyrus. Vellum, primarily calfskin, differed from parchment as the entire skin was used in the manufacturing process. Unlike leather, neither material is tanned. While parchment in book form essentially halted around 1500, its durability extended its use into the 19th century.

To prepare parchment, the skin of the animal is washed and steeped in lime to remove hair. Then,

using a convex blade, it is scrapped and washed again. The skin is then stretched over a frame, scrapped again and dusted with chalk. The skin is then rubbed with powdered pumice. You can distinguish the outer side of parchment from the flesh side by a rougher surface texture, a faint yellowing, and the appearance of hair follicles.

For calligraphers, parchment was the ideal surface. Patent officers, in both Great Britain and in the United States, also relied on the material. While Thomas Jefferson's rough draft was "laid" all-rag paper, the officially signed Declaration of Independence was parchment. Today the term "vellum" refers to any fine parchment made from young animal skin, although technically it applies only to calfskin.

Molds

The Use of Early Hand-Molds

The greatest challenge faced by early papermakers was creating a device cable of picking up the fine fibers from the surface of the water. The invention had to allow for the drainage or removal of the water while maintaining a level of fiber uniformity. The tool developed was known as a papermaking mold. Studying these molds helps us piece together the long history of papermaking. Not unlike the manufacture of other types of materials, papermaking evolved and with it, many varieties of molds were created and improved.

The "Wove" Mold

Few artifacts from the first half-century of papermaking in the Far East have survived, thus much speculation still surrounds the process. Most speculate that a coarsely wove cloth, held in place by a

An actual "wove mold" used for making paper by hand.

bamboo frame was either dipped into a vat, or had the fibrous mixture poured upon it. The mold was then placed in the sun for drying. Once the paper had dried it was removed easily from the mold. Both the vertical (warp) and horizontal (woof) fibers of the mold would have left impressions on the paper similar to modern watermarks.

Wove molds evolved, and eventually fabric gave way to rhea (Chinese grass) fastened to four bamboo bars. The lack of supports or ribs underneath the wove rhea limited the size of the paper produced.

The "Laid" Mold

While it is unclear as to when the "laid" mold came into existence, most believe it was not long after the wove mold. The benefit of the laid mold was that the wet sheet of paper could be removed while still moist. This was due to the use of a mold covering, which was placed on the mold frame. Both the frame and flexible cover was dipped into the fiber vat, then removed. The material was lifted free from the mold-frame, with the wet layer of paper deposited flat upon another sheet. The cover was then rolled up from the top edge to the bottom, leaving only the moist sheet behind.

The convenient covering was made of thin strips of rounded bamboo set side by side, then stitched or laced together at intervals with a variety of material from silk to horse hair. Paper made by this method is easily identifiable by the mark left in the paper. "Laid-lines" are left by the horizontal bamboo strips and "chain-lines" are left by the vertical stitching material. While paper can be identified by counting both the "laid-lines" per inch and measuring the intervals between chain-lines, much variation existed in both the ancient bamboo and later metal-wire molds.

Metal would eventually replace earlier materials. This process is believed to have taken place in Europe not long after the 12th century. Naturally the evolution of molds also varied by country once this form of papermaking was introduced. If you collect autographs and manuscripts originating from a specific country such as Korea, Japan, or India, you should reference resources that cover papermaking in these countries.

European Molds

The Spanish first used bamboo molds in Europe during the 12th century. Since bamboo was not a commodity in Europe, metal wires were eventually substituted in laid molds. Another change was the adoption of a rigid mold over the Oriental flexible mold. This change was necessitated by the Europeans preference for rag fibers. The Europeans also modified the process of keeping the newly formed paper within bounds by adding a "deckle" or "fence." This deckle was joined permanently at the corners and placed on the mold prior to forming then removed prior to the couching of the paper. Therefore, the deckle also was critical to determining the size of the paper. Similar to their Orient predecessors, the Europeans had little consistency to the number of laid-lines to the inch or uniformity of chain lines.

It is believed that John Tate founded the first paper mill in Hertford at the end of the 15th century. The lack of consistency of lines found in old papers, makes it nearly impossible to determine the time and place of origin. Therefore, authenticators are forced to utilize other characteristics to date paper.

One noted characteristic of European paper made prior to about 1800, was the heavier deposits of pulp along each side of every chain-line in the paper. The darker streaks are immediately noticeable when examining samples from this era. The elimination of these dark streaks was done by the addition of wires in fashion to reduce suction as the mold was lifted from the vat. This type of paper is correctly referred to as

An actual "laid mold" used for making paper by hand.

Housing occupied by the Pietists of Germany and located in Ephrata, Pennsylvania. Nearby these building was one of America's first paper mills.

"antique laid", although as years passed the term "medieval laid" has become synonymous.

Claim for the origination of the "wove" mold-covering was first attributed to John Baskerville the famed printer of Birmingham, then later to the Balston Paper Mill in Maidstone, Kent. The latter manufacturing genuine "wove" paper for a book in 1759. In this book, the mill's distinct watermark of "W" can be found. Baskerville had been seeking a smoother paper for his book printing. It is believed he suggested the modifications to the wove covering. A fine non-rusting brass screen was created on a loom and when used left an indistinct impression similar to fabric. Baskerville made his mark in the printing industry with the release of "Virgil" in 1757, the first European book to utilize "wove" paper—a paper that would be popular for the next three decades.

These small changes and distinctions have aided authenticators in determining the approximate date, country of manufacture and process in which a paper sample was created. With over 200 sizes of handmade European paper identified, size in some cases can be helpful, but generally not a key factor in authentication. Often authenticators, while examining a piece of European wove paper, have the good fortune of discovering a year watermarked in the sample. But if such a situation isn't the case distinguishing paper from one century to the next or from one country to the next could provide a significant challenge to the authenticator.

American Molds

In the late 17th century, the American colonies were introduced to papermaking. Because there were no wire workers in this country, molds had to be imported from Europe. It was Isaac Langle, of Germantown, Pennsylvania, who became America's first mold-maker. Langle would cater to the tremendous need of Pennsylvania papermakers, specifically the early needs of the Ephrata mill in Lancaster County (c.1740). Langle was followed later by Nathan Sellers, an artisan of paper molds, around 1770. It was Sellers who was supplying molds for the Wilcox mill of Pennsylvania—a premier supplier to the government.

Characteristics of Early Paper

- Production demand and expense limited paper sizes in Europe during the 15th and 16th century.
- With the exception of the deckle edges, paper was seldom cut.
- All old paper, and even modern handmade paper, can vary considerably in thickness and finish.
- The absence of chemicals and modern day processes prevented older paper from having a uniform tone.
- Prior to fabric bleaching, not used until the late 18th century, paper assumed the tone of the rags used in its manufacture.
- Many samples of early American-made paper appear muddy due to the lack of water clarification.
- The tints in paper can help identify origin, as early English paper (until late 17th century) often appeared gray, while in France a blueing agent was used to counter discoloration.
- It is not uncommon to find translucent spots, made by water droplets, in early paper samples. This is caused through mishandling by workers, and as such, these spots often occur near edges and in corners. Other mishandling characteristics include blurred chain-lines, foreign artifacts such as hair, insects, etc. and discoloration.
- While size could vary, early European paper typically falls below 15" x 20".

Watermarks

Early Watermarks

Thousands of watermarks have graced paper since the 13th century, with little attention paid to this ancient craft until some five hundred years later. During the 19th century, the lore of watermarks attracted scholars from all over Europe. As antiquaries rushed to be the first to document the history of watermarks in their country, many speculated as to the theory of their inception and the need for these unique marks.

The use of watermarks has been attributed to everything from papermaker trademarks to religious propaganda, and even a correlation with paper mold size. For many their meaning will have gone to the grave with their originator. While other scholars simply believe their use was as an extension of the art of papermaking and an additional form of creativity. Whatever the case, this fascination with watermarks has led to extensive research and documentation. Volumes of works have been written about watermarks, leaving some exceptional resource tools for authenticators.

As the first paper molds were constructed of bamboo, a material that did not lend itself to the unique process of watermarking, ancient Oriental papers contained no watermarks. In fact, it wasn't until the 13th century that the first use of watermarks occurred in Italy and blossomed so fast that by the time printing was introduced into Europe (c.1450) the art was now centuries old. Examination of a 15th century work, quickly concludes that it is not unusual for a single book to contain over a dozen different watermarks.

Wires fastened to the "laid" surface of a mold originally created watermarks. These wires, often of simple design, formed indentations in the paper. As all European paper prior to the 18th century was made on "laid" molds, the design of the watermark would appear with those left by "laid" and "chain" wires. The term "watermark" is as deceiving as speculation regarding the use of these designs, as water in and of itself is not responsible for the design.

While watermarks can be helpful to the authenticator in determining origin, they have serious pitfalls. One issue precluding exact dating and sourcing is that not all watermarks include dates. Dates are often only an indication of when paper was printed and not when it was used or sold. Many papermakers didn't bother with changing the date on molds, and they were often sold to other papermakers. Additionally, forgers often duplicated other papermakers' watermarks.

Scholars often group early watermarks by their subject or design. The art of watermarks evolved from simple symbols (From origin to nearly the end of the 13th century) to human figures, then onto vegetation

---

Common Early European Watermark Designs

- Foolscap
- Britannia
- Pots
- Jugs
- Arms
- Hands
- Glove (often with initials of papermaker)
- Post-horn

---

and animals (c. 1300). Knowing when a certain design was introduced can be extremely helpful to the authenticator. For example, the earliest watermark of Jesus Christ appeared as a portrait at the end of the 14th century (France). To find the origin of a specific design you may want to consult your library or a specific historical society, the latter of which can often contain many early samples of regional paper.

Foreign watermarks were introduced into American papermaking by skilled artisans who had migrated to the New World and by the use of foreign molds. Watermarks flourished in America during our first fifty years of papermaking, but by the middle of the 18th century, our views changed and less interest was paid to this art.

Later Watermarks

One need only look as far as the new changes in American currency to understand the evolution and application for watermarks. The 19th and 20th century saw advancements in the watermark manufacturing process and improved imagery. From colored watermarks, to shaded (light and shade) images watermarks took on an entirely different look.

Machine-made paper led to the construction of a "dandy-roll." This large cylinder supports a wire gauze, which in turn supports the water-marking material. The paper stock passes below this water marking roll leaving either a laid or wove impression. The roll on

---

Common Early American Watermark Designs (1690-1835)

- Indians
- Eagles
- Ships
- Crossed Arrows
- Horse Head & Plow
- Cherry Leaf
- A Deer
- Flowers
- Clover
- The U.S. Capitol
- A Bust of George Washington
- The Arms of Virginia
- Other State Arms (numerous)
- Numerous variations of initials, dates, companies, etc.

Note:
- Printed copies of the Declaration of Independence are watermarked "J. Honig & Zoonen", prominent Holland papermakers.
- George Washington, who was interested in the papermaking process, used writing and ledger paper bearing the watermark of a plow, upon which was seated the figure of Liberty. This was framed with a double circle bearing the president's name and surmounted by an eagle.

which the image is wired must be remade for each pattern, thus adding an additional cost to the process.

The process of documenting modern watermarks can be an arduous, but indeed valuable task. Fortunately for collectors and authenticators many valuable resources on this topic already exist and for your convenience will be listed in the bibliography portion of this book.

Just how valuable can watermarks be to authenticators, let me offer the 1918 legal case of a contested will of a Mr. Edward B. Jennings, involving a nice round sum of $6,000,000. In this case a will offered by a Mr. Edward C. Koester in which he claims to be the sole heir of the fortune is unmasked as a forger by the watermark in the paper. It was proven that the watermark in the paper was not produced until two years after the forged will was dated.

Early American Paper Mills

- Rittenhouse Mill, Germantown, Pennsylvania (1690) Watermark examples include: "Company", "WR/clover, shield, crown w/ "Pensilvania"

- William De Wees Mill, Germantown, Pennsylvania (1710) Watermark examples include: did not use watermarks

- Thomas Wilcox Mill, Delaware County, Pennsylvania (1729) Watermark examples include: "TMW w/dove & olive branch", "ivy leaf"

- Pietists of Germany, Ephrata, Pennsylvania (1736) Watermark examples include: "(large) 4 w/"RF", "FB", "Cross design w/Efrata"

The Evolution of Papermaking

Early Materials

Both American and European papermakers utilized linen and cotton rags until nearly the end of the eighteenth century. The cellulose content of these materials, in particular cotton, was key to the lasting and durable quality of early paper. Cellulose is the chief substance in the cell walls of plants, used in making paper, textiles, etc. Increased paper consumption during the first half of the eighteenth century created a problem for papermakers because they could not procure a sufficient number of rags to meet the demand. The demand for rags was so critical that everything from, posters, newspaper advertisements and even watermarks routinely called out to the population with cries to "Save Your Rags."

When it became clear that the supply for linen would not meet the demand of papermakers, the search for new fibers to replace the rags began. Supply, cost and ease of use became primary factors, with quality taking a backseat to quantity. The first and logical place to begin the quest for a new paper alternative fiber began with those substances high in cellulose content, hemp, jute, etc. The use of wood as an alternative was first and formally suggested by Rene Antoine Ferchault de Reaumur of France in 1719. The

impetus for Reaumur's suggestion was drawn from observations he made of wasps building a nest. Other scholars and scientists, not yet sold on all the benefits of wood, also continued experimentation with alternative materials. These materials ranged from asbestos to swamp moss. Of paramount importance at this time was the research of Jacob Christian Schaffer of Bavaria, who led experiments into a variety of paper making alternatives. His research, often referenced by his predecessors, was both inspirational and integral to the developments in papermaking in the years that followed.

It would be Matthais Koops of Great Britain, however, who would take the first step in using various vegetable fibers in paper making at a large commercial scale. It was his mill, in operation only from 1801-1804, that first offered Europeans a viable alternative to linen and cotton rags.

Automating the Papermaking Process

All papermaking was essentially made from hand until the beginning of the 19th century when the advent of the paper machine slowly became a viable alternative. It would be the Frenchman Nicholas-Louis

Robert, working in the mill of Francois Didot, who would create the first papermaking machine. Inspired ironically by the complaints of co-workers, rather than the frustration of developing a cheaper and more abundant paper, Roberts labored through various versions of his machine until he finally developed a sound design and applied for a patent in 1798 (granted 1799).

Roberts machine employed all the elements of traditional papermaking. The added advantage was that his paper was not limited to the size of a mold, but rather had endless length limited only by the width of his machine. As printing had always developed with papermaking, this new paper-machine with its continuous web of paper was a stimulus for the development of the rotary press. By 1799, the Fourdrinier brothers of England had transformed the

principles of Robert's machine. Similar to Robert's their design was exploited by others who would eventually build their own variations. Ironically, for all the hard work by numerous individuals, few found significant financial reward.

In England (1809) at the mill of John Dickinson, of Dickinson paper fame, another type of machine, the cylinder was being utilized and perfected. His invention, only one of many of his patents pertaining to paper, fed a continuous thread of cotton, flax, silk or alternative materials into the endless web of paper. The paper Dickinson manufactured caught the eye of the philatelic community who used it for envelopes and even stamps. Dickinson prospered from his work and eventually retired in 1859.

America's first efforts at machine papermaking began with a cylinder-like machine operated in 1817 by

Key Dates Useful For American Paper Authentication

Date	Event
1638	In Cambridge, Massachusetts the first printing press is established.
1690	William Rittenhouse establishes first paper mill in America near Germantown, Pennsylvania.
1690	First paper money used in British American colonies.
1704	The earliest permanent newspaper in America is established in Boston, the *Boston News Letter*.
1718	First colored printing in America (red & black).
1795	Wove paper appears for the first time in an American book.
1797	Embossed paper is first patented, but will not become common until the 19th century.
1817	First paper-machine in use at the mill of Thomas Gilpin.
1821	Gilpin prints first important book on machine-made paper.
1830	Perceived to be the first year that wood-pulp paper was used in printing a newspaper.
1840s	Paper mill embossments become common to the end of the century.
1849	The earliest known American photograph on paper.
1851	First useful chemical wood fiber for paper.
1852	Earliest coating of paper on one side.
1860	First general use of American Christmas Cards.
1875	Earliest coating of paper on both sides.
1880	First half-tone used in a New York newspaper.
1881	First commercially available coated paper.
1887	Monotype invented in America.
1903	First use of corrugated fiber containers.
1905	Gassine paper introduced in the United States.
1906	First paper milk bottles made in San Francisco, CA.
1909	First craft (sulfate pulping process) paper manufactured in America.
1910s	During this decade paper begins to be used as a food wrapper.
1929	Establishment of The Institute of Paper Chemistry
Mid-1940s	Plastic begins to challenge papers market position.
1957	First patent describing confocal microscopy was filed by Marvin Minsky. Eventually this process will be used in the three-dimensional evaluation of paper surfaces.
1960s	Paper attacks the textile markets with "disposable" concept. Market consolidation through mergers and acquisitions redirects production and applications
1970s	Production upgrades and expansions now allow paper production to surpass the 5000 feet per minute threshold for some grades.

Key Early Dates Useful For European Paper Authentication	
Date	**Event**
BC 250	Camel's hair brush invented
AD 400	Invention of true ink from lamp-back.
770	Earliest instance of text printed upon paper.
868	The Diamond Sutra becomes the earliest printed book.
1041-9	Chinese invention of movable type.
1109	Oldest European manuscript on paper.
1282	Watermarks used in Europe for the first time.
1309	First use of paper in England.
1450-5	The Gutenberg bible is produced igniting European printing.
1450	The use of bookplates is noted.
1486	First English book printed on paper.

Thomas Gilpin at a mill along the Brandywine Creek just a few miles from Wilmington, Delaware. Gilpin's work so impressed those around him that he was quickly servicing the needs of many of the fine printers of Philadelphia including that of Matthew Cary and Son. Newspapers also delighted in Gilpin's work and his clients included Poulson's American Daily Advertiser. Gilpin would dominate his field until the emergence of John Ames of Springfield, Massachusetts. Ames, a mechanical engineer of sorts, had a gift for improving many of Gilpin's designs, eventually producing a better machine.

By 1827, the first Fourdrinier designed paper machine found its way to America. This machine was imported by Henry Barclay of Saugerties, New York and it quickly, as anticipated by the English, created a rash of imitators. Drying cylinders in use in 1821 were really not perfected until 1839. By now the evolution of American papermaking was in full swing.

Not until 1867 in Curtisville, Massachusetts, was ground-wood paper first produced commercially, although it had been done so some two decades prior in Europe. The problem with wood pulp is that it contains lignin, a natural binder, which unless chemically treated has a degrading effect. Because of this, other processes needed to be experimented with, the first being a soda process used in England in 1851. Cheapness and speed would continue to dominate quality and durability during the next century.

Paper Examination

The scientific study of the paper properties of a questioned document can prove invaluable as evidence. Despite the thousands of sheets that are created nearly identical each day, many papers can dramatically differ from one another and be positively identified. Forensic laboratories all over the world study the final product to determine its content and the process used to create a piece of paper.

You now know that paper is comprised of finely matted fibers of rag and specially treated wood fibers. Rag makes up the finer writing papers, while the special treated wood fibers attack less expensive applications. Some applications may include the use of both or the addition of another component such as straw, esperato grass or many others.

A sulfite process is used to break down the wood into pulp. Other processes also include grinding the wood into fine particles or cooking them in either a caustic soda or a sodium sulfide solution.

Water and variety of other materials, such as bleach, loading materials and dyes, are added until the mix reaches about 99% water content. The recipe is then run through the paper machine, extracting materials such as water, forming a continuous web. The fibers, having been shaken on a screen in order to mat them together, are then lifted from their position and rolled. More water is extracted as the fibers are dried. The variables involved up to this point differ depending upon the desired output. Many papers are then finished or coated to achieve a better acceptance in their application.

It then is up to the forensic scientist to reconstruct this process with only the aid of the paper. A number of techniques are used for paper examination, they include microscopic, physical, ultraviolet, visual and micro-chemical testing. All but the latter are recommended as micro-chemical is a destructive form of testing—it requires a sample.

Paper Examination

- Application—Does the paper fit the application? Is it of the proper size?
- Edge analysis—Has the paper been torn or cut? Is the paper handmade?
- Fold analysis—Has the paper been folded? Is the fold indicative of something, such as was it done so to create an envelope that could be sealed?
- Measurements
- Length
- Width
- Thickness—using a micrometer
- Printed material—Examine all of the printing on the paper. Is the printing indicative of the era? Is the paper ruled?
- Surface texture—as seen by transmitted light, often over a light box.
- Thread analysis—often threads are added to prevent forgery
- Ultraviolet radiation—to determine the color and fluorescence quality.
- Watermarks—useful for dating and determining manufacturer

Notes:
* These exact measurements will assist you in determining if two sheets were cut at the same time. Microscopic striations, from nicks in the cutting blade will also be useful in this determination.

Modern Advances in the Surface Analysis of Paper

The surface characteristics of paper are paramount when determining the wide-variety of applications for its use. While many elements of traditional papermaking have remained essentially the same over the years, the production process has evolved. To better understand the nature and behavior of paper, scientists have employed new techniques, many enhanced through new and affordable technology. Powerful new software packages are capable of generating multi-dimensional images and are now used for surface analysis by many major paper manufacturers.

Microscopic, spectroscopic and other emerging technologies are areas of interest for those advancing the study of paper surfaces. While traditional terms such as roughness, porosity and compressibility still apply, their analysis has been enhanced by many of the new techniques applied through the available technology.

The Printed Word

For the advanced autograph collector the study of type and printing has proved invaluable for the authentication of documents and manuscripts. Knowledge in this area has put some of the best forgers ever behind bars. Forgers who thought that they had taken into consideration every element to make the perfect masterpiece, met their demise through someone knowledgeable about print.

The distribution and preservation of man's knowledge evolved from the written word to the printed word by the middle of the 15th century. Practical printing became a viable form of communication through the development of movable metal type. The full range of alphabetic and numeric characters, along with punctuation marks, allowed movable type to create consistent text, now composed and printed faster than any other available process. Printing quickly became the key form of communication, a title it would not relinquish until the development of radio.

Through print, learning was simplified and knowledge was shared, preserved and efficiently distributed. Calligraphers and illuminators were in essence replaced with the typesetter, whose craft it was to arrange type, first by hand, then by machine into a readable form. While always seeming to be

---

Straight To The Point

As all type is specified in "points," authenticators should memorize these key measurements:
- ONE POINT = 0.01383 INCHES (0.35128 MM)
- AN INCH = ABOUT 72 POINTS (25.4 mm)
- A PICA = 12 POINTS

Spacing material is based on an "em"—a unit of measurement that is a square of the typeface's point size:

A 10 point em = 10 points high, 10 points wide.

A half of an em = an en.

A lead = (2 points thick)

A slug = (6 points thick)

---

governed by the advancements in papermaking, typographers found new creative freedom through movable type. Printed pieces, be it a book, broadside or whatever, now took on entire new forms of design.

Type

Type Founding

Type founding, the accurate manufacturing of type, is credited to the German Johann Gutenberg. Using a hard metal punch, a character was engraved in relief, then driven into a softer form of metal, creating what was termed a matrix. This matrix was then placed into an adjustable type mold. A molten metal was then poured into the mold as the material quickly became hard. The relief image, identical to that on the punch, then underwent some fundamental finishing operations, such as filing, before it was ready to use. This simple process essentially remained consistent into the 19th century.

Type Terminology

As printing evolved, new terms were added, while most traditional words remained the same. All upper and lowercase letters of the alphabet are considered a font of type. The word case was derived from one of the tools in a print shop, a printer's type case or cabinet. This hinged double box was where one could find all the capital letters housed above, in the upper case—along with small capitals and various special characters, while in the adjacent or lower case was small letters, numerals and spacing material. The sloping frame design of the case is efficient for the compositor—who often works in a standing position, and convenient for type storage.

A compositor uses a handheld adjustable frame called a "stick." The adjustable stick, calibrated in picas (12 points), allows the compositor to easily assemble the type upside down (the letters are in reverse), right-to-left. Justification—the tight fitting of

type, along with divisions between words and sentences is completed by adding spacing material. The term "leading," or space between lines of type, is derived from the thin metal strips called "leads" which were used by printers. Once several lines have been composed they are transferred to a metal tray, with an opening on one end, called a "galley." The galley serves as the storage unit until the pages are completed. Once the lines of type have been "leaded out" and alterations in design made, "galley proofs" are printed by hand. Once these proofs are approved, by an editor or client, the type is locked into position in preparation for printing.

Typeface Development

Understanding the origin and evolution of typefaces has also unmasked numerous forgeries. While this has always been a necessary education of archivists, librarians, book collectors and dealers, it had been less essential to many autograph collectors. The increase in quality forgeries however, now necessitates such an education. From military appointments and land grants, to broadsides and even photographs, autograph collectors have been increasingly exposed to typefaces.

Pen-drawn letters of early artisans were the inspiration for Gutenberg's typefaces. As the popularity of printing increased the popular formal black letter styles of Germany were replaced with new styles, some even inspired by popular handwriting. Early Roman faces were naturally very popular as uppercase letters were derived from Roman tablets of the first and second century.

By the middle of the 16th century French typefaces dominated book printing, not giving way to Dutch types until the 17th century. The Dutch types were highly sought be English printers who found the contrast and vertical design elements far more appealing than there French predecessors. By the 1720's, English printers shifted their interest homeward, to the gifted type founder William Caslon. The Dutch influenced Caslon had an eye for simplification and as such his typefaces became increasingly popular with printers.

"Old-style Romans" lost its appeal to what has been defined as transitional typefaces in the 18th century. The transitional faces featured greater line contrast, increased vertical emphasis and lighter serifs—the line at the of upper and lower strokes. As the century closed the elegant serifs of Parisian Firmin Didot and Italian Giambatista Bodini were at the forefront type design.

The 19th century was both innovative and competitive for type foundries who found production levels at all-time highs. As the competition increased, driven by the needs of a broad base print market, type founders became ruthless in copying their competitors products. With no copyright protection on typeface design the benefit far exceeded the risk.

By the 20th century, many key movements in both art and architecture, sparked interest in the development of type design. This concern would continue into the next century, spurred by technology, but always with great reverence for the past.

Developments In Typesetting

During the 19th century the need for reliable and efficient mechanical typesetting became paramount in the print market. Ottmar Mergenthaler became the first to answer this need with his Linotype machine (c.1880's). This along with the Monotype relied first on metal typecasting, but the fall of letter press relief printing in favor of offset encouraged the development of composition systems.

By 1946, the U.S. Government Printing Office was experimenting with an Intertype Fotosetter. The Fotosetter used film negatives that were imaged onto photosensitized paper that could then be used for the creation of printing plates. Font storage eventually transformed from a spinning film matrix to a digitally stored image, as imaging evolved from a cathode ray tube, to a laser.

The Typewriter

As a collector you realize that knowing something about this fascinating machine will assist you in dating and authenticating some of the documents you encounter. Since thousands of model typewriters have been produced by hundreds of manufacturers, it is beyond the scope of this book and that of the collector to identify each model and what features may link it to certain types of output. Worth noting however, is that the features of some models are so unique, or unusual for their time period, that output from these devices can be traced to its origin. For example, The Automatic Typewriter (circa 1880s) employed proportional spacing—different widths for different characters, as did the Columbia index manufactured by The Columbia Typewriter Co. (1885). The Remington Portable No. 3B (1935) used a lowercase "L" to replace the "1" key and a capitol "O" to replace the zero key.

The Oliver No. 5 (1906) even included a pencil holder that allowed the operator to draw a straight line on the paper.

The early 1970s saw the introduction of word processing systems. At first simply a typewriter and information storage, these systems evolved quickly. From adaptations to the Selectric typewriter, to word processing systems such as the Xerox 800, today's products were tomorrow's trash.

"Daisy wheel" impact printers (350 words per minute) now doubled the word output available on the Selectric (150-180 words per minute). While these new impact printers were fast, they were also loud and did little for the concentration needs of executives. Soon impact printers would give way to alternate forms of technology as ink-jet, thermal and laser printers were right around the corner.

Unmasking Forged Typewritten Documents & Manuscripts

Linking A Letter To Its Source

As an advanced autograph collector you can become pretty good at unmasking a forged typewritten letter or document, but it will require some practice to train your eye to the anomalies inherit in the device.

The individuality of a typewriter is determined by a number of factors including type size, type style, font design and availability, output defects (printing) and inherent defects (machine).

Manufacturers often produced several different fonts within a variety of type sizes and styles.

Therefore, knowing which ones were available and when, can be useful to linking a letter to a particular machine. Font design is an art in itself and not all characters are created equal. Between manufacturers, the same font can vary in design; for example serifs can be left off a stroke, or altered in size. Often when a machine is first introduced it will have limited font availability. Once it is determined that the product is going to be a success in the market, the expense of adding more fonts is then incurred.

Output defects are evident in printing. Here the alignment of the characters or defects in the typeface reveal much about the source. We know that a typewriter is designed to place a uniformly printed character, on an imaginary baseline centered within a designated unit. Since this is seldom the case, especially with older manual typewriters, certain anomalies of a device become identifying traits. They can include characteristics such as both vertical and horizontal misalignment, improper slant (varying right or left from the desired 90 degree position), nonuniform printing (as a result of unevenly striking the paper surface; the ink is heavier in certain areas of the impression) and even printing a double impression. Typeface defects can be the result of improper manufacture or can occur through use. Typically the latter prevails, as most manufacturers have a quality control function to catch manufacturing errors. Defects that can result from use include cracks, chips, etc.

To identify these traits, an advanced autograph collector must carefully examine a questioned typed document under magnification. Forensic scientists use test plates to pick up on alignment defects, but many of these defects can be identified with the tools that are common to advanced autograph collectors. Machine defects or peculiarities, such as improper spacing, can also assist in linking a document to a source, but only if the repetition is consistent over a series of examples.

Variations can occur in a manual typewriter, especially heavily used older models. They can range from those as a result of a worn platen to that of a worn ribbon. A dirty typeface, like that of a worn ribbon, can be corrected and because of this will not prove as useful in the identification procedure as alignment or typeface defects. As long as the variations you identify are repeated and not due to chance, they can be considered in the identification of a typewriter.

The anomalies in typewriting have applied mainly to type bar machines—the original method for producing typewriting. As most of you know, it evolved from manual to electric, and with it other changes took place. Changes such as the inclusion of two typefaces on each type bar—a capital and lowercase letter. The electric typewriter worked in the same fashion as its predecessor, only the type bar movement was activated electrically.

Manufacturers were excited about the electric typewriter and a battle quickly ensued to make units in all shapes and sizes. The introduction of IBM's Executive, the first successful proportional spacing typewriter would change the way document examiners would view typewriting. Proportional spacing meant that each letter would no longer occupy the same horizontal space. Examiners could no longer use the alignment test plates they had used for standard typewriting but would have to reconfigure the units to match that of the new spacing configurations. The goal was for the typewritten page to mimic as closely as possible that of one printed. Other manufacturers would follow IBM including Remington Rand, Underwood, Olivetti, Olympia and Hermes.

IBM's introduction of the Selectric typewriter in 1961 introduced an entirely new class of machine, the type ball or single element typewriter. Since the Selectric would be the only single element machine available until 1974, examiners could at least limit their focus to one manufacturer of this type of technology. When the elements or type balls became interchangeable, the approach to typewriting examination had to change.

Now one of the first steps a document examiner takes is determining whether a document was created on a single element machine or another class of typewriter. This is done by examining the paper. If the characters emboss the paper it was created on a type bar or type wheel machine. Typically the type ball unit will not emboss the paper. Other clues that a document were created with a type ball is superior uniformity or the presence of small hairline flairs projecting from a character.

For most advanced autograph collectors, studying the IBM Selectric pica fonts will probably be as far as they will want to go researching the typewriter. Because the Selectric fonts are among the most common found, some study will prove helpful, but the days of the typewriter were slowly drawing to close, as word processing was just around the corner—IBM released its Mag Card Executive Typewriter as part of the company's word processing unit in 1972. While the alignment defects of a single element machine are slight, almost nonexistent when compared to their predecessors, when they are repeated enough times they can be sufficient to identify the source.

What Clues Or Habits Of The Typist Can Be Found In The Output?
The identification of a typist can be a difficult task, but here are some things to look for:

Capitalization
Content—phraseology, salutations, closings, etc.
Corrections—type, familiarity
Format—where does the page begin and end, margins, etc.

Hyphenation
Markings—stenographic, proofreading, etc.
Mistakes—common and uncommon
Punctuation
Spelling
Symbols—distinct and common

Printing

The definition of a print, like printing is dynamic. A print can be a mark made on a surface by pressing or stamping or cloth printed with a design. A print can be the impression of letters, designs, etc. made by inked type or from a plate block, etc. A print can be a photograph made from a negative. Initially made by hand, prints were utilitarian in nature, serving the needs educators, politicians, explorers and even entertainers. As other forms of printing evolved, the hand printmaking process became more exclusive, catering primarily to the fine arts market.

A print's identity as a multiple became its most important characteristic. Artists had complete control over the amount of impressions, or editions of prints to be struck. While it is now traditional for artists to limit an edition size and to number and sign the prints. This was not always the case, as some printing techniques subject the image to deterioration, such as drypoint. In these destructive printing methods, earliest impressions are the sharpest and thus the most valuable. Printers, while artisans, often view their forms as output. While quality is a concern, so is profitability.

Printing has been so dynamic that a number of processes today involve no ink. While it's hard to imagine that such could be the case, technology has taken us far beyond the traditional methods. The core of printmaking/printing is three traditional processes: relief, intaglio, planographic (lithography).

Relief Printing

The output from a raised printed surface is a relief print. Portions of the block or plate meant to take the ink are raised, while areas not to be printed are removed or cutaway below the surface. Relief printing, in its most common form is a woodcut. The artist draws a design on a piece of wood, then removes the non-image areas with specially designed tools. The raised images are inked with a roller, then a paper is placed on the block, and then the back of the paper is rubbed to pick up the image. Variations of this method include linoleum block printing (linocut) and wood engraving.

Intaglio Printing

Contrary to relief is intaglio printing, where the image areas are depressed below the surface of the

This hinged double box was where a printer would find all the capital letters housed above, in the upper case - along with small capitals and various special characters, while in the adjacent or lower case was small letters, numerals and spacing materials.

The paper was placed over this bed of inked type then compressed to create an image (Relief Printing).

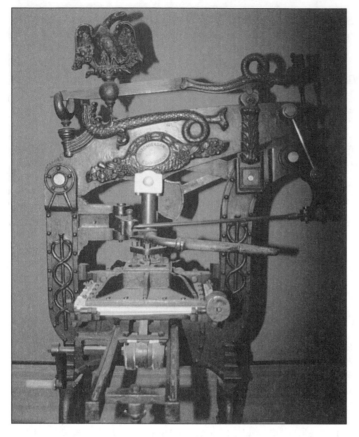

The printing press revolutionized communication and was a paramount key to uniting the colonies of America.

plate. Lines are engraved or cut into a metal plate or some similar surface using sharp tools or acids. The plate is then inked by the printer. The engraved or cut lines hold the ink, after the surface is wiped clean. The depressed image is then picked up by paper forced into the lines. Common forms of intaglio printing include aquatint, drypoint, engraving, etching and mezzotint.

Planographic

Planographic, is a type of printing where the image surface is flat. Lithography is the most common form of planographic printing. This process relies on the repellent chemical reaction between grease and water. Artist use grease pens to draw on lithographic stones or plates. The grease attracts the ink, while the undrawn areas are treated to repel it. It has become the most common of the three major processes.

Lithographic printing has been extended to include the offset principle. Instead of paper being placed upon the stone and the ink then transferred by the pressure of a scraper, both the paper and plate lie flat. With both aligned along the bed of the press, a rubber-covered offset cylinder rolls over the inked plate (metal), picking up the ink. It then moves on to roll over the paper, depositing the ink. The advantages to the process are clear, the image no longer has to be in reverse on the plate and the registration is improved. The latter occurs because it is easier to place a sheet of paper accurately on the bed of a modern press than to lower it face down over an inked plate.

Other Images

Screen print

Silk screen or screen printing, adapted from basic-stencil-making, is known as Serigraphy. Images are drawn on a mesh made up of silk or nylon. The non-image areas are made non-porous, so that as a squeegee is pulled across the screen, ink flows into only the image area, then onto the paper that is placed directly underneath.

Other techniques include monotype and cliche-verre, xerography, laser printing and various other forms of impact and non-impact printing.

Printing Overview

The Three Major Types of Printing

1. Relief Printing

Types: woodcut, linocout, ukiyo-e—a classic Japanese woodcut technique, and wood engraving.

Other Approaches: cut block, small block, stamped, embossed, metal relief, plaster, reduction block, cardboard relief and linoleum prints.

2. Intaglio

Types: drypoint, engraving, mezzotint, etching and aquatint.

Metal plates: copper, zinc, brass, aluminum, magnesium, and steel

Other Approaches: embossed (ink less intaglio), chine colle, photoetching, photogravure, collograph and the metal collage print

3. Planographic

Types: lithography, photolithography and serigraphy (screen printing)

Relief Printing

The most direct of the four major printmaking processes is relief printing. The raised surface of the block can be created by cutting away either the positive (areas to be printed) or negative areas (areas not to be printed), or by adding objects or pieces to a flat surface. The earliest printed images were relief prints—often woodcuts. Wooden stamps have even been traced back to Egypt and clay seals have been found in Rome. Since paper was invented in China on or about AD 105, one could assume that the popularity of relief printing grew exponentially in the years that followed.

One of the earliest known Chinese woodcuts, found by Sir Aurel Stein in 1907, is the 17-foot long Diamond Sutra (AD 868) housed in the British Museum in London. After viewing this piece it becomes clear that relief printing in China was in a mature state during this period. In fact, it was so advanced that it would take centuries before western woodcuts would attain such precision and artistry.

A surviving French woodcut, Bois Protat, in the collection of Emile Protat has been dated to about 1380 and probably was used in a textile application, as the total block would have been too large for paper milled during this era. Religious and secular imagery in print was not prominent until about 1400, when paper was finally available in sufficient quantities.

During the 15th century, Germany was a hub for woodcut printing. Many surviving handcolored examples highlight their crisp designs. Nowhere is an example of this better exemplified than in a surviving print "rest on the Flight into Egypt" (c.1410) found at the Albertina Graphische Sammlung in Vienna. Since religion played such a pivotal role in 15th-century life most early woodcuts bear religious imagery. During this era (1450-1470) prints were also used to simulate illuminated manuscripts and textiles, but few examples survived due to the process (paste prints). Using glue, other materials began being embedded in the prints, including, cloth, precious stones and gold leaf. Card games were also extremely popular and as a result many examples of cheaply printed cards, from the early 1400s, have survived.

In the early 15th century there was no movable type, so an alteration of the woodcut technique was used to illustrate books. This new form, block books, contained text and illustrations cut into the same block. One of the first books to combine printing from text and wood block images was the "Speculum Humanae Salvationis" (Mirror of Man's Salvation, Germany—c.1473) which is housed in the Metropolitan Museum of Art in New York. The second half of the 15th century also saw the emergence of the metal cut or dotted print. This print used a metal plate made from lead, pewter and copper. The plate was adorned using tools more familiar to a goldsmith than an etcher. Designs were patiently and meticulously created through cuts, stamps, and punches. The end of the 15th century finally found the Italian artists developing their own style of wood cutting and not surprisingly it exemplified the innovative elements of the Italian Renaissance.

The woodcut would not be elevated to the level of fine art, were it not for the distinguished painter and printmaker Albrecht Durer. Executing his first woodcut in 1492, Durer quickly raised the quality of the imagery to a level of detail and form never thought possible. His primarily black-and-white images inspired his contemporaries including Hans Burgkmair, Lucas Cranach, Urs Graf, Albrecht Altdorfer, Hans Baldung Grien, Lucas van Leyden and Hans Holbein.

While Germany and the Low Countries mastered relief printing during the 15th and 16th centuries, the French and the Italians did not go unnoticed. Of those Geoffrey Tory, Giuseppe Scolari and the master painter Titian inspired those who followed.

After the 16th century, wood cutting slipped into the background, as engraving and etching were assuming a more prominent role in art. Applications for wood cutting, during the 19th century centered around book and magazine illustration, reaching a pinnacle in the mid and latter part of the century. Among those who distinguished themselves were Thomas Bewick—known for his delicate boxwood woodcuts, John Tenniel—best remembered as the illustrator of Lewis Carroll's *Alice's Adventures in Wonderland* (1865), Caspar David Friedlich—a landscape painter, and Wilhelm Busch—a cartoonist whose images of Max and Moritz, a forerunner to comic strips, had a profound influence on illustrators. *Harper's Weekly,* a popular periodical at the time, often included the wood engravings of Winslow Homer and Thomas Nast. While both these artists brought a new meaning to the art, not even the sensitivity of Homer could stop the photography from supplanting the print as the medium of choice.

Intaglio Printing

The precision and vitality of the intaglio process gives this printing process an identity all its own. The Italian word itself means to engrave or cut into. An impression is created when the paper comes in contact with the ink that has filled the finely formed depressions and recesses that have been cut into a metal plate. Types of intaglio prints include drypoint, engraving, mezzotint, etching and aquatint. The cuts made on the metal plate can be created in a number of ways. In etching and aquatint, these depressions are created with acid. In line and stipple engraving a burin or graver forms the recesses and in drypoint it is simply the direct scratching or scoring.

Intaglio prints include works such as collagraphs and epoxy prints, that are made in a similar fashion but use additive techniques. To make an intaglio print, the printmaker first applies a soft ink to the surface of the plate, carefully being sure that it is rubbed into all the recessed areas. The surface ink is then removed, leaving behind only the ink in the incised areas. A dampened piece of paper is then applied to the plate. An etching press is then used to apply pressure to the paper, forcing it into the recessed areas where it will then come in contact with the ink. The types of metal used for intaglio plates include copper, zinc, brass, steel aluminum and magnesium.

Intaglio printing has a rich history tracing back to the 15th century when armorers and goldsmiths began their transformation from metal to paper. Religious imagery and secular themes were common, and if not printed on a sheet paper, might find their way onto playing cards. Although the styles differed, German and Italy were the epicenters for the development of engraving. The first significant engravers in northern Europe were often anonymous, recognized mainly from the images on playing cards.

The last half of the century focused considerably on the Italian masters, many of which were residing in Florence, the city in the forefront of the Italian Renaissance. Engraving was divided into two schools in Florence, the Fine Manner; which seems to have evolved from the silversmith's process known as niello and the Broad Manner; influenced by the artisan works of the Renaissance. Noted etchers of the day included: Martin Schongauer, Maso Finiguerra, Antonio Pollaiuolo, and Andrea Mantegna.

The work of German artist Albrecht Durer was the primary inspiration of intaglio printing during the 16th century. Not only would Durer elevate relief printing to new levels, but he would also make new strides in engraving, etching and drypoint. Other artists who left significant contributions to intaglio printing during this era included Lucas van Leyden (Dutch), Francesco Mazzouli (Italian), and Hendrik Goltzius (Northern Europe).

Engraving and etching reached its pinnacle as an art form during the 17th century. Noted French practitioners of the era included Claude Mellan, Robert Nanteuil, Claude Gellee (Lorrain) and Jacques Callot. The latter of which introduced two notable changes in etching techniques, a harder and more uniform varnish and the use of the echoppe—a steel cylinder with an angular point, as a replacement for the traditional pointed needle.

Engraving in the North, Flanders and Holland, was dominated by the master, Rembrandt. Although known first as a painter, his abundant etchings and drypoints are conclusive evidence of his mastery of intaglio. Long after his death, his work continued to circulate in the art market, as his plates continued to be recut and reprinted.

The mezzotint, invented by Ludwig von Siegen and refined by Prince Rupert of the Palatinate, became popular for its soft continuous overall tone. This look was achieved by using a small spike-toothed wheel, that when applied to the plate left behind a cluster of dot like abrasions, similar to the half tone process. In America the mezzotint is often linked to Peter Pelham, who upon bring the process to our shores, created many outstanding portraits.

Intaglio printing during the 18th century saw artists such as Giovanni Battista Tiepolo (Italy), Antonio Canale (Canaletto, Italy), Giovanni Battista Piranesi (Italy), William Hogarth (England), Thomas Rowlandson (England), James Gillray (England), William Blake (England) and Francisco de Goya y Lucientes (Spain), explore new avenues for the media. Gillray, more of a political satirist and cartoonist, than engraver perhaps, poked fun of the royalty and bourgeoisie through efforts in intaglio. Poet William Blake illustrated his eccentric writings with equally fascinating engraved images. Spanish royal court painter Goya, used the power of his imagery to depict the atrocities of warfare, while also elevating aquatint from a technical process to an expressive medium.

The 19th century would see intaglio influenced by The Barbizon School (France), French Impressionists and American Expartriates. Artists such as Jean-Francois Millet, Theodore Rousseau, Edgar Degas, Mary Cassatt and James Abbott McNeill Whistler experimented with intaglio to capture the essence of their subjects.

During the 20th century, intaglio was the chosen form for everything from social commentary to Cubism. No longer was the artist's perceptions limited by visual reality. In Europe, Kathe Kollwitz, Max Beckmann, Jacques Villon, Henri Matisse and Pablo Ruiz y Picasso, took the complexity out of etching and replaced it with emotion. In America, isolationism, experimentation and color embodied the works of Edward Hopper, Jasper Johns, James Rosenquist, Robert Rauschenberg, Jim Dine, Gabor Peterdi, and Mauricio Lasansky.

Planographic

German Aloys Senefelder discovered the principle of lithography in 1798. While it was used for music printing early on, it wasn't until about the 1820s that its versatility and ease of use really emerged through commercial printing. Artists and printers found working on a lithographic stone far easier than using the tools of previous processes. Senefelder, now the ambassador of his invention, carried it to London in 1800. There the artist Benjamin West tried his hand at the technique. Senefelder's strategy was to commission prominent artists to create works that would draw attention to the medium.

By the time lithography would reach the hands the era's fine artisans, it was no longer a novelty. It was quickly transformed into a major medium by technicians such as the French printer Godefroy Engelmann. He would eventually develop the first "process printing" using primary colors to produce a full chromatic range, later known as a chromalithograph (color lithography).

In England, Charles Hullmandel set up the first important lithographic press (1919). It would become the leading force in English lithography until the mid-19th century. Hullmandel would also distinguish himself as having a major influence on attracting prominent artists to the process.

All across Europe artists were drawn to the lithographic technique. In Spain, it was welcomed by a 73-year old Francisco Goya, while in France, Jean-Auguste-Dominique Ingres experimented and pushed the process. Goya would have a strong impact on the artists of the Romantic movement in France, including Theodore Gericault. Eugene Delacroix, also part of the movement, would use lithography to illustrate works by those authors popularized by Romantics, such as Byron, Goethe, Scott and of course Shakespeare. Later, other French artists, such as Eugene Isabey, Eugene Ciceri and Paul Huet, used landscapes to exhibit their strength of the medium.

What Durer did for the woodcut and what Rembrandt did for the etching, was matched by Honore Daumier with lithography. He would become the undisputed master of the process and influence many who would follow.

Outside France others were feeling the repercussions of the Romantic movement, including the Englishman Richard Parks Bonington who worked on the monumental twenty-volume, *Voyages pittoresques dans l'ancienne France*.

Lithography didn't reach America until the early 19th century. Here one of the earliest lithographic shops was established in New York by Nathaniel Currier in 1834. He would use the medium to depict current events. In 1852, Currier would join forces with James Merritt Ives, henceforth "Currier & Ives." The subjects of their lithographs had no bounds, and became so popular that they needed a large staff to maintain production. Ironically, few of the firm's prints were chromolithographed, instead they opted for an assembly-line type production of hand coloring.

During the latter half of the nineteenth century artists such as Edouard Manet, Edgar Degas, Rodolphe Bresdin, Odilon Redon, James Abbott McNeill Whistler and Edvard Munch found lithography perfect for their subjects. The medium was also attracting attention for its use in advertisement, the popular form of which was the poster. Frenchman Jules Cheret revived the chromolithograph, printing brilliant colors with three or four stones. Other poster artists followed including Alphonse Mucha and Henri de Toulouse-Lautrec.

The twentieth century saw lithography used by Henri Matisse, Pablo Picasso, Georges Braque, Marc Chagall, Joan Miro, Thomas Hart Benton, George Bellows Arthur B. Davies, Graham Sutherland, Robert Rauschenberg and Jasper Johns, to name only a few.

Distinguishing The Printed Word

Printing Illustrated Books
Since signatures can be found both in books and on prints, a brief overview of the printing methods that were most commonly used should prove helpful.

1460-1550
Virtually every book with printed illustrations used woodcuts. Most often you will find them combined on a page with text.

1550-1650
During this period engravings began to compete with woodcuts, despite the fact that to combine them with text required passage through the intaglio press. Engraving was also growing in popularity. They were often used as plates that would later be bound into a book.

1650-1790
This era saw intaglio printing dominant in its use for book illustration. Common forms include line engravings, pure engravings or etchings and also mezzotints.

1790-1825
Similar to the previous period, line engravings dominated book illustration. In expensive works, however, it is not uncommon to encounter hand-colored aquatints. Relief printing, in the form of wood engravings was also briefly revived.

1825-1850
As steel gradually displaced copper as the plate of choice, line engravings continued to enjoy enormous popularity. But a new threat appeared on the horizon, lithography. This form began to be widely used by the 1820s, especially for books with separate plates. A decade later would also see the tinted lithograph replace the hand-colored aquatint. Wood engravings also found a home at the low-end of the market.

1850-1900
This highly transitional period saw certain applications began to favor more efficient forms of printing. Steel engravings and lithographs dominated monochrome (one color) production until about the 1870s, when photolithography, collotype and

photogravure became more practical. For color plates the alternatives included tinted lithography, chromolithography, and chromoxylography. Low-end production, such as magazines, continued their use of wood engravings. This would later be replaced the line block, followed by the halftone block at the end of the period.

1900-1950

A majority of the book illustrations during this period were printed relief, with some higher-end collotype and photogravure in the early years. The use of halftone blocks required high-gloss paper for optimal results, so unlike blocks that worked well with text, they would most often appear in a separate section. For the same reason, most of the color plates you will encounter will be tipped-in (glued along one edge and inserted on blank text pages) to the book. Unlike book production, magazine manufacturers would ignore complaints about how hard it was to read text on glossy paper and print with halftone blocks. Gradually magazine production was moving toward gravure.

1950-1970

For monochrome book illustrations during this period the choice was gravure. Plates could be found in separate sections or interspersed between pages of letter press text because gravure was another process that could not meet both the needs of illustration and text. Despite the lack of text quality with this process, it did become a low-cost alternative. All top-shelf books had gravure images combined with relief text necessitating another pass through the press. By the 1960s, offset lithography was clearly coming into its own and a decade later would have no rival.

1970-Date

Book illustrations are now dominated by offset lithography. Metal type has long given way to photographic typesetting and the problem of successfully merging both text and halftone illustration has been solved. Traditional methods of prepress have now evolved to the desktop.

So how can you tell how a piece of text was printed? Here are some clues and points of information:

Relief Text

- With relief text the letters will appear to have been pushed into the paper or you will see evidence that the ink has pushed to the edge of each letter.

Intaglio Text

- Early seventeenth century lettering was somewhat primeval and uneven, while by the late seventeenth century execution had improved dramatically.

- Early nineteenth century artist's etchings typically did not include text and when it does appear it is often primitive looking because it had to be written backwards.
- The ink appears as if it is rising up from the paper.
- Differing intensity of inks in lines of similar width.

Planographic Text

- Planographic text can be distinguished only by the way the ink lies on the paper, which is deposited smoothly and without pressure.

Screen Process Text

- Gravure text is most commonly distinguished by its jagged edges.
- Offset lithography has smooth edges—in comparison to other forms, with consistent ink distribution.

Signatures on Prints

Once an artist completes an edition of prints he carefully reviews each one to remove those that are defective or inconsistent with the desired quality. If the artist does not print the edition himself, he will review

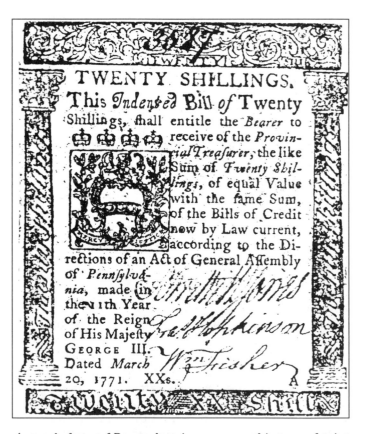

An early form of Pennsylvania currency, this type of printing can include the signatures of many early American patriots.

The signature of patriot John Hancock appears on this Faneuil-Hall lottery ticket.

the edition with the printer. The prints that are rejected are typically destroyed. After completing this process he will commence numbering and signing the edition, a standard practice since the 1930s. While the signature is often found in the lower right hand corner and the number in the lower left corner, no firm rules for signature placement exist.

The method used to print the edition will determine the difference between the first and last print pulled. While there is often no difference in lithography, such was not the case with drypoints, mezzotints and aquatints, where a slight deterioration might be found. With the latter it is important for the sequence of numbering to be correct, as it is important to a collector or dealer.

A print edition typically includes a printer's mark, the publisher's mark, the workshop mark and sometimes a copyright seal. These are placed on the prints by means of blind stamping (embossing or debossing) on the front or by wet stamping on the back (when the artist does not want the surface of the print altered). These "chop marks" are beneficial for tracking down the origin of a particular print and the collaborators and for counterfeit protection. While the placement of the mark is made by the artist, most fall on the lower border near the artist's signature.

Types Of Print Proofs

Artist's Proofs (epreuve d'artiste)
Although the figure can vary, about ten percent of the edition is reserved for artist's proofs. Identical to the edition prints, these proofs are for the artist's personal use.

Bon a' Tirer Proof
The first impression that meets all of the artist's standards, as well as the printer, is the bon a tirer, or "right to print" proof.

Cancellation Proof
An impression taken after a plate has been effaced, at the end of the run, is known as the cancellation proof. This acts as proof that no further prints can be made.

Presentation Proofs
Presentation proofs, identical to those of the edition, are dedicated to an individual and typically not sold.

Printer's Proof
Printers who collaborate with an artist are often given printer's proof. These can be personalized or marked as "Printer's Proof."

Progressive Proofs
A series of impressions made for multicolor prints, exhibiting each color separately and in combination with each of the other colors are progressive proofs.

State Proofs

Trial Proofs
Attempts, in color or black & white, exhibiting alterations in an incomplete image are called trial proofs. All trial proofs are made prior to the bon a tirer proof.

The type of printed item and the cost effectiveness of its duplication will no doubt play a factor in how frequently an advanced autograph collector may encounter a forgery. As you are already aware, printing technology has changed dramatically over the last few decades. High-grade printing has migrated from letter press to the more versatile offset printing. Both methods, as you are now aware, involve two distinctly different techniques.

Note:

Worth noting is that many standard forms have printing codes that identify their source.

Photography

The signed photograph has always been one of the most popular forms of autograph collecting, particularly in certain areas of the hobby, such as sports and entertainment. While collector's eyes often start first with the analysis of a signature to determine the authenticity of such an item, I have seen more than one instance where a forgery was immediately concluded as a result of dating the photograph alone.

As a collector or dealer how often have you been asked the following questions: "Who was the first U.S. President to sign a photograph?" "Did Babe Ruth ever sign a color photograph?" "What is an autographed carte-de-viste?" "What U.S. Presidents could have signed color photographs?" These questions are just a few examples of why as advanced autograph collectors we must better acquaint ourself with this technology.

Of greatest interest to most autograph collectors is early portrait photography. The often formal setting of the studio appealed to most subjects, many of which were celebrities, because the output was typically a flattering portrait. With photography in its infancy and subjects still impressed by the technology, the addition of a signature slowly became a natural occurrence. As exposure times improved for both daguerreotypes and calotypes (c.1839) photographic studios began appearing across both the United States and Europe.

The reflective surface of the detailed daguerreotypes was impressive, but certainly not conducive for a signature. In contrast, calotypes exhibited far less detail but were printed on photogenic drawing paper. By the mid-1840s most portrait photographers were opting for calotypes over daguerreotypes, but changes were on the horizon, including portraits made from wet collodion-on-glass negatives and the invention of the carte-de-viste.

Five types of photographic images were being produced in the mid-1850s: daguerreotypes, ambrotypes, tintypes, calotypes and albumen paper prints (using glass negatives). It was the French photographer Nadar (Gaspard Felix Tournachon), following the opening of his studio in 1853, who would bring the lifestyles of the rich and famous into the forefront with his portraits. For two decades Nadar, now the preeminent portrait photographer, captured timeless images of prominent artisans.

By 1854, however, portrait photography would find itself affordable to the middle class through the invention of the carte-de-viste by Frenchman Andre Disderi. Using a standard glass negative the photographer made portraits small enough (3.5" x 2.5") to fit on calling cards (4" x 3"). The new cost effective form of photography quickly became popular with socialites. In fact, cartes de vistes flourished for nearly five decades from 1857 to 1900. While this form waned at the turn of the century, it did endure into the 1920s. As Disderi photographed the well-known celebrities of the day, the public swept up the huge editions of his popular subjects like children waiting in line for baseball trading cards. His patented method allowed Disderi to produce up to ten images on a single photographic plate.

An early tintype that could be mounted and then autographed below.

An early tintype that could be mounted and then autographed below.

Definitions Of Popular Early Photographic Images

Pre-Paper Photography

Daguerreotypes

Daguerreotypes, invented by the Frenchman Louis-Jacques-Mande Daguerre, were images produced on a silver-coated copper plate. They were first introduced in 1839 and reached peak popularity during the early 1850s. By the mid-1850s the popularity of the process began to wane and the technology would soon be replaced by collodion on glass. Although numerous artisans would continue the process, it fell out of favor by 1865.

Ambrotype

The ambrotype, invented by the Englishman Frederick Scott Archer, was introduced in 1854. A negative image was produced on a glass plate and when a black backing was added, the picture resembled a positive. Popular during the late 1850s and popularized in the United States by James Cutting, the technology began to fall out of favor by 1861 and was essentially obsolete by the middle of the decade.

Tintype (Melainotype or Ferrotype)

The tintype, invented by Hamilton Smith, was a negative image produced on a very thin iron plate. When a black varnish was added as an undercoating, the image appeared as a positive. Introduced in 1856 and patented in the United States by Peter Neff, the technology's peak production years were from 1860 to about 1863. The technology fell out of favor by the end of the decade, with the last tintypes contained in cases produced about 1867. Other variations of the technology would continue over the next half century.

Photography on Paper (1839-1900)

Calotype

Introduced in 1841, the calotype was a positive photographic image produced on a salted paper. Invented by the Englishman W. H. Fox Talbot, the image was popular during the mid-1850s. By the 1860s, the process was obsolete.

Albumen

From a glass negative, a positive print was produced on paper coated with egg whites. The albumen print, invented by the Frenchman L.D. Blanquart-Evard, was introduced in 1850 and remained popular during the latter half of the century. The technology waned during the 1890s, but remained significant for its historical value.

Carte-de-visite

A carte de visite is a small (2-1/2" x 3-1/2") albumen print mounted to a popular sized card (2-1/2" x 4"). Introduced in 1854 and revolutionized by Frenchman Andre-Adolphe-Eugene Disderi, it was enormously popular during the early 1860s. The form, although continued into the next decade, waned in popularity during the 1870s.

Cabinet Cards

The cabinet card, popularized by Windsor & Bridge in Britain, was a photographic print (4" x 5-1/2") mounted on a larger cardboard mount (4-1/4" x 6-1/2"). Introduced in 1863, this form was popular for three decades, finally falling out of favor at the turn of the century.

Stereographs

Introduced in 1851, and popular for over a half century, stereographs are two photographs—often taken with a binocular camera, mounted together for three-dimensional viewing. The viewing was done on a stereoscope. Images were produced by nearly every photographic process available.

Gelatin Print

Introduced by Englishman Richard Maddox in 1871, an image was printed onto a gelatin-coated paper. With the addition of a dry plate, this form was very popular among professional photographers by the mid-1890s. While images could be enlarged, they were typically contact-printed and mounted in a style similar to the cabinet card. This early process evolved into modern photography.

Note:

Introduced in 1839, wood frame based cases were covered with a variety of materials including paper, leather and cloth. By the mid-1850s, a mixture of sawdust and shellac was molded into popular high-relief patterns that could be produced in a variety of shapes. Both wood-frame and plastic cases were produced in large quantities during the Civil War.

Celebrity Carte-de-vistes

Because so many autographed Carte-de-vistes have entered the market, including some bearing facsimile and forged autographs, both autograph collectors and dealers have had to familiarize themselves more with this form of photography than any that had preceded it. Autographed Carte-de-vistes now routinely find their way into dealer catalogs and auctions. Creating great interest, most of these examples are quickly purchased by the public with what seems to be little regard for authenticity. I say this because most of the purchasers I have encountered know little about the photographic process, the quantities produced or even how to date the image.

Collecting Carte-de-visites

- The carte de visite grew in popularity from 1854 to 1957 in Europe, but did not spread to America until about 1858.

- One of the major promoters of this form in America was Charles D. Fredericks. His imprint was "C.D. Fredericks & Co., NEW YORK".

Spurred by the untimely death of Prince Albert in December of 1861, photographers turned out over one hundred thousand Carte-de-viste portraits of him in the few weeks that followed. This was certainly no surprise to many, as most had witnessed the American

A carte-de-viste of President Andrew Johnson signed on the back. Note the presence of a tax stamp adhered to the back. This was required from August, 1864 to August, 1866.

photographer John Mayall, while working in England, produce an extremely popular (60,000 sets) Royal Family album in 1860. Needless to say the boom in this form of photography had begun.

Photographers quickly scrambled to publish hundreds of celebrity portraits while publishers hurried to develop trade lists—negative files and even catalogs listing available titles. Notable photographers, such as Matthew Brady, copied their daguerreotypes on Carte-de-viste negatives and hooked up with publishers. In Brady's case, it was E. Anthony (1860). Both these gentlemen purchased extensively from other photographers and in some instances even pirated images. When and if an image of a famous notable could not be found, a financial agreement would be struck between the subject and the photographer.

Another example of a carte-de-viste

The Mail order Carte-de-vistes became big business. Just how big you ask? Well, there were cases as high as three hundred thousand copies of a single image being sold. E. & H.T. Anthony issued an impressive catalog of 2000 portraits in 1862. The catalog also included hundreds of war scenes converted by Brady. The eleven subjects listed in the catalog represented the most extensive grouping of American images to date.

The United States followed its counterparts in Europe, producing the portraits of many notables from 1860-1866. When the sale of notable Carte-de-vistes waned, alternative subjects filled the void— scoundrels, circus figures, Siamese twins, etc. These often vulgar images, appearing as early as 1870, dominated carte sales from the mid 1870s to the mid 1880s.

During carte's early period, many large-scale publishers worked out of Boston and New York, while others could be found in San Francisco, Washington, St. Louis and Philadelphia. Notable New York publishers included: E. & H.T. Anthony, D. Appleton & Co., A. Bogardus., M. Brady, C.D. Fredericks, J. & Son Gurney, Hallett & Bro. and G.C. Rockwood. Of those listed, "E. & H.T. Anthony" will probably be the first images a collector might encounter, followed by Gurney & Son and Fredericks. Naturally, location affects availability; if you live in Hawaii images of H.L. Chase and M. Dickson will probably be the first encountered.

During the next two decades, Napoleon Sarony would become the premier American portraitist. His hallmark became his beautiful portraits of theatrical performers in full costume. Working in both cabinet and Carte-de-viste format, autographed images of theatrical stars, produced by Sarony, represent one of the most sought after forms in the hobby.

Sarony's apprentice, Mora established his own studio in 1870. His images mirror Sarony but are less creative in composition. Images from both are highly sought and typically easy to identify through their printed mounts—"Sarony (cursive) 680 BROADWAY, N.Y.", "Mora (cursive) 707 BROADWAY, N.Y."

Of those photographers most identified with carte's second period of popularity was Charles Eisenmann (New York). His catalog of unusual portraits rivaled in quality that of E. & H.T. Anthony. From acrobats to dwarfs, Eisenmann profited from the shift in popularity of Carte-de-vistes.

Popular celebrities whose images adorned thousands of Carte-de-vistes included: Benjamin Disraeli, Giuseppe Garibaldi, Louis Aqassiz, Brigham Young, Adelina and Carlotta Patti and Tom Thumb. So easy is it to find the latter image, that when this author stopped in the first antique shop in quest of the image, he quickly found one—an "E. & H.T. Anthony" image.

Counterfeit cartes are common and easily identified by the lack of a photographer or publisher imprint. This does not mean, however, that counterfeit imprinted images of celebrities can not be found. A carte de viste image of Lincoln, imprinted from a photographer in Reading, PA, would naturally arouse some suspicion regarding authenticity. The author advises the pursuit of genuine autographed images over pirated versions.

Images of personalities of the past produced from artwork can often be found in Carte-de-viste form. Portraits of Washington, Adams and Jefferson are common. Like all forms of photography, knowing when a particular form was introduced can help you authenticate an autographed image. If you ran across two autographed photographs of President Zachary Taylor, one a carte-de-viste and the other a calotype, which one would most likely be authentic? Just food for thought!

Two autographs can be found on carte-de-vistes, that of the subject and occasionally the photographer. Often astute photographers would approach personalities, such as those of theater and ask them to autograph a quantity of images. These images were then sold at a premium. Unfortunately, these images are often confused with printed signatures that appear on the bottom front of the carte-de-viste or on the back of the mount. Some of these facsimiles are so realistic that they are often mistaken as being authentic. So buyer beware!

Often overlooked by the autograph collector, until now, is that some revenue stamps were canceled with the signature of the photographer. These should not be confused with facsimile reproductions of the photographer's signature that have appeared as part of the back imprint of an image.

Theatrical photography brought actors and actresses from stage and screen into our homes well before the advent of radio and television. The albumen (a coating placed on paper to enhance longevity) images of Sarah Bernhardt by Nadar, were just some of many prompting the use of photography for theatrical promotion. Carte-de-viste images of your favorite celebrity quickly found their way into theater lobbies where they were sold to the public. As the demand for carte-de-vistes waned during the turn of the century, imagery shifted from portraits to specific productions. By the 1920s photographically illustrated programs prompted the need for greater dramatic imagery in photography. All this was only a prelude to the massive distribution of today's glossy (often 5" x 7" or 8" x 10") and the traditional "photo call" among stage actors.

Cabinet Cards

The larger cabinet cards were a natural extension to that of the carte-de-viste. Created with a similar process, this format (four times larger than its predecessor) was introduced in 1863 by Windsor & Bridge (London). It consisted of a 4" x 5-1/2" albumen print adhered to a 4-1/4" x 6-1/2" heavy cardboard mount. Because no photo albums existed when this format was released many found their way into the confines of the drawing room cabinet.

Collecting Images Of The Civil War

- By most accounts, cartes-de-visites make up the largest percentage—in form, of Civil War images, followed next by tintypes.
- While both stereographs and ambrotypes are scarce, the most difficult form to find from this era is large albumen prints and daguerreotypes.
- Tintypes are commonly found without their original case. Those images with original cases can command higher prices.
- The frequency of ambrotype images decreased during the war. Images in this form are typically early scenes or young officers, the latter of which is highly sought by collectors.
- Massive quantities of carte-de-visites were produced during the war and often mailed back and forth between acquaintances and family members.
- Images produced by the eras finest photographers—Brady, O'Sullivan and Gardner, were mass produced both as cartes and stereographs and distributed by the E. and H.T. Anthony and Co.
- As many Civil War uniforms were difficult to recognize, collectors should familiarize themselves with the styles of the era in order to better identify images.
- The U.S. government instituted a law requiring that a tax stamp be adhered to the back of specific types of photographs from August 1864 until August 1866. The stamp denominations were in proportion with the cost of the photograph. The stamps were canceled by the seller with an identifiable ink stamp—sometimes dated or simply with a mark of ink.

The photos, produced in pairs on a full plate negative, soon became the format of choice and gradually displaced the carte-de-viste. By 1866, the new format had found its way to America. Because of the larger negative, photographers made retouching an integral part of the process along with the use of backgrounds and accessories.

The popularity of this format began to wane by the end of the 1880s due to the development of the halftone printing process. Albumen prints however, did sustain themselves for many years after the advent of gelatin-based papers. Cabinet cards can be found dating up to the beginning of World War I, but they are far less prevalent than those of the prior century.

Most of the autographed cabinet cards a collector encounters are those bearing imprints of Brady, Disderi, Mora, Nadar and Sarony because these were the photographers noted for shooting important subjects.

Stereographs

Stereographs, also called stereo cards, stereotypes, stereoscopic views or stereoviews, were a pair of photographs, created by a myriad of processes, mounted for three-dimensional viewing in a stereoscope. Charles Wheatstone envisioned the concept, but it wasn't popularized until 1851 when Sir Charles Brewster invented a stereoscope that was exhibited at the Crystal Palace Exhibition.

Early images were made by taking two exposures at different angles with the same camera, or by using two cameras sitting side by side. Brewster's stereoscope gave way to that of American John Mascher in 1855. By this time companies were scrambling to produce and stockpile thousands of different stereo images. Some of the first commercial stereograph businesses were the Langenheim Brothers of Philadelphia, the London Stereoscopic Company, Gladwells, and Negretti & Zambra all of Great Britain. Later E. and H.T. Anthony and Company would also play a leading role in the manufacture of stereographs.

Not only were the images being refined, but so were the stereographic viewers. One of the most popular in America was the Holmes-Bates Stereoscope, promoted by none other than the well-known physician and author himself, Oliver Wendell Holmes.

By the late 1860s, stereograph manufacturers had evolved into selling a complete set or several sets of cards revolving around a single theme. These sets included Niagara Falls, the Johnstown Flood and even a staged series such as Little Red Riding Hood.

The era of the "Victorian Television," which in retrospect really describes the period, would be popular until about 1810 when it began to falter amidst new technology.

Dry Plates and Gelatin Prints

Despite the popularity of the collodion wet-plate process it was hampered by complaints of it being a messy process, which it indeed was. You could always pick out the photographer in a group because his hands were stained from contact with the silver nitrate. A dry-plate process seemed a logical alternative and was heavily experimented with during the 1860s and 1870s. Commercial dry-plate production would not commence until the end of the 1870s, when improvements were made to the 1871 concept of the gelatin-based photographic plate introduced by Richard Maddox, a British physician.

Because of the initial poor results of the process, photographers were slow to embrace this new dry-plate process. Even an endorsement from the Photographic Association of America, could not enhance the transition that was slowed also because plates had to be purchased from the manufacturers.

Emphasis then shifted to the amateur photography market and was enhanced by the entrance of George Eastman (Kodak) who would invest his life savings to produce dry plates for E. and H.T. Anthony and Co. Eastman not only competed successfully in the dry-plate business, but also ventured into the development of gelatin roll film (1884) and the popular Kodak detective camera (1888).

During this period as well, experiments were being conducted in Britain with a new type of printing paper that had a similar gelatin-based emulsion. This bromide or silver-bromide paper would not be embraced in America until a court battle was settled between Eastman and Edward Anthony, both claiming patent infringement over the manufacture of the new paper.

Because many problems still existed with the early gelatin papers, migration was slow, as photographers turned to other options which included velox, carbon prints or sticking with albumen. The advantage of velox, a gelatin-chloride paper, was its flexibility—it was less sensitive, but the disadvantage was cost. Carbon, having been around for half a century, was always an option, as was albumen. During this time there were also new developments in the platinum print process, forerunners of the modern photographic process.

With the new century came options, as the new question was roll film, plate or both. Dry-plate had remained the staple until roll film came into extensive use. We most often associate the image of the photographer inserting the dry-plates one by one into his camera with this era.

Contact printing was still popular, as enlargers were just coming into use. Paper was in two forms, developing (exposed with a gaslight) or printing-out (exposed by the sun). Photography was now also coming into focus, and with it an entirely new definition of the photographer and his art.

Infrared Photography

Infrared photography is of interest to many, including advanced autograph collectors, because it produces images that are not possible with conventional photographic films. Enhancing its appeal is that it does not differ dramatically from normal photography. Because of this, the same cameras and light sources can be used and even the same processing solutions. What this form of photography does is allow the film to record what the eye cannot see. The infrared range of the electromagnetic spectrum lies beyond the red—a portion that is invisible to human eyes.

While infrared photography has many applications in the forensic lab, it was not until the 1930s that it became a common tool of the document examiner. It can reveal engravings, photographs and printed matter that have been damaged by dirt or age. Mechanical and chemical erasure can be revealed even if overwritten*. Infrared photography has also replaced other forms of study in determining the authenticity of works of art.

* The overwriting must be of an ink transparent to infrared.

Brief Photographic Processes

Selected Developments 1900-Date

Year	Event
1948	Polaroid Black & White, peel-apart diffusion transfer material
1955	Kodak Type C Ektacolor paper
1955	Kodak Type R Ektachrome paper
1963	Polacolor peel-apart color diffusion transfer
1972	Polaroid SX-70 integral diffusion transfer color material
1976	Kodak Instant Print film
1979	Cibachrome "A" Pearl surface resin coated paper
1981	Kodak Ektaflex PCT one-solution color print making system
1982	Kodak Disc-film camera, film and processing system
1983	Polaroid Polaprinter, instant one minute full-color prints
1984	Kodak Elite Fine-Art Paper
1991	Kodak Photo CD

Identification of Handlettering and Numerals

Inexperienced autograph collectors pay little attention to the details of a signed document, opting instead to go straight to the source of their delight, a signature. Advanced autograph collectors know better and spend just as much time looking at numerals and even printed letters as much as a signature. The reason is a simple one, both handlettering and numerals can be extremely revealing to a questioned document. More than one criminal has been put behind bars for forging accounting books, bank deposit slips, engineering drawings, gambling sheets, medical records, receipts, and time logs.

Handlettering

Handlettering is a disconnected form of writing and often a predecessor to cursive in our educational systems. Our use of it is often not limited to medical visits, as handlettering can play an integral part in some various specific occupations, such as architects, engineers and draftsman. If handlettering were not as common as we think, there wouldn't be as many cases of fraud and deception in our legal system.

Handlettering is a disconnected form of communication taught under various systems in our schools or at home. Depending upon the individual, some aspects of the learned system may or may not follow him throughout his life. Whatever the case, however, each individual will develop a unique handlettering system.

Many of the same factors that are used to analyze handwriting can also be applied to handlettering. These factors include number of strokes per form, proportion, size, stroke direction, stroke sequence, and slant. Writing qualities such as the precision of execution along with coordination elements such as speed, pressure and tremulous strokes can all be examined relative to handlettering. Because the letters are disconnected a primary consideration must be the continuity of each letter, or how many strokes are used to create each letter. Because it is a puzzle, different analytical methods are used to better understand the entire picture. Copies are made of known and questioned documents, similar words, word combinations and letter combinations are removed, enlarged and compared side by side. Unique character formations are identified, enlarged and then compared side by side. It is important to realize that a sufficient enough number of individual characteristics must be identified and common to both sets, so that little if any doubt remains. If you are trying to prove the opposite scenario this would also be the case.

The key to the above comparison is finding known examples written under similar circumstances. Hastily written handlettering can differ from that created in a normal environment. It is important to remember, however, that even under dramatic conditions in which the subject is trying to disguise his handwriting, with enough known comparisons a positive or near positive identification can be made. Often individuals who resort to handlettering in attempt to disguise their identity think that this form precludes detection and as such they make little attempt to alter their common writing characteristics.

With practice, you can become proficient at the identification of handlettering. In fact, most of you will find it both intriguing and challenging. Like many form of document analysis you will need tools, such as a protractor, ruler, magnification glass, access to a copier with enlargement features, etc., which many of you might already have close at hand.

The ABC's Of Handlettering

A Checklist of Concerns

A	Number of strokes, slant, curvature, size, cross-bar form
B	Number of strokes, slant, curvature, size, stroke intersection, flamboyance
C	Design, slant, curvature, size, flamboyance
D	Number of strokes, slant, curvature, size, stroke intersection, flamboyance
E	Number of strokes, slant, curvature, size, stroke intersection, stroke size pattern
F	Number of strokes, slant, curvature, size, stroke intersection, stroke size pattern
G	Number of strokes, slant, curvature, size, (LRHC)
H	Number of strokes, slant, size, stroke intersection, stroke height
I	Slant, size
J	Slant, curvature, size, flamboyance
K	Number of strokes, slant, curvature, size, stroke intersection, flamboyance
L	Number of strokes, slant, size, stroke intersection, flamboyance
M	Number of strokes, slant, curvature, size, stroke intersection, stroke sizes *
N	Number of strokes, slant, size, stroke intersection, stroke sizes *
O	Slant, curvature, size, stroke intersection or closure
P	Number of strokes, slant, curvature, size, stroke intersection, formation
Q	Slant, curvature, size, stroke intersection, flamboyance, (LRHC)
R	Number of strokes, slant, curvature, size, stroke intersection, (LRHC)
S	Symmetry, slant, curvature, size, flamboyance
T	Number of strokes, slant, size, stroke intersection and height
U	Slant, curvature, size, stroke intersection, height of beginning and ending stroke
V	Number of strokes, slant, size, height of beginning and ending stroke
W	Number of strokes, slant, size, stroke intersection & size, symmetry
X	Slant, size, stroke intersection, stroke length, symmetry
Y	Number of strokes, slant, curvature, size, stroke intersection, flamboyance
Z	Number of strokes, slant, size, stroke intersection & size, stroke length, symmetry

(LRHC) - Pay close attention to lower right hand corner of letter, * if not continuous; in many cases above I am assuming that the formation is not continuous. Form is a primary consideration of all characters.

Numerals

If you collect autographed sports memorabilia then you already know that numerals can be useful in identification. A common practice of both amateur and professional athletes is to include their number as part of their signature. Racecar driver Mark Martin integrates his racecar number "6" into the final stroke of his signature.

Since numerals involve fewer characters they can present a greater challenge, but trust me when I say they alone have unmasked many cases of deception. In addition to numerals, don't ignore symbols as a source of hidden identity. Naturally, symbols pertain to specific applications, so bear this fact in mind.

Changes in form and movement are often an indication that a document has multiple authors. The examiner pays close attention the numerals beginning and ending strokes— pen position, the flamboyance of the stroke, form—is it complex or simplified? , slant, speed, alignment, proportion and positioning in relation to other numerals, strokes and the page itself. Consistencies and inconsistencies should be identified, marked—obviously not on the original and recorded. All these factors will be combined with distinctions in the writing to form an individual case, or set of numerals, symbols and habits indicative of a single source. These distinctions could range from joining certain pairs of numerals or making some numerals consistently smaller than others or perhaps always aligning decimal points or underlining negative numbers.

Similar to handlettering, a level of natural variation—within certain tolerances, is to be expected. Trying to be sure that the known samples were created in a similar environment as that of the document in question will help control these variations. It is not uncommon to run into an individual that forms the same numeral differently on a single page, but this variation will be consistent if it is indeed genuine.

Numeral problems occur primarily around applications for their existence, such as accounting records, bank deposits, time logs and architectural and engineering diagrams. While not all these applications are common to the autograph market, many have indeed surfaced in dealer catalogs over the past twenty years. Advanced autograph collectors who acquaint themselves with the characteristics of both handlettering and numerals will eventually reap big dividends, so just be patient.

By The Numbers

A Numerals Checklist

1	Form, slant, curvature, size
2	Form, number of strokes, slant, curvature, size, stroke intersection *
3	Form, number of strokes, slant, curvature, size, symmetry
4	Form, number of strokes, slant, curvature, size, stroke intersection
5	Form, number of strokes, slant, curvature, size (especially top stroke)
6	Form, slant, curvature, size, stroke intersection **
7	Form, number of strokes, slant, curvature, size (especially top stroke)
8	Form, number of strokes, slant, curvature, size, stroke intersection, symmetry **
9	Form, number of strokes, slant, curvature, size, stroke intersection **
0	Form, slant, curvature, size, stroke intersection **

Symbols

@	Form, number of strokes, slant, curvature, size, stroke intersection, flamboyance
#	Form, number of strokes, slant, curvature, size, stroke intersection
$	Form, number of strokes, slant, curvature, size, stroke intersection, symmetry
%	Form, number of strokes, slant, curvature, size, stroke intersection, symmetry

* Because of the formation of the number "2" its relationship to the baseline should always be considered; ** The numerals 6,8,9, and 0 have loop, or ovals as part of their construction. These areas should be carefully examined for size, closure and flamboyance.

Chapter 3

Thwarting Forgeries

The Single Signature

Autograph collectors often find themselves authenticating a simple signature on an item rather than a handwritten letter filled with helpful holographic samples. The act of signing one's name is common and routine, thus taking on certain characteristics indicative of this process. A person's signature becomes a hallmark of the individual, be it flamboyant and careless, or simple and meticulous. While parallels can be drawn between a person's handwriting and the copybook writing that the individual studied, how one signs his name has less of an association. This is why collectors will often find many similarities in the handwriting of family members schooled in the same manner, yet differences in their signatures.

How a subject signs his name depends upon a number of factors such as the environment, the individual's health (includes age and its factors), personality, temperament, even what the individual is signing and how many times he's signing it—writing frequency. All these factors, most of which are transparent to the subject, play important roles in the authentication of a single signature.

It is important to consider the environmental conditions in which an item was signed. For example, Mark McGwire can sign an item differently when he's approached by fans near a dugout in contrast to being mobbed while trying to get on the team bus. A Ken Griffey, Jr. signature acquired during a sports memorabilia show, where the subject is paid for the task, will often be more meticulous than an autograph acquired from "Junior" at a restaurant. Too often this factor is forgotten while purchasing or authenticating an autograph.

Seasoned collectors know that health is a factor that can effect a signature. This factor is exhibited in the signatures of many individuals including John Adams, John Quincy Adams, Ben Hogan, Earl Averill, and Sandy Saddler. An individual whose signature was once flamboyant and meticulous can suffer from an illness that can detract from the simple task of signing his name. Numerous anomalies can appear such as tremulous writing and lack of character definition. Depending upon the writing instrument, the ink distribution can be uneven or uncommonly heavy, all as a result of poor health.

The personality and flamboyance of an individual can reek havoc on a signature, for example the often dynamic and flamboyant signatures of Michael Jackson, Tom Wolfe, Dennis Rodman, and Madonna. Celebrities are human too and as such exhibit emotion. After winning an NBA championship, Academy Award, or PGA tournament, the exhilaration can lead to flamboyant flourishes in one's signature.

Signature Variations

There are many factors that can cause a signature to vary such as age, illness, drugs and alcohol use, and mood. Some celebrities can get very irritated with autograph collectors and can even exemplify that temperament in a signature that is sloppy and illegible. I have witnessed this characteristic in-person numerous times with celebrities in all fields. I have seen members of the Rolling Stones sign a bunch of circles on an album that look more like accidental marks than a signature. I have even watched baseball players sign someone else's name on a team ball.

While baseball players are used to signing balls, hats, bats, etc., other prominent individuals in other fields are not, therefore, their signature can vary when it appears on these items. Authenticating a signature on a non-flat item is a study unto itself, especially if the subject is unfamiliar with signing such an item. Because of the characteristics inherent in a golf ball, basketball, hat, helmet or uniform, this task is best left to a professional authenticator.

Writing frequency is a factor that can affect a single signature. Individuals differ in the frequency to which they sign their name during a given day. While a celebrity may sign their name often, an average person or lesser known celebrity may go days or even weeks before rendering a signature. And what about the celebrities who sign autographs at shows or conventions? After signing over 500 items, few individuals can maintain interest yet alone concern themselves with the placement and formation of your signature, even if they are being paid.

Most of us strive for a consistency in our signature, if only to protect us from forgery. The execution of this process is the invisible combination of both the macro and micro factors, all of which can have an affect on the outcome. While minor variations are normal, significant differences are not.

How much a signature varies depends upon the individual and the environment in which it was accomplished. When you are comparing a single signature to known (authentic) examples in your file, be sure that these exhibits exemplify all of the subtle variations of the individual in question. For example, Babe Ruth signatures exemplify fine variations, such as the formation of the "R", slant and height of the "b" and even the ending stroke—which on limited occasions could double back. To draw a conclusion on authenticity an examiner must be able to exhibit the anomalies in known samples.

For a collector, natural changes or repeated occurrences in an individual's signature are easier to study than irregular variations. This is because natural variations occur more often. While I am more comfortable talking about the natural variations of a signature, I would be remiss if I didn't touch upon irregular variations.

Genuine signatures can exhibit an accidental or rare variation. Because this phenomena is not a common occurrence, it may require meticulous documentation. Examples of variation may occur when signatures are penned hastily on receipts or are signed under the influence of alcohol or narcotics. Other variations of signatures happen under extreme stress and during the declining years of ones life. Because of this, you must be able locate known authentic examples signed by the subject under these conditions.

Baseball Hall of Fame signature collectors often include in their files examples of Roy Campenella's signature before and after his serious automobile accident, samples of a youthful and aging Carl Hubbell,

---

A Brief Inspection Checklist For A Single Signature

Macro factors
- Beginning and ending strokes
- Continuous writing
- Interrupted writing—stops, pen lifts
- Letter connections
- Letter dynamics—smooth, sharp
- Pen position
- Stroke emphasis and shading
- Stroke retouching—habitual or unusual
- Writing pressure
- Writing rhythm—fluent, tremulous
- Writing speed

Micro factors
- Character formation & slant
- Character ornamentation or enhancements & flourishes
- Character size—capitals, lower case, ascender & descender height
- Signature balance

Note: These factors are dependent upon the writing instrument used and its movement combined with the physical factors involved in the completion of the process.

along with examples of Buck Leonard's signature before and after his 1986 stroke. For years U.S. Presidential autograph collectors have been fascinated by the transitions in Richard Nixon's signature during the Watergate crisis—an intriguing subject! A point worth noting is that genuine variations, unlike forgeries, make no attempt to improve or alter these variations.

Collecting single signatures that can be dated is a common practice among advanced autograph collectors. The practice is of particular assistance when variations occur as a result of old age or illness. Football great Amos Alonzo Stagg lived to be 102 and by that time his signature had changed greatly due to his age. Complicating this task is that many individuals in this condition are probably under some sort of medication that could have a powerful impact on their signature. I have seen more than one forensic scientist squirm, while testifying as an expert witness, that he was not aware of the medication taken by a subject. Nor was he aware of its possible side effects or even its effect on a subject's signature at various dosages under specific time periods.

Pencil And Pencil Erasures

The pencil has always been a popular writing device mainly because changes and revisions can be made easily by erasing unwanted strokes. Its popularity has even extended itself to the unscrupulous, who have used the tool to alter or forge documents. As an advanced collector it will be useful for you to familiarize yourself with how to identify if there has been an erasure and if there was, what was originally written?

The writing stroke of a pencil is produced by friction and unlike ink, cannot penetrate the paper fiber itself. The stroke a pencil produces is also not a solid line and varies through writing pressure, lead hardness and paper fiber. The pressure on the point and its sharpness also leaves an artifact in the form of a groove or embossing. This embossing can also be an artifact of material underneath the paper that is being written upon. How often have you written a note on a pad of paper with a pencil and lifted up the next sheet only to find that writing has transported itself into the next sheet? The extent of this embossing will depend on all the factors associated with the pencil stroke.

For years the typical way a pencil erased was with a rubber eraser found on most wooden pencils or mechanical pencils. Artists often use soft art gum that is slow, but effective, in erasing lighter pencil strokes without disturbing the fibers. Erasing typically removes the stroke from the paper, but often leaves

artifacts behind. Evidence of an erasure is often a disturbance of the paper fibers, a noticeable change in the papers finish or even small bits of the material used, such as graphite left behind.

Graphite is a form of carbon and as such cannot be bleached or eradicated. The graphite pencil stroke is not as easily removed as one might think, therefore, it is typical to find letter fragments in conjunction with a writing groove left behind. What remains are the clues for the authenticator, the missing puzzle pieces.

Determining if an erasure has been made will require a series of visual examinations. While not all erasures are alike, most are very obvious. Slightly discolored areas often appear where the paper has been obviously altered or pencil stroke fragments can be found under limited magnification. Erasures on printed forms or applications can often be picked up through the elimination of a line below where a person is to write. The key to erasure detection is having the right tools available for such a determination and knowing what characteristics to look for.

First the tools. Good lighting with the ability to alter both the angle and intensity of the beams is needed, along with various magnification tools. While most consider a light box or light table a nonessential, I find it a must. A set of color filters can be useful when dealing with colored pencil erasures. Weak color fragments can be enhanced with the addition of a complimentary color filter placed over the light source. Filtered ultraviolet radiation works great for certain types of erased ink, but is less effective with pencil erasures.

Under magnified study and low angle illumination, surface alterations and stray markings can become easily apparent to the authenticator. Writing indentations, which despite erasure often contain graphite fragments, can be deciphered from impressed writing, which are graphite free, made by another piece of paper.

The reverse side of a document should also be examined, as the process of erasing, can cause smears and smudges to appear. If any discoloration appears on the back of the questioned document, the suspected area should then be carefully examined from the front of the paper.

For most, the visual examination of a document alone is sufficient to locate pencil erasures. An advanced autograph collector should realize that additional chemical and physical tests can be performed by qualified forensic document examiners. Since some of these tests have destructive consequences, they are typically not associated with the hobby of autograph collecting. The chemical test most common to collectors is fuming the document with iodine. Rubber eraser marks appear as yellow

---

Characteristics Of An Erasure

- Alterations to the reflective surface of the paper
- Disruption of paper fibers
- Indentations, aligned with existing writing
- Paper discoloration in suspected areas
- Partially erased letters or words
- Portions of adjacent letters erased
- Small pieces of graphite found in suspected area
- Unexplainable paper thinning

---

stains versus a typical iodine stain when fumed in a chamber. The fumes are created by heating iodine crystals leaving your document discolored. When first viewed by a collector this procedure can cause near panic, but the discoloration partly disappears or can be chemically removed.

Other tests also exist, from dyed lycode powders and powdered graphite to even fluorescent powder. Most collectors will find few, if any, instances when chemical and physical tests will be necessary.

Providing handwriting examples is an area where autograph dealers and collectors are particularly beneficial to document examiners. Often a forensic examiner will have few specimens, or perhaps only the document itself as examples of the author's handwriting. The uniqueness of writing lends itself to the examination of how an individual structures characters, numbers and even words.

Photography can be extremely useful to both a document examiner and an autograph collector. Many techniques have evolved through experimentation with both film and light. While some techniques will require special equipment and materials, many will not. Black and white photography is the film of choice for decipherment. Among standard emulsions, moderate contrast films have exhibited excellent results. With each case unique, light angles, light sources, film types and print size are often experimented with in order to maximize the best result.

Oblique and low angle lighting have provided excellent results in many cases and for many years. Controlling the angle at which the light strikes the paper being the key to a good photograph. It is the author's suggestion that photographs be taken at chosen angle increments from every side, through the rotation of the document. Techniques using vertical illumination and low intensity light have also proven valuable and should be experimented with.

Infrared photography is common and used primarily when unerased pencil elements remain on the document or in situations where overwriting needs to be eliminated. Any writing tool containing infrared absorbing elements, such as carbon will have its trace elements intensified with the use of this method. For optimum lighting conditions, filter use, shutter speeds, etc. you should consult the many photographic resources available through numerous publishers and corporations, especially Eastman Kodak. Keep in mind that with this method you will have limited choice in emulsion, film format and processing (E-4). All advanced autograph collectors should experiment with infrared as a tool in their authentication arsenal.

If the erased writing was made by a color pencil, techniques such as the use of certain photographic filters or infrared luminescence can be employed. Unlike black pencil graphite, colored pencils often have luminescence properties—a reflective shine, and since this form of writing tool is often difficult to erase, examiners can often find fragments left on the document.

Once the film leaves your camera and enters a photography lab, numerous enhancements can be made to your images through varied developers, filters, etc. Naturally not all labs are the same, so you will have to consult with each individually in regard to the techniques they can employ.

The use of ESDA, or Electrostatic Detection Apparatus, has been very popular with document examiners. This device is extremely sensitive to impressions and invisible writing pressures. Using a vacuum bed, a piece of film is placed over the questioned document, then charged leaving an image corresponding exactly to the compression variances in the paper. The benefit of this technique is the ability to record very weak impressions on paper. ESDA, like all methods is not without its drawbacks. Results have been impacted through changes in the procedure and the testing environment. Because ESDA may pose a destructive threat to a pencil document it should be one of the last methods employed for decipherment.

Because of the many destructive characteristics surrounding the use of chemicals to aid in the decipherment of a document, it is not a recommended procedure. As an autograph collector just be aware that techniques such as iodine fuming do exist.

Physical decipherment techniques, such as dusting with powders, plastic and silicone rubber replicas can be useful but rarely do they uncover all that has been erased. Additionally these techniques could deface a document and therefore restrict any subsequent examinations. Unlike the movies, you should NEVER try to uncover indentations through rubbing the surface with the flat side of a soft leaded pencil.

Studying writing impressions involves many of the same techniques used in analyzing erasures and alterations. Oblique lighting is extremely useful as is magnification. Remember a writing impression will not have the small pencil carbon fragments common in erasures. As such ESDA could certainly be an alternative, as could properly chosen fluorescent powders, but I would only recommend to autograph collectors visual examination.

Occasionally journals, notebooks and other bound documents are offered in the autograph market. Some of these may include writing indentations that could assist you in determining if any alterations were made to the previous page, or if pages were removed.

The autograph collector as document sleuth must try to put themselves into the shoes of the forger. A careful and detailed examination of the front and back of every document , from every angle, is a mandatory procedure. In a multiple page document patterns should be noted, as changes in dates, time and amounts often require related changes in a document. Certain terms, abbreviations and symbols relate to specific fields such as shorthand, navigation, chemistry and physics. If the questioned document uses specific nomenclature, be sure to familiarize yourself with it or consult an expert.

If you are not certain if a particular test or examination is going to have any effect on the questioned document or perhaps exclude some form of future testing, consult a professional. Since it may be conceivable that no alterations have been made to the questioned document, it would be disastrous to put it through rigorous or unneeded testing.

Associated items can be of assistance to collectors, especially photocopies. By monitoring the autograph market—watching what items are offered for sale in dealer catalogs and advertisements, I have found on more than one occasion a fraudulent handwritten pencil note added to an authentic letter. An authentic letter from a famous writer's wife was offered for sale, and since I have a personal interest in the writer I photocopy all items relating to him that enter the market. Boy was I shocked when just months later- now decades since the writer's death, a handwritten note from him miraculously appeared at the bottom of the exact letter. The meaning and thus value of a document can be altered by the addition of writing just as quickly as an erasure.

Alterations in a person's handwriting, writing instrument (pencil dulls with use), crowding of words, unusual margins, unusual folds or creases should be noted, then investigated.

The Detection Of Changes Or Removed Writing

A document examiner often finds alterations (changes) and obliterations (signs of handwriting removal), or even ink variation within a questioned document. Since this is evidence of a second writing instrument, authentication is immediately questioned.

Often these types of details are uncovered through low magnification and under a variety of lighting conditions. Using various types of color filters, some in combination, the document examiner is able to go beyond what can be seen by the naked eye. If this examination is not enough, he will go deeper into his arsenal of tool and perhaps use a stereo microscope to uncover subtle changes in shading or evidence of secondary lines. Also available is photography or Video Spectral Comparison (VSC) used to enhance selective portions of the light spectrum.

Infrared imagery, although not new, has played a valuable role in uncovering details not seen by the unaided eye. Inks that appear similar under normal lighting conditions now reveal their true identity. The luminescence or glow of the ink can be observed and the ink could disappear or even appear unchanged. This process can be recorded for court purposes in the form of photography or VSC.

Thin-layer chromatography, explained in detail below, has also proved invaluable for the examination of inks. Because TLC is a form of destructive testing it may not appeal to an autograph collector, but in cases where this type of examination will not impact the value of a document, it can be helpful.

Combining these methods, with methods specific to a particular form of writing instrument can yield dramatic and conclusive results. For example, if a ball-point pen was used as the writing instrument, under microscopic observation the stria (furrow, channel), or lack thereof conclusions can be drawn about a particular pen.

The First Steps Of Unmasking Deception

- Evidence of Artifical Aging
- Feathering—the spreading of new ink applied to old paper
- Inconsistent Writing Style & Form
- Off-scale Writing—writing too big or too small
- Retouching *
- The Wrong Writing Materials
- Tremuous Writing **
- Uncommon Form—"Abe Lincoln" instead of "A. Lincoln"
- Unnatural Handwriting
  * **Note:** I have seen retouching as habit with only a few individuals.
  ** **Note**: subject dependent

Mechanical & Facsimile Signatures

One of the most challenging areas of autograph collecting has been the constant monitoring of the use of machine-generated signatures. The idea is far from new; just visit Monticello and view in-person Thomas Jefferson's polygraph. Even in Jefferson's era, the demands of a public official often necessitated making copies of certain documents and any device that could help the president save time was be appreciated.

For decades, public officials, who often receive thousands of pieces of mail weekly, had sought solution to the overwhelming task of responding to the needs of their constituents. To tackle the problem of answering mail, they turned to machines such as the **Autopen** or **Signa-Signer**. Both of these machines proved very useful in signing the hundreds of stock letters on file in a politician's office.

Tamkin Color/Studio Fan Mail is a company familiar to all autograph collectors, as they respond to mail sent to many celebrities. While the facsimile signed items sent by the firm are easy to distinguish as such, I have found some listed on the popular web site ebay identified as authentic signatures.

The limitations of the early machines, such as storing only one matrix pattern - one style of signature, were elevated by advances in storage technology. Autograph collectors soon realized that they could win a few battles against this nemesis, such as identifying certain patterns because the signatures superimposed at certain portions of the signature, but to win the war would be a long and arduous task.

Those of you who have ever seen a pen plotter work can easily envision such a device. These machines can easily replicate a person's signature, initials and even handwriting. While the patterns of the past can be easily identified by the tremulous strokes and the replication of a near identical signature, the machines of today have improved considerably. Entire books have and will continue to be written that identify machine-generated signature and handwriting patterns for autograph collectors. For example, John F. Kennedy's robust use of such a machine led autograph sleuth Charles Hamilton to pen *The Robot that Helped to Make a President*. Hundreds of machine-signed letters and cards surface on the market each year.

Ironically, most people today, many of whom are familiar with the advances in output technology, still can't believe that an elected official would resort to such an option. As collectors we need only look as far as our own collection to view many examples of these signatures. From John F. Kennedy and Lee Trevino, to Jack Kemp and Oprah Winfrey, machine-generated signatures have proved to be cost effective. A "common sense" approach to this dilema will avoid many mistakes. Consider the popularity and work schedule of the individual, along with the content/importance of the letter or document or likelihood of an in-person signing opportunity.

While as a hobby we certainly view any technology that can reproduce a signature as a nemesis, not everyone feels the same way. Many court cases have even held that mechanically reproduced signatures were acceptable in place of genuine signatures in some instances.

Since technology has now given us so many different ways to put a signature on a piece of paper, we are going to have to spend more time, money and energy evaluating the signature habits of our subjects. This means more letters, more examples of both authentic and facsimile signatures and bigger and bigger files on our subjects. We are also going to have to keep up with advances in technology. Collectors are going to have to be able to identify signatures created by laser copiers and pen plotters and understand the current limitations in optical scanning.

"Ghost" Signers

Thousands of celebrities, athletes, businessman and politicians have used legal forgers, also known as "ghost" signers, to put the pen to paper on their behalf. While the process was not new in concept, it really gained popularity during the 20th century, especially with the emergence of motion pictures, television and even athletes as entertainers. With time a precious commodity, it only made sense and besides a facsimile was a warmer and more personal approach than using that of a rubber stamp or mimeograph machine.

Often this approach was used when a celebrity was involved in a fund raising event, marketing contest or charity effort. Little did dad realize that the photo of Harry James he received from Chesterfield cigarettes, "Best Chesterfield Wishes Harry James" was actually the work of a legal forger and mom's Bing Crosby signature from that Swans Down Cake Flour, well, yeah that was also a ghost signature.

The role of ghost signer has been filled by relatives, secretaries and even batboys. So where does this leave the autograph market? Both dealer and collectors are forced to rigorously evaluate any signature acquired indirectly. To do so however, requires a strong understanding of handwriting

identification. A task that is not easy and one that is being performed less and less by those entering the hobby.

Celebrities Known To Have Used Ghost Signers

Below is just a partial list of celebrities known to use others to sign on their behalf:

Winthrop W. Aldrich	Albert Goldman	Robert Redford
Gene Autry	Jean Harlow	Martin Revson
Lucille Ball	Averill Harriman	Quinton Reynolds
Mrs. August Belmont	June Havoc	Grantland Rice
Jack Benny	Arthur Garfield Hayes	Eddie Rickenbacker
Evangeline Booth	Helen Hayes	Paul Robeson
Pearl Buck	William Randolph	Nelson Rockefeller
Eddie Cantor	Hearst	Winthrop Rockefeller
Al Capp	Bob Hope	Eleanor Roosevelt
Dale Carnegie	Lena Horne	Theodore Roosevelt
Rosemary Clooney	Harry James	Helena Rubenstein
Glen Close	Georgie Jessel	Jane Russell
Claudette Colbert	Sammy Kaye	Babe Ruth
Perry Como	Kay Kayser	Steven Seagal
Sean Connery	W.K. Kellogg	Vincent Sheehan
Kevin Costner	Gene Kelly	Dinah Shore
Jamie Lee Curtis	Grayson Kirk	Frank Sinatra
Lily Dache	Fiorello H. LaGuardia	Alfred Smith
Charles De Gaulle	Herbert H. Lehman	Kate Smith
Jay Hanna "Dizzy"	Claire Booth Luce	Nathan Strauss
Dean	Bela Lugosi	Barbra Streisand
Thomas E. Dewey	Mickey Mantle	Arthur H. Sulzberger
Joseph P. DiMaggio	Dean Martin	Elizabeth Taylor
Melvyn Douglas	Steve McQueen	Shirley Temple
Hugh Downs	Marilyn Monroe	Lowell Thomas
Clint Eastwood	Edward R. Murrow	Dorothy Thompson
James A. Farley	Paul Newman	John Travolta
Marshall Field	Dorothy Parker	Claire Trevor
Lynn Fontanne	Jack Paar	Henry A. Wallace
Helen Forest	Brock Pemberton	Mike Wallace
Lou Gehrig	Mary Pickford	Thomas Watson
Arthur Godfrey	Brad Pitt	John H. Whitney

On-Site Authentication

Autographed sports memorabilia has been area that has been plagued by problems of forgery. As a result some parties have embraced the issue and offered some possible solutions.

PSA

Professional Sports Authenticator (PSA), established in 1991, is the world's largest grading and authenticating service in the trading card industry. The company followed in the steps of its parent PCGS, Incorporated, a collectibles service company that

provides quality verification, publications and other associated products and services to a broad area of the collectibles market. While PSA began by grading sports cards, they have now expanded their service to include non-sports trading cards. The way the company has chosen to approach the market is through its PSA Authorized Dealer Network, which is comprised of card dealers authorized by PSA to accept trading cards from the public and submit them to the corporation for grading and authentication. PSA authorized dealers also buy, sell and trade cards through auctions, direct sales and dealer-to-dealer transactions.

PSA Card Grading Service

Cards are submitted to PSA through the PSA Authorized Dealers Network or by members of the PSA Collectors Club. The club, established in 1996, was formed after many collectors requested direct submission privileges to PSA. Once a card is received, and they receive many (about 70,000 per month), it's graded and sealed with a certification insert in a state-of-the-art, tamper-evident holder.

The company uses a ten point grading system from Gem-Mint (GEM-MT 10) to Poor to Fair (PR-FR1). The firm also protects the customer and the hobby by not encapsulating cards that are altered or counterfeit. They also conveniently offer a number of grading services based on turn-around time. These include: Two-Day Express Service, Regular Service, Economy Service and Commons Service. This service is backed by the firm's Guarantee of Grade, Originality and Authenticity.

DNA Technologies is one of the premier corporations using the vital building blocks of life as a way to authenticate items. They currently manufacture pens used by many individuals to help thwart forgeries.

Dedicated to the Task

The company's commitment to the hobby is also exhibited through its newsletters and reports to assist sports card collectors, dealers, and investors interested in PSA and collecting. They include: Sportscard Market Report, a buying guide for PSA graded sports trading card; PSA Population Report, a census on every sports card graded, authenticated and encapsulated by PSA and PSA Grading Report, which spotlights specific cards, trends or the latest information in the sports card industry.

On August 8, 1998, PSA announced that it had contracted with DNA Technologies of Los Angeles, to introduce autograph authentication to its list of services. This logical extension of the company's services, which is known as PSA/DNA Guaranteed Authentic, combines the resources of the firm with the world's leading anti-counterfeiting technology company.

All items certified will also be tagged with an invisible and non-damaging DNA trace liquid that is unique to the service. This invisible DNA mark can be read and confirmed using a handheld infrared laser device.

Each item authenticated will bear a non-transferable tamper-evident label displaying a unique certification number as well as the logo of the service. This high-security adhesive label is constructed using proprietary laminant, adhesive and optical technologies. When properly verified, any photo substitution, alteration or removal of information can be detected.

The technology is currently used on autographs signed in the presence of a PSA/DNA Guaranteed

Authentic representative, with hopes that in the future it may extend to previously signed material. The service is available for public and private signings with prices per autograph authentication ranging from $2—$7.

PSA/DNA Guaranteed Authentic, P.O. Box 6180, Newport Beach, CA 92658

Phone: (949) 833-8824, (800) 325-1121, Fax: (949) 833-7955

Email: info@psacard.com, Website: www.psadna.com
Contacts: Steve Rocchi, PSA President, Miles Standish or Jason Micheletto

Total Sports Concepts

Total Sports Concepts of Clarks Summit, PA has received a patent on an authentication system that involves digital photos of every item being signed. The photos are placed onto a driver's license-looking certificate of authenticity along with the owner's name and address. The certificate includes three photographs—the item being signed, the item by itself and a blowup of the autograph. Each card includes a tracer code that can be entered into TSC's database to find the history of the signature, while each item carries an unremovable hologram.

In 1995, the company was started by CEO William G. Fleming Sr., as a publishing company for limited edition lithographs. TSC believe that it can provide its service for both public and private signings and hopes that its ability to provide a new certificate card for every ownership change will enhance its presence in the market. For additional information you can contact: (717) 587-1675

Super Star Greetings

Super Star Greetings of Livingston, N.J., which is affiliated with Prince of Cards, offers products authenticated with a new system. The firm places matching numbered holograms on the item, certificate of authenticity and a photo of authenticity. The concept was derived from Prince of Cards, known for including photographs with its autographs acquired during private signings. The company has already used the system for many signings including photographs obtained by the company from noted *Sports Illustrated*

photographer Neil Leifer. For further information you can contact: (973) 994-2784

Even if you do not agree with the concept of on-site authentications, you have to applaud the efforts of any firm who is willing to go an additional step to thwart forgery. As for which system or systems will prove most viable, only time will tell. The one area/method that has attracted considerable attention with advanced autograph collectors has been research in the field of DNA. So let's dig a little deeper into the realm of DNA.

The Signature as a Forgery

Traced Forgeries

During the 1980s, when the boom in autographed sports memorabilia was just taking off, it wasn't a difficult task to find bogus signatures at dealer's tables. One Central New York dealer became notorious for tracing signatures and passing them off as cuts—or portions cut from documents. While his initial efforts were primitive, he did get pretty good at it over time. But there was one problem, while his disjointed tracing strokes got smoother, he continued using the same examples, thus when you were able to hold two or more of his offerings up to the light they appeared identical, similar to machine-signed signatures. Knowing he didn't have the financial resources to continue buying authentic originals, I was able to draw the conclusion that he was tracing the signatures. Ironically, at the next show, he brought in his originals—as he was confronted about forgery at the previous show, and tried to sell them to another dealer. Upon close inspection you could see the indentations as a result of tracing over the originals. While it's hard to believe that this really happened, it's even harder to believe that the dealer is still in business.

Because this approach is more like drawing a signature rather than writing one, this technique is easy to identify as such. Often a forger will even go back into a stroke and attempt to retouch it, these markings can be picked up through magnification by an experienced autograph collector. When porous tip pens are used with this method, stroke stoppages—with the pen still in contact with the paper can produce easily identified absorption points. One dealer in the area of rock 'n' roll autographs uses this method but lays down a series of dots placed strategically to guide his pen through the stroke. He uses this method because he wants to maintain the correct path, but with a far smoother stroke. I purchased some of his

signatures as examples of this method. Unfortunately, I believe he is also still in business.

While traced forgeries are a joke, they are still used. Collectors can still be enticed by even crude imitations. Carbon tracings used to be extremely popular with forgers, but have fallen off over the years as dealers become more proficient at recognizing them as such. This method fails on many accounts:

- The carbon leaves a haloing effect around the ink.
- Erasing the marks after an ink signature is laid down can damage the ink and show up under magnification and finally.
- The one most often used in court, infrared photography can penetrate most inks, leaving only the carbon outline.

If you're not already running to your safe deposit box to check to see if any of those Lou Gehrig cuts you purchased are actually forgeries, perhaps you should!

While some old methods of forgery do occasionally surface, most have given way to improved methods. However, the old tracing a guideline first with a stylus method, followed by a pen over trace of the indented line does rear its ugly and identifiable head on occasion. Thankfully as a hobby we made it over some of these humps. If you're involved in a litigation where a traced original is suspected, although it may be difficult to do, try to get a hold of the original that was used. It will be extremely helpful in proving your case in court. Here's how one collector did it:

A collector had purchased a series of traced baseball Hall of Fame cuts from an unscrupulous dealer. After confronting the dealer directly about the counterfeits, but having no success at getting his money back, he chose an indirect path. He had another dealer confront the alleged forger. This dealer was excellent at enticing the other dealer's attention and even better at eliciting fear. To make a very long story

---

The Detection Of A Freehand Forgery

Characteristics to Examine

- Awkward character formations—Are the characters formed properly?
- Awkward pen lifts—Does the stroke abruptly stop in an uncommon area?
- Degree of execution—How closely does it reflect an authentic sample?
- Direction changes—Are there any awkward changes in stroke direction?
- Hesitant stroke—Are there any areas of the signature that do not flow freely?
- Patching & repair—Under magnification has any retouching been done?
- Pen position—Does the stroke begin and end at relatively the same position as an original?
- Rhythm—Songs have rhythm, so do signatures!
- Signs of hesitation—Does any aspect of the stroke look apprehensive?
- Stroke continuity— Are there any inadvertent skips in the stroke?
- Stroke emphasis—Does the signature contain the proper stroke emphasis?
- Stroke firmness—Is the pressure of the stroke indicative of the subject?
- Tremulous strokes—Are there any tremulous strokes in the signature?
- Writing speed—Is the writing speed indicative of that of the subject?

---

short, the scared unscrupulous dealer later sold the originals to the dealer who approached him. That dealer then passed them along to the collector. Whether the collector ever got his money back, I do not know, but what I am certain of is that he now had one heck of a case.

If a questioned signature bears no likeness to that of the subjects, then perhaps it was just a careless forgery or a ghost signer. I have seen numerous payroll checks hit the market that were not signed by a subject, but by his wife. Many of these examples are covered in my other books.

Freehand Forgeries

Only the best and most skillful forgers use freehand imitations for deception. Integral to his with this method is his ability to mimic all elements of his subject's signature. He does so without his own inherit writing characteristics getting in the way, or at least he thinks so! Many freehand forgeries look more drawn than signed. They are primitive with far more emphasis on character definition than stroke.

Identifying the Forger

Identifying who executed a forgery is a difficult, but not impossible task. A common method used involves acquiring enough exemplars of the party in question to construct a strong case against the individual. This is done by cutting and pasting known examples together that bear a resemblance to a particular disputed signature. In some cases, the identity of an individual was uncovered through an anomaly he had in his own handwriting, be it a unique character construction or the common addition or deletion in character pair constructions. Whatever the approach, most require a substantial amount of research often without enough known examples to prove anything.

Initials

As an advanced autograph collector there are times when you will encounter items signed with initials only, such as "F.D.R." or "R.N." Some individuals and dealers in the hobby have done an excellent job at dissecting the anomalies inherent in certain individual's initials, such as Franklin D. Roosevelt and Richard M. Nixon. Initials can be authenticated through all the elements previously mentioned; the difficulty in doing so, is typically finding enough known examples to complete the process.

Technology

Since nearly everything created can be autographed, advanced autograph collectors have to keep up with technology and its byproducts. A signature that appears on an item that was not created during the subject's lifetime, should be a dead giveaway—pardon the pun, that the item is not authentic.

Technology Time Line

1822	Joseph N. Niepce (1765-1833) produces earliest form of the photograph.
1835	William H.F. Talbot (1800-1877) invents photographic negative using silver chloride.
1837	Samuel F.B. Morse (1791-1872) patents first commercially successful version of the telegraph.
1839	Louis J.M. Daguerre (1789-1851) announces his process for making photographs, called daguerreotypes.
1846	Richard M. Hoe (1812-1896) invents rotary printing press.
1867	Latham Sholes (1819-1890) and two others invent first practical typewriter.
1937	Chester F. Carlson (1906-1968) invents xerography, the first method of photocopying.
1969	ATMs and bar-code scanners introduced.
	ARPANET, the first part of the Internet, is set up to link Defense Department contractors.
1975	IBM introduces first laser printer.
1985	Apple's LaserWriter printer and Aldus Corp.'s PageMaker program usher in the age of desktop publishing.

Electrophotography

With over one trillion documents copied each year through the combination of light and electricity—electrophotography, it is probably fair to assume that at least some of these copies will become an autographed item through the simple addition of a signature. Although many different processes exist within the framework of electrophotography, the most popular systems seem to be those that involve electrostatically charged particles on insulator surfaces. This concept was patented in 1942, by Chester F. Carlson who had the distinction of making the first xerographic image in 1937.

The term "electrophotography" quickly evolved into "xerography," which means dry writing, but most of us became familiar with another word Xerox. The Halloid Company of Rochester, New York, licensed by The Battelle Memorial Institute in Columbus—who was working with Carlson, developed and marketed the first copying machine based on the new technology. The Halloid Company used the name Xerox to describe its equipment. The name became so synonymous with the technology that the company altered its name first to Halloid Xerox in 1958, followed by the Xerox Corporation in 1961. (A good example of how corporate name changes on letterheads can assist the document examiner in determining the age of an item.)

Prior to the advent of electrophotography, the Halloid Corporation sold photocopying machines based only on wet chemical processes. Xerography, as a form of electrophotography, has had its share of competitive technologies including Electrofax, Persistent Internal Polarization and Photoconductive Pigment Electrophotography. To date, none has been able to compete successfully against xerography's quality, cost and output rates. This technology, which is used in virtually all commercial copiers, has also become widely used in printing.

As the hobby of autograph collecting evolves, so does the technology around us. Many of the signed items that will appear in the autograph market over the next few decades will have been created using fairly advanced technologies and materials. All of these advancements must be noted in order to ease the difficulty of authentication.

Many security agencies have been well aware of advances in xerography. Manufacturers have worked with various governmental agencies, such as the FBI and the Treasury Department. As the quality of xerography advanced, so did mechanisms enabling these agencies to trace the origin of fraudulent documents created through the process. When caught, forgers choosing to use this process to create and distribute their counterfeits will be easily prosecuted and convicted, ironically through detection systems that have been in place for years.

In future editions I will try to include a comprehensive listing of product introductions, so that you will know that the first direct electrostatic process machine using zinc oxide paper was introduced by Apeco in 1961 or that the 3M dual spectrum Copier was introduced in 1963. You can already see the benefit of having this data.

The first time a dealer offers a copy of The Constitution, printed from a laser printer and signed by the entire Supreme Court under Warren E. Burger, what do you think is going to be the first question asked to an authenticator? Was it possible at the time for such a document to be created? Well, was it?

The Internet

The Internet now makes access to autographs, both authentic and forged, simple. Since advanced autograph collectors take numerous precautions prior to purchasing items, I need not remind you about guarantees, etc. If you are not familiar with a dealer, ask questions! Also remember that reputable autograph dealers can be found both "on" and "off" the Internet. So I wouldn't draw any conclusions based upon whether or not a dealer has a web site.

The Internet is just another marketing tool for dealers and another acquisition channel for collectors. Internet autograph sites vary tremendously in ease-of - use, style, format, and convenience. Some dealers include pictures of the items for sale, so at least the form of the signature can be viewed. That is, of course, if the picture is really the signature you are going to receive when you purchase the item. Naturally, the only way a collector would buy an item he has not seen is if he is dealing with a reputable dealer he knows.

Some dealers do an outstanding job maintaining their sites, adding new features and links to other locations, as well as providing detailed descriptions of items and the purchasing process. On the contrary, some other web sites are a disaster and miss the boat completely in their design. Some are just too slow, hard to read, include incomplete descriptions and don't have simple functions like a global search of the site— "Hello?"

The good news for collectors is some of the dealers are waking up to our needs. No doubt with a little exploring you will find the site that best suits your needs by using America OnLine (AOL) and Yahoo! as a search engine. Global searches can link "autographs" to well over 15,000 sites, another testament to the popularity of our hobby. Below I have listed a few sites that I visited while writing this chapter and added my comments.

In addition to visiting the many web sites dedicated to autograph collecting, collectors should also visit institutional sites. For example, the John Hopkins University Special Collections Main Page includes a listing of rare books, historical manuscripts, sheet music, and other interesting material. Within the historical manuscripts section you will find an overview, manuscript registers, collection development policy and related university archives. Inside each collection (Manuscript register), you will find detailed information about the archive, such as size, provenance, permission and other details.

The Internet is an excellent tool for the advanced autograph collector and a logical and must addition to his collecting arsenal.

ebay

On-line commerce does not exclude the autograph business, therefore, numerous sites feature autographed material for sale. One of the most popular sources for signatures is "ebay", which not only provides an auction platform for the sale of autographs but just about everything else imaginable. Like any internet site that features autographs, the integrity and knowledge of the dealer or seller is paramount. Similar to buyers, not all sellers are created equal, so you must first determine just who are you dealing with. A novice who just found an old John Travolta autographed photo in a trunk and decided to part with it? or an experienced dealer who routinely sells this type of item and is familiar with the many nuances in the hobby? Typically the way an item is being described is the first indication of the caliber of the seller. An experienced dealer utilizes traditional hobby terms and is very specific with every element, accurately indicating the size of the item, details surrounding the subject's signing habits and clearly stating references or hobby affiliations.

The biggest mistake most buyers make is putting too much faith in the seller's expertise in the hobby. This hobby is no longer simple and to represent yourself as a knowledgeable dealer requires education. Dealers must be familiar with facsimile signatures, ghost signed items and machine generated examples. Unfortunately, many are not and as a result many vautographed items find there way onto auction sites and are represented as authentic, when they are not. As the buyer, you must take precautions! If you don't know ask, and if the person selling the item can not give you an answer to your question find someone who can.

As a collector, I need not lecture you again on protecting yourself against fraud, but be careful. Make sure you are completely comfortable with any item you purchase on-line and understand what level of guarantee you have with the item. Nothing short of one hundred percent satisfaction, including a lifetime guarantee of authenticity should be acceptable. References and previous buyer feedback should be checked on every seller before making your purchase. Also, if a scanned image of an item is provided, be sure that is indeed the piece that you will be receiving upon purchase. Take nothing for granted, especially the knowledge of the person who sold it to you. Do not rely upon the COA (certificate of authenticity) as the final confirmation of authenticity. Anyone can offer one! This document is only as good as the person who signs it.

Many quality autograph and manuscript dealers also sell on e-bay and often they have links to their website, so explore! Take a look at what they have to offer on their personal site and get a sense of the type

Useful Internet Sights For Autograph Collectors

Selected Sights—Not Intended to be Comprehensive

Alexander Autographs (http://www.alexautographs.com)
Alexander Autographs sponsors a mail, phone, fax and internet auction approximately every four months featuring autographs in all fields of collecting. I like the site and found it easy it use and understand.

Alfies Autographs of Hollywood (www.alfies.com)
If you like flashy web sites, Alfies is for you! Users can browse through his "Autograph Finder," "Attractions," "Press Clips" or view his "In-Person Star Collection." The popular site includes sections on actresses, female celebs, actors, male celebs and specials. The site was fun and easy to read.

Auction Universe (www.auctionuniverse.com)
This must have been a new site or was under construction when I visited it, as it didn't appear complete. Under autographs was 49 items being auctioned off, most of them autographed sports memorabilia. The site seems to have considerable potential and was easy to read.

Cordelia and Tom Platt (http://www.ctplatt.com)
A colorful and organized web site that is divided as follows: "About Us," "Products & Services," "Projects," "Schedule," "Contact Us," and "What's New." The site is operated by Cordelia and Tom Platt, established and knowledgeable dealers. I enjoyed the site and liked their selection of inventory, which was very diverse.

Early American History Auctions, Inc. (www.EarlyAmerican.com)
Early American History Auctions, Inc. offers six catalogs (auctions) at $36 per year. Their web site was simple, easy to understand and included some very nice items.

Mastros Fine Sports Auctions (www.mastrofsa.com)
Mastros is an excellent source for fine sports collectibles and their catalogs alone are worth a subscription. Tap into their web site for a look!

Max Rambod Inc. (www.maxrambod.com)
Max Rambod is an established and knowledgeable dealer, so I wasn't surprised to see a well-organized and easy-to-use site. It is divided as follows: "About Max Rambod Autographs," "About Autographs," "About Autograph Prices," "About Autograph Authenticity," "Sell Us Your Autographs." The site had a strong inventory of items in a number fields and was enjoyable to visit.

Moments in Time (http://www.momentsintime.com)
Moments in Time does a great job describing their inventory which is often impressive.

Odyssey Group (http://www.odysseygroup.com)
Odyssey Group is familiar to most of us through their fabulous periodical, *Autograph Collector.* If you like the magazine, you'll love this site. It is divided up as follows: "Price Guide," "*Autograph Collector,*" "*Pop Culture Collecting,*" "Forum," "Contact Us," "Order Books for Collectors," "Subscribe to AC," "Subscribe to *Pop Culture,*" and "Unsubscribe to On-line Newsletter." The site was informative, colorful and enjoyable to visit.

Photo Classics (www.photoclassics.com)
A great site if you need to purchase photographs!

Profiles in History (www.profilesinhistory.com)
Profiles in History is a well organized site that is convenient and easy to understand. It is divided as follows: "Home," "Collecting," "F.A.Q.," "Hollywood," "Autographs," "eBay Link," "P.I.H. Email" and "Catalog Orders." Their inventory was impressive both in content and variety!

R&R Enterprises (www.rrauction.com)
R&R runs an impressive monthly autograph auction!

Stanley Gibbons Autographs—Incorporating Fraser's (http://www.stangib.com/frasers/)
A enjoyable site to visit, well organized, easy to read, illustrated and their current inventory was very impressive.

Steven S. Raab Autographs (need information here)
One of the most popular web sites for autographs on the internet, it is divide as follows, "Home," "Catalogs & Publications," "Autographs," "Premier Offerings," "Order Form," "Gallery," "Find-It Service," "What's New," "Civil War," "Entertainment List," "Sounds of History," and "Feedback." This site is very easy to use, well organized and includes an impressive inventory of autographed items.

University Archives (UniversityArchives.com)
The University Archives web site is easy-to-use, detailed and well organized. Not only is their current catalog on-line, but it conveniently tells you which items have been sold. The site includes a well-described inventory that is also very impressive.

Note: Refer to the "Limit of Liability/Disclaimer of Warranty" in the front of this book.

of individual or firm you are dealing with. Are they selling choice items on their own site? Historical pieces where authentication is of minimal concern? What protection from fraud do they offer their buyers? Are there autographed items for sale that you know are questionable? What references do they provide? Ask questions, and get answers that will give you the feeling of confidence in your purchase.

Now, another element that you may face is on-line authentication services, so here are the facts. Only a certified forensic laboratory, familiar with document analysis can provide you with information that is admissible and conclusive in court. That's it! Cursory overviews and certificates of any kind are essentially worthless. In fact, you are better off today asking a qualified dealer for his opinion than opting for the many services willing to authenticate your on-line purchase. For an autographed item to be properly authenticated it must be in the hands of the forensic laboratory. Representation in any other form will not be definitive. An "Authentication & Grading Overview for Autographs" is provided on e-bay and it utilizes the services of PSA/DNA—a firm covered in another portion of this book. Familiarize yourself with the service and understand precisely how they determine authenticity.

Finally, have fun, as e-bay has brought a whole new level of excitement to our hobby. So, can you find great buys? Of course you can, just understand the pitfalls and rewards and bid. Utilizing the numerous pricing resources you now have available, determine the value of an item, develop a logical and unemotional bidding strategy and attack!

Digital Color Prepress

As an advanced autograph collector you are going to have to acquire some knowledge about digital color prepress. This is because the traditional prepress method of the process has evolved to the desktop where it is now more accessible and far more cost effective. Forgers can now easily reproduce those Hollywood stills, by scanning them into their system, make whatever corrections are needed to mask them as counterfeits, then output them. Some have even tried adding scanned signatures or scanning the signature separately as an independent file for output as a machine generated autograph. If these facts scare you, they should!

Famous Hoaxes In Document History

The names of those who have altered American history through forgery could easily fill this book. Bogus letters from prominent individuals can be found in both the collections of institutions and private collectors. During my lifetime alone I have witnessed numerous hoaxes from the Hitler Diaries to the Howard Hughes-Clifford Irving affair. So compelling are these frauds that the media often becomes totally obsessed with the situations. Perhaps the intrigue can be attributed to a dichotomy of human emotions, the thrill of discovering a pivotal piece of history, contrasted with the intrigue in unraveling the puzzle and proving it is nothing more than a hoax.

While in the past an autograph collector need only acquaint himself with the works of some key forgers, this is not the case today. Autograph forgery, particularly in the area of sports and entertainment is rampant. The problem is so bad, that with certain individuals, the public is more familiar with forgeries than with the actual signature of the individual. Because of this trend, the advanced autograph collector must know how to unmask a forgery. He must be given the proper tools and correct information to be able to make a judgment on his own.

Studying the forgers and hoaxes of the past can certainly be helpful. While it will not protect you against all forgeries, it may protect you from some.

A Handful Of Infamous Known Forgers Of The Past

Joseph Cosey (Martin Coneely)

If there were a Hall of Fame for forgers, Joseph Cosey would certainly be included. While many of his early attempts at forgery failed due to lack of attention to detail, his later examples were outstanding.

Hallmark: Ben Franklin, Edgar A. Poe

Noted forgeries: George Washington, Benjamin Franklin, Abraham Lincoln, U.S. Grant, Aaron Burr, Patrick Henry, James Madison, Mark Twain, Signers, etc.

Common forms: Handwritten documents, manuscripts and letters

Common mistakes: character spacing, character formation

Hints: To unmask a Cosey forgery, one must be familiar with all aspects of the subject's handwriting. Cosey paid little attention to details such as how a person's signature evolves with age or the writing tools available to a subject. To unmask his renditions of George Washington's signature I look for three characteristics: 1. Does the beginning stroke of the "t" begin at, or near the signature's baseline? 2. Does the descending stroke of the "g" exhibit a more condensed formation? 3. Is the crossing of the "t" shorter and more subdued in flamboyance? If the answer to all three of these questions is "yes," I would pass on purchasing the document.

Eugene Field II

The son of the famed poet and author of "Little Boy Blue," Eugene Field II inherited his father's creativity, but expressed it in a different form. While it is uncertain just how many forgeries left the hand of Field, numerous examples of his work have found their way into the market. While an advanced collector would certainly not be fooled by Field's Theodore Roosevelt or Henry W. Longfellow signature, a novice might. Field's renditions of Mark Twain's handwriting were outstanding and have fooled more than one advanced collector, so pay particular attention to details.

Hallmark: Eugene Field (his father), Mark Twain

Noted forgeries: Eugene Field, James Whitcomb Riley, Mark Twain, Bret Harte, Frederic Remington, Henry W. Longfellow, James Russell Lowell, Theodore Roosevelt

Common forms: Signed books, often claimed to be from his father's library, multiple signed books

Common mistakes: character formation, adding phrases and drawings that bore little significance to the subject.

Hints: Field had a tendency to add greater detail to his character formations and paid little attention to other aspects such as signature breaks.

Robert Spring

Working out of Baltimore, Philadelphia and briefly in Canada, Robert Spring established himself as one of the greatest forgers of the late nineteenth century. He died in 1876, leaving behind what most estimate to be hundreds, if not thousands, of bogus handwritten letters from America's founding fathers.

Hallmark: George Washington

Noted forgeries: George Washington, Thomas Jefferson, Benjamin Franklin, Martin Luther, John Paul Jones

Common forms: Revolutionary passes, holograph checks of George Washington, Washington handwritten letters

Common mistakes: Character formation, slant, character spacing, and character size

Hints: Spring made one consistent mistake—his common words (the, and, etc.) were often nearly identical from one letter to another. With George Washington's signature you should compare the "Go:W" formation. An original Washington signature has sharp peaks in the "W" and greater space between the "G" and the "W." For John Paul Jones I use the "Dear Sir" word combination which Spring often enhanced the character formation and increased the character spacing.

Charles Weisberg

Weisberg worked out of the Philadelphia area during the 1930s and 1940s. His forgeries were often outstanding and could fool some of the best collectors. While it is not known just how many pieces he created, I still have found examples of what I believe to be his work in auction and dealer catalogs today.

Hallmark: Abraham Lincoln, George Washington

Noted forgeries: Abraham Lincoln, George Washington, Katherine Mansfield

Common forms: Handwritten letters, surveys, book inscriptions

Common mistakes: Character spacing, character formation

Hints: In numerous Washington examples he flattens out the bottom of the "G" which often dips below the signature's baseline. In his Lincoln examples he pays little attention to the slant of his lower case letters and adds more space between the "o" and the "l".

Henry Woodhouse

Socialite, financier, publisher, and aeronautics advisor, Henry Woodhouse was often seen with some of the most famous people of his era. Ironically, instead of asking them to autograph a few items for him, he simply added the signatures himself. His forgeries seldom fool the advanced collector, but may take a tool on a novice.

Hallmark: Presidents, signers, aviators, explorers

Noted forgeries: Walt Whitman, John Adams, Theodore Roosevelt, Woodrow Wilson

Common forms: Aero Club of America postal covers, items sold through Gimbel's department store in New York

Common mistakes: Character formation, tremulous strokes, slant, character spacing, adding signatures in new ink to old paper

Hints: Woodhouse often added signatures to authentic period items such as documents, books, and newspapers. Any autographed unusual association pieces and multiple signed aviation covers should be questioned.

While these are only a handful of the better-known forgers, numerous sources available to collectors can further acquaint you with other unscrupulous individuals.

How To Deal With The Work Of Known And Unknown Forgers

As an autograph collector, to counter the work of known and unknown forgers you must do three things. First, you must maintain a library of actual and facsimile signatures. Second, you must monitor the items being sold in the autograph market and third, you must monitor or research the signing habits of individuals you collect. While all three of these tasks may take some time, they will be well worth the effort. At your disposal is also a wealth of information in the form of outstanding periodicals like Autograph Collector and Autograph Times, as well as book such as the Collectors Guide to Celebrity Autographs, all of which can assist you in all three tasks.

My library of actual and facsimile signatures consists of index cards that are filed away alphabetically. Contained on the cards is the name of the individual, source of the signature and date. In addition to the actual and facsimile signatures of the individual, I also keep any stamped returned address or other identifying marks. In cases where it is clear that the celebrity also addressed the letter, I also retain it with the same information.

As part of my library of actual and facsimile signatures, I also keep samples of known or suspected forgeries. In the case of prominent individuals or celebrities that I have a greater interest in, I keep these counterfeit signatures on clear acetates that I use as templates. These templates can be placed over a document for signature comparison. If you are collecting an individual who has been a constant subject for forgers, such as Abraham Lincoln, John F. Kennedy, George Washington, etc., this technique could prove extremely useful. I also store known mechanical signature patterns in the same way. If I find a questioned signature being offered in a dealer catalog, using a copier, I add the signature to my template.

As an autograph collector you already know that the hobby is filled with misinformation and rumors. To separate fact from fiction you must monitor the items being sold in the autograph market. By doing so you will be able to draw numerous conclusions, such as: which dealers specialize in certain areas; which dealers work with each other to get rid of inventory; what items are routinely offered in the market; what items are most dealers buying or selling; which documents are currently circulating in the market, which dealers are overpriced, etc. Since the autograph market is very volatile and can react quickly to certain forms of information or misinformation, the advanced autograph collector must be prepared to respond to these changes. Because I am the author of a price guide, I also log every catalog or advertisement I receive into a computer database. By doing so, I can monitor autograph price changes, evaluate by percentage what types of inventory certain dealers handle, sort dealer catalogs by price, etc. All this information can be extremely helpful to a collector.

The task of monitoring or researching the signing habits of individuals who interest you will not only allow you to refute rumors, but will also save you money. Numerous times I have seen items that I have received via mail, to recent autograph requests, appearing in dealer catalogs priced at unrealistic levels. Remember, while dealers buy and sell autographs, few actually make an effort to acquire a signature in-person or via a mail request. The reason for this is pure economics, as it is just not cost effective for most of them to do so.

Other tasks can also assist you in not becoming a victim of a forger's pen. They include joining an autograph organization, sustaining a positive relationship with some of the hobbies premier dealers or collectors and maintaining a research library at your fingertips.

Famous Cases Of Forgery

The Hitler Diaries

On April 22, 1983 the editors of the West German photo-weekly Stern announced that they had discovered 62 volumes of Adolph Hitler's alleged secret diaries. The book bound in black imitation-leather covers, documented the Nazi Fuhrer's years from 1932 to 1945.

Stern, as one might imagine, hailed the discovery and offered serialization of the diaries at up to $3 million. A media frenzy ensued as firms such as Rupert Murdoch's News Corp., Paris Match and Panorama (Italy) quickly signed on the dotted line. But with the discovery came an international concern over the authenticity of the diaries.

Stern's response as to where the documents originated from, revolved around their correspondent Gerd Heidemann, who acquired the documents but could not reveal his source. Apparently the documents had been recovered from an airplane crash near Dresden on April 21, 1945. The airplane was just one in a fleet that was carrying Hitler's staff and cargo from the Bunker in Berlin. The diaries were pulled from the wreckage just over a week before the Fuhrer would decide to kill himself. Surprisingly well preserved, the diaries had been concealed in a nearby hayloft.

Historians, Nazi scholars and even autograph collectors were quick to point out the unbelievability of the discovery. Hitler was known to detest writing and preferred dictation. Not to mention the challenges of war, that left him with little time for such an exercise and even physically challenged following a 1944 assassination attempt.

Despite the concerns Stern placed their confidence totally with the assessment of Cambridge Historian Hugh Trevor-Roper (*The Last Days of Hitler*) who had vouched for the volumes authenticity following a personal examination. Others, including *Newsweek* magazine were skeptical despite a consultant's review.

Stern published the first installment of the diaries one day prior to West Germany's Interior Minister Friedrich Zimmermann's denunciation of the authenticity of the volumes. The conclusion was made following the Federal Archive's chemical analysis on the paper, labels, glue, cover, and bindings of a few of the volumes. It was the archive's belief that much of the contents had been taken from a book, "Hitler's Speeches and Proclamations 1932-45, written by Max Domarus in 1962.

Polyester threads were found in the binding that weren't invented until after World War II. The chemical analysis also revealed that the glue used on the labels of the books contained postwar chemicals. Other discrepancies followed from aging anomalies to content errors.

Ashamed, Stern then vowed to find the source of the forgery. Vindicated were the many scholars who concluded that the diaries were fraudulent before the chemical analysis, one of which was the noted Autograph Dealer Charles Hamilton. Both Hamilton and autograph analyst Kenneth Rendell—who examined the documents for *Newsweek* magazine, exhibited the value of a trained autograph eye to spot a forgery.

As to the motive of the fraud, one would certainly assume money would have been the paramount factor, but with such a historical twist, one could not be certain. While hindsight is always 20/20, many were quick to ask why were so many people so gullible?

The Lincoln Love Letters

In 1928 the *Atlantic Monthly* decided to produce a series of articles based on some newly found letters about Abraham Lincoln. The cache of letters, nine in total—three from Abraham Lincoln to Ann Rutledge, two from her to him and four written by the President about her, would form the basis for "Lincoln the Lover." Historians had always speculated that the two were sweethearts when both were in their twenties and now they had the foundation to prove it, or so they thought.

The fact that Ellery Sedgwick, the well-educated and respected *Atlantic* editor, accepted the letters was proof enough to many that the letters were indeed authentic. Just to be sure, Sedgwick turned to the services of Lincoln scholar Rev. William E. Barton. Although Barton had some initial concerns, it appears as if he fell for the charming source of the letters, a one Wilma Frances Minor. The former actress and writer Minor seemed to fill a bit of the emptiness left behind in Rev. Barton, who had been lonely following the death of his wife.

Even the famed Lincoln biographer Carl Sandberg was taken by the appeal of the letters, and he was not alone. But the shine quickly dimmed following Atlantic's first published installment, as the critics came out of the woodwork to denounce the letters as forgeries. The mistakes often quoted surrounded the content of the letter. Lincoln had mentioned "Kansas," not a state at the time, cited incorrect land survey data and even had signed the letters to Rutledge "Abe," a nickname he was known to abhor.

Minor had claimed that the letters were handed down through her family by her mother Mrs. Cora DeBoyer, who was later proven to be the originator of the hoax. Minor later stated that her mother had composed the letters based on spiritual messages sent to her by both Lincoln and Rutledge. Although neither Minor nor her mother were prosecuted, it left a black eye that *Atlantic Monthly* would have to give time to heal.

Cracks In The Hughes Foundation

- Irving did not have enough known examples to execute a more deceptive document.
- Irving was using the same samples that the authenticators were using
- Irving did not pay enough attention to character formation within the text, resulting in very sloppy mistakes.
- Irving paid far more attention to structure, albeit inefficiently, rather than to flow. A common trait in a forged document.

Mussolini's Diaries

In 1957, the Rome office of *Life* magazine had been approached by the mother-daughter team of Rosa and Amalia Panvini who offered the respected periodical the diaries of Benito Mussolini. Natives of northern Italy, the Panvinis, who had also offered the diaries to an Italian newspaper, stated that they needed to raise some money. Daughter Amalia, claimed that the diaries had been given to her father.

Mussolini family members verified that the writing was indeed that of the former dictator, as did other experts who even performed numerous tests on the diaries. Before a purchase could be arranged however, the Italian police raided the Panvini home, seized some of the diaries and proclaimed charges of forgery and fraud. Both women were given suspended sentences following Rosa's admission that she had produced the diaries.

The famed autograph sleuth Charles Hamilton claimed that he would often see the same forgery again years after his initial encounter with the piece. Proof of Hamilton's point, the *London Sunday Times* bought the remaining diaries in 1968. Although the *Times* aborted the publication, they were short considerable cash.

The Howard Hughes-Clifford Irving Affair

In 1971 writer Clifford Irving approached the publishing firm McGraw-Hill and convinced the company that Howard Hughes, alive at the time, had asked him to help write his biography. Irving supported his claim with forged letters. These correspondences from Hughes to himself were so convincing that a contract of $750,00 was drawn up. Freelance writer Irving would produce the 230,000-word biography, which would even be excerpted in *Life* magazine.

Irving insisted that the McGraw-Hill check payments be made out to a "H.R. Hughes," which stood for "Helga R. Hughes" an alias Irving's wife Edith was using to operate her Swiss bank account. Irving and his co-conspirator Richard Suskind were insistent upon a solid foundation for the manuscript, which they found when they gained access to a manuscript by James

Phalen and the accompanying transcript of his interviews. Phalen was working with a former Hughes associate, Noah Dietrich, so naturally the credibility would be there. While other research materials had been pursued, including *Time-Life* library files and that of the *Library of Congress*, the Phalen link was critical to their success.

Preserving absolute secrecy with all the parties involved was critical to Irving's success and of course not considered unusual considering Hughes reclusive nature and passion for privacy. The hoax remained solid for an entire year—from conception, until the autobiography was announced on December 7th.

Officials of the Hughes Tool Company claimed immediately that the book was a hoax and threatened legal action. McGraw-Hill and *Life* then headed for the highly respected writing analysis firm of Osborn Associates with every scrap of paper they could find with known authentic handwriting from Howard Hughes. The firm reported that the evidence was "overwhelming" that all were written in the same hand. Now what?

Then the unheard of happened, Howard Hughes emerged after years of silence, albeit only on a speaker telephone, and declared to those who knew his voice that the whole Irving affair was a hoax. Irving claimed the voice was someone else and remained confident. Then during the first week of January 1972, McGraw-Hill and *Life* began an investigation into the Swiss bank account to which three checks to "H.R. Hughes," for a sum of $650,000, had been deposited. Once they learned that H.R. Hughes wasn't the person they thought, the scheme unraveled quickly.

An admission to conspiracy and grand larceny landed Irving and his wife in prison for 18 months. Ironically, in hindsight Irving's plan was executed with considerable success and of course, luck. Irving, who had written a book "Fake!" (the story of a brilliant art forger named Elmyr de Hory), was well aware of what elements needed to be present in order to succeed with a hoax. Conceived with passion and set on a grandiose scale, Irving was convinced he could succeed. The difference in completing successfully or unsuccessfully a large and complex puzzle, lies only in a single piece.

As for authentic examples of Howard Hughes handwriting, those voids were filled first by *Newsweek* running a small reproduction of handwriting in an issue covering the pioneer aviators departure from Las Vegas and then ironically with a color reproduction of an entire letter reproduced in *Life* magazine. I guess what goes around really does come around.

The Oath Of A Freeman

The story of Mark Hofmann's machinations and murderous deceptions is both sad and intriguing. Hoffmann, a specialist in Mormon document forgeries, was the first known forger to possess an extensive knowledge of chemistry. Hoffmann put together an extraordinary run of "discovered documents," rivaling that of the finest collectors of autographs. His near-perfect scam was aimed at undermining the Mormon church for his own monetary gain.

From the Anthon Transcript find in 1980, to the incredible "White Salamander" letter in 1985, Hoffmann was building a reputation as this century's greatest treasure hunter. His scam was simple at first, produce historical documents that were must purchases for his clients. Historical documents, one-of-a-kind pieces, so significant and perhaps even controversial, that once acquired they would be locked in a vault and accessible to only a few.

The "White Salamander" letter to Martin Harris, which Hoffmann unveiled in 1985, was said to have been written in 1830. The letter connected Joseph Smith to folk magic and self-fulfilling economic gain, rather than angelic revelation. The letter undermined the *Book of Mormon* and the origins of the Church of Latter-Day Saints. If the founder of Mormonism, Joseph Smith was indeed led to the gold tablets by a "white salamander" and not by an angel, one could only wonder the affect it would have on the religion.

Steven Christensen, a Mormon bishop, purchased the "white salamander" letter from Hoffmann for $40,000. On October 15, 1985, Christensen was killed by an exploding package originating from Hoffmann. Apparently he may have reneged on payments for the letter, so the forger took matters into his own hands. Another Hoffmann bomb intended for Christensen business associate Gary Sheets, killed his wife instead. Both men were investigating the letter's authenticity. Hoffmann eventually confessed to two counts of second-degree murder and two counts of theft by deception.

But why was Mark Hoffmann so successful at fooling the members of the Mormon hierarchy and numerous other document and forgery experts? His knowledge of history and chemistry was astounding, as were his technical skills. He chose the paper

originating from the proper time periods, mixed his own ink or purchased it, added sizing to the paper to avoid the feathering created by the addition of ink, then removed the sizing through the use of a hydrogen peroxide solution. In addition, he chose the proper writing instrument of the era and then executed the writing with incredible precision. He was always well aware of the anomalies in the handwriting of his subjects. For example, in his rendition of the handwriting of Joseph Smith, he duplicated Smith's use of double consonants.

Hoffmann even mastered the skill of aging a document, at least until forensic scientists discovered his technique and were able to mimic his process. The scientists were tipped off by the peculiar minute cracks that appeared in the ink.

One of Hoffman's masterpieces, or so it seemed that way initially, was his attempt at "The Oath of Freeman." This document, perhaps the first piece of printed matter produced in North America, is known to have existed by January 1639 according to known references; none are known to survive. The "Bay Psalm Book" (1640), of which there are eleven copies, is the first surviving piece of printed matter in North America. Since this item had sold for over $150,000 in 1951, it wasn't hard for Hoffmann to fantasize about how much "The Oath of a Freeman" could bring.

Like any rare find, Hoffmann knew a stage had to be set in order to make his unearthing of such a rare document believable. He started first by building a provenance for the piece. He targeted the well-known Argosy Book Store in New York City, a haven for nineteenth century ephemera and other unique items. Since he hadn't created the document yet, he couldn't simply plant it in a book. Instead he altered a ballad about Abraham Lincoln, by removing it's title and substituted "The Oath of a Freeman." He photographed, altered, then rephotographed and finally printed a new document. The newly altered ballad, printed on a sheet of paper from 1860, was then planted in a box at the store. Finding the document he had planted, the ballad was then sold to Hoffmann and invoiced under the new title.

Now having a genuine invoice, Hoffmann then went about the task of creating "The Oath of a Freeman." Using an excellent facsimile of the Bay Psalm Book, he then undertook the tedious task of photographing and then cutting up individual characters from the source. After creating the entire text of "The Oath of a Freeman," he altered the document to the necessary size to make a process line block. Because this process can be distinguished from genuine type impressions— the type height is different, Hoffmann had to alter the block. Like other forgers, Hoffmann made his own ink—beeswax, carbon and linseed oil. To be sure that the carbon would date to the period, he burned paper removed from a book of the era. He then printed his document on a blank end leaf that had been removed from a book. A common practice among forgers is removing old paper from books dating to the desired period of the forgery.

The results were convincing, so good in fact, that it fooled many a trained eye. While the document could pass many of the common tests given to documents, it could not withstand the critical eye of those who understood printing. The printing of the document failed in numerous ways. The alignment of the lines was better than what was indicative of the period, letters overlapped between lines, characters misaligned or aligned where they shouldn't have, characters were too big or too small, a word was lifted exactly from the Bay Psalm Book, a word was misspelled and he even left small indications on the print that photography had been used.

Despite the flaws in the document it had a profound affect on document analysis. It proved that despite all the technological wonders available to the forensic community, an examiner has to know what to look for. This is why I believe that the advanced autograph collector, along with experts in other fields, can play a pivotal role alongside the forensic scientist.

Operation Foulball

It is estimated that the sales of sports memorabilia now exceeds $3 billion a year. Unfortunately for collectors, with this dramatic rise has been an exponential growth in forgery. Enter the FBI and Operation Foulball, the first federal crackdown on counterfeit sports memorabilia.

The first big bust occurred in Chicago, Illinois, where the FBI brokeup a ring operated by six men, each of which was given sentences of 18-1/2 months in prison to four years of probation for bilking collectors out of as much as $5 million.

The agent heading up the case, Mike Bassett first nabbed a Chicago sports-collectible dealer named Anthony Alyinovich. For two years, Alyinovich peddled bogus balls, bats, jerseys bearing the forged autographs of professional athletes. The subject went so far as to even admit that during one five-week period he distributed more than 1,700 items. As they say in, Chicago, "Holy Cow!"

Heading up the list of forgery targets, you guessed it, Michael Jordan. "His Airness" (who seldom signs autographs), is selected precisely for this reason. In the sports memorabilia market, if the athlete won't sign, someone will sign for him to meet the demand for his signature. It has become so ridiculous, that many collectors are more familiar with the forgeries than with the actual signatures themselves.

Following interviews with some key athletes regarding their signature policy, such as Jordan, Pippen and Frank Thomas, the "G-Men" began staking out all the sporting-goods stores around Chicago. The first clue that they may be headed in the right direction occurred when they discovered the shortage of Air Jordan basketball shoes, size 13 (MJ's size).

With the assistance of store owners, the FBI marked merchandise to link it to the forgery ring. Using search warrants they visited delivery services to open packages, inspect the contents, then reseal the packages for delivery. Also used in the operation were wiretaps and concealed cameras.

What they found ranged from a list designating which forger signs which member of the Bull's signature, to bogus certificates of authenticity. Naturally, when questioned the suspected forgers gave the now typical dealer responses of, "I pay hawkers to obtain the signatures in hotels or outside the arena" and of course, "I know someone close to the athletes."

A total of six men were convicted. All of the individuals, while clearly motivated by greed, ironically seemed to have a passion for collecting sports memorabilia. As for the confiscated memorabilia, an agent is assigned the duty of erasing and obliterating the signatures. But like any story of good versus evil, there is a silver lining, as the FBI is donating thousands of the sports items, now stamped "OPERATION FOULBALL" to Chicago's Boys & Girls Clubs and the Cabrini Green Little League. As Harry would say, "How about that!"

The Files Of Lawrence X. Cusack

In 1994, Pulitzer Prize-winning journalist Seymour Hersh received a phone call from a Capitol Hill source, which steered him toward some intriguing documents. The papers are alleged to have come from the files of Lawrence X. Cusack, a prominent New York attorney. Cusack, who had died in 1985, had links to many well-known clients including Francis Cardinal Spellman and may have even done some work for John F. Kennedy.

As the story goes, one of his sons, Lawrence or "Lex," a paralegal came across documents, many of which were written in the handwriting of J.F.K., while searching through some his father's legal papers. The papers appeared to link the late president to both the mob and Marilyn Monroe, both of which have for years been speculated upon. Cusack then took the papers to a leading autograph dealer, who then offered them for sale through a different outlet.

The merchant dealing the documents stated that five "top experts" had verified the authenticity of the documents, some of which had already been sold to Steve Forbes, who houses the largest private collection of presidential documents. When Hersh heard that more documents were available, he salivated and urged the merchant for an invitation, which he received.

Hersh's visit to the southern merchant yielded over fifty pages of mouth-watering material. Startling material so powerful, that it would rewrite the pages of history. From hiring mobster Sam Giancana to a payoff to silence Marilyn Monroe—signed by both her and J.F.K., the materials would surely be the find of the century, that is of course if they were original. Hersh, who was in the process of writing a book about John Kennedy, needed copies of the materials. Six months later he would receive them, but with some stipulations.

Collaborator and J.F.K. assassination researcher, Michael Ewing worked with Hersh. It would be Ewing who would press for hardcore forensic analysis before using the papers. It was August of 1995, when the Cusack story began to unravel.

Two things happen after every document hoax. First, experts come from out of nowhere claiming "I told you so" and quickly stating, "How could anyone be so gullible?" and second, numerous individuals, from autograph dealers to crime lab-specialists to even forensic scientists, take undeserved credit for unearthing the truth. The real truth is that even the finest autograph dealers and document examiners of their day have been fooled. This book, like so many others that have been written about the study of document and handwriting analysis, should be proof enough that this is a very challenging science.

Remember while there is no perfect forgery, there is also no perfect autograph collector, dealer or forensic scientist. The quality of a forgery varies depending upon the ability and knowledge of the forger, two common elements shared with a document examiner. All forgers make mistakes, and all of these can be unmasked through knowledge, persistence and patience.

How The Cusack J.F.K. Papers Are Revealed As Forgeries

- Janet De Rosiers, who briefly worked for J.F.K., was the only living witness to one of the contract amendments included in the Cusack papers. De Rosiers would contradict all the aspects surrounding the amendment—she had never met Marilyn Monroe and the signature that appeared on the amendment was not hers.
- Available firsthand sources, along with logical secondhand intimates, denied the existence of any contracts.
- The credibility of the source of the papers, Cusack began to fall apart—claims could not be substantiated.
- More and more documents emerged from the source, as previous ones were questioned.
- No evidence of J.F.K. handling the disputed papers was uncovered by a respected crime-lab specialist. But could the fingerprints have worn off?
- The letterhead used for a transfer payment dated January 9, 1961 (on Cusack's stationery and written by J.F.K.) included a ZIP code. ZIP codes did not exist until 1963 and were not commonly used until 1965. Could the materials have been backdated?
- A document examiner discovered that some of the typed characters had been lifted off and replaced with a "single-element/ball-style" IBM Selectric typewriter not invented until 1973. Also found was the use of a plastic ribbon, also not available during the time the documents originated, along with incompatible fonts and proportional spacing.
- Bills provided by Cusack's law firm confirmed that the stationery in question had not been purchased until 1965. The firm also turned up two drafts of the ZIP coded documents in a room occasionally used by Cusack.

If It Pleases The Court

As an advanced autograph collector you are well aware of the fact that our hobby has been littered with forgery. Like any market that becomes lucrative, we have attracted individuals and corporations wishing to exploit it for their own benefit. Unfortunately, when the demand couldn't be met for authentic merchandise, we opted for the alternative, a forgery. Most of us did so unconsciously, because we were not able to distinguish between the forgery and an authentic example.

While twenty-five years ago most could empathize with this situation, today, we can not. Autograph collectors now have numerous quality resources available to them to assist in all their authentication needs. While we have lost some of the pioneers in our field recently, we have developed an entire new base of reputable dealers and knowledgeable collectors. Many of the individuals now participating in our hobby are some of the most knowledgeable we have ever had.

As an advanced autograph collector you are probably familiar with many of them already, as most are dealers. I say this because it is hard not to run across them if you are buying quality merchandise. However, we are less likely to know the names of the private collectors or institutions that specialize in certain fields. They too can bring a wealth of knowledge to the table about autograph collecting. Many of these parties can be reached through organizations who are familiar with the collecting

habits of their members. Those who write in this field, myself included, can be reached through their publisher. As an advanced autograph collector you should take advantage of every possible resource.

Initially, when I designed the table of contents for this material I was very reticent about including this information, but having been asked to be an expert witness in a number of court cases and understanding a collector's apprehension with the legal system, I changed my mind. So here are my observations.

The Past —The Collector versus the Forensic Scientist

For years some of the traditional methods used in document examination have included deciphering, handwriting analysis, and obliterated and indented writing. While these methods were useful, many fell short of providing more conclusive evidence. Alternatives needed be invented, but were slow in coming because few document examiners were comfortable outside their realm of handwriting and typewriting evaluation and nearly all adhered to the principle that a questioned document must be preserved in its original state. As forensic science evolved, formal training in chemical and physical methods led to significant developments in the area of forgery detection.

As a hobby some of our participants contributed greatly to many of the earlier areas of signature analysis, but as forensic science evolved it grew away from autograph collecting for many reasons. The first reason was simple, the technology had limited appeal to the average collector. While some collectors have formal education in the sciences and could understand the terms and methodology, most did not. Next, was our failure as a hobby to keep up with forensic advances and educating our collectors on new ways to battle forgery. Finally, the forensic community began to look down on the field of autograph collecting for the lack of organization, education, and self-regulation. Since the hobby was unaware of the advances in

technology, we were making foolish and often avoidable mistakes.

Nowhere is the dichotomy between autograph collector and forensic scientist better exemplified than in the courtroom. Both can provide valuable information to a case and often compliment eachother's strengths. While a forensic scientist can present TLC data on ink analysis, he can't provide information about the signing habits of particular individuals. He won't be able to tell you how often the person has been accessible to the public, or the frequency of which certain documents and manuscripts have entered the market. The forensic scientist may not be able to provide address and signature changes, or present samples in a wide variety of forms and spanning a long period of time. In a court of law, if a case involves the authentication of a Mickey Mantle autographed baseball or a contract signed by Walt Disney, the issue needs to be addressed from both sides with expert witnesses.

As an advanced autograph collector you are encouraged to study cases involving document analysis and how the testimony of a forensic scientist or autograph expert impacted the result of the case. Here are only a handful, of the thousands of cases that involve document fraud. Presenting these actual cases that involve document fraud should be enough to make any forger uncomfortable. The technology now exists to detect even the best forgeries.

Related Case Studies

Cases

Md. v. Doe (1)

A fascinating case for any forensic scientist or advanced autograph collector is Md. v. Doe. This case involved documents prepared by a medical doctor suspected of Medicaid fraud. The documents exhibited "peculiarities" that were characteristic of artificial aging. Under UV light, contrasting images of streaks were evident. These markings were often inconsistent from page to page. It was concluded that the marks were the result of heating the document on an oven rack. There have been studies that indicate that oven aging, under certain specific conditions can equal years of normal aging. The process also can be modified to eliminate the streaks and alter the chemical balance in the paper. Ink can also be altered during a heating process, resulting in a different chromatogram (TLC) from that of unheated standard inks. *

The Howard Hughes Will (2)

This case involved the disposition of the vast fortune amassed by the flamboyant and controversial Howard Hughes. Being investigated on the charges of fraud and forgery was an individual by the name of Melvin Dumar. In question was a will that may have been backdated, so the attorney general's office contacted the BATF. The organization determined the ink formula and when a particular dye was available, which happened to fall within the timeframe of the origin of the document. Ink appearing on envelopes that housed the will also matched that of the document. Document personnel also determined that the will was not written in the hand of the late pioneer aviator. Worth noting here and something that will be brought up later in this chapter, is that the attorneys for the Hughes interests retained three experts who testified that the document was fraudulent.

The Downfall of a Vice President (3)

Spiro T. Agnew, former Governor of the state of Maryland and vice president under Richard M. Nixon, was investigated for possible conspiracy, extortion, bribery and tax evasion. Records of kickbacks were contained in diaries and pocket-sized ledgers maintained by an associate of Agnew. These extensive records were examined by the BATF and matched to inks available during the time period. The notations, made in several colored inks, incriminated Agnew. Entering a plea of nolo contendere—a plea by the defendant in a criminal prosecution that without admitting guilt subjects him to conviction but does not preclude him from denying the truth of the charges in a collateral proceeding, regarding the criminal charges, he later resigned his high office (October 10, 1973)

People v. Corona (2)

In a highly publicized trial Juan V. Corona stood accused of perpetrating what was believed to be the largest mass murder in the history of the United States. Again signature analysis played an important role, as an expert witness identified Corona's writing that appeared in a ledger book. The writing in the ledger gave the names of the victims of this gruesome crime. Also a ball-point pen , owned by Corona, was identified as the source of the writing in the ledger.

Stoller v. U.S. (3)

A monumental case, as this was the first time the ATF used their systematic approach to ink identification and ink dating as part of formal testimony in a case. They used their findings as a rebuttal to impeach the testimony of the defendant. The authenticity of the dairies in question in the case were determined to have been written ink that was not yet commercially available.

U.S. v. Bruno (4)

In this case, analysis by the ATF revealed that the ink used to sign a document was not available commercially until years after its date. In this case however, the presiding judge ruled that the evidence was not conclusive. Concern that the field of ink identification had not reached a reasonable degree of scientific certainty was given in the judge's opinion.

U.S. v. Meyers (5)

Ink and handwriting analysis indicated that loan application forms had been prepared by a bank official rather than a loan applicant The bank official was accused of illegally awarding loans to small business concerns.

U.S. v. Mitchell (6)

Disputed in this case was the age of a document—had it been prepared at the alleged date or earlier. Both paper and ink analysis were used during the investigation. Ink analysis confirmed the availability of the ink during the period in question, however the investigation into the paper uncovered a different result. The manufacturer of the paper was identified through a watermark. Upon contacting the manufacturer, the investigator was told that the chemistry of the paper had been altered on a specific date, nine months after the date of the disputed document.

U.S. v. Sloan (7)

In this case ATF ink analysis acted as primary evidence and it led to a conviction of perjury. The ATF presented evidence that a unique dye identified in the ink was not available during the date of an agreement.

U.S. v. Wolfson (8)

In this case claims that a seven page document had been altered were disproven through findings that included paper analysis, ink testimony and watermark examination.

State v. Bulna (9)

In this case a conviction was reversed because of the exclusion of a test of the document examiner testifying for the state.

State of New Jersey v. Bruno Hauptmann (10)

In this case it is worth noting that eight document examiners testified for the state.

Notes:

1. Md. v. Doe, 1981, 2. People v. Corona, CalApp3d 684, 23CrL 2212, (1980), 3. Stoller v. U.S., 69-974-CIV-CA, S.D. F.a., Miami, FL (1969), 4. U.S. v. Bruno, 333 F. Supp. 570, L.D. PA, (1971), 5.U.S. v. Meyers, N.Y., N.Y., (1970), 6. U.S. v. Mitchell, S.D. FL., 1975, 7. U.S. v. Sloan, CR-69-137, W.D. TN., (1970), 8. U.S. v. Wolfson, 437 F.2d 862 (2d Cir. 1970), 9. The Appellate Division, 46 N.J. Super. 313, 134 a. 2d 738, App. Div. 1957 recognized that the expert could not be discredited without clear proof of the authorship of the test specimen used. The Appellate Division's decision was affirmed by the Supreme Court of New Jersey.

Chapter 4

Enjoyable Areas of Autograph Collecting

As part of each edition of this book, I am going to provide the reader with a brief overview of several different areas of the hobby that he/she may want to consider venturing into, such as the signatures of American authors. While some of the areas included here are logical first choices, such as the signatures of U.S. Presidents, others are not. Naturally, entire books can and have been written about certain areas and topics, so I will refer to them for more specific information. I hope you enjoy this first installment.

American Authors

During the nineteenth century American literature flourished, with many scholars even describing the mid-century mark as "The American Renaissance." Thanks to collectors such as Mr. Clifton Waller Barrett, J. Pierpoint Morgan, J.P. Morgan and Stephen H. Wakeman, to name a few, the autographs and manuscripts of many of America's great writers during this period did not get overlooked.

American Literary Autographs

Louisa May Alcott (1832-1888)
Author and reformer, Alcott's work has entertained generations of boys and girls. From *Jack and Jill* to *Little Women* her stories have struck a chord with many Americans. She was a prolific writer and many of her correspondence have found homes in institutions, such as the Harvard University Library and the Alderman Library (University of Virginia). Her work is scarce in the autograph market in all forms but a simple signature.

Thomas Bailey Aldrich (1836-1907)
A gifted writer in many forms and editor (*The Atlantic Monthly*), Aldrich is commonly associated with

The Story of a Bad Boy. His papers can be found at the Harvard University Library. Aldrich autographed material does occasionally appear in the autograph market and is often in the form of an AMS. His writings associated with the title mentioned above can command solid prices.

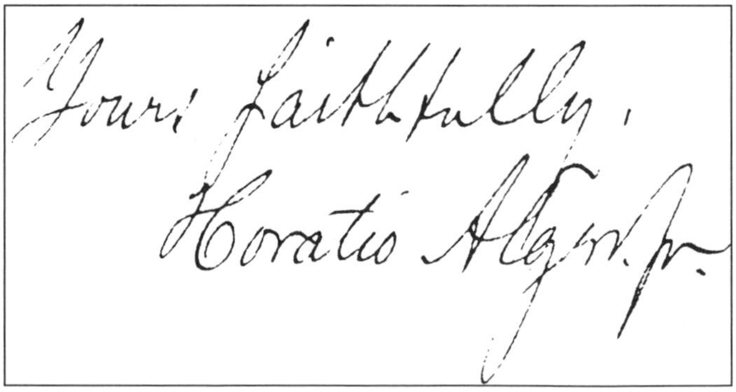

Horatio Alger

Horatio Alger (1834-1899)

Author and clergyman, Alger was a prolific writer, penning over one hundred books for boys, including Luck and Pluck and Tattered Tom. He spent much of his time as chaplain to the Newsboys' Lodging House in New York City. It was there that the altruistic author gained much of his inspiration. Despite his success as a writer he died a poor man. His papers can be found in the Huntington Library. His writings in any form other than a simple signature are not common in the autograph market.

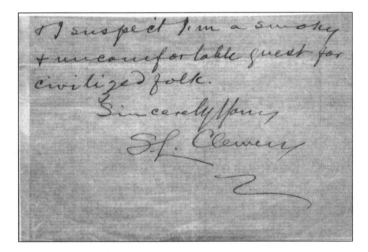

Ambrose Bierce

Ambrose Bierce (1842-1914)

Satirist, author and journalist, Bierce wrote for numerous publications during his lifetime. He is perhaps best remembered for his work, *Can Such Things Be?* which he penned in 1893. Some of his manuscripts can be found in the Huntington Library. Autographed material in any form from Bierce is not common in the market.

Robert Montgomery Bird (1806-1854)

Physician, novelist and editor, Bird is perhaps best known for his play *The Gladiator* which he penned in 1831. He edited the Philadelphia North American, which he was part owner of right up until the time of his death. Many of his writings can be found at the University of Pennsylvania Library, but surprisingly few are found in the autograph market.

Charles Brockden Brown (1771-1810)

Brown gave up the legal profession to become America's first author. His novels included *Alcuin*, *Wieland*, *Ormond* and others, before he turned toward journalism. Brown's handwriting was very legible with distinctive character formations often found in the letters, "g", and "y." The ascenders in letters such as "h", "f" and "k" were typically very high, and often the highest points in an entire line of handwritten text. Brown's signature in all forms is scarce. Samples of his writing can be found in the Library of the Historical Society of Pennsylvania.

Orestes Augustus Brownson (1803-1876)

Clergyman, journalist and author, Brownson was a controversial figure both as a writer and speaker. *His New Views of Christianity, Society and The Church* was one of the seminal books in American Transcendentalism. While a large group of his writings has found a home at the University of Notre Dame, few find their way into the autograph market.

William Cullen Bryant (1794-1878)

Poet, essayist, activist and editor, William Cullen Bryant authored the first great American poem, "Thanatopis" at the young age of 15. His work surfaces

periodically in the autograph market. While an average handwritten letter might run over $500, those of strong content can command nearly four times this amount. Most distinctive of his handwriting is the presence of connected words in phrases such as "tobe", "ofthe", "isnot." Bryant is well represented in the collections of many institutions including The New York Public Library and the Huntington Library.

John Burroughs (1837-1921)

A prolific writer, lecturer and critic, Burroughs had a passion for natural history. He became popular through his work and association, as he was a good friend of Walt Whitman. His papers can be found in numerous repositories throughout the country. Surprisingly few of his autographed items have appeared in the market.

Samuel L. Clemens

Samuel Langhorne Clemens (Mark Twain) (1835-1910)

Perhaps America's greatest author and certainly one of the most popular, Clemens penned numerous classics. His papers reside in many institutions including the Yale University Library and the University of California Library (Stanford). His signature in any form is highly sought by both autograph dealers and collectors. Because of the constant demand, autographed items routinely appear in the market and command significant prices. He has been the target of forgers for years and many of these bogus examples are almost routinely encountered by major dealers.

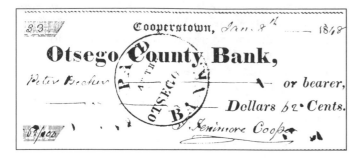

James Fenimore Cooper

James Fenimore Cooper (1789-1851)

One of Americas first internationally recognized novelists, James Fenimore Cooper is best remembered for his Leather-Stocking tales including the book *The Last of the Mohicans*. For decades collectors have had a chance to own his signatures that appear routinely in the autograph market in the form of bank checks drawn from the Otsego County Bank. Demand for his signature has remained consistent in all forms, with the most sought examples being handwritten letters of strong content. Examples of his work can be found in the Yale University Library.

Stephen Crane (1871-1900)

A gifted writer in many forms, Crane died at the young age of twenty-nine. Left behind was a large body of work that secured his place in American literature. Typically associated with *The Red Badge of Courage*, Crane handwriting of any kind is scarce. His papers can be found in a few institutions, such as Syracuse University and Columbia University Library.

Richard Henry Dana (1787-1879)

A poet, essayist and critic, Dana is best remembered as author of *Two Years Before the Mast*. His work is often overlooked in an autograph market more interested in the correspondence of his son. Little of his material has surfaced in the market over the past decade. Although his writing is often legible, letters can be small. A good character formation for comparison is the "th" combination, which often looks like a crossed "M." Samples of his work can be found in the Harvard University Library and the Massachusetts Historical Society Library.

Emily Dickinson (1830-1886)

Emily Dickinson, perhaps the finest woman poet, had only seven poems published during her lifetime but wrote nearly 2000. Her autograph in any form is extremely scarce. Unfortunately, she has been a target for forgers who prey on public demand. Her writing is very distinctive and easy to authenticate, so most will not be fooled by a bogus signature. The Houghton Library houses a vast majority of her papers.

Mary Mapes Dodge (1831-1905)

Author of children's books and editor (*St. Nicholas*), Dodge is typically associated with *Hans Brinker*. Both her work and the magazine made her very popular during her era. Her papers can be found in the Alderman Library at the University of Virginia and in several other institutions. Her correspondence appears occasionally in the autograph market where most will find her writings surprisingly affordable.

Paul Laurence Dunbar (1872-1906)

A gifted poet and the first to write in black American dialect, Dunbar is best remembered for *Lyrics of Lowly Life*. He was a prolific writer, even while serving as an assistant in the Library of Congress. Dying at such a young age certainly contributes to the scarcity of his work. Dunbar's autograph in any form is very rare.

Finley Peter Dunne (1867-1936)

Humorist and author, Dunne is best known for his series of Mr. Dooley books. Dooley became extremely popular with Americans for his political humor. Dunne's autographed material is scarce in all forms.

Ralph Waldo Emerson (1803-1882)

Clergyman, poet, philosopher and transcendentalist, Ralph Waldo Emerson penned many works including, *The American Scholar* and *The Conduct of Life*. He was a prolific writer and an obliging signer of autographs. When requested he would even transcribe his poems for autograph collectors. His writing is very distinctive and easy to authenticate. Letters of significant content have disappeared in the market, most are now part of private collections. Emerson letters and manuscripts are part of the holdings of many institutions, with a principal depository being at The Houghton Library at Harvard University.

Eugene Field (1850-1895)

A gifted writer in many forms, Field is typically associated with work while on the staff of the Chicago Morning News. His work appears in the repositories of many institutions and does occasionally appear in dealer catalogs. He was the target of numerous forgeries, many of which still surface in the autograph market. All of his material should be carefully scrutinized.

James T. Fields (1817-1881)

Author, poet and editor (*The Atlantic Monthly*), Fields also made a name for himself in the publishing field as partner of Ticknor & Fields. Both he and his wife befriended many of the leading writers of the day and as such it is not unusual to find a letter from Fields to a prominent author. The Harvard University Library houses many of his papers.

John Fiske (1841-1901)

Historian, philosopher, and lecturer, Fiske is encountered by many through his work, *The American Revolution*. His work is found in numerous institutions across the country. Surprisingly, his signature in any form is not common in the market.

Clyde Fitch (1865-1909)

A gifted playwright, Fitch is best known for his work *Beau Brummell*, which he penned in 1890. He was one of the first playwrights to release a consistent number of works. Surprisingly little of his autographed material has found its way to market.

Margaret Fuller (1810-1850)

Social reformer, teacher, author and editor (*The Dial*), Fuller was a gifted woman of letters. She was accepted into the Concord transcendentalist circle where she was welcomed by both Thoreau and Emerson. The Harvard University Library houses a nice collection of her papers. Her signature and correspondence have appreciated significantly in recent years.

William Lloyd Garrison

William Lloyd Garrison (1805-1879)

Radical abolitionist and author, Garrison was the founder and editor of *The Liberator* (1831-1865). His writings have entered the market in the form of his "The Free Mind", a poem which he often penned for autograph collectors. His letters can be found in many institutions including the Boston Public Library.

Edward Everett Hale (1822-1909)

Clergyman, historian and author, Hale is most remembered for his book, *The Man Without a Country*. He was a prolific writer and was active in numerous causes. His autograph does periodically surface in the market in a variety of forms. His papers can be found in numerous institutions, including the Harvard University Library.

Fritz-Greene Halleck (1790-1867)

Banker and poet, Fritz-Greene Halleck became popular for his works *The Croaker Papers* and *Marco Bozzaris*. Halleck was prominent in New York City banking and considered his writing more of an avocation. He spent numerous years working as confidential clerk to John Jacob Astor. His papers are represented in many libraries and collections. He was very responsive to autograph requests and while popular during his day, has now been somewhat forgotten.

Joel Chandler Harris (1848-1908)

Joel Chandler Harris is typically associated with his ten *Uncle Remus* books. He was a quiet man who found solace in his home state of Georgia. His papers can be found in the Emory University Library in Atlanta. Harris autographed material, in nearly all forms, and is not common in the market.

Bret Harte (1836-1902)

A gifted writer in many forms, Harte is typically associated with *The Luck of Roaring Camp* and *Ah Sin*. He was an early American expatriate who found greater comfort as part of English society. His papers can be found at the Huntington Library and his writings periodically appear in the autograph market. He has a flair for writing very small and his letters can be difficult to read. He was obliging to autograph seekers and when he had time would write out portions of poetry.

Julian Hawthorne (1846-1934)

Son of Nathaniel, Julian Hawthorne is typically associated with his family biographies. His autographed material is not common in the market and unless family related has limited appeal to most collectors.

Nathaniel Hawthorne

Nathaniel Hawthorne (1804-1864)

Novelist and short-story writer, Hawthorne penned such classics as *The Scarlet Letter* and *The House of the Seven Gables*. He was a prolific writer and kept numerous journals during his life, most of which can be found at The Pierpoint Morgan Library. Similar to

Thoreau and Melville, his autograph in any form has always been in demand. Because of this he is the occasional target of a forger. Some of his materials have entered the market in DS form, most signed as surveyor of Salem Port or as U.S. consul at Liverpool.

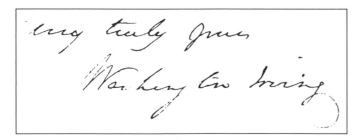

Oliver Wendell Holmes (Sr)

Oliver Wendell Holmes (1809-1894)

A physician, teacher and poet, Holmes was a prolific writer. He is perhaps best remembered for his poem "Old Ironsides", which when printed nationally thrust him into the literary spotlight. Holmes papers can be found in many institutions including John Hopkins University and the Harvard University Library. His signature surfaces periodically in the autograph market and shouldn't prove to be too difficult of an acquisition.

Julia Ward Howe (1819-1910)

Author and reformer, Howe is perhaps best remembered for penning *The Battle Hymn of the Republic*. Like all those who fought for women's suffrage, interest in her work and her writings has increased dramatically over the past two decades. Considering her wonderful work, most feel her signature is undervalued in the autograph market. Her papers are found in many institutions including the Harvard University Library.

William Dean Howells (1837-1920)

Diplomat and writer in numerous forms, Howells is often associated with two periodicals *Atlantic* and *Harper's Magazine*. His writings appear in numerous institutional holdings and are common in the autograph market. He often signed "W.D. Howells" and patient collectors should be able to pick up a nice ALS or two at affordable prices.

Washington Irving

Washington Irving (1783-1859)

A gifted historian, essayist and biographers, Washington Irving is perhaps best remembered for *Rip Van Winkle* and *The Legend of Sleepy Hollow*. While his handwritten letters are often legible, many of the character formations can be very small. Irving was a prolific writer, with the most common form found in the autograph market being an ALS. He served as U.S. Minister to Spain from 1842 to 1846 and also served as the first president of the Astor Library (now a part of The New York Public Library). Although Irving is popular with autograph collectors, his signature remains very affordable. Numerous examples of his work can be found in the Yale University Library, Harvard University Library, The New York Public Library and the University of Virginia.

Helen Hunt Jackson (1830-1885)

Poet and novelist, Jackson is most remembered for her novel, *Ramona*. She fought for the cause of the Indians and was very moved by their plight. The Huntington Library houses many of her papers. An occasional autograph of hers finds its way to market and attracts limited interest.

Henry James (1843-1916)

Perhaps the greatest novelist ever, James penned classics such as *Daisy Miller* and *The Portrait of a Lady*. Born in New York City, but educated in Europe (where he would make his home), James became a prolific writer. The Harvard University Library houses much of his work and autographed material of his in any form is scarce. His handwriting varied significantly during his life and is well worth advance study prior to the purchase of any of his autographed material.

Sarah Orne Jewett (1849-1909)

A gifted writer in many forms, Jewett achieved a solid reputation through her short stories which appeared in numerous major periodicals. Her papers can be found at a number of institutions, including the Harvard University Library. Jewett autographed material appears sporadically in the market.

John Pendleton Kennedy (1795-1870)

Author and statesman, John Pendleton Kennedy wrote *Swallow Barn*, *Horse-Shoe Robinson*, *Rob of the Bowl* and *Quodlibet*. Most of his writings that surface in the autograph market are examples from his days in the U.S. House of Representatives or as Secretary of the Navy. Not overly-popular with autograph collectors, examples of his work remain inexpensive.

Sidney Lanier (1842-1881)

A poet and musician, Lanier's quest was to combine both in what he felt would be a profound experience. Known more as a Southern poet and a gifted flute player, his papers can be found in the John Hopkins University Library. His handwriting is easily recognized for his unique capitalization—in particular his "S." His autographed material in any form is seldom found on the market.

Emma Lazarus (1849-1887)

A fine poet, Lazarus is typically associated with her words on the pedestal of the statue of liberty, "Give me your tired...," part of *The New Colossus*. Her short life no doubt contributes to the scarcity of her holograph material of which there is little.

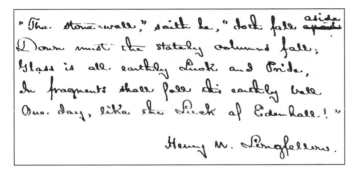

Henry W. Longfellow

Henry Wadsworth Longfellow (1807-1882)

A gifted poet who penned many outstanding works, Longfellow was a prolific and willing autograph signer. Despite the generosity with his signature, he has been a subject of numerous forgeries. His letters were often lengthy, so be wary of short correspondence. His handwriting, particularly the capitalization, is very distinctive thus many forgeries can be unmasked under the proper conditions. The Harvard University Library houses many of his papers.

James Russell Lowell (1819-1891)

A prolific writer, teacher and diplomat (U.S. Minister), Lowell autographs often enter the market from his years as U.S. Minister. His autograph, not uncommon, does carry a far greater price tag than one might expect. The Harvard University Library houses much of his work, not a surprise since he taught French and Spanish at the college for thirty years.

Lafcadio Hearn (1850-1904)

Author and gifted writer of prose, Hearn mimicked the style of his favorite French writers. He finally settled in Japan and taught English at a nearby university. His reflections on Japanese life were some of the first glimpses many had into the culture of the West. His papers can be found in many institutions, but they seldom appear in the autograph market.

Herman Melville (1819-1891)

Novelist, short-story writer and poet, Melville is typically associated with *Moby Dick*. The lack of recognition during his lifetime contributes greatly to the lack of surviving Melville material estimated at fewer than 300 letters. His papers are housed at The Houghton Library (Harvard) and The New York Public Library. To date, he has not been the target of a great number of forgeries. Most advanced autograph collectors agree that you have a better chance seeing Moby Dick than actually encountering an authentic Melville letter.

Francis Parkman (1823-1893)

An outstanding historian, Parkman authored many important works including *The California and Oregon Trail*. He suffered numerous ailments during his life, and some even inhibited his correspondence. Surprisingly little of his autographed material has entered the autograph market.

John Howard Payne (1791-1852)

Dramatist, actor and diplomat, John Howard Payne, wrote, translated or adapted over 50 plays. Perhaps best remembered for his opera "Clari" and the immortal "Home, Sweet Home", Payne was also interested in the plight of the American Indian. Payne autographs still periodically surface in the autograph market, where a handwritten letter of strong content can command over $500. His work can be found as part of collections in the Huntington Library and Columbia University Library.

James Gates Percival (1795-1856)

Poet, lexicographer, musician and scientist, James Gates Percival was a Renaissance man. Perhaps best remembered for *Zamor, The Dream of a Day* and the poem "Prometheus." Admired in his day, Percival has been much forgotten today in the autograph market. His work seldom surfaces and may present a challenge to some who would like to add his illegible handwriting to their collection. His work is well represented in Yale University Library.

Edgar Allan Poe (1809-1849)

Gifted poet and short-story writer, Poe is often associated with his famous poem "The Raven." While many are familiar with the handwriting he used in his formal letters and manuscripts, his casual pen was quite different and will take study to be fully understood by collectors. Poe also penned manuscripts in "roman script." Perhaps the most highly sought autograph of all American literary figures, his very scarce signatures command significant price levels. Because of this, it will come as no surprise to the advanced autograph collector that his signature has often been a target of forgery. Exercise extreme caution when buying any Poe material because if it's not forged it may be stolen. Poe manuscripts are housed in many repositories including The New York Public Library, the Morgan Library and The Free Library of Philadelphia.

William S. Porter

William Sydney Porter (O. Henry) (1862-1910)

A gifted writer in many forms, Porter led an interesting life. Fame came to him gradually and later in life—not until he moved to New York City. His papers can be found in numerous institutions, especially those found in the state of Texas. His autographed material does surface periodically in the market and typically carries a hefty price tag.

William Hickling Prescott (1796-1859)

Both a scholar and historian, Prescott was a detailed writer with a flair for the dramatic narrative. Due to the loss of an eye and failed eyesight, the author wrote with the aid of a noctograph, which is a writing case for the blind. Using a stylus and carbon paper he penned his manuscripts, most of which are housed in the Massachusetts Historical Society Library. While his signature is not expensive, at least by today's standards, few find their way into the autograph market.

Thomas Buchanan Read (1822-1872)

Both a poet and an artist, Read is perhaps best remembered for his poem "Sheridan's Ride." His papers can be found in The Historical Society of Pennsylvania. While an occasional autograph surfaces in the market, few generate the interest one might expect.

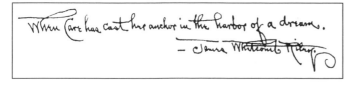

James W. Riley

James Whitcomb Riley (1849-1916)

"The Hoosier Poet" was best known for his dialect verse. Riley loved to combine both verse and prose and did it often. His papers can be found in many institutions, including the Lily Library (Indiana University). His autographed material often appears in the autograph market, with some commanding nice price levels. Since he has been the target of forgers, collectors are advised to exercise caution with their purchases.

Edward Arlington Robinson (1869-1935)

A poet, Robinson is best remembered for his works "Lancelot" (1920) and "Tristram" (1927). His papers can be found in numerous institutions, and periodically surface in the autograph market.

Lydia Huntley Sigourney (1791-1865)

A prolific poet and writer, Lydia Huntley Sigourney was one of the most popular writers of her day. Unfortunately, while she has been represented in many American Institutions such as the Yale University Library, her work appears sporadically in an autograph market that appears to have long forgotten her. Her right-slanted writing is distinctive, graceful and pronounced, with long ascenders and descenders in letters such as "f", "g" and "p."

William Gilmore Simms (1806-1870)

Poet, novelist and editor, Simms was a prolific writer and the leading man of letters not only in his wonderful hometown of Charleston, South Carolina, but all around the South. Many of his writings were lost during a fire at his plantation home, thus much of what is found in the market has been penned later in his life. The University of South Carolina Library houses much of his work

Francis Hopkinson Smith (1838-1915)

An engineer and author, Smith found the latter late in his life. He wrote and illustrated many works based on his travels. While you may find an occasional letter in an institutional holding, Smith is scarce in any form in the autograph market.

Jared Sparks (1789-1866)

Historian, educator, editor and clergyman, Jared Sparks was a promoter of American history, both as a professor and president at Harvard University. His writing is both legible and distinctive. Examples of his work can be found in Harvard University Library and The Historical Society of Pennsylvania. Examples of his work are often inexpensive and overlooked in the autograph market, perhaps due to lack of familiarity with his role in history.

Frank Stockton (1834-1902)

Author and artist, Stockton is best remembered for his novel *Rudder Grange* and his short-story *The Lady or the Tiger*. Many of his papers can be found at the Alderman Library (University of Virginia). Stockton's writing in any form is not common in the autograph market, and when they do appear generate little interest.

Harriet Beecher Stowe

Harriet Beecher Stowe (1811-1896)

Novelist best remembered *for Uncle Tom's Cabin*, Stowe was quite prolific. Her handwritten letters or signed documents periodically enter the autograph market but most examples encountered will be signed cards. Signed books and photographs are two scarce forms for her signature. The Huntington Library houses a nice collection of her papers.

Bayard Taylor (1825-1878)

An historian, poet and novelist, Taylor is perhaps best remembered for *Views A-Foot*. Taylor traveled extensively and wrote about his encounters. The Cornell University Library houses much of his papers. While an occasional autograph does find its way to market, few attract the interest one might expect.

Henry David Thoreau (1817-1862)

Naturalist and poet, Thoreau is best remembered for his work *Walden; or, Life in the Woods*. His signature in any form is extremely scarce, no doubt attributable to the lack of fame he received during his lifetime. Contrary to public opinion, he wasn't a total recluse! Unsigned pages of his journal, that used to occasionally surface, have all but disappeared. Any item that does surface should receive careful analysis. Thoreau has not only been a target of forgery, but as his papers have grown in value, institutions have been prone to thievery. The comprehensive collection of his work can be found in the Morgan Library. The Huntington Library houses the seven drafts for Walden and the author's corrected proof for the work.

Henry Timrod (1828-1867)

Often referred to as "Poet Laureate of the Confederacy," Timrod was celebrated by the South for the promotion of their cause during the Civil War. The University of South Carolina Library houses most of his papers. Timrod material is scarce in all forms, but one can only speculate as to the demand.

Lew Wallace

Lew Wallace (1827-1905)

Diplomat, author and a major-general during the Civil War, Lew Wallace is best remembered for his epic *Ben-Hur: A Tale of the Christ*. His autograph is highly collected by both literary and Civil War buffs, both of which prize his signature. The Lily Library at Indiana University houses much of his papers, including the manuscript of Ben-Hur.

Noah Webster (1758-1843)

An author, scientist, public official and humanitarian, perhaps best known for *An American Dictionary*, Webster carried the banner for Americanism. His penmanship is generally legible with distinctive character formations found in the letters "T", "F" and "d." Autographed material in all forms, except signatures, is scarce. Samples of his writing can be found in The Pierpoint Morgan Library and The New York Public Library.

Walt Whitman

Walt Whitman (1819-1892)

One of our most gifted poets, Walt Whitman is typically associated with *Leaves of Grass*. Whitman lived a modest life in Camden, New Jersey during the end of his lifetime. An 1873 paralytic stroke did much to inhibit his travels. His prolonged popularity has consistently driven autographed material to new price levels. When a signed Whitman piece enters the market it is often a signed photograph or book. Whitman has for years been a target for forgers, so it is best to carefully scrutinize any material you find in the market. His works are included in many institutional collections, including the Library of Congress and The New York Public Library.

John G. Whittier

John Greenleaf Whittier (1807-1892)

Poet, author and editor, Whittier penned many a memorable verse including, "The Tent on the Beach." He edited several periodicals, but never for a prolonged period of time. His autograph appears periodically in the market, but often only in simple letters or as signatures. The Essex Institute houses many of his papers.

Samuel Woodworth (1784-1842)

Dramatist, journalist and poet, Samuel Woodworth is perhaps best remembered for his poem "The Old Oaken Bucket." His penmanship is often legible and distinctive by the "T", "th", "p" and "B" character formations. Samples of his writing can be found in The Harvard University Library and The New York Public Library. Not overly popular with collectors, his signature can still be found at about the $50 price level.

American Composers

The beauty of music is its lack of cultural boundaries. If we can't understand a particular language, we can communicate through the emotion and imagery created by music. As a young nation, the United States became a melting pot for cultures, who brought with them their musical influences. Music quickly took root in various forms throughout this great land and the tradition of American music was born.

Collecting American musical manuscripts has been popular for decades. Many quality pieces have already found homes in private or institutional collections. As musical manuscripts diminished from the market, autograph collectors turned to alternative forms such as a signed photograph, piece of sheet music or program.

The most popular form however, quickly became the autograph musical quotation signed, AMQS. This is often a small sheet (8vo), with a few bars of music drawn by the composer, followed by a signature. While this form is clearly not a musical manuscript, it is probably the closest many autograph collectors will come to acquiring one. Unlike the rich history of music in many other countries, American music is only a few hundred years old, thus many artifacts from its evolution including autographed items, still find their way into the market. Below is a brief collector overview of a few popular American composers.

Samuel Barber (1910-1981)

Samuel Barber (Adagio for Strings, Vanessa) is one of the true romantics of last century's composers. His autographed material in some forms has been found in an autograph market that still hasn't warmed up to its value. As his place in music history begins to solidify, Barber material should begin to catch up with the appropriate price levels.

Leonard Bernstein (1918-1990)

Leonard Bernstein (West Side Story), was always obliging to autograph requests in-person or through the mail. His signatures can be found in many forms in the market including AMQS.

Aaron Copland (1900-1990)

Aaron Copland (Billy the Kid, Appalachian Spring) was a gracious and willing signer. Whether acquired in-person or through the mail, his signature seemed to be one of the first sought for any collection of American composers. Many of his letters have already been swallowed up by institutions and private collectors, but a few choice AMQS can still be found periodically in the autograph market.

Duke Ellington

Duke Ellington (1899-1974)

Duke Ellington (Mood Indigo, Take the A Train) was a gracious signer in-person, however, I never had much luck through the mail. His autographed material is very popular with collectors in all forms. Vintage signed photographs remain favorites with collectors, with most commanding a significant price. The Smithsonian Institution and the Library of Congress house many of his papers.

Stephen C. Foster (1826-1864)

Autographed material from Stephen C. Foster (My Old Kentucky Home, Oh! Suzzanna) is scarce in all forms. While a collector may at some time be lucky enough to encounter a signature for sale, all other forms would be rare occurrences. Most of his holograph material is within institutional walls, such as that of the University of Pittsburgh.

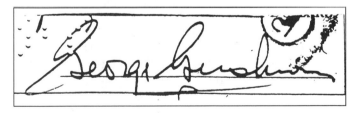

George Gershwin

George Gershwin (1898-1937)

George Gershwin (An American in Paris, Porgy and Bess), working with his brother Ira, collaborated on some of the finest examples of American music. He was an outstanding signer right up until his death in 1937. Musical manuscripts and handwritten letters are rare, and most AMQS and DS forms have also been swallowed up by collectors. A collector's best bet now is a signature. Much of his work is housed in the Library of Congress.

Charles Ives (1874-1954)

Charles Ives (Song for Harvest Season, Johnny Poe) autographed material, in a variety of forms, still occasionally finds its way into the autograph market. Most, if not all, musical manuscripts have been absorbed by institutions, in particular, Yale School of Music.

Scott Joplin (1868-1917)

Scott Joplin (Maple Leaf Rag) thrust ragtime into the forefront of American music. While an occasional autograph or two finds its way into the market, it has never been enough to fulfill the demand. Considering all aspects of his life getting a Joplin signature at under a four-digit sum is still a value!

Jerome Kern (1885-1945)

Jerome Kern (Show Boat, The Way You Look Tonight), himself a book and manuscript collector, played an important role in the development of 20th century American music. While a signature and occasional DS can appear in the autograph market, most musical manuscripts and letters are safe within the walls of The Library of Congress.

Edward MacDowell (1860-1908)

Edward MacDowell (Woodland Sketches, Sea Pieces), an early American composer, is in my opinion one of the most overlooked musicians in the autograph market. His material in all forms is still obtainable at reasonable price levels.

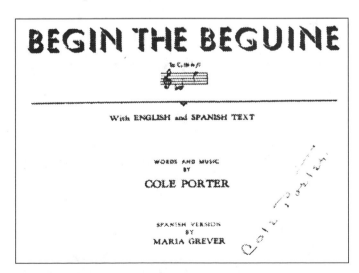

Cole Porter

Cole Porter (1891-1964)

Cole Porter (Kiss Me, Kate, Can-Can) was fairly receptive to autograph requests and as such, his signatures do appear routinely in the market. Collectors should be forewarned that the public seems to have an insatiable appetite for his signature, especially on quality vintage pieces, so act fast! Most of Porter's musical manuscripts are housed at his alma mater, Yale University.

Richard Rodgers (1902-1979)

Richard Rodgers (Oklahoma!, The Sound of Music) was always a gracious signer in-person and through the mail! While his musical manuscripts have been absorbed by institutions, his signature can still be found in other forms. Handwritten letters remain difficult to find, but signed cards, the way in which he responded to most autograph mail requests, are common.

John Philip Sousa

John Philip Sousa (1854-1932)

John Philip Sousa (The Stars and Stripes Forever, El Captain) autographed material is still affordable for most collectors. While most of his musical manuscripts have found solace inside institutional walls, such as the Library of Congress, some autograph items do find their way into the market. His once obtainable AMQS are slowly being absorbed by the market, so if you spot one you should act fast!

Andrew Lloyd Weber (1948-)

Andrew Lloyd Webber (Cats, Evita) is an elusive signer in-person and does not comply with written autograph requests. Because there are few authentic examples, many forgeries have entered the market, so collectors should exercise caution when purchasing his signature.

John Williams (1932-)

John Williams (Summon the Heroes, Star Wars) is a gracious signer in-person and through the mail!

Not on this list yet, but certainly worth mentioning, are those many composers who delight us with their wonderful soundtracks, individuals such as James Horner, John Barry, Jerry Goldsmith, Bill Conti, Alan Silvestri, Randy Newman and Danny Elfman.

A Brief Aviation Overview

Boyington, Gregory "Pappy"

The top Marine ace, Boyington led "The Black Sheep Squadron" during World War II. The winner of the Congressional Medal of Honor, his signature is very legible and is considered common.

Werhner von Braun

Braun, Wernher von

Along with Walter Domberger, he was brought to the United States from Germany to begin the space

program. He was a willing signer and as the public became more and more aware of his contributions to rocketry popular with autograph collectors. His signature is considered uncommon.

Curtiss, Glenn

Signed material from Curtiss is in demand with those building a serious aviation collection. The rarity of his signature has prompted forgeries, so collectors should carefully inspect all material.

Doolittle, Jimmy

A brilliant pilot and the man who led the raid on Tokyo early in the war, Doolittle has always been extremely popular with autograph collectors. He was a very willing signer both in-person and through mail requests. His signature is considered common.

Mrs Jameson.
Miss E. Hoar. London.

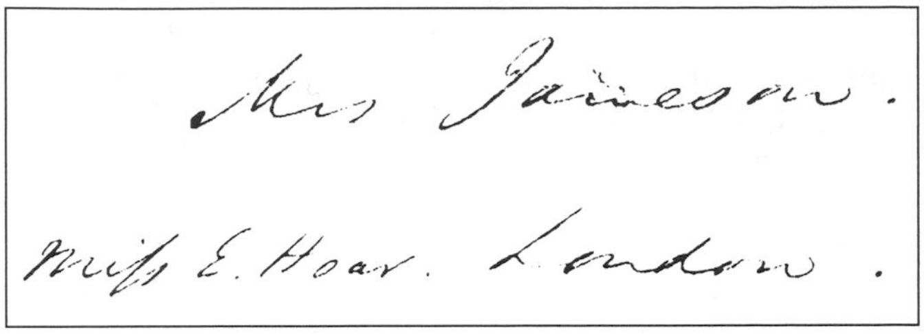

Amelia Earhart

Earhart, Amelia

As the first woman to fly the Atlantic, Amelia Earhart became an extremely popular figure and a must signature addition to any serious aviation collection. Her untimely disappearance during an around-the-world flight attempt in July of 1937, has been speculated upon for many years. Her signature is scarce and the rarity of it has prompted many forgeries. If an authentic example does enter the market it is often a signed book.

Fokker, Anthony

A pivotal contributor to aircraft design, Fokker was an obliging signer however is signature is considered scarce today. He came to the United States in 1922 from Germany and centered his corporation in New Jersey.

Hinton, Walter

As the first person to fly the Atlantic, Hinton's signature will always be in demand. When examples enter the autograph market they are often found on envelopes rather than any other form. While tougher to find in letters, his signature is considered common.

Langley, Samuel P.

Both an astronomer and airplane pioneer, Langley intensely studied solar radiation and flight as Secretary of the Smithsonian Institution in Washington, D.C. His signed material is rather uncommon and when it does surface it is typically from his days at the Smithsonian.

Lindbergh, Charles A.

He made the first solo nonstop transatlantic flight from Roosevelt Field, New York to Le Bourget Air Field in Paris, France (May 20-21, 1927) and became a national hero. His signature has been sought ever since and continues to be a key indicator in the hobby. Despite signing many items Lindbergh has also been a target of forgers, so be cautious of all material. During his later years mail requests for his signature went unanswered, but fortunately for collectors his often expensive signed items do periodically surface in the market.

To
Bob Guggenheim
Patriot and Sportsman
With whom it has been
a great pleasure to be
associated in developing
our ideas of both
Patriotism and Sportsmanship.
Wm. Mitchell
Boxwood
Middleburg, Va.
1/4/27

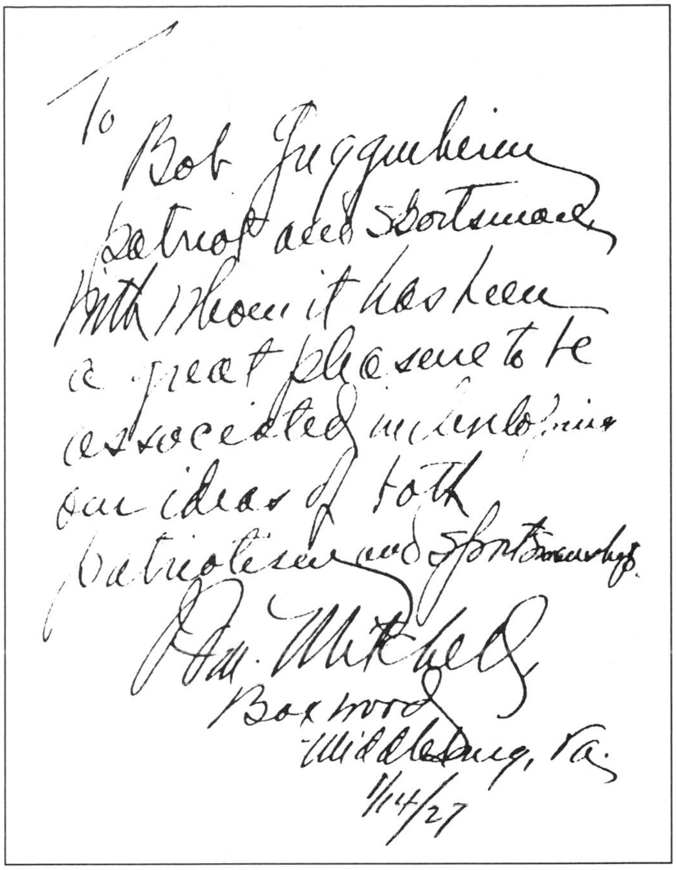

William "Billy" Mitchell

Mitchell, Billy

An outspoken advocate of air power, Mitchell was a controversial figure in American aviation. Because of this his signature is uncommon, yet key to a comprehensive collection of aviation signatures.

Post, Wiley

He made the first solo flight around the world and proved the value of instrument flight. Post died tragically in an airplane crash with Will Rogers. His signed material, often in the form of air mail covers, surfaces occasionally in the market and often at a significant cost.

Rickenbacker, Edward V.

An American aviator and industrialist, Rickenbacker was obsessed with speed be it on a race track or in the sky. He was a brilliant flyer and his victories earned him the Congressional Medal of Honor. Rickenbacker was always an obliging signer in-person and often through the mail. At times mail was answered with a stamped signature. Highly sought by collectors are photographs of him in uniform and when found are typically the image of him that appears on his autobiography. His signature is considered common.

Rutan, Dick

Along with Jeana Yeager, Rutan completed the first around-the-world nonstop and nonrefueled flight. He is a responsive signer and his autograph is considered common.

Sikorsky, Igor

The developer of the first practical American helicopter, Sikorsky set numerous flight records. He came to the United States in 1919 and founded the Sikorsky Aero Engineering Corporation, which he headed until his retirement in 1957. As a must addition to any aviation autograph collection, his signature has become increasingly expensive and tougher to find in recent years.

Spaatz, Carl

An American air force officer, Spaatz initiated daylight bombing of German-occupied Europe in 1942. His signature is considered common.

Orville Wright

Wilbur Wright

Wright, Orville and Wright, Wilbur

The Wright brothers made the first successful flight in a motor-powered airplane at Kill Devil Hills, near Kitty Hawk, North Carolina on December 17, 1903. The two held numerous aviation patents, most of which they utilized in the manufacture of their own flight machines. Wilbur died from typhoid fever in 1912 and his signature is scarce. Orville sold his interest in the airplane manufacturing company (American Wright Company) in 1915 and survived his brother by over three decades. Orville's signature, more common than his brother's, is considered uncommon. Both signatures are must additions to any collection, but can be costly. Because of their achievements they have also been a target of forgeries, so it is best to opt for canceled checks which appear occasionally.

Yeager, Chuck

A modern-day hero, Yeager was the first to break the sound barrier. He is a brilliant pilot and while his peers chose the spotlight of the space program, he opted to forge his own path. Yeager has always been a responsive signer both in-person and through mail requests for his signature.

Yeager, Jeana

Copilot of the Voyager in the first nonstop, nonrefueled around-the-world flight, Yeager is an obliging signer. Her signature is considered common.

In This Corner—Collecting Boxing Autographs

The establishment of a legitimate and recognized International Boxing Hall of Fame has been one of the contributing factors to the increased interest in collecting boxing autographs. Boxing autograph collectors can now focus their interest on a finite set of elite individuals, critical to the appeal of many areas of collecting.

Boxing Hall of Fame Members

Members of the International Boxing Hall of Fame are currently divided into four classes: Modern (68), Old Timer (68), Pioneer (24) and Non-Participant (48). These classes mimicked those created by *The Ring* magazine's Boxing Hall of Fame instituted in 1954. Obtaining at least one signature of every member of a particular sports Hall of Fame is popular with baseball, football, basketball and hockey collectors. However, it is not a viable task to the boxing autograph collector. Boxing as a popular sport, unlike the other four modern-day sports, dates back to the early 1700s, making some autographed material quite scarce. To better understand the challenges in collecting boxing Hall of Fame autographs, let's review each of the classes.

Pioneer

Most of the pioneer members in the Boxing Hall of Fame, died before 1900 and four even died before the year 1800. If this alone is not enough of a deterrent to collecting these boxing signatures add a location factor to the equation. Most of the members are

English, therefore, limiting access to much of the material that may exist if you live in the United States.

Some of the members died before the age of thirty: Belcher, Burke, Duffy, Figg, Pearce and Sayers. Paddy Duffy, an American, died at the young age of 26 and is by far the scarcest signature of the six.

Ben Brain, Jack Broughton, Tom Johnson, and James Figg all died before the year 1800. Of these three I feel the coalminer Ben Brain, who died suddenly at the age of 41, is the scarcest of the three signatures. Both Figg, Johnson and Broughton were very popular in their day and are believed to have signed more material. Broughton lived to the age of 85 and was very well respected. Ward lived to the age of 83 and was accessible to many of his fans.

Of all the pioneers, I have found the signature of John L. Sullivan easiest to obtain. As one might expect, an autograph from any member of this group can command a significant price.

Non-Participants

A few of the non-participant members in the Boxing Hall of Fame, died before or during the year 1900—John G. Chambers, Pierce Egan, & John S. Douglas. Of these three members, Chambers is by far the most difficult signature to find. Egan was a prolific writer and some of his material has even found it's way into the British market. A handwritten note from John S. Douglas was sold by Remember When Auctions, Incorporated in their October 10, 1994 auction.

From 1901 to 1950, some non-participant members died—Thomas S. Andrews, Jack Blackburn, James W. Cofforth, Lord Lonsdale, Tex Rickard, and James J. Walker. Of these members, Lord Lonsdale is by far the most difficult signature to find. The easiest of the six to find is two-time New York City mayor and former state senator James J. Walker. Despite being a journalist, Andrew's material still seems quite scarce. Blackburn, a former fighter recognized for his work with Joe Louis, has had some of his signatures surface in old turn-of-the-century autograph books. Of the promoters Cofforth and Rickard, the latter was the more popular and thus more acquired by collectors. As promoters, their signatures adorned many fight contracts, most of which will eventually find their way into the hands of collectors.

Most of the members in this category who died after 1950, or who are still living, should be easy signatures to add to your collection. Over time expect more signatures from this group to surface in the boxing memorabilia market, particularly as it gains increased legitimacy. I often view the boxing non-participants members, similarly to umpires who are in the Baseball Hall of Fame, in that their signatures are often found only on flat items, such as photographs, contracts, or slips of paper, but are seldom found in other forms. After all, when was the last time you found a Tex Rickard autographed boxing glove for sale?

Old Timers

Many boxing autograph collectors agree that the ten toughest signatures in this Hall of Fame category are: Les Darcy, Jack Dempsey (The Nonpareil), Stanley Ketchel, Pancho Villa, Terry McGovern, George Dixon, Joe Gans, Tiger Flowers, Peter Jackson and Harry Greb. Les Darcy was a very popular Australian boxer who turned professional at the age of sixteen. Darcy came to America during World War I, but was never given a legitimate opportunity to box. He became ill and died on May 24, 1917, at the young age of twenty-one. Although the Boxing Hall of Fame has a lock of Darcy's hair, they do not possess any samples of his signature. Jack Dempsey (The Nonpareil) died at the age of thirty-two in 1895. Autographed material from Dempsey is also scarce, although some samples have changed hands during the last few years. A Dempsey signature on the reverse of a business card appeared in an auction (11/92) with a minimum bid of $2,500.

At the age of twenty-four, Stanley Ketchel was shot to death by Walter Dipley on October 15, 1910, cutting short what looked to be a great career and leaving behind little autographed material. Ketchel was on holiday at a ranch in Conway, Missouri when Dipley, jealous over the affections displayed between his girlfriend and the fighter, shot him. Very little authentic autographed material exists from this fighter.

In another unexpected death, Pancho Villa died on July 14, 1925 from blood poisoning caused by an infected tooth following his fight with Jimmy McLarnin. At the age of thirty-two Harry Greb died from an eye operation; he had gained most of his popularity by defeating both Johnny Wilson and Gene Tunney. Some autographed Greb material has entered the market, but it still remains difficult to find. He did respond to mail requests for his signature during his life.

Tiger Flowers also died from the effects of an operation at the age of thirty-two, and ironically was Greb's last ring opponent. A cut signature of Flowers can command a significant price. Joe Gans died on August 10, 1910 from tuberculosis, at the young age of thirty-five. Some Gans autographed material has found it's way into the memorabilia market, but it also remains difficult to find.

Terry McGovern became so mentally ill that he had to be confined to a sanitarium. He passed away at the age of 37 on February 26, 1918. McGovern's physical state during the last years of his life cast much doubt about his writing legibility. George Dixon fought his last bout on December 10, 1906 and died three years later. Dixon autographed material has been scarce over the years. Peter Jackson autographed material is also scarce, but a few autographed theater pieces have changed hands. In addition to doing boxing exhibitions, Jackson became a stage actor and even toured in "Uncle Tom's Cabin."

In addition to the ten members I have mentioned, Jim Driscoll, Young Griffo, Sam Langford, Charles (Kid) McCoy, Packey McFarland, Philadelphia Jack O'Brien, Tommy Ryan, and Joe Walcott (Barbados) will also present a significant autograph acquisition challenge.

Signatures from James J. Corbett, Jack Dempsey, Bob Fitzsimmons, James J. Jeffries, Jack Johnson and Gene Tunney have appeared in the market over the last few years with some carrying a significant price tag.

Many of the members of this classification were excellent signers throughout their lifetime such as Jack Dempsey, Jack Sharkey and Gene Tunney. Many boxing autograph collectors seem to loose sight of some of the lighter weight classes. Don't overlook the autographs of fighters such as Mike Gibbons and Battling Nelson.

Modern

For any collector attempting to complete a full set of Boxing Hall of Fame signatures, this category will be by far the easiest. Most collectors agree that the toughest signatures in this group to acquire are Marcel Cerdan, Sonny Liston, Dick Tiger and Salvador Sanchez.

Cerdan was killed in an airplane crash on October 27, 1949 on his way back to America for a return bout against Jake LaMotta. The twenty-seven year old Cerdan had lost the World Middleweight Championship to LaMotta on June 16, 1949 while fighting in Detroit. A difficult signature to acquire not only because of a tragic death at a very early age, but also due to fighting locations. Of the 115 total bouts Cerdan fought, only eight fights (7%) were fought in the United States, and this was only from 1946-1949.

Sonny Liston, was by some accounts, the most disliked heavyweight the United States had since Jack Johnson in 1919. Liston had a difficult childhood that resulted in prison time for robbing a service station. Despite winning the 1952 Golden Gloves title and then turning professional, the past continued to haunt him. He was arrested again in 1956 for assaulting a policeman and that resulted in having his boxing license revoked. Association with many alleged organized crime figures, primarily through his manager Joseph "Peppy" Barone, also scarred his image. In February of 1962, Liston took on a new manager and finally secured a title shot against Floyd Patterson. Seven months after defeating Patterson twice, Liston would face Cassius Clay.

Following his defeat to Cassius Clay, he continued to fight, but was never considered a contender. Five

years later on January 5, 1971, Charles Liston was found dead in his Las Vegas home. Although much mystery still shrouds the cause of his death, some narcotics were found in his kitchen. Confusion not only surrounds his death, but also his signature. Liston was believed to have been somewhat illiterate, casting doubt upon some of his writing examples found in the market. Liston's wife was rumored to have handled much of his correspondence during his life. All collectors are advised to exercise caution when purchasing any Liston autographed material.

Dick Tiger had an outstanding career as a fighter and retired from the ring on July 19, 1971 at the age of 41, he died later that same year of cancer. The Nigerian began fighting in the United States in 1959. Of Tiger's eighty one career bouts, less than half took place on American soil. Surprisingly, little autographed material of Tiger's has been sold in the boxing memorabilia market.

Sanchez successfully defended his featherweight crown nine times, before being killed in an automobile accident. Such a tragic death before reaching his mid-twenties contributes to the lack of autographed memorabilia available in the market.

The most popular signatures in this category are those of Muhammad Ali, Joe Louis, Rocky Marciano and Sugar Ray Robinson. All of these fighters remained popular throughout their career and into their retirement. All four would be considered prolific signers, the least of which being Marciano.

During the last few years, Ali has been a familiar face signing autographs at sports collectible shows. I have heard of some recent mail requests for his signature answered after thirteen months of waiting. Ali, who is perhaps the greatest heavyweight fighter of all-time and certainly the most popular, remains a prolific signer. His signature has shown some significant variation throughout the years, primarily due to his health.

Joe Louis signed numerous autograph requests throughout his life. Often his signature adorns banquet programs, books, and autograph album pages. He was simplest to acquire following his retirement from the ring, although many samples signed during his time in the military service (1942-1944) have also been sold in the market. I have seen many autographed items from Joe Louis's Restaurant that opened up in Harlem on September 4, 1946.

Rocky Marciano was also congenial to autograph requests, especially outside of the fighting arena. My father played professional baseball with Rocky's brother in the early 1950s with the Three River Yankees. Driving back home from Key West my father stopped by "Marciano's" restaurant. He found the fighter sitting in the back of the restaurant, talking with a bunch of his friends. After some brief introductions,

Marciano sat down with my father at the bar, treating him like he had known him for years and sharing many wonderful stories. This story is just one of many that I have heard, about a fighter who cared greatly for his fans. Marciano was killed in an airplane accident in Newton, Iowa on August 31, 1969, the day before his forty-sixth birthday.

"Sugar" Ray Robinson, pound for pound, may have been the best fighter of all-time. He was an elusive signer during his fighting years. Most mail sent to him went unanswered or was returned with a "ghost" signature. During his retirement he became gracious toward autograph requests, until his later years when Alzheimer's disease forced him to curtail his signing. Mail requests answered between 1986 and 1989 may include a secretarial signature, rather than an authentic signature. Autograph collectors should be wary of material during this period of the fighter's life.

Autographs of fighters living outside the United States can provide an acquisition challenge, signatures such as Nino Benvenuti, Eder Jofre and Carlos Zarate. Fortunately for collectors, some of these fighters return to Canastota for the annual Boxing Hall of Fame Induction Weekend or are very good at responding to mail requests for their signature.

Two deceased fighters that I have also found surprisingly little autographed material from are Flash Elorde and Fritzie Zivic—Elorde is the tougher of the two. Both of these fighters died in the mid-1980s, yet little autographed material from them surfaces in the boxing memorabilia market.

The popularity of certain fighters in this category along with the demand for their signature can be volatile. Should a fighter such as Muhammad Ali decide that he will no longer sign at collector's shows, the value of his signature will skyrocket, if only temporarily. Additionally, supply is also a key factor in determining value. Should the supply of certain fighter's signature increase, due to one or more private signings, the value will be temporarily decreased until the demand has been meant, at which time, it should level at an appropriate price.

The risk of forgery, although it exists, has not been as bad in boxing, as it has been in other sports. Perhaps it's due to the fluctuating popularity of the sports or simply a result of the unfamiliarity of collectors with this segment of the hobby. Whatever the case, it still remains somewhat untouched by deception. We'll see just how long it lasts!

International Boxing Hall of Fame 1999, Total Members—208

Modern
Muhammad Ali, 1990 *, USA, H

Sammy Angott, 1998, USA, L
Alexis Arguello, 1992 *, Nicaragua, L, F,, SF
Henry Armstrong, 1990, USA, W, L. F
Carmen Basilio, 1990 *, USA, W, M
Wilfred Benitez, 1996 *, USA, JW, W
Nino Benvenuti, 1992 *, Italy, JM, M
Jackie (Kid) Berg, 1994, England, JW
Jimmy Bivens, 1999 *, USA, LH, H
Joe Brown, 1996, USA, L
Charley Burley, 1992, USA, M
Miguel Canto, 1998 *, Mexico, FL
Marcel Cerdan, 1991, Algeria, M
Antonio Cervantes, 1998 *, Columbia, JW
Ezzard Charles, 1990, USA, H
Billy Conn, 1990, USA, LH
Gabriel (Falsh) Elorde, 1993, Philippines, JL
Bob Foster, 1990*, USA, LH
Joe Frazier, 1990 *, USA, H
Gene Fullmer, 1991*, USA, M
Khaosai Galaxy, 1999 *, Thailand, JB
Kid Gavilan, 1990 *, Cuba, W
Joey Giardello, 1993 *, USA, M
Wilfredo Gomez, 1995 *, Puerto Rico, SB, F, JL
Billy Graham, 1992, USA, W
Rocky Graziano, 1991, USA, M
Emile Griffith, 1990 *, Virgin Islands, W, M
Marvelous Marvin Hagler, 1993 *, USA, M
Masahiko (Fighting) Harada, 1995 *, Japan, FL, B
Beau Jack, 1991, USA, L
Lew Jenkins, 1999, USA, L
Eder Jofre, 1992 *, Brazil, B, F
Harold Johnson, 1993 *, USA, LH
Jake LaMotta, 1990 *, USA, M
Sugar Ray Leonard, 1997 *, USA, W-LH
Sonny Liston, 1991, USA, H
Joe Louis, 1990, USA, H
Rocky Marciano, 1990, USA, H
Joey Maxim, 1994 ^, USA, LH
Bob Montgomery, 1995 *, USA, L
Carlos Monzon, 1990, Argentina, M
Archie Moore, 1990 , USA, LH
Matthew Saad Muhammad, 1998 *, USA, LH
Jose Napoles, 1990 *, Cuba, W
Ken Norton, 1992 *, USA, H
Ruben Olivares, 1991 *, Mexico, B, F
Carlos Ortiz, 1991 *, Puerto Rico, JW, L
Manuel Ortiz, 1996, USA, B
Floyd Patterson, 1991 *, USA, H
Eusebio Pedroza, 1999 *, Panama, B, F
Willie Pep, 1990 *, USA, F
Pascual Perez, 1995, Argentina, FL
Aaron Pryor, 1996 *, USA, JW
Sugar Ray Robinson, 1990, USA, W, M
Luis Rodriguez, 1997, Cuba, W
Sandy Saddler, 1990*, USA, F, JL
Vicente Saldivar, 1999, Mexico, F
Salvador Sanchez, 1991, Mexico, F

Max Schmeling, 1992 *, Germany,H
Michael Spinks, 1994 *, USA, LH, H
Dick Tiger, 1991 , Nigeria, M, LH
Jose Torres, 1997 *, Puerto Rico, LH
Jersey Joe Walcott, 1990, USA, H
Ike Williams, 1990 , USA, L
Chalky Wright, 1997, Mexico, F
Tony Zale, 1991, USA, M
Carlos Zarate, 1994 *, Mexico, B
Fritzie Zivic, 1993, USA, W

Old-Timers
Lou Ambers, 1992, USA, L
Abe Attell, 1990, USA, F
Max Baer, 1995, USA, H
Jack Britton, 1990, USA, W
Panama Al Brown, 1992, Panama, B
Tommy Burns, 1996, Canada, H
Tony Canzoneri, 1990, USA, F, L,JW
Georges Carpentier, 1991, France, LH
Kid Chocolate, 1991, Cuba, JL, F
Joe Choynski, 1998, USA, H
James J. Corbett, 1990, USA, H
Johnny Coulon, 1999, Canada, P, F, B
Les Darcy, 1993, Australia, M
Jack Delaney, 1996, Canada, LH
Jack Dempsey (The Nonpareil), 1992, Ireland, M
Jack Dempsey, 1990, USA, H
Jack Dillon, 1995, USA, LH
George Dixon, 1990, Canada, B, F
Jim Driscoll, 1990, Wales, F
Johnny Dundee, 1991, Italy, F, JL
Bob Fitzsimmons, 1990, England, M, H, LH
Tiger Flowers, 1993, USA, M
Joe Gans, 1990, USA, L
Frankie Genaro, 1998, USA, F
Mike Gibbons, 1992, USA, M
Tommy Gibbons, 1993, USA, H
Harry Greb, 1990, USA, M
Young Griffo, 1991, Australia, F
Pete Herman, 1997, USA, B
Peter Jackson, 1990, West Indies, H
Joe Jeannette, 1997, USA, H
James J. Jeffries, 1990, USA, H
Jack Johnson, 1990, USA, H
Stanley Ketchel, 1990, USA, M
Johnny Kilbane, 1995, USA, F
Fidel LaBarba, 1996, USA, FL
Sam Langford, 1990, Canada, H
Kid Lavigne, 1998, USA, L
Benny Leonard, 1990, USA, L
John Henry Lewis, 1994, USA, LH
Ted (Kid) Lewis, 1992, England, W
Tommy Loughran, 1991, USA, LH
Benny Lynch, 1998, Ireland, FL
Jack McAuliffe, 1995, Ireland, L
Charles (Kid) McCoy, 1991, USA, M

Packey McFarland, 1992, USA, L
Terry McGovern, 1990, USA, F, B
Jimmy McLarnin, 1991 *, Ireland, W
Sam McVey, 1999, USA, H
Sammy Mandell, 1998, USA, L
Freddie Miller, 1997, USA, F
Battling Nelson, 1992, Denmark, L
Philadelphia Jack O'Brien, 1992, USA, LH
Maxie Rosenbloom, 1993, USA, LH
Barney Ross, 1990, USA, W, JW, L
Tommy Ryan, 1991, USA, W, M
Jack Sharkey, 1994, USA, H
Freddie Steele, 1999, USA, M
Young Stribling, 1996, USA, LH, H
Lew Tendler, 1999, USA, B, F, L, W
Gene Tunney, 1990, USA, H
Pancho Villa, 1994, Philippines, FL
Joe Walcott (Barbados), 1991, Brit. West Indies,W
Mickey Walker, 1990, USA, W, M
Freddie Welsh, 1997, Wales, L
Jimmy Wilde, 1990, Wales, FL
Kid Williams, 1996, Denmark, B
Harry Wills, 1992, USA, H

Pioneer
Jem Belcher, 1992, England
Ben Brain, 1994, England
Jack Broughton, 1990, England
James Burke, 1992, England
Tom Cribb, 1991, England
Mike Donovan, 1998, USA, M
Paddy Duffy, 1994, USA, W
James Figg, 1992, England
John Jackson, 1992, England
Tom Johnson, 1995, England
Tom King, 1992, England
Nat Langham, 1992, England, M
Jem Mace, 1990, England
Daniel Mendoza, 1990, England
Tom Molineaux, 1997, USA
John Morrissey, 1996, Ireland
Henry Pearce, 1993, England
Bill Richmond, 1999, USA, H
Dutch Sam, 1997, England
Tom Sayers, 1990, England
Tom Spring, 1992, England
John L. Sullivan, 1990, USA, H
William (Bendigo) Thompson, 1991, England
Jem Ward, 1995, England

Non-Participants
Thomas S. Andrews, 1992, USA, writer, publisher
Ray Arcel, 1991, USA, trainer
Bob Arum, 1999 *, USA, promoter
Giuseppe Ballarati, 1999, Italy
Jack Blackburn, 1992, USA, trainer
William A. Brady, 1998, USA, manager
Teddy Brenner, 1993, USA, matchmaker

John Graham Chambers, 1990, England, rules
Gil Clancy, 1993 *, USA, trainer, manager
James W. Coffroth, 1991, USA, promoter
Cus D'Amato, 1995, USA, manager
Arthur Donovan, 1993, USA, referee
Mickey Duff, 1999 *, Poland, matchmaker
Angelo Dundee, 1992 *, USA, trainer
Chris Dundee, 1994 , USA, manager, promoter
Don Dunphy, 1993, USA, broadcaster
Lou Duva, 1998 *, USA, trainer, manager
Pierce Egan, 1991, England, historian
Nat S. Fleischer, 1990, USA, writer, publisher
Richard K. Fox, 1997, Ireland, writer, publisher
Eddie Futch, 1994 *, USA, trainer, manager
Charley Goldman, 1992, Poland, trainer
Ruby Goldstein, 1994, USA, referee
Murray Goodman, 1999, USA, publicist
Joe Humphreys, 1997, USA, announcer
Jimmy Jacobs, 1993, USA, manager, film historian
Mike Jacobs, 1990, USA, promoter
Jimmy Johnston, 1999, England, promoter
Jack Kearns, 1990, USA, manager

Don King, 1997 *, USA, promoter
A.J. Liebling, 1992, USA, writer
Lord Lonsdale, 1990, England, patron
Harry Markson, 1992 , USA, publicist, promoter
Marquess of Queensberry—J.S. Douglas, 1990 **
Arthur Mercante, 1995 *, USA, referee
Wiliam Muldoon, 1996, USA, trainer, official
Tom O'Rourke,1999, USA, manager, official
Gilbert Odd, 1995, England, writer
Dan Parker, 1996, USA, sports editor, columnist
George Parnassus, 1991, Greece, promoter
George (Tex) Rickard, 1990, USA, promoter
Irving Rudd, 1999 *, USA, publicist
George Siler, 1995, USA, referee
Jack Solomons, 1995, England, promoter
Emanuel Steward, 1996 *, USA, trainer, manager
Sam Taub, 1994, USA, broadcaster
Herman Taylor, 1998, USA, promoter
James J. Walker, 1992, USA, politician

Notes: Member, induction yr., country, wt. class/desig.
* = living, **—England, patron. Inaugural class in
italics

The Civil War

C.S.A. Generals

Collectors of signatures from generals of the American Civil War, find themselves involved in a fascinating area that is both established and fairly well understood. While some collectors choose sides, many also collect both Union and Confederate States of America (CSA) signatures. The latter quest is typically more expensive—often double that of their counterparts and a far greater task to complete. Both sectors are not only fun for autograph collectors, but also still fairly reasonable in price compared to other signatures in the market.

Over a century has passed since shots rang out across the fields of Gettysburg, yet we remain infatuated, if not obsessed, with the only war fought on American soil. Fortunately for collectors, many outstanding resources have been produced in this area that may assist you in your pursuit of a specific signature. These fine resources are listed in the bibliography section of this book and many can still be purchased at a reasonable price.

Values in this area are based upon what is known in regard to supply and public demand of an individual's signature. When I examined this area in 1998 for my reference & value guide, *The Standard Guide to Collecting Autographs*, I found many discrepancies in both pricing and the accurate evaluation of supply. A

dealer's knowledge in this area accounts for most discrepancies in price, while the supply of many general's signatures has been debated for years. Many past assumptions in this area have been defeated when a newly unearthed supply of signatures from a specific general is uncovered. Advanced autograph collectors in this area typically have a library of resources to refer to, highlighted by the accepted definitive resource, *Generals in Gray* by Ezra J. Warner, as well as some involvement with the many Civil War clubs and organizations. They also spend considerable time evaluating the items that find their way into the autograph market and their price.

The prominent generals of the C.S.A. often command the greatest attention, these include but are not limited to, Patrick Cleburne, Nathan B. Forrest, Robert Garnett, A.P. Hill, Stonewall Jackson, Jeb Stuart, George Pickett, James Longstreet, Albert S. Johnston, and of course Robert E. Lee. While the signatures of many lesser-known generals, whose signatures are tougher to find, can often command a far greater price than some of those listed above, they appeal to a much smaller general base of collectors.

Having a passion for controversy and a love for statistics and equations, I thought it would be interesting to rank the signatures of CSA generals by scarcity using a formula that would include age, known

The Generals Of The C.S.A.

The 40 Most Difficult Signatures to Acquire

1. Barnard Elliott Bee	1824-1861	21. William Edwin Starke	1814-1862
2. John Herbert Kelly	1840-1864	22. Abner Monroe Perrin	1827-1864
3. John Caldwell C. Sanders	1840-1864	23. Elisha Franklin Paxton	1828-1863
4. Johnson Kelly Duncan	1827-1862	24. Preston Smith	1823-1863
5. Patrick Ronayne Cleburne	1828-1864	25. John Decatur Barry	1839-1867
6. William Dorsey Pender	1834-1863	26. John Stevens Bowen	1830-1863
7. James Dearing	1840-1865	27. Otho French Strahl	1831-1864
8. James Barbour Terrill	1838-1864	28. Lewis Addison Armistead	1817-1863
9. Turner Ashby	1828-1862	29. Mosby Monroe Parsons	1822-1865
10. Lawrence O'Bryan Branch	1820-1862	30. Stephen Elliott, Jr.	1830-1866
11. Thomas Reade Rootes Cobb	1823-1862	31. Thomas Jonathan Jackson	1824-1863
12. Ben McCulloch	1811-1862	32. Albert Sidney Johnston	1803-1862
13. Adley Hogan Gladden	1810-1862	33. Albert Gallatin Jenkins	1830-1864
14. Phillip St. George Cocke	1809-1861	34. John Astin Wharton	1828-1865
15. John Carpenter Carter	1837-1864	35. Jean Jacques A.A. Mouton	1829-1864
16. John Bordenave Villepigue	1830-1862	36. William Henry C. Whiting	1824-1865
17. Charles Sideny Winder	1829-1862	37. Leonidas Polk	1806-1864
18. Victor Jean Baptiste Girardey	1837-1864	38. John Adams	1825-1864
19. Lewis Henry Little	1817-1862	39. Walter Husted Stevens	1827-1867
20. James McQueen McIntosh	1828-1862	40. Richard Waterhouse	1832-1876

Note:

This chart is based on the author's data base prepared for this book, and includes information on age, known writing frequency/exposure, education, date of death, and a variety of market data. The current market value for a general's signature was not factored into the equation, nor was demand.

writing frequency/exposure, education, date of death, and market data. The current market value for the general's signature was not factored into the equation. As an advanced autograph collector, put your list together and match it against the list included here. While we may not agree with the order, I bet the names are very similar!

Union Generals

Collecting the signatures of generals of the Union is a far easier task than their counterparts in the CSA, but similar to the latter can provide some challenges. The sheer number of generals in the Union Army, over 580, offers collectors a number of price levels. The dilution of the rank (brigadier, major and lieutenant general) as well as the availability of Union documents over those of the South contributes to a lower cost per signature, typically about half of what you may pay for a similar CSA document.

The Union did have its fair share of notable generals. In fact, four went on to serve as President. Those signatures most sought after include, Joshua L. Chamberlain, George A. Custer, Abner Doubleday, Andrew Johnson, James A. Garfield, Ulysses S. Grant, Rutherford B. Hayes, Joseph Hooker, George B. McClellan, George G. Meade, Philip Sheridan, and W.T. Sherman.

Many resources about the Civil War can be extremely helpful to advanced collectors of Union general signatures. A good place to begin is with Ezra J. Warner's *Generals in Blue,* while others can be found in the bibliography section of this book. Below is my list of the fifty most difficult signatures to acquire of Union generals. Like many of you, I also had relatives who fought in this great war, one of which was a general. Since he stuck his neck out, so shall I.

The Generals Of The Union

The 50 Most Difficult Signatures to Acquire

1. George Dashiell Bayard	1835-1862		26. Robert L. McCook	1827-1862
2. Edmund Kirby	1840-1863		27. William R. Terrill	1834-1862
3. Elon J. Farnsworth	1837-1863		28. Strong Vincent	1837-1863
4. William Nelson	1824-1862		29. James S. Jackson	1823-1862
5. Michael Corcoran	1827-1863		30. Francis E. Patterson	1821-1862
6. Thomas G. Stevenson	1836-1864		31. William W.H.L. Wallace	1821-1862
7. Joshua W. Sill	1831-1862		32. Edward N. Kirk	1828-1863
8. Philip Kearny	1815-1862		33. Pleasant A. Hackleman	1814-1862
9. Edward P. Chapin	1831-1863		34. Conrad F. Jackson	1813-1862
10. Thomas E.G. Ransom	1834-1864		35. William H. Keim	1813-1862
11. Jesse L. Reno	1823-1862		36. Charles F. Smith	1824-1862
12. William P. Sanders	1833-1863		37. Louis Blenker	1812-1863
13. Daniel McCook Jr.	1834-1864		38. Henry Bohlen	1810-1862
14. George C. Strong	1832-1863		39. George W. Taylor	1808-1862
15. Israel B. Richardson	1815-1862		40. Thomas A. Smyth	1832-1865
16. Alexander Schimmelfennig	1824-1865		41. William H. Lytle	1826-1863
17. John Buford	1826-1863		42. Charles R. Lowell	1835-1864
18. Stephen G. Champlin	1827-1864		43. Thomas Welsh	1824-1863
19. David Bell Birney	1825-1864		44. Isaac I. Stevens	1818-1862
20. Hiram Burnham	1814-1864		45. Joseph B. Plummer	1816-1862
21. Alexander Hayes	1819-1864		46. Thomas Williams	1815-1862
22. Charles D. Jameson	1827-1862		47. Samuel K. Zook	1821-1863
23. Nathaniel Lyon	1818-1861		48. Stephen H. Weed	1831-1863
24. Isaac P. Rodman	1822-1862		49. James C. Rice	1829-1864
25. Edward Dickinson Baker	1811-1861		50. Ormsby M. Mitchell	1809-1862

Note:

This chart is based on the author's database, prepared for this book and includes information on age, known writing frequency/exposure, education, date of death, and a variety of market data. The current market value for a general's signature was not factored into the equation, nor was demand. Old market data would position George Armstrong Custer third on this list, however the author's research does not support these older claims.

Hollywood Stars

A very popular area of autograph collecting is acquiring the signatures of prominent individuals in the area of the performing arts. Whether we have seen them on the silver screen, on the stage or in our living room on television, our fascination with actors, actresses and those around them seems relentless.

Understanding the impact of the performing arts on our society, and even that of certain entertainers in pivotal roles, will help you gage the demand for, and value of certain autographs. This is why you will quickly understand when a simple signed photograph of Clark Gable sells for $700 and a similar signed photograph of the actor, only this time as "Rhett Butler" sells for $1,200 to $1,400. For pricing information consult *The Standard Guide to Collecting Autographs,* written by this author and published by Krause Publications.

While the signed photograph is certainly the most popular form of collecting in this niche, numerous other forms do enter the market. Contracts, canceled personal checks, signed movie programs and posters, and on occasion letters are even found in dealer catalogs. Autograph albums, album pages and collections of 3" x 5" index cards are also extremely common.

Due to its popularity, collecting in this area has many pitfalls. Forgery is rampant, particularly with newer stars and the established legends. If you think all those ads you see in collector magazines advertising signed photos of Brad Pitt, Harrison Ford and Bruce Willis are authentic, you better think again! Many of these stars are impossible to get signatures from in-person, even from aggressive collectors and via mail, forget it! In the past thirty—five years that I have sent autograph requests to Paul Newman—literally hundreds of letters, I have only received one authentic signature, just one. Facsimiles and "ghost" signatures are also common in the performing arts, so you will have to acquaint yourself with these examples. If you thought collecting sports autographs was challenging, you just wait!

This market is very dynamic, so much so in a study of the market I rated it unstable. Prices are driven by screen legends and those stars who are currently popular. Also anticipate paying more for those signatures received in-person or examples that are clearly authentic. Pricing varies significantly and by my study averages 25.6% between sources.

Presented here is useful information that you can use to authenticate, identify or even use to assist you in determining a value for a specific item. This will be particularly useful to collectors just beginning to venture into this area. While I began writing to many of the individuals presented in this section almost four decades ago, it's never to late to start collecting!

Abbreviations Key

AAW—Academy award winner, CS—Common salutations, OP—Often personalized items, RS—Responsive signer to mail requests, FA—Facsimile/Forgery alert, PF—Popular forms in the market

Bud Abbott & Lou Costello

Abbott & Costello

One of the most popular comedy teams ever, the signatures of both in any form is highly sought. FA, watch out for secretarial signatures and examples where both signatures were signed by one person. Highly sought is Universal Pictures signed publicity photographs. PF—autograph album pages. Abbott's signature was typically very large, sometimes twice the size of Costello's.

Acquanetta (1920-)

A Cheyenne Indian actress, with a signature often constructed of ten strokes, her autograph is easy to authenticate. PF—autograph album pages.

Aherne, Brian (1902-1986)

The forever-charming British gentleman, Aherne was an obliging signer with a distinct autograph—very vertically constructed with little slant. The first loop of the letter "B" is typically very thin, resembling an upside down thin "U". He often added an underline beneath his name. Occasionally his signature may appear with that of actress Joan Fontaine, whom he was married to. PF—autograph album pages.

Albert, Eddie (1908-)

With a very distinctive and flamboyant signature, Eddie Albert has always been a reluctant signer in-person and nearly impossible to acquire via mail. Earlier examples of his signature are characterized by the enormous formation of the "E", whose flamboyant structure is often twice the height of the "A". Surprisingly little of his material is available in the market. Occasional documents and canceled checks remain affordable. His signature has gotten far less flamboyant with age. Occasionally his signature may appear with that of actress Margo, whom he was married to.

Albertson, Frank (1909-1964)

A highly sought character actor, Albertson was an obliging signer in-person. I wrote to him near the end of his life and did not receive a response. His signature always appeared hurried, with the "F" often resembling a "P". His signature is distinctive as it appears printed with flamboyant character connections—"an", "be" and "ts", PF—autograph album pages, index cards.

Alexander, Ben (1911-1969)

A popular child actor in the era of silent film, Alexander is often associated with the TV series "Dragnet" where he appeared as Officer Frank Smith. OP, CS—"Frank Smith", PF—autograph album pages, index cards. Surprisingly little of his autographed material has entered the market.

Allan, Elizabeth (1908-1990)

A British beauty who came to Hollywood during the thirties, Allan had a huge fallout with MGM after being replaced in a leading role. Her signature is often illegible with only the "All" formation recognizable. OP, very tough to authenticate. PF—autograph album pages, index cards.

Allen, Gracie (1902-1964)

Half of the Burns-Allen comedy team, Gracie was a very obliging signer. Her signature is typically legible, with the "G"—which resembles a large "g", the most distinctive characteristic. Despite her being a responsive signer, her signature is uncommon today. Naturally, collectors would prefer a vintage piece signed by both members. If found be sure that the piece was actually signed by both and not just one member writing both names. PF—autograph album pages, index cards.

Allen, Tim (1953-)

"Tim the Tool Man Taylor" emerged into the spotlight with "Home Improvement" and thus Tim Allen became a big Hollywood star. Approachable in-person for a signature, Allen uses a fan mail service to answer autograph requests. His signature is often illegible and difficult to authenticate. PS—"Be good to your tools", FA, PF—photographs.

Anderson, Eddie "Rochester" (1905-1977)

Anderson emerged from vaudeville to link up with Jack Benny as his valet. Both on radio, then on TV (1937) Anderson was a hit with audiences. As a regular on "The Jack Benny Show" he was catapulted to star status. He remains very popular with autograph collectors today especially on signed photographs. CS—"Hello From Rochester". At one point he signed publicity photos (bw, 5" x 7") bearing a facsimile "Regards Rochester", to which he added a salutation and his full name in a light part of the picture. RS, FA, PF—autograph album pages, index cards, photographs.

Andrews Sisters, The

This popular singing group seemed to dominate the forties silver screen. The toughest signature to acquire was that of Laverne. Maxene's signature is often the boldest and it is not uncommon for her to add a salutation. Patricia commonly signed "Patty", RS, OP, PF—autograph album pages, index cards, photographs.

Andrews, Julie (1935-)

Forever associated with film classics such as "Mary Poppins" and "The Sound of Music", Julie Andrews made her mark on both stage and screen. While she is a willing signer in-person after a play, through the mail she responds with a facsimile signed photograph. Most sought after are autographed photographs from her in one of her key roles. PF—autograph album pages, index cards, photographs .

Arbuckle, Roscoe "Fatty" (1887-1933)

Silent screen comic actor, Roscoe "Fatty" Arbuckle is commonly associated with an event off-screen rather than on. A 1921 party he gave in San Francisco's St. Francis Hotel turned tragic when a promising actress died. Allegedly she had been assaulted by Arbuckle behind closed doors, however the star was finally acquitted of charges after three long trials. Because of

his contribution to early cinema his signature is highly sought by collectors. RS, OP, CS—"Sincerely yours", PF—autograph album pages, index cards, photographs.

Arden, Eve (1908-1990)

Comic actress who appeared in numerous films including "Mildred Pierce" and "Anatomy of A Murder", Arden is perhaps most remembered for her television work. Her single stroke signature often starts out large and gradually becomes smaller. RS, PF—autograph album pages, index cards, photographs.

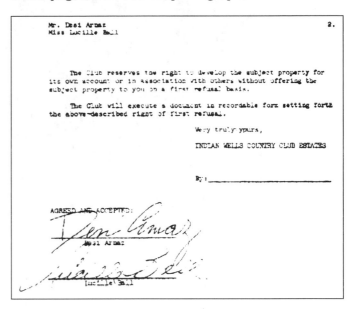

Desi Arnaz & Lucille Ball

Arnaz, Desi (1917-1986)

Cuban singer and bandleader, Desi Arnaz appeared in a few films, but is forever associated with his wife Lucille Ball and the popular television show, "I Love Lucy". His signature is highly sought by collectors who are aware of his significant contribution to television. A responsive signer in-person, he was allegedly a prolific writer during his later, however despite repeated attempts via mail I was never successful at obtaining a signature from him. PF—autograph album pages, index cards, photographs.

Arno, Sig (1895-1975)

German comedian and character actor, Arno appeared in films such as "The Great Dictator", "The Mummy's Hand" and "Up in Arms." He often included a quick sketch as part of his signature. PF—autograph album pages, index cards, photographs.

Arthur, Jean (1900-1991)

A talented comedic actress, Arthur appeared in film such as "Mr. Smith Goes to Washington", "Shane", and "The More the Merrier". Ironically, her screen persona was far different from her personal life that was shrouded in privacy. She did not like signing autographs at all and often went out of her way to avoid doing so. Her signature is far scarcer than many realize. PF—autograph album pages, index cards, photographs.

Fred Astaire

Astaire, Fred (1899-1987)

The screen's greatest dancer, Astaire's charm and fancy footwork won the hearts of all who saw his brilliant performances. He appeared in films such as "Top Hat", "Easter Parade", "Swing Time" and "Funny Face". It's not unusual to find his signature alongside that of his wife's Adele or next to one of his dancing partners such as Ginger Rogers, Leslie Caron or Rita Hayworth. He was very obliging to signature requests in-person, however I had sporadic luck with him through the mail. His signature is fairly common in the market and has shown consistent demand since his death. RS, CS—"Sincerely", PF—autograph album pages, index cards, photographs.

Astor, Mary (1905-1987)

A talented and beautiful actress , Astor gave many memorable performances in films such as "The Maltese Falcon", "The Great Lie" and "Little Women". Her signature will always be sought by Oscar collectors and should continue to exhibit strong appreciation. AAW, RS, PF—autograph album pages, index cards, photographs.

Autry, Gene (1907-1998)

The first successful Hollywood singing cowboy, Autry made over 90 films and sold millions of records. He was always a responsive signer right up until the

last years of his life. His signature exhibited some variation over his lifetime most notably in the letter "A". It is not unusual for his signature to adorn everything from a baseball to a guitar, so if your patient you'll probably find the form you are most looking for. While is signature is not scarce, more and more dealers are purchasing vintage pieces from his western days at Mascot, Republic and Columbia Pictures.

Bacall, Lauren (1924-)

The actress with "The Look", Bacall appeared in many films including "To Have and Have Not", "Key Largo" and "How to Marry a Millionaire". She has been a responsive signer throughout her life and a classic example of how a Hollywood screen legend should behave. RS, PF—autograph album pages, index cards, photographs—especially those with Bogart.

Baldwin, Alec (1958-)

The most successful thus far among the Baldwin Brother Dynasty, Alec has appeared in many memorable films such as "The Hunt for Red October". He is a very accommodating signer in-person, however mail requests for his signature are often unanswered. PF—autograph album pages, index cards, photographs.

Lucille Ball

Ball, Lucille (1911-1989)

Perhaps Hollywood's finest clown, Ball was a comedic genius. While she was great in film, her legacy will always be her roles on television especially during her series "I Love Lucy" (1951—1957). She was an obliging signer in person, however fan mail requests for signatures were often answered with facsimile signed photographs. While early signature examples will bear her full name, later pieces will be signed "Love Lucy". Collectors obviously prefer the earlier variety, however they are scarce. Because her signature has shown significant collector interest, the "Love Lucy" variety has been forged so be careful! CS— "Love", OP (early examples only), FA, PF—autograph album pages, index cards, photographs—especially those with Desi which are very uncommon.

Bara, Theda (1890-1955)

Often called Hollywood's first "vamp", Bara was both charming and romantic. She appeared in films such as "A Fool There Was", "Under Two Flags" and "Romeo and Juliet". She died in 1955 and is highly collected by early film buffs who recognize her contribution to the medium. Her signature is uncommon and little is known of her signing habits. Occasionally her autograph turns up in old autograph albums. PF—autograph album pages, index cards.

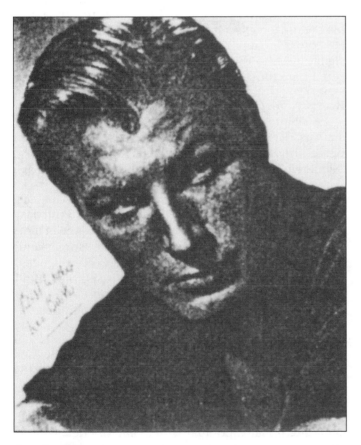

Lex Barker

Barker, Lex (1919-1973)

An athletic actor, Barker appeared in numerous films, but is probably remembered most as Tarzan. He replaced Johnny Weissmuller and did five films for RKO. His signature often appears next to two actress Arlene Dahl and Lana Turner, both of whom he married. His signature has shown consistent appreciation since his death because of the "Tarzan Factor". RS, PF—autograph album pages, index cards, photographs.

John Barrymore

Barrymore, John (1882-1942)

"The Great Profile", Barrymore was nothing short of magnificent on the stage and on the silver screen. He appeared in memorable silent films such as "Sherlock Holmes" and "Beau Brummel", then went on to talkies in films like "Grand Hotel", "Dinner at Eight" and "Reunion in Vienna". He had times off the screen where he was often unpredictable, especially near the end of his life. AAW, PF—autograph album pages, index cards, photographs.

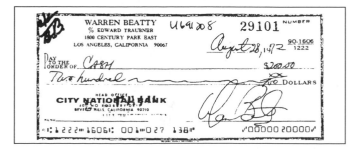

Lionel Barrymore

Barrymore, Lionel (1878-1954)

A prolific character actor and eldest brother of John and Ethel, Lionel appeared in hundreds of films including "A Free Soul", "Dinner at Eight", and "It's a Wonderful Life". He is often remembered fondly for his role as Dr. Leonard Gillespie in the "DR. Kildaire" films of the late thirties and forties. AAW, RS, PF—autograph album pages, index cards, photographs.

Bassinger, Kim (1953-)

A popular actress, Bassinger has appeared in numerous films including "Never Say Never Again", "Nine and a Half Weeks" and "Batman". She is a responsive signer in-person, however mail requests for signature often go unanswered. Her signature, or should I say initials, is often illegible. Because she is not a prolific signer and her autograph is an authenticity nightmare, her signature is often forged especially on color photographs of her in "Batman". PF—photographs.

Warren Beatty

Beatty, Warren (1937-)

One of Hollywood's gifted leading men, Beatty has appeared in many popular films including "Reds", "Bonnie and Clyde" and "Shampoo". He is not a fan of autograph collectors and seldom responds to in-person requests. Forget about getting a signature via mail also, as requests often go unanswered. His signature is often illegible and difficult to authenticate., AAW, FA, PF—autograph album pages, index cards, photographs.

Beavers, Louise (1902-1962)

A very popular character actress, Beavers is commonly associated with her television role as "Beulah" during the early fifties. While she was a responsive signer, little of her material surfaces in the autograph market. RS, OP, "Sincerely", PF—autograph album pages, index cards, photographs—especially from her thirties film roles are scarce.

Belushi, John (1942-1982)

A gifted comedian, Belushi was thrust into the limelight when he was chosen as an original cast member of "Saturday Night Live". From television success came film offers, including "Animal House", "The Blues Brothers", "Neighbors" and "Continental Divide". He was a responsive signer in-person, however mail often went unanswered. His tragic death quickly escalated the price of his signature. Some of his personal checks have surfaced in the market giving collectors an opportunity to purchase a legitimate signature. FA, PF—index cards, photographs—highly sought are those portraying him in a memorable role.

Beery, Noah (1883-1946)

A silent screen villain, Beery appeared in films such as "The Mark of Zorro", "The Sea Wolf" and "Beau Geste". His signature in any form is scarce, CS— "Sincerely", PF—autograph album pages, index cards.

Beery, Wallace (1885-1949)

A terrific screen actor of the twenties and thirties, Beery gave numerous memorable performance in films such as "The Champ", "Grand Hotel", "Treasure Island" and "Tugboat Annie". The Oscar winner often signed "Wally Berry" and his last name often resembles "Buy" because of its minimal character definition. AAW, PF—autograph album pages, index cards, photographs.

Benny, Jack (1894-1974)

Star of radio, television and film, the versatile Jack Benny was a comedic genius. His films include "The Big Broadcast of 1937", "To Be Or Not To Be" and "It's in the Bag". While he was a gracious signer in-person, I never had any luck via mail, although others had. His signature remains popular with collectors decades after his death. PF—autograph album pages, index cards, photographs.

Bergen, Edgar (1903-1978)

The father of actress Candice Bergen, Edgar was a talented ventriloquist who popularized his wooden dummy Charlie McCarthy. Bergen appeared on radio, film and later television. RS, CS—"and Charlie McCarthy", PF—autograph album pages, index cards, photographs.

Ingrid Bergman

Bergman, Ingrid (1915-1982)

A talented and beautiful Swedish actress, Bergman gave many memorable performances in films such as "Casablanca", "Gaslight", "Anastasia" and "Murder on the Orient Express". A multiple Oscar winner, her signature remains very popular with both dealers and collectors. While she was responsive in-person to autograph requests, many mail requests went unanswered. Her signature is characterized by large capitalization and the very deep descenders in the letter "g". FA, PF—autograph album pages, index cards, photographs—especially from Casablanca.

Berle, Milton (1908-)

Everyone's Uncle and "Mr. Television", Berle appeared in a number of films, but dominated the medium of television. A reluctant but obliging signer in-person, Berle hasn't responded to mail requests for his signature in years! CS—"Sincerely", PF—autograph album pages, index cards, photographs—especially from his early television days.

Bickford, Charles (1889-1967)

A brilliant character actor, Bickford's career spanned half a century. He appeared in films such as "Anna Christie", "The Song of Bernadette" and "A Star is Born". He was a responsive signer in-person and with the exception of the "C", "B", "h", "l", "k" and , "f" the character formations in his signature were often very small or difficult to decipher. RS, PF—autograph album pages, index cards, photographs.

Blandick, Clara (1880-1962)

A gifted character actress, Blandick appeared in numerous films, including "Tom Sawyer", "Shopworn" and "Gentleman Jim", however will always be associated with her role as Aunt Em in "The Wizard of Oz". It is her appearance in the latter film that has continued to drive the price of her very scarce signature upward. She was responsive to autograph requests early in her career, but health problems eventually led her to discontinue the practice. FA, OP, PF—autograph album pages, index cards, photographs.

Humphrey Bogart

Bogart, Humphrey (1899-1957)

Hollywood legend and brilliant actor, "Bogey" left his legacy in films such as "The Maltese Falcon", "Casablanca" and "The African Queen". A very reluctant, but occasionally compliant signer, Bogart authentic material is scarce. For years his secretaries handled his mail. Due to his popularity and the little authentic signed material that has surfaced in the market, he has been a target for forgers. Many dealers will suggest that you consult and expert first before buying and if possible try to purchase an unquestionably authentic document—if you can find one! AAWFA, PF—autograph album pages, index cards, photographs—especially from his premier roles.

Ray Bolger

Bolger, Ray (1904-1987)

A versatile actor, Ray Bolger appeared in numerous films including "The Great Ziegfeld", "Sweethearts", and "The Harvey Girls", but he is best remembered for his role as the Scarecrow in "The Wizard of Oz". Although he was a prolific signer throughout his life, even at Oz conventions and for dealers, his signature is always in demand as newer generations discover the classic film. Because of this he has also been a target of forgers, so exercise caution when purchasing his signature. FA, OP, PF—autograph album pages, index cards, photographs—especially OZ related.

Bond, Ward (1903-1960)

A favorite of both John Ford and John Wayne, Bond appeared in hundreds of films including "Tobacco Road", "Wagonmaster" and "Gone With the Wind". His latter association and his untimely death both contribute to the value of his signature. He was a responsive signer in-person of a very legible signature. PF—autograph album pages, index cards, photographs.

Marlon Brando

Brando, Marlon (1924-)

A screen legend, Brando established his legacy in films like "On the Waterfront", "A Streetcar Named Desire" and "The Godfather". While he would reluctantly sign some items early in his career, it wouldn't take him long to simply refuse all requests. A recluse, he opts to live on his own island and shun the limelight completely. Because his signature is so uncommon, it has been a target of forgers for years. Most of what is on the market today is fake and will probably remain that way until action is taken, or the actor opts for a new autograph policy. AAW, FA, PF—autograph album pages, index cards, photographs—especially from his role in The Godfather.

Bronson, Charles (1921-)

A talent actor, Bronson has appeared in numerous films but is most associated with his "Death Wish" series. A responsive signer in-person, however much of his mail is often ghost signed. Some checks and documents have entered the market and are a good source for collectors. FS, PF—autograph album pages, index cards, photographs.

Brosnan, Pierce (1952-)

"Bond, James Bond", so many Bonds but Brosnan is the latest. He has appeared in numerous films including "Golden Eye", "Dante's Peak" and "Mrs. Doubtfire". He showcased his talent in the hit television series "Remington Steele", before setting his sights on the silver screen. Brosnan is delightful in-person and very accommodating to autograph requests, however via mail, if you do manage to get a response, it is probably not from Brosnan but from whoever answers his mail. FA, PF—autograph album pages, index cards, photographs—especially Bond related.

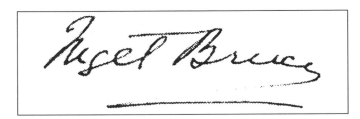

Nigel Bruce

Bruce, Nigel (1895-1953)

Bruce appeared in 14 "Sherlock Holmes" films as the character Dr. Watson. While he is typically associated with the series he did appear in other films including "Rebecca", "The Bluebird" and "Suspicion". He was a responsive signer in-person and would often take extra time to personalize requests. His signature is not common so collectors will have to be patient until one enters the market. RS, OP, PF—autograph album pages, index cards, photographs—especially "Sherlock Holmes" related.

Billie Burke

Burke, Billie (1885-1970)

A delicate actress, Burke had memorable roles in numerous films including "Topper", "Dinner at Eight" and "The Man Who Came to Dinner", but will forever be associated with "The Wizard of Oz". In the picture she played Glinda, "The Good Witch of the East".

She was a responsive signer in-person, however I never had much luck getting a signature from her by mail. PF—autograph album pages, index cards, photographs—especially "Oz" related which are very scarce.

George Burns

Burns, George (1898-1996)

A charismatic comedian, Burns conquered radio, film and television. The latter being the one he is commonly associated with for the series "The George Burns and Gracie Allen Show". Burns was accommodating to in-person autograph requests throughout most of his life, however in his later years mail was answered by secretaries. FA, PF—autograph album pages, index cards, photographs.

Burr, Raymond (1917-1993)

Burr is commonly associated with his role in the hit television series "Perry Mason", but he did appear in numerous films including "Rear Window", "A Place in the Sun" and "Walk a Crooked Mile". While he was responsive to autograph requests in-person, he seldom answered requests for his signature by mail. OP, CS—"My Very Best", PF—autograph album pages, index cards, photographs—especially as Perry Mason.

Burton, Richard (1925-1984)

A dramatic Welsh-born actor, Burton made the transition from stage to screen and appeared in many successful films including "Cleopatra", "The Sandpiper" and "Who's Afraid of Virginia Woolf?". His on again, off again, relationship with actress Elizabeth Taylor kept both in the tabloids and drove each more into seclusion. He was a reluctant but occasionally obliging signer in-person, however mail requests nearly always went unanswered. His signature includes distinctive character formations in the letter "d", which includes three loops, and the combination "rt" in Burton, which is often disproportionately large. FA, PF—autograph album pages, index cards, photographs.

Nicholas Cage

Cage, Nicolas (1964-)

Changing his last name from Coppala to Cage, this talented actor set out to become a big star, which he has. Cage has appeared in numerous films including "Raising Arizona", "Guarding Tess", "Moonstruck", and "Leaving Las Vegas". Cage is very responsive to in-person autograph requests and still responds to mail requests. RS, PF—autograph album pages, index cards, photographs.

James Cagney

Cagney, James (1899-1986)

A versatile and gifted actor, Cagney became a Hollywood legend and left behind a legacy of outstanding films including, "The Public Enemy", "White Heat" and "Yankee Doodle Dandy". He was an elusive signer in-person, however I had tremendous success writing to him during his retirement years. He would often respond with a small autographed photo, typed letter or with one of his postcards. The common form of his signature is "J. Cagney" and it can bear a striking resemblance to that of his sister's Jeanne Cagney. During the last decade the market has witnessed an increased number of his forged signature, so exercise caution. AAW, RS, PF—autograph album pages, index cards, photographs—especially in major roles.

Carradine, John (1906-1988)

A prolific character actor, Carradine appeared in hundreds of films including "Stagecoach", "The Grapes of Wrath" and "The Last Hurrah". He was an obliging signer in-person, however mail requests for his signature often went unanswered. His signature can be illegible and prove difficult to authenticate. PF—autograph album pages, index cards, photographs.

Carrey, Jim (1962-)

"The Man of a Thousand Expressions", Carrey has successfully made the transition from television to film. His films have included "The Mask", "Ace Ventura: Pet Detective" and "Batman Forever". He is an elusive but occasionally obliging signer in-person, however by mail he still sends out those "Spank You Very Much" facsimile signed photographs. FA, PF—autograph album pages, index cards, photographs—especially those from "Batman Forever".

Nancy Carroll

Carroll, Nancy (1904-1965)

One of the talkies first big stars, Carroll made numerous films including "The Shopworn Angel" and "The Devil's Holiday". She retired in the late thirties and signature is uncommon. PF—autograph album pages, index cards.

Chaney, Lon (1883-1930)

A silent era star who could transform himself into any role, Chaney made numerous films including "The Hunchback of Notre Dame", "The Phantom of the Opera", and "The Miracle Man". He became a legend among horror film buffs who still marvel at his ability to use makeup to alter himself. He was not a responsive signer, choosing instead to selectively pass along autographs to friends and co-workers. His signature is uncommon in any form and when a signed photograph does surface it is typically a signed studio still often from "Tell It To the Marines". FA, CS—"Most Sincerely" or lengthy personal salutation, FA, PF—autograph album pages, index cards, photographs—scarce.

Chaney, Lon, Jr. (1906-1973)

Following in his father's footsteps, Creighton Chaney changed his name to Lon Chaney, Jr. While his signature is not nearly as rare as his father's, demand for his autograph in any form has been consistent for decades. He was far more accessible to his fans both in-person and through the mail, however I never had any luck with the latter. His performances in "Of Mice and Men" and "The Wolf Man" are typically sited when people hear his name. FA, RS, PF—autograph album pages, index cards, photographs.

Charlie Chaplin

Chaplin, Charlie (1889-1977)

"The Little Tramp" captured our hearts and became a testament to the power of film and the incredible talent of Sir Charles Chaplin. His films included "The Tramp", "Modern Times", "The Great Dictator" and "The Circus". Highly sought are the signatures from his early days in film, where he would sign "Charlie" or "Charles", later he would opt for "C. Chaplin" or "Chas. Chaplin". Age took its toll on Chaplin and his signature deteriorated with his health. Collectors prefer earlier examples, where he may on rare occasion add a drawing to his signature. He was an elusive signer in-person and mail requests, many of which were mine, went unanswered. His popularity and lack of authentic examples in the market has contributed to the great number of forgeries a collector may encounter. Exercise caution and opt for vintage signatures only! AAW, OP, CS—"Faithfully", PF—autograph album pages, index cards, photographs—as "The Tramp" are "top shelf" and will forever be in demand.

Cher

Cher (1946-)

Is there anything that she can't do? Cher has proven herself time and time again. A great singer, fabulous performer and brilliant actress, Cherilyn Sarkesan has won our approval in numerous roles including film, where she has appeared in "Moonstruck", "Mask" and "Silkwood". She is an obliging signer in-person and during the sixties and seventies even answered her fan mail. Today, she is best to acquire in-person as mail requests for her signature typically go unanswered. AAW, PF— autograph album pages, index cards, photographs.

Chevalier, Maurice (1888-1972)

Legendary singing Frenchman, Chevalier enticed us with his rendition of "Thank Heaven for Little Girls" in the film "Gigi". Decades earlier he gave impressive performances in "The Love Parade", "One Hour With You" and "The Merry Widow". He was a responsive signer in-person and very friendly to all his fans. He became reclusive later in life and such most material encountered in the market will reflect his early days in Hollywood. PF—autograph album pages, index cards, photographs.

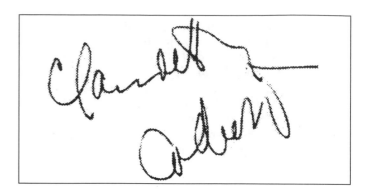

Claudette Colbert

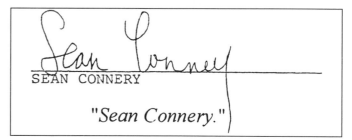

Montgomery Clift

Clift, Montgomery (1920-1966)

A character actor who took on a cult status following his death, Clift appeared in films such as "Red River", "From Here to Eternity" and "The Misfits". He was unpredictable in-person to autograph requests, while mail attempts for his signature often went unanswered. He always seemed to sign small and the few authentic examples I have seen on the market have been documents or programs. He died tragically young at the age of 45. FA, PF—autograph album pages, index cards.

Coburn, Charles (1877-1961)

A prolific and wonderful character actor, Coburn appeared in numerous films including "The More the Merrier", "The Lady Eve" and "Kings Row". He was a responsive signer in-person of a very legible signature. Distinctive in his signature is his character formation of letters with long ascenders, such as "h" and "b", which are often created with two strokes rather than a single stroke. AAW, PF—autograph album pages, index cards, photographs.

Colbert, Claudette (1905-1997)

A versatile actress, Colbert delivered many memorable roles in films such as "It Happened One Night", "The Sign of the Cross" and "I Met Him in Paris". A very responsive signer in-person, I had little luck with acquiring her signature later in life via a mail request. She lived in Barbados and responded sporadically to fan mail. Her signature is very distinct and easy to authenticate. AAW, PF—autograph album pages, index cards, photographs.

Coleman, Ronald (1891-1958)

A very popular actor, Coleman appeared in numerous films including "The Dark Angel", "Arrowsmith" and "A Double Life". He was a responsive signer and his signature was very elongated with small character formations. Unless you are familiar with his autograph it can be difficult to identify. He also used ghost signers to respond to his mail. AAW, FA, RS, PF— autograph album pages, index cards.

Sean Connery

Connery, Sean (1930-)

Connery made his mark as James Bond, then went on to do many more outstanding films including 'The Hunt for Red October", "Highlander" and "The Untouchables". An actor who rarely responds to autograph requests, Connery may sign an item in-person but via mail an authentic signature is nearly impossible. He has often utilized the services of others to respond to his considerable volume of fan mail. Connery is a far more difficult signature to acquire than most think and because of this he has been a target of forgers. AAW, FA, PF—autograph album pages, index cards, photographs—especially as James Bond, but these are scarce.

Gary Cooper

Cooper, Gary (1901-1961)

An outstanding actor, Cooper left behind an impressive body of film work including "Sergeant York", "High Noon", "A Farewell to Arms" and "Pride of the Yankees". A multiple Oscar winner, his signature has been popular with collectors for decades. He was a responsive yet occasionally reluctant signer in-person. Characteristic of his signature is the large "g" formation in his first name and the "op" combination in Cooper which connects often at capitalization height. AAW, FA, OP, CS—"Best Wishes", PF—autograph album pages, index cards, photographs—especially from key roles.

Costner, Kevin (1955-)

A versatile actor, Costner has appeared in numerous popular motion pictures including "Bull Durham", "Dances with Wolves" and "The Untouchables". Costner hates signing autographs and if pushed to do so in-person will typically sign just a "K" with a line. Secretaries often respond to his fan mail and if you get a response at all it is typically from them. Since he signs very little material, he has been a target of forgers for years. Exercise extreme caution when purchasing any material that he supposedly has signed. AAW, FA, PF—autograph album pages, index cards, photographs.

Joan Crawford

Crawford, Joan (1904-1977)

Joan Crawford had a long and very distinguished career in film. Some of her performances became classics such as her title role in "Mildred Pierce" and as Sadie Thompson in "Rain". She was very responsive to her fans throughout her life and a prolific writer. Common are her typed letters on blue stationery, most of which you will find signed simply "Joan". Crawford was not bashful and many of the letters that I have from her are loaded with tabloid gossip or biting remarks. AAW, RS, PF—autograph album pages, index cards, photographs.

Crisp, Donald (1880-1974)

A gifted and prolific director of silent films, Crisp also became a notable character actor. He appeared in "Broken Blossoms" and "How Green Was My Valley", the latter of which earned him an Oscar. His signature is often illegible and can be difficult to identify. AAW, PF—autograph album pages, index cards, photographs.

Bing Crosby

Crosby, Bing (1901-1977)

Crosby sold millions of records and appeared in numerous films including the "Road" pictures with Bob Hope, "Going My Way" and "The Bells of St. Mary's". He was a responsive signer both in-person and to mail requests for his autograph. I received many responses from him on his personal stationery. RS, PF—autograph album pages, index cards, photographs—especially in key roles.

Cruise, Tom (1962-)

One of Hollywood's top leading men, Cruise has appeared in many popular films including "Top Gun", "Rain Man" and "A Few Good Men". Early in his career he was very responsive to autograph requests and his signature was legible. Now that he's a big star it's difficult to get to him in-person and when he does sign it is often a quick two strokes of the pen that bear little resemblance to his early signature. Mail requests go unanswered so "Save Your Stamps!" Unfortunately, Cruise forged color photographs are rampant in the market. Be cautious of any example of his signature that you run across. FA, PF—autograph album pages, index cards, photographs.

Curtis, Jamie Lee (1958-)

From "B" movie horror flicks to bona fide major productions, Jamie Lee Curtis has made the transition successfully. Her resume now includes "Perfect", "True Lies" and "Trading Places". A private person, she has never enjoyed signing autographs and her fan mail, if you get a response at all, is allegedly signed by her mom, Janet Leigh. Her authentic signature is often illegible with only the "J" showing any sign of a character formation. Fortunately, some contracts signed by her have surfaced in the market, finally giving collectors an opportunity to purchase an authentic Curtis signature. FA, PF—autograph album pages, index cards, photographs.

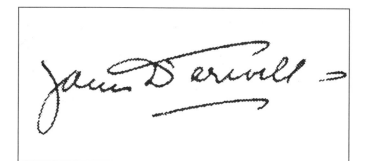

Jane Darwell

Darwell, Jane (1879-1967)

An outstanding character actress, Darwell appeared in numerous films including "Mary Poppins", "Gone With the Wind" and "The Grapes of Wrath". An Oscar winner for the latter film, her signature is also in demand for her appearance in "Gone With the Wind". Her autograph is uncommon, like that of numerous character actors and actresses. Her signature is characterized by the large "J" and the two-looped "D". PF—autograph album pages, index cards, photographs—especially those from "Gone With the Wind."

Bette Davis

Davis, Bette (1908-1989)

A screen legend, Davis left behind a plethora of outstanding performances in films such as "Dangerous", "Jezebel" and "What Happened to Baby Jane". She was very responsive to her fans and always took time to answer in-person requests for her signature and her fan mail! AAW, RS, PF—autograph album pages, index cards, photographs.

Davis, Sammy, Jr. (1925-1990)

The multi-talented Davis was the complete package, a great singer, talented actor and superb dancer! A member of the infamous "Rat Pack", he filled rooms routinely in Las Vegas for his shows. While he was a responsive signer in-person, fan mail often went unanswered. PF—autograph album pages, index cards, photographs.

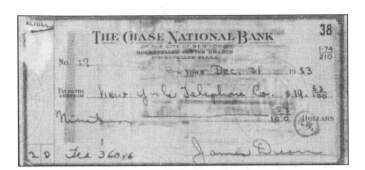

James Dean

Dean, James (1931-1955)

A Hollywood legend after only three films, Dean was a teen idol in films such as "East of Eden", "Rebel Without a Cause" and "Giant". He died tragically at the age of 24 in an automobile accident. His signature in any form is rare. Some checks and documents have entered the market over the years and given collectors an opportunity to purchase an authentic example, even if it is at a very significant price level. FA, PF—autograph album pages, index cards, contracts, personal checks, and photographs.

Marlena Dietrich

Dietrich, Marlene (1901-1992)

A versatile actress, Dietrich appeared in numerous films including "The Blue Angel", "Shanghai Express" and "Destry Rides Again". A responsive signer in-person, I had little luck with her via mail, however others were successful. Her distinctive signature eventually evolved into a combination that looked like "M, line, Setric". Because of this her later signatures can be tough to authenticate. PF—autograph album pages, index cards and photographs—especially from "The Blue Angel."

Douglas, Kirk (1916-)

A versatile actor, Douglas portrayed many memorable characters in films such as "Champion", "The Bad and the Beautiful", "Gunfight at the OK Coral", and "Spartacus. A responsive signer in-person for years, Douglas did for a period of time sporadically answer fan mail, however in later years he responded with facsimile signed photographs. His signature with its trademark large capitalization is very distinct and easy to authenticate. FA, PF—autograph album pages, index cards and photographs.

Eastwood, Clint (1930-)

From "spaghetti" westerns to major Hollywood productions, Eastwood's career has spanned decades and brought with it many memorable performances. As detective Harry Callahan in "Dirty Harry", Eastwood redefined the term fearless in a series of successful motion pictures. While he has been responsive to requests in-person, most of his fan mail is allegedly ghost signed. Early in his career his signature was legible and he often even took the time to personalize requests. Today, his signature has been abbreviated to "Cl Eastwood" with the "E" crossing the "t" in his last name. He is currently responding to most mail requests with a facsimile-signed photograph. AAW, FA, PF—autograph album pages, index cards and photographs—especially in key roles.

Douglas Fairbanks, Sr.

Fairbanks, Douglas, Sr. (1883-1939)

A screen legend, Fairbanks appeared in such classics as "The Mark of Zorro", "Robin Hood", "Thief of Baghdad" and "The Black Pirate". He married America's sweetheart, Mary Pickford who was also a screen favorite. Fairbank's signature is uncommon in any form and always in demand. It is not unusual to find his signature in an autograph album near or alongside that of his wife's. FA, PF—autograph album pages, index cards and photographs.

W.C. Fields

Fields, W.C. (1880-1946)

A vaudeville veteran, Fields made a successful transition to film and became a public favorite. His films included "My Little Chickadee", "The Bank Dick" and "David Copperfield". Fields became identified with his portrayal of cantankerous old character who had a passion for the bottle. A character many claim not to be too far away from Fields himself. He was a very reluctant signer and allegedly responded to little if any fan mail. PF—autograph album pages, index cards and photographs—which are scarce.

Barry Fitzgerald

Fitzgerald, Barry (1888-1961)

A charming character actor, Fitzgerald appeared in numerous films including "Ebb Tide", "How Green Was My Valley", "The Naked City" and "Going My Way". His memorable performance as Father Fitzgibbon in the latter film earned him an Oscar. He was a responsive signer in-person of a signature that can often be difficult to read. PF—autograph album pages, index cards and photographs—especially from "Going My Way."

Errol Flynn

Flynn, Errol (1909-1959)

A Hollywood action hero, Flynn starred in films such as "Captain Blood", "The Adventures of Robin Hood" and "The Charge of the Light Brigade". His passion for working hard, then playing harder eventually took its toll on the actor who died at the age

of 50. He was an obliging signer in-person but allegedly paid little, if any, time responding to his fan mail. His signature is often flamboyant, with the "E" the largest character. The signature breaks in his last name are often inconsistent, as is the formation of the "F". While signed photographs are scarce they do turn up on occasion. Often they are large (11" x 14") black and white portraits or a still from one of his movies. He often added an underline beneath his signature. FA, , OP, CS—"All my good wishes", "Very kindest regards", PF—autograph album pages, index cards and photographs.

Henry Fonda

Fonda, Henry (1905-1982)

A screen legend, Fonda starred in many films including "Young Mr. Lincoln", "The Grapes of Wrath", "12 Angry Men" and "On Golden Pond". He was a responsive signer both in-person and via a mail request for his signature. AAW, PF—autograph album pages, index cards and photographs.

Fonda, Jane (1937-)

An accomplished actress, Fonda has appeared in numerous films including "China Syndrome", "The Electric Horseman" and "On Golden Pond". Like her father, she has been very responsive to fans when asked for a signature and still responds favorably via a mail request. RS, PF—autograph album pages, index cards and photographs.

Harrison Ford

Ford, Harrison (1942-)

One of Hollywood's leading men, Ford has already put together a fantastic film resume. His pictures include "Star Wars", "Indiana Jones and the Temple of Doom" and "The Fugitive". Unfortunately for collectors he is a very difficult signature to acquire. Ford rarely signs in-person and does not respond to mail requests for his signature. If you do indeed find an authentic example, it will appear more like "I am Sorry", than resemble his name. Because demand is so high and his signature is so scarce he has been a target of forgers for years. Most of what is in the market is fake, so buyer beware! FA, PF—autograph album pages, index cards and photographs—especially in Star Wars or as Indiana Jones.

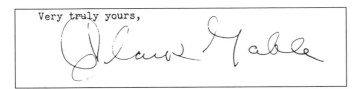

Clark Gable

Gable, Clark (1901-1960)

A Hollywood legend, Gable didn't just play a role, he immortalized it. His films included "Mutiny on the Bounty", "It Happened One Night", "The Misfits" and of course "Gone With the Wind". He was a responsive signer in-person and his signature is always in demand. Some personal checks signed by him turned up in the market a few years ago and they are a good source for his signature. Signed photographs are scarce and when they do turn up they are usually a posed portrait, rather than the actor in a role.

I would be highly suspect of any signed photographs of him from "Gone With the Wind". He has been a target of forgers for years especially on photographs or as cut signatures. FA, OP, CS—"With my kindest wishes always", PF—autograph album pages, index cards and photographs.

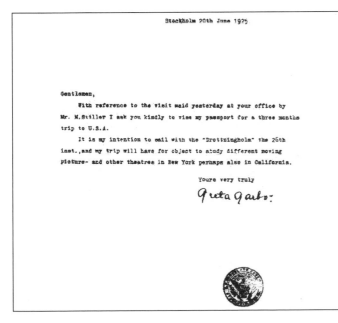

Greta Garbo

Garbo, Greta (1905-1990)

A screen legend, Garbo appeared in many great films including "Anna Christie", "Grand Hotel" and "Ninotchka". Intensely private, her catch phrase became "I want to be alone" and she did exactly that becoming a recluse in retirement. She signed autographs rarely and only during the height of her Hollywood fame. Garbo also never responded to autograph requests by mail. A few documents and personal checks have entered the market, but they are also very scarce and expensive. She hasn't been a target of forgers, because most collectors realize that she never signed anything she didn't have to. PF—autograph album pages, personal checks and documents.

Gardner, Ava (1922-1990)

Glamorous and seductive, Gardner appeared in numerous films including "The Killers", "Show Boat" and "The Sun Also Rises". She was a responsive signer in-person, but answered autograph requests via mail sporadically. PF—autograph album pages, index cards, personal checks, and photographs.

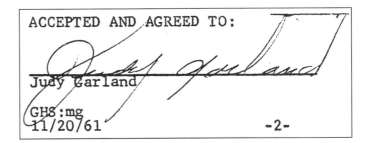

Judy Garland

Garland, Judy (1922-1969)

A talented actress and singer, Garland captured our hearts as Dorothy in "The Wizard of Oz". Her other films were also successful including "Meet Me In St. Louis", "The Pirate" and "Easter Parade". She was a responsive signer in-person, but mail requests for her signature often went unanswered—many of which were mine. Her signature varied dramatically during her lifetime and can be very difficult to authenticate. A few personal checks and documents have surfaced in the market and can command a significant price. Although "Oz" related items are in demand, she signed very few from her classic role. During the filming of the movie, she did sign some photographs for those in the film who asked, but they were black and white portraits (8" x 10"). She also responded to some requests with MGM studio portraits, most of which are larger in size (typically 11" x 14"). FA, CS—"kindest wishes", "sincerely", PF—autograph album pages, index cards and photographs.

Gleason, Jackie (1916-1987)

Primarily associated with his work in television, Gleason did appear in some films, such as "Requiem for a Heavyweight", "The Sting II", and the "Smokey and the Bandit" series. While he was an accommodating signer in-person, I never had much luck with him through the mail. Highly sought are signed photographs of him in "The Honeymooners" as that is the show he is typically associated with. PF—autograph album pages, index cards and photographs.

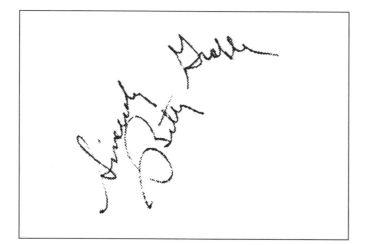

Betty Grable

Grable, Betty (1916-1973)

World War II's number one pin-up girl, Grable was a stunning actress who could catch any ones attention with her looks. She appeared in many films including "Down Argentine Way", "Tin Pan Alley" and "Mother Wore Tights". She was a responsive signer in-person and mail requests for her signature were sporadically answered. RS, CS—"Sincere best wishes", PF—autograph album pages, index cards and photographs—especially her classic photograph from behind.

Cary Grant

Grant, Cary (1904-1986)

A handsome actor with superb talent, Grant was every man's idol. His films included "Bringing Up Baby", "The Philadelphia Story" and "To Catch a Thief". He was an obliging signer in-person, but fan mail often went unanswered. PF—autograph album pages, index cards and photographs.

Jack Haley

Haley, Jack (1898-1979)

A talented comedic actor, Haley will forever be known as The Tin Woodsman in the film "The Wizard of Oz". He did appear in other films during the thirties including "Sittin Pretty", "Pigskin Parade" and "Rebecca of Sunnybrook Farm". He was a responsive signer and even appeared at numerous "Oz" events. RS, PF—autograph album pages, index cards, personal and business checks, and photographs—especially "Oz" related.

Hamilton, Margaret (1902-1985)

A gifted character actress, Margaret Hamilton was nothing short of unforgettable as the Wicked Witch of the West (WWW) in "The Wizard Oz". What surprises many is that she was one of the warmest and most caring individuals you would ever want to meet, just extraordinary! She was extremely responsive to her fans throughout her entire life. I wrote her many, many times and she always took time to send back a delightful response. She appeared in other films including "My Little Chickadee", "Guest in the House" and "State of the Union". Near the end of her life she would respond with either an "Oz" still or a picture of her as "Cora" from her coffee commercials that would always be signed. The "Oz" photos often included "WWW" underneath her signature exemplifying how proud she was of her work. RS, OP, PF—autograph album pages, index cards and photographs—especially "Oz" items.

Hanks, Tom (1956-)

One of Hollywood's leading box office attractions, Hanks has successfully made that transition from television to film in change that most would have said "it could never happen". His film resume now includes some of the biggest films of all-time, "Forrest Gump", "Philadelphia" and "Apollo 13". He is a reluctant but obliging signer in-person, however getting a signature from a mail request is nearly impossible. Because supply has not met demand, he is now a target of forgers. Unfortunately, most of what appears in the market today is fake. Unless Hanks starts signing, or the forgers get caught, the trend is likely to continue. "Sorry Forrest!", AAW, FA, PF—autograph album pages, index cards and photographs—especially as Forrest Gump.

Jean Harlow

Harlow, Jean (1911-1937)

A "Blonde Bombshell", Harlean Carpenter transformed herself into Jean Harlow and with it a legend was created. She appeared in films like "Hell's Angels", "Dinner at Eight" and "Bombshell". She had a considerable impact in a very short period of time and died at the young age of 26. She was a responsive signer in-person, however fan mail was often ghost signed. Her simple, often primitive looking signature is scarce in any form and should prove to be a challenging acquisition. FA, PF—autograph album pages, index cards.

Hayward, Susan (1917-1975)

An outstanding actress, Hayward gave many Oscar-worthy performances in films such as "Smash-Up" and "My Foolish Heart". Cancer unexpectedly claimed her life in 1975. While her signature does surface in the market periodically, it is not common and therefore can command a significant price. The formation of the "H" can vary, however her signature remained relatively consistent during her lifetime. AAW, OP, CS—"Sincerely", PF—autograph album pages, index cards.

Hayworth, Rita (1918-1987)

Forever glamorous, Hayworth ignited the screen with performances in films such as "Gilda" and "The Lady From Shanghai". She was in failing health during the last decade of her life and was unable to answer fan mail. Her signature often appears very hasty and can vary dramatically in formation especially in her last name. The connection between the "a" and the "H", which can vary in flamboyance, is a trademark. Her signature may appear with that of Orson Welles, her second husband.

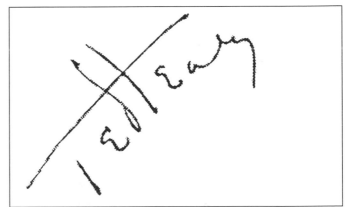

Ted Healy

Healy, Ted (1896-1937)

The originator of the "Three Stooges", Healy made appearances in films such as "Bombshell" and "Reckless". His signature is very distinct with is trademark crossing of the "T" also the formation for the middle of the "H". His signature is not that common and may prove to be a challenging acquisition. PF—autograph album pages.

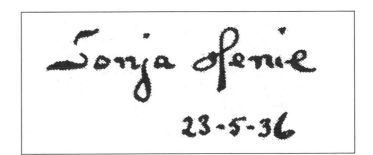

Sonja Henie

Henie, Sonja (1912-1969)

A gold medalist in three consecutive Winter Olympics, Henie also skated her way to Hollywood to appear in numerous light romantic films including "Thin Ice" and "Sun Valley Serenade". Her signature, which appears printed, is very distinctive. Some pencil forgeries have been turned up in the market. RS, FA, PF—autograph album pages, index cards.

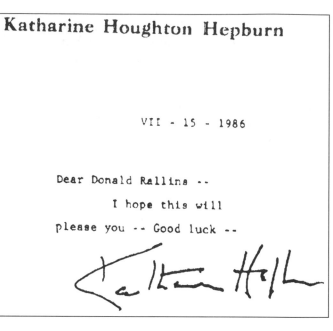

Katharine Hepburn

Audrey Hepburn

Hepburn, Audrey (1929-1993)

One of Hollywood's most popular leading ladies, Hepburn captured American hearts with her roles in Breakfast at Tiffany's, GiGi and My Fair Lady. Her signature is very distinctive with the large formation of the "r" in Audrey and the "H" which resembles more of a "U" in Hepburn. While she was a responsive signer in-person, via mail she was nearly impossible to get a response from. I tried for many years unsuccessfully. Her signature is highly sought by collectors and continues to have enormous appeal. AAW, OP, FA, PF—autograph album pages, index cards, photographs.

Hepburn, Katharine (1907-)

One of the most compelling actresses of her time, Hepburn is a screen legend. Her passion for privacy includes not answering mail requests for her signature. Material signed by her does appear periodically in the autograph market and can command significant price levels. Her signature has shown deterioration due to health and can add to authenticity concerns. Serious collectors prefer vintage signatures over those signed in later years. There are many authenticity concerns surrounding her signed material and unless you are very familiar with her signing habits, you should consult an expert first before buying! AAW, FA, PF—autograph album pages, index cards, photographs, letters. She often signs simply "Kate" or "K. Hepburn."

Alfred Hitchcock

Hitchcock, Alfred (1899-1980)

A legendary director, Hitchcock scored hits with films such as "Psycho", "Rebecca" and "Rear Window". Despite being a prolific signer, his material is highly sought by collectors and has shown considerable appreciation since his death. OP, RS, FA, PF—autograph album pages, index cards, photographs.

Dustin Hoffman

Hoffman, Dustin (1937-)

A reluctant but obliging signer in-person, but you can forget about trying to get an authentic signature via a mail request. He responds with facsimile-signed photographs. Popular ever since "The Graduate", demand for signature seems to increase with each new role. He has been a forgery target for years so exercise extreme caution when purchasing his material, especially signed color photos from his films "Tootsie", "Hook", and "Rain Man". AAW, FA, PF—autograph album pages, index cards, photographs.

Holden, William (1918-1981)

A brilliant actor who could conquer any role he chose, Holden is associated with many films including "Stalag 17" and "Sunset Boulevard". He was reluctant but obliging signer in-person but unresponsive to mail requests for his signature. Surprisingly little of his material has appeared in the autograph market. PF—autograph album pages, index cards, photographs.

Holliday, Judy (1923-1965)

A very witty actress, Holliday is typically associated with the film "Born Yesterday". Characteristic of her signature is the "falling off the baseline" ending "y"s in her name. Her last name can also be difficult to read or interpret as such. AAW, RS, OP, PF—autograph album pages, index cards, photographs.

Holmes, Phillips (1909-1942)

A striking leading man, Holmes appeared in numerous films during the early thirties.

While serving in WWII, he was killed in an air disaster. His signature is scarce and when does surface in the market it is often an autograph album page. PF—autograph album pages.

Hope, Bob (1903-)

An American legend and gifted comedian, Hope is commonly associated with his series of seven "Road" pictures or his entertaining of U.S. servicemen. He has always been an obliging signer in-person, but in later years would resort to using his secretary to answer autograph requests. During the early years he would often personalize items and add his trademark "Thanks for the Memories." During the sixties, Hope would answer mail requests with facsimile signed vintage photographs. Failing health forced him to eventually stop signing entirely. AAW, CS—"Thanks for the Memories", OP, FA

Horne, Lena (1917-)

Horne broke the color barrier in film with her long-term MGM contract. She has been a responsive signer throughout her entire life. CS—"Most Sincerely", RS, PF—autograph album pages, index cards, photographs.

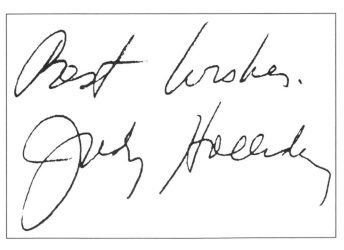

Juday Holliday

Leslie Howard

Howard, Leslie (1893-1943)

A charming gentlemen, Howard is commonly associated with his role as Ashley Wilkes in "Gone With the Wind". Because of the association his single-stroke signature has never lost its demand and has continued to show significant appreciation. Howard was killed in a tragic air disaster in 1943. RS, FA, PF—autograph album pages, index cards, photographs.

Hudson, Rock (1925-1985)

A top Universal star of the fifties, Hudson scored with numerous films, but is commonly associated with his comedies opposite Doris Day. While he was a responsive signer in-person, mail requests for his signature often went unanswered. His material surfaces periodically in the autograph market in a variety of forms. OP, CS—"Sincerely", FA, PF—autograph album pages, index cards, photographs.

Hunter, Jeffrey (1925-1969)

A screen idol of the late fifties and early sixties, Hunter captured roles in numerous films including "The Last Hurrah", "King of Kings" and "The Longest Day". He was a very responsive signer who would often take time to personalize and give a warm salutation with each signature. he died tragically at the age of 43 following a mysterious fall. Is signed material is uncommon in the autograph market. RS, OP, CS—numerous, PF—autograph album pages, index cards, photographs.

Jessel, George (1898-1981)

America's "Toastmaster General", Jessel was an entertainer, actor, songwriter and even producer. He was married to actress Norma Talmadge at one point. His signature could be illegible at times and while he would sign in-person, mail request for his signature often went unanswered. PF—autograph album pages, index cards, photographs.

Johns, Glynis (1923-)

Johns really moved into the spotlight following her role as a mermaid in the film "Miranda" (1948). Her signature can be illegible at times especially her last name.

PF—autograph album pages, index cards, photographs.

Al Jolson

Jolson, Al (1886-1950)

Forever linked to the film "The Jazz Singer"—the world's first feature talkie, Jolson appeared in numerous popular films. His single stroke signature has remained popular with collectors for years, most preferring it on a photograph from one of his key roles. He was married to actress Ruby Keeler. RS, PF—autograph album pages, index cards, photographs.

Jones Carolyn (1929-1983)

Fifties movie actress who is often associated with the film "House of Wax", Jones is also familiar for her later television role as Morticia in "The Addams Family". Her printed style form of signature is appealing to horror film buffs especially since she played alongside Vincent Price. RS, PF—autograph album pages, index cards.

Jones, Jennifer (1919-)

A brilliant actress, Jones is often associated with her Oscar winning role as Bernadette Soubirous in "The Song of Bernadette". Her signature has changed over time but is still popular among collectors. AAW, OP, CS—"With best wishes", PF—autograph album pages, index cards, photographs.

Kane, Helen (1903-1966)

The "Boop-Boop-A-Doop Girl", Kane made her mark singing a high-pitched version of "I Wanna Be Loved by You" in the musical "Good Boy". OP, CS—"Sincerely", RS—often added the words "Boop-Boop-a-do" underneath her signature, PF—autograph album pages, index cards.

Boris Karloff

Karloff, Boris (1887-1969)

"The King of Hollywood Horror Films", Karloff was a prolific actor, appearing in over 100 films. He also appeared on Broadway and hosted a television series. His signature, especially on photographs from "Frankenstein" and "The Mummy", are highly sought by collectors. Karloff was a responsive signer in-person however I was never able to get a response from him via a mail request. Be cautious of forged signatures where Karloff appears in character. He preferred sending out posed signed photos of himself out of character. RS (in-person), CS—"Sincerely", PF—autograph album pages, index cards, letters, photographs.

Kaye, Danny (1913-1987)

Kaye became very popular for the zany characters he often portrayed. He appeared in films such as "Up in Arms", "Wonder man", and "The Secret Life of Walter Mitty". Kaye was a responsive signer in-person, however I never had much luck with him responding to my mail requests for an autograph. PF—autograph album pages, index cards, photographs.

Keaton, Buster (1895-1966)

The king of deadpan humor, Keaton was one of silent films greatest comedians. His best work was made during the twenties and included films such as "The General" and "The Paleface". He was responsive to requests in-person, however mail requests often went unanswered. His scarce signature is very popular with collectors. PF—autograph album pages, index cards.

Keaton, Michael (1951-)

A popular actor, Keaton really stepped into the forefront following his role as Batman, however ever since his popularity seems to have waned. He is an obliging signer in-person, but mail requests will go unanswered. Since signed photos of him as Batman are the most sought after form, they are also the most forged. PF—autograph album pages, index cards, photographs.

Kellaway, Cecil (1893-1973)

A talented character actor, Kellaway appeared in many films including "Wuthering Heights", "The Postman Always Rings Twice" and "The Luck of the Irish". RS, PF—autograph album pages, index cards, photographs.

Kelly, Gene (1912-1996)

Charming actor, dancer and choreographer, Kelly appeared in numerous films including "For Me And My Gal", "An American in Paris" and "Singin in the Rain" . The scene of him dancing with his umbrella in the latter film is now a Hollywood classic. As such signed photographs of Kelly in this scene are extremely popular with collectors. he was an obliging signer in-person however utilized a variety of methods to answer his fan mail including facsimile and ghost signed photographs. He did answer some requests personally, however it was far less than many other sources claim. PF—autograph album pages, index cards, photographs.

Grace Kelly

Kelly, Grace (1929-1982)

Elegant and charming, Grace Kelly married Prince Ranier III of Monaco in 1956 to become Princess Grace de Monaco. The event put an end to her film career which included roles in "High Noon", "Rear Window" and "The Country Girl". It also put an end to her signing "Grace Kelly". She was a responsive signer during her days in Hollywood and has a signature that is very distinct. She was fairly prolific in her letter writing while in Monaco so some do surface in the market. Often these are signed simply "Grace" or "Grace de Monaco". The market for the latter signature is about half of that for her vintage "Grace Kelly". Since the demand for her signature is so great she is a forgery target so buy with caution. AAW, FA, RS, PF—autograph album pages, index cards, photographs.

Kilbridge, Percy (1888-1964)

Percy Kilbridge is commonly associated with his role as the farmer Pa Kettle, in the highly successful film series. He did appear in other films, including "State Fair", put the public just couldn't shake Pa Kettle from their memory. All autographed items associated with the popular film series are sought by collectors. RS, OP, PF—autograph album pages, index cards.

Kilmer, Val (1959-)

A gifted actor and great signer in-person, Val Kilmer hit pay dirt with his role as Batman, following the departure of Michael Keaton, and with his portrayal of Jim Morrison in "The Doors". While mail requests for his signature go unanswered, at least he signs in-person. Because the supply doesn't meet the demand for his signature, Kilmer has been a forgery target, especially on color photographs portraying him as Batman. His authentic signature is often illegible with only the "V" recognizable, thus it is an authentication nightmare. FA, PF—autograph album pages, index cards, photographs.

Bert Lahr

Lahr, Bert (1895-1967)

A veteran stage actor who turned his attention to film, Lahr is typically associated with his classic role as the Cowardly Lion in MGM's film "The Wizard of Oz". His other films include "Love and Hisses", "Ship Ahoy" and "Rose Marie". While signed photographs of Lahr in "The Wizard of Oz" are highly sought, they are extremely rare and if found should be highly scrutinized. Photographs bearing his signature are

often out of character posed shots. His signature in any form is always in demand. RS, FA, PF—autograph album pages, index cards, photographs.

Lake, Arthur (1905-1987)

A character actor who is typically associated with his role as Dagwood Bumstead, Arthur Lake transformed his long running "Blondie" film series to television in 1957. His signature was often illegible with only the "A", "L" and "e" bearing any resemblance to a character, Since he commonly added a drawing of Dagwood to his signature it became a source of identification. RS, PF—autograph album pages, index cards, photographs.

Lake, Veronica (1919-1973)

A glamorous actress, Lake co-starred in numerous films with Alan Ladd such as "This Gun For Hire" and "The Glass Key". She also landed roles in other films including "Hold Back the Dawn" and "I Married a Witch". CS—"with my sincere best wishes", RS, PF—autograph album pages, index cards, photographs.

Lamarr, Hedy (1913—2000)

A gorgeous actress who arrived in Hollywood in the late thirties, Lamarr appeared in films such as "Lady of the Tropics", "Boom Town" and "Samson and Delilah". She was a responsive signer during her film years, but since retirement has only occasionally responded to autograph requests. PF—autograph album pages, index cards, photographs.

Lamas, Fernando (1915-1982)

A talented Argentine leading man, Lamas made numerous films including "This Gun For Hire", "The Glass Key", and "I Married a Witch". His signature may appear on occasion with his former actress wives Arlene Dahl or Esther Williams. PF—autograph album pages, index cards, photographs.

Lamour, Dorothy (1914-1996)

"The Queen of Island Pictures", Lamour appeared in numerous films including "The Jungle Princess" and "The Hurricane". She is most commonly associated with her seven "Road" films she did alongside Bob Hope and Bing Crosby. She was responsive to in-person autograph requests and in her later years even did some private signings. RS, OP, PF—autograph album pages, index cards, photographs.

Lanchester, Elsa (1902-1986)

A talented stage and screen actress, Lanchester made numerous film appearances including "David Copperfield", "The Bride of Frankenstein" and "Come to the Stable". The wife of actor Charles Laughton, it's not unusual to find both signatures adorning the same or similar items. Her signature is popular among horror film collectors for her role in "The Bride of Frankenstein". Any signed items from this film can bring twice the amount of an unassociated piece. RS, PF—autograph album pages, index cards, photographs.

Carole Landis

Landis, Carole (1919-1948)

She arrived in Hollywood as a teenager and her striking looks caught the eyes of many including her numerous husbands. Landis appeared in films such as "Topper Returns", "Moon Over Miami" and "Orchestra Wives". Unfortunately before her career could move up a level, she committed suicide at the young age of 29. Her signature is scarce today and if it turns up at all it is typically on the page of an autograph album. PF—autograph album pages, index cards.

Laughton, Charles (1899-1962)

A brilliant British character actor, Laughton appeared in films such as "The Private Life of Henry VIII", "Mutiny on the Bounty" and "Witness for the Prosecution". As Henry VIII he captured a Best Actor

Oscar. His is signature is often illegible and hastily written. AAW, PF—autograph album pages, index cards and photographs.

Stan Laurel and Oliver Hardy

Laurel and Hardy

Perhaps films greatest comedy team, Stan Laurel (1890-1965) and Oliver Hardy (1890-1957) have been popular for decades and will continue to be as new generations discover their work. During the pinnacle of their success they used just about every method known to handle the enormous amounts of fan mail. From facsimile signatures to ghost signers, you name it they probably tried it. Often authentic signatures from them both appear on autograph album pages. If photos are encountered that have both signatures often it is a posed black & white studio portrait, often 11" x 14". Independently, the used other sized photographs to sign also. Typically inscriptions were handled by Stan, who often printed something appropriate such as "Our Best Wishes Always". Later in life, Laurel did answer some fan mail but it was sporadic. Often his letters are signed simply "Stan" rather than in full. Because they were so popular supply has never met demand and prices have escalated through the years. Surprisingly, I have encountered very few questionable pieces and when found and as anticipated, they were cut signatures in pencil. Always better to be safe than sorry. FA, OP, PF—autograph album pages, index cards and photographs.

Sincerely yours,

VIVIEN LEIGH

Vivien Leigh

Leigh, Vivien (1913-1967)

British stage and screen actress, Leigh is often associated with her role as Scarlet O'Hara in the film classic "Gone With the Wind". Her other memorable films include "Waterloo Bridge", "The Hamilton Woman" and "A Streetcar Named Desire". Her signature has been in constant demand and as such can command a significant price. She was responsive signer in-person of an autograph that can often be illegible. Combine all these factors with her tragically early death and you can see why signature has also been a target of forgers. AAW, FA, PF—autograph album pages, index cards and photographs—especially as "Scarlet O'Hara".

Lloyd, Harold (1893-1971)

A silent film genius, Lloyd appeared in numerous films including "Grandma's Boy", "The Freshman" and "Safety Last". The latter film being the film where dangles from a building holding on to nothing but the big hands of a clock. Lloyd was always responsive to his fans and often took plenty of time to sign autographs or respond to fan mail. PF—autograph album pages, index cards and photographs.

Lorre, Peter (1904-1964)

A talented character actor, Lorre had a passion for sinister characters. He appeared in such films as "M", "The Maltese Falcon" and "Casablanca". He was often a reluctant but obliging signer in-person and I never had any success with mail requests for his autograph. His uncommon signature can also be illegible and will take some experience to authenticate. PF—autograph album pages, index cards and photographs.

Bela Lugosi

Lugosi, Bela (1884-1956)

The actor who will always be "Dracula", Lugosi became a horror film legend. His films included "Ninotchka", "Dracula", "The Return of the Vampire" and "The Raven". While he would sign in person, most of his fan mail was ghost signed. Unless you can tell the difference it is probably best to stick with another form, if you can find one. FA, PF—autograph album pages, index cards and photographs—especially as Dracula.

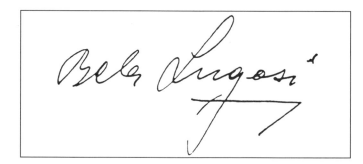

Hattie McDaniel

McDaniel, Hattie (1895-1952)

Best remembered for her role as "Mammy" in the film classic "Gone With the Wind", McDaniel is one of the toughest cast signatures from the movie. She appeared in other films including "The Little Colonel", "In This Our Life" and "Thank Your Lucky Stars", but it's in "Gone With the Wind" where she will always be immortalized. Her signature in any form is very tough and when does hit the market typically sells quickly. FA, OP, RS, PF—autograph album pages, index cards, documents and photographs.

McQueen, Steve (1930-1980)

A brilliant actor, McQueen appeared in some great films including "The Great Escape", "The Magnificent Seven", "Papillion", and "The Sand Pebbles". He was an elusive and reluctant signer in-person and impossible via a mail request. If you did get a mail response from him it was probably ghost signed! A real McQueen signature is often characterized by the large and flamboyant "St" letter combination and the "cQ" combinstion appears more like a "Y". FA, PF—autograph album pages, index cards, documents and photographs.

Dean Martin

Martin, Dean (1917-1996)

An actor and singer, Martin paired up with Jerry Lewis and made 16 films together including "My Friend Irma", "Artists and Models", and "The Caddy". A member of Sinatra's "Rat Pack", Martin's career endured in other mediums including stage and television. He was a responsive signer throughout his life and because of this his signature is common. RS, OP, PF—autograph album pages, index cards, and photographs.

Martin, Steve (1945-)

A musician, comedian and actor, Martin scored first on television before making the transition to film. His film resume now includes "Father of the Bride", "Leap of Faith" and "All of Me". He is an elusive signer in-person, but will answer fan mail! Ironically, off stage he is a completely different person, very private and quiet. RS, PF—autograph album pages, index cards, and photographs.

Marvin, Lee (1924-1987)

A very talented actor, Marvin appeared in many films including "Cat Ballou", "The Dirty Dozen" and "Paint Your Wagon". Throughout his life he was a very difficult person to get a signature out of and never answered his fan mail! Because of this his signature is not only tough to find, but expensive. PF—autograph album pages, index cards, and photographs.

The Marx Brothers

The Marx Brothers

The original Marx Brothers consisted of Chico (1886-1961), Groucho (1890-1977), Harpo (1888-1964), Gummo (1897-1977) and Zeppo (1901-1979). The latter two brothers would essentially step aside before the trios film career would begin, although Zeppo was in their first five films. The genius of the three would shine brightly in films such as "Animal Crackers", "Duck Soup", "A Day at the Races" and "A Night at the Opera". Incredibly popular, all were asked for their autographs often, and always complied. Of the trio, Harpo's signature appears less and can command a greater value. If a single item was signed by all of them, it was commonly first names only, the exception being those penned early in their career. The most prolific in all forms was Groucho. He was very responsive to his fans and I corresponded with him often. In later years, Groucho would often comply to requests for his signature with an autographed black and white photograph (8" x 10"). RS, FA—be cautious of photos, PF—autograph album pages, index cards, and photographs.

Merman, Ethel (1909-1984)

An actress and singer, Merman appeared in numerous films including "Anything Goes", "Alexander's Ragtime Band" and "There's No Business Like Show Business". She was an obliging signer in-person, however most of my mail requests went unanswered. PF—autograph album pages, index cards, and photographs.

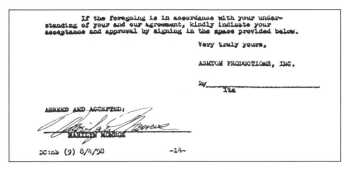

Marilyn Monroe

Monroe, Marilyn (1926-1962)

An enduring screen icon, the beautiful Marilyn Monroe appeared in films such as "The Seven Year Itch", "Bus Stop", "Some Like It Hot" and "The Misfits". Her stunning looks and tragic early death have immortalized her and the public fascination with her life seems boundless. From being linked to the Kennedy family, to her tragic and often public relationships, she remained charming and constantly in the public spotlight. She was often compliant to an in-person autograph request, however the problem was getting to her. She was often mobbed and rushed by those around her through crowds as fast as possible. Her voluminous fan mail required the services of others to respond to it, which they often did with ghost signed autographs. Purchasing a Monroe signature is best left to an expert. Fortunately, some documents have entered the market and they circulate regularly and at higher and higher values. Checks are quite popular and a bit more common, frequently appearing in auctions, but still command a high price. Photographs signed by Monroe are quite scarce and expensive. FA, PF—autograph album pages, index cards, documents, and photographs.

Demi Moore

Moore, Demi (1962-)

A talented actress, Moore has appeared in the films "Ghost", "Striptease" and "A Few Good Men", to name only a few. Along with her marriage to Bruce Willis, she also inherited some of his reluctance toward autograph seekers. Now that they have parted their ways, perhaps she'll be more compliant to requests. Mail requests for her signature are not even answered, so "Save Your Stamps!". A rare signature in-person will often appear printed rather than cursive. Much of what is currently offered in the market is fake, so until she starts signing by mail, your only logical alternative is in-person or hope a document of two surface. FA, PF—autograph album pages, index cards, and photographs.

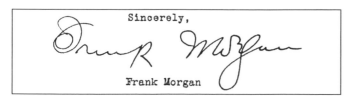

Frank Morgan

Morgan, Frank (1890-1949)

"Pay no attention to the man behind the curtain!", but if you did you would find out that The Wizard of Oz was actually Frank Morgan. In fact he played numerous roles in the film! And while his signature has remained forever in demand because of these portrayals, he did appear in other films including "The Great Ziegfeld", "Bombshell" and "The Courage of Lassie". He was responsive to in-person autograph requests, however his signature varied in its legibility and can be tough to identify. PF—autograph album pages, index cards, and photographs—which if found signed will often be a formal MGM studio portrait.

Murphy, Audie (1924-1971)

The most-decorated American soldier of WWII, Murphy was a real hero who returned home to try his luck at acting in motion pictures. He appeared in many films including "To Hell and Back", "The Red Badge of Courage" and "The Quiet American". Murphy died tragically in a plane crash in 1971. While he was a very compliant signer in-person, his shortened life has made his signature uncommon. His signature often appears deliberate and can appear questionable. OP, CS—"My luck to you", PF—autograph album pages, index cards, and photographs.

Paul Newman

Newman, Paul (1925 -)

A Hollywood icon, Newman has appeared in many memorable films including "Butch Cassidy and the Sundance Kid", "The Sting" and "The Verdict". While he can be friendly in-person, he detests signing autographs and will often go out of his way to avoid the task. He has employed a variety of methods to answer his fan mail during his career including responding with facsimile signed photographs and even using ghost signers. Much of the Newman autographed material being sold in the market is fake or signed by a ghost signer. His authentic signature is uncommon and collectors should opt for documents that enter the market or attempt an in-person signature, possibly at the race track where he often can be found. FA, PF—autograph album pages, index cards, documents, and photographs.

Nicholson, Jack (1937-)

A talented actor, Nicholson has delivered some classic performances in films such as "One Flew Over the Cuckoo's Nest", "A Few Good Men" and "Terms of Endearment". He is a responsive signer in-person—most catch him at a home Lakers basketball game, and even sporadically answers mail requests for his autograph. RS, PF—autograph album pages, index cards, and photographs—in classic roles like as the Joker in "Batman".

Mary Pickford

Pickford, Mary (1893-1979)

"America's Sweetheart", Pickford was the queen of silent film. A prolific artist she appeared in many films including "Rebecca of Sunnybrook Farm", "Pollyanna" and "Coquette". Her performance in the latter film earned her an Oscar. Always a responsive signer, during her retirement years she often corresponded with her fans. Numerous stamp signature appear on the market. The character formation of the "P" in Pickford is the trademark of her signature. PF—autograph album pages, index cards, and photographs.

Pitt, Brad (1963-)

A popular current star, Pitt has appeared in films such as "A River Runs Through It", "Interview with a Vampire" and "Legends of the Fall". As a "Hollywood Heartthrob" he attracts considerable attention both from fans and the tabloids. He is nearly impossible to acquire in-person and even if you get a response from a

mail request, which is rare, it will be a ghost signature. Adding to the complexity of acquiring a real autograph is the lack of consistency in his signature, which is often illegible and abbreviated. Unfortunately, most signed photographs of him being offered in the market are fake. If you need his signature be patient as eventually documents will surface. FA, PF—autograph album pages, index cards, and photographs—especially from "Legends of the Fall".

Power, Tyrone (1913-1958)

A popular actor of the late thirties and early forties, Power appeared in films such as "Jesse James", "The Mark of Zorro" and "The Razor's Edge", The son of actor Tyrone Power, Sr., he was obliging to signature requests in-person. His signature was often hastily written and can be illegible at times. PF—autograph album pages, index cards, and photographs.

Vincent Price

Price, Vincent (1911-1993)

A gifted character actor, Price became known for his work in horror films, such as "House of Wax", "The Fly" and "Return of the Fly". He was also impressive in Roger Corman's Edgar Allen Poe film series. Price later turned to television work and even played a villain on the series "Batman". He was an obliging and friendly signer in-person, however through the mail in his later years responses were sporadic. RS, OP, CS—"Sincerely", PF—autograph album pages, index cards, and photographs—especially in one of his horror roles.

Redford, Robert (1937-)

An established actor, Redford is typically associated with his roles alongside Paul Newman in films such as "Butch Cassidy and the Sundance Kid" and "The Sting". He has delivered many memorable performances in films such as "The Natural", "All The President's Men", and "Out of Africa". Redford's enormous popularity meant having to deal with requests for his signature. Occasionally responsive in-person, his mail has been handled in numerous ways from facsimile-signed postcards to ghost signatures. Unfortunately, because Redford has signed so little and the demand for his signature has been so great , he has been a target of forgers. Most Redford signed material in the market is not authentic and therefore collectors should opt for documents that do surface periodically. FA, PF—autograph album pages, index cards, and photographs.

George Reeves

Reeves, George (1914-1959)

A talented character actor, Reeves is typically associated with his television role as Superman in the popular hit series "Adventures of Superman". He appeared in numerous films including "Torrid Zone", "The Strawberry Blonde" and "Gone With the Wind". The fact that he appeared in the latter film only adds to the increased demand for his signature. So popular in his role as Superman, he was forced to employ the services of others to sign the enormous stacks of fan mail. Reeves was very obliging in-person to autograph requests and had a genuine appreciation for all his fans. Some photographs of him in costume have surfaced signed simple "Best Wishes, Superman" and are not as appealing as those signed with his full name. His untimely death from a gunshot wound ended his career far too soon. FA, OP, CS—"Best Wishes", PF—autograph album pages, index cards, documents, and photographs—especially as Superman.

Roberts, Julia (1967-)

A current and very popular actress, Julia Roberts has appeared in film such as "Pretty Woman", "The Pelican Brief" and "Runaway Bride". While she's popular on screen, off screen her attitude toward her fans has been far from favorable. Roberts distances herself as much as possible from the general public and hates the thought of having to sign autographs. Her reluctance to sign has only proven to be an enticement for forgers. With the exception of only a few documents, nearly everything available in the autograph market is fake. FA, PF—autograph album pages, index cards, and photographs.

Robinson, Edward G. (1893-1973)

A talented and popular character actor, Robinson appeared in numerous films including "Little Caesar", "Key Largo", and "The Ten Commandments". He was a responsive signer in-person, however I had little luck with mail requests for his signature. PF—autograph album pages, index cards, and photographs.

Ginger Rogers

Rogers, Ginger (1911-1995)

A versatile actress, Rogers is typically associated with her dance roles alongside Fred Astaire. her film resume includes "42nd Street", "Stage Door" and "Kitty Foyle". Rogers won a Best Actress Oscar for her role in the latter film. She was a responsive signer throughout her life, even answering her fan mail! Her early signatures are very different from the flamboyant later examples and this often confuses collectors. AAW, RS, OP, CS—"Sincerely", PF—autograph album pages, index cards, and photographs—especially dancing with Astaire.

Rogers, Roy (1912-)

A very popular singing cowboy, Rogers starred in many "B" westerns. Later he would become famous to most with his hit television series "The Roy Rogers Show". Both he and wife Dale Evans were gracious signers for many years until health problems finally forced Roy to stop. His signature remains very popular with collectors. RS, CS—"Happy Trails" (may also add Triggers name), PF—autograph album pages, index cards, and photographs.

Will Rogers

Rogers, Will (1879-1935)

A witty and versatile entertainer, Rogers appeared in a few films including "They Had to See Paris", "State

Fair" and "Steamboat Round the Bend". Rogers died tragically in a plane crash that also claimed the life of noted aviator Wiley Post. Roger's signature is uncommon, but does surface occasionally. RS, PF—autograph album pages, index cards, and photographs.

Ryan, Meg (1961-)

A current popular actress, Ryan has appeared in many popular films including "Top Gun", "When Harry Met Sally" and "Sleepless in Seattle". She can be an elusive, yet occasionally accommodating signer in-person, yet does occasionally signs fan mail. PF—autograph album pages, index cards and photographs.

Scott, Randolph (1898-1987)

A prolific character actor, Scott appeared in many films including "Jesse James", "Virginia City" and "The Spoilers". He was typically associated with westerns and they did represent some of his best work. He was an obliging signer in-person, however fan mail often went unanswered. PF—autograph album pages, index cards and photographs.

Sellers, Peter (1925-1980)

A gifted comedy actor, Sellers appeared in many films including "Being There", "Lolita" and "The Pink Panther". It is however for his role as Inspector Clouseau in the "Pink Panther" series of films that he will forever be associated with. He was a reluctant but obliging signer in-person and despite claims that he never answered his fan mail, I always had tremendous success writing to him. RS, OP, PF—autograph album pages, index cards and photographs.

Shearer, Norma (1900-1983)

MGM's "First Lady of the Silver Screen", Shearer appeared in many films including "The Divorcee", "The Barretts of Wimpole Street" and "Romeo and Juliet". She was a responsive signer in-person during the height of her career, but when she retired in 1942 little of her fan mail was ever answered. AAW, PF—autograph album pages, index cards and photographs.

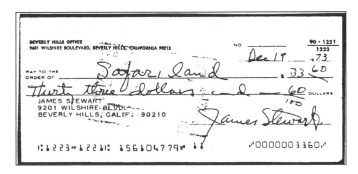

Jimmy Stewart

Stewart, James (1908-1997)

One of Hollywood's beloved actor, James Stewart's screen resume represents some of the finest films ever made including "Mr. Smith Goes to Washington", "Rear Window" , "Vertigo", and "It's a Wonderful Life". He was a responsive signer throughout his life and even took time to respond to fan mail. Stewart always loved his role in "Harvey" and for many years he would add a sketch of the imaginary rabbit to his signature. Unfortunately, these sketches have also been forged so collectors must be cautious when purchasing one. AAW, RS, PF—autograph album pages, index cards and photographs.

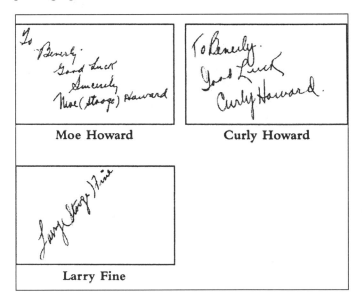

The Three Stooges

The Three Stooges

Originally formed in 1925, The Three Stooges consisted of Moe Howard (1897-1975), his brother Shemp Howard (1895-1955), and Larry Fine (1902-1975). In 1932, Shemp was then replaced by his brother Curly Howard (1903 -1952). When health problems forced Curly to leave the group, Shemp rejoined in 1946. When Shemp died in 1955, Joe Besser (1907-1988) replaced him. Joe De Rita ("Curly Joe", 1909-1993) then replaced Besser in 1959. The most sought after iteration of the group is Moe, Larry and Curly Howard and it is also the most expensive even when they signed only their first names, which was typical. Individually, the signature of Curly Howard is worth more than that of both Moe and Larry's combined. When each member signed separately, they often used their last name. In combination, this seldom was the case. As new generations discovered their work, a greater demand and thus greater price tag was placed on their signatures. RS, FA, PF—autograph album pages, index cards and photographs.

Elizabeth Taylor

Taylor, Elizabeth (1932-)

A stunning actress, Taylor has an impressive film resume including "Cat On A Hot Tin Roof", "Cleopatra", "Butterfield 8" and "Who's Afraid of Virginia Woolf?". She was responsive to signature requests early in her career, however when her popularity skyrocketed you could forget it! Once her personal life became front-page tabloid news she, along with whomever she was with at the time—often Richard Burton, became reclusive. Throughout her career she has used various methods to respond to her fan mail including stamped signatures, facsimile signed photos and even ghost signers. While documents that include her signature are often expensive, they may be your only alternative for getting an authentic signature. FA, PF—autograph album pages, index cards, documents, and photographs—especially as Cleopatra.

Shirley Temple

Temple, Shirley (1928-)

A child actor of the thirties, Shirley Temple captured our hearts in numerous films including "The Little Colonel", "Curly Top" and "The Little Princess". While she went on to other film and even television roles, we never forgot her as the curly headed little girl with that wonderful smile. She had always been an obliging signer until just recently when she decided to discontinue the practice. Since her 1950 marriage to Charles Black, she has always signed "Shirley Temple Black". Most sought by collectors are early examples of her signature—just "Shirley Temple", especially on photographs. She has not only had an incredible film career, but also a prestigious public service role as an Ambassador of this country. Her signature will forever be in demand as new generations of fans discover her work. RS, OP, PF—

autograph album pages, index cards, documents, and photographs—especially in vintage roles.

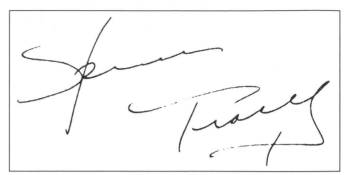

Spencer Tracy

Tracy, Spencer (1900-1967)

A sensational actor, Tracy appeared in many films including "Captains Courageous", "Boy's Town" and "Guess Who's Coming to Dinner". A multiple Oscar winner, back-to-back in fact, Tracy seemed to endure while other actors faded from the spotlight. He rarely signed autographs in-person and fan mail often went unanswered. His signature is considerably more difficult to find than people realize. AAW, PF—autograph album pages, index cards, and photographs.

Travolta, John (1954-)

A versatile and very popular current actor, Travolta survived the transition from television to film and even endured while his career faced many challenges. Popular for films like "Grease" and "Saturday Night Fever", he resurfaced in the films "Get Shorty" and "Pulp Fiction" and set his career back on course for the next decade. Travolta's response to his fans is extraordinary, always taking the time to talk with them and to sign autographs. During a time when many stars won't give you the time of day, Travolta has found the key to longevity and as such his career will endure. Until which time other stars will follow his example, numerous other actors and actresses will fade into obscurity wondering what happened— "Hello"! The actor had allegedly used ghost signers to respond to much of his fan mail, but after seeing him sign in-person recently I have to refute much of that claim. RS, PF—autograph album pages, index cards, and photographs.

Turner, Lana (1920-1995)

A glamorous actress, Lana Turner appeared in many films including "They Won't Forget", "The Postman Always Rings Twice" and "Peyton Place". An obliging signer in-person, Turner also occasionally answered her fan mail. PF—autograph album pages, index cards, and photographs.

Valentino, Rudolph (1895-1926)

A silent film legend, Valentino died suddenly in 1926, leaving behind millions of fans. His films included "Blood and Sand", "The Eagle", "The Sheik" and "Son of the Sheik". Through his work he became the first great lover of the silver screen and captured the hearts of every women who was mesmerized by his looks. Fame came quickly for the actor and such he was mobbed everywhere he went and seldom even had the opportunity to stop and sign an autograph. His signature is very scarce and can prove to be a very challenging acquisition. PF—autograph album pages, index cards, and photographs.

John Wayne

Wayne, John (1907-1979)

"The Duke" was a screen icon and gave many brilliant performances in films such as "Stagecoach", "Sands of Iwo Jima" and "True Grit". He was a prolific actor who appeared in hundreds of films during his lifetime. His enormous popularity attracted an abundance of fan mail, which was handled in a variety of ways, from facsimile-signed photographs to ghost signatures. Wayne was often unpredictable in-person to autograph requests and could simply walk away or comply depending upon his mood at the time. He was more obliging to requests later in life than earlier in his career. I look for two things in an original Wayne signature. First the double backed formation of the "o" in John, which is often cited by autograph collectors, and the "yn" combination in Wayne. The creation of the latter often finds the "n" dipping below the signature baseline creating another level to his autograph. AAW, FA, PF—autograph album pages, index cards, and photographs.

Weissmuller, Johnny (1904-1984)

Olympic medalist and champion swimmer, Weissmuller made the transition from sports icon to screen heartthrob. His film legacy centers around his role as Tarzan. He appeared in numerous films, opposite many "Janes" including Maureen O'Sullivan. His signature is not only in demand because of his role as Tarzan, but also a favorite of Olympic collectors who are impressed with his five gold medals. He was an obliging signer in-person, however much of his fan mail went unanswered. FA, PF—autograph album pages, index cards, and photographs—especially as Tarzan.

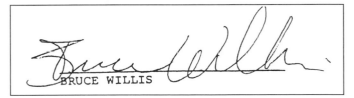

Orson Welles

Welles, Orson (1915-1985)

Acclaimed director and respected actor, Welles often appeared in his own films, including "Citizen Kane", "Macbeth" and "Touch of Evil". His legacy will forever surround his radio dramatization of "War of the Worlds" and his film "Citizen Kane", considered by many as the best of all-time. He was a reluctant but obliging signer in-person, however fan mail was often simply ignored. His autograph could exhibit significant variation, so exercise caution before purchasing his signature. PF—autograph album pages, index cards, and photographs—especially "Citizen Kane" related.

Williams, Robin (1952-)

A comedy genius and talented actor, Williams has appeared in numerous films including "Good Will Hunting", "What Dreams May Come", "Mrs. Doubtfire", and "Dead Poets Society". His popularity seems to grow with each new project he pursues. He receives an enormous amount of fan mail and thus has had to resort to alternatives in order to answer letters. While he may occasionally respond to some mail requests for his autograph, most responses will be ghost signed. Fortunately for collectors he is a very gracious signer in-person. AAW, FA, PF—autograph album pages, index cards, and photographs.

Bruce Willis

Willis, Bruce (1955-)

A popular character actor, Willis has appeared in many films including "12 Monkeys", "Pulp Fiction" and Hudson Hawk", but is associated most with his appearances in the "Die Hard" series of films. He hates signing autographs and will go out of his way to avoid the task. All of his mail is handled by a fan mail service that responds with a facsimile signed photograph. Because Willis doesn't sign autographs, forgers sign for him and the market is littered with fake material, most of which are on photographs. Collectors will just have to be patient and hope that documents surface in the market. FA, PF—autograph album pages, index cards, and photographs.

Natalie Wood

Wood, Natalie (1938-1981)

A brilliant actress, Natalie Wood appeared in some very popular films including "Miracle on 34th Street", "Rebel Without a Cause", "West Side Story" and "Splendor in the Grass". She was very responsive to her fans and signed autographs both in-person and through mail requests. Unfortunately, she died far to young during an accidental drowning. Her signature is highly sought by collectors and continues to reach new price levels each year. RS, CS—"Sincerely", PF—autograph album pages, index cards, and photographs.

First Ladies

The United States of America cherishes the Office of the President of the United States, and with it, the role of the First Lady. We are fortunate as a country to have been graced with so many wonderful women who have contributed not only to the reputation of their husband, but immensely to our country. As we review their origins we see that they are from all walks of life and are as diverse geographically, socially and academically as their husbands.

Ironically, as a finite set of autographs, they are a far greater challenge than acquiring the signatures of their husbands. Many signature samples are so scarce, that only a few are even known to exist. Because of this, collectors must understand the challenges they face when trying to complete such a set.

Abundant

Johnson, Claudia "Lady Bird" Alta Taylor (1912-)

Charming, and intelligent, "Lady Bird" Johnson brought good old-fashioned Texas hospitality to the White House. She did her best to ease the pain of a nation torn by the tragic death of John F. Kennedy. Active in numerous causes, including many conservation efforts and the Head Start program for preschool children, Lady Bird retired to the confines of the LBJ Ranch where the President died in 1973. For years she was accommodating to autograph requests, but has since stopped signing. Her signature is fairly plentiful and should not prove difficult to acquire.

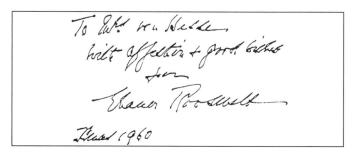

Eleanor Roosevelt

Roosevelt, Anna Eleanor Roosevelt (1884-1962)

One of the most loved and reviled women of her generation, Anna Eleanor R. Roosevelt transformed the role of First Lady. Intelligent, dedicated and incredibly socially conscience she broke down barriers and set her own standards. She was a prolific writer, and her correspondence output as First Lady far exceeds that of her predecessors.

Eisenhower, Mamie Geneva Doud (1896-1979)

Devote and outgoing, Mamie Geneva Doud Eisenhower was a gracious and popular First Lady. A courageous military wife, she seemed equally dedicated to her country, children, and husband. A prolific writer, she took great pride in handling her own correspondence and was always obliging to autograph requests.

Common

Clinton, Hillary Rodham (1947-)

Well-educated, articulate and energetic, Hillary Rodham Clinton has been a dedicated First Lady. Despite all the adversity that has faced the first family, she has been a pillar of strength. Her work on behalf of protecting the rights of children and families has been exemplary. A multifaceted woman with enormous talents, Hillary Rodham Clinton is destined to have a significant impact after leaving the White House. To date, her correspondence has remained scarce in the market, but this should change with administrations and any future politcal role.

Barbara Bush

Bush, Barbara Pierce (1925-)

Warm, compassionate, keen and hard working, Barbara Bush championed many causes, but none more than the promotion of literacy. During her reign as First Lady, she won the hearts of all she came in contact with, so much so, that by the time she was ready to leave the White House she seemed to be at the pinnacle of her popularity. Like those before her in the White House, correspondence was often answered with machine generated signatures. Today she does respond to in-person requests and occasionally mail requests will be answered with an authentic signature.

Nancy Reagan

Reagan, Anne Frances "Nancy" R. Davis (1921-)

Nancy Davis was an actress who appeared in 11 films from 1949 to 1956, the last playing opposite her husband Ronald Reagan. As First Lady she returned a sense of elegance to the White House that had not been seen since the Kennedy Administration. She was active in numerous causes from the Foster

Grandparent Program to drug and alcohol abuse, all while she exhibited a steadfast dedication to her husband. Like many modern-day First Ladies, she took full advantage of using machines to sign her correspondence. First Lady collectors are best to opt for an autographed item from her days in Hollywood.

Rosalyn Carter

Carter, Rosalynn Smith (1927-)

Dedicated, articulate and active, Rosalynn Carter was an extremely hard working First Lady. She served as the President's personal emissary to Latin America, committed herself to numerous programs aimed at the less fortunate and was the Honorary Chairperson of the President's Commission on Mental Health. After leaving the White House, the couple returned to Georgia where both remained extremely active in community service. Most of the autographed material of hers that has entered the market has been pre-presidential. She is a reluctant signer of autographs and not as prolific a writer as her husband.

Ford, Elizabeth Bloomer Warren "Betty" (1918-)

Dignified and self-confident, Betty Ford brought a new meaning to the role of First Lady. She became an advocate for many individuals in special need, such as those suffering from breast cancer or drug and alcohol addiction. Her supports of the arts and human rights has gone beyond what many of us could have expected and as the years have passed the respect for her work has continued to grow. Her machine-signed correspondence far exceeds authentic examples.

Nixon, Thelma Catherine Patricia Ryan (1912-1993)

A gracious First Lady and a charming envoy, Pat Nixon helped add more of an international flavor to her duties in the White House. She championed many charitable causes worldwide and promoted the fine arts. Not as prolific as one might think, her letter writing slowed considerably following her husband's departure from the White House.

Truman, Elizabeth Virginia "Bess" (1885-1982)

Elizabeth Virginia Wallace Truman did not particularly care for the role of First Lady, yet conscientiously fulfilled her obligations when needed.

The Trumans, who lived in Blair House during the second term, preferred to keep their home life simple. After her husband's death, she continued to live in their family home in Independence, Missouri. Although she generated far fewer letters than she answered, Bess Truman was always obliging to autograph requests or inquiries.

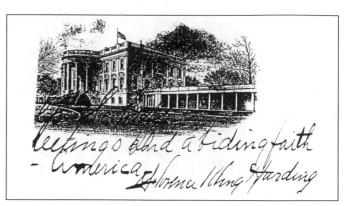

Florence K. Harding

Harding, Florence King De Wolfe (1860-1924)

Dedicated, yet independent, Florence Harding was an integral part of her husband's career. She was an energetic First Lady both at home in the White House and while traveling. Illness and sorrow dominated the time after her husband's death and she would survive him by only just over a year. Having destroyed most of her own papers, her signature can occasionally be found in the form of calling cards and brief notes.

Lou Henry Hoover

Hoover, Lou Henry (1875-1944)

Lou Henry Hoover took her role as First Lady very seriously and adhered to the details of the role. Elegant and refined, she wasn't afraid to turn toward tradition and spent much of her time recreating period rooms in the White House. Lou Hoover also served as president of the Girl Scout movement. She was a fine writer, but less prolific than one might think.

Edith Bolling Wilson

Wilson, Edith Bolling Galt (1872-1961)

Charming, intelligent and dedicated, Edith Wilson played a pivotal role as First Lady. When her husband's health failed in 1919, she handled many of his routine duties. Acting as his personal secretary, she handled much of his correspondence. Her signature can still be found periodically in the market, but collector's should be conscious of her use of a rubber stamp for some mail.

Taft, Helen Herron (1861-1943)

Independent, persistent and elegant, Helen Taft relished the role of First Lady. She brought to the White House her charm and social splendor. A lover of travel and the fine arts, she remained in Washington after her husband's death in 1930. She was the first First lady to ride in the Inaugral parade, and the first to be buried in Arlington Cemetary and was later followed by Jacqueline Bouvier Kennedy.

Roosevelt, Edith Kermit Carow (1861-1948)

Edith had been a friend of the Theodore's since infancy and married him following the death of his first wife Alice. She was a dignified and cultured First Lady who played an active role in the 1902 renovation of the

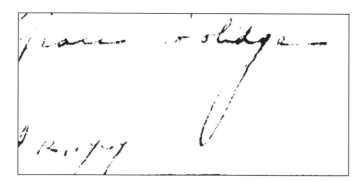

Grace Coolidge

Coolidge, Grace Anna Goodhue (1879-1957)

Grace Coolidge's dignity and charm served only to enhance her appealing simplicity. As First Lady she was extremely popular and exhumed her love for people, the outdoors, and animals. A prolific writer, her correspondence reflected the simplicity of her life.

White House. Following her husband's death, Edith returned to Sagamore Hill at Oyster Bay, Long Island where she spent much of her time reading, writing or participating in various charities. Examples of her signature periodically find their way into the autograph market.

Harrison, Mary Scott Lord (1858-1948)

Mary Scott Lord Dimmick married Harrison in 1896. She survived him by almost 47 years and was his first wife's widowed niece and former secretary.

Francis F. Cleveland

Cleveland, Frances Folsom (1864-1947)

Frances F. Cleveland was the first bride of a President to be married in the White House. During fifteen months of his first term, Rose Elizabeth Cleveland was hostess for her bachelor brother. During her time as First Lady, Francis Cleveland became extremely popular as our nation's hostess. Following the death of the President, she married a university professor, Thomas J. Preston, Jr., and the two became figures in the Princeton social community. She was always a gracious signer and such examples of her signature periodically surface in the autograph market.

Garfield, Lucretia Rudolph (1832-1918)

Dedicated, intellectual, and graceful, Lucretia Garfield respectfully filled the role of First Lady. When her husband was shot, she was in frail health, yet traveled to be by his side at his time of need. Following his death, she returned home to the family farm in Ohio, where she led a very private life for another 36 years. She was obliging to many autograph requests until finally overwhelmed by mail, Lucretia resorted to rubber-stamped signatures.

Hayes, Lucy Ware Webb (1831-1889)

Gracious, wise and articulate, Lucy Hayes was the first First Lady with a college degree. Because she was a temperance advocate, liquor was banned at the White House resulting in her earning the nickname "Lemonade Lucy." She was obliging to autograph requests, most of which found their way onto album pages or note cards.

Grant, Julia Boggs Dent (1826-1902)

Julia Grant weathered adversity but remained loyal to her husband. She enjoyed entertaining which she did so with style and grace. She always dressed the part and was lavishly trimmed with the finest accessories of the day. She considered her correspondence not a chore but a responsibility of her role as First Lady, thus samples of her cards and letters do occasionally appear in the autograph market.

Polk, Sarah Childress (1803-1891)

Strict and well-educated, Sarah Polk was the niece of Andrew Jackson. As First Lady she was active in her husband's affairs and steadfast in her Presbyterian beliefs. She was very responsive to autograph requests, most of which were answered in the form of small note cards. A typical response was signed "Mrs. James K. Polk, Polk Place." Polk Place was the name of her retirement home in Nashville.

Tyler, Julia Gardiner (1820-1889)

Julia Tyler, the "Rose of Long Island," secretly married the President in 1844. The First Lady, thirty years younger than the President, reigned for the last eight months of her husband's term. She was a charming First Lady and filled the role with grace. She was rather prolific, with soft and nearly illegible handwriting.

Can Be Difficult To Find

Wilson, Ellen Louise Axson (1860-1914)

Dignity, grace and style were exhibited by Ellen Louise Wilson as First Lady. She championed concerns for the poor and her advice was cherished by her husband. A gifted artist, she had a studio with a skylight installed at the White House in 1913. She died of Bright's disease during her husband's term on August 6, 1914.

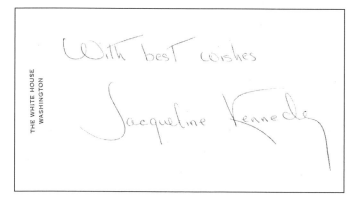

Mary Lincoln

Lincoln, Mary Todd (1818-1882)

Mary Todd Lincoln's fascinating personality, elegance and wit, was often shrouded by sarcastic innuendoes that could bring some of the finest conversations of the day to a swift halt. Her role as First Lady sparked constant criticism, creating a lasting legacy for the very misunderstood figure. As a prolific writer of often interesting correspondence, Mary Todd Lincoln's letters have been well absorbed by institutions and Lincoln collectors.

Jacqueline Kennedy

Kennedy, Jacqueline Lee Bouvier (1929-1994)

The most popular First Lady since Eleanor Roosevelt, Jacqueline Lee Bouvier Kennedy brought Camelot to the White House. Young and beautiful, she was raising the first young children of a President in half a century inside the walls of the White House. The public quickly fell in love with the Jackie, as her elegance and charm captivated everyone she came in contact with. Following the tragic death of her husband, she tried hopelessly to retreat from public life. She was hounded by the press until her death in 1994. Her correspondence in any form is highly sought and continues to bring strong prices.

J. M. Pierce

Pierce, Jane Means Appleton (1806-1863)

Like some of her predecessors, Jane Pierce was not fond of Washington and opted instead for the beauty of Concord, New Hampshire. She fainted at the news that the Democratic party had chosen her husband as their candidate for President. Tragedy struck as the last of her three sons was killed before her, during a train derailment just two months before her husband's inauguration. Her intense bereavement was further intensified by the loss of others. Her role as First Lady was very limited to selective events. She corresponded with family members, and much of that well-written correspondence now resides at the Library of Congress.

Anna Harrison

Harrison, Anna Tuthill Symmes (1775-1864)

Illness prevented Anna Harrison from joining her husband in Washington, so the President-elect asked his daughter-in-law Jane Irwin Harrison, widow of his namesake son, to join him and act as hostess. Because the President died exactly one month after his inauguration, Anna never made it to the White House. She often responded to requests for her husband's signature. Examples of her shaky signature can occasionally be found in the market.

Dolly P. Madison

Madison, Dorothea "Dolley" Payne Todd (1768-1849)

A socialite and extremely popular, Dolley Madison transformed the role of the First Lady into that of an occasional social butterfly. She was a prolific letter writer, with distinct block script. Demand for this signature has been consistently strong, as her legend continues to grow.

Adams, Abigail Smith (1744-1818)

A prolific and gifted writer whose letters are often polished and insightful. Collectors will find her signature a challenge, as many of thousands known to exist have been absorbed by institutions. She had a voracious appetite for reading and cherished her role as the First Lady. Demand for her material is high in any form.

Adams, Louisa Catherine (1775-1852)

The only First Lady born outside the United States, Louisa Adams was a darling hostess, but by the time she had reached the White House, was in poor health. She preferred quite evenings reading or composing music, as she was also a gifted harp player. An educated and occasionally prolific writer, few letters of hers survive outside of those at the family home in Quincy, Mass.

Very Difficult To Find

McKinley, Ida Saxton (1847-1907)

Ida Saxton McKinley, suffered from a variety of illnesses, yet was committed to her role as First Lady. Her social inadequacies were ignored by guests, many of whom were aware of Ida's health problems. Following the death of her husband, by an assassin's bullet, she returned to Canton, Ohio and was cared for by her younger sister. If you are lucky enough to happen across a scarce signature of hers, it will probably be as a franked envelope.

Harrison, Caroline Lavina Scott (1832-1892)

Active, articulate and a lover of the arts, Caroline Lavinia Scott Harrison was an active First Lady. She served as President General of the National Society of the Daughters of the American Revolution, while focusing toward the traditional role of the White House. She established the collection of china, now so much associated with White House, as well as the annual Christmas tree. She died of tuberculosis during her husband's term in October of 1892. Following her death, her daughter Mary Harrison McKee acted as hostess for her father.

(Buchanan) Lane (Johnston), Harriet (1830-1906)

President James Buchanan did not marry, so the role of White House hostess fell to his orphaned niece Harriet Lane. As hostess she added color to a White House that was faltering with threats of state succession. While her life was later filled with despair following the deaths of her uncle, her husband, and two young sons, Harriet persevered. She amassed a sizeable art collection that she later bequeathed to the government and continued numerous altruistic pursuits. Much of her correspondence can be found at the Buchanan family home, Wheatland, in Lancaster, Pennsylvania.

Jackson, Rachel Donelson Robards (1767-1828)

Far more comfortable at The Hermitage, than the thought of having to live in the White House, she died a few months before her husband's inauguration. Poorly educated, writing was not a pleasure, but a chore. Most of her letters were lost in a fire at The Hermitage. The role she would have had as First Lady was filled by Emily Donelson, wife of her nephew and later by Sarah Yorke Jackson, wife of Andrew Jackson, Jr.

Washington, Martha Dandridge Custis (1731-1802)

Neither a prolific or gifted writer, only a few hundred of her letters are known to exist, many of which are illegible. There were occasions in which her husband signed on her behalf, but they are scarce. When George died Martha burned their correspondence. Demand for her material is high in any form.

Virtually Nonexistent

Taylor, Margaret Mackall Smith (1788-1852)

"Peggy" Taylor abhorred the thought of the White House over her Mississippi plantation. As First Lady she did not participate in formal social functions. She chose to greet her own family in the confines of her upstairs sitting room and passed on the role of hostess to her youngest daughter Mary Elizabeth "Betty" Bliss. The signatures of both the First Lady and the hostess are scarce in all forms.

Tyler, Letitia Christian (1790-1842)

Already confined to an invalid's chair for two years prior to her husband's unexpected role as President, Letitia Tyler felt far more at home in Williamsburg than anywhere else. She did find some solace in a second-floor room at the White House, but passed the roll of hostess to her daughter-in-law Priscilla Cooper Tyler. Letitia Tyler was the first President's wife to die in the White House. Her signature is scarce in all forms.

Van Buren, Hannah Hoes (1783-1819)

Hannah Van Buren, a respected lady of the Christian faith, died before her 36th birthday, 18 years before her husband became President. The President's eldest son

Abraham served as his private secretary. Abraham married Angelica Singleton, who would become hostess of the White House for her father-in-law.

Hannah Van Buren's signature in any form is virtually nonexistent. A South Carolina library houses the Singleton family papers in which some examples of Angelica's signature can be found. Her signature should provide a significant challenge to collectors.

Monroe, Elizabeth Kortright (1768-1830)

Elizabeth Monroe's poor health curtailed many of her responsibilities as First Lady. She did manage to transform the White House back to a more formal atmosphere, one of European flavor over the Virginia social style popularized by her predecessor. Like that of many, her correspondence with her husband was burned following her death. Her signature in any form is a rarity.

Jefferson, Martha Wayles Skelton (1748-1782)

Martha died nearly two decades before her husband entered the White House and little is known of writing habits. The role of First lady was filled on occasion by Dolley Madison, but also by the President's daughter Martha "Patsy" Jefferson—Mrs. Thomas Mann Randolph, Jr. and her writings are very difficult to find.

Fillmore, Abigail Powers (1798-1853)

Abigail Powers Fillmore had a passion for education and continued to teach even after her marriage to husband Millard Fillmore. Assuming the role of First Lady following the death of Zachary Taylor, Abigail brought to the White House a more subdued environment. The routine social responsibilities were passed to the Fillmore's daughter Mary "Abby" Abigail Fillmore. Suffering from chronic poor health, she developed pneumonia following President's Pierce's inauguration and died a few weeks later. All her family correspondence was later burned, leaving her signature in any form scarce.

Fillmore, Caroline McIntosh (1813-1881)

Millard Fillmore later married Caroline McIntosh Fillmore. Her signature in any form is also very difficult to find.

Johnson, Eliza McCardle (1810-1876)

A courageous Eliza Johnson was in poor health when she entered the White House and thus passed on the hostess responsibilities to her daughter Martha Patterson. She withdrew to a second-floor room where accessibility was limited to only family members. Her signature in any form is scarce.

Arthur, Ellen Lewis Herndon (1837-1880)

Ellen Lewis Herndon Arthur died ten months before her husband's election to the Vice Presidency. The President then asked his youngest sister Mary Arthur McElroy to assume certain social duties and to attend to his daughter Ellen. Years later, the Arthur family papers were destroyed, making her signature scarce in any form.

Roosevelt, Alice Hathaway Lee (1861-1884)

Alice Hathaway Lee Roosevelt died four years after her wedding to Theodore, leaving behind her husband and an infant daughter Alice. Little is known of her signature habits, as is the existence of any examples.

All That Jazz

One of the most fascinating areas of autograph collecting is picking an area of the hobby that few focus upon, such as the field of Jazz. While the field of autograph collecting is knowledgeable about many areas of the hobby, such as the signatures of United States presidents, it is not entirely comfortable with jazz. While the signing habits—supply & demand, of the key players are understood, little is known about the minor or often overlooked contributors.

Maybe the reason more people don't collect jazz autographs, is because they don't understand the music and its rich history. So let's take a brief, but closer look. Jazz, as the only indigenous American musical form, has had a profound affect on the Western world. Black musicians in the late 19th century blended harmonics and forms with African inflections. Using improvisation, syncopation and intonation, jazz music drew from within the soul and took those who sang it back into their roots, be it a field holler with a classic work song, or a classic spiritual.

Jazz was transformed from a musical approach to a musical form. Nowhere was this more evident than witnessing a funeral procession through the streets of New Orleans. Somber black marching bands, such as Henry "Red" Allen's Brass Band, played slowly to traditional hymns as they marched toward the cemetery at the edge of town, then as if the gates of heaven had opened, the same band returned with upbeat, jazz infused versions of the same songs. The sound centered around the rhythm section of drums or string bass, then spread to the trumpet or coronet to carry the melody. Other instruments, such as the clarinet and trombone filled in, and as the music matured more instruments were added.

Dixieland

We were headed toward the roaring twenties and before the White Sox could throw the pennant, The Original Dixieland Jazz Band headed by Nick La Rocca began their Victor recording career in a New York studio. It was 1917, and in order to capture this new sound, bands had to travel to two cities, New York or Chicago—the hubs of the recording business during the era. La Rocca had sewn his roots in New Orleans, learning how to play jazz from black musicians, while playing in places like the Haymarket Cafe.

A half decade later, in April of 1923, King Oliver's Creole Jazz Band would enter the studio to lay down the first significant recordings by black musicians. King Oliver was raised in New Orleans and had toured and gigged with numerous bands before forming his own band. He attracted some of the finest talent in New Orleans including Louis Armstrong, Johnny Dodds, "Baby" Warren Dodds and Honore Dutrey. The band loved to play in Chicago and it wasn't long before others saw their future between the chords of Oliver's music.

Bix Beiderbecke joined The Wolverines in October of 1923. Having fashioned his sound aboard the Great Lakes Steamers sailing between Michigan City and Chicago, Beiderbecke enriched the polyphonic texture known as Dixieland. While the smaller bands of Chicago felt at home in ballrooms and inns, the New York jazz scene preferred bigger groups that catered to the needs of vaudeville shows and larger venues. The Jazz Age of the roaring twenties seemed to have no bounds, whether it was it was due to the indispensable factor of improvisation in the music or simply attributable to the times, it was clear that America had a new art form.

Other than Armstrong, collecting signatures from this jazz era can be a challenge. While Beiderbecke's autograph has surfaced a couple times during the last decade, the same can't be said for the other key players. Collectors will just have to be patient and hope that someone, be it a collector or dealer, stumbles across some autograph examples.

New York Jazz

As jazz evolved during the Twenties it became more formal. Written arrangements evolved from no notations at all and the proficiency of new young talent set the groundwork for soloists. Musicians such as Louis Armstrong, Sidney J. Bechet, Coleman R. Hawkins, James P. Johnson, and F.L. "Jelly Roll" Morton now stepped forward to fill their new positions. The emergence of soloists, now meant celebrity status and with the new position came autograph requests. Collectors could now target both the bandleaders, and his key players for signatures.

The new big band sound of New York was led by "Smack" Fletcher Henderson (with arranger Don Redman) and Edward Kennedy "Duke" Ellington. From his residency at the Roseland Ballroom of New York, Henderson intertwined call-and-response patterns with various other elements to define a performance style known as swing. Meanwhile, Ellington was defining the role of bandleader to include composition. Working the New York club scene, Ellington finally took residency at the Cotton Club on December 4, 1927 and stayed until February 1931. The club offered the bandleader the perfect element to test his new compositions during their revues. Not only would many of his songs become hits, but they would also set a new benchmark for the bandleaders that would follow.

Also emerging from the jazz scene was the blues singer, adding vocals as a commentary between sung phrases. Setting the standard for this musical element was Bessie Smith who quickly became one of the highest paid artists on the theater circuit.

Signatures of the jazz musicians of this era are highly sought in the autograph market, particularly those of Louis Armstrong and Duke Ellington. Although both Ellington and Armstrong were gracious signers, their timeless appeal continues to draw collectors and fans to their work. Both the signatures of "Jelly Roll Morton" and Bessie Smith are scarce in all forms, the former being more so than the latter. The signatures of Fletcher Henderson and Don Redman, while harder to find than most might expect, are also less valuable.

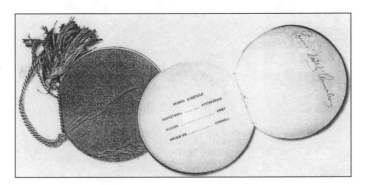

Louis Armstrong

Duke Ellington

Swing

Swing would flourish during the next two decades as the big band sound filled dance halls across the country. The movement was led by Tommy and Jimmy Dorsey, Benny Goodman, Woody Herman, Glenn Miller and Artie Shaw. Countering the complex big band arrangements was the Kansas City swing style of swift tempos, repetition, and blues vocabulary. Carrying this element was Count Basie and Bennie Moten, along with numerous soloists including Lester Young.

Autograph collectors drawn to the big band sound were often treated to signatures from their favorite artists, most of which were prolific signers. As a result many signed items from this era routinely find their way into the autograph market. The signature of Glenn Miller—a responsive signer, is always in demand and difficult to obtain due to his untimely death. He has

remained popular with collectors for decades. All the participants of the Kansas City swing style are less prevalent than the mainstream big bands. Basie, also a good in-person signer, surfaces periodically in autograph dealer catalogs, but others will take some serious autograph hunting.

Bebop

Jazz, like all forms of music, has its revolutionaries, the first of which really emerged during the 1940s. The lack of intimacy among band members and restrictive arrangements were shed in favor of smaller groups with increased interplay among members. Soloists

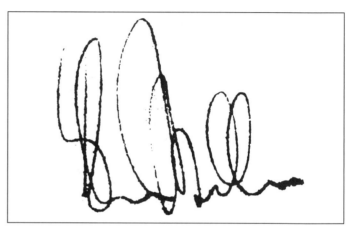

Glenn Miller

Tommy and Jimmy Dorsey

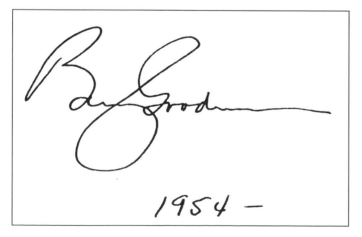

Benny Goodman

Charlie Parker

flourished as complex rhythms favored the ears of the audience rather than their feet. Bebop musicians, despite the sophistication of the sound, were considered radicals and as a result rejected from the mainstream.

Fueling bebop was Dizzy Gillespie, Thelonious Monk and Charlie Parker. While most of the musicians from this genre were obliging to autograph requests, they received far fewer than what most think. Quality autographed material, therefore, appears only sporadically in the autograph market and typically attracts considerable interest.

Cool Jazz & Third Stream

Rejecting the often pompous sophistication of bebop, cool jazz streamlined the range of their music, focusing upon the middle register. The music wasn't directly assaulted, but instead gradually attacked. This movement, a return to the fundamentals of swing was led by Miles Davis and his gifted academic performers. Although new instruments seemed to be introduced at the same frequency as new members of the ensembles, they provided a fresh sound with little vibrato.

Cool would later combine with some classical forms in a style known as "third stream." The polyphony texture was best exemplified in the work of The Modern Jazz Quartet.

Davis attracted most of the attention from autograph seekers, as getting his signature in-person was the primary acquisition mode. Miles Davis was an elusive signer later in life, with autograph requests via mail often unanswered.

Free Jazz—The 1960s

Not only did rock music mirror the turbulent 1960s, but so did jazz. Setting the foundation of the decade was Ornette Coleman. Through his 1960 album Free Jazz, he echoed the need for unrestricted creativity. Others, such as Cecil Taylor followed and pushed jazz further toward the edge.

It was John Coltrane however that really took jazz down a path that few thought it could return from. Coltrane improvised with seemingly reckless abandon toward tonality. Few had seen jazz pushed to such emotional levels, but if you could see past the passion and the simplicity of a single scale structure, you would realized the intent. The trouble came when many refused to recognize or understand the new path of the art and slowly drifted away from jazz.

Autograph collectors during this era virtually ignored this sector, despite many enjoying the music. Coltrane, who died young, was an elusive signer making his signature far more valuable than most realize.

The Big Band Renaissance—The 1970s

The fans lost during the 1960s, revisited jazz again a decade later. This time, it was the rebirth of the big band. College students once again danced to the sounds of Count Basie and Woody Herman. Even the New Orleans Preservation Hall Jazz Band was met with a young and enthusiastic audience. Collecting jazz autographs flourished during this decade, as most of the musicians were easy targets during their tours.

Those musicians who couldn't look back, moved forward toward a fusion of rock and jazz, they included George Benson, Chick Corea, Miles Davis, Herbie Hancock and Wayne Shorter. Jazz was electric, robust and melodic and as a result, a new legion of fans were drawn toward the art. Unlike the old bandleaders, some of these musicians were tough targets for autograph collectors, such as Miles Davis. George Benson has been elusive to autograph requests, with most sent through the mail stamped with a facsimile signature. Chick Corea and Herbie Hancock have always been great toward responding to autograph requests both in-person and through the mail.

Never a form to stay within the lines, jazz once again experimented. This time it was with a touch of spiritualism in the sounds of Anthony Braxton and Sun Ra. The signatures from both these artists are tougher to find than one might think.

Chick Corea

The Eclectic Eighties & Nineties

Latin-American, South American, and African music added a new dimension to jazz during the Eighties as a new stream of classically-trained musicians entered the jazz scene. An increased interest in the complex structures of the past, along with an appreciation of improvisation permeated recordings and performances.

Musicians such as George Benson; Arty Blakey; Michael Brecker; Ruth Brown; Gary Burton; Benny Carpenter; Betty Carter; Natalie Cole; Harry Conick, Jr.; Chick Corea; Miles Davis; Bill Evans; Ella Fitzgerald; Pete Fountain; Joe Henderson; Lena Horne; Etta James; Al Jarreau; Quincy Jones; Stan Getz; Dexter Gordon; John Hendricks; Dr. John; Cleo Laine; Branford & Wynton Marsalis; Bobby McFerrin; Oscar Peterson; David Sanborn; Doc Severinson, Diane Schuur, Joe Williams; and groups like; Mahatten Transfer; McCoy Tyner Big Band; Phil Woods Quartet; Rob McConnel and the Boss Brass; 2 + 2 Plus; Take 6; Yellowjackets; Gil Evans and the Monday Night Orchestra; and the Pat Metheny Group would help guide jazz to the end of the millennium; although not all would see it.

My favorite jazz signers during the last two decades include: Michael Brecker; Chick Corea; Pete Fountain—"The Best"; Lena Horne; Etta James; Branford & Wynton Marsalis; Bobby McFerrin and Doc Severinson. Many of these musicians go to great lengths to please their fans who request autographs. Those on the "Save Your Stamps" list include: George Benson (stamps his signature); Harry Conick, Jr. (facsimile signed photograph); the deceased Ella Fitzgerald (facsimile signed photograph); and Quincy Jones (facsimile signed photograph).

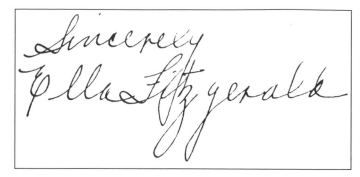

Ella Fitzgerald

Things To Come

While parallels to the popularity of jazz music and that of collecting autographs of its participants can certainly be drawn, one element has remained consistent, it has been a favorite of relatively few collectors. Because of this, however, it has a unique appeal. While many mainstream autograph dealers are always willing to purchase signatures of Glenn Miller, Louis Armstrong and Duke Ellington, they often overlook those of Billy Strayhorn, Henry "Red" Allen, Chick Webb and many, many others. An educated jazz autograph collector or historian can still find some very difficult signatures at prices far below their market value. In fact, if you glance through many autograph price guides, few even bother to list a majority of the musicians listed below.

Similar to collecting the signatures of those great baseball players of Negro Leagues, jazz autographs just may be a diamond in the rough. While those who wait to start a jazz autograph collection will soon be singing the "Canal Street Blues", other experienced collectors will be whistling "If You Could See Me Now."

Jazz & Blues Autograph Directory

A

Name	Years	Price	Notes
Adderley, Julian "Cannonball"	1928-1975	Price Range: $40—75	Alto sax player
Armstrong, Louis "Satchmo"	1900-1971	Price Range: $265—500	Singer, trumpet player, "scat" vocalist

Although fairly easy to find, his signature is always in demand; a responsive signer in-person; very distinct signature with the letter "g" almost always twisted inward

B

Bailey, Mildred	1907-1951	Price Range: Undetermined	Blues singer, uncommon.

She suffered from diabetes and heart trouble and spent the last part of her life in a Poughkeepsie, NY hospital.

Baker, Chet	1929-1988	Price Range: $30—$65	Trumpet player
Basie, Count	1904-1984	Price Range: $80-$250	Orchestra leader, piano player.

Although fairly easy to find, his signature is always in demand. A must for every collection!

Bechet, Sidney	1897-1959	Price Range: $135—?	Soprano sax player, jazz pioneer.

Hard to determine the pricing of many unique items. Bechet toured the U.S. extensively, but made his home, from the Summer of 1951, in France.

Name	Years	Price	Notes
Beiderbecke, Bix	1903-1931	Price Range: $5500—?	Composer, cornet and piano player.

Scarce in all forms with only a few being offered in the market over the past few decades; very distinct signature.

Beneke, Tex	1914-	Price Range: $20—$45	Sax player; featured with Glenn Miller.

Has always been responsive to autograph requests via mail until recently; later signatures are very tremulous and will eventually prove difficult to authenticate.

Benford, Tommy	1906-1994	Price Range: $20-$50	Drummer
Berigan, Bunny	1908-1942	Price Range: Undetermined	Trumpet player, singer; scarce in all forms.

Worked with Tommy Dorsey, had small band residency at 47 Club in New York (1940).

Bigard, Barney	1906-1980	Price Range: $70-$135	Clarinet player; brother of Alex.

Worked with King Oliver, Duke Ellington; during the 1970s he played numerous festivals in both the U.S. and Europe.

Blanton, Jimmy	1918-1942	Price Range: Undetermined	Bass; played with Duke Ellington.

Became seriously ill in 1941; spent the last few months of his life in the Duarte Sanitarium; scarce in all forms.

Bolden, Charles "Buddy"	1877-1931	Price Range: Undetermined	Cornet player; jazz band pioneer.

His behavior was erratic during the final years of his life; was admitted to an Insane Asylum in 1907 and spent the rest of his life there; scarce in all forms.

Brown, Clifford	1930-1956	Price Range: Undetermined	Trumpet player.
Byas, Don	1912-1972	Price Range: $25-$45	Tenor sax; played in Lionel Hampton's Big Band.

Also played with Count Basie, Dizzy Gillespie, Benny Carter; lived his final years in Europe; played Newport (1970)

C

Calloway, Cab	1907-1995	Price Range: $35-$150	Band leader.

Responsive in-person and via mail to autograph requests

Carney, Harry	1910-1974	Price Range: $30- $70	Baritone sax; worked with Duke Ellington
Catlett, "Big Sid" Sidney	1910-1951	Price Range: Undetermined	Drummer; composer.

Died suddenly of a heart attack; surprisingly little of his material has surfaced in the autograph market.

Cheatham, Doc	1905-1997	Price Range: $15—$30	Big band trumpeter.

Played with Cab Calloway, Fletcher Henderson and Benny Goodman. Worked many free-lance recording sessions; played at President Carter's Jazz Party in 1978; toured relentlessly.

Cherry, Don	1937-1995	Price Range: $20-$40	Lyrical jazz trumpeter.
Christian, Charlie	1919-1942	Price Range: Undetermined	Guitar player; played with Benny Goodman.

Diagnosed with tuberculosis in 1941; spent rest of his brief life in Seaview Sanitarium; scarce in all forms.

Clarke, Kenny	1914-1985	Price Range: $30-$60	Modern drum pioneer.

Worked with Louis Armstrong, Ella Fitzgerald, Benny Carter and Dizzy Gillespie; founding member The Modern Jazz Quartet; moved to Europe in 1956

Clayton, Buck	1911-1991	Price Range: $30-$55	Trumpet player; arranger.

Played with Count Basie, Sidney Bechet, Eddie Condon and many others; arranged for Basie, Benny Goodman and Harry James; played at numerous festivals during the last two decades of his life; taught at Hunter College in the early 1980s.

Cleveland, James	1931-1991	Price Range: $25-$45	Gospel singer.
Cohn, Al	1925-1988	Price Range: $25-$50	Tenor sax player, composer.
Cole, "Cozy" W.R.	1909-1981	Price Range: $20-$40	Drummer; recorded with Jelly Roll Morton.

Played with Cab Calloway; worked with Benny Goodman; started drum-tuition school with Gene Krupa; featured on numerous television shows.

Name	Years	Price	Notes
Coltrane, John	1926-1967	Price Range: $350-$1250	Innovative tenor sax player; a tough signature!
Condon, Eddie	1904-1973	Price Range: $45-$100	Band leader, guitar player.

Owned his own club in New York where he signed numerous autographs.

D

Name	Years	Price	Notes
Dameron, Tadd	1917-1965	Price Range: $30-$60	Piano player, composer.

Wrote for many bands including Harland Leonard's, Dizzy Gillespie's and Jimmie Lunceford; played with Miles Davis; spent time in jail in 1958.

Name	Years	Price	Notes
Davis, Eddie "Lockjaw"	1921-1986	Price Range: $30-$50	Tenor sax player
Davis, Miles	1926-1991	Price Range: $175-$500	Trumpet player, pioneer of "cool" jazz.

A tough signature; he could be an illusive signer!

Name	Years	Price	Notes
Davison, Wild Bill	1906-1989	Price Range: $40-$100	Cornet player, Chicago jazz pioneer.

Guested with many bands; was a regular at Eddie Condon's club; toured Europe extensively.

Name	Years	Price	Notes
Desmond, Paul	1924-1977	Price Range: $35-$60	Alto sax player
Dickenson, Vic	1906-1984	Price Range: $30-$50	Trombone player, composer.

Played with Benny Carter, Count Basie and many others.

Name	Years	Price	Notes
Dodds, Johnny M.	1892-1940	Price Range: $50-$80	Clarinet player.

Played with Kid Ory, King Oliver; a prolific free-lancer; owned apartment block at 39th and Michigan in Chicago where he was often obliging to autograph requests.

Name	Years	Price	Notes
Dodds, Warren "Baby"	1898-1959	Price Range: $40-$50	Drummer; played with King Oliver.

Extensive free-lancer; often featured on the "This is Jazz" radio series; played sporadically at the end of his life due to failing health.

Name	Years	Price	Notes
Dorsey, Jimmy	1904-1957	Price Range: $40-$300	Band leader, clarinet & alto sax player.

Was one of the first jazz groups to broadcast; extensive studio worker; featured in numerous films; a responsive signer!

Name	Years	Price	Notes
Dorsey, Tommy	1905-1956	Price Range: $50- $250	Band leader, trombone player.

Played with his brother Jimmy; featured with his brother in "The Fabulous Dorseys'"

E

Name	Years	Price	Notes
Eldridge,Roy	1911-1989	Price Range: $30-$75	Trumpet player, drummer, singer.

A multi-talented musician; "Little Jazz" played with Fletcher Henderson, Gene Krupa; Artie Shaw, Benny Goodman, Coleman Hawkins, Ella Fitzgerald and Count Basie; featured in first national J.A.T.P. tour; worked regularly at Jimmy Ryan's Club.

Name	Years	Price	Notes
Ellington, Duke	1899-1974	Price Range: $225-$1000	Band leader, composer, piano player.

One of the greatest composers ever; had residency at the Cotton Club 1927-1931; toured extensively later in life; died of cancer; responsive to in-person autograph requests, while in later years mail requests for his signature were often ignored.

Name	Years	Price	Notes
Evans, Bill	1929-1980	Price Range: $25-$50	Piano player
Evans, Gil	1913-1988	Price Range: $20-$45	Composer, arrange, piano player.

Worked with Miles Davis; extensive free-lancer; led his own big band for many years.

F

Name	Years	Price	Notes
Fitzgerald, Ella	1918-1996	Price Range: $50-$125	Jazz vocalist.

Often elusive to autograph requests in later years, all mail requests answered with facsimile signed photos; played with Chick Webb; gained international recognition as solo artist; her signature changed significantly during her lifetime

G

Name	Years	Price	Notes
Garland, "Red"	1923-1984	Price Range: $25-$50	Piano player
Garner, Erroll	1921-1977	Price Range: $85-$165	Piano, composer
Getz, Stan	1927-1991	Price Range: $100-$250	Tenor sax player

Name	Years	Price	Notes
Gillespie, Dizzy	1917-1993	Price Range: $75-$250	Composer, trumpet player.

Worked with Cab Calloway, Fletcher Henderson, Benny Carter, Duke Ellington, and Charlie Parker; leading exponent of "be-bop"; worked relentlessly; often unresponsive to autograph request via mail.

Goodman, Benny	1909-1986	Price Range: $75-$265	Band leader, clarinet player.

Responsive to autograph requests; prolific free-lancer; extensive radio work; featured on "Let's Dance" radio show; gained national then international fame with his own band; long residence at the Congress Hotel in Chicago; featured in numerous films; worked with Lionel Hampton, Gene Krupa and Teddy Wilson.

Gordon, Dexter	1923-1990	Price Range: $30-$60	Tenor sax player.

H

Hackett, Bobby	1915-1976	Price Range: $30-$60	Trumpet and cornet player; led his own big band.

Prolific free-lancer, worked with Horace Heidt, Glenn Miller, Benny Goodman and Tony Bennett; was staff musician at NBC.

Handy, W.C.	1873-1958	Price Range: $300-$800	Composer, "St. Louis Blues"; "Father of the Blues".

Went blind in the early 1920s; was a semi-invalid following a 1943 accident; a tough signature!

Hawkins, Coleman	1904-1969	Price Range: $150-$265	Tenor sax player; led his own big band.

Played with Fletcher Henderson; a prolific free-lancer; made numerous appearances late in life at the Village Vanguard in New York.

Henderson, Fletcher	1898-1952	Price Range: $25-$50	Orchestra leader, arranger.

Worked with Ethel Waters and Benny Goodman; very responsive to autograph requests; very legible and flamboyant handwriting.

Herman, Woody	1913-1987	Price Range: $25-$100	Band leader, clarinet and alto sax player.

Led his own series of bands known as various herds, The First Herd etc.; was responsive to in-person autograph requests.

Higginbotham, Jay C.	1906-1973	Price Range: $40-$60	Trombone player.

Worked with Chick Webb, Fletcher Henderson, Benny Carter and the Louis Armstrong Big Band.

Hines, Earl "Fatha"	1905-1983	Price Range: $40-$275	Piano player; opened his own club.

Worked with Louis Armstrong; worked regularly, despite ill health, until his death.

Hodges, Johnny	1907-1970	Price Range: $40-$60	Alto sax player.

Prolific freelance artist; worked with Sidney Bechet, Chick Webb and Duke Ellington

Holiday, Billie	1915-1959	Price Range: $750-$2000	Blues singer, "Strange Fruit".

Responsive in-person signer; worked all the best jazz performers and band leaders; in later years worked as solo attraction; made final public appearance on May 25, 1959 at The Phoenix Theater in New York.

Hooker, John Lee	1917-40	Price Range: $100-$125	Guitarist and blues singer, no longer signs.
Hopkins, Sam "Lightnin"	1912-1982	Price Range: $40-$125	Guitarist and blues singer.
Howlin' Wolf	1910-1976	Price Range: $300-$850	Guitarist, harmonica player, blues singer.

J

Jackson, Mahaila	1911-1972	Price Range: $100-$200	Gospel singer.
Jefferson, Blind Lemon	1897-1930	Price Range: $1250-$2500	Guitarist, blues singer; a very difficult signature!
Johnson, Bunk	1879-1949	Price Range: $225-$600	Cornet and trumpet player; jazz pioneer.

Made first issued recordings in 1942; held various jobs including truck driver, music teacher while playing; played first concert on April 12, 1943; was a semi-invalid following his 1948 stroke; a difficult signature.

Johnson, James P.	1891-1955	Price Range: $140-$500	Composer, piano player.

Worked with Bessie Smith and Ethel Waters; collaborated with poet Langston Hughes; lead his own orchestra; after suffering a severe stroke in 1951 was an invalid for the rest of his life; common signature form "James P. Johnson", with a distinctive letter "P."

Name	Years	Price	Notes
Johnson, Robert	1912-1938	Price Range: Undetermined	Guitarist, singer, songwriter.
Jones, Jo	1911-1985	Price Range: $30-$50	Drummer.

Played with Bennie Moten and Count Basie; prolific free-lancer; recorded with many jazz greats including Billie Holiday, Duke Ellington, Harry James and Benny Goodman.

Jones, Philly Joe	1923-1985	Price Range: $25-$40	Drummer.
Jones, Thad	1923-1986	Price Range: $25-$75	Trumpet and cornet player; a responsive signer.
Joplin, Scott	1868-1917	Price Range: $700-$2250	Ragtime composer.

The most famous of the ragtime pianists and composers; a prolific songwriter; his signatures are scarce.

Jordan, Louis	1908-1975	Price Range: $35-$70	Singer, alto sax player.

An enormous recording success; worked with Louis Armstrong, Bing Crosby and Ella Fitzgerald; his signatures appear occasionally in the autograph market.

K

Kenton, Stan	1912-1979	Price Range: $50-$125	Orchestra leader, composer, piano player.

Conducted numerous jazz clinics at universities during the 1970s; following a serious operation in 1977 performed only on a limited basis, such as Newport (1978); responsive signer.

King, Albert	1923-1992	Price Range: $20-$50	Blues guitarist.
Krupa, Gene	1909-1973	Price Range: $50-$200	Band and combo leader, drummer.

Starred with Benny Goodman; ran a drum-tuition school in New York; responsive signer.

L

LaFaro, Scott	1936-1961	Price Range: Undetermined	Bass player.
Ledbetter, Huddie "Leadbelly"	1888-1949	Price Range: $5000-?	Guitarist, blues singer; scarce in all forms.
Lewis, Mel	1929-1990	Price Range: $20-$75	Orchestra leader, drummer; responsive signer.
Lunceford, Jimmie	1902-1947	Price Range: $45-$150	Band leader, sax player.

Residency at the Cotton Club in 1934; one of the most sought after prewar big bands; collapsed while signing autographs during an appearance and died shortly afterwards; responsive signer.

M

McPartland, Jimmy	1907-1991	Price Range: $30-$55	Trumpet player.

Worked with The Wolverines, Art Kassel, Ben Pollack, Russ Colombo; led his own band; married musician Marian Page; toured extensively.

McRae, Carmen	1920-1994	Price Range: $20-$45	Jazz singer.
Miller, Glenn	1904-1944	Price Range: $200-$750	Band leader, Trombone player.

Worked in Max Fischer's Band and the Dorsey Brothers' Orchestra; also worked with Ben Pollack; gradually gained enormous popularity; his band was featured in two films, "Sun Valley Serenade" and "Orchestra Wives"; led A.E.F. Orchestra during WWII; reported missing after flight from England to France in 1944; was responsive to autograph requests.

Mingus, Charles	1922-1979	Price Range: $135-$250	Composer, bass player.
Monk, Thelonius	1920-1982	Price Range: $100-$200	Piano player, composer, bop developer.

Worked with Lucky Millinder, Cootie Williams and Coleman Hawkins; led his own big band; toured with "The Giants of Jazz"; an elusive signer.

Montgomery, Wes	1925-1968	Price Range: $40-$60	Guitarist.
Morton, "Jelly Roll"	1890-1941	Price Range: $500-$750	Composer, singer, piano player.

Recorded with The New Orleans Rhythm Kings; worked with W.C. Handy; led his own band.

Moten, Bennie	1894-1935	Price Range: Undetermined	Piano player.

Led his own band- after death Count Basie took over the remnants.

Mulligan, Gerry	1927-1996	Price Range: $20-$50	Baritone sax player, songwriter.
Murphy, Turk	1915-1987	Price Range: $25-$65	Band leader, trombone player. Led his own band; was a responsive signer!

N

Name	Years	Price	Notes
Navarro, Theodore "Fats"	1923-1950	Price Range: Undetermined	Trumpet player.
Nichols, Red	1905-1965	Price Range: $40-$75	Cornet player.

Worked with many band leaders; participated in countless free-lance recording sessions; led his own very popular band; featured on a regular radio series and also in film.

O

Oliver, King	1885-1938	Price Range: $400-$800	Cornet player, band leader.

Worked with Kid Ory, Bill Johnson and Lawrence Duhe; outstanding composer; worked in a Savannah, Georgia fruit stall for a while and even as a pool-room attendant in his later years.

Oliver, Sy	1910-1988	Price Range: $35-$80	Composer, conductor, arranger.

Worked with Zack Whyte, Jimmie Lunceford and Tommy Dorsey; led his own band in residency in New York City during the final decades of his life.

Ory, Kid	1886-1973	Price Range: $125-$250	Trombone player, "Muskrat Ramble".

Worked with King Oliver, Louis Armstrong, Dave Peyton and Clarence Black; led his own very successful band; from 1954-1961 played at his own club in San Francisco, called On The Levee; appeared in numerous films; spent final years living in Hawaii.

P

Parker, Charlie	1920-1955	Price Range: $375-$3250	Composer, alto sax player, improviser.

Often unpredictable; an obliging signer.

Pass, Joe	1929-1994	Price Range: $20-$45	Guitarist.
Pepper, Art	1925-1982	Price Range: $35-$70	Alto sax player.
Pettiford, Oscar	1922-1960	Price Range: $45-$75	Bop bassist.
Powell, Bud	1924-1966	Price Range: $100-$200	Piano player, modern jazz pioneer.
Pullen, Don	1942-1995	Price Range: $20-$40	Percussive piano player.

R

Ra, Sun	c.1915-1993	Price Range: $25-$60	Bandleader, composer, pianist.
Rainey, Gertrude "Ma"	1886-1939	Price Range: $475-$1275	Blues singer; successful recording artist.

Headed her own show with her Georgia Jazz Band; did theater and tent shows; spent final years in Rome, Georgia.

Redmon, Don	1900-1964	Price Range: $20-$60	Composer, arranger.

Worked with Fletcher Henderson, Louis Armstrong, Jimmy Dorsey, Count Basie, and Harry James; his first band formed in 1931—long residency at Connie's Inn; featured on many radio shows; rarely played in public during his final years; responsive signer.

Reinhardt, Django	1910-1953	Price Range: $65-$125	Influential European guitarist.
Rich, Buddy	1917-1987	Price Range: $40-$150	Band leader, drummer.

Worked with Harry James, Artie Shaw, Tommy Dorsey, Benny Carter, Count Basie and Les Brown; formed his own band in 1945; had international success; appeared on many television shows; responsive signer.

Rodney, Red	1928-1994	Price Range: $20-$40	Trumpeter.
Rosolino, Frank	1926-1978	Price Range: $25-$40	Trombone player.
Rowles, Jimmy	1918-1996	Price Range: $15-$30	Composer, accompanist.

Worked with Benny Goodman, Woody Herman, Les Brown, Tommy Dorsey; active free-lancer; led own small group; played on numerous recordings.

Rushing, Jimmy	1903-1972	Price Range: $30-$60	Blues singer.

Worked with Jelly Roll Morton, Walter Page, Bennie Moten, and Count Basie; recorded with Benny Goodman, Bob Crosby and Johnny Otis; played many jazz festivals; worked regularly at the Half-Note in New York; responsive signer.

Name	Years	Price	Notes
Russell, Pee Wee	1906-1969	Price Range: $25-$50	Clarinet player.

Worked with Herb Berger, Joe Johnson, Bix Beiderbecke, Eddie Condon and Red Nichols; became critically ill in 1950 but recovered; played numerous jazz festivals; played at President Nixon's inaugural ball (1969).

S

Name	Years	Price	Notes
Sims, Zoot	1925-1985	Price Range: $30-$60	Tenor, alto sax and clarinet player.
Singleton, Zutty	1898-1975	Price Range: $25-$45	Drummer.

Worked with Louis Armstrong, Earl Hines, Dave Peyton, Fats Waller, Carroll Dickerson, Eddie Condon and Joe Marsala; led own band; often featured on Orson Welles' radio shows; appeared in a few films.

Name	Years	Price	Notes
Smith, Bessie	1894-1937	Price Range: $550-$2000	Blues singer; one of the era's highest paid artists.

Featured in the film "St. Louis Blues"; had radio series; killed in an automobile accident.

Name	Years	Price	Notes
Smith, Clarence "Pinetop"	1904-1929	Price Range: Undetermined	Boogie Woogie pioneer, piano player, singer.

Played with Ma Rainey; shot during a disagreement; a scarce signature in any form.

Name	Years	Price	Notes
Smith, Willie "The Lion"	1897-1973	Price Range: $85-$150	Stride pianist; did many free-lance recordings.

Led own band; a highly successful teacher; played numerous festivals.

Name	Years	Price	Notes
Spanier, Muggsy	1906-1967	Price Range: $40-$75	Band leader, coronet player.

Worked with Ted Lewis, Ben Pollack, Miff Mole, and Earl Hines; organized own band; appeared in a few films.

Name	Years	Price	Notes
Stitt, Sonny	1924-1982	Price Range: $20-$40	Alto, tenor sax player.
Strayhorn, Billy	1915-1967	Price Range: $40-$80	Composer, piano player.

Gifted Ellington arranger and composer; rarely appeared with orchestra in public.

T

Name	Years	Price	Notes
Tatum, Art	1910-1956	Price Range: Undetermined	Piano player; worked with Adelaide Hall.

Talented soloist; did prolific recordings later in life.

Name	Years	Price	Notes
Taylor, Art	1929-1995	Price Range: $20-$40	Bandleader, drummer.
Teagarden, Jack	1905-1964	Price Range: $75-$135	Trombone player, singer.

Worked with Doc Ross, Ben Pollack; recorded with Benny Goodman, Red Nichols, Louis Armstrong and Eddie Condon; made many free-lance recordings.

Name	Years	Price	Notes
Tough, David	1908-1948	Price Range: Undetermined	Drummer.
Tristano, Lennie	1919-1978	Price Range: Undetermined	Piano player, composer.
Turner, Joe	1911-1985	Price Range: $50-$150	Blues singer; sang with Duke Ellington's Band.

Opened Blue Room Club in Los Angeles with Pete Johnson in 1945; scored with "Chains of Love"; appeared at numerous jazz festivals.

V

Name	Years	Price	Notes
Vaughan, Sarah	1924-1990	Price Range: $50-$275	Singer.
Venuti, Joe	1903-1978	Price Range: $55-$125	Pioneer jazz violinist; MGM studio musician.

Appeared in many films; led his own band; Newport Hall of Fame (1975)

W

Name	Years	Price	Notes
Walker, T-Bone	1910-1975	Price Range: $50-$125	Electric guitar pioneer.

Made record debut as "Oak-cliff T-Bone"; worked with Ma Rainey and Les Hite; worked long solo residences in Los Angeles.

Name	Years	Price	Notes
Waller, Thomas "Fats"	1904-1943	Price Range: $350-$800	Piano player, composer, singer.

Began recording career in 1922; collaborated successfully with lyricist Andy Razaf; worked with James P. Johnson, Fletcher Henderson, Jack Teagarden, and Ted Lewis; had his own CBS radio show; made several films; responsive signer with very legible and distinct signature; key letter formations "F" and the "W."

Name	Years	Price	Notes
Washington, Dinah	1924-1963	Price Range: $140-$225	Singer.
Waters, Ethel	1896-1977	Price Range: $50-$175	Jazz and blues singer.

Very successful recording artist; recorded with Duke Ellington and Benny Goodman; worked as film actress and appeared on television.

Watson, Johnny	1935-1996	Price Range: $25-$125	Guitarist (R&B).
Webb, Chick		1902-1939	Price Range: Undetermined

Band leader, drummer; led the Harlem Stompers. Appeared often at the Savoy Ballroom; worked with Ella Fitzgerald; died young and his signature in any form is difficult to find.

Webster, Ben	1909-1973	Price Range: $140-$250	Tenor sax player.

Worked with Bennie Moten, Fletcher Henderson, Benny Carter, Cab Calloway and Duke Ellington; led his own small groups; appeared often in New York; moved to Copenhagen in the late 1960s.

Whiteman, Paul	1890-1967	Price Range: $70-$240	Orchestra leader.

Employed numerous successful solo artists including Bix Beiderbecke, Tommy & Jimmy Dorsey and Joe Venuti; also featured vocalists Bing Crosby and Mildred Bailey; featured in many films.

Williams, Charles "Cootie"	1910-1985	Price Range: Undetermined	Band leader, trumpet player.

Played with Chick Webb, Fletcher Henderson, Duke Ellington and Benny Goodman; formed own big band.

Williams, Mary Lou	1914-1981	Price Range: Undetermined	Composer, piano player.

Arranged for Benny Goodman, Louis Armstrong (band), Earl Hines, Tommy Dorsey and many others; featured in many jazz festivals.

Wilson, Teddy	1912-1986	Price Range: $50-$125	Composer, piano player.

Worked with Louis Armstrong, Jimmie Noone, Benny Carter and Benny Goodman; recorded with Billie Holiday; led his own big band; gifted teacher.

Winding, Kai	1922-1983	Price Range: Undetermined	Composer, trombone player.

Y

Yancey, Jimmy	1894-1951	Price Range: Undetermined	Piano player.

Worked for many years as a groundsman at Comiskey Park; worked often around the Chicago area; suffered from diabetes later in life

Young, Lester "Prez" & "Red"	1909-1959	Price Range: $90-$175	Composer, tenor sax player.

Worked with Bennie Moten, King Oliver, Count Basie, and Fletcher Henderson; recorded with Billie Holiday; suffered from poor health for over a decade; worked in his later years as a soloist.

Note: For updated pricing refer to *The Standard Guide to Collecting Autographs*. Prices have been included only in this section to give better perspective to a misunderstood area of collecting.

Nobel Peace Prize Winners

The Nobel Prizes, first awarded in 1901, were created through a bequest of $9.2 million from Alfred B. Nobel (1833-1896) and by a gift from the Bank of Sweden. A Swedish chemical engineer, Nobel was the inventor of dynamite and other explosives. In his will, Nobel directed that the interest from the fund be divided among people who have made significant discoveries or inventions in the fields of chemistry, medicine and physics. He also singled out authors, "who produce the most outstanding work of an idealistic tendency" and peacemakers, "who have done the most or the best work for fraternity between nations, for the abolition or reduction of standing armies and for the holding and promotion of peace congresses." On the 300th anniversary of the Bank of Sweden (1968), an additional annual prize was added for outstanding work in the economic sciences and was awarded the following year.

The prizes continue to be funded today, through the assistance of the Bank of Sweden. The Royal Swedish Academy of Sciences in Stockholm makes the decisions in the field of chemistry, economics and physics, while the Nobel Assembly at the Karolinka Insititute in Stockholm chooses the recipients for physiology and medicine. The award for literature is chosen by the Swedish Academy, Stockholm, and the choice for peace made by the Norwegian Nobel Committee in Oslo.

The annual prizes are awarded on December 10, the anniversary of Nobel's death. All of the prizes are presented by the King of Sweden in Stockholm, except the peace prize which is given in Oslo. The interest from the fund is what determines the amount of the awards. In 1998, it was approximately $1 million for each recipient. Each winner receives a diploma, a gold medal and a gift of money during a formal ceremony.

Collecting the signatures of Nobel Peace Prize recipients has grown in popularity over the past few decades. While collecting the signatures of those winners in other fields is certainly a viable option, the charter of the peace award, as well as the notoriety given the recipient seems to attract the majority of autograph collectors.

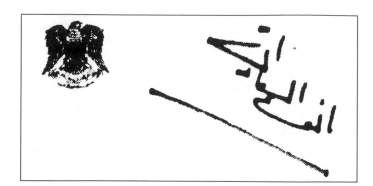

Anwar Sadat

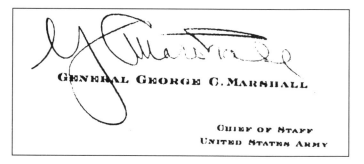

Martin Luther King, Jr.

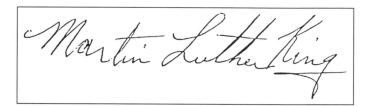

George C. Marshall

Brisquier avec mes bonnes pensées
albert Schweitzer

Albert Schweitzer

MEMOIRS

MIKHAIL GORBACHEV

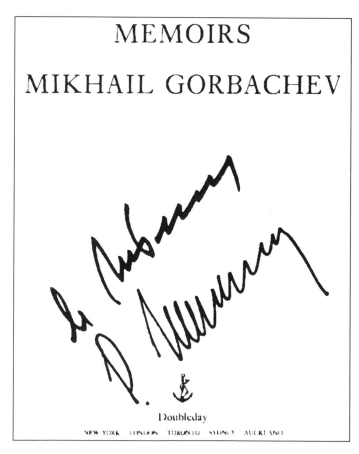

Doubleday

NEW YORK   LONDON   TORONTO   SYDNEY   AUCKLAND

Mikhail Gorbachev

February 3...1908.

Approved in accordance with the provisions of Section 28 of the Act of April 26, 1906 (34 Stat.L., 137), provided that it may be terminated at any time in the discretion of the Secretary of the Interior.

T. Roosevelt

Theodore Roosevelt

Nobel Peace Prize Recipients

Year	Winner	Country	Comments
1997	The Inter. Campaign to Ban Landmines, Jody Williams	U.S.	J. Williams has been an obliging signer.
1996	Bishop Carlos X. Belo	Australia	
	Jose Ramos-Horta	E. Timor	
1995	Joseph Rotblat	U.K.	
1994	Yitzhak Rabin	Israel	Rabin was always an obliging signer.
	Shimon Peres	Israel	An obliging signer.
	Yasir Arafat	PLO	A tough signature!
1993	Pres. F. W. de Klerk		
	Nelson Mandela	South Africa	Has always been a tough signature!
1992	Rigoberta Menchu	Guatemala	
1991	Daw Aung San Suu Kyi	Myanmar	
1990	Mikhail S. Gorbachev	USSR	Signs for the mighty dollar!
1989	Dalai Lama	Tibet	A very tough signature!
1988	United Nations Peacekeeping Forces		
1987	Oscar Arias Sanchez	Costa Rica	
1986	Elie Wiesel	Rom./U.S.	A very responsive signer!
1985	Inter. Phys. for the Prev. of Nucl. War	U.S.	
1984	Bishop Desmond Tutu	S. Africa	A very responsive signer!
1983	Lech Walesa	Poland	Was elusive for years, but has begun signing again!
1982	Alva Myrdal	Sweden	
	Alfonso Garcia Robels	Mexico	
1981	Off. of U.N. High Commis. for Refugees		
1980	Adolfo Perez Esquivel	Argentina	
1979	Mother Teresa of Calcutta	India	Always responsive to autograph requests!
1978	Anwar Sadat	Egypt	Was always a very tough signature!
	Menachem Begin	Israel	Occasionally responsive to requests.
1977	Amnesty International		
1976	Mairead Corrigan	N. Ireland	
	Betty Williams	N. Ireland	
1975	Andrei Sakharov	USSR	A very elusive signature!
1974	Eisaku Sato	Japan	
	Sean MacBride	Ireland	
1973	Henry Kissinger	U.S.	A notorious non-signer!
	Le Duc Tho (Prize declined)	N. Vietnam	
1971	Willy Brandt	W. Germany	A responsive signer!
1970	Norman E. Borlaug	U.S.	
1969	International Labor Organization		
1968	Rene Cassin	France	An inexpensive signature!
1965	U.N. Children's Fund (UNICEF)		
1964	Martin Luther King Jr.	U.S.	A very valuable and elusive signature!
1963	International Red Cross (League of Red Cross Societies)		
1962	Linus C. Pauling	U.S.	Was always a very responsive signer!
1961	Dag Hammarskjold	Sweden	Was a responsive signer!
1960	Albert J. Luthuli	S. Africa	
1959	Philip J. Noel-Baker	British	An inexpensive signature!
1958	Georges Pire	Belgium	
1957	Lester B. Pearson	Canada	An inexpensive signature!
1954	Office of the U.N. High Commis. for Refugees		
1953	George C. Marshall	U.S.	A responsive signer!
1952	Albert Schweitzer	France	Diff. in auth. form! Lots of ghost-signed ex.!
1951	Leon Jouhaux	France	

Nobel Peace Prize Recipients (continued)

Year	Recipient	Country	Note
1950	Ralph J. Bunche	U.S.	Was a responsive signer!
1949	Lord John Boyd Orr of Brechin Mearns	Great Britain	
1947	Friends Service Council	Great Britain	
	American Friends Service Commission	U.S.	
1946	Emily G. Balch	U.S.	
	John R. Mott	U.S.	An inexpensive signature!
1945	Cordell Hull	U.S.	Was a responsive signer!
1944	International Red Cross		
1938	Nansen Int. Off. for Refugees		
1937	Viscount Cecil of Chelwood	Great Britain	
1936	Carlos de Saavedra Lamas	Argentina	
1935	Carl von Ossietzky	Germany	
1934	Arthur Henderson	Great Britain	
1933	Sir Norman Angell	Great Britain	
1931	Jane Addams	U.S.	Cons. inter. in her work is beg. to raise prices!
	Nicholas Murray Butler	U.S.	
1930	Nathan Soderblom	Sweden	
1929	Frank B. Kellogg	U.S.	Was a responsive signer!
1927	Ferdinand E. Buisson	France	
	Ludwig Quidde	Germany	
1926	Aristide Briand	France	
	Gustav Stresemann	Germany	
1925	Sir J. Austen Chamberlain	G. Britain	Still an inexpensive signature!
	Charles G. Dawes	U.S.	Material routinely available.
1922	Fridtjof Nansen	Norway	
1921	Karl H. Branting	Sweden	
	Christiain L. Lange	Norway	
1920	Leon V. A. Bourgeois	France	
1919	Woodrow Wilson	U.S.	Material routinely available!
1917	International Red Cross		
1913	Henri La Fontaine	Belgium	
1912	Elihu Root	U.S.	Was a very responsive signer!
1911	Tobias M. C. Beernaert	Belgium	
	Alfred H. Fried	Austria	
1910	Permanent Inter. Peace Bureau		
1909	Auguste M. F. Beernaert	Belgium	
	Paul H. G. G. d'Estournelles de Constant	France	
1908	Klas P. Arnoldson	Sweden	
	Fredrik Bajer	Denmark	
1907	Ernesto T. Moneta	Italy	
	Louis Renault	France	An inexpensive signature!
1906	Theodore Roosevelt	U.S.	Material routinely available!
1905	Baroness Bertha von Suttner	Austria	
1904	Institute of International Law		
1903	Sir William R. Cremer	Great Britain	
1902	Elie Ducommun	Switzerland	
	Charles A. Gobat	Switzerland	
1901	Jean H. Dunant	Switzerland	
	Frederic Passy	France	

Note:

There were no awards given for the years omitted (1940-1942). The official web site for the awards is http://www.nobel.se/.

On The Ballot

Many outstanding Americans have run for President of the United States, but not all have been elected to the cherished office. Signatures of those who ran but lost are an interesting and fun set to collect. Yes, I realize that nobody ever remembers who came in second and that some of these individuals did go on to eventually win the office, but how about those who did not? Not only were some of these individuals extremely popular, but many historians have often pondered the "what if?" question. Where would America have been if Henry Clay had defeated Andrew Jackson, or if Thomas Dewey had defeated Franklin Roosevelt?

Those Who Lost A Presidential Election

Aaron Burr

Year	Candidate, DOB/DOD	Party	Winner
1796	Thomas Pinckney, 1750-1828	Federalist	J. Adams

Comments:
His signature appears periodically in the autograph market; Governor of South Carolina (1787-89); U.S. minister to Great Britain (1792-94); diplomat; USHR (1797-1801); major general; brother of Charles.

1800 — Aaron Burr, 1756-1836 — Dem./Rep. — T. Jefferson

Comments:
The signature of Aaron Burr, once generally available, now periodically surfaces in the market; when they are found it is often in the form of a check. USS (1791-97); vice president of the U.S. (1801-05); mortally wounded Alexander Hamilton in a duel (1804); arrested and acquitted (1807).

1804 — Charles C. Pinckney, 1746-1825 — Federalist — T. Jefferson

Comments:
The signature of Charles C. Pinckney appears occasionally in the autograph market. Since he signed the Constitution his holograph is always in demand; aide to George Washington; brigadier general; member Constitutional Convention; minister to France (1796); brother of Thomas.

George Clinton

1808 — George Clinton, 1739-1812 — Dem./Rep. — J. Madison

Comments:
His signature has been periodically available to collectors, often in document form; Continental Congress (1775); brigadier general; Governor of New York (1777-95, 1801-04); vice president of U.S. (1805-12)

1812 — DeWitt Clinton, 1769-1828 — Dem./Rep. — J. Madison

Comments:
His signature appears periodically in theautograph market and is also expensive; USS (1802-03), mayor of New York City; governor of New York (1817-23, 1825-28).

Year	Candidate, DOB/DOD	Party	Winner
1816	Rufus King, 1755-1827	Federalist	J. Monroe

Comments:
His signature is periodically offered for sale by autograph dealers; member Continental Congress (1784-87); signed Constitution; USS (1789-96, 1813-25); U.S. minister to Great Britain (1796-1803, 1825-26).

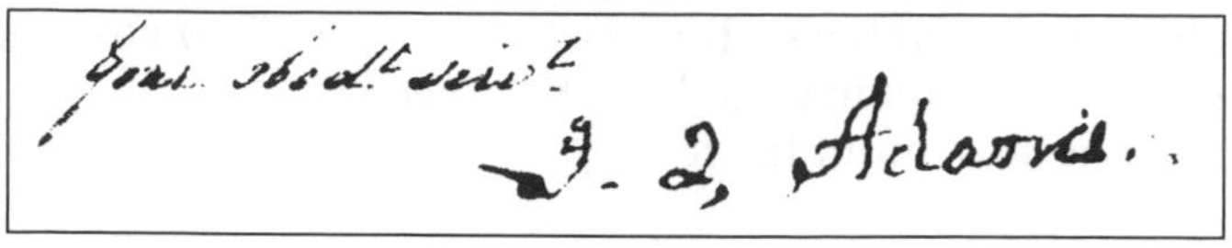

John Quincy Adams

1820	John Quincy Adams, 1767-1848	Federalist	J. Monroe

(See U.S. Presidents)

1824	William H. Crawford, 1772-1834	Dem./Rep.	J.Q. Adams

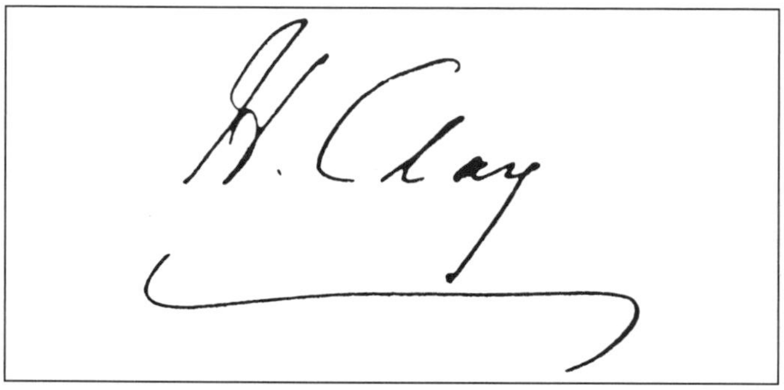

Henry Clay

	Henry Clay, 1777-1852	Dem./Rep.	J.Q. Adams

Comments:
The signature of the "Great Pacificator" appears periodically in the market and often in the form of legal documents; USS (1806-07, 1810-11); USHR (1811-14, 1815-21, 1823-25); U.S. secretary of state (1825-29), USS (1831-42).

1828	John Quincy Adams, 1767-1848	Federalist	A. Jackson

(See U.S. Presidents)

1832	Henry Clay, 1777-1852	Dem. Rep.	A. Jackson

Comments:
The signature of the "Great Pacificator" appears periodically in the market and often in the form of legal documents; USS (1806-07, 1810-11); USHR (1811-14, 1815-21, 1823-25); U.S. secretary of state (1825-29), USS (1831-42).

Daniel Webster

1836	Daniel Webster, 1782-1852	Whig	M. Van Buren

Comments:
The signature of this lawyer and statesman appears regularly in autograph dealer catalogs; USHR (1813-17, 1823-27); USS (1827-41); U.S. secretary of state (1841-43, 1850-52). All material surrounding his arguments in front of the Supreme Court are highly sought by collectors.

	Hugh L. White, 1773-1840	Whig	M. Van Buren

Comments:
The signature of this lawyer and politician is rare; USS (1825-40).

Year	Candidate, DOB/DOD	Party	Winner
1840	James G. Birney, 1792-1857	Liberty *	W.H. Harrison

Comments:
The signature of this antislavery leader is rare; founded KY Anti-slavery Society (1835); published Philanthropist (1836-37).

Year	Candidate, DOB/DOD	Party	Winner
1844	James G. Birney, 1792-1857	Liberty *	J. Polk

Comments:
The signature of this antislavery leader is rare; founded KY Anti-slavery Society (1835); published Philanthropist (1836-37).

	Candidate, DOB/DOD	Party	Winner
	Henry Clay, 1777-1852	Dem./Rep.	J. Polk

The signature of the "Great Pacificator" appears periodically in the market and often in the form of legal documents; USS (1806-07, 1810-11); USHR (1811-14, 1815-21, 1823-25); U.S. secretary of state (1825-29), USS (1831-42).

Year	Candidate, DOB/DOD	Party	Winner
1848	Lewis Cass, 1782-1866	Whig	Z. Taylor

His signature appears periodically in autograph dealer catalogs; brigadier general; U.S. secretary of war (1831-36); U.S. minister to France (1836-42); USS (1845-48); USS (1849-57); U.S. secretary of state (1857-60)

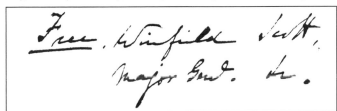

Daniel Webster

Year	Candidate, DOB/DOD	Party	Winner
1852	Winfield Scott, 1786-1866	Whig	F. Pierce

Comments:
The signature of "Old Fuss and Feathers" appears periodically in autograph dealer catalogs; commander in Mexican War; lieutenant general (1852).

John C. Fremont

Year	Candidate, DOB/DOD	Party	Winner
1856	John C. Fremont, 1813-1890	Rep.	J. Buchanan

Comments:
An explorer, army officer and politician, he was a prolific writer, thus his signature is common; USS (1850-51); major general in Civil War; governor Territory of Arizona.

Stephen A. Douglas

Year	Candidate, DOB/DOD	Party	Winner
1860	Stephen A. Douglas, 1813-1861	Dem.	A. Lincoln

Comments:
His signature, when included in many autograph catalogs, is found in document form. Most letters have been purchased by institutions; USHR (1843-47); USS (1847-61).

	Candidate, DOB/DOD	Party	Winner
	John C. Breckenridge, 1821-1875	S. Dem.	A. Lincoln

Comments:
His signature surfaces periodically in the autograph market; USHR (1851-55); vice president of U.S. (1857-61); USS (1861); major general CSA (1862); secretary of war CSA (1865).

Year	Candidate, DOB/DOD	Party	Winner
	John Bell, 1797-1869	Const. Un.	A. Lincoln

Comments:

His signature surfaces on occasion in the autograph market; USHR (1827-41); speaker (1833-35); U.S. secretary of war (1841); USS (1847-59).

| **1864** | George McClellan, 1826-1885 | Dem. | A. Lincoln |

Comments:

His signature surfaces periodically in the autograph market; buyers should be cautious of forgeries; major general (1861); Governor of New Jersey (1878-81).

| **1868** | Horatio Seymour, 1810-1886 | Dem. | U.S. Grant |

Comments:

Has been a scarce signature for a long period of time; governor of New York (1853-55, 1863-65).

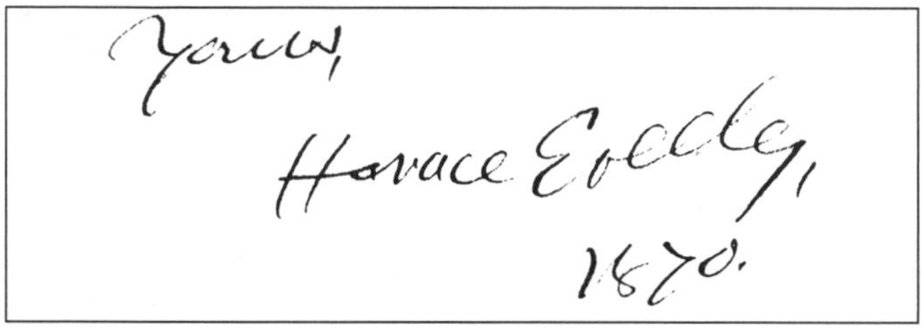

Horace Greeley

| **1872** | Horace Greeley, 1811-1872 | Dem./Lib. R. | U.S. Grant |

Comments:

Greeley's handwriting is often indecipherable and letters can confuse many as to the content; founded and edited The New Yorker (1834-41); founded New York Tribune (1841). His material is frequently offered in dealer catalogs.

| | Victoria C. Woodhull, 1838-1927 | Equal Rights | U.S. Grant |

Comments:

Her signature surfaces occasionally in the market and has shown significant appreciation in recent years. Her work as an American reformer is now highly respected.

| **1876** | Samuel J. Tilden, 1814-1886 | Dem. | R. B. Hayes |

Comments:

His signature surfaces periodically in the market; governor of New York (1875-76).

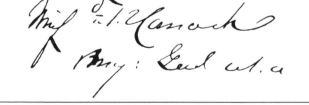

Winfield S. Hancock

| **1880** | Winfield S. Hancock, 1824-1886 | Dem. | J. Garfield |

Comments:

His signature surfaces periodically in the market; brigadier general; major general (1862); commander of II Corps, Army of the Potomac (1863-65).

| **1884** | James G. Blaine, 1830-1893 | Rep. | G. Cleveland |

Comments:

His signature still surfaces regularly in the market; USHR (1863-76); speaker; USS (1876-81); U.S. secretary of state (1881, 1889-92).

Grover Cleveland

Year	Candidate, DOB/DOD	Party	Winner
1888	Grover Cleveland, 1837-1908	Dem.	B. Harrison
(See U.S. Presidents)			
	Belva A. Lockwood, 1830-1917	Equal Rights	B. Harrison

Comments:
A scarce signature in any form; lawyer; first woman admitted to practice before U.S. Supreme Court (1879); U.S. delegate to peace congress in Europe (1906, 08, 11).

1892	Benjamin Harrison, 1833-1901	Dem.	G. Cleveland

Benjamin Harrison

(See U.S. Presidents)

	James B. Weaver, 1833-1912	People's **	G. Cleveland

Comments:
A scarce signature, that like so many others does surface on occasion; brevet brigadier general (1864); USHR (1879-81).

William Jennings Bryan

Year	Candidate, DOB/DOD	Party	Winner
1896	William J. Bryan, 1860-1925	Dem.	W. McKinley

Comments:
Has been available in many forms in the market and remains popular with certain dealers; USHR (1891-95); U.S. secretary of state (1913-15); notable courtroom debate with Clarence Darrow (1925).

	Eugene V. Debs, 1855-1926	Socialist	W. McKinley

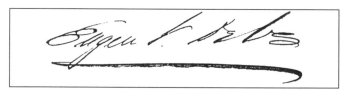

Eugene V. Debs

Comments:
A hard-to-find signature that does surface periodically. You'll need patience to acquire an example; founder and first president of American Railway Union (1893); Organized Social Democratic party of America (1897); indicted for violation of Espionage Act (1918), convicted, sentenced, later released by a Presidential order.

1900	William J. Bryan, 1860-1925	Dem.	T. Roosevelt

Comments:
Has been available in many forms in the market and remains popular with certain dealers; USHR (1891-95); U.S. secretary of state (1913-15); notable courtroom debate with Clarence Darrow (1925).

1904	Alton B. Parker, 1852-1926	Dem.	T. Roosevelt

Comments:
A very elusive signature and far harder to acquire than one might anticipate; well-known jurist in New York courts.

1908	William J. Bryan, 1860-1925	Dem.	W.H. Taft

Comments:
Has been available in many forms in the market and remains popular with certain dealers; USHR (1891-95); U.S. secretary of state (1913-15); notable courtroom debate with Clarence Darrow (1925).

Year	Candidate, DOB/DOD	Party	Winner
1912	Theodore Roosevelt, 1858-1919	Bull Moose	W. Wilson

(See U.S. Presidents)

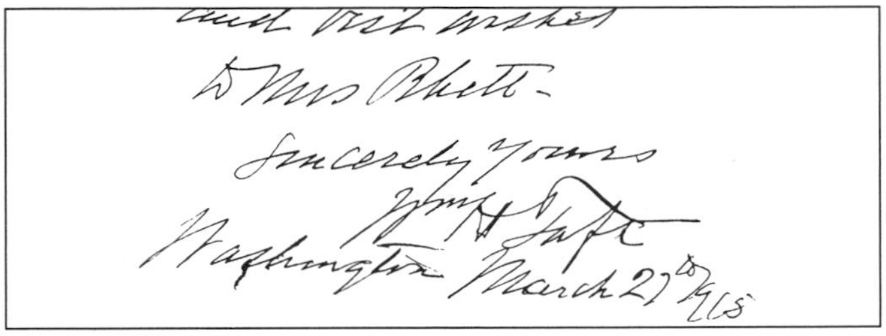

William H. Taft

	William H. Taft, 1857-1930	Rep.	W. Wilson

(See U.S. Presidents)

Charles Evans Hughes

1916	Charles E. Hughes, 1862-1948	Rep.	W. Wilson

Comments:
Sought by Supreme Court collectors he was a prolific writer and his material is considered common; governor of New York (1907-10); associate justice U.S. Supreme Court (1910-16); U.S. secretary of state (1921-25); member of Hague Tribunal (1926-30); Chief justice U.S. Supreme Court (1930-41).

1920	James M. Cox, 1870-1957	Dem.	W. Harding

Comments:
Was once generally available, however has surfaced far less in recent years; newspaper publisher; USHR (1909-13); Governor of Ohio (1913-15, 17-21).

1924	John W. Davis, 1873-1955	Dem.	C. Coolidge

Comments:
Surface periodically in the market and remains an inexpensive signature; USHR (1911-13); U.S. solicitor general (1913-18); U.S. ambassador to Great Britain (1918-21).

	Robert M. La Follette, 1855-1925	Progressive	C. Coolidge

Comments:
Was once generally available, however has surfaced far less in recent years; USHR (1885-91); Governor of Wisconsin (1900-06).

	William Z. Foster, 1881-1961	Communist	C. Coolidge

Comments:
Was once generally available, however has surfaced far less in recent years; author; active in Communist party.

1928	Alfred E. Smith, 1873-1944	Dem.	H. Hoover

Comments:
Available to collectors in many forms; governor of New York (1919-20, 23-28).

	Norman Thomas, 1884-1969	Socialist	H. Hoover

Comments:
Available to collectors in many forms; author; helped found American Civil Liberties Union (1920); chairman of Postwar (WWII) World Council.

Herbert Hoover

Year	Candidate, DOB/DOD	Party	Winner
1932	Herbert Hoover, 1874-1964	Rep.	F. Roosevelt

(See U.S. Presidents)

1936	Alfred M. Landon, 1887-1987	Rep.	F. Roosevelt

Comments:
Although his material appears in many dealer catalogs, he was not responsive to autograph requests in his later years—or at least I never had any luck.

	Earl R. Browder, 1891-1973	Communist	F. Roosevelt

Comments:
Available to collectors in many forms and also inexpensive.

1940	Wendell Wilkie, 1892-1944	Rep.	F. Roosevelt

Comments:
Available to collectors in many forms.

1944	Thomas E. Dewey, 1902-1971	Rep.	F. Roosevelt

Comments:
Available to collectors in many forms; governor of New York (1943-55).

	Gerald L.K. Smith, 1898-1976	America 1st	F. Roosevelt

Comments:
A lot tougher to find than one might think!

1948	J. Strom Thurmond, 1902-	States Rights	H. Truman

Comments:
Lots of examples, many autopen, available to collectors; USS.

	Henry A. Wallace, 1888-1965	Progressive	H. Truman

Comments:
Generally available with patience; editor; secretary of agriculture (1933-40); vice president of U.S. (1941-45); secretary of commerce (1945-46).

1952	Adlai E. Stevenson, 1900-1965	Dem.	D. Eisenhower

Comments:
Can still be found in the market in various forms.

	Douglas MacArthur, 1880-1964	America 1st	D. Eisenhower

Comments:
Very popular with both dealers and collectors, his autographed material is common in market catalogs. His signature is not inexpensive!

1956	Adlai E. Stevenson, 1900-1965	Dem.	D. Eisenhower

Comments:
Was responsive to autograph requests; governor of Illinois (1949-53); U.S. ambassador to UN (1961-65).

Richard Nixon

1960	Richard M. Nixon, 1913-1994	Rep.	J. F. Kennedy

(See U.S. Presidents)

Year	Candidate, DOB/DOD	Party	Winner
1964	Barry Goldwater, 1902-1998	Rep.	L.B. Johnson

Comments:

Very responsive to autograph requests during his retirement; USS.

1968	Hubert H. Humphrey, 1911-1978	Dem.	R.M. Nixon

Comments:

Lots of machine-signed signatures, so be careful! HHH was responsive to in-person requests for his signature; USS (1949-64, 70-78); U.S. vice president (1965-69).

	George C. Wallace, 1919-1998	Amer. Indep.	R.M. Nixon

Comments:

Very responsive to autograph requests during his retirement. His autograph changed dramatically near the end of his life; governor of Alabama.

1972	George S. McGovern, 1922-	Dem.	R.M. Nixon

Comments:

Very responsive to autograph requests now; USS.

Gerald Ford

1976	Gerald R. Ford, 1913-	Rep.	J.E. Carter

(See U.S. Presidents)

Jimmy Carter

1980	Jimmy Carter, 1924-	Dem.	R.W. Reagan

(See U.S. Presidents)

	John B. Anderson, 1922-	Indep.	R.W. Reagan

Comments:

Lots of facsimile signatures while he was running for office, but is now very responsive to autograph requests.

1984	Walter F. Mondale, 1928-	Dem.	R.W. Reagan

Comments:

A responsive signer in-person, but often machine-signed through the mail.

1988	Michael Dukakis, 1933-	Dem.	G.H.W. Bush

Comments:

An obliging signer, in-person or through request by mail, of an illegible autograph.

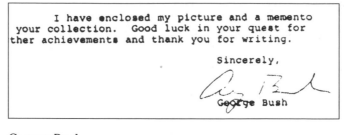

> I have enclosed my picture and a memento
> your collection. Good luck in your quest for
> ther achievements and thank you for writing.
>
>   Sincerely,
>
>   *George Bush*

George Bush

Year	Candidate, DOB/DOD	Party	Winner
1992	George H.W. Bush	Rep.	W.J. Clinton
(See U.S. Presidents)			
1996	Robert Dole	Rep.	W. J. Clinton

Comments:
An obliging signer in-person, but numerous machine-signed items routinely find their way into the autograph market.
Could be a sleeper if his next title is First Gentleman!
*—Prohibitionist, **—Populist,

From the Oval Office

This set of autograph subjects has always been popular with collectors and should remain so through the next millenium. Naturally as our country gets older many of the earlier pieces will increase in value. So when collecting presidential signatures beware of forgeries, secretarial signatures, and autopens. Take the time to do some research.

Presidential Overview

George Washington

With his attractive calligraphy, prolific and insightful output, George Washington, who seldom signed his full name—opting instead for "Go. Washington", was a prolific president. The variance in content of his letters is best reflected in the exponential price ranges they command. Thus each individual letter from Washington will necessitate some research to accurately determine price. Washington, extraordinary during his own era and extremely popular, will not be as common as one might think in a clipped signature form. Generally these will only appear in the market when an established collector is trying to upgrade his set or a lazy forger is trying to pass off his latest creation. Washington forgeries are common and often examples done by Robert Spring (mid 1800s) or later those of Joseph Cosey. Collectors are advised to seek the tremendous research materials published by autograph sleuth and collecting pioneer Charles Hamilton for further information on bogus Washington examples.

Worth noting is that Alexander Hamilton acted as Washington's secretary during the Revolutionary War. Therefore, many LS examples found were actually

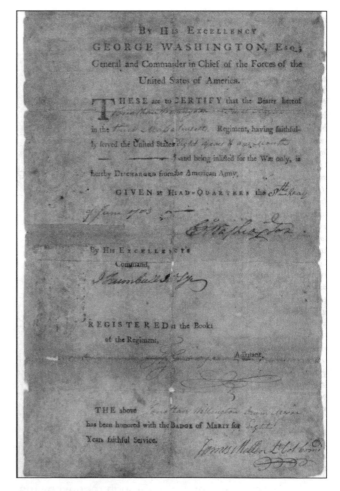

George Washington

penned by the future president. Washington did personally sign all war discharges, however, finding an example in "investment" condition is difficult.

Although the language of diplomacy during this era was French, Washington never learned the language and did not attend a university.

Johns Adams

John Adams

Prolific and insightful, the letters of John Adams typically exemplify an asymmetric quality to his calligraphy. Size and character formations vary regularly, with his signature decreasing in proportion and legibility with age. Considered by many to be the rarest of the early Presidents, term dated material is scarce and certainly attributable to his single service in office. His hands shook with palsy by the time he became president. The transformation in his signature, to nearly illegible prior to his death, has led to much confusion among collectors. Adams was a voracious reader and often added handwritten notes in the margins of his books. He was also a prolific writer and diarist, recording the many details of the people he met and the places he visited. Common forms: "John Adams", "J. Adams".

Thomas Jefferson, DS, 1779, Appointment of a bobacco inspector.

Thomas Jefferson

Consistent and often fascinating in content, the letters of Thomas Jefferson are highly sought by both collectors and institutions. His handwriting varied little over his life. Similar to Washington, authentic clipped signatures remain scarce and enter the market typically when collections are upgraded. Forgeries are

Thomas Jefferson, 1791, Congressional Act, beautifully framed.

common, especially with regard to signatures and handwritten letters. Many of the Jefferson documents that appear in the market are land grants or ships' papers, some of which also bear the signature of James Madison. Although Jefferson also wrote in French—he also knew Greek and Latin, few examples of such are rare domestically. He was a meticulous record keeper and an avid book collector. In fact, a library of his books was sold to the government after the British destroyed the Library of Congress. Perfect copies of much of Jefferson's correspondence were created through the use of a polygraph that reproduced precisely the hand movements of a writer. Common form: "Th. Jefferson".

James Madison

James Madison

The letters and documents of the "Father of the Constitution" are in great demand by both collectors and institutions. While insightful handwritten letters are rare, even his prolific and mundane correspondence is getting increasingly difficult to acquire. Tremulous later examples are common as an arthritic Madison fought valiantly against the disease. His wife Dolley authored many a letter for her suffering husband during the latter years, most of which were adorned by his print-like signature. Many ships' papers, bearing both Madison and Monroe signatures, have been available to collectors throughout the years, with even a few franks surfacing. Military commissions and land grants are two other viable alternatives for acquiring his authentic signature. Be wary of cuts and exercise all the typical cautions associated with such a purchase. Madison was crippled by rheumatism during the last six months of his life and confined to his room. Madison kept a comprehensive journal on the Constitutional Convention and was also proficient in Latin. Common form: "J. Madison" (exception legal documents), rare as "James Madison, Jr."

James Monroe

James Monroe

Succinct and often routine, the letters of James Monroe exhibit many handwriting variances over his lifetime. Examples of his authentic signature can still be found in many forms especially documents such as land grants. It was common for land to be transacted in lieu of cash during his era. Monroe had the uncommon proclivity of having his handwriting increase in size over the body of a correspondence and similar to other presidents, his script lost legibility due to age. Unlike many presidents, his writings rarely mentioned his religious faith. Common form: "James Monroe", also "J. Monroe", rare in other forms.

John Quincy Adams

John Quincy Adams

Similar to his father, Adams' handwriting transformed with age due to illness. While his early correspondence is consistent, insightful, small and legible, the latter was in stark contrast. Adams was also a poet, and while an occasional manuscript poem may be unearthed, it is now uncommon. Having been a single term president, that lends itself to the rarity of associated material, although alternatives are certainly available to collectors in the form of documents, such as land grants and even an occasional frank. Daniel Brent was Adams' secretary and his handwriting bore a stark similarity to the president, thus determining an ALS from a DS might provide collectors with a research challenge. Adams was proficient in a number of languages including Latin, Greek, Dutch, French and somewhat with Spanish. He was also the only former president to serve as a U.S. representative. Common forms: "John Quincy Adams", "J.Q. Adams" and later "J.Q.A".

Andrew Jackson

Andrew Jackson

Although the eloquence of his letters is far cry from his predecessors, Andrew Jackson's bold and succinct correspondence with its large signatures are attractive to collectors. A truly charismatic figure, Jackson's candid letters often contained a fair share of spelling and grammatical errors, however, few could claim it detracted from his message. While his handwriting and typical full signature changed little throughout his life, he did much to alter the signing habits of the presidency. Jackson discontinued signing land grants during his second term and bequeathed much of his signatory power to liberate himself from administrative details. Andrew Jackson Donelson, the president's nephew and secretary, handled many of these tasks that over time have led to much identification confusion in the autograph market. From bank checks to land grants, Donelson adequately adorned the signature of his uncle as needed. Collectors are advised to exercise caution when purchasing any Jackson autographed second term items. Common form: "Andrew Jackson"—bold.

Martin Van Buren

Although the first president born an American citizen had the capability to fire off an insightful correspondence, Van Buren seldom utilized this talent. Instead he opted for politically correct and often mundane communications. His script also transformed from small and legible to large and often unintelligible with age. Unfortunately for collectors, examples of his

Martin Van Buren

signatures are scarce in many forms and will require some patience before certain items find their way into the market. Likely this will be a document signed by Van Buren as Andrew Jackson's Secretary of State. As a youth Van Buren studied at the law firm of Francis Sylvester and often had the duty of making copies of documents. Collectors should pay particular attention to Van Buren land grants, which often bear proxy signatures. Common forms: "M. Van Buren", "M.V.B." or "M.V. Buren".

William Henry Harrison

William Henry Harrison

The most difficult signature to obtain on material authored while he was in the oval office, William Henry Harrison reflects a dichotomy of sorts as his non-presidential autographs are fairly common. Harrison's handwriting evolved during his life and reached its pinnacle in form and substance during his quest for the presidency. Common forms: "Wm. H. Harrison", "Willm. Henry Harrison" and "W.H. Harrison".

John Tyler

John Tyler

Following the death of William Henry Harrison, John Tyler became the first vice president to assume the Oval Office. Tyler brought to the office greater administrative control and took great comfort in handling most of his correspondence. Typically his letters varied in length, legibility and content due to both his attitude and the materials he chose to write with. His often succinct and forceful script is best exemplified with examples during his term in office, with the most revealing in content those to his friends and relatives. While both handwritten letters and franks are somewhat common, documents and signed letters can be more elusive. Characteristic of his signature is the addition of a decorative line to which a date is often added nearby. During his last years he served as chancellor of his alma mater, the College of William and Mary. Tyler was the only president to join the Confederacy. Advanced autograph collectors should pay particular attention to Tyler land grants, which often bear proxy signatures. Common form: "J. Tyler".

J.K. Polk

James Know Polk

The eleventh President of the United States, James K. Polk, a former House Speaker and Governor of Tennessee, is perhaps most commonly associated with his elaborate, distinctive and often embellished signature. Of the documents that have surfaced in the market, appointments which often include the signature of Secretary of State James Buchanan, have drawn interest. Handwritten letters as Speaker of the House, and Congressman have also surfaced, while term-related pieces remain elusive. Dictated letters also remain evasive, a few impressive multiple page early legal documents have found themselves in collector hands in the past five years. Considered by many historians as the greatest one-term president, it remains a shock to many that his writings do not command a greater price in the autograph market. Common form: "James K. Polk"

Zachary Taylor

Serving only fifteen months in office before his death, Zachary Taylor presidential autographed material presents a significant acquisition challenge for the collector. Surfaced pre-presidential autographed items have been typically signed

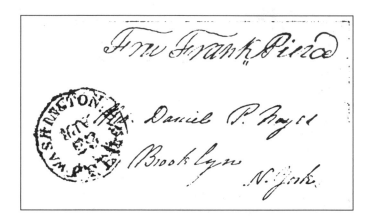

Zachary Taylor

documents. Bold, clean, and attractive handwritten letters, particularly those substantive in content remain elusive and in demand. Taylor at his literary finest, is represented best in correspondence during his Indian-fighting days. "Old Rough and Ready" fought in the War of 1812, the Black Hawk War and the Seminole War. He was a poor speller during his entire life. Common forms: "Z. Taylor"

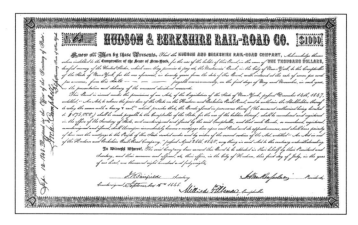

Millard Fillmore, DS, 1848, railroad coupon bond.

Millard Fillmore

Upon Zachary Taylor's death in 1850, Whig party member and vice-president Millard Fillmore became our 13th President. A prolific person who penned precise, prudent and prosaic communications, his lack of available presidential autographed materials is countered in the market by numerous non-presidential examples. Partly printed signed documents are perhaps the most common form offered, many of which relate to his days practicing law in Buffalo, New York. Fillmore also served in the House of

Representatives (1833-35, 1837-43) and became the New York State Comptroller in 1848. Although other Presidents had been photographed, Fillmore marks the first president to become familiar with the task of inscribing his name to a carte de viste. Common forms: "Millard Fillmore"

Franklin Pierce

Franklin Pierce

Often illegible and seldom intriguing in content— with the exception of friends and relatives, the letters of Franklin Pierce were far from literary masterpieces. Collectors will find handwritten letters, naval commissions and even perhaps a "Warrant for a Pardon" before any other forms. Clipped signatures, franks and signed photographs have always been scarce. Because Pierce repealed the Missouri Compromise and passed the Kansas-Nebraska Act— which ultimately fueled the Civil War, he was not particularly popular after leaving office. Common forms: Franklin Pierce", also "Frank Pierce", "F. Pierce" and "Fr. Pierce"

James Buchanan

James Buchanan

With his ornate calligraphy, Buchanan rivaled only Washington for the most attractive, yet precise handwriting of any President. Buchanan's signature varied little over his life, with perhaps the most notable example the increase in his signature's size as he grew in prominence. His typical single page correspondences have been offered for years in the autograph market and although examples have been exemplary of most of the periods of his life—with the slight exception being his term, interest has been generally moderate or below average. Now considered slightly controversial, as greater details of his personal life have been unearthed over the years, one can now anticipate some additional interest. Advanced autograph collectors should pay particular attention to Buchanan land grants, which often bear proxy signatures. During his retirement he was a very prolific writer. Common form: "James Buchanan"

Abraham Lincoln

Abraham Lincoln

Insightful and succinct, yet gracious and charming, the letters of Abraham Lincoln are the most sought after form for inclusion in autograph collections. The demand for Lincoln material far exceeds the supply, as well as the demand for material from any other U.S. President. His pre-presidential material is also scarce as are his legal briefs, many signed with the firm's name. "Draft Calls" and "Military Appointments" (which include the signature of Edwin M. Stanton, Secretary of War), do surface in the market, but like all Lincoln material carry a hefty price tag. Full signatures appear on official documents and formal papers signed as President, ninety-nine percent of all other examples in this form should be questioned. Most experts believe that less than ten and as little as two, authentic signed photographs of Lincoln are known to exist. If you understand the man you can certainly believe this to be true. Unfortunately, demand and the lack of significant variation in his handwriting has led to numerous forgeries ever since his death. Abraham Lincoln was the first president to introduce "Executive Mansion" stationary (octavo sheets). Collectors are advised to consult an expert before making any Lincoln autograph purchases. Advanced autograph

collectors should pay particular attention to Lincoln land grants, which often bear proxy signatures. Common form: "A. Lincoln"

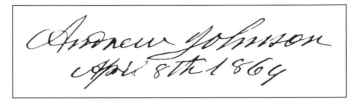

Andrew Johnson

Andrew Johnson

Johnson assumed the office following the death of Abraham Lincoln, although Johnson believed in the former president's policies, he lacked the efficiency and skills to fulfill them. His conflict with radical Republicans led to his impeachment, which fell short by only a single vote. Following his term in office he was again elected to the Senate, where he had previously served from 1957 to 1862. Johnson was also a former member of the House of Representatives (1843-54) and Governor of Tennessee (1853-57). Johnson's handwritten letters are typically routine and short in length, due to his lack of education and bad right arm, but nevertheless in demand because of their scarcity. He also used secretaries, his son and even a rubber stamp to fulfill the demand for his signature. Commissions, pardons and land grants typically enter the market and are good sources for an authentic example. While Johnson photographs (c.d.v.s) are not common, they have occasionally appeared in the market with an appropriate hefty price tag. Collectors should familiarize themselves with all of Johnson's facsimile signatures before attempting to purchase an authentic example. Some forms, such as franks, were often signed by his son and can be tricky to identify. Common forms: "Andrew Johnson", and occasionally "A. Johnson" or "And. Johnson"

Ulysses S. Grant

The 18th President of the United States, Ulysses S. Grant, formerly "Cadet U.H. Grant", changed his name early in life. Grant's finest handwritten letters were authored during his war years, and as such have remained in demand for decades. A weak cabinet, disorganized policies and corrupt intimate associates scared much of his presidential legacy. Common in all forms, collectors are most likely to first encounter handwritten letters and signed documents. Although Grant introduced the formal "Executive Mansion" card, no doubt for short and expedient notes, ironically only few examples with signature are known to exist. Signed Grant photographs, both cabinets and c.d.v.s, also

Ulysses S. Grant

occasionally surface in the market. Near the end of his life he lost his voice and was forced to communicate by notes. Common form: "U.S. Grant"

Rutherford B. Hayes

Rutherford B. Hayes

Although much of his material has found its way into the hands of institutions, the autographed material of Rutherford B. Hayes has never been overly popular with collectors. Some of the institutional draw to artifacts of the Hayes administration has been attributed to interest in his economic recovery, civil service reform, and conciliation of the Southern states. Hayes handwritten letters typically fill the page, with some variations in legibility. Hayes was also prone to an occasional underline to emphasize a particular point. Collectors are more apt to encounter the president's signature on handwritten letters or commissions over many other forms. Hayes did occasionally make use of "Executive Mansion" cards for brief notes. Common forms: "R.B.Hayes", "Rutherford B. Hayes"

For additional information contact: The Rutherford B. Hayes Presidential Center, Fremont, Ohio, 800-998-7737, also www.rbhayes.org

James A. Garfield

James A. Garfield

Having been assassinated just four months after taking office, Garfield's term-related letters and documents are extremely scarce. However, fortunately for collectors his pre-presidential is quite common in many forms. Numerous fine manuscript signed letters, on House of Representatives letterhead, have found their way into the market, as have a few franks. Garfield did employ a secretary by the name of J. Stanley Brown, during the year prior to his election, whose handwriting bore a stark resemblance to the president's. Collectors purchasing handwritten material from this era should exercise caution. Garfield is scarce on "Executive Mansion" cards, as well as all other examples authored during his term. Common forms: J.A. Garfield"

Chester A. Arthur

Chester A. Arthur

Perhaps the easiest of all presidential handwriting to identify, Chester Arthur was not an advocate of lifting his pen off the paper once he began writing, therefore, most of his words are connected. Non-presidential Arthur material is common, with many handwritten letters found on "Custom House, New York, Collector Office" letterhead or "Law Offices of Arthur, Phelps, Knevals & Ransom" stationery. Of the scarce presidential items collectors are likely to encounter, military appointments seem to hit the market occasionally, along with a signed manuscript letter or card. The latter being the engraved depiction of the White House which he introduced in a convenient card format. These cards were in addition to the already used "Executive Mansion" version. Worth noting is that Arthur was the first president to utilize a typewriter as part of his daily routine (1881-1885). He was bedridden in his final months and during this time he directed that all of his public and private papers were to be burned. Common forms: "C. A. Arthur", "Chester A. Arthur"

Grover Cleveland

Grover Cleveland

Both the 22nd and 24th President of the United States, Grover Cleveland was also an assistant district attorney, sheriff, mayor and governor. Although he wrote so small that many of his letters were difficult to read, he was always insightful, formal, polite and often charming. Abundant in many forms, collectors can anticipate finding signed appointments, handwritten letters and even photographs—the most prevalent being the profile bust cabinet photo by Gutekunst of Philadelphia. As president he also used "Executive Mansion" cards, which required a stamp since he never had franking privilege. Cleveland was said to have answered all of his mail personally into his final years, a statement confirmed by the numerous examples I have seen over the years. Cleveland also authored numerous articles for the Saturday Evening Post from 1900-1906. Common form: "Grover Cleveland"

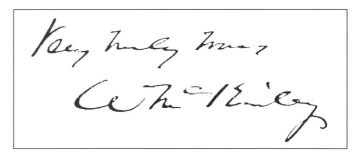

Benjamin Harrison

Benjamin Harrison

Grandson of William Henry Harrison, Benjamin Harrison's pro-protection platform won him election as the 23rd President of the United States. Harrison served in the Union army, was active in Grant's presidential campaign, involved in state politics and elected U.S. Senator for Indiana. His handwriting varied significantly over his lifetime, losing much of its legibility in his later years. Handwritten letters of Harrison are fairly scarce with most pre-presidential on "Porter, Harrison & Fishback, Attorneys at Law" letterhead and signed "Benja. Harrison." Some pre-presidential personal checks drawn from "Fletcher's Bank" in Indianapolis, IN have also found their way to the autograph market over the past decade. Photographs of Harrison are scarce and may command a significant price. Much of his post-presidential material is in TLS or LS form on his personal stationery: "BENJAMIN HARRISON, 874 NORTH DELAWARE STREET, INDIANAPOLIS, IND." During his retirement he also penned numerous articles for national magazines. Common form: "Benj. Harrison"

William McKinley

William McKinley

McKinley served in Congress and was also Governor of Ohio, before becoming a Republican Presidential candidate. Although Cleveland and Harrison were no strangers to the typewriter, McKinley seemed to be the first president truly comfortable with the machine. Therefore, many pre-presidential TLSs have turned up in the market. Handwritten letters of William McKinley as president are scarce, although some examples before he took office have been available. Collectors will typically encounter authentic signatures of McKinley in document form in the market. These will range from military commissions and appointments to simple appointments as Marshall of the United States. "Executive Mansion" cards and signed photographs can also be found. Common forms: "William McKinley"

Theodore Roosevelt, SP, 1917.

Theodore Roosevelt

Despite the lack of gracefulness to his script, this "Roughrider' wrote clear, crisp and forceful letters. A prolific writer, whose handwriting varied little over his lifetime, Roosevelt spent time in the New York Legislature (1884), was President of the New York Police Board (1895-97), Assistant Secretary of the Navy (1898), Governor of New York State (1898-1900) and Vice-President in 1901, before assuming the presidential office after the assassination of McKinley. His signature habits included the use of a rubber stamp as Governor of New York, as well permitting his secretary to sign on his behalf—as Governor and vice-president. While obtainable in all forms, collectors will typically cross paths with his signatures first on typed letters and documents. As president he changed the format of the "Executive Mansion" cards, to "White

House" in hopes of presenting a different image. He was the first president to be known popularly by his initials. During 1910-1914 he was associate editor of Outlook magazine. The demand for his material has remained strong over the years, while exhibiting some nice price appreciation. Common forms: Theodore Roosevelt", "T. Roosevelt"

William H. Taft

William Howard Taft

The 27th President of the United States, William Howard Taft is perhaps best remembered as the only man to serve time both in the oval office and also as the Chief Justice of the U.S. Supreme Court (1921-1930). A prolific man of letters, his material has been common in many forms for years, the only exception being handwritten letters as President and "White House" cards. Many signed photographs, which were initially thought to be scarce, have surfaced from private collections over the years. These signed photographs depict Taft as both President and Chief Justice. Ironically, many collectors find his correspondence as Chief Justice far more interesting and appealing. After leaving the oval office he accepted an appointment as Kent professor of law at Yale University (1913-1921). As the first president to take up golf, keep your eye out for signed scorecards! Common forms: "Wm. H. Taft", and to friends and relatives "Bill", "Bill Taft"

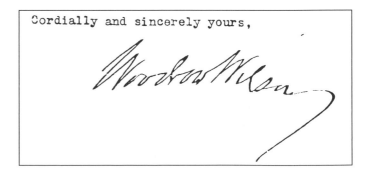

Woodrow Wilson

Woodrow Wilson

A gifted wordsmith, who also happened to have legible handwriting, Wilson wrote magnificent letters, particularly early in his life. As his responsibilities increased, so did the demand on his correspondence.

He began limiting himself to brief notes, while also finding solace behind a typewriter. His signed typed letters will be some of the first examples collectors will encounter in the market, followed by military appointments. As Governor of New Jersey and during his run for the office, Wilson resorted to the use of a rubber stamp on correspondence. Wilson signed photographs do occasionally appear in the market as have a couple scarce canceled checks from his days at Princeton. Signed "White House" cards are also scarce and the ones that have entered the market have been signed at the top of the card. Following his 1919 stroke, his signature picked up a few slight variations. He was virtually blind in his final years. Common form: "Woodrow Wilson"

Warren G. Harding

Warren G. Harding

An interest in journalism led Warren Harding to purchase the Marion Star and as its editor, the paper prospered. A prolific Harding quickly caught the attention of Republican politicians. As a Lieutenant Governor (1904-06), then Senator (1914), he honed his political skills, before becoming his party's dark-horse nominee. While he was easily elected to the Presidency, the infrastructure of his Cabinet was filled with ineptness and corruption. During his rise to prominence his handwriting varied significantly, losing considerable legibility. While his autographed material is uncommon and even scarce in some forms, the demand for such items has been weak over the past decades. Harding did use a rubber stamp to answer correspondence and even employed a secretary who mimicked his handwriting. After Harding died unexpectedly in San Francisco, his wife burned his papers, adding much speculation to her reasoning. Common forms: "W.G. Harding"—almost always connected, Warren G. Harding"

Calvin Coolidge

Coolidge was a man who believed that if you don't have anything good to say, well, why bother saying or even writing anything at all. Certainly one of the least profound and insightful presidents, his autographed material has been relatively common and in little demand. He had a knack for filling a page, even if it was far from necessary. His handwritten letters are scarce, as are term-authored documents. Coolidge did have secretaries signing his name, although most are easily

Calvin Coolidge

distinguished as such. During his retirement he wrote numerous articles for many national magazines. Common form: "Calvin Coolidge"

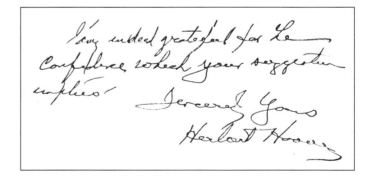

Herbert Hoover

Herbert Hoover

Common in numerous autographed forms, particularly signed typed letters, Herbert Hoover will no doubt be one of the first signatures in your presidential collection. Handwritten letters are nearly impossible to acquire, as even according to Hoover himself he wrote very, very few. While his letters in general were far from interesting, he was a prolific writer who authored many intriguing books. Hoover did authorize his secretary to sign his name, therefore causing some confusion for collectors who often confuse the facsimile with an authentic signature. "White House" cards are attainable, but not common. Franks are even more difficult to encounter. In his final years he resided often at the Waldorf-Astoria Hotel in New York, and was virtually deaf and blind. Common form: Herbert Hoover

For additional information contact: Herbert Hoover Presidential Library and Museum, West Branch, Iowa, 319-643-5301, also www.hoover.nara.gov

Franklin D. Roosevelt

Franklin D. Roosevelt

Polite, yet platitudinous, amicable, yet aseptic, perhaps best characterizes Franklin Roosevelt's correspondence, with the only exception those letters he wrote to intimate friends and relatives. Handwritten letters, particularly as president, are difficult to come by and when you do find one, it is typically pre-presidential. Roosevelt also often signed his correspondence with initials only, and since he used proxy signers, many facsimiles can be difficult to distinguish. Roosevelt, also an autograph collector, varied his signature often and even used a rubber stamp as Governor of New York. Although "White House" cards and even "New York State" cards were commonly found in the market, they too have dissipated somewhat with the increased interest in the hobby. Many of the proxy signatures of FDR have fooled both novice and experienced collectors, so exercise caution. Common forms: "FDR", "Franklin D. Roosevelt"

For additional information contact: Franklin D. Roosevelt Library and Museum, Hyde Park, N.Y., 914-229-8114, also www.academic.marist.edu/fdr

Harry S. Truman

Harry S. Truman

If you're just wild about Harry, it probably had little to do with the content of one his letters. Often formulaic, Truman rarely displayed his passionate feelings in written form, but when he did, you knew he meant it. Handwritten letters are scarce and when they do hit the market can command a significant price. Post-presidential typed letters signed have been common for years, with the demand increasing steadily over the past two decades. As Senator, Truman authorized secretaries to sign his letters so exercise caution when purchasing material from this era. Truman also used facsimile holograph letters on occasion, with all lacking a formal salutation to the recipient. After the Presidency, Truman dated nearly every autograph he signed, which can make for an interesting study on signature variations. Common forms: " Harry Truman", "Harry S. Truman", "HST"— presidential memorandums

For additional information contact: Harry S. Truman Library and Museum, Independence, MO., 800-833-1225, also www.trumanlibrary.org

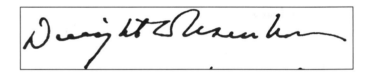

Dwight D. Eisenhower

Dwight D. Eisenhower

An extremely popular American general and the 34th President of the United States, Dwight Eisenhower has always been popular among autograph collectors. While dictated letters and typed letters signed have been generally available, those handwritten by "Ike" have not—the only exception an occasional letter he wrote to his wife. Signed photographs, particularly those of him in uniform, seem never to fill the demand, while routine presidential poses meet with less appeal. Eisenhower was the first president to introduce facsimile signatures on "White House" cards and thankfully they were identified as such on the back of the card. Some war-dated correspondences bear secretarial signatures, so collectors beware! Numerous proxy signatures have also adorned items obtained during his first presidential campaign. Common form: "Dwight D. Eisenhower", "D.E."—to friends, "Ike" very rare other than to his wife.

For additional information contact: Dwight D. Eisenhower Library, Abilene, Kansas, 785-263-4751, also www.eisenhower.utexas.edu

John F. Kennedy

Books have been written about the signature habits of John F. Kennedy, who is by far the most the

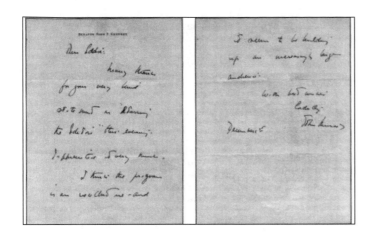

John F. Kennedy, ALS, as Senator

THE WHITE HOUSE
WASHINGTON

June 13, 1961

Dear Governor Clyde:

I know in the past you have been good enough to serve as Honorary State Chairman for the USO and in my capacity as National Honorary Chairman, it is my pleasure to extend to you a warm invitation to serve again in this capacity.

I know that the morale and welfare of the men and women in our Armed Forces is close to your heart. Through your cooperation, added impetus will be given to the USO's comprehensive program. It reflects America's concern for the welfare of our service personnel wherever they might be, at home or in the many foreign lands where needed on behalf of the security of freedom in this world.

As you may know, USO, a federation of six civilian agencies representative of the three major faiths of the nation, is supported principally through contributions to Community Chests and United Funds. For this reason, your utmost cooperation in these drives will be most effective and welcome at this time.

Sincerely,

Honorable George D. Clyde
Governor of Utah
Salt Lake City, Utah

John F. Kennedy, TLS, 1961

most unpredictable signature in history. The irony, of course, is that Kennedy himself was an autograph collector. His signature was unpredictable, inconsistent in slant, character formation, signature breaks, etc. The only consistent elements to his signature have been the numerous machine signed patterns, secretarial facsimiles, and forgeries. Because the demand for authentic Kennedy material has always been high and the variables in his signature numerous,

he has constantly been a target for forgeries. Even the finest handwriting experts in the country have been deceived by forgeries, therefore, collectors are at an incredible risk when purchasing his material. Handwritten letters are scarce as are examples found on "Air Force One" stationery. Collectors will typically encounter typed letters signed, signed photographs, or a variety of examples signed while Kennedy was campaigning. While some pre-presidential material was dictated, JFK often felt obligated to add a handwritten postscript. His prolific use of the autopen has frustrated many a collector. Those of you who wish further information on the device should purchase a copy of Charles Hamilton's book The Robot That Helped to Make a President. Doodles and notes from Kennedy have also found there way to the market, but they too are difficult to authenticate. Common forms: "John Kennedy"

For additional information contact: John F. Kennedy Library and Museum, Boston, MA, 617-929-4500, also www.cs.umb.edu/jfklibrary

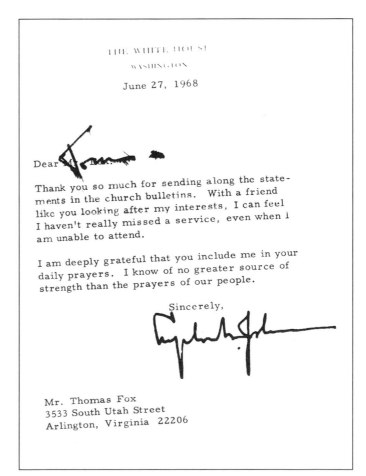

THE WHITE HOUSE
WASHINGTON

June 27, 1968

Dear Mr. Fox:

Thank you so much for sending along the statements in the church bulletins. With a friend like you looking after my interests, I can feel I haven't really missed a service, even when I am unable to attend.

I am deeply grateful that you include me in your daily prayers. I know of no greater source of strength than the prayers of our people.

Sincerely,

Mr. Thomas Fox
3533 South Utah Street
Arlington, Virginia 22206

Lyndon B. Johnson, TLS, 1968; scarce in authentic form as President

Lyndon B. Johnson

Following Kennedy's assassination, Johnson carried out many of JFK's policies including his philosophy on correspondence. Secretarials, machine signed and facsimile examples of Johnson's signature are common in the market. Authentic Johnson signatures are scarcer than what collectors first thought. Post-presidential items found in the market are often dictated letters signed by "LBJ." Collectors wishing to purchase an authentic Johnson example may best to turn to signed books or photographs. The lack of interest in his autographed material over the past two decades seems to be dissipating somewhat as more information regarding his administration becomes declassified. Johnson's image has as been enhanced greatly by the release of many of his taped phone conversations. Common forms: "Lyndon B. Johnson", "Lyndon", "LBJ"

For additional information contact: Lyndon B. Johnson Library and Museum, Austin, Texas, 512-916-5137, also www.lbjlib.utexas.edu

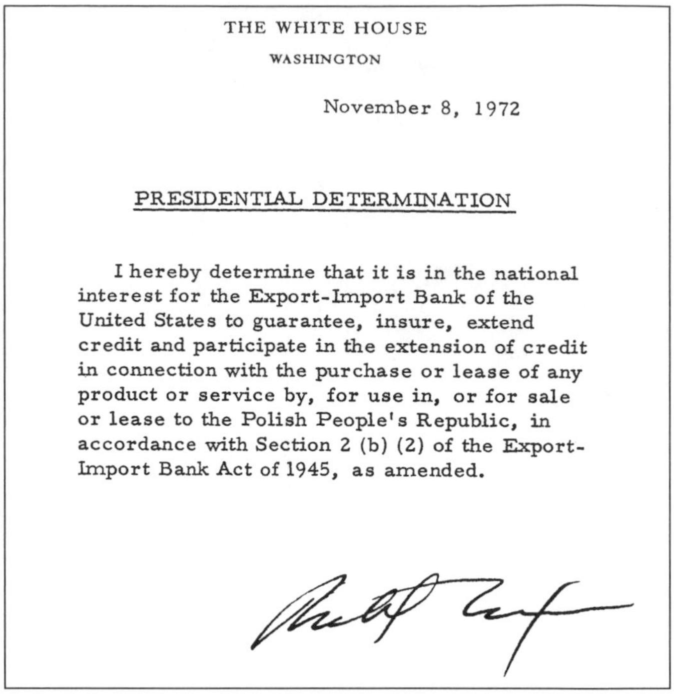

THE WHITE HOUSE
WASHINGTON

November 8, 1972

PRESIDENTIAL DETERMINATION

I hereby determine that it is in the national interest for the Export-Import Bank of the United States to guarantee, insure, extend credit and participate in the extension of credit in connection with the purchase or lease of any product or service by, for use in, or for sale or lease to the Polish People's Republic, in accordance with Section 2 (b) (2) of the Export-Import Bank Act of 1945, as amended.

Richard Nixon, DS, 1972, Presidential Determination.

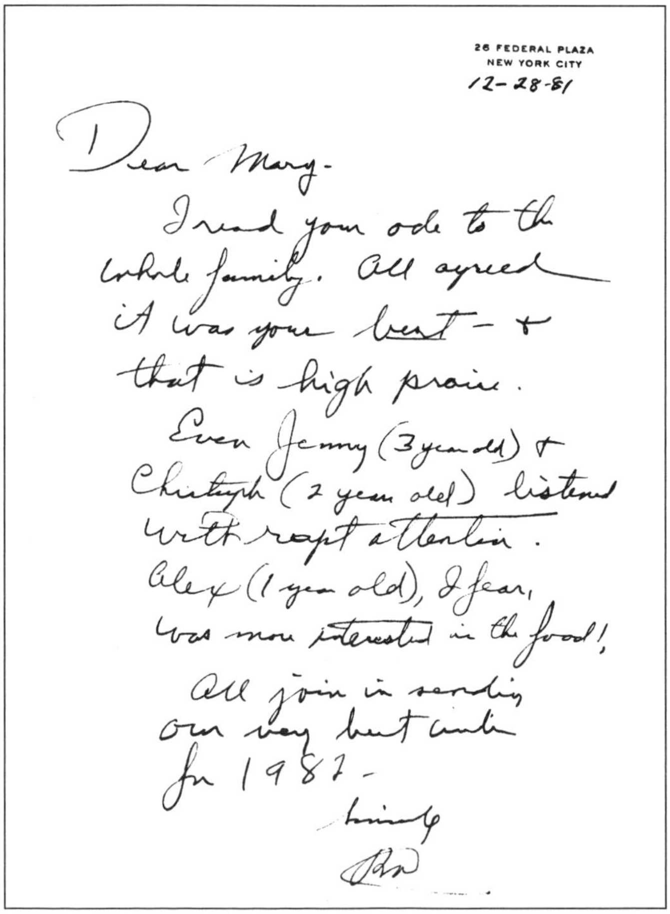

26 FEDERAL PLAZA
NEW YORK CITY
12-28-81

Dear Mary-

I read your ode to the whole family. All agreed it was your best - & that is high praise.

Even Jenny (3 year old) & Christopher (2 year old) listened with rapt attention. Alex (1 year old), I fear, was more interested in the food!

All join in sending our very best wishes for 1982-

Sincerely
RN

Richard Nixon, ALS, 1981, signed with his "RN" monogram.

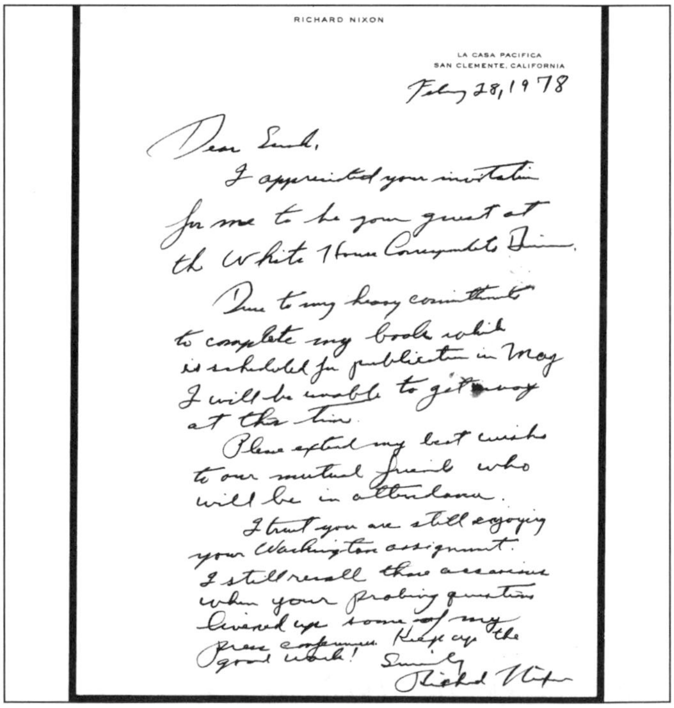

RICHARD NIXON

LA CASA PACIFICA
SAN CLEMENTE, CALIFORNIA

Feby 28, 1978

Dear Sarah,

I appreciated your invitation for me to be your guest at the White House Correspondents Dinner.

Due to my heavy commitments to complete my book which is scheduled for publication in May I will be unable to get away at this time.

Please extend my best wishes to our mutual friends who will be in attendance.

I trust you are still enjoying your Washington assignment. I still recall those occasions when your probing questions livened up some of my press conferences. Keep up the good work!

Sincerely
Richard Nixon

Richard Nixon, ALS, 1978.

Richard M. Nixon

Authentic letters from the first President to submit his resignation are scarce, with the few surfacing being from his later years. Secretarial and autopen samples are common, particularly on "White House" cards. Most authentic signed pieces from his presidency have been with his initials. Collectors wishing to complete a set may want to turn to a signed book authored by Nixon after leaving office. Common forms: "R. Nixon"—early, "Richard Nixon", "R.N.", and "Dick" or "Dick Nixon" to friends.

For additional information contact: Richard M. Nixon Library and Birthplace, Yorba Linda, California, 714-993-3393, also www.nixonfoundation.org

Four U.S. Presidents, SP, Richard Nixon, Gerald R. Ford, Jimmy Carter, and Ronald Reagan

Gerald R. Ford

Like all modern presidents, Ford made extensive use of the autopen and secretarial signatures. While he is considered scarce in handwritten letters, a few do occasionally enter the market. Collectors will most likely run across authentic signed photographs or books before any other forms. Common forms: "Gerald R. Ford", "Gerald Ford", and "Jerry" or "Jerry Ford" to friends.

For additional information contact: Gerald R. Ford Museum, Grand Rapids, Michigan, 616-451-9263, also www.ford.utexas.edu

Jimmy Carter

Jimmy Carter

By the time Jimmy Carter was elected to office, machines were being created that could reproduce an entire handwritten letter. Both machine generated and secretarial facsimiles of Carter's signature are commonly found in the market. Carter remains scarce in authentic handwritten letters, which typically began with a "To" salutation. Carter, who has become an outstanding humanitarian and prolific author, is probably best to obtain in a signed book form to complete a collection. Common forms: "Jimmy", "Jimmy Carter", "J. Carter"—later

For additional information contact: Jimmy Carter Library, Atlanta, Georgia, 404-331-3942, also carterlibrary.galileo.peachnet.edu

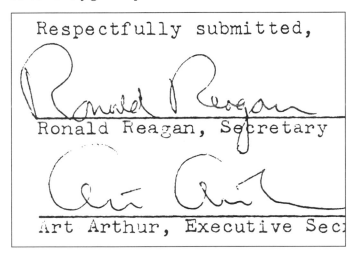

Ronald Reagan

Ronald Reagan

As both a film star and politician, Reagan utilized proxy signers. As the 40th President of the United States he signed very little, opting instead for all the now accepted alternatives. Fortunately for collectors, Reagan was passionate about maintaining old relationships through handwritten correspondence, many of which have found their way into the autograph market. Most of these are warm and friendly in content and often signed "RR", "Ron" or "Dutch." A few of his handwritten drafts as Governor have also appeared in the market, typically they have a red slash drawn across the sheet to indicate that they have been typed in final form. Despite this alteration—a commonly accepted office procedure, these drafts are also extremely popular with collectors. Following his presidency, Reagan withdrew quickly from the public spotlight, which has been attributed by most as his reaction to battling Alzheimer's disease. Common forms: "Ronald Reagan"

For additional information contact: Ronald Reagan Presidential Library, Simi Valley, California, 800-410-8354, also www.reagan.utexas.edu

George Bush

For additional information contact: George Bush Presidential Library and Museum, College Station, Texas, 409-260-9554, also www.csdl.tamu.edu/bushlib

Bill Clinton

George Bush

While Bush is common in authentic post-presidential forms, many of his pre-presidential signatures are secretarial or autopenned. As president, authentic forms of his signature were at first scarce, but with each passing year they have become more prevalent. Bush seems to have always had a passion for note cards and as president even introduced a new form. Since leaving office he has even done private signings for dealers, thus his material is readily available to collectors. Common forms: "George Bush", "George"

Bill Clinton

In-person he has always been charismatic, charming and even warm to autograph requests, however by mail it is a completely different picture. Since the President receives about 15,000 letters a day, a majority are destined for a printed response by form letter or a personalized form letter that has been machine-signed. Clinton has always made excellent use of machine signed signatures and it is doubtful it will discontinue. Like most modern Presidents it will take a few years out of office before a variety of material will surface in the marketplace. Common forms: "Bill Clinton", "Bill"

Rock 'n' Roll/Country Music Autographs

Abba

The best way to acquire the group's signatures is in-person, as the band does not sign autographs via mail requests. An occasional engagement contract or two surfaces periodically, making this form another viable option.

AC/DC

Australia's premier metal band for decades, the group has faced its fair share of triumph and tragedy. Bon Scott (1946 - 1980) signed items, often those associated with "Highway to Hell", are most sought after.

Aerosmith

America's own "bad boys from Boston", Aerosmith has rocked on for decades (Since 1970). The band has always been very gracious signers in-person and that is how I would suggest you acquire their signatures. Signed material from the band in many forms is common in the market.

The Allman Brothers

A band that sustained the loss of two members, both from motorcycle accidents, The Allman Brothers endured in memory of Duane Allman and Berry Oakley. Greg Allman, Dicky Betts and Jaimoe remained the core nucleus in a lineup that would change numerous times over the past three decades. Pieces signed by both brothers are considerably harder to find than most think.

Tori Amos

Tori Amos really broke out in 1992, first with her single "Crucify", followed by being named by many polls as best new female artist. She has a very dedicated and large following, both of which contribute to the appeal of her memorabilia. Amos can be a temperamental signer in-person and often unresponsive to mail requests for her signature.

The Animals

Formed in 1962, the Animals were part of the sixties "British Invasion". Eric Burden is the key signature and while he is often unresponsive to mail requests, in-person he can be an obliging signer. The original lineup, which includes "Chas" Chandler (1938-1996), is sought on signed sixties vintage items. Some signed engagement contracts have surfaced in recent years and have commanded significant prices.

Badfinger

Signed to Apple Records by Paul McCartney, Badfinger struck gold in the early seventies with hits such as "Come and Get It" and "Day After Day". After the band jumped to Warner Brothers business problems essentially led to their demise. Both Pete Ham and Tom Evans committed suicide ending Badfinger's aspirations of a possible resurrection in popularity. Signed material from the band, that includes both Ham and Evans, is scarce.

The Band

The Band established a very large following despite their lack of singles and airplay. All the members were responsive to in-person requests, however mail requests were often unanswered. Richard Manuel died in 1986 and Rick Danko passed away in 1999. Signed items of the entire band are scarce, however because some of them appeared at record store signings, including Danko and Manuel, you have a shot at getting an item signed by all. That is of course if you can find an item in the market.

The Beach Boys

The sun, surf, sand and summer have all become synonymous with The Beach Boys. All members are responsive signers in-person, however Dennis Wilson was always temperamental. With the exception of Brian Wilson, the band toured endlessly. I have had success with both Brian Wilson and Al Jardine through mail requests. With both Carl and Dennis Wilson now deceased, it's hard to say how much longer the others might go on.

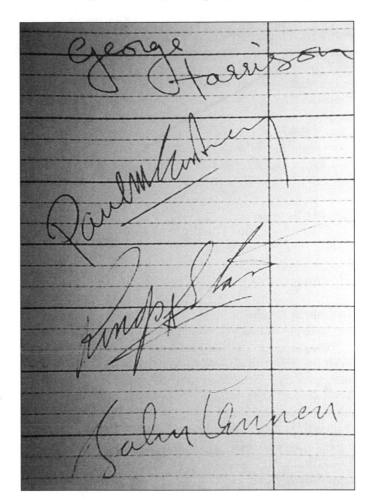

The Beatles

The Beatles

Authentic Beatles signatures are not very common. In addition to being highly forged, many other individuals signed on the band's behalf including their road manager Neil Aspinall, Mal Evans (The Fifth Beatles) and many secretaries. Little material was actually signed following 1963 and since the band ceased live performances in 1966, they were primarily together as a group only during recording sessions (until August 1969). The band only sat down and signed autographs on three occasions: at Dawson's Music Shop (UK, 1962), Brian Epstein's NEMS Record Store (UK, 1963) and The Beatles London Fan Club Convention (UK, 1963). I would be incredibly skeptical of any signed item after 1963 and I wouldn't even go near item signed after 1966. Beatles signatures require an expert opinion to be certain of their authenticity.

The Bee Gees

Barry Gibb and his twin brothers Robin and Maurice moved from the U.K. to Australia with their parents in the late fifties. The Bee Gees triumphed first in Australia then internationally. Their career has gone through many stages and through it all they have endured. They respond to mail request for their autographs with a facsimile signed photograph. It's best to catch them in-person; your best shot probably being Miami Beach, Florida where they spend much of their time.

Chuck Berry

The father of rock 'n' roll hates autograph collectors and refuses to sign in-person or answer mail requests for his signature.

The Big Bopper

J.P. Richardson (The Big Bopper) was an obliging signer. He died in the same crash that took the lives of Buddy Holly and Ritchie Valens. His signature is scarce and commands a big price tag.

The Blues Brothers

Late seventies and early eighties satire group started by Saturday Night Live actors Dan Aykroyd and John Belushi, the Blues Brothers hit pay dirt with songs such as "Soul Man" and "Gimmie Some Lovin". Aykroyd has always been obliging to both in-person and mail requests for his signature. Belushi, who died tragically young, was responsive in-person to autograph requests.

David Bowie

"The Chameleon" has endured for decades with his artistic prowess and ability to transform himself into whatever image is most desirable at the time. He is a very reluctant signer in-person and does not answer mail requests for his signature. His signature is also illegible, both as David R. Jones and as David Bowie, making it very difficult to authenticate. I have witnessed three items signed during the same period all of which appear very different.

Jimmy Buffet

"King Parrot Head", Buffet has amassed an empire and proved that you can still sing at Captain Tony's Saloon in Key West and make it! He's obliging in-person to signature requests, but I have never received an authentic signature through the mail!

The Byrds

Folk rock pioneers with their hallmark harmonies, guitar hooks, and screaming Rickenbacker riffs, The Byrds have inspired many rock bands for generations. Of the original lineup, Gene Clark departs the band in 1966, while David Crosby and Michael Clarke leave the following year. McGuinn, Clark and Hillman reunite during the late seventies and even tour. Gene Clark died in 1991 and Michael Clarke passed away in 1993. I

The Byrds

never met Crosby or Clarke, but all the other members of the band were very obliging to signature requests in-person. I have never had any luck getting any of them to respond to a signature request via mail.

Mariah Carey

An elusive and reluctant signer who seldom autographs anything in-person and responds to mail request for her signature with fan club info or a facsimile signed postcard. Beware of forgeries especially on color photographs.

The Carpenters

One of the most gifted duos in rock history, The Carpenters put together a run of 17 consecutive Top 30 hits! Both were outstanding signers in-person and very responsive to their fans. Richard Carpenter has always answered mail requests for his signature and is a true gentleman. Contracts signed by both have surfaced in the market in recent years and have commanded a significant price.

The Carter Family

The pioneer family of country music, The Carters were America's most popular band from 1926 until they disbanded in 1943. Material signed by all three is scarce with Alvin Carter (1891 - 1960) being the key signature.

Harry Chapin

One of music's genuine gifts, Harry Chapin managed to accomplish much in his far too short time here on earth. While we remember his hits such as "Taxi", we will never forget his work for world hunger.

Chapin was very responsive to his fans and often signed autographs for fans after the show. He often signed tour programs and typically personalized most.

Ray Charles

The author of many R& B classics, Ray Charles seems to conquer every barrier put in front of him. He does sign items on occasion, but much of what you will receive from him via mail will be ghost signed.

Eric Clapton

Eric Clapton

A rock 'n' roll disciple and a blues god, Eric Clapton has had a prolific career. His body of film work alone is an entire career! He is a reluctant but accommodating signer in-person and believe it or not if you are patient, you may receive an authentic signature from your mail request. I once waited a year and a half for a positive response.

Patsy Cline

Patsy Cline

The first woman solo artist elected to the Country Music Hall of Fame, Patsy Cline was killed in a plane crash at the young age of 30. She was always responsive to her fans and thus some signed material has entered the market in recent years. Watch out for forgeries, many of which appear as cut signatures.

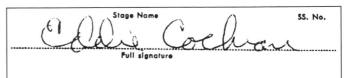

Eddie Cochrane

Eddie Cochran

With songs such as "Summertime Blues", "Sittin' in the Balcony" and "C'mon Everybody", Eddie Cochran made a considerable impression in a very short period of time. He was killed in a tragic auto accident in 1960, months short of his twenty-second birthday. Because his signed material is scarce, few authentic pieces have entered the market. Be careful of forgeries and cautious of all clipped signatures.

> THE USE OF THIS CHECK BY PAYEE IS ACKNOWLEDGMENT OF RECEIPT OF THE APPENDED VOUCHER AND PAYMENT IN FULL OF THE ACCOUNT THEREIN DESCRIBED

Sam Cooke

Sam Cooke

Late fifties early sixties singer, Sam Cooke left behind a legacy of classic hits such as "You Send Me", "Chain gang" and "Shake". His controversial death, just prior to his thirtieth birthday, in 1964 shocked music audiences worldwide. His signature is scarce, but a few autographed programs and contracts have surfaced over the past five years.

Elvis Costello

The son of a successful big-band singer, Costello emerged as a star during the late eighties. He has sustained himself over the years by not limiting himself to only a single form of music. He is a very responsive signer both in-person and through mail requests for his signature.

Cream

A three-member band that had a profound effect on music for a very short period of time, Cream popularized the thundering trio with hits like "Sunshine of Your Love" and "White Room". All members are accommodating to signature requests in-person and some even by mail. The group has done a private signing with a dealer who heavily advertised the signed photographs. Watch out for forgeries!

Credence Clearwater Revival/John Fogarty

The kings of "swamp rock" or "bayou blues", CCR revolved around the talented John Fogarty. Fogarty just kept writing hit after hit until the other band members began taking issue with his talent. Vintage-signed material is scarce, especially those bearing Tom Fogarty's signature.

Jim Croce

Early seventies singer who died tragically in a plane crash at age thirty, Jim Croce left behind an incredible legacy of hits such as "Operator", "Bad, Bad Leroy Brown" and "Time in a Bottle". Signed material of his is scarce and little has surfaced in the market.

Crosby, Stills and Nash

Crosby, Stills, Nash and Young

Volatile sixties, seventies and eighties band whose high harmonic sound put to largely acoustic-based songs became their hallmark, CSN & sometimes Y scored with anthems such as "Woodstock" and "Ohio". The best signer in the group is Graham Nash and the worst is Neil Young. Stephen Stills' signature is often illegible and David Crosby, like Neil Young is unpredictable. Getting the signatures of all four in-person is a challenge and unfortunately the only way to achieve such a goal. Fortunately, some contracts have surfaced in the market bearing some if not all of their signatures.

Bobby Darin

Late fifties and early sixties teen idol, Bobby Darin scored with hits such as "Beyond the Sea", "Lazy River", and "You Must Have Been a Beautiful Baby". Plagued throughout his life with heart problems, Darin died on December 20, 1973 following surgery to repair a heart valve. Signed material of his is uncommon.

Miles Davis

Miles Davis played a role in every major jazz development from the forties until his death in 1991. He was an elusive artist and often unresponsive to signature requests in any form.

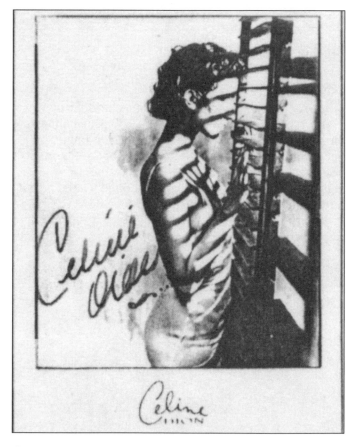

Celine Dion

Celine Dion

Celine Dion peaked with "My Heart Will Go On (Love Theme From 'Titanic')" before a self-imposed retirement from the limelight. Clearly, she is a woman of priorities and convictions, for which all of her fans have learned to adore her that much more. She is a responsive signer in-person, however mail requests for her signature often go unanswered.

Willie Dixon

A pivotal Mississippi bluesman who influenced the key contributors of early rock and roll, Willie Dixon is best remembered for songs such as "You Shook Me", "Little Red Rooster", "Back Door Man", and "I Just Wanna Make Love to You".

The Doors

The Doors

A major act of the sixties, The Doors had many hits, but are commonly associated with "Light My Fire". The key signature here is obviously Jim Morrison who died in 1971. The remaining living members are very obliging to signature requests both in-person and through the mail. In addition to being a tough signature to find, Morrison was seldom sober; thus his signature can vary significantly. He often signed "Cheers, J. Morrison". A typical characteristic of his signature is that all the letters are often close, or identical in height (as measured from the baseline). Common signature breaks fall between the "M" and "o" and between the "r" and "i" in Morrison. The finishing stroke of the "n" in his name also had a tendency to fall below the baseline. Morrison's autograph has remained popular with collectors for decades and because of this forgeries are not uncommon. Often they will appear on plain sheets of paper or as cut signatures. Fortunately, checks and documents signed by him do periodically surface.

Bob Dylan

Bob Dylan

A rock legend, Bob Dylan has attracted the attention of generations with songs like "Blowin' in the Wind", "Like a Rolling Stone" and "Tangled Up in Blue". Because he has become a spokesman for these generations he has sustained enormous popularity. He does sign autographs in-person, often reluctantly, and responds to fan mail with facsimile-signed photographs. Because he is such a difficult signature to acquire his authentic autograph can command a significant price. Unfortunately, he has also been the target of forgers so exercise caution when purchasing a signed Dylan item.

The Eagles

One of the premier acts of the seventies, The Eagles landed with hits such as "Best of My Love", "Lyin' Eyes" and "Hotel California". Generally speaking all of the band members are good signers in-person and most even respond to fan mail, the exceptions being Don Henley and Glen Frey. Hell froze over in 1994 and the group reformed and toured, giving autograph collectors a shot at getting an item signed by all the original members.

Emerson, Lake and Palmer

An enduring band that successfully fused rock and classical music, ELP became very popular despite not being a singles band. All three members are excellent signers in-person and have even done signing sessions with a few dealers.

Eurythmics

A British synth-pop act of the eighties, the Eurythmics are Annie Lennox and Dave Stewart. Both are responsive signers in-person and Lennox even answers fan mail!

Everly Brothers

The most influential duo in rock history, The Everly Brothers gave us hits like "Bye Bye Love", "Wake Up Little Susie" and "Cathy's Clown". While both can be reluctant but obliging to autograph requests, neither answers fan mail! Both are a tougher signature than most think!

Fleetwood Mac

Formed in 1967, by the time the group really struck it rich only two of the original members remained, John McVie and Mick Fleetwood. The late seventies belonged to Fleetwood Mac and its members, McVie, Fleetwood, Christine McVie, Stevie Nicks and Lindsey Buckingham. The album "Rumours" alone had four Top Ten hits. The only way to acquire their signatures is in-person as most fan mail goes unanswered. In-person Nicks is the most willing signer if she's in the right mood. The most reluctant signer is Buckingham!

The Grateful Dead

"The Immortal Living Caravan", The Grateful Dead has been a constant reminder of just how good the sixties really were. Despite personnel changes in the group, the key signatures have always been Jerry Garcia and Bob Weir. All the band members were generally very responsive to autograph requests in-person. Garcia, Ron "Pigpen" McKernan, Keith Godchaux and Brent Myland are all now deceased. Any autographed items from the original lineup, which included McKernan, could command a significant price.

Guns 'N' Roses

Late eighties hard rock and self-destruction band, Guns 'N' Roses had hits with songs like "Sweet Child o' Mine" and "Welcome to the Jungle". Eventually the band became known for more of what they did off stage, rather than on. All the members of the band were and still are unpredictable so take your chances. Slash will sign items in the right environment, but his signature is often so illegible that no one would believe

it's actually his. If Rose signs anything it will often be printed rather than cursive.

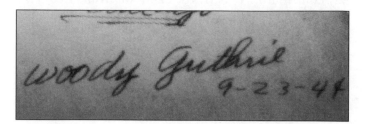

Woody Guthrie

Woody Guthrie

A pre-World War II folk icon, Guthrie gave us many memorable songs including "This Land Is Your Land", "Pastures of Plenty" and "So Long, It's Been Good to Know You". Many including Bob Dylan revered him. His signature in any form is scarce.

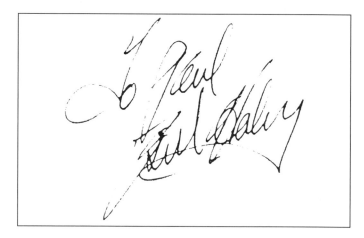

Bill Haley

Bill Haley

A genuine rock pioneer, Bill Haley along with His Comets gave us hits like "Rock Around the Clock", "Shake, Rattle and Roll" and "See You Later Alligator". While he was responsive later in life to in-person autograph requests, he seldom answered fan mail. During his years as a teen idol, you couldn't even get near him to ask for a signature.

Heart

Late seventies and eighties power-pop group, Heart, led by the Wilson sisters, hit pay dirt with numerous songs including "Magic Man", "Barracuda", "These Dreams" and "Alone". All the band members are responsive in-person, with only Ann and Nancy Wilson occasionally reluctant. Fan mail requests for their signature often go unanswered.

Jimi Hendrix

Jimi Hendrix

A guitar god, Jimi Hendrix took music to an entirely new level with songs like "Purple Haze" and "Foxey Lady", to name only a few. He was a very obliging signer in-person and often added inscriptions such as "Stay Kool", "Be Sweet" and Be Groovy". The hallmarks of his signature are the two-stroke "J", the descending peaks of the lower case stroke of "imi", the large two or three stroke "H", and the large "e" in Hendrix. His signature has been in demand ever since his untimely death and can command a significant price. Unfortunately, his signature has also been a target for forgers who typically pen his name to a blank sheet of paper. Buyer beware!

Buddy Holly and the Crickets

Buddy Holly and the Crickets

It's hard to believe that nearly a half-century after his death, Buddy Holly could continue to have such an enormous impact upon music, but it's true. The hits came fast and furious, "That'll Be The Day", "Peggy Sue", and "Oh Boy", were only a few of the classics he would leave behind. Both he and the Crickets were very obliging signers in-person. Unlike some other artists, Holly was not prone to inscriptions or personalizations. On album pages where the signatures of the entire band appear, his is typically the largest. Hallmarks of his signature include consistent character slants, long ascenders in the "dd" and "ll" letter combinations and the lack of formation in the "y". As one might expect forgeries can be encountered so be cautious when purchasing his autographed material.

Whitney Houston

Late eighties and early nineties pop diva, Houston's extraordinary musical ability was showcased in songs such as "Saving All My Love for You", "Greatest Love of All" and "I Will Always Love You". Arguably the greatest voice in popular music, Houston has also pursued an acting career. She is an elusive, yet occasionally obliging signer in-person, however fan mail is hardly ever answered. If she does sign, it will often be a salutation and "Whitney" only! A far tougher signature than most think!

INXS

A late-eighties Aussie funk-rock pop band, INXS scored big with hits such as "New Sensation", "Never Tear Us Apart" and " Suicide Blonde". The tragic death of David Hutchhence has essentially put an end to the group. While all band members were occasionally responsive to autograph requests, Hutchhence could be a challenge.

The Isley Brothers

The Isley Brothers first came to light in the late fifties with the hit single "Shout". They would later go on to give us a number of hits including "This Old Heart of Mine", "It's Your Thing" and "The Lady (Part I)". The group went through numerous member changes and some members are now deceased. All of the living members are responsive signers in-person and some even respond to mail requests for their signature.

The Jackson Five/Michael Jackson

The Jackson Five dominated the pop charts in the early seventies with hits like "ABC", "I'll Be There" and "I Want You Back". Later, Michael Jackson would opt for a solo career that would crown him "The King of Pop". Breaking every conceivable sales record, Michael Jackson would redefine music with his release of "Thriller". The album would spend a record thirty-seven weeks at the top of the U.S. album chart. Armed with a heavy security staff, it is nearly impossible to close enough to Michael Jackson to ask for an autograph. Fortunately for fans he does occasionally respond to fan mail and if you're lucky and patient you just might get an authentic autograph.

Janet Jackson

A pop diva, Janet Jackson was thrust into the spotlight following the 1986 release of her album "Control". From that period until today, the hits just kept coming including "Miss You Much", "Black Cat" and "That's the Way Love Goes". She is often an obliging signer in-person if you can get close enough to her to ask. Fan mail however, often goes unanswered.

Jan and Dean

Sixties surf duo, Jan and Dean gave us many classics including "Surf City", "Dead Man's curve" and "The Little Old Lady (from Pasadena)". Both Jan Berry and Dean Torrence are very responsive to their fans and don't mind signing autographs both in-person and via mail requests. They both typically sign only their first names.

Jefferson Airplane/Jefferson Starship

Jefferson Airplane defined the psychedelic era of the sixties with hits such as "White Rabbit" and "Somebody To Love". Later iterations of the band were also extremely successful during the seventies and eighties. All members of the group are very responsive to autograph requests in-person and most also respond to mail requests.

Jethro Tull

Jethro Tull, a name taken from an 18th century agriculturist, has essentially been both Ian Anderson and Martin Barre. The group, formed in 1967, has given such hits as "Locomotive Breath", "Thick as a Brick" and "Bungle in the Jungle". All the members of the band are obliging signers in-person, however fan mail often goes unanswered.

Billy Joel

The late seventies and eighties saw Billy Joel dominate the record charts. His hits include "Piano Man", "It's Still Rock and Roll To Me" and "Tell Her About It". In-person he is very responsive to his fans but through the mail autograph requests are machine or ghost signed.

Elton John

A prolific and talented artist, Elton John has had enormous success in the music business. His hits include "Your Song", "Crocodile Rock", "Island Girl" and "Candle in the Wind". Because he is so popular it is often difficult to get close enough to him to ask for an autograph. Mail requests are answered with facsimile-signed photographs. Because the supply of his autograph has not met the demand, an authentic signature is not only hard to find but also costly.

Forged Elton John color photographs are also commonly encountered so choose your purchases wisely!

Quincy Jones

Perhaps the most important figure in modern music, Quincy Jones has carved out a legacy which few, if any, could follow. He has been a successful jazz musician, bandleader, composer, arranger and producer. He is also a very difficult autograph to obtain. He is elusive to requests in-person and if you get a response to a request by mail, it will be a facsimile signed photograph.

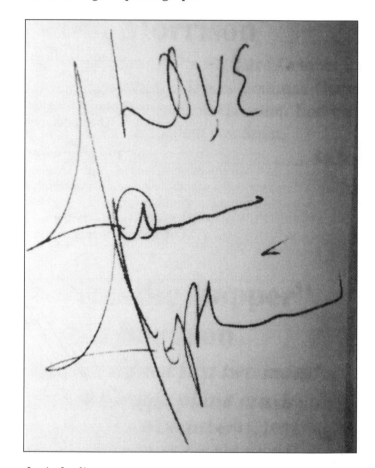

Janis Joplin

Janis Joplin

A rock music legend, Janis Joplin could mesmerize an audience with songs like "Down On Me" and "Piece of My Heart". Her tragic death in 1970 came far to soon and nowhere was this more evident than with the posthumous album release of her unfinished recording sessions, simply titled "Pearl". While she was very responsive to her fans in-person, her death at such a young age has made her signature scarce, expensive and very much in demand. Often she would add an inscription to her autograph, such as "Love" or "Peace". The capitalization in her signature often resembles the number "4" because of its formation and typically the "a" and "op" are the only legible lower case letters. Forgeries do exist, so be cautious!

The Judds/Wynonna

The Judds, a mid-eighties mother and daughter act, dominated the country charts with songs such as "Mama He's Crazy", "Why Not Me" and "Cry Myself to Sleep". Their enormous popularity forced them to explore the alternatives to answering fan mail. They have used everything from personalized facsimile photographs to machine generated signatures. Only recently has Wynonna begun to answer her fan mail personally. We all hope the trend continues.

B.B. King

A modern day blues legend, B.B King has given us many classic recordings including "Three O'Clock Blues", "You Didn't Want me", and "Please Love Me". He has always been very responsive to his fans and signs autographs both in-person and via mail requests.

KISS

One of the most popular rock acts ever, KISS will soon be entering their fourth decade. The band has given us hits such as "Rock and Roll All Nite", "Shout It Out Loud", "Beth" and "I Was Made For Lovin You". The band has always been obliging to signature requests in-person, however fan mail typically goes unanswered. The original lineup is most sought by autograph collectors, however the autograph of Eric Carr, who died tragically from cancer, is also valuable. Watch out also for forgeries!

Led Zeppelin

One of the most influential forces in rock music, Led Zepplin has left behind an impressive legacy. Their enormous popularity kept most of them away from the public while not on stage. Security around the band was always very tight, with the chances of getting an autograph practically impossible. John Bonham's death in 1980 essentially put an end to the group. Items signed by all the members of the band are scarce and highly sought by collectors. Of the surviving members both Jimmy Page and Robert Plant are the easiest signatures to acquire; in fact I caught Robert Plant taking a commercial flight to New York. Both Page and Plant have toured together, thus bringing another opportunity to collectors. The toughest living member is John Paul Jones who has remained elusive to collectors. None of the former band members answers fan mail.

Little Richard

One of rock 'n' roll's apostles, this exotic late-fifties performer seemed to harbor his rebelliousness until he hit the stage. Little Richard gave us the classic hits

"Tutti Frutti", "Long Tall Sally" and "Good Golly, Miss Molly". Unfortunately for fans, Richard has never warmed up to autograph requests under any circumstances. Many collectors have never even seen his signature.

Lynyrd Skynyrd

Lynyrd Skynyrd followed the Allman Brothers successful recipe and helped ignite interest in the "Southern Rock Movement". They landed hits with "Sweet Home Alabama", "Free Bird" and "What's Your Name". A tragic 1977 plane crash claimed the lives of six people including band members Ronnie Van Zant and Steve Gaines. In 1990, Allen Collins passes away from pneumonia. Signed items from the height of their career are rare. The remaining members of the band, who have regrouped often, are obliging signers in-person.

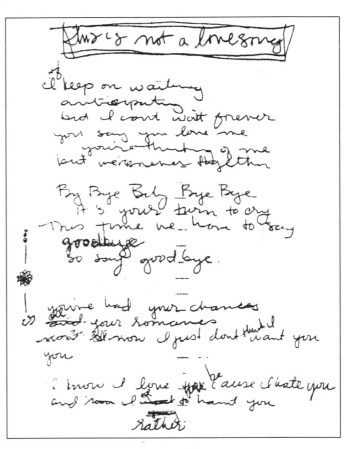

Madonna, lyrics

Madonna

The "Material Girl", Madonna has been a creative force in the industry constantly pushing all boundaries, be it sexual or social. Her hit songs include "Like a Virgin", "Live to Tell", "Open Your Heart" and "Justify My Love". Never boring or predictable, she continues to push herself and her audience to new levels of expectation. Nearly always accompanied by heavy security, if you can get close enough to her to ask for an autograph, she will often comply. She does not sign mail requests for her signature or answer her fan mail. Fortunately for collectors numerous documents and even handwritten lyrics have entered the market giving you an addition source for her signature. Because she is so popular and signs little material, Madonna has been a target of forgers. Many of the signed photographs being offered in the market are fake, so be cautious. She signs simply "Madonna" and her signature can be an authentication nightmare because of variations.

The Mamas and the Papas

A late sixties Greenwich Village folk pop act, The Mamas and the Papas scored hits with "California Dreamin", "Monday, Monday", "I Saw Her Again" and "Creeque Alley". Lasting a mere three years, the band did try to reform in 1971, but failed. Years after the death of Cass Elliot, the band regrouped again in 1981. All the remaining members are obliging to autograph requests in-person, however mail requests are often ignored. Fortunately for collectors some appearance contracts have entered the autograph market, giving collectors the rare opportunity to purchase the signatures of all the original members.

Bob Marley and the Wailers

An icon in the world of reggae music, Bob Marley was an international star and a Jamaican hero. He is best remembered for the songs "No Woman, No Cry", "Exodus", and "Is This Love". His signature is extremely scarce and anything signed by the entire band is also rare. Peter Tosh, Carlton Barrett and Marley are all deceased.

Johnny Mathis

A very popular singer who rose to prominence in the late fifties, Mathis is typically associated with the songs, "Wonderful Wonderful", "It's Not for Me to Say" and "Chances Are". He is very responsive to his fans and has always taken time to sign autographs both in-person and through the mail.

Curtis Mayfield

A gifted singer, songwriter and producer, Mayfield is commonly associated with the songs "Superfly", "Freddie's Dead" and "People Get Ready". A horrible accident in 1990 left him permanently paralyzed from the neck down. His signature is uncommon.

Metallica

The "Lords of Metal", Metallica has a large and very dedicated following. The two songs they are commonly associated with are "One" and "Enter Sandman". All the members are obliging signers in-person, however fan mail often goes unanswered. The key signatures are James Hetfield and Lars Ulrich.

Bill Monroe

"The Father of Bluegrass", Monroe gave us songs like "Kentucky Waltz", "Footprints in the Snow" and "Blue Moon of Kentucky". He was very responsive to his fans throughout his entire career and responded to autograph requests both in-person and through the mail.

The Moody Blues

Initially formed as a blues band in the sixties, The Moody Blues gave us hits like "Go Now", "Nights in White Satin", and "The Story in Your Eyes". Following the departure of Denny Laine and Clint Warwick, Justin Hayword and John Lodge were added to what would become the most popular lineup. The band is obliging to signature requests in-person, however request through the mail often unanswered.

Van Morrison

Early sixties Irish pop icon, Morrison became popular for songs like "Gloria", "Brown Eyed Girl" and "Domino". He has not warmed up to the hobby of autograph collecting and hates to sign anything. Requests for his signature via mail are also unsuccessful.

Rick Nelson

An American teen idol, Nelson had hits with "I'm Walkin", "Stood Up" and "Garden Party". Prior to his untimely death in a 1985 air crash, he was a very responsive signer both in-person and through the mail. As a member of the Rock and Roll Hall of Fame, his signature will only continue to grow in demand and is far from cheap to acquire.

Nirvana

A Seattle grunge act, Nirvana gave the nineties an anthem called "Smells Like Teen Spirit". The band became incredibly popular, so successful in fact that it began to take a toll on its members. Front man Kurt Cobain eventually ended his own life on April 8, 1994. The band had to reluctantly deal with autograph requests and when and if they signed would typically only use their first name. Cobain also signed his first name as "Kurdt" on occasion, so don't let that throw you. Since Cobain's death many forged examples have entered the market, so exercise caution when purchasing any signed Nirvana pieces.

Oasis

Led by the Gallagher brothers, Liam and Noel, Oasis has been far more popular in their native Great Britain than in the United States. "Wonderwall" and " D'You Know What I Mean" are the two songs most associated with the band. The band is reluctant but obliging to autograph requests in-person, however mail requests often go unanswered.

Roy Orbison

A rock legend, Orbison became popular for songs such as "Only the Lonely", "Crying" and "Oh, Pretty Woman". He was a responsive signer in-person, however mail requests for his autograph often went unanswered. Orbison signed material is much harder to find than one might think.

Wilson Pickett

Late-sixties soul singer, Pickett gave us hits such as "In the Midnight Hour", "Land of 1,000 Dances" and "Funky Broadway". He is an obliging signer in-person, however request made through the mail are seldom answered. His induction into the Rock and Roll Hall of Fame will always guarantee a market for his signature.

Pink Floyd

The entire face of rock music was transformed with the release "The Dark Side of the Moon" by Pink Floyd in 1973. The album catapulted the band into stardom and spent 741 weeks on the album charts. The band followed with numerous other successful albums including "Wish You Were Here", "The Wall" and "A Momentary Lapse of Reason". The band has been through some changes over the years, but the lineup most sought by collectors is that of Wright, Waters, Mason and Gilmour. I have been told that the members are obliging signers in-person, but know that they don't answer autograph requests via mail.

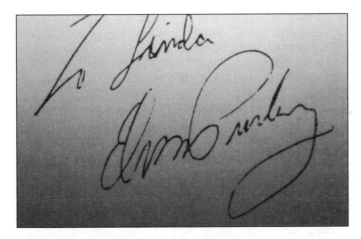

Elvins Presley

Elvis Presley

"The King", Elvis Presley, as popular as he was, often took time to sign autographs for his fans. During his lifetime he employed many techniques to respond to his enormous stacks of fan mail, from facsimile signed photographs to ghost signed items. Also worth noting is that Presley associates often signed for him, although these are fairly easy to identify as such. His signature varied greatly during his lifetime, primarily in

capitalization, character formation and flamboyance. Most notable is the lack of flamboyance when signing legal documents, as compared to a simple in-person request for an autograph. By the late seventies, his handwriting exhibited significant degradation making these examples very difficult to authenticate. As one might anticipate forgeries have also been encountered so be careful.

Prince

Sexy, mysterious, controversial and cutting-edge, "The Symbol" has brought us hits such as "Let's Go Crazy", "Purple Rain" and "Raspberry Beret". He does not like signing autographs and will only do so if it is the only alternative. Through the mail he will respond with backstage passes, which are cool but not signed. A tough signature!

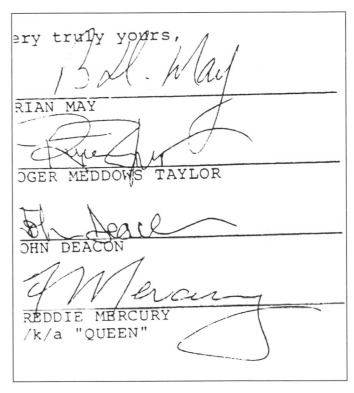

Queen - Brian May, Freddie Mercury, Roger Taylor, John Deacon

Queen

One of the most successful bands of the seventies and eighties, Queen gave us numerous hits including "Bohemian Rhapsody", "We Are the Champions/We Will Rock You" and "Crazy Little Thing Called Love". The untimely death of Freddie Mercury put an end to the band in 1991. The band was often obliging signers in-person, the problem was getting to them to ask. Mail requests often went unanswered and still do to living members.

Otis Redding

An outstanding sixties soul singer, Redding scored hits with "These Arms of Mine", "(Sittin' on) The Dock of the Bay", and "I've Been Loving You Too Long". He died tragically in a 1967 plane crash. He was an obliging signer in-person, however very little of his signed material ever enters the market. His signature is considered uncommon and is in constant demand.

R.E.M.

Eighties and nineties pop rockers, R.E.M. caught our attention with songs such as "The One I Love", "Fall On Me", "Superman" and "Its the End of the World as We Know It (and I Feel Fine)". The band's popularity grew gradually and to a level never dreamed of by either the band or their record company. While three of the original four members will reluctantly sign autographs, Michael Stipe will not. The forever-eccentric lead singer has shunned autograph seekers for years and will probably continue to do so. Now that Bill Berry has left the group, one wonders what the chances are of getting all four of the original members to sign an item, probably not good. The band does not sign autograph requests via mail!

Cliff Richard

Britain's Elvis Presley, Richard has placed more than one hundred hit singles in the U.K. Top Forty, including "Move It", "Living Doll" and "Travelin' Light". Truly a living rock and roll legend, Cliff Richard is a must addition to any autograph collection.

The Rolling Stones

Simply "The World's Greatest Rock and Roll Band", The Rolling Stones have given us numerous hits including "Jumping Jack Flash", "Brown Sugar" and "(I Can't Get No) Satisfaction". Their enormous popularity has made it extremely difficult for any of the members to live a normal life. Ironically, Mick Jagger, who always has security members close by, is the most obliging to autograph requests. All the other members are very reluctant but obliging signers. Vintage signed pieces that include all the original members are always in demand. The band does not sign autograph requests via mail!

Linda Ronstadt

Linda Ronstadt

The beautiful voice of Linda Ronstadt has given us many hits including "You're No Good", "When Will I Be Loved" and "Blue Bayou". She is somewhat apprehensive when people approach her for autographs. Once she realizes that you are sincere, she is more than happy to oblige. Mail requests for her signature are typically unsuccessful.

Diana Ross/The Supremes

Sixties Motown female vocal group, The Supremes landed numerous hits including "Stop! In The Name of Love", "You Can't Hurry Love" and "You Keep Me Hangin' On". All of the members of The Supremes have been very responsive signers both in-person and through mail requests. Florence Ballard, who left the group in 1967, died in 1976. Her signature is the most sought, followed by Ross.

Rush

A Canadian power trio, Rush is often associated with the songs, "Limelight", "Tom Sawyer" and "Freewill". The band has always been responsive to their fans in-person and all willingly sign autographs. Geddy Lee is an avid sports fan and is often sighted at baseball spring training camps or at a professional hockey game. Drummer Neil Pert often does drum clinics and you may be able to pick up a signature from him during a session. Alex Lifeson is a pilot, so when he's not on stage, try the airport. Mail requests for autographs are often unanswered.

Pete Seeger

A pivotal figure in American folk music, Pete Seeger is typically identified with the songs "If I Had a Hammer", On Top of Old Smokey" and "Goodnight Irene". He is one of only a few who have worked with both Woody Guthrie and his son Arlo. He has been a responsive signer throughout his life both in-person and to mail requests for his autograph.

Bob Seger

A blue-collar rocker, Bob Seger has given hits like "Night Moves", "Still the Same", "Like a Rock", and "Old Time Rock and Roll". He is a responsive signer in-person and still responds to his fan mail!

The Sex Pistols

A band that changed the course of rock and roll, The Sex Pistols did so during a very short and turbulent career. They produced only one studio album, "Never Mind the Bollocks Here's the Sex Pistols", but it ranks as one of the most important records ever. They also did only one very short U.S. Tour before the band began unraveling. Johnny Rotten quit the band, Sid Vicious is arrested and charged with murder and later dies of a heroin overdose. Living former band members only recently have really warmed up to autograph requests. Items signed by Rotten, Steve Jones, Paul Cook and Vicious are very rare. A few appearance contracts have surfaced but rarely include all signatures.

Paul Simon and Art Garfunkel

Paul Simon/Simon and Garfunkel

After giving us classic songs such as "Bridge Over Troubled Water", "Sounds of Silence" and "The Boxer", both these performers went on to successful solo careers.

Both Paul Simon and Art Garfunkel are very temperamental and can be reluctant yet obliging to in-person signature requests. Simon responds to mail requests for his signature with facsimile signed photos. Garfunkel will respond to letters if they exhibit some creativity, but routine requests often go unanswered.

Frank Sinatra

Frank Sinatra

A talented singer and actor, "Ol' Blue Eyes" went through many phases in his long and prestigious career. From his early days with the Harry James Orchestra to the Capitol Record Years with Nelson Riddle, the hits just kept coming. Sinatra even picked up a 1953 Oscar for his role in the film "From Here to Eternity", giving collectors another reason to acquire

his signature. Throughout most of his career he was either mobbed by fans or protected by security, making it difficult to get close enough to him for a signature. Mail requests for his signature during the sixties and seventies were answered with facsimile signed photographs. Most of the mail requests for his signature over the next years of his life often went unanswered. Sinatra's signature did change during his life. It was very flamboyant in his early years, but later in life appeared much stiffer. Because of his enormous popularity, he has been a target of forgers, so exercise caution when purchasing any autographed items.

Sly and the Family Stone

Late-sixties Bay area founders of funk, Sly and the Family Stone was led by the dynamic Sly Stone (Sylvestor Stewart). The group gave us numerous hits including "Dance to the Music", "I Want to Take You Higher" and "Hot Fun in the Summertime". Group members are generally obliging in-person but I have had little luck via mail requests. Some appearance contracts have surfaced in the market. Sly's reputation took some hard hits with drug arrests and even a jail sentence.

Cher

Sonny and Cher

Late sixties husband and wife duo, Sonny and Cher gave us songs like "I Got You Babe", "The Beat Goes On" and "Baby Don't Go". Following their 1975 divorce,

Sonny went on to an acting career, various other ventures and eventually a seat in the Congress, while Cher went on to create a legacy in both music and film. Little material signed by both rarely surfaced before Sonny's tragic death, and now afterwards it has been even harder to find an item. Both were obliging signers in-person during their early years, however later I only had luck with Cher answering mail requests. Later in his life Sonny Bono was very responsive to in-person autograph requests.

Bruce Springsteen

Bruce Springsteen

"The Boss", Bruce Springsteen has given us anthems like "Born to Run", "Born in the U.S.A." and "Dancing in the Dark". He has been popular for decades now, always attracting new generations of fans. As one might expect, Springsteen is very obliging to in-person signature requests and even will drift outside concert halls to sign for his fans! Mail requests for his signature typically go unanswered.

Steely Dan

Seventies concept pop group, Steely Dan scored hits with "Do It Again", "Reeling in the Years", "Peg" and "Hey Nineteen". The problem with getting their signatures is that they rarely toured, so you never had access to either Walter Becker or Donald Fagen. Mail requests for their signatures often go unanswered. The group did finally tour again in the nineties, but it was on a limited basis.

Rod Stewart

A true megastar, Rod "The Mod" Stewart has had a long and prolific career. His hits have included "Tonight's the Night (Gonna Be Alright)", "Da Ya Think I'm Sexy", and "Forever Young". While his attitude toward autograph requests has varied over the years, he is currently very obliging to both in-person and requests via mail.

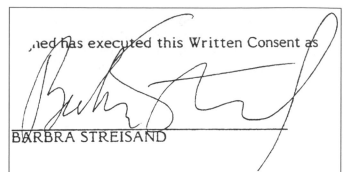

Barbra Streisand

Barbra Streisand

Having sold more than 50 million albums in the U.S. alone, it's not hard to understand why Barbra Streisand is the top-selling female artist in history. From the Broadway stage to appearances in over a dozen films, this multi-faceted artist continues to impress her fans. During her long career she has handled mail requests for her autograph with everything from facsimile-signed photos to ghost signed items. She doesn't like signing autographs and will rarely do so. If she does sign it will often be only "Barbra". Fortunately for collectors numerous documents signed by her have appeared in the market. As a collector I would be skeptical about all signed Streisand material with the exceptions of documents.

The Temptations/David Ruffin/Eddie Kendricks

A dominating male vocal group of the sixties and early seventies, The Temptations went through numerous personnel changes. The group brought us songs such as "My Girl", "Beauty's Only Skin Deep" and "I Wish It Would Rain". Many of the early members of the band are now deceased and items signed by one of the key lineups, especially Ruffin and Kendricks are uncommon.

Ike and Tina Turner/Tina Turner

Late sixties and early seventies soul revue, Ike and Tina Turner scored hits with "It's Gonna Work Out Fine", "Proud Mary" and "Nutbush City Limits". After the marriage ended, Tina went on to a successful solo career, however Ike Turner had a string problems including a prison sentence. I have been told that Tina is a responsive signer in-person, however she does not sign mail requests for her autograph.

U2

The eighties spawned many successful bands, but perhaps none has gained as much widespread acceptance as U2. The group has brought us hits such as "With or Without You", "I Still Haven't Found What I'm Looking For" and "Desire". The enormous popularity of the band has meant increased security, making it harder and harder to approach the band for autographs. The group does not sign autograph requests via mail! Of all the band members Bono Vox (Paul Hewson) is generally the most public and if you can get to him, he will sign. Watch out for forgeries!

Ritchie Valens

During a very short period of time, Ritchie Valens scored hits with "Come On, Let's Go", "Donna" and "La Bamba" before having his career cut short in a tragic plane crash that also claimed the lives of the Big Bopper and Buddy Holly. He was a very obliging signer in-person and did so often for friends around the San Fernando Valley area of California. The problem is that the supply of his signature never met the demand and with his tragic death at such a young age, you have a very scarce autograph.

Van Halen

Van Halen rose to prominence in the late seventies and scored hits with songs such as "Dance the Night Away", "Panama" and "Why Can't This Be Love". The band put a whole new meaning to the term power rock and with it Eddie Van Halen's guitar prowess vaulted him into a "Guitar God". Surprisingly, despite their fame, the band has remained fairly down to earth and doesn't mind taking some time to sign autographs both in-person and through mail requests.

Stevie Ray Vaughan

A blues icon, Stevie Ray Vaughan was really just coming into his own, when he died in a helicopter crash. He was very obliging to autograph requests and very fond of his fans. Vaughan also didn't mind doing record store autograph signings as well. He had a very flamboyant signature and wasn't hesitant to inscribe a line such as "Soul to Soul" to an item. As his legend continues to grow so will the price of his signature.

Muddy Waters

A rock disciple, Muddy Waters has influenced nearly every major artist that has followed him. He is associated with many songs including "I'm Your Hoochie Coochie Man", "Manish Boy" and "Forty Days and Forty Nights". Surprisingly little of his signed material has entered the market and when it does it usually attracts significant interest.

The Who

Early sixties band who broke with songs like "My Generation" and "I Can See For Miles", The Who made their first serious statement with the release of "Tommy". By the time "Who's Next" was released in 1971 the band's place in rock history was solidifying with songs such as "Won't Get Fooled Again" and "Baba

O'Riley". Band members have always been pretty accommodating when it comes to signing autographs and in recent years a few have even done private signings with dealers. Vintage items signed by Townshend, Entwhistle, Daltry and Moon are the most sought. Following Moon's death in 1978, Kenny Jones filled in on drums. Moon's signature is very difficult to authenticate and is best acquired in document form. None of the living members answer requests for their signature via mail! Long Live Rock!

Hank Williams

Hank Williams

Williams was country & western music's most influential artist with hits such as "Cold, Cold Heart", "Hey Good Lookin'" and "Your Cheatin' Heart". Unfortunately, he died from a heart attack before his thirtieth birthday. His signature is very scarce in any form.

Stevie Wonder

Blind since birth and inspired by the golden voice of Ray Charles, Stevie Wonder released his first single at the age of twelve. He later went on to give us songs such as "Superstition", "You Are the Sunshine of My Life" and "You Haven't Done Nothin'". His signature is his thumbprint, and he replies to mail requests for his signature with a facsimile signed photograph that includes his thumbprint.

The Yardbirds

Best known as a band whose alumni have gone on to do bigger and better things, The Yardbirds did score hits with "For Your Love", "Heart Full of Soul" and "I'm a Man". The Yardbirds was a home for Eric Clapton, Jeff Beck and Jimmy Page, but only the latter two played together. Signed items from the band will vary in value depending upon the lineup at the time.

Yes

Seventies art rock group, Yes was primarily an album and concept act, rather than a singles producer. Known for songs such as "Roundabout" and "Owner of a Lonely Heart", the group has had its fair share of personnel changes and perhaps this is why the band never seemed to loose their creative edge. Most collectors prefer signed material from the lineup of Bruford, Anderson, Squire, Howe and Wakeman. The band is obliging to signature requests in-person however I have never had any luck with any of them through mail requests.

Neil Young

An eloquent singer and songwriter, Neil Young's appeal has transcended generations with songs such as "Heart of Gold", "Old Man" and "Cinnamon Girl". Highly creative, albeit a bit off the walls at times, Young is also unpredictable. Never a person who has warmed up to autograph requests, Young will only sign items if he is in the mood or there is no other alternative. When he does sign an autograph it is often illegible, with only the "Y" and "o" in Young distinguishable as characters.

Frank Zappa

Frank Zappa/Mothers of Invention

A prolific artist and composer, Frank Zappa pushed his art about as far as anyone could during a single lifetime. Always fairly accessible to his fans, he often signed "F. Zappa" or "Frank Z.", but seldom his full name.

Sports Memorabilia

For over two decades the thriving sports memorabilia market has defied its critics, many of whom have long predicted that the apocalypse was near. The end of the century saw record prices in all niches of the hobby, from game-worn uniforms to sports trading cards. The Mastro FineSports Auction held on November 19-20, 1998 set an all-time record of $5.4 million and eclipsed the $4.6 million sale total of the famed Copeland Collection in 1991.

The Mastro Auction included more than 100 lots that totaled $10,000 or more including top-graded sports trading cards and rare memorabilia. Many individual records were also set as items sold for prices three, four, or five times normal levels.

The auction included: Mickey Mantle 1951 rookie year jersey ($73,386), Lou Gehrig bat ($61,226), a 1933 Sports Kings Ty Cobb ($50,600), a pair of PSA-8s 1933 Goudey Lajoies ($61,226 and $56,026), a PSA-9 1951 Bowman Mickey Mantle rookie ($56,023), a 1952 Topps Andy Pafko ($49,302), a 1933 Goudey Benny Bengough graded at PSA-8 ($46,000) and a 1952 Topps Mantle ($46,302).

Also sold was: 1938 Goudey Heads Up DiMaggio graded at PSA-9 ($40,250), 1941 Play Ball DiMaggio PSA-8 ($41,745), Babe Ruth game-worn hat ($39,637), Mark McGwire All-Star uniform ($27,782), 1903 World Series program ($43,671), Lou Gehrig signed ball ($37,950), Dan Brouthers signed ball ($36,991) and Steve Carlton's 1977 Cy Young Award ($32,754). The McGwire jersey was part of a run of 51 lots of Major League Baseball All-Star uniforms that raised a total of $95,500 for BAT—Baseball Assistance Team.

As if this sale alone wasn't enough to curtail any skepticism in the sports memorabilia market, on January 12, 1999, Guernsey's auction house offered Mark McGwire's 70th home-run ball for sale. When the gavel fell, this baseball sold for a record $2.7 million plus a $305,000 (11%) commission. The previous mark of $93,000, paid by actor Charlie Sheen for the "Mookie Ball"—the baseball hit by Mookie Wilson that went through Bill Buckner's legs in the 1986 World Series, had been shattered only a few weeks prior when the first home-run ball Babe Ruth hit at Yankee Stadium sold for $126,000.

Autograph collectors also delighted when on December 19, 1998, Ron Oser Enterprises auction featured 883 lots including a 1927 Yankees World Series team baseball, signed by the Bronx Bombers with handwritten inscription "World Series 1927" by Babe Ruth, which brought $29,853—a record price for a team-signed baseball. A single-signed Babe Ruth baseball was also sold at the auction for $18,047—one of the highest recorded prices for a single-signed Ruth ball.

The sports memorabilia boom has been a key market driver for the autograph market. Just pick up a copy of *Autograph Collector* magazine and you will witness for yourself an enormous influx of autograph sports memorabilia dealers. The November, 1998 issue alone contained 39 full-page advertisements offering products and services related to the sports memorabilia market. More and more dealers are also migrating from sports into other areas of the hobby such as entertainment autographs. While the degree to which these dealers will succeed during this transformation remains uncertain, a key to survival will certainly be education. Experienced dealers in the core autograph market realize it takes more than knowing how to spot a legitimate Joe DiMaggio autograph to survive.

Top Ten Current Stars Driving The Autograph Sports Memorabilia Market In 1999

1. Mark McGwire

"Big Mac" remains the biggest thing in sports and interest in his memorabilia has driven the memorabilia market into the next millennium. Although every time you see a picture of him he is either watching a ball sail out of the park or he's signing autographs, the latter scenario has done little to satisfy the enormous demand for his signature. Unlike many star athletes he has not participated in a large autograph signing in years. Much misinformation regarding McGwire's signing habits exist—don't believe everything you hear! Collectors wanting to add an authentic signature to their collection should anticipating paying around $200 for a signed baseball, $75 for an autographed photograph (8" x 10") and $275 for a bat. Hard to believe—not; a replica McGwire signed A's jersey from 1987 sold at a November 12-13 Lelands auction for $3,521.

2. Michael Jordan

Yes, I know he's retired, but what person in their right mind wouldn't put him on the vintage star list. Jordan's relationship with Upper Deck Authenticated (UDA) has provided much of the supply of autographed "Air" products found in the market. Until he alters his signing habits, there will be far more forgeries in the market than authentic signatures. Unless you personally handed an item to Mike and witnessed him signing it, I wouldn't bother with any other form of acquisition. Signed basketballs have run about $400, while an autographed photograph costs about $100.

3. Brett Favre

A good signer in-person, Favre hasn't done enough signings to completely fulfill demand. As a sports celebrity, demand for his signature seems to vary significantly, as it does with many, with his appearances in major championships. An authentic signed football can cost a collector about $200, while an autographed photograph can run $50.

4. Ken Griffey, Jr.

Like his game, demand for Ken Griffey, Jr.'s signature has been fairly consistent. His autograph material has remained accessible through marketing contracts with firms such as Upper Deck Authenticated. You can anticipate paying about $30-$40 for an autographed photograph, while an official league baseball can run between $60-$75.

5. Sammy Sosa

His home run heroics have forever linked him to the Summer of 1998. Currently demand still outstrips supply, but this should eventually level off, but when? It's all up to Sammy and his signing habits. He needs to find a legitimate avenue for his signature to make it accessible to the general public. If he can't sign, the forgers will and have signed for him! Like McGwire, I would wait until some of the home run legacy fades, before hunting for a legitimate Sosa signature.

6. Wayne Gretzky

For two decades "The Great One" has lifted professional hockey to a new level of play and established himself as the best to ever lace up a pair of skates. He thankfully has made his signature accessible to the public through corporate affiliations such as Upper Deck. Because of this, more collectors have familiarized themselves with his signature and been less prone to purchasing a forgery. Over the years he has employed numerous options to answer the enormous amount of mail requests for his signature. Despite all his efforts he still remains a target for forgers, partly due to the common variations in his signature. Collectors should only purchase his signatures through reliable sources or attempt a request in-person.

7. John Elway

His recent Super Bowl victories have only served to intensify the demand for his signature which far exceeds the supply of genuine examples. Collectors have tried for years to get genuine signatures through mail requests, but few, if any succeed. Collectors will encounter forged Elway material, particularly on photographs. Variations in his signature throughout the years have not helped authentication efforts, so be cautious when purchasing an autographed item. Similar to Wayne Gretzky, we will see how retirement alters his signature habits.

8. Terrell Davis

After only four seasons, Terrell Davis has risen to superstar status. Letting his performance on the field speak for itself, he's racking up numbers almost as fast as he is acquiring new fans. He has been accessible to collectors through shows and private signings, and even through the mail. At times his signature can appear sloppy, depending upon the signing environment—as when he's in a hurry to catch the team bus. Both he and Jamal Anderson look like the running backs of the future, so get both their signatures while you can!

9. Randy Moss

From written off NFL prospect, to all pro status in a single season! Moss can catch anything thrown to him, except a Sharpie if he's not in the mood to sign autographs. Moss has been accessible through private signings and autograph shows. Despite his availability, demand still exceeds supply, thus the entrance of some forged material. Best to catch him at a signing or other convenient places where the players hang out after the game!

10. Payton Manning

Manning's signature was in greater demand before his professional career started. Similar to Ryan Leaf's autograph—but not nearly as bad, his popularity and thus demand for his signature waned with each Colt loss. But now that he has brought the Colts into the playoff picture everything changed. He was a good signer throughout college; we'll have to see if he'll continue the practice or not—too soon to tell!

Source: *SportsCards Magazine and Price Guide*, Krause Publications (1/99)

Top Ten Vintage Stars Driving The Autograph Sports Memorabilia Market In 1999

1. Roger Maris

Not a surprise considering all the hoopla surrounding the great home run race of 1998, that the name Roger Maris is now seen in an entirely new and appreciative light. The humble Roger Maris received far less accolades for breaking Ruth's single season record, but it was during a far different time. I wrote Maris often when he was alive and he was always a gracious signer. During the 1980s a flood of fake Maris balls poured into the market creating considerable confusion. Exercise extreme caution when buying the items you find in the market as the forgeries of his signature have been very deceptive!

Roger Maris

2. Joe DiMaggio

Now that the "Yankee Clipper" has passed on, a flood of hoarded autographed merchandise—much of it fake, will enter the sports memorabilia market from all directions. He has always been a major target of forgers, with far more fakes in the market than authentic signatures. Besides the obvious reasons for forgers to target DiMaggio was his limited public and private signing sessions. As most are aware, he was an extremely quite and refined gentleman. DiMaggio's privacy meant more to him than the value of a business opportunity. Relatives assisted him

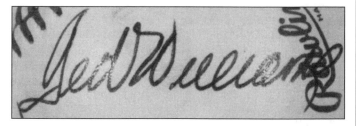

Joe DiMaggio

often with answering his mail, some of which were even proficient at imitating his signature. It's very unfortunate that the signature of Joe DiMaggio will remain under constant scrutiny for the many decades to follow, but his signing habits were exemplary of exactly what superstar athletes should not do to meet the public demand for their signature. Purchase his items only from credible dealers and try to stick to vintage signatures that can be dated or legal contracts.

3. Ted Williams

Another one of the primary targets for forgers, although not quite as bad as DiMaggio, has been Ted Williams. During the 1980s, the amount of his forged signatures was underestimated, while in recent years it has been over exaggerated. I have witnessed Williams himself deny that a signature of his that I saw him sign personally, was actually a legitimate example. Naturally, this scenario could apply to many celebrities who sign thousands of items a year, but it is a good example of just how

Ted Williams

confusing this market can be. Fortunately, albeit many would differ with me, Ted Williams was smart enough to begin marketing his own autographed material directly. You are a far higher target of forgery if authentic examples of your signature are not available to the general public—despite the price!

4. Mickey Mantle

Similar to the names above, Mickey Mantle has been a target of forgers for years. Like DiMaggio, he refused to sign certain items, such as bats for a number of years. While there have been some exceptionally good DiMaggio and Williams forgeries in the market, Mantle versions have been far inferior to his authentic signature. Like the names above be very cautious when purchasing any of his autographed material. Also, don't fall for the numerous stories dealers give you about how they obtained the signature. Any dealer who has an authentic Mickey Mantle signature doesn't need to talk anyone into buying it, as the item will sell it self.

5. Babe Ruth

Facsimiles, forgeries and ghost-signed items are common occurrences when an individual is in pursuit of an authentic Babe Ruth signature. While Ruth was always a gracious signer, the demand for his signature still outweighs the supply. Finding an autographed Babe Ruth baseball won't be a problem, put paying for it might! As you will see in the chart provided in this chapter, those official league baseballs in top condition with a dark, clear and crisp signature on the sweet spot can command a significant price. Most of the Ruth forgeries I have seen, including a machine scanned photograph signed with a porous tip pen, have been ridiculous and could never fool an advanced autograph collector. Since his signature is not scarce, take your time and purchase the best dateable item you can!

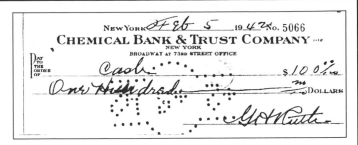

Babe Ruth

6. Joe Namath

While I personally wouldn't place Broadway Joe at number six on this chart, that is where he falls with both collectors and dealers. Whenever the Jets do well during the season, Joe's name is evoked in reverence. Joe was the consummate superstar, always bigger than life and very popular with fans. While demand for his autograph is often sporadic, he still has been able to maintain a significant amount of interest with collectors. Unlike the names above, you will encounter far less forgeries in the market. Signed helmets with the vintage Jets logo have always been popular with collectors.

7. Joe Montana

A gentleman and perhaps the best quarterback to ever play the game, Montana has maintained a good autograph regiment. He's obliging in-person, signs sporadically through the mail and has always made his signature accessible to the public through corporate affiliations such as Upper Deck. The only drawback is that his signature is prone to forgery because of its style. His signature has been inconsistent in size, form and character definition, making it difficult to authenticate.

8. Larry Bird

Now in the Hall of Fame and recipient of a Coach of the Year award, Bird has flown back into the minds of collectors. While his signature has always been accessible to collectors through corporate affiliations such as Upper Deck, he himself is a reluctant signer. Bird, similar to Namath, has maintained some level of interest in the autograph market; however, it has had a tendency to be sporadic. Unfortunately for collectors, you will run across some Bird forgeries in the autograph market, most of which seem to be on combination photographs, such as him with Magic Johnson.

9. Hank Aaron

Probably the most undervalued signature of any player ever to perform in the Major Leagues, Hank Aaron baseballs and photographs still remain at affordable levels. While how long this phenomenon is likely to last is uncertain, collectors should take full advantage of the situation, because when it changes it will likely be dramatic. His signature seems to have always been available in the market, and he has been a relatively good signer throughout the years. Collectors will encounter some forgeries and even some ghost-signed examples, but many of these will be easy to determine as such.

10. Willie Mays

While not the most popular guest of all-time at autograph shows, Willie Mays has at least made his signature available. Collectors had some success with mail requests during the 1970s, but he has never been a consistent signer. Arguably the greatest all-around player, his signature is also currently undervalued in the market. Collectors will come across their fair share of forgeries, most of which will adorn "500 Home Run Club" items, be it bats, balls or artwork. The transition in his signature over the years will make some items difficult to authenticate so refer to the many excellent resources available in the marketplace for signature comparison.

Source: *SportsCards Magazine and Price Guide*, Krause Publications (1/99)

The Quest for the Single Signed Baseball

The key market driver for all autographed sports memorabilia is the single signed baseball. This came about as the result of the sports memorabilia explosion of the 1980s. No one sector in any area of sports memorabilia is more indicative of the strength of the hobby. While many believe it is also the driving force in the entire hobby of autograph collecting, many traditional dealers refute these claims.

Although it is the most sought after form by collectors of autographed baseball memorabilia, it is also the most scrutinized. Value can vary dramatically due to the condition of the baseball, strength & position of the signature and whether it is on an official league baseball or not. Condition is an important factor in determining the value of a particular baseball. Near Mint and Excellent condition autographed baseballs often bring dramatically higher prices than those of lesser condition do. The exception to this rule is obviously a lesser condition ball signed by an obscure and very difficult player to find in this form.

Not all inks are created equal, as you will certainly realize when you get to the chapter about this unique writing fluid. As such many fade quicker than others and are less resilient to a variety of environmental conditions. The strength of a signature, which is often due the ink's lead component, also plays a critical factor in determining value. Collectors favor dark, crisp, clean signatures and are not very tolerant of flaws. The "sweet spot," the narrow point between the two seams—often opposite the ball's logo and the facsimile signature of the league president or commissioner, is the primary area for the placement of a single signature on a baseball. Those signatures appearing on or close to this position bring the higher prices in the market.

While many manufacturers make and have made baseballs in all styles and sizes, only the "official baseballs" manufactured for Major League Baseball are desired for autographs. Autographed official leagues baseballs are identical to those used by the major leagues, with most being easily dated by the appearance of the facsimile signature of the league president or commissioner. To better understand how all these elements impact value, please refer to the chart concerning autographed Babe Ruth baseballs. The information that appears in this chart is courtesy Mastro Fine Sports Auctions, 1515 W. 22nd St., Suite 125, Oak Brook, Illinois, 60523. Bill Mastro, owner of the firm, has over 35 years of hobby experience and no single individual has handled more sports cards and memorabilia. There are no finer sports auction catalogs than those published by Mastro! If you pride yourself on your knowledge of sports collectibles and your personal collection, the subscription to the firm's catalog is an absolute must.

The ultimate single signature collection of autographed baseballs is one that includes the authentic examples of all members of the Baseball Hall of Fame. Similar to other autograph collecting feats, this task will not only present a significant challenge to you and your wallet, but will do much to challenge your authentication skills and your patience. Since this niche has now been popular for decades, few bargains will be had, but an occasional find may come your way.

No one sector in any area of sports memorabilia is more indicative of the strength of the hobby, than autographed baseballs

Single Signed Baseballs

Player	SP	TOB	LOT	Price Realized
Ty Cobb	Side	UN	398	$11,635
Honus Wagner	SS	ONL	400	$2,952
Babe Ruth	SS	OAL	399	$17,869 *
Tris Speaker	SS	OAL	402	$6,197
Cy Young	SS	OAL	403	$6,193
G.C. Alexander	SS	UN	404	$6,962
George Sisler	SS	OAL	405	$2.711
Babe Ruth	SS	OAL	407	$9,936 **
Lou Gehrig	Side	OAL	409	$37,950
Rogers Hornsby	Side	OAL	406	$3,884
Frankie Frisch	SS	ONL	408	$738
Mickey Cochrane	SS	OAL	410	$16,421
Mel Ott	Side	ONL	411	$9,276
Dizzy Dean	Side	ONL	415	$1,117
Ted Lyons	SS	OAL	416	$337
K.M. Landis	SS	ONL	421	$1,743
Dan Brouthers	SS	ONL	423	$36,991
Connie Mack	SS	OL	420	$2,558
Roger Bresnahan	SS	ONL	422	$15,481
Jack Chesbro	SS	OAL	424	$24,033
Ed Walsh	Side	OAL	425	$3,283
Ray Schalk	SS	OAL	427	$1,191
Elmer Flick	Side	OAL	429	$897
Red Faber	Side	ONL	430	$794
Casey Stengel	SS	OAL	431	$898
Tommy Connolly	SS	OAL	426	$1,969
Satchel Paige	Side	OAL	432	$1,310
Roger Maris	SS	OPL	435	$3,884

Abbreviations:

SP- Signature placement, TOB-Type of Baseball, SS-"Sweet Spot," OAL-Official American League, ONL-Official National League, OPL-Official Pro League, LOT-Lot number it appeared in auction catalog, PR -Price realized

Data taken from Mastro & Steinbach, Fine Sports Auctions, sales 1198.

Autographed Babe Ruth Baseballs

Baseball type	SS	SP	BC	L	PR
Off. Spalding NL mini	5	SS	EX-MT	1353	$1,493
ML model	6	IS	EX	1329	$2,243
OAL	10	SS	NM	1313	$24,020
Unofficial	4/5	IS	G/VG	1244	$1,112
OAL	9	SS	EX	1210	$13,214
OAL, some use	5	SS	U	419	$3,251
OAL	7	IS	EX	413	$2,781
OAL	U	SS	NM	407	$9,936
OAL	10	SS	NM	399	$17,869
Off. Spalding NL mini	7	SS	NM	6	$1,265
Unofficial, used	U	SS	U	768	$4,331
D&M Official League	U	Side	NM	1207	$2,780
Worth Official League	4/5	SS	G	1209	$2,021
Official League	U	IS	EX	549	$3,000
OAL	7	SS	U	552	$3,860
OAL	3/4	SS	G	1333	$2,126
Blank	U	IS	NM	1394	$4,392

Abbreviations:

SS-Signature Scale-subjective, SP-Signature placement, SS-"Sweet Spot," IS-Inscribed to someone on the side of the baseball, BC-Baseball Condition-subjective, EX-Excellent, NM-Near Mint, G-Good, U-Undetermined, L-Lot number it appeared in auction catalog, PR-Price realized

Data taken from Mastro & Steinbach, Fine Sports Auctions, sales 1198 (1-9 items above), 0798 (10-13), 1197 (14-17)

Notes:

Average signed NL mini baseball	$1,379
Average baseball price (-minis)	$6,462
Average OAL, 9-10-SS, NM/EX	$18,367

Dating An Official League Baseball

Using this convenient chart you can determine if it was possible for a particular player to sign an official league baseball, as the league president's facsimile signature appears opposite the "sweet spot."

Major League Baseball league presidents:

National League
Morgan G. Bulkeley, 1876
William A. Hulbert, 1877-1882
A.G. Mills, 1883-1884
Nicholas Young, 1885-1902
Henry Pulliam, 1903-1909
Thomas J. Lynch, 1910-1913
John K. Tenner, 1914-1918
John A. Heydler, 1934 *
Ford Frick, 1935-1951
Warren Giles, 1951-1969
Charles S. Feeney, 1970-1986
A. Bartlett Giamatti, 1987-1989
William B. White, 1989-1994
Leonard S. Coleman, 1994-present

American League
Byron Bancroft Johnson, 1901-1927
Ernest S. Barnard, 1927-1931
William Harridge, 1935-1959 *
Joseph E. Cronin, 1959-1973
Leland S. MacPhail Jr., 1974-1983
Robert W. Brown, 1984-1994
Gene A. Budig, 1994-present

* The National League began using facsimile league president signature baseballs around 1934, while the American League followed the following year. Prior to this effort the league's president's signature was occasionally stamped on the side of a ball.

Autographed Team Baseballs

Year	Baseball Team	C	#Sigs.	Lot	PR
1918	Cincinnati Reds	U	19	710	$6,325
1925	St. Louis Cardinals	EX	U	455	$741
1931	St. Louis Cardinals	7	25	456	$3,391
1933	New York Yankees	U	20	458	$1,808 *
1936	Boston Red Sox	NM	22	460	$949
1937	Chicago Cubs (UN)	NM	24	988	$596
1937	New York Yankees (UN)	U	23	461	$1,503 *
1938	New York Yankees (UN)	NM	28	462	$3,934
1939	Chicago White Sox	NM/M	27	463	$417
1942	St. Louis Cardinals	EX/M	24	464	$1,193
1945	St. Louis Browns	EX	25	465	$522
1946	New York Yankees	EX/M	27	466	$1,193
1948	Boston Braves	NM	29	467	$1,020
1949	Philadelphia Athletics	NM	25	469	$721 *
1950	Philadelphia Phillies	VG	19	470	$682
1952	Cleveland Indians	NM/M	25	471	$656
1954	Brooklyn Dodgers	EX/NM	23	319	$1,035
1954	Chicago Cubs	EX/M	24	989	$566
1954	New York Giants	NM	30	472	$555
1955	Brooklyn Dodgers	NM	23	325	$3,275
1955	New York Yankees	EX/M	24	473	$575
1957	Milwaukee Braves	M	31	1367	$1,020
1957	New York Yankees	M	27	474	$612
1957	Milwaukee Braves	NM	27	475	$459
1958	Kansas City Athletics	NM/M	32	476	$417
1959	Chicago White Sox	EX/M	36	477	$738
1962	New York Mets	EX/M	25	478	$840
1966	Baltimore Orioles	NM	32	479	$983
1969	Oakland A's	NM/M	30	480	$542
1972	Cincinnati Reds	NM	29	481	$611
1989	Oakland A's	NM/M	33	482	$1,161

Data taken from Mastro & Steinbach, Fine Sports Auctions, sales 1/98

Facts About MLB's Rookie Of The Year Award

* It was first awarded in 1947 to Jackie Robinson.

* For the first two years only a single player received the award.

* The year 1949 was the first year that a single player was chosen from each league.

* There has only been two years, 1976 (NL) and in 1979 (AL), when a tie allowed co-recipients of the award.

* Of the 104 chosen from 1947 to 1998, only 10 (although not all are eligible yet) went on to enter the Baseball Hall of Fame. Even though there are clearly many recipients who will certainly get inducted into the Hall, less than 10% often shocks many followers of the game.

The Rookie Craze

No baseball prospect is a sure thing, but looking through the many pages of the Spring Training and Fantasy Baseball magazines, it's certainly not hard to find 100 prospects that just might have a shot at being the early-next century's hottest young rookie. So I sat down and compiled my list of players, some of which had already had a cup a coffee in the show, and decided to take a shot at writing to them for some autographs. Every prospect received the same letter, four index cards and a S.A.S.E. (self-addressed stamped envelope). All requests were mailed out at the same time and in the same fashion.

I wish I had a dime for every piece of misinformation in this hobby, but unfortunately I do not. I have heard numerous times from both dealers and collectors, that baseball players are no longer worth contacting for autographs via mail requests. While in some cases I believe that this is indeed true, I wasn't sure about the leagues top prospects? The future rookies of the year, you know the Wally Moons and Herb Scores of tomorrow.

Before I go any further let's set the record straight about winners of Major League Baseball's coveted Rookie of the Year honors, as I have heard more incorrect information regarding this award than perhaps any other.

Back to the study, I contacted each player during Spring Training (1999). Not only is this an exciting time of year for all the players, but it is also the only time when all player levels have an opportunity to interact with each other. Therefore, despite where the player ends up following the session, I have a chance to reach him at the same time as all the other potential prospects who will end up at various levels within Major League Baseball.

By the end of Spring Training, I had received 63% of my requests. All were favorable responses ranging from one autograph to four. The most common number of signatures that I received was three. Not all the signatures were legible, but thankfully I had coded each S.A.S.E. to be able to trace the envelope back to the specific request. In a few instances the player also enclosed an autographed sports trading card— although I did not ask for one or send him a card. Only one player responded with a small note. To my knowledge none appear to be "ghost" or mechanically signed.

I figured the cost of my project to be about $71.75, not including my time. By the end of Spring Training, I had received 183 signatures. This breaks down to $.39 per signature. I never anticipated such a high response rate, so I was pleasantly surprised by the return. The study also puts to rest claims by dealers that many of the prospects don't bother signing autographs.

Whether or not this rookie signing trend continues, the study proved worthwhile and most of all fun. I didn't have to purchase expensive trading card packages looking for the signed premium cards or buy an item from a satellite shopping station, I just had to put a little time, money and effort into an enjoyable project.

Top, left to right: Jeremy Giambi, Eric Chavez, Alex Gonzalez, Nick Johnson. Bottom: Michael Barrett, Gabe Kapler, Matt Riley, Brad Penny

The Study Results—Major League Baseball's Top 100 Prospects

(In Alphabetical Order)

Player	Pos./Team	Rank/Comments	Signing Habits
Anderson, Ryan	LHP, Seattle Mariners	5, "The Little Unit," 6'10" powerful lefty!	Unresponsive
Ankiel, Rick	LHP, St. Louis Cardinals	2, Led all minor leaguers in K's during 1998	Unresponsive
Armas, Tony	RHP, Montreal Expos	45, Was 12-8 in Jupiter with 136Ks!	Unresponsive
Barrett, Michael	3B, Montreal Expos	12, A great bat, hit .320 in Harrisburg!	Unresponsive
Bell, Rob	RHP, Cincinnati Reds	22, Posted 197 K's with Danville in 1998!	Responsive signer!
Belliard, Ronnie	2B, Milwaukee Brewers	31, Hit .321 at Louisville in 1998!	Responsive signer!
Beltran, Carlos	OF, Kansas City Royals	73, Hit .352 at Wichita in 1998!	Unresponsive
Benson, Kris	RHP, Pittsburgh Pirates	57, The 1996 draft's top pick!	Responsive signer!
Bergeron, Peter	OF, Montreal Expos	63, Hit .317 at San Antonio in 1998	Responsive signer!
Berkman, Lance	OF, Houston Astros	6, A .306 hitter, twice hit 3 homers in a '98 game	Unresponsive
Bradley, Milton	OF, Montreal Expos	83, Hit .302 At Cape Fear in 1998!	Responsive signer!
Bradley, Ryan	RHP, New York Yankees	24, Went from A ball to Yankees in 1998!	Responsive signer!
Branyan, Russell	3B, Cleveland Indians	28, Hit 79 HRS combined '96 & '97 season!	Responsive signer!
Brown, Dermal	OF, Kansas City Royals	41, Youngest player in American League in 1998!	Unresponsive
Burnett, A.J.	RHP, Florida Marlins	71, The minors' highest K/IP rate in 1998, 14.07!	Responsive signer!
Burrell, Pat	1B, Philadelphia Phillies	21, Hit .303 in Clearwater!	Responsive signer!
Burroughs, Sean	3B, San Diego Padres	76, Son of 1974 AL MVP Jeff Burroughs!	Responsive signer!
Butler, Brent	SS, St. Louis Cardinals	62, Third round pick in 1996 draft!	Responsive signer!
Chavez, Eric	3B, Oakland A's	3, AL leading ROY contender	Responsive signer!
Chen, Bruce	LHP, Atlanta Braves	4, Went 13-7 at 3.29 for Greenville.	Unresponsive
Clement, Matt	RHP, San Diego Padres	14, Led al AAA in K's in 1999 with 160!	Unresponsive
Crede, Joe	3B, Chicago White Sox	39, MVP Carolina League in 1998, hit .315!	Responsive signer!
Cuddyer, Mike	SS, Minnesota Twins	59, First round pick in 1997 draft!	Responsive signer!
Curtice, John	LHP, Boston Red Sox	29, One of the league's best power pitchers at 18!	Responsive signer!
Davis, Ben	C, San Diego Padres	27, Hit .286 at Mobile in 1998, .327 on the road!	Responsive signer!
Dotel, Octavio	RHP, New York Mets	85, Posted 1.97 ERA at Binghamton in 1998	Responsive signer!
Drew, J.D.	OF, St. Louis Cardinals	1, Hit .417 in 14 games with cards in 1998	Unresponsive, signs at shows
Encarnacion, Mario	OF, Oakland A's	95, Hit .272 at Huntsville in 1998!	Responsive signer!
Escobar, Alex	OF, New York Mets	10, Hit .310 at Cap. City, with 27 HRs!	Responsive signer!
Febles, Carlos	2B, Kansas City Royals	32, A .530 slugging average in 1998!	Responsive signer!
Garcia, Freddy	RHP, Seattle Mariners	69, Was part of Randy Johnson trade!	Unresponsive
Giambi, Jeremy	OF, Kansas City Royals	8, Led all pro baseball in batting in 1998-.372!	Responsive, (2) only!
Gibson, Derrick	OF, Colorado Rockies	43, Hit .429 after being called up in 1998!	Unresponsive
Giles, Marcus	2B, Atlanta Braves	34, Led Sally League in HRs, RBIs, Rs, TB, ...!	Responsive signer!
Goetz, Geoff	LHP, Florida Marlins	88, Part of Mike Piazza trade, a flame thrower!	Unresponsive
Gold, J.M.	RHP, Milwaukee Brewers	89, Posted 2.61 ERA at Ogden in 1998!	Responsive signer!
Gonzalez, Alex	SS, Florida Marlins	9, Spectacular fielder, hit .277 at Charlotte in 98'	Responsive signer!
Guillen, Carlos	2B, Seattle Mariners	86, Hit .333 with Seattle in 1998!	Responsive signer!
Guzman, Cristian	SS, Minnesota Twins	91, Hit .277 at new Britain in 1998!	Responsive signer!
Halladay, Roy	RHP, Toronto Blue Jays	11, Youngest pitcher in AL in 1999, great stuff!	Unresponsive
Hermansen, Chad	OF, Pittsburgh Pirates	18, Hit 28 HRS, only 20 yrs. old and in AAA!	Responsive signer!
Hernandez, Ramon	C, Oakland A's	82, Won CA League batting crown at .361 in	1997, Responsive signer!
Jimenez, D'Angelo	SS, New York Yankees	53, Hit .270 at Norwich in 1998	Responsive signer!
Johnson, Nick	1B, New York Yankees	13, Hit .317 in Tampa with .466 OBP!	Responsive signer!
Jones, Jacque	OF, Minnesota Twins	70, Hit .330 with 16 Hr's on road in 1998!	Responsive signer!
Kapler, Gabe	OF, Detroit Tigers	15, Hit .322 In Jacksonville with 28 HRS!	Responsive signer!
Kearns, Austin	OF, Cincinnati Reds	94, Hit .315 at Billings in 1998!	Unresponsive
King, Cesar	C, Texas Rangers	80, A top defensive prospect!	Unresponsive
Kinney, Matt	RHP, Minnesota Twins	75, Posted 1.33 ERA in Maryland Fall League !	Responsive signer!
Koch, Bill	RHP, Toronto Blue Jays	64, Was 14-7 at Dunedin with 108 K's in 1998!	Unresponsive
Ledee, Ricky	OF, New York Yankees	74, Went 6 for 10 in 1998 World Series!	Responsive signer!
Lee, Carlos	3B, Chicago White Sox	48, Hit .302 in Birmingham in 1998!	Unresponsive
Lilly, Ted	LHP, Montreal Expos	67, Averages 10Ks per game!	Responsive signer!
Lombard, George	OF, Atlanta Braves	23, Hit .308 at Greenville with 22 HRS in 1998	Unresponsive

Looper, Braden	RHP, Florida Marlins	42, Had 20 saves in Memphis, 43 Ks in 40 innings	Unresponsive
Lopez, Felipe	SS, Toronto Blue Jays	90, Hit .373 at St. Catherines in 1998!	Unresponsive
Lowell, Mike	3B, New York Yankees	44, Hit .304 in Columbus in 1998!	Unresponsive
Marquis, Jason	RHP, Atlanta Braves	68, At 19 years old, posted 135 K's in 1998!	Unresponsive
Martinez, Willie	RHP, Cleveland Indians	46, Had 117Ks in 1998 at Canton-Akron!	Unresponsive
Mateo, Ruben	OF, Texas Rangers	7, Hit .309 at Tulsa in 1998, 20 years old!	Unresponsive
McDonald, Darnell	OF, Baltimore Orioles	56, Hit .261 at Delmarva in 1998!	Unresponsive
McGlinchy, Kevin	RHP, Atlanta Braves	77, Posted 2.91 ERA at Danville in 1998!	Unresponsive
Meche, Gil	RHP, Seattle Mariners	66, Had 168Ks in 149 Innings in 1998!	Responsive signer!
Melian, Jackson	OF, New York Yankees	84, A third year key prospect at the age of 18!	Unresponsive
Meluskey, Mitch	C, Houston Astros	30, Hit .353 in New Orleans in 1998!	Unresponsive
Mills, Ryan	LHP, Minnesota Twins	99, Posted 1.80 ERA at Fort Myers in 19981	Responsive signer!
Morris, Warren	2B, Pittsburgh Pirates	52, Hit .331 at Tulsa in 1998!	Responsive signer!
Mulder, Mark	LHP, Oakland A's	37, Top rated pitcher out of Michigan State!	Responsive signer!
Myette, Aaron	RHP, Chicago White Sox	98, Posted 2.01 ERA at Winston-Salem in 1998	Responsive signer!
Nixon, Trot	OF, Boston Red Sox	72, Hit .320 at Pawtucket, also a 20-20 player!	Responsive signer!
Ortiz, Ramon	RHP, Anaheim Angels	55, In 1997 led in SO, CG and Ks in Mid. League	Responsive signer!
Ozuna, Pablo	SS, Florida Marlins	26, Led all minor leaguers in hits in 1998-192!	Responsive signer!
Patterson, Corey	OF, Chicago Cubs	51, Only 1998 two-time high school All-American	Responsive signer!
Patterson, John	RHP, Arizona Diamondbacks	33, Led CA League in ERA in 1998!	Unresponsive
Pena, Angel	C, Los Angeles Dodgers	61, Hit .335 at San Antonio in 1998	Responsive signer!
Pena, Carlos	1B, Texas Rangers	79, Hit .325 at Savannah in 1998!	Responsive signer!
Penny, Brad	RHP, Arizona Diamondbacks	17, Fourth in minors in Ks in 1999!	Responsive signer!
Perez, Odaliz	LHP, Atlanta Braves	38, Had 143Ks in Greenville in 132 innings!	Unresponsive
Petrick, Ben	C, Colorado Rockies	40, Great overall catching prospect!	Responsive signer!
Pickering, Calvin	1B, Baltimore Orioles	49, A .587 four year slugging average!	Responsive signer!
Prokopec, Luke	RHP, Los Angeles Dodgers	81, A 1.38 ERA at San Antonio in 1998!	Responsive signer!
Ramirez, Alex	OF , Cleveland Indians	96, Hit .299 at Buffalo in 1998!	Responsive signer!
Ramirez, Julio	OF, Florida Marlins	25, Outstanding defensive player!	Unresponsive
Restovich, Mike	OF, Minnesota Twins	47, Hit .355 at Elizabethton in 1998!	Responsive signer!
Riley, Matthew	LHP, Baltimore Orioles	16, A 1.19 ERA last season in Delmarva!	Responsive signer!
Rivas, Luis	SS, Minnesota Twins	100, Hit .281 at Ft. Myers in 1998!	Responsive signer!
Rivera, Juan	OF, New York Yankees	78, Hit .333 with GCL Yankees in 1998!	Unresponsive
Roberts, Grant	RHP, New York Mets	50, Was 1997 Sally pitcher of the year!	Responsive signer!
Rose, Brian	RHP, Boston Red Sox	54, Organization's best pitching prospect!	Responsive signer!
Seguignol, Fernando	1B, Montreal Expos	58, Hit .288 at Harrisburg with 25 HR's in 1998	Responsive signer!
Soriano, Alfonso	SS, New York Yankees	36, Played in Japan, strong defensively!	Unresponsive
Stenson, Dernell	OF, Boston Red Sox	20, Youngest player in AA all-star game in 1998!	Unresponsive
Veras, Wilton	3B, Boston Red Sox	93, Hit .291 at Trenton in 1998!	Responsive signer!
Ward, Daryle	OF, Houston Astros	35, Hit .305 in New Orleans with 96 RBIs!	Unresponsive
Webb, Alan	LHP, Detroit Tigers	97, Batters hit only .181 off him in 1998!	Unresponsive
Wells, Vernon	OF, Toronto Blue Jays	65, Hit .285 at Hagerstown in 1998!	Responsive signer!
Werth, Jayson	C, Baltimore Orioles	92, Drafted in first round of 1997 draft!	Unresponsive
White, Matt	RHP, Tampa Bay Devil Rays	19, Was country's top high school player!	Responsive signer!
Wilson, Enrique	SS, Cleveland Indians	87, Hit .322 with Cleveland in 1998	Responsive signer!
Yarnall, Ed	LHP, Florida Marlins	60, Was 9-0 with 1.02 ERA before Charlotte in 1998	Unresponsive

Honorable Mention: OF Norm Hutchins, RHP Jeff Weaver, 3B-OF Willie "Mo" Pena, and RHP Joe Nathan

Source: Author's data base/research

The Top Dozen Signers

* Morris, Warren	* Lilly, Ted	* Bradley, Milton
* Benson, Kris	* Hermansen, Chad	* Penny, Brad
* Seguignol, Fernando	* Johnson, Nick	* Burroughs, Sean
* Riley, Matthew	* Kinney, Matt	* Ortiz, Ramon

Note:
The dozen players listed above were the first to respond to my mail requests.

Chapter 5

Autograph Organizations, Periodicals & References

As a dedicated autograph collector sharing your knowledge with others in your field is paramount. A logical forum for such an interchange is certainly an autograph organization. Fortunately for collectors there are many outstanding organizations to choose from. As you read the brief overviews of the organizations (listed below in alphabetical order). I am certain that you will find one or more that will suit your needs.

Autograph Organizations

IACC/IADA—International Autograph Collectors Club & Dealers Alliance

Mike Frost and Stephen Koschal founded the IACC/DA in October of 1997. The organization includes over 100 dealer members and four times the number of collector members. Catering to both collectors and dealers, this nonprofit organization boasts that it is the largest club of its kind in the world devoted exclusively to autograph collecting.

The official headquarters of the group is located in Hollywood, Florida. Both members and non members are welcome to visit or write to the address for information. While visiting you can chat about autographs with one of the board members or scan the collection of authentic signatures that the group maintains.

The group also conducts private signings and offers to its membership autographs at prices well below market value. For example, a black & white photograph (8" x 10") signed by boxing legend and Hall of Famer Kid Gavilan can be purchased by members for $9.50.

Samples of items produced by International Autograph Collectors Club and Dealer Alliance.

The club's outstanding publication called *Eye's, Ears And Voice Of The Hobby* is published six times a year and sent to the entire membership. For many, this publication alone is worth the cost of a membership. Interesting articles adorn the pages of this periodical, from comprehensive overviews of U.S. Presidential signatures to industry tidbits and even alerts about stolen merchandise.

For dealers joining the club, it will involve more than just filling out a membership form. Each will have to provide for the club a sponsor, as well as two recognized dealer references. Not until this process is complete, will the membership committee then review the application for acceptance. The club feels that only through this process can they guarantee that dealers have earned every credential that they bestow upon them.

The club also publishes annually the IACC/DA DEALER DIRECTORY. This handy periodical includes only dealers that have lived up to the club's stringent code of ethics. The 1998 IACC/DA DEALER DIRECTORY contained 61 dealers.

Impressive also is the club's commitment to education. They offer members courses led by some of the hobbies finest scholars. All members attending these courses receive a certificate of completion signed by the instructor. Many of these courses are held in conjunction with the club's Show Calendar of five national events.

In 1998 the club proposed the establishment of the Autograph Hall of Fame, so that the many outstanding contributors of can be recognized for their contributions to the hobby. The presidents of the major autograph clubs were on the ballot committee. Members of the club participated in the election of the first inductees during the early part of 1999.

You may contact this club at: IACC/DA, 4575 Sheridan St., Ste. #111, Hollywood, FL 33021. Internet website: http://www.ewol.com/autos.

International Autograph Collectors Club And Dealers Alliance

1999 Membership Information

Collector Membership, US Zip Codes	$17.50
All Foreign Countries, USD	$25.00
Renewal Dealer Membership	$60.00
New Dealer Membership	$70, includes $10 appl. fee

U.A.C.C.—Universal Autograph Collectors Club

Founded in 1965, the UACC has become a strong resource for collectors worldwide. Members of the Universal Autograph Collectors Club benefit a number of ways from the club. Perhaps the most visible is the group's award-winning bimonthly journal *The Pen and Quill*. It features articles on all aspects of collecting, from autographic studies and auction updates to information on autographic fakes.

The UACC is doing much to enhance the hobby including presenting awards to distinguished contributors. Here is UACC Treasurer Al Wittenbert presenting the first Outstanding Autograph Dealer Award to Joe Rubinfine in 1997.

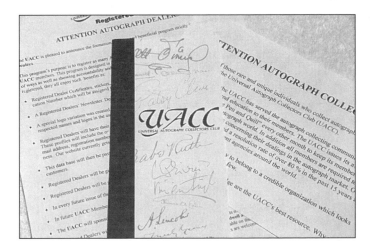

Items sent out to potential members of the Universal Autograph Collectors Club.

The club also sponsors autograph shows that feature educational displays, seminars and celebrity guests. The club regulates its dealers who must comply with the group's strict Code of Ethics. The group also conducts auctions, as well as offering special autographed premium items to members at cost.

The UACC gives its members a forum to interact with fellow collectors and even provides opportunities to purchase low-cost reference materials from many of the leading autograph experts. The organization also caters to the needs of dealers through programs like the one presented here in the chart below.

It's easy to join UACC. Simply request a membership application from: UACC, Dept. AAC, P.O. Box 6181, Washington, DC 20041-6181, or visit the club's website at www.uacc.org.

The UACC Registered Dealer Program

Includes:

* Registered dealer certificates, stickers and promotional kits along with a Dealer Identification Number which is assigned for the duration of the dealer's membership.
* A Registered Dealers' Newsletter. Designed specifically for dealers.
* A special logo variation created specifically for the group.
* Registered Dealers will have their profiles listed on the UACC website and free link capabilities. These profiles include the owner's name, company name, address, telephone and fax numbers, e-mail address, registration number and other important information that tells collectors about your business. The site, which receives hundreds of hits a day, is also linked to other web search engines for maximum exposure.
* Registered Dealers are given discounts on tables at UACC shows and on address labels.
* Registered Dealers receive advertising discounts in the club's publication "The Pen and Quill." This publication also profiles one Registered Dealer in each issue.
* Registered Dealers are also listed separately in UACC Membership Directories.
* The UACC sponsors promotions for dealers only.
* All Registered Dealers have complete access to the UACC Ethics Files.

Note:
All applicants must be UACC members. Dues for registered dealers : $25 per year. For application profiles contact: JD Bardwell at P.O. Box 324, York, ME 03909 or pick up a copy on the club's website. All dealers who have been members of the UACC for the last three years are welcome to join.

International Autograph Dealers Alliance Directory

- ADS Autographs, P.O. Box 8006, Webster, NY 14580, (716) 671-2651
- Alexander Autographs, 100 Melrose Avenue, Ste. 202, Greenwich, CT 06830, (203) 622-8444
- Michael J. Amenta, 28 Helene Avenue, Merrick, NY, 11566, (516) 868-9208
- Autograph Avenue, 34545 Chope Place, Clinton Twsp., MI 48035, (810) 791-5867
- Autos & Autos, P.O. Box 280, Elizabeth City, NC 27909, (919) 335-1117
- Jack Bacon & Co., 4602 Canyon Ridge Ln., Reno, NV 89503, (702) 746-6310
- Walter R. Benjamin Autographs, Inc., P.O. Box 255, Hunter, NY 12442, (518) 263-4133
- Beverly Hills Autograph Co., 264 So. La Cienga #1265, Beverly Hills, CA 90211, (310) 826-3595
- John Blumenthal Autographs, 2853 Rikkard Dr., Thousand Oaks, CA 91362 (805) 493-5070
- Bob Buckleys Red Door Sports Gallery, 912 Fairview Ave., Feasterville, PA 19053, (215) 357-0712
- William J.B. Burger-Historical Americana, P.O. Box 832, Pine Grove, CA 95665, (209) 296-7970
- Frederick Castaing Autographs, 13 Rue Chapon, Paris, 75003, France, 01 427 46909
- Celebrity Coin & Stamp, 4161 S. Howell Ave., Milwaukee, WI, 53207, (800) 522-6037
- Classic Rarities, P.O. Box 29109, Lincoln, NE 68529, (402) 467-2948
- Collectables of the Stars, 6806 Stirling Rd., Hollywood, FL 33024, (954) 963-5238
- Collectibles Unlimited, 245 Somerset Way, Weston, FL 33024, (954) 963-5238
- Bill Corcoran, 9228 Sunflower Dr., Tampa, FL 33647, (813) 973-4727
- Deco Memorabilia, P.O. Box 5358, Scottsdale, AZ 85261, (602) 657-7448

- E.A.C. Gallery, 838 Willis Ave., Albertson, NY 11507, (516) 248-4163
- E.V.S. Memorabilia, Shop 3, 136 Pakington St., Geelong West, Victoria, 3218, Australia, 03 52218999
- Federal Hill Antiquities, P.O. Box 600, Phoenix, MD 21131, (410) 584-8329
- David W. Foudy Collectibles, Inc., P.O. Box 224, Demarest, NJ 07627, (201) 385-1199
- Frasers, 399 Strand, London, WCZ ROLX, England, 011 44 1718369325
- G&P Autographs, International, P.O. Box 2082, Middletown, NY 10940, (914) 343-3362
- G&P Handel International, Wendlinger Strasse 7, D-72622, Nurtingen, Germany, 011 49 7022 560237
- Great Lakes Autographs, 8903 Southmoor Ave., Highland, IN 46322, (219) 923-8884
- Roger Gross Ltd., 225 East 57th St., New York, NY 10022, (212) 759-2892
- Jack W. Heir Baseball Autographs, P.O. Box 88, Manalapan, NJ 07726, (732) 446-4758
- Mike Hirsch Autographs, 11 Philips Mill Dr., Middletown, NJ 07748, (732) 787-1202
- History Makers Inc., 4040 E. 82nd St., C-10, Indianapolis, IN 46250, (800) 424-9259
- David J. Holmes, Autographs, P.O. Box 548, Collingswood, NJ 08108, (609) 854-8570
- Houle Rare Books & Autographs, 7260 Beverly Blvd., Los Angeles, CA 90036, (213) 937-5858
- J. & J. Lubrano, Music Antiquarians, 8 George St., Great Barrington, MA 01230
- Susan Kerville Autographs, 28 Dixon Dr., Pimpama, QLD, 4209, Australia, 61 7 5546 7740
- Stephen Koschal Autographs, P.O. Box 1581, Boynton Beach, FL 33425, (561) 736-8409
- Kottie Autographs, Bergblickstr 7, 87672, Rosshaupten, Germany, 8367 1060
- La Scalia Autographs, Inc., P.O. Box 715, Pennington, NJ 08534, (609) 737-8778
- Main Street Fine Books & Manuscripts, 206 North Main St., Galena, IL 61036, (815) 777-3749
- J.B. Muns, Fine Art Books & Musical autographs, 1162 Shattuck Ave., Berkeley, CA 94707, (510) 525-2420
- F. Don Nidiffer, P.O. Box 8184, Charlottesville, VA 22906, (804) 296-2027
- One Of A Kind Collectibles, 7615 SW 6nd ave., Miami, FL 33143, (305) 661-4244
- Patton, P.O. Box 441175, Kennesaw, GA 30152, (770) 419-7897
- Linda Payne Autograph Company, P.O. Box 081336, Racine, WI 53408, (414) 633-7478
- Peachstate Historical Consulting, Inc., 2625 Piedmont Rd., Suite 56-106, Atlanta, GA 30324, (770) 754-4717
- Piece of the Past, Inc., 2240 Palm Beach Lakes Blvd., #310, West Palm Beach, FL, 33409, (561) 689-7079
- P&P Autographs, 92 Main St., Hampton, CT 06247, (860) 455-0784
- Max Rambod Autographs, 16161 Ventura Blvd., #756, Encino, CA 91436, (818) 784-1776
- Rancourts Autographs, 1750 Georgia Ave., NE, St. Petersburg, FL 33703, (813) 521-1539
- Remains To Be Seen, 3520 South Ocean Blvd., Palm Beach, FL 33480, (561) 547-3786
- Kenneth W. Rendell, Inc., P.O. Box 9001, Wellesley, MA 02181, (781) 431-1776
- R. H. Classics, Post Box Weidstrasse 174, 4317 Wegenstetten, Switzerland, 061 8710240
- Rocky Mountain Rarities, Ltd., Inc., P.O. Box 303, Bountiful, UT 84011, (801) 296-6276
- R&R Enterprises, 5 Chestnut Dr., Bedford, NH 03110, (800) 937-3880
- Harris Schaller Autographs & Collectibles, P.O. Box 746, Dubuque, IA, 52004, (319) 583-2757
- SearleÆs Autographs, P.O. Box 9369, Asheville, NC 28815, (704) 299-0512
- Signed Sealed Delivered, 7320 Ashcroft #204, Houston, TX 77081, (713) 995-0272
- Star Shots, 5389 Bearup St., Port Charlotte, FL 33981, (941) 697-6935
- Christophe Stickel Autographs, P.O. Box 569, Pacific Grove, CA 93950, (408) 656-0111
- Time Again Collectibles, P.O. Box 8042, Hilton Head, SC 29938, (803) 842-6616
- University Archives, 600 Summer St., Stamford, CT 06901, (203) 975-9291
- Walls of Fame Autographs, P.O. Box 1053, Neptune, NJ 07753, (732) 988-0315
- Michael Wehrmann Autographs, 70-40 Juno St., Forest Hills, NY 11375, (718) 261-4183
- The Written Word Autographs, P.O. Box 490, Tamworth, NH 03886, (603) 323-7563

The Manuscript Society

The Manuscript Society is an international organization of persons and institutions devoted to the collection, preservation, use, and enjoyment of autographs and manuscripts. Founded in 1948 as the National Society of Autograph Collectors, The Manuscript Society has grown to an impressive international membership of over 1,700. Their membership is surprisingly diverse and includes dealers, private collectors, scholars, authors, archivists, curators and librarians. The society also appeals to historical societies, museums and both special and academic libraries.

The Manuscript Society also publishes two impressive quarterly publications, *Manuscripts* and *The Manuscript Society News,* which are sent to each member at no charge. With an established reputation, *Manuscripts* is a delight for any collector in pursuit of autographs. This journal includes numerous educational articles covering many aspects of the hobby. Auction results, dealer advertisements and even a list of new members can also be found in the journal. *The Manuscript Society News* is a must for the serious collector. Inside of it readers will find information regarding recent discoveries, acquisitions, trends, disasters, preservation, upcoming sales, legal issues, thefts, forgeries and exhibitions. Also useful to its readers is a section where scholars and collectors can advertise their interest in specific material.

A five-day annual meeting is also held by The Manuscript Society. The programs held during this event include tours, exhibitions, panel discussions, and speakers. Plenty of opportunities are provided for social interaction between attendees. The locations for these annual meetings have been quite diverse, ranging from smaller domestic communities to international sites, such as London (1970, 1986), Ottawa (1978), Dublin (1991) and Edinburgh (1996).

Membership in The Manuscript Society has been so successful that numerous chapter groups have spun off, including the Twin Cities, Washington and Southern California. Membership in these chapters is for all in good standing with the organization.

The contribution to the hobby by The Manuscript Society has been nothing short of monumental. In 1978, the book *Autographs and Manuscripts: A Collector's Manual* was published under their auspices by Charles Scribner's Sons. This was the first title to really dissect the hobby through useful topics authored by some of the most respected participants in the hobby. Now considered a classic, if there was a hall of fame for autograph books, this book would be in it.

Manuscripts: The First Twenty Years was published by Greenwood Press in 1984 and is kind of a "best of" anthology of articles from the Society's journal. For collectors this publication will provide hours of enjoyable reading.

In 1990, The Manuscript Society published *The Autograph Collector's Checklist,* providing valuable lists to aid collectors in a number of popular collecting fields. A primary goal of every successful collector organization has always been meeting the demands and needs of their membership and clearly The Manuscript Society has never fallen off track.

As part of our nation's bicentennial, a traveling exhibit was sponsored by the Society in cooperation

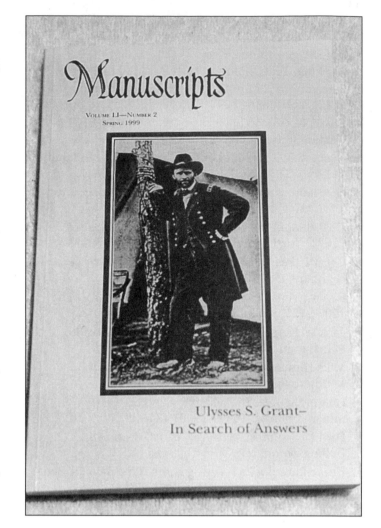

The Manuscript Society has done so much for the hobby that they deserve an award. Here is a copy of their outstanding seasonal publication Manuscripts that is available to all members.

with the Smithsonian Institution. The exhibit included documents written during the early months of the American Revolution, which were loaned for the purpose by members of The Manuscript Society. From their own private collections, individuals sacrificed artifacts of freedom and with it not only educated and entertained those who viewed the exhibit, but brought respect to the hobby of autograph collecting.

The Manuscript Society has also gotten involved in numerous aspects of litigation that face the hobby. While no organization welcomes litigation, I have seen some turn away from conflict. The Manuscript Society is not an organization that looks the other way, when they are needed in the hobby, they participate.

New members are welcomed by The Manuscript Society. You may contact this club through: David R. Smith, Executive Director, The Manuscript Society, 350 N. Niagara Street, Burbank, CA 91505-3648.

The Manuscript Society

1999 Membership Information

Annual Membership Fees

Institutional Membership. $35
Regular Membership $35
Contributing Membership $70
Sustaining Membership $100
Life Membership. $1000

Resource Price List

Manuscripts (quarterly journal): Most back issues from 1976 to date and many earlier issues available—$7.00 each. Generous discounts for long runs.

Manuscript Society News (quarterly newsletter): All back issues available $3 each

Index to Manuscripts Vol. I-XXVIII (1948-1976) $7

Index to Manuscripts Vol. II XXIX-XL (1977-1988) $7

1998 Manuscript Society Membership Directory $7

Airmail delivery of Manuscripts to other countries $10/year

Manuscript Society Mailing List—the current membership roster supplied on pressure-sensitive mailing labels in ZIP-Code order—$200.00 (plus $10 extra for airmail delivery to other countries)

History In Your Hand: Fifty Years of The Manuscript Society (Praeger) John M. Taylor's lively history of the Society, told in the larger context of autograph collecting in general over the past century, hardcover, illustrated, postpaid price—$45.00

The Autograph Collector's Checklist—useful manual covering 22 of the most popular collecting topics, with lists of names, commentary, and ranking by scarcity—postpaid price $17.20

The Manuscript Society Criteria For Describing Manuscripts and Documents—$2.00

George Washington's Expense Accounts—facsimile edition of Washington's Revolutionary War expense accounts (1775-1783); published for the manuscript Society by William R. Coleman on the occasion of the 200th anniversary of the conclusion of the war—$10.00

Prepayment required on all orders:

David R. Smith, Executive Director, The Manuscript Society, 350 N. Niagara Street, Burbank, CA 91505-3648.

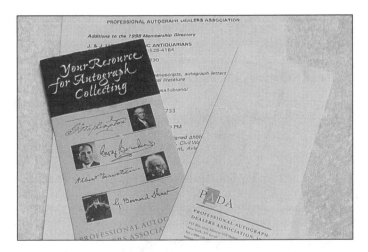

PADA, Professional Autograph Dealers Association, Inc. has tried to increase interest in the hobby by holding dealers to a strict code of ethics.

PADA—The Professional Autograph Dealers Association

The Professional Autograph Dealers Association, PADA, is a source for dealers who are experienced, knowledgeable, dedicated to customer service and committed to a strict code of ethics. Here are just some of the ways a PADA dealer can serve the need of a collector:

Inventory: PADA dealers offer the largest and most diverse assortment of autographs available anywhere, in all price ranges and of all types. They are an unrivaled source for fine and important autographs.

Expertise: PADA dealers—most of whom have decades of experience—can guide you in all aspects of collecting. They can help you decide what to collect, explain the factors involved in determining autograph prices, and answer any questions in a courteous, informed and professional manner.

Authentication: PADA dealers authenticate every autograph in your inventories, drawing on their many years of research and expertise. They can help you determine the authenticity of autographs in your collection. (Many individuals had secretaries sign for them; others used stamped, facsimile, or autopen, i.e., machine-generated, signatures.)

Conservation: PADA dealers will gladly advise you on the proper methods for storing or displaying your autographs. They can direct you to sources for archival storage materials and framing, and can help you find an expert conservator should your autographs require professional repair.

Appraisals: PADA dealers can evaluate your autographs for insurance, donation, tax, or estate purposes. Their knowledge of the market will assure you of an accurate and fair assessment of the worth of your material.

Auction representation: PADA dealers can act as your agent at auction, inspecting pieces prior to the sale and checking their authenticity, condition, and content against the auction catalogue's description. They can advise you on values and bid for you at the sale, endeavoring to purchase the autographs you want at the lowest prices.

Selling your autographs: PADA dealers represent a significant market for purchasing autographs, whether single items or entire collections. They can buy autographs outright, offering you a fair price and immediate payment. If you prefer, a PADA dealer can act as your agent for selling material or can take items on consignment, after fully discussing the terms with you. A PADA dealer can also suggest other options for selling your autographs or donating them to an institution.

In *Your Resource for Autograph Collecting brochure*, PADA includes "Five Guidelines for Buying Autographs"

1. Buy autographs that capture your interest. Avoid fads and autographs presented as "great" investments or sold through pressure tactics.

2. Learn as much as you can about what makes an autograph authentic and important.

3. Use common sense when buying an autograph. If a price seems too good to be true, it probably is.

4. Buy only what you can afford.

5. Buy only from reputable dealers, who will help you avoid risks and problems. PADA makes it easy for you to find an entire group of dealers on whom you can rely. Please consult a recent membership list.

If you are an interested dealer, you can get a free brochure and membership directory by writing to: *The Professional Autograph Dealers Association,* P.O. Box 1729-A, Murray Hill Station, New York, NY 10156 or visit the group's web site: http://www.padaweb.org.

The organizations presented here are listed in the order in which I received an answer to my inquiry about the organization. I have tried to present each fairly and in their own words. All four of these organizations provide a wonderful service to the hobby and to that we are all deeply indebted. As an advanced autograph collector or dealer, you may find joining one or more of these clubs a valuable experience, as each is unique in its own way. Perhaps someday there will be a time or forum in which all four of these organizations could unite as one to tackle some of the difficult issues facing the hobby.

PADA—Professional Autograph Dealers Association

Mission Statement
To establish an autograph marketplace in which collectors can buy and sell with confidence and receive knowledgeable, accurate, and experienced advice.

Code of Ethics
PADA's Code of Ethics is the most stringent in the trade and is strictly enforced. The code requires all PADA dealers:
- Conscientiously authenticate and accurately describe all autographs
- Provide a money-back guarantee of authenticity to the original purchaser, without time limit, for every autograph sold
- Strictly adhere to the payment terms agreed upon with the seller when purchasing autographs;
- Conduct business honestly, fairly, and with integrity;
- Treat each customer with respect and make every effort to promote customer satisfaction.

PADA—1998 Membership Directory

- Abraham Lincoln Book Shop, Inc., 357 W. Chicago Ave., Chicago, IL 60610; Daniel R. Weinberg, (312) 944-3085, http://www.ALincolnBookShop.com
- *ADS Autographs, P.O. Box 8006, Webster, NY 14580-8006; Joseph R. Sakmyster, (716) 671-2651
- Alexander Autographs, P.O. Box 101, Cos Cob, CT 06807; Basil A. Panagopulos, (203) 622-8444, http://www.alexautographs.com
- Archives Historical Autographs, 119 Chestnut Hill Rd., Wilton, CT 06897; Warren Weitman, (203) 226-3920
- Catherine Barnes, P.O. Box 30117-MB, Philadelphia, PA 19103; (shop) 2031 Walnut St., Suite 308, Philadelphia, PA 19103. Catherine Barnes, (215) 854-0175
- Robert F. Batchelder, Inc., ! W. Butler Ave., Ambler, PA 19002-5701; Robert F. Batchelder, (215) 643-1430
- Walter R. Benjamin Autographs, Inc., P.O. Box 255, Hunter, NY 12442-0255; (shop) 664 Scribner Hollow Rd., Hunter, NY 12442-0255; Christopher C. Jaeckel.
- Beverly Hills Autograph Co., 264 S. LaCienga Bl., Suite No. 1265, Beverly Hills, CA 90211; Ray Anthony, (310) 826-3595, http://websites.earthlink.net/2beverly hills/
- Edward N. Bomsey Autographs, Inc., 7317 Farr St., Annandale, VA 22003-2516; Edward N. Bomsey, (703) 642-2040, http://www.abaa-booknet.com/usa/bomsey
- Books & Autographs, 287 Goodwin Rd., Eliot, ME 03903; Sherman R. Emery
- Gary Combs Autographs, Inc., 3 Sheridan Sq., 7-H, N.Y., N.Y. 10014; Gary Combs, (212) 242-7209
- Bruce Gimelson, P.O. Box 440, Garrison, NY 10524-0440; Bruce Gimelson, (914) 424-4689
- Roger Gross Ltd., 15 W. 81st St., N.Y., N.Y. 10024; (office) 225 E. 57th St., N.Y., N.Y. 10022; Roger Gross, (212) 759-2892, http://padaweb.org/rgross/
- Gary Grossman, 7 Dell Drive, E. Rockaway, N.Y. 11518; Gary Grossman, (212) 532-3730
- Golden Age Autographs, P.O. Box 20408, Park West Finance Station, N.Y., N.Y. 10025; Tom Kramer, (212) 866-5626
- David J. Holmes, Autographs, P.O. Box 548, Collingswood, NJ 08108; David J. Holmes, (609) 854-8570
- Houle Rare Books & Autographs, 7260 Beverly Blvd., Los Angeles, CA 90036; George Hule, (213) 937-5858, http://www.quikpage.com/H/houlebooks
- La Scala Autographs, Inc., P.O. Box 715, Pennington, NJ 08534; James Camner, (609) 737-8778, http://members.aol.com/scala
- Kenneth R. Laurence, 1007 Kane Concourse, Bay Harbor, FL 33154; Kenneth Laurence, (800) 345-5595
- Lion Heart Autographs, Inc., 470 Park Avenue S., Penthouse, N.Y., N.Y. 10016; David H. Lowenherz, (212) 779-7050, http://www.lionheartinc.com
- James Lowe Autographs, Ltd., 30 E. 60th St., Suite 304, N.Y., N.Y. 10022; James Lowe, (212) 759-0775
- Nancy L. McGlashan, Inc., P.O. Box 303, Kew Gardens, N.Y. 11415; Nancy L. McGlashan, (718) 849-0020
- Noble Enterprises, 3709 Blain Dr., Rowlett, TX 75088-6077; Donnell Noble, (972) 463-2424
- North Shore Manuscript Co., Inc., P.O. Box 458, Roslyn Heights, N.Y. 11577; Susan Levin Hoffman, (516) 484-6826
- Les Perline & Company, Two Gannett Drive, Suite 200, White Plains, NY 10604; Les Perline, (800) 567-2014
- Steven S. Raab Autographs, P.O. Box 471, Ardmore, PA 19003; (shop) 143 Charles Drive, Havertown, PA 19083; Steven S. Raab, (800) 977-8333, http://www.raabautographs.com
- Max Rambod, Inc., 16161 Ventura Blvd., #756, Encino, CA 91426; Max Rambod, (818) 784-1776, www.maxrambod.com
- Kenneth W. Rendell, Inc., P.O. Box 9001, Wellesley, MA 02481; Kenneth W. Rendell, (781) 431-1776
- 46 Eliot Street, S. Natick. MA 01760; (gallery) 989 Madison Ave., NY., N.Y. 10021, (212) 717-1776
- Safka & Bareis Autographs, P.O. Box 886, Forest Hills, N.Y. 11375; Bill Safka, (718) 263-2276, http://idt.net/-sbautog/
- Seaport Autographs, 6 Brandon Lane, Mystic, CT 06355; Norman F. Boas, (860) 572-8441
- Barry A. Smith, Inc. Historical Americana, P.O. Box 38306, Greensboro, NC 27438; Barry A. Smith, (336) 288-4375
- R.M. Smythe & Co., Inc., 26 Broadway, N.Y., N.Y. 10004; Diana E. Herzog, (212) 943-1880, http://www.rmsmythe.com
- Christophe Stickel, P.O. Box 569, Pacific Grove, CA 93950; Christophe Stickel, (408) 656-0111
- Gerard A.J. Stodolski, Inc., 555 Canal Street, Manchester, NH 03101; Gerard Stodolski, (603) 647-0716
- Tollett & Harman, 175 W. 76th St., N.Y., N.Y. 10023; Robert Tollett, (212) 877-1566
- Scott J. Winslow Assoc., Inc., P.O. Box 10240, Bedford, NH 03110; Scott J. Winslow, (800) 225-6233
- J&J Lubrano, Music Antiquarians, 8 George St., Great Barrington, MA 01230; John Lubrano, (413) 578-5799, abaa-booknet.com/usa/lubrano

Note:

This list is as of April, 1999

Periodicals

As an advanced autograph collector you are going to want to monitor the hobby and the best way to do so is through some of its outstanding publications. I must warn you however, that not everything printed about the hobby has been accurate, therefore you're going to have to occasionally separate fact from fiction. Also since, both dealers, writers and collectors contribute articles, you may be forced to set aside some propaganda—known as literary license in the writing trade, in order to understand the agenda of some articles. Using myself as an example, when I contribute articles and I have written and published many, I always pitch my latest project, so just let it go and wait for a strike! The two premier publications for collectors are *Autograph Collector* and *Autograph Times*.

Autograph Collector

As an advanced autograph collector there is no better place to put your hard earned money than into a subscription to *Autograph Collector* magazine. Under the umbrella of Odyssey Publications, Incorporated, this magazine has transcended the expectations of even some of the most insightful dealers and collectors. It has emerged into the forefront of the hobby as a primary source of information.

Under the watchful eye of Ev Phillips, Editor-in-Chief, the magazine boasts one of the finest staff of contributing editors in the hobby, including Jeffrey M. Ellinport, Kevin Hasely, Scott Johnson, James Lowe, Joseph Maddalena, Anthony Record, John Reznikoff, Steve Ryan, John E. Schlimm II, Barry Shuck, Tiny Urban, Jeffrey Woolfe and Yvonne Woolf. If this alone were not enough, since its inception it has also heard and published stories from some of the better known and published writers on the hobby including Charles Hamilton, George Sanders, Kevin Martin, and yes, I happened to sneak one in also.

There is not a single collector who doesn't eagerly await their next issue of *Autograph Collector* magazine. The April 1999 issue alone filled 136 pages at an 8-1/2" x 11" format. Full color is cost effectively intermingled into each issue, often in the form of impressive advertising. Each issue includes two to four feature articles, ten departments and about ten informative columns. The features, or the heart of the issue, are typically detailed articles dedicated to a particular segment of the hobby. Amidst the features you will often find the cover story typically authored by one of the better known names in the hobby.

Autograph Collector phone: (800) 996-3977 or (909) 734-9636; website: www.AutographCollector.com

Autograph Times

As an advanced autograph collector you will also find *Autograph Times* to be a very useful publication. *Autograph Times, Inc.* is published monthly by The Marlan Publishing Group, Ltd. of Mesa, Arizona. The black & white, down-sized publication is starting to move toward a color cover as it continues to modify its format to better meet the demands of collectors.

The periodical is published under the wing of Marty Marsh and editors Barbara Bingham and Ardith Wilson. Contributing editors include Gene Bondy, Steven Buchanan, Jeff Curtis, Melanie Francisco, Michael W, Peterson, Jim Sargent and Larry Smith. *Autograph Times* is not only informative, but encourages collector and reader participation. The publication uses their dialogue column to publish letters to the editor and staff and always seem to go out of their way for reader feedback.

Autograph Times phone: Toll-Free 877-860-0349; fax: 480-777-0844; email: AutoTimes@aol.com

As a hobby we don't realize just how lucky we are to have these two outstanding publications dedicated to autograph collecting. Add to this the many peripheral publications that address specific niches in the hobby, such as *Sports Collectors Digest, Sports Cards, Tuff Stuff*, and the numerous Beckett publications, and you can see why the modern day autograph collector is so thoroughly informed.

Other useful periodicals, both of the past and present, include: *L'amateur d' autographs, American Antiquarian, American Archivist, American Book Prices Current, American Clipper Monthly Catalogue of American Historical and Literary Material, Autograph News, Biblio, The Book Collector/The Collector, Cohasco Report, The Collector, History News, Manuscripts, The Month (at Goodspeeds), and Pen and Quill.*

References

As an advanced autograph collector you will not only want to enhance your collection, but also invest in a library's worth of outstanding research materials. A good research library should include books (both in and out of print), pamphlets, catalogs (auction, dealer, exhibition, etc.), magazines, periodicals, related articles, advertisements, etc. Below is a partial listing of some of the references that I believe you should consider adding to your library.

Autograph Collector's Checklist. John M. Taylor ed. Burbank, CA: The Manuscript Society, 1990

Baker, Jay Newton. *The Law of Disputed and Forged Documents.* Charlottesville, Virginia: Michie, 1955

Baker, Mark A. *The Baseball Autograph Handbook., 2nd ed.* Iola, WI: Krause Publications, 1991

_____. *Team Baseball,* Iola, WI: Krause Publications, 1992.

_____. *All Sport Autograph Guide,* Iola, WI: Krause Publications, 1994.

_____. *Auto Racing Memorabilia and Price Guide,* Iola, WI: Krause Publications, 1996.

_____. *Collector's Guide To Celebrity Autographs,* Iola, WI: Krause Publications, 1996.

_____. *Goldmine Price Guide to Rock 'n' Roll Memorabilia,* Iola, WI: Krause Publications, 1997.

_____. *The Standard Guide to Collecting Autographs,* WI: Krause Publications, 1999.

Benjamin, Mary. *Autographs: A Key to Collecting,* New York: R.R. Bowker, 1946; rev. ed., 1963.

_____. *The Presidents: A Survey of Autograph Values.* New York: Walter R. Benjamin Autographs, Inc., 1965

Binns, Norman E. *An Introduction to Historical Bibliography.* London: Association of Assistant Librarians, 1962.

Bordin, Ruth B., and Robert M. Warner. *The Modern Manuscript Library.* New York: Scarecrow Press, 1966

Bresslau, Harry. *Handbuch der Urkundenlebre, 3rd ed.* 3 volumes. Berlin: Walter de Gruyter & Co., 1958.

Briquet, Charles M. *Les filigranes.* Amsterdam: Paper Publications Society, 1968

Broadley, A.M. *Chats on Autographs.* New York: Frederick A. Stokes Co., 1910

Brotherhead, William, ed. *The book of the Signers: Containing Facsimile Letters of the Signers of the Declaration of Independence.* Philadelphia: W. Brotherhead, 1861

Brumbaugh, Thomas B. "Pursuing the Documents of Art" Auction 2, no. 6. February, 1969: 10-13

Cahoon, Herbert, Thomas V. Lange, and Charles Ryskamp, eds. *American Literary Autographs.* New York: Dover, 1977

Charnwood, Lady. *An Autograph Collection and the Making of It.* New York: Henry Holt, 1930

Carr, Paul K. *The Autographs of President Gerald R. Ford,* New York: UACC, 1974

Carvalho, David N. *Forty Centuries of Ink, or a Chronological Narrative Concerning Ink and Its Background.* New York: Banks Law Publishing Co., 1904

Charvay, Etienne. *Faux autographes; affaire Vrain-Lucas; etude critique sur la collection vendue a M. Michel Chasles et observations sur les moyens de reconnaitre les faux autographes.* Paris: J. Charavay aine, 1870.

Chu, Petra Ten-Doesschate. "Unsuspected Pleasures in Artists' Letters." Apollo: A Journal of the Arts, 104, October, 1976.

William L. Clements Library. *Facsimiles & Forgeries: A Guide to a Timely Exhibition...,* Ann Arbor, Michigan:, 1950.

Croft, Peter J. *Autograph Poetry in the English Language.* 2 volumes. New York: McGraw-Hill, 1973

Dawson, Giles Edwin, and Laetitia Kennedy-Skipton. *Elizabethan Handwriting.* New York: Norton, 1966

Deuel, Leo. *Testaments of Time: The Search for Lost Manuscripts and Records.* New York: Knopf, 1965.

Diringer, David. *Writing.* New York: Prager, 1962

Draper, Lyman C. *An Essay on the Autograph Collections of the Signers of the Declaration of Independence and of the Constitution.* New York: Burns & Son, 1889.

Duckett, Kenneth W. *Modern Manuscripts: A practical Manual for Their Management, Care and Use.* Nashville, Tennessee: American Association for State and Local History, 1975.

Elsevier's Lexicon of Archival Terminology. Amsterdam-London-New York: Elsevier, 1964

Farrer, James Anson. *Literary Forgeries.* London-New York: Longmans, Green and Co., 1907

Freidel, Frank and Richard K. Shoman, eds. *Harvard Guide to American History,* 2 vols., Cambridge, Massachusetts: the Belknap Press of Harvard University Press, 1974.

Friendenthall, Richard. *Letters of the Great Artists From Ghiberti to Gainsborough and Letters of the Great Artists from Blake to Pollack.* London: Thames and Hudson, 1963

Geigy-Hagenback, Karl. *Album von Handschriften beruhmter Personlichkeiten vom Mittelalter bis zur neuzeit.* 1925.

Gerigk, Herbert, *Neue Liebe zu alten Schriften. Von Autogrammjager zum Autographensammler.* Stuttgart: Deutsche Verlags-Anstalt, GmbH., 1974

Goodspeed, Charles. *Yankee Bookseller.* Boston: Houghton Mifflin, 1937

Gratz, Simon. *A Book About Autographs.* Philadelphia: William J. Campbell, 1920

Grebanier, Bernard D.N. *The Great Shakespeare Forgery.* New York: Norton, 1965

Greg, Walter Wilson. *English Literary Autographs, 1550-1650.* 3 vols. Oxford: Oxford University Press, 1925-1932

Hamilton, Charles. *Collecting Autographs and Manuscripts.* Norman, OK: University of Oklahoma Press, 1961.

_____. *The Robot That Helped to Make a President.* New York: Self-published, 1965.

_____. *Scribblers and Scoundrels.* New York: Paul S. Eriksson, Inc., 1968.

_____. *The Book of Autographs*. New York: Simon & Schuster, 1978.

_____. *The Signature of America*. New York: Harper & Row, 1979.

_____. *Great Forgers and Famous Fakes*. New York: Crown, 1980.

_____. *American Autographs*. 2 vols. Norman: University of Oklahoma Press, 1983

Hamilton, Charles and Diane Hamilton. *Big Name Hunting: A Beginner's Guide to Autograph Collecting*. New York: Simon & Schuster, 1973.

Harris, Robert. *Selling Hitler*. London: Faber and Faber, 1986.

Harrison, Wilson R. *Suspect Documents: Their scientific Examination*. London: Sweet and Maxwell, 1958.

_____. *Forgery Detection: A Practical Guide*. New York: Prager, 1963.

Haselden, Reginald Berti. *Scientific Aids for the Study of Manuscripts*. Oxford: Oxford University Press for the Bibliographical Society, 1935.

Heawood, Edward. *Watermarks, Mainly of the 17th and 18th Centuries*. Hilversum, Netherlands: Paper Publications Society, 1950.

Hector, Leonard Charles. *Paleography and Forgery*. York, England: St. Anthony's Press, 1959

_____. *The Handwriting of English Documents*. 2nd ed. London: E. Arnold, 1966

Hill, George B. *Talk About Autographs,* New York: Houghton Mifflin, 1896

Hunter, Dard. *Old Papermaking*. (Chillicothe, Ohio), 1923

_____. *Papermaking: The History and Technique of an Ancient Craft*. New York: Knopf, 1943.

_____. *Papermaking by Hand in America*. Chillicothe, Ohio: Mountain House Press, 1950.

Jahans, Gordon A. "A Brief History of Paper." *Books Collectors Quarterly,* 15, July-September, 1934

Johnson, Allen, et al., eds. *Dictionary of American Biography*. 11 volumes and 3 supplements. New York: Scribners, 1928-1977

Joline, Adrian H. *Meditations of an Autograph Collector*. New York: Harper & Bros., 1902

Jung, Herman. *Ullstein Autographenbuch. Vom Sammeln handschriftlicher Kostbarkeiten*. Frankfurt-am-Main, 1971.

Labarre, E.J. *Dictionary and Encyclopedia of Paper and Papermaking, 2nd ed.,* Amsterdam: Swets & Zeitlinger, 1952

Leisinger, A. H., Jr. "The Exhibits of Documents." *American Archivist*, 26, January, 1963: 765-86

Lescure, M. de. *Les autographes et le ... France et a l'etranger*. Paris: V. Gay, 1865

Madigan, Thomas F. *Word Shadows of the Great*. New York: Frederick A. Stokes, 1930

Manuscripts: The First Twenty Years. Taylor, Priscilla S., ed. Westport, CT: Greenwood Press, 1984.

Mecklenburg, Gunther. *Von Autographensammeln: Versuch einer Darstellung seines...,* Marburg: J.A. Stargardt, 1963

Mitchell, Charles A. *Inks, Their Composition and Manufacture. 4th ed.,* London: C. Griffin, 1937

Muir, Percival H. *Minding My Own Business*. London: Chatto & Windus, 1956

Munby, Alan N.L. *The Cult of the Autograph Letter in England*. London: Athlone, 1962.

Nash, Ray. *American Penmanship 1800-1850: A History of Writing and a Bibliography of Copybooks From Jenkins to Spencer*. Worcester, MA: American Antiquarian Society, 1969.

Netherclift, Joseph. *Autograph Letters, Characteristic Extracts, and Signatures, From the Correspondence of Illustrious and Distinguished Women of Great Britain, From the XIVth to the XIXth Century*. London: J. Netherclift, 1838

Nickell, Joe. *Pen, Ink & Evidence*. Lexington: University Press of Kentucky, 1990.

Nichols, John G. *Autographs of Royal, Noble, Learned, and Remarkable Personages Conspicuous in English History*. London: J.B. Nichols and Son, 1829

Notlep, Robert. *The Autograph Collector: A New Guide*. New York: Crown. 1968.

Osborn, James M. *Neo-philobiblon: Ruminations on Manuscript Collecting*. Austin, TX: Humanities Research Center for the University of Texas, 1973

Patterson, Jerry E. *Autographs: A Collector's Guide*. New York: Crown, 1973

Quaritch, Bernard. *Facsimiles of Choice Examples Selected From... and Illustrated Books of Early Date. 4 volumes*. London: B. Quaritch, 1890

Rawlins, Ray. *Four Hundred Years of British Autographs*. London: J.M. Dent, 1970.

_____., *The Guinness Book of World Autographs*. Enfield, Middlesex, England: Guiness Superlatives, Ltd., 1977

_____., *The Stein and Day Book of World Autographs*. New York: Stein and Day, 1978.

Reed, Ronald. *The Nature and Making of Parchment*. Leeds, England: Elmete Press, 1976

Rendell, Diana J. and Kenneth W. Rendell. *Fundamentals of Autograph Collecting*. Somerville, MA: Kenneth W. Rendell, Inc., 1972.

Rendell, Kenneth W. *Forging History.* Norman: University of Oklahoma Press, 1994

The Rendells, Inc. *Autograph Letters, Manuscripts, Drawings—French Artists & Authors.* Newton, MA: The Rendells, Inc., 1977

Reese, Michael II. *Autographs of the Confederacy.* New York: Cohasco, Inc., 1981.

Ricci, Seymour de. *English Collectors of Books and Manuscripts (1530-1930) and Their Marks of Ownership.* Cambridge, England: Cambridge University Press, 1930, 1960

Rosenbach, Abraham S. Wolf. *Books and Bidders.* Boston: Little Brown, 1927

_____. *A Book Hunter's Holiday: Adventures With Books and Manuscripts.* Boston: Houghton Mifflin, 1936

Scott, Henry T., and Samuel Davey. *A Guide to the Collector of Historical Documents, Literary Manuscripts and Autograph Letters.* London: S.J. Davey, 1891

_____. *Autograph Collecting: A Practical Manual for Amateurs and Historical Students.* London: L.U. Gill, 1894.

Sims, George R. *Among My Autographs.* London: Chatto & Windus, 1904

Shorter, Alfred H. *Paper Mills and Paper Makers in England, 1495-1800.* Hilversum, Holland: Paper Publications Society, 1957.

Sowards, Neil. *The Handbook of Check Collecting.* Fort Wayne, IN: self-published, 1976

Stevens, Benjamin Franklin. *Facsimiles of Manuscripts in European Archives Relating to America, 1773-1783.* 24 volumes. London: Malby & Sons, 1889-1895

Stevens, Robley D. *Enjoy Your Leisure Time: Autograph Collecting Guide.* Ann Arbor, MI,: Edward Bros., 1955

Stevenson, Allan Henry. *Paper as Bibliographical Evidence.* London: The Bibliographical Society, 1962.

Sullivan, George. *The Complete Book of Autograph Collecting.* New York: Dodd, Mead, 1971.

Taylor, John M. *From the White House Inkwell.* Rutland, VT: Charles E. Tuttle, 1968, rev.ed. Modoc Press, 1989

Tessier, Georges. *Diplomatique royale francaise.* Paris: Editions Picrad & Co., 1962

Thomas, George C. *Autograph Letters and Autographs of the Signers of the Declaration of Independence.* Philadelphia: privately printed, 1908

Thompson, H. Keith, and Henry strutz. *Doenitz at Nuremberg: A Re-appraisal.* New York: Ambler, 1977

Warner, Sir George Frederick, ed. *Facsimiles of Royal, Historical, Literary and Other Autographs in the Department of Manuscripts, British Museum.* London: British Museum, 1899

_____. *Universal Classic Manuscripts.* London-Washington, D.C.: M.W. Dunne, 1901

Waters, C.E. *Inks.* Circular C426 of the National Bureau of Standards, U.S. Department of Commerce, Washington, D.C.: U.S. Government printing Office, 1940

Weeks, Lyman H. *A History of Paper-Manufacturing in the United States, 1690-1916.* New York: Lockwood Trade Journal Co., 1916.

William, Henry Smith. *The History of the Art of Writing.* London: Hooper & Jackson, 1902

Winsor, Justin. *Narrative and Critical History of America.* New York: Houghton Mifflin, 1884-1889

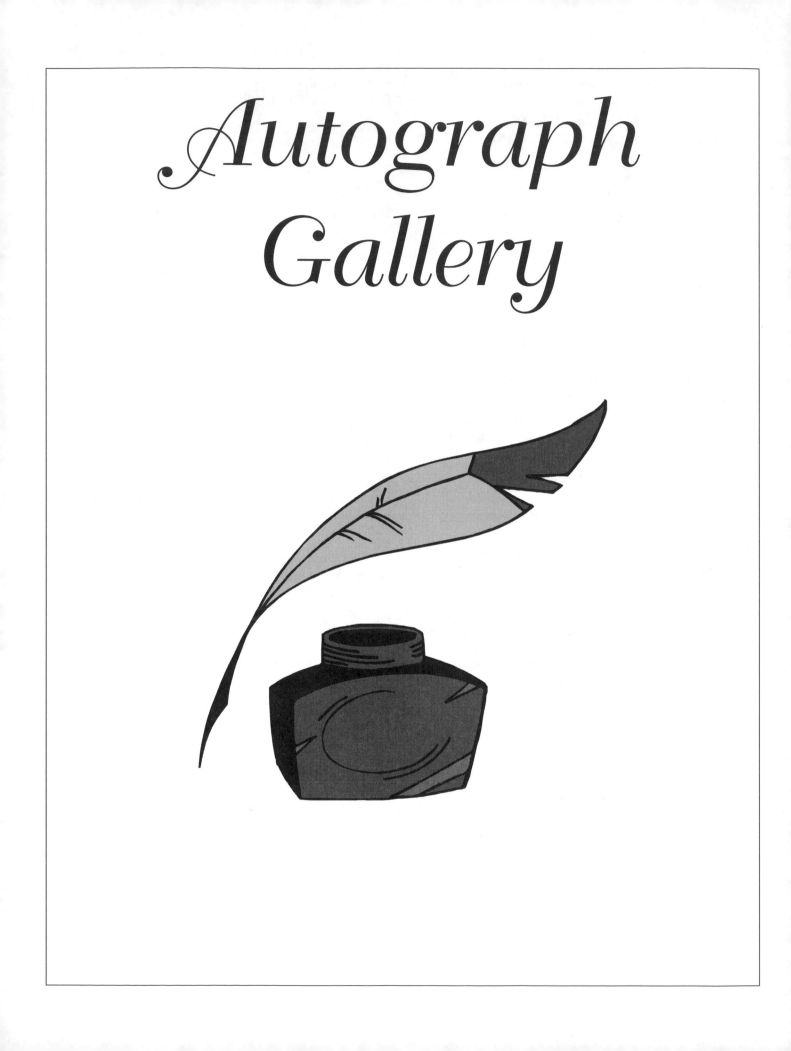

A

Lee Aaker

This copy of *Yosemite and the Range of Light* by Ansel Adams is one of a special edition prepared for Time/Life Books subscribers with the signature of the photographer.

Carmel, California
1981

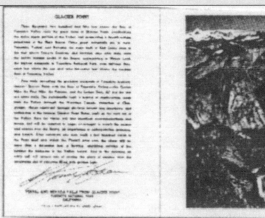

Ansel Adams

Bud Abbott & Lou Costello

Charles F. Adams

Harold M. Abrahams

John Adams

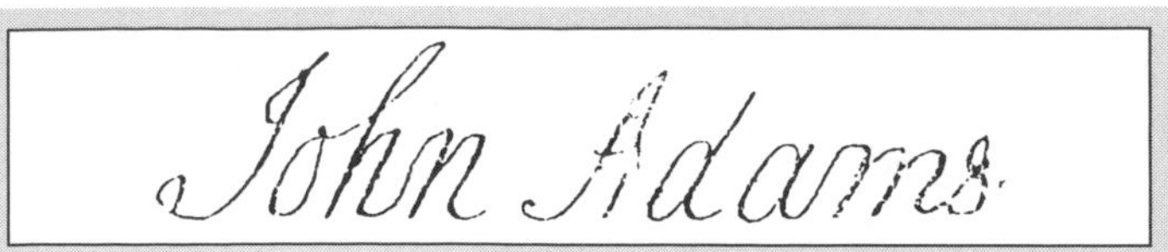

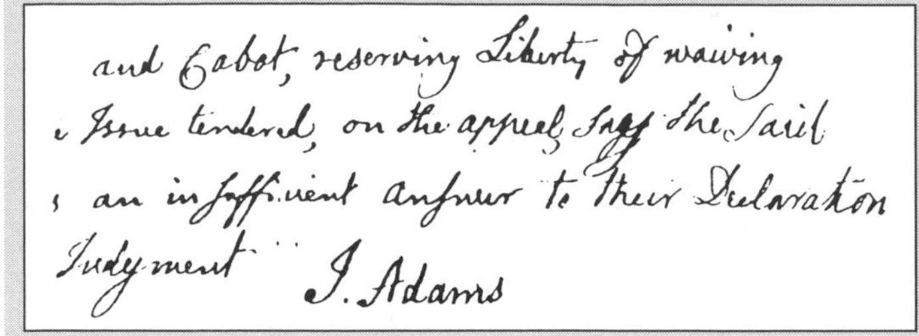

John Adams

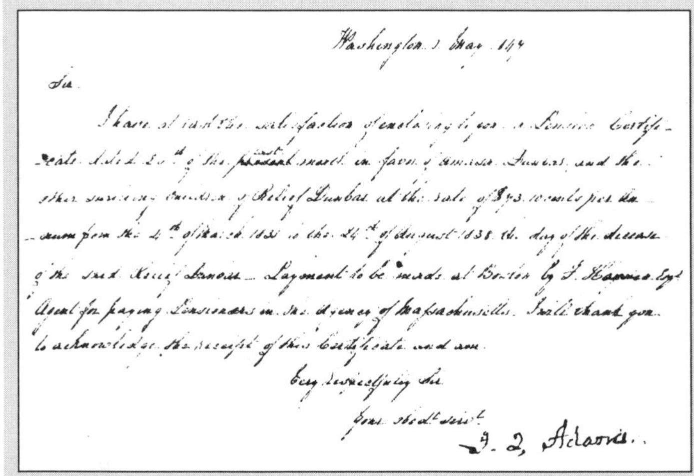

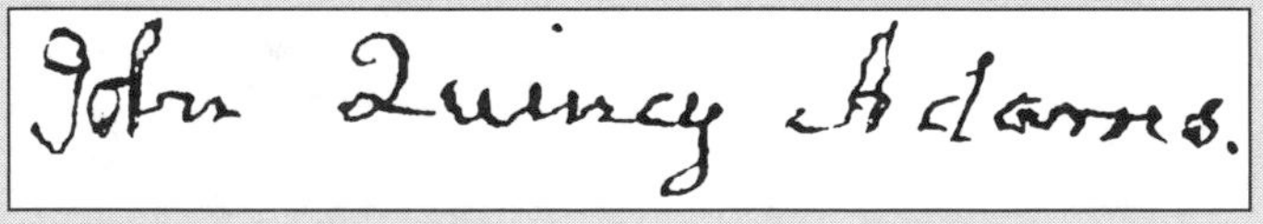

and Cabot, reserving Liberty of waiving
Issue tendered, on the appeal, Say the Said
an insufficient answer to their Declaration
Judgment   J. Adams

John Adams

[handwritten letter]

Washington. 1 May 14

John Quincy Adams

John Quincy Adams

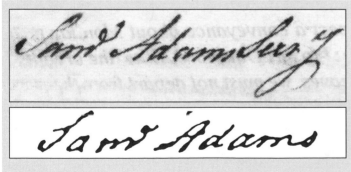

Saml Adams Secy

Saml Adams

Samuel Adams

[signature]

Alfred Adler

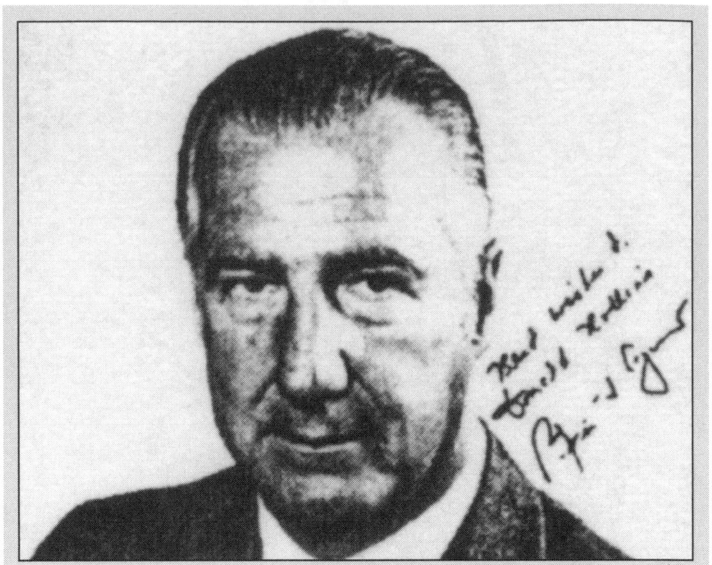

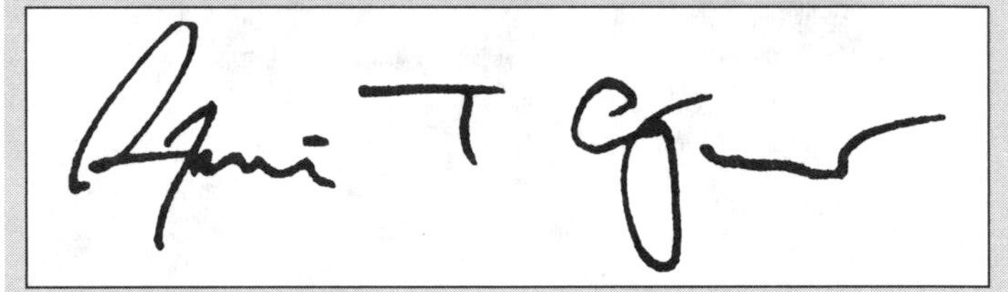

[photograph with signature]

Spiro T. Agnew

Spiro T. Agnew

Albert

Albert (Husband of Queen Victoria)

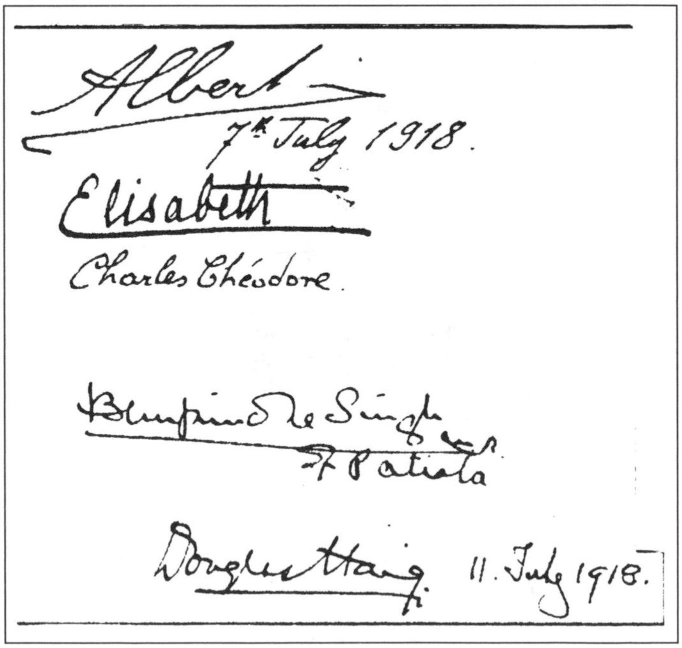

Albert   7th July 1918.
Elisabeth
Charles Théodore.

[signatures]
Douglas Haig   11. July 1918.

Albert (Husband of Queen Victoria)

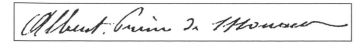

Prince Albert of Monaco

John W. Alcock & A. Whitter Brown - Aviators

Amos B. Alcott

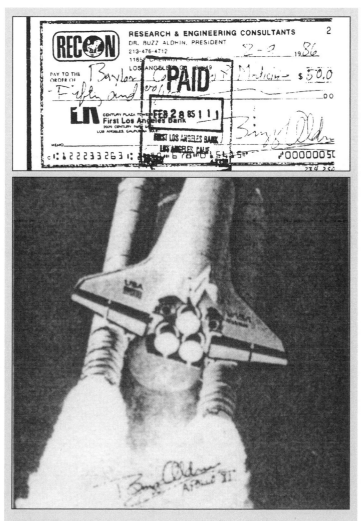

Buzz Aldrin

John Alexander

Alexander I (Russian Emperor)

Horatio Alger

Lord Horatio Alger

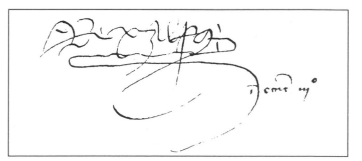

Henry Red Allen

King Alphonso V (Aragon)

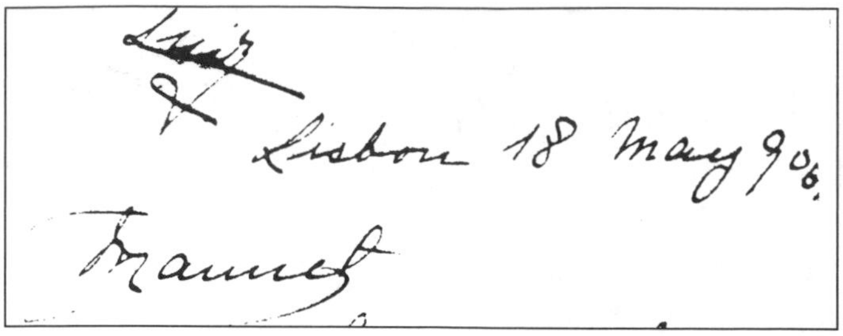

Queen Amalia & King Manuel of Portugal

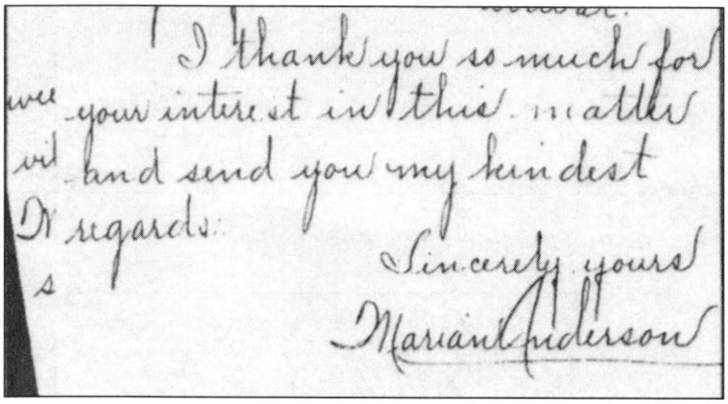

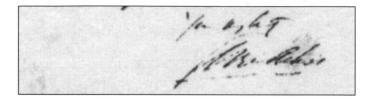

Eddie Arcaro

Marion Anderson

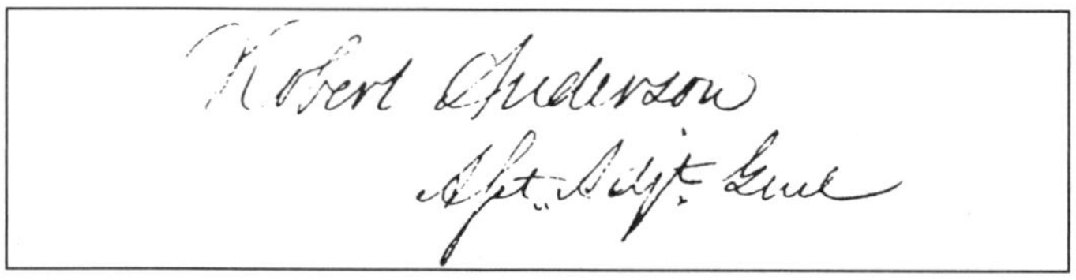

George Arliss

Robert Anderson

Louis Armstrong

John Andre

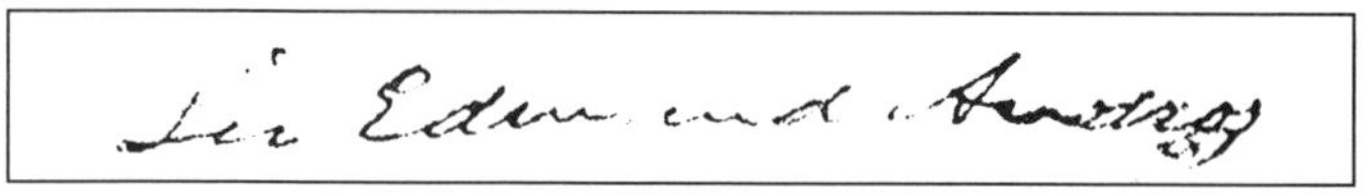

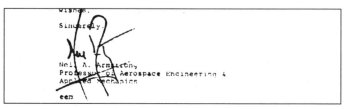

Neil Armstrong

Sir Edmond Andros

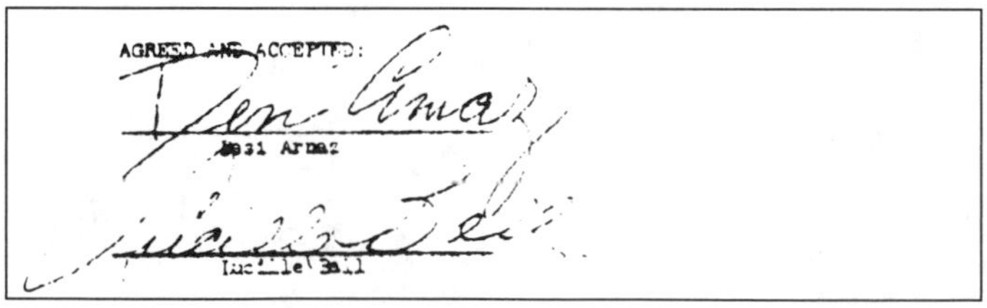

Desi Arnaz & Lucille Ball

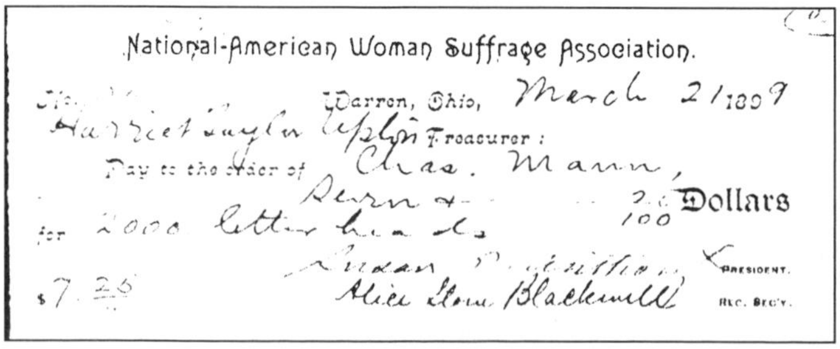

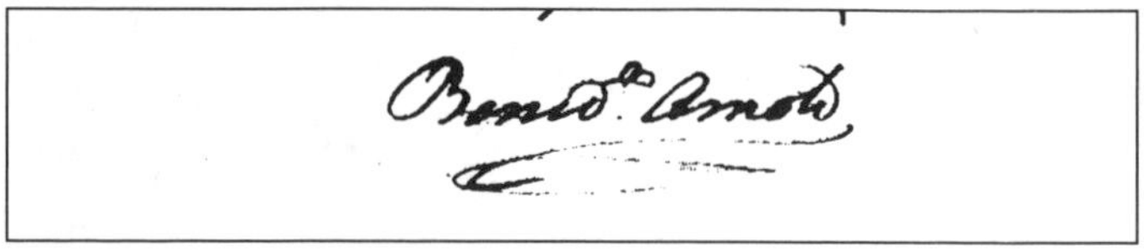

Susan B. Anthony & Alice S. Blackwell

Benedict Arnold

Benedict Arnold

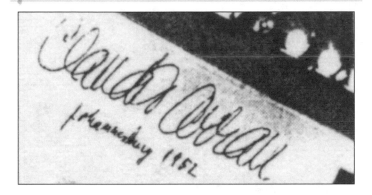

Claudio Arrau

Jean Arthur

Fred Astaire

John Jacob Astor

Astronauts - Apollo 11 - Armstrong, Aldrin & Collins

Asttronauts - Apollo 15 - Scott, Irwin & Worden

Chester A. Arthur

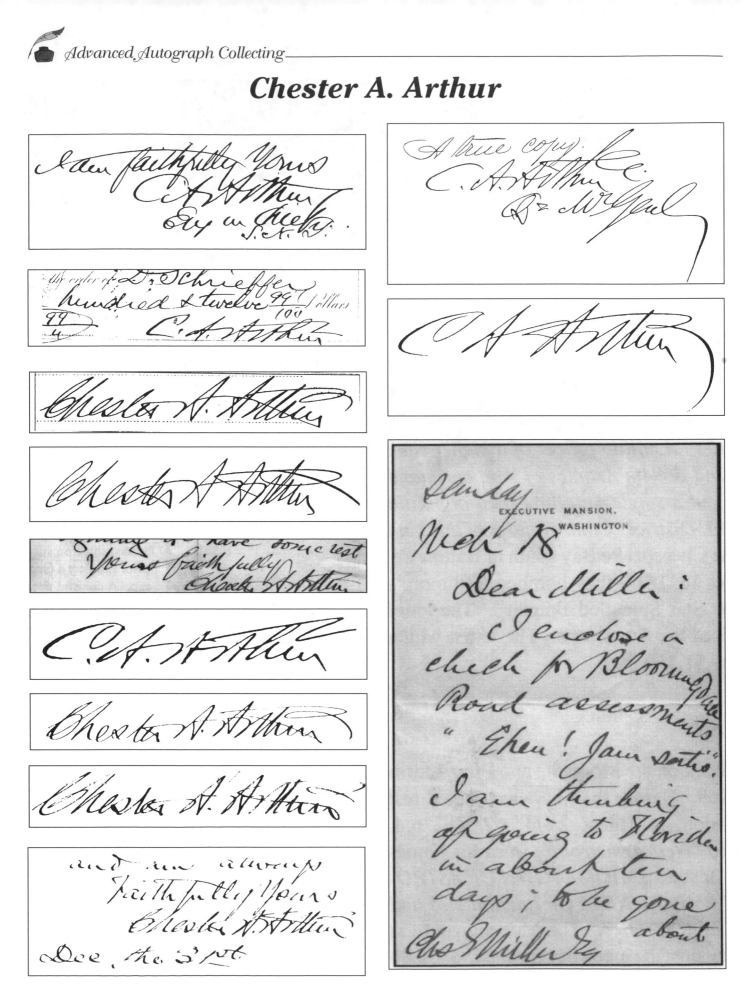

Astronauts - Women

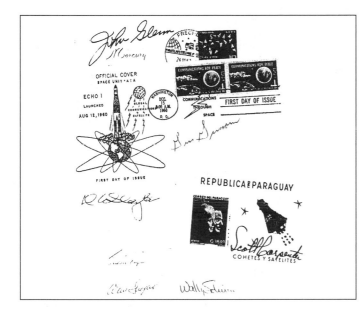

Astronauts - Mercury

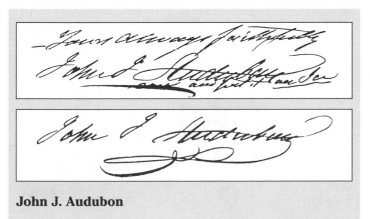

Jess Altmiller

John J. Audubon

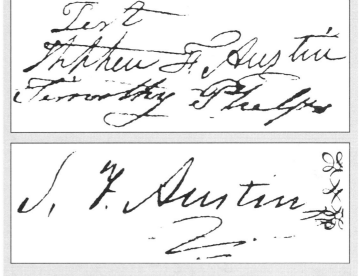

Jane Austen

Stephen F. Austin

Gene Autry

John L. Baird

Richard Bache

Robert Baden-Powell

Sir Robert Baden-Powell

Abraham Baldwin

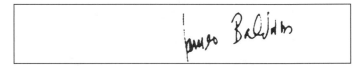

James Baldwin

Arthur James Balfour

Max Baer

Lucille Ball

Lucille Ball

Anne Bancroft

Rex T. Barber

Sabine Baring-Gould

Lex Barker

Gerard Barkhorn

Gen. Francis C. Barlow

P.T. Barnum

Phineas T. Barnum

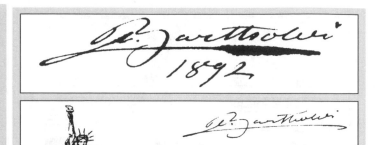

Frederick Auguste Bartholdi

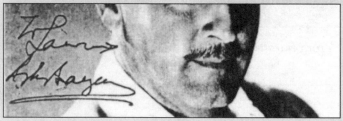

John Barrymore

Josiah Bartlett

Bela Bartok

Clara Barton

Count Basie

Lionel Barrymore

Kim Basinger

David H. Bates

Edward Bates

Warren Beatty

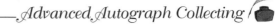

P.G.T. Beauregard

Fontaine Beckham

Alexander Graham Bell

The Beatles

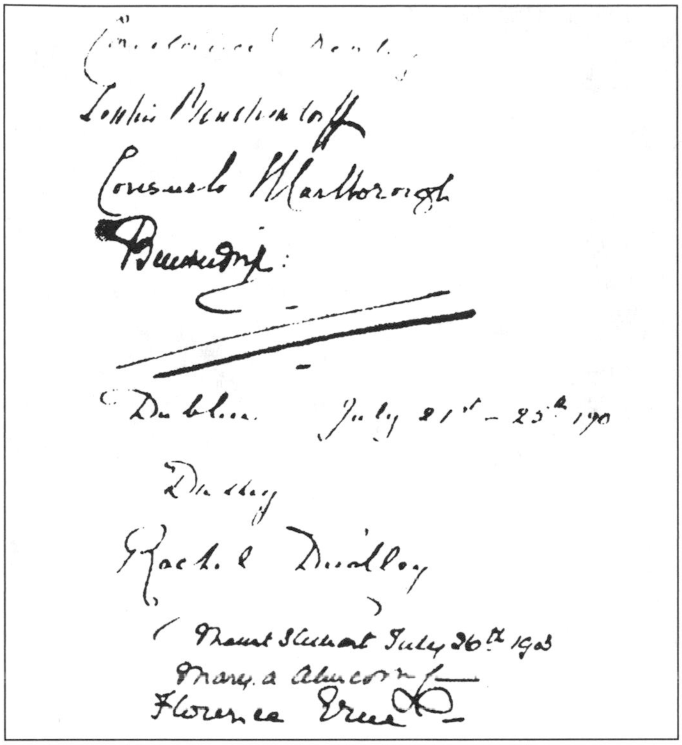

Count Benckendorff & Consuelo Vanderbilt Marlborough

Chief Bender

Eduard Benes

Stephen Vincent Benet

David Ben-Gurion

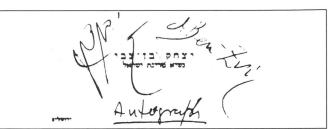

Yitzhak Ben-Zvi

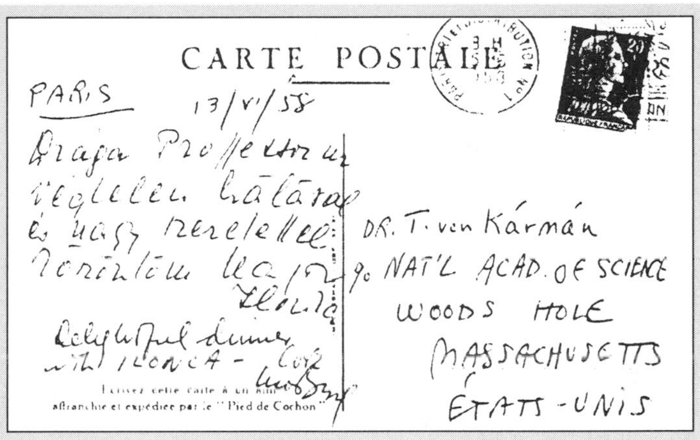

Moe Berg

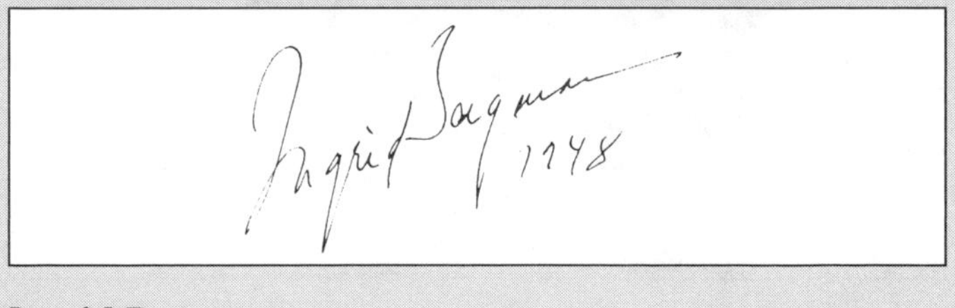

Ingrid Bergman

Irving Berlin

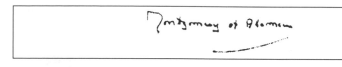

Viscount Bernard of Alamein

Henry Bessemer

Ambrose Bierce

Albert Bierstadt

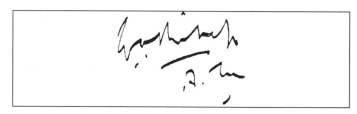

William A. Bishop

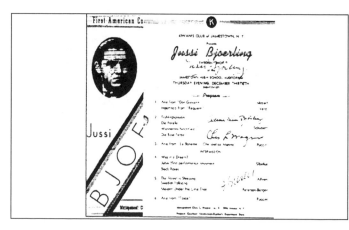

Jussi Bjoerling

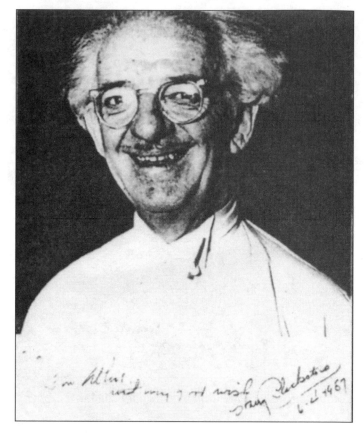

Harry Blackstone

John Blair

Montgomery Blair

William Bligh

Joan Blondell & Dick Powell

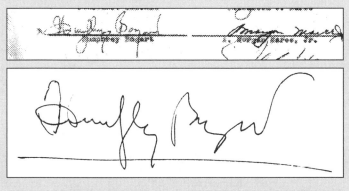

Humphrey Bogart

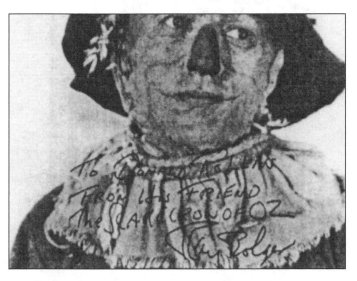

Ray Bolger

Simon Bolivar

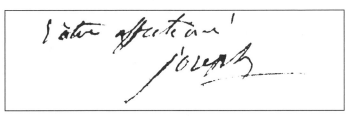

Joseph Bonaparte

Napolean Bonaparte, 1811

Richard Boone

William Booth

William Booth

Max Born

Fernando Botero

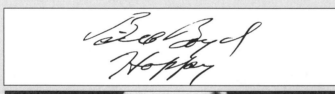

William Boyd

General of the Army

Gen. Omar Bradley

Johannes Brahms

Louis D. Brandeis

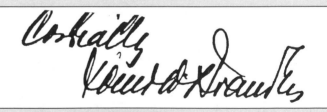

Marlon Brando

Marlon Brando

Carter Braxton

John C. Breckinridge

Walter Brennan

Joseph Brandt

Georges Braque

Benjamin Britten

Helen Broderick

Helen Broderick

Phillips Brooks

Phillips Brooks

A. Roy Brown

A. Roy Brown

John Brown

KNOW ALL MEN BY THESE PRESENTS, That we *John Brown, Stow & Wetmore, William Wetmore, Himan Oviatt and Frederick Brown* are jointly and severally bound to the President, Directors and Company of the WESTERN RESERVE BANK, as principal debtors, in the sum of *six thousand* dollars, to be paid, with interest, to the said President, Directors and Company of the WESTERN RESERVE BANK, at their Banking House, in Warren, in *sixty* days from the date hereof, or at any subsequent day or days to which the payment may from time to time be extended by the Directors of said Bank. TO WHICH PAYMENT, well and truly to be made, we bind ourselves, or heirs, executors, and administrators, firmly by these presents. Scaled with our seals, and dated the *second* day of *August* Anno Domini, 183*7*

$6000

John Brown

Johnny Mack Brown

Johnny Mack Brown

Joe E. Brown

Joe E. Brown

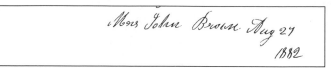

Mrs John Brown. Aug 27 1882

Mary Ann Brown (wife of John Brown)

Mary Ann Brown (wife of John Brown)

Tom Brown

Tom Brown

Francis E. Brownell

Francis E. Brownell

Song from "Pippa Passes"

Give her but a least excuse to love me!
When — where —
How — can this arm establish her above me,
If fortune fixed her as my lady there,
There already, to eternally reprove me?
("Hist!" — said Kate the Queen; (reproves,
But "Oh"— cried the maiden, binding her
"Tis only a page that carols unseen,
crumbling your hounds their messes!")
Is she wronged? — To the rescue of her honour,
My heart!
Is she poor? — What costs it to be styled a donor?
Merely an earth to cleave, a sea to part.
But that fortune should have thrust all this upon her,
("Nay, list!" — bade Kate the Queen;
And still cried the maiden, binding her tresses,
Tis only a page that carols unseen,
Fitting your hawks their jesses!")
Nov. 8. '87. *Robert Browning.*

Robert Browning

Robert Browning

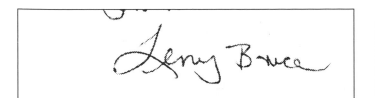

Lenny Bruce

Nigel Bruce

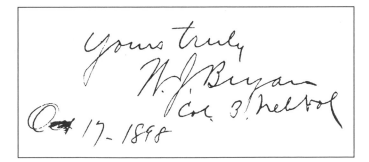

Virginia Bruce

William Jennings Bryan

Paul "Bear" Bruyat

William Jennings Bryan

Yul Brynner

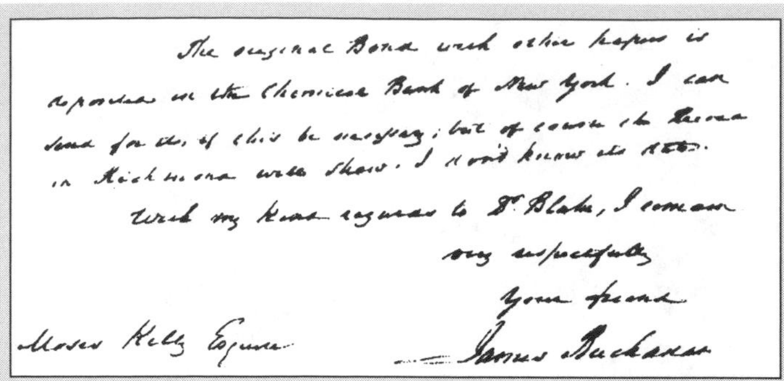

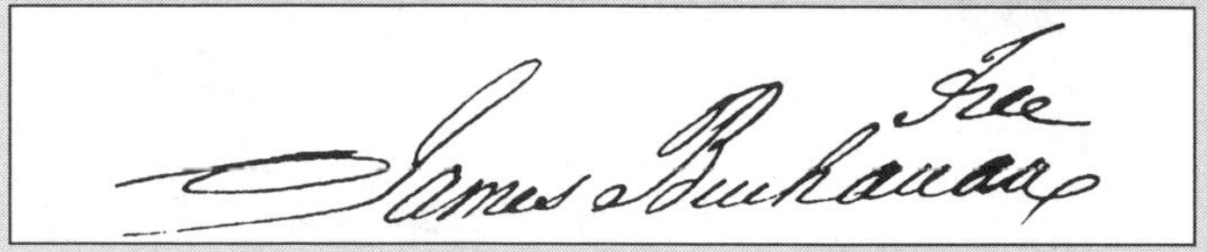

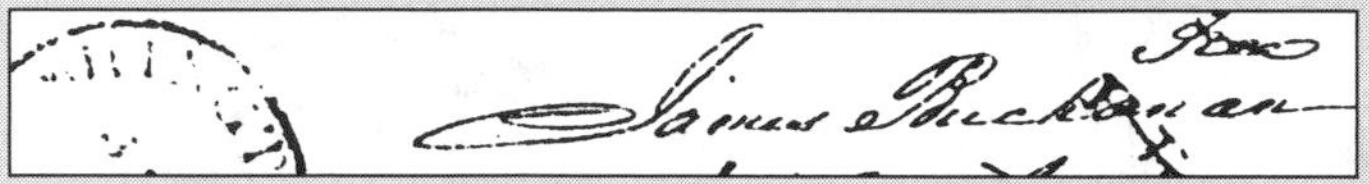

The original Bond with other papers is reposed in the Chemical Bank of New York. I can send for this, if this be necessary; but of course the record in Richmond will show. I don't know its N[o].

With my kind regards to D[r] Blake, I remain very respectfully Your friend

James Buchanan

Moses Kelly Esquire

James Buchanan

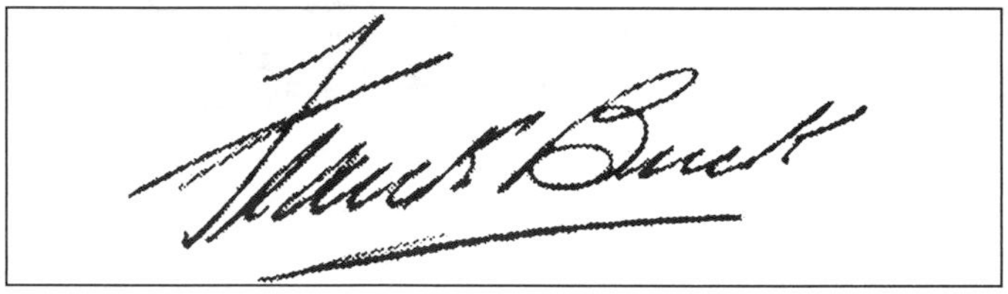

Frank Buck

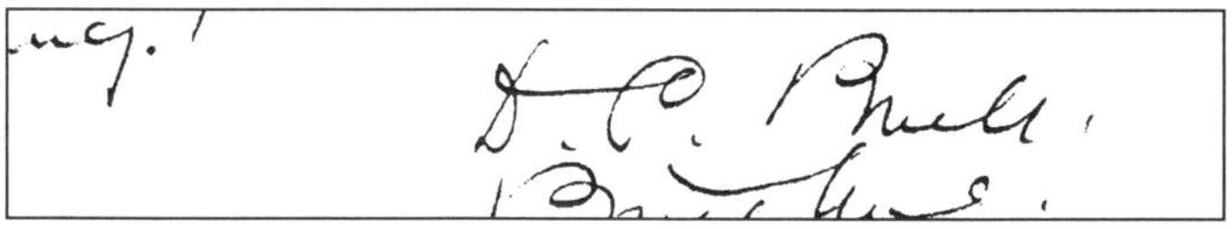

Gen. Don Carlos Buell

Morgan Bulkeley

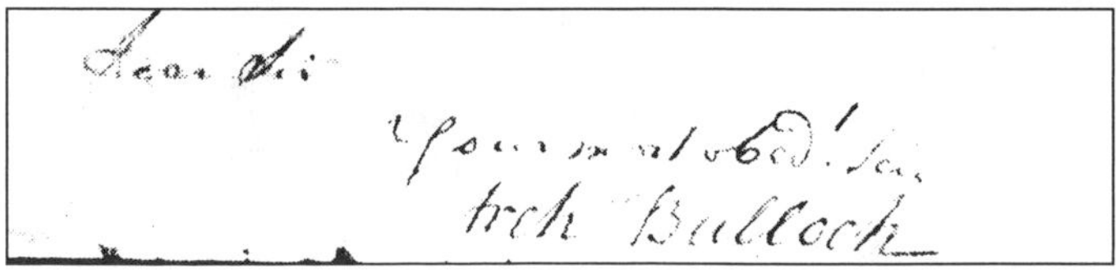

Archibald Bulloch

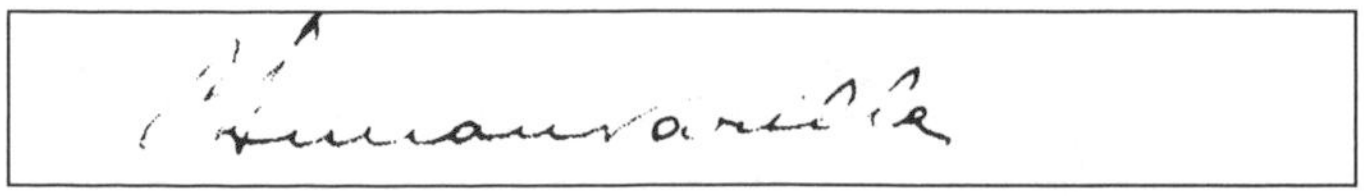

Phillippe Bunau-Varilla

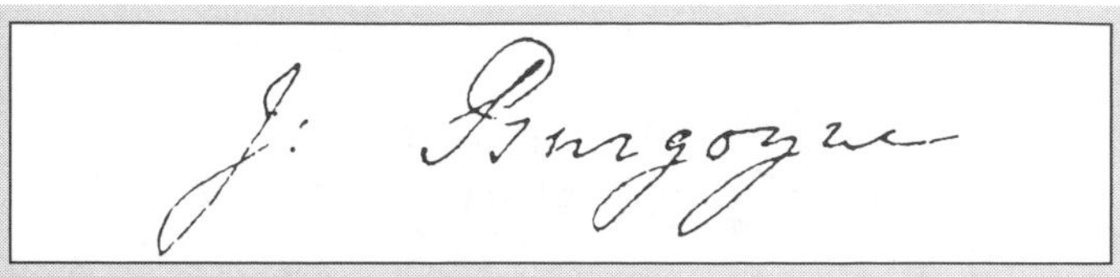

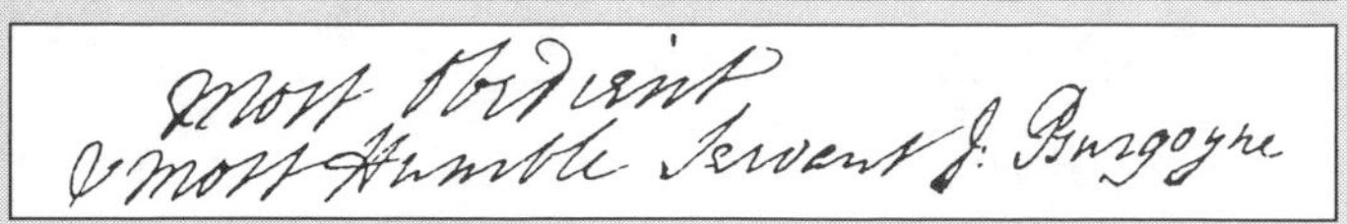

Gen. John Burgoyne

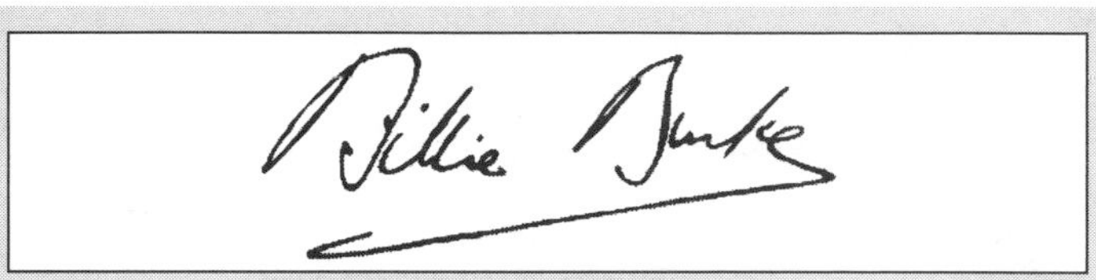

Most Obedient, & Most Humble Servant J. Burgoyne

Billie Burke

Deep —— riv-er, my home is over

Compliments o—

H. Burleigh

Oak Bluffs, Mass. Aug. 21st 1944

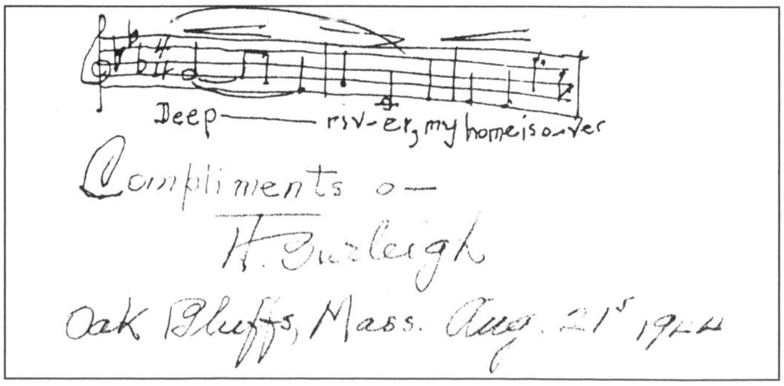

Henry T. Burleigh

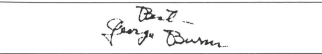

George Burns

Gen. Ambrose E. Burnside

Edgar Rice Burroughs

Barbara Bush

Aaron Burr

George Bush

Benjamin F. Butler

Edgar Rice Burroughs

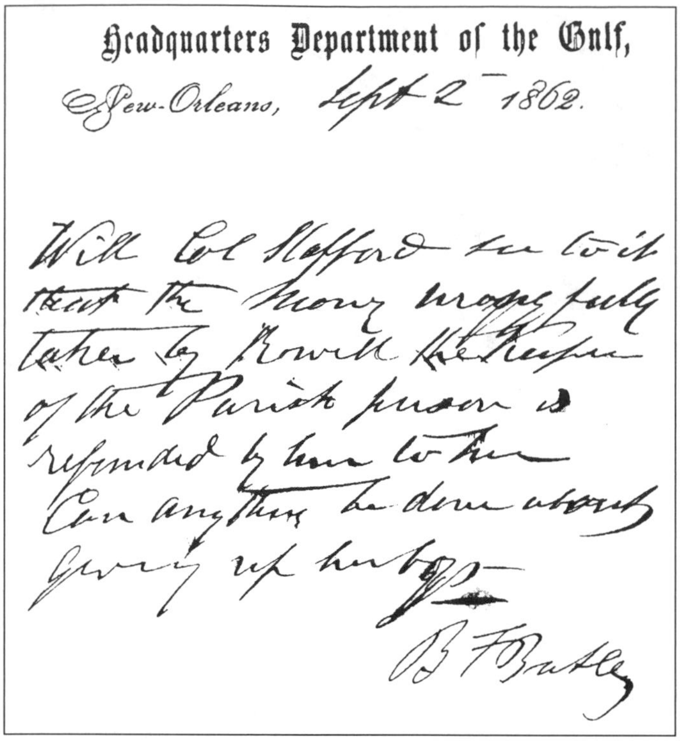

Headquarters Department of the Gulf,

New-Orleans, Sept 2ⁿ 1862.

[handwritten letter]

B. F. Butler

Gen. Benjamin Butler

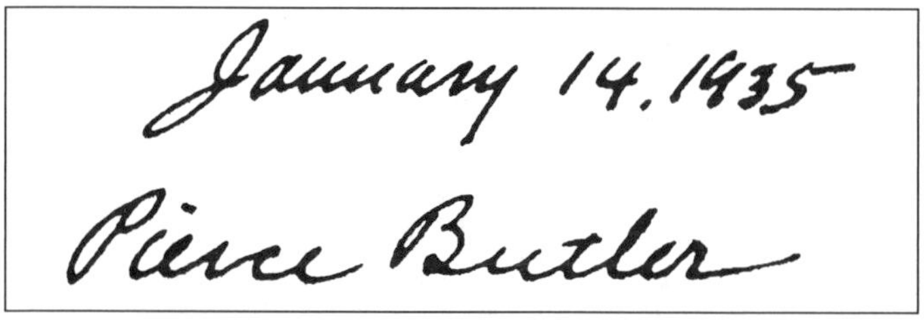

January 14. 1935

Pierce Butler

Pierce Butler

Chas. F. Butterworth

Charles Butterworth

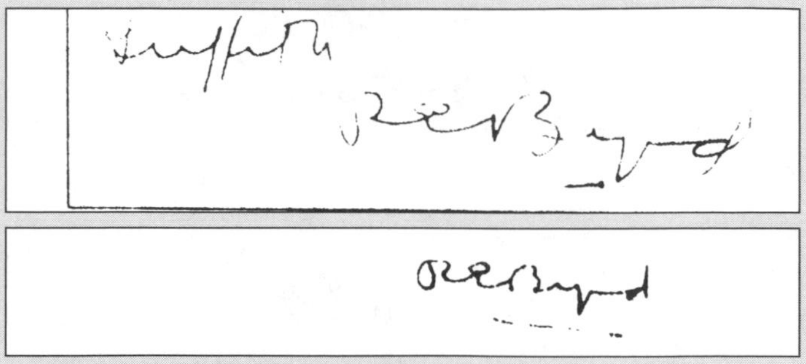

Ricahrd E. Byrd

The Byrds

Bruce Cabot

Nicholas Cage

James Cagney

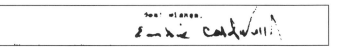

Alexander Calder

Sandy Calder

Erskine Caldwell

John C. Calhour

Maria Callas

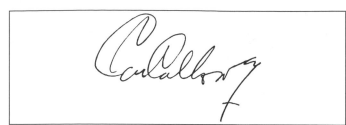

Cab Calloway

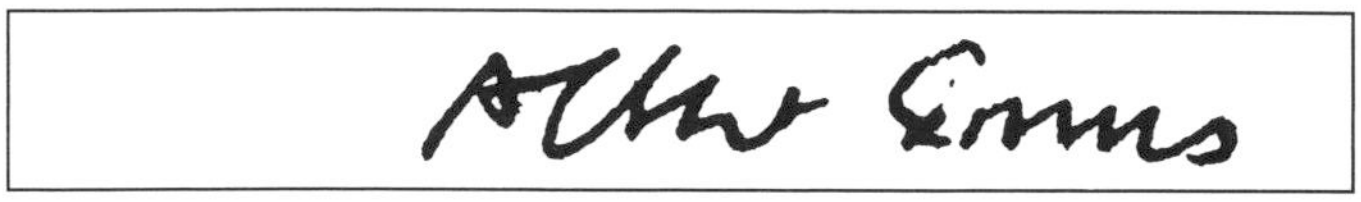

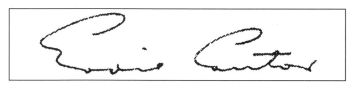

Albert Camus

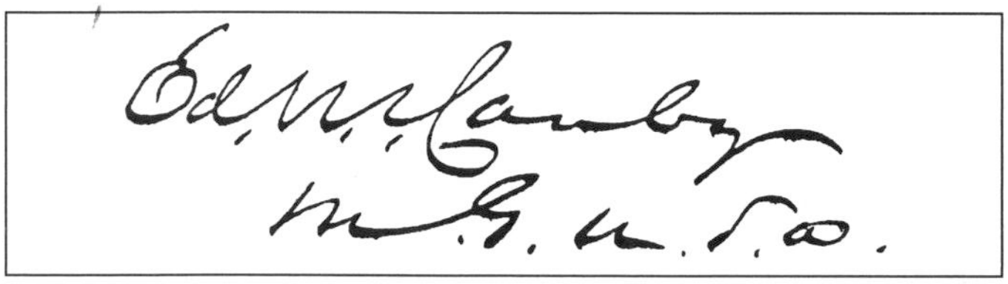

Gen. Edward R.S. Canby

Eddie Cantor

Washington
May 25, 1937

Charles Schwager, Esq.
Dear Mr. Schwager,

Many thanks, sir, for your cordial message —

Very truly yours
Benjamin Cardozo

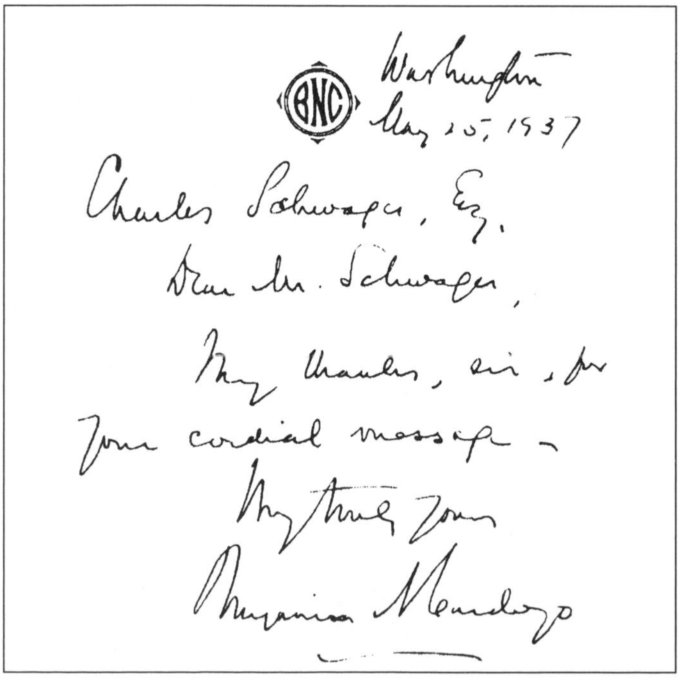

Benjamin N. Cardoza

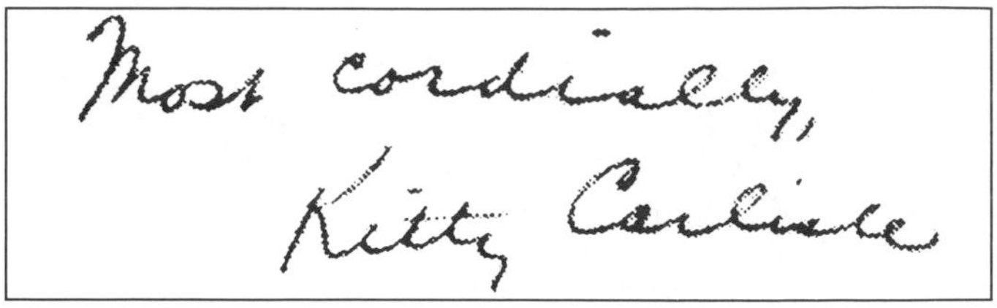

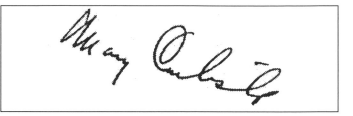

Kitty Carlisle

Mary Carlisle

Hogey Carmichael

Brick House
Noroton, Connecticut

Please tell the President that for a "True Hero" there is no such word as finis and he is both Hero and Prophet.

Yours Ever
Andrew Carnegie

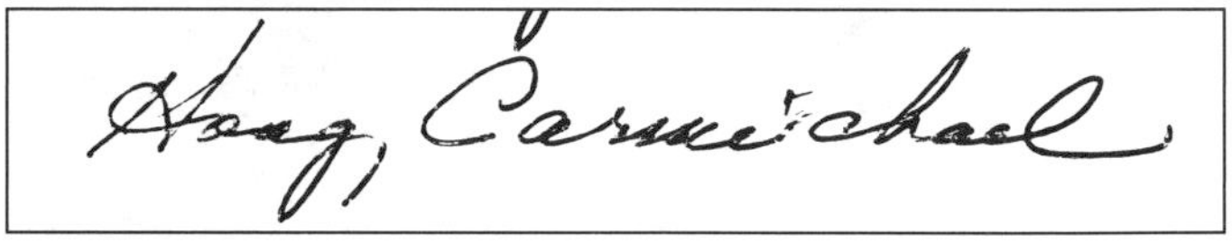

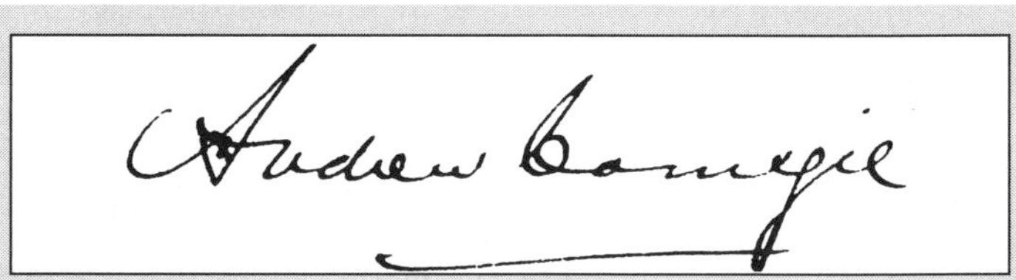

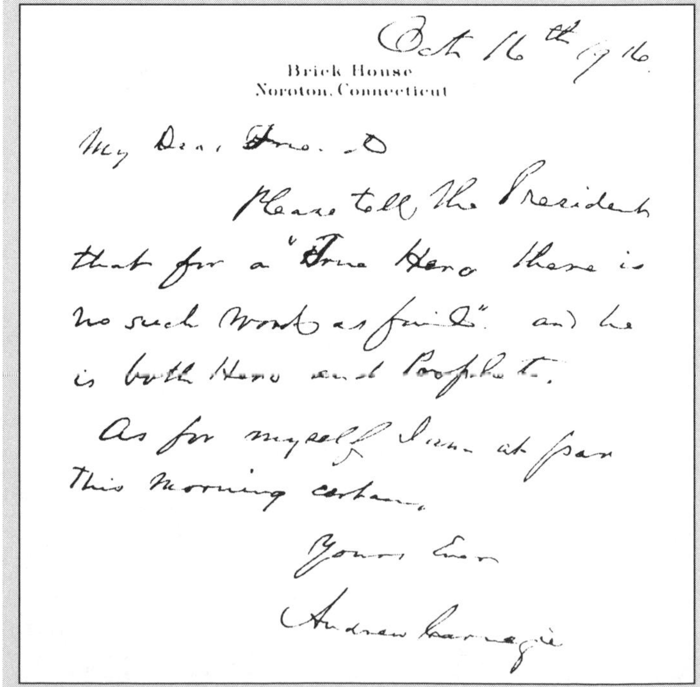

Andrew Carnegie

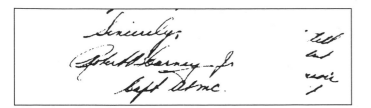

Robert Carney, Jr.

Leo Carrillo

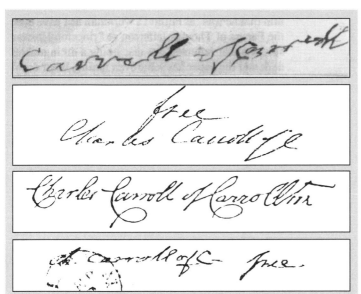

Charles Carroll of Carlton

Madeline Carroll

Nancy Carroll

Rachel Carson

Jimmy & Rosalyn Carter

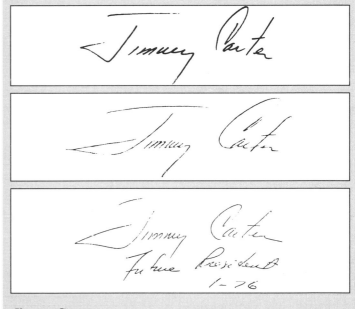

Jimmy Carter

Cartoonists - Charles Schulz, Walter Lantz, Chuck Jones

Cartoonists - Schulz & Ketchum

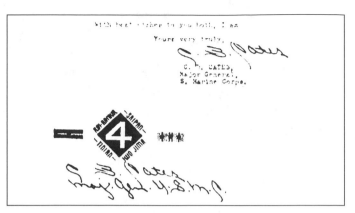

Clifton B. Cates

Enrico Caruso

Catherine II the Great, Empress of Russia

Eugene Cernan

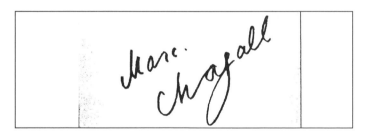

Marc Chagall

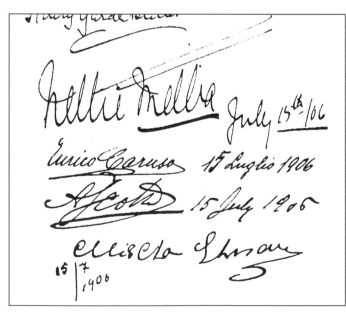

Enrico Caruso, Nellie Melba, Antonio Scotti, Mischa Elman

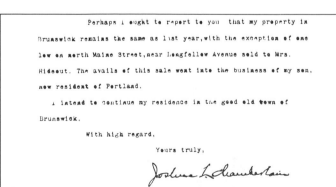

Gen. Joshua L. Chamberlain

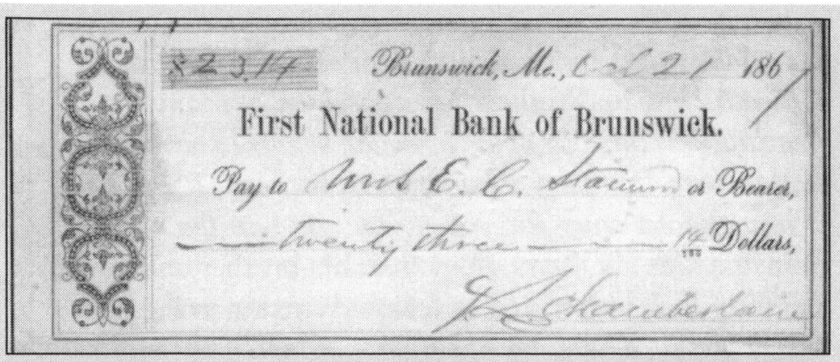

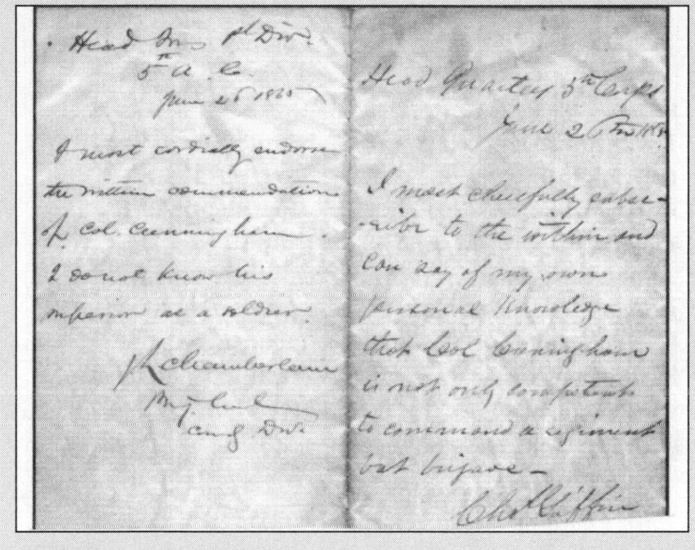

Joshua Chamberlain

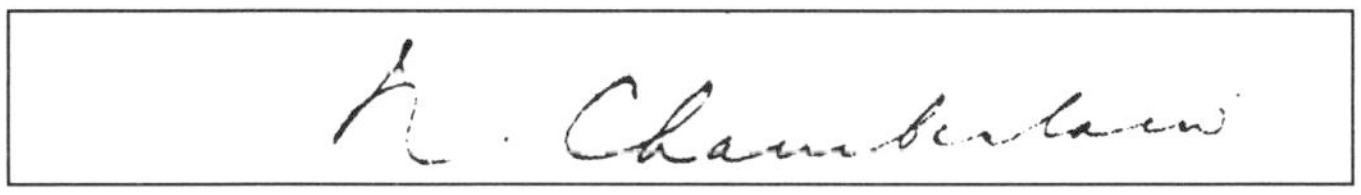

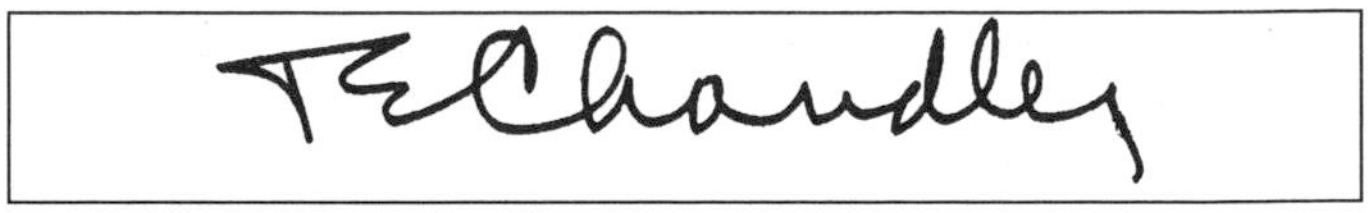

Theodore E. Chandler

Cecile L. Chaminade

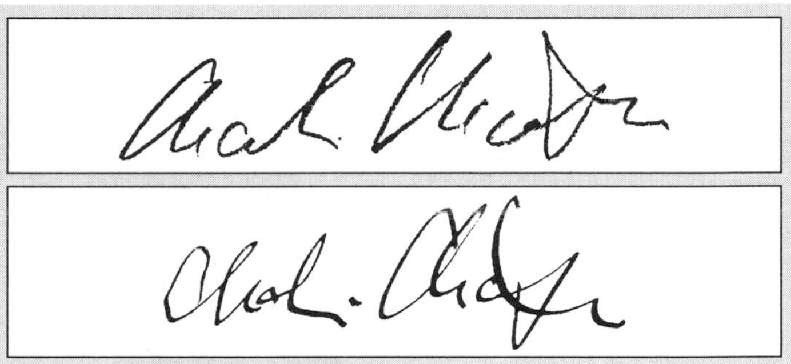

Charlie Chaplin

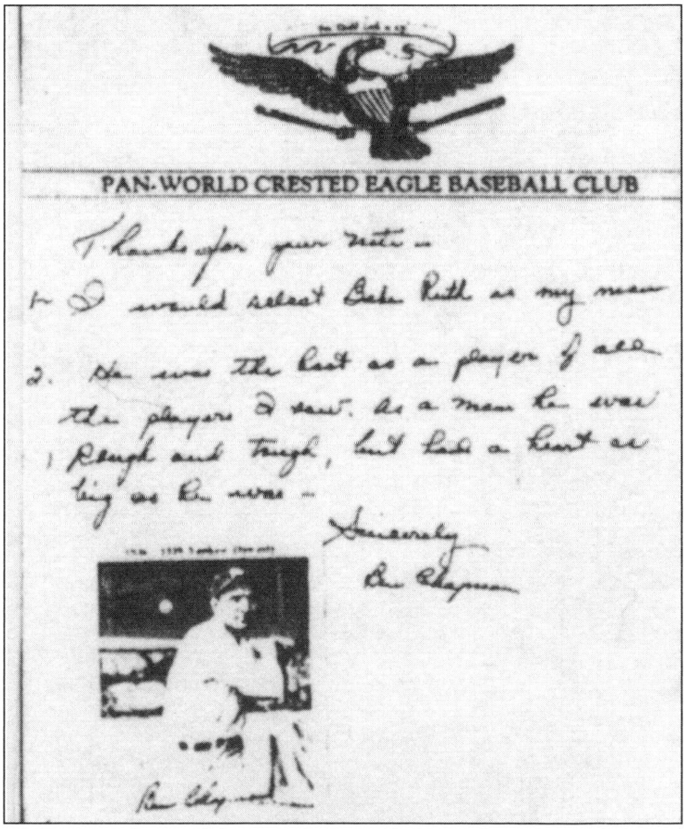

Neville Chamberlain

Neville Chamberlain, Stanley Baldwin, Richard B. Bennett

Ben Chapman

Charles I of England

Charles IX, King of France

Prince Charles and Diana Spencer

Gustav Charpentier

Ilka Chase

Samuel Chase

Ruth Chatterton

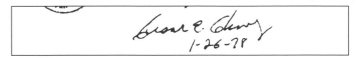

Cesar Chavez

Claire Chennault

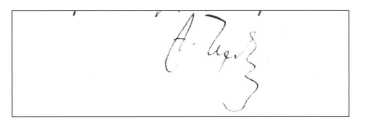

Anton Chekhov

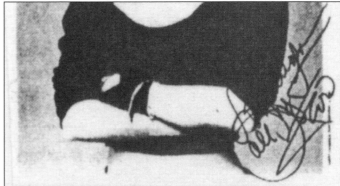

Cher

Luigi Cherubini

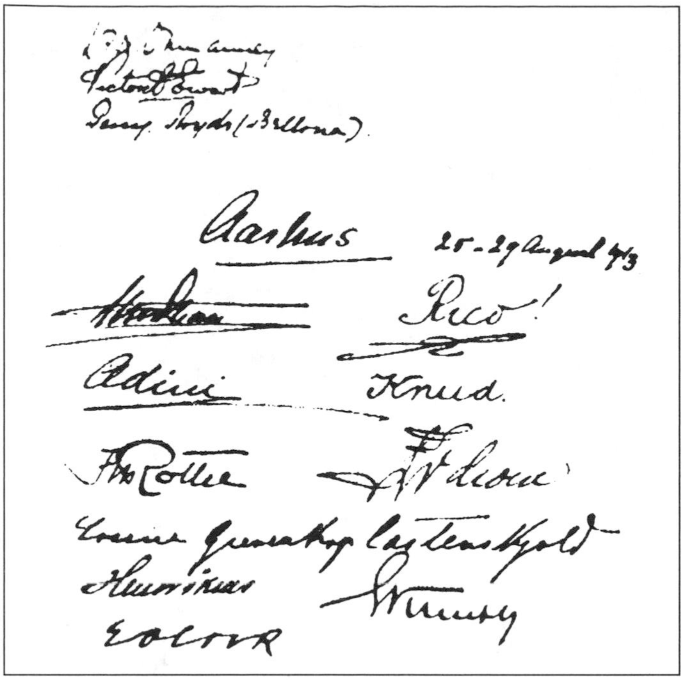

King Christian X, King Frederick IX, Queen Alexandrine - Denmark Royalty

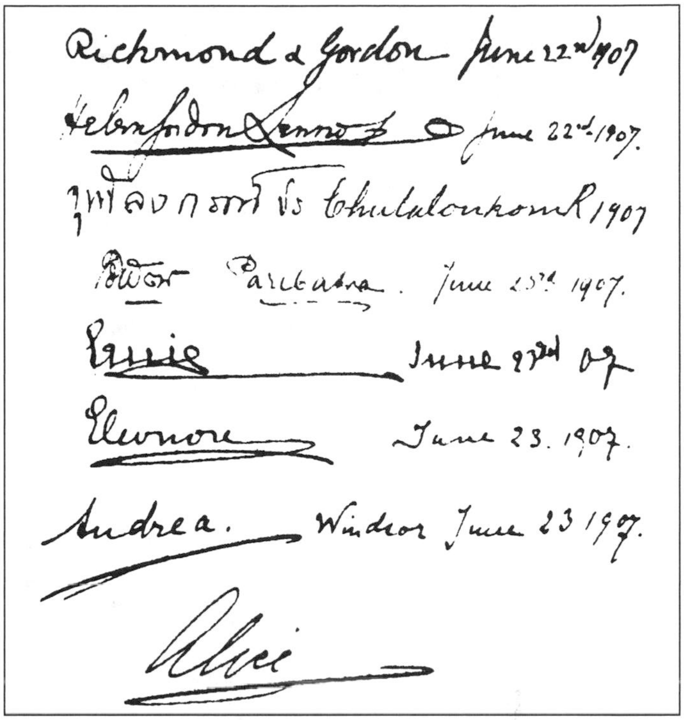

King Chulaholkorn of Thailand, Grand Duke & Duchess Ernst & Ealeanor of Hesse, Prince and Princess Andrew and Alice of Greece

Mady Christians

Agatha Christie

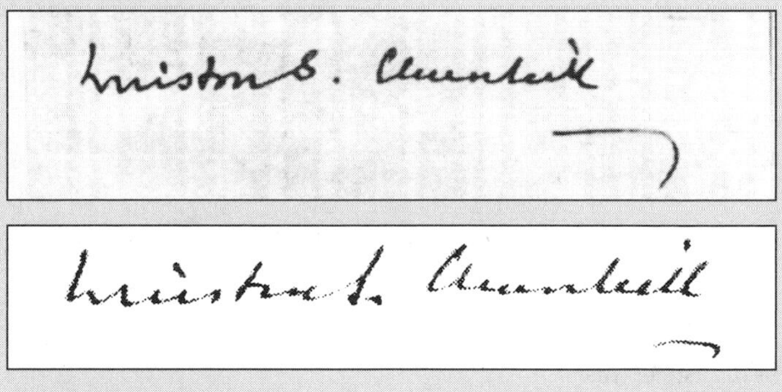

Winston Churchhill

Walter Chrysler

Eric Clapton

Abraham Clark

Bobby Clark

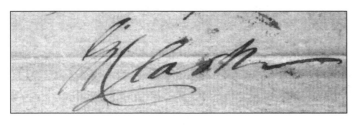

George Rogers Clark

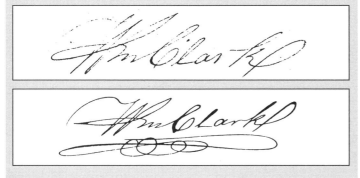

William Clark

Henry Clay

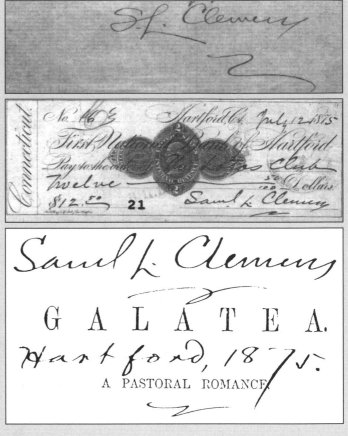

Samuel L. Clemens

Francis F. Cleveland

Grover Cleveland

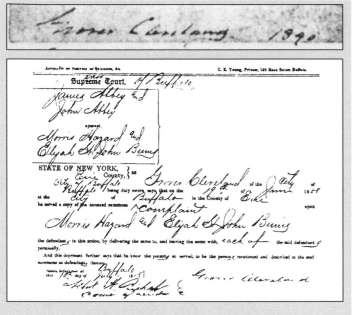

Grover Cleveland

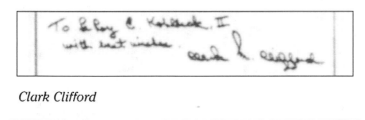

Rose Elizabeth Cleveland

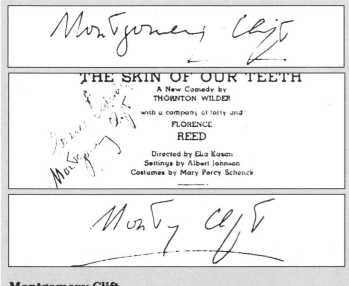

Clark Clifford

Montgomery Clift

Patsy Cline

Bill Clinton

George Clinton

Baron Clive

George Clymer

Erwin S. Cobb

Ty Cobb

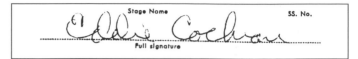

Mickey Cochrane

Eddie Cochrane

William F. Cody

George M. Cohan

Claudette Colbert

Nat King Cole

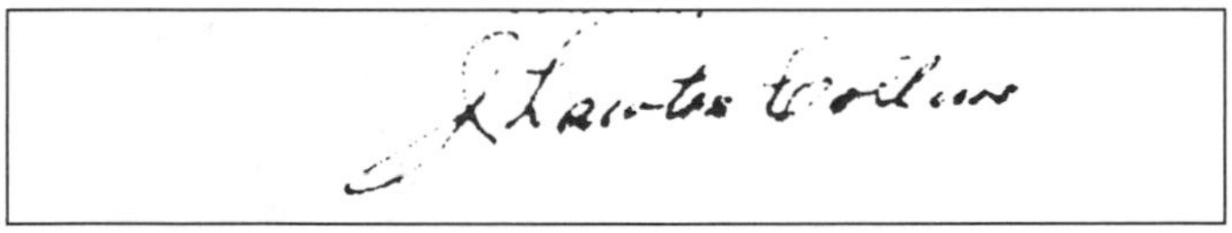

J. Lawton Collins

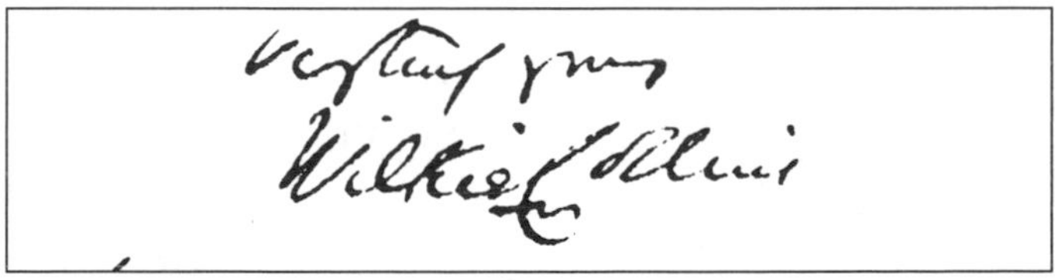

Wilkie Collins

Samuel Colt

Carl T. Compton

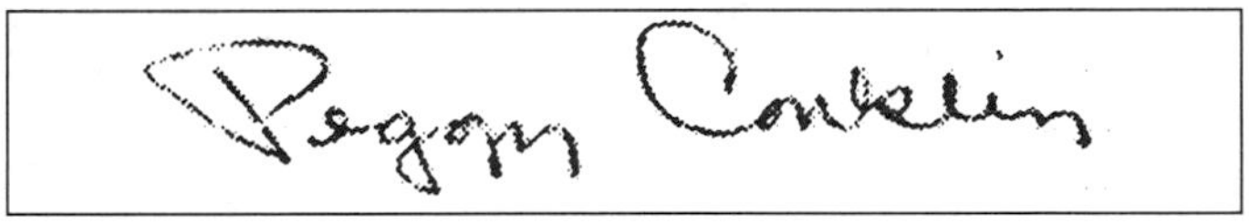

Peggy Conklin

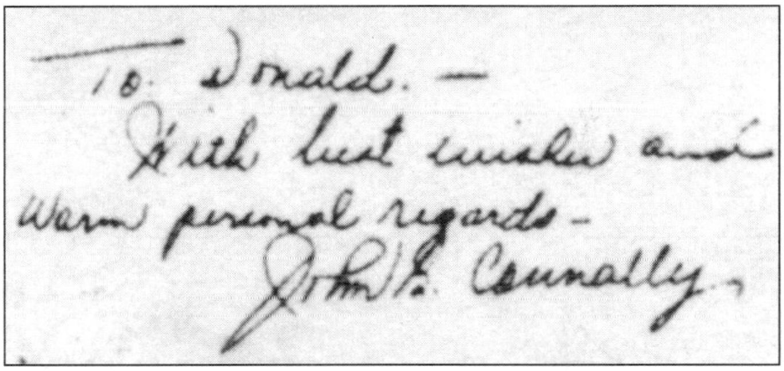

John Connelly

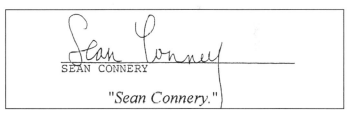

Sean Connery

Jackie Coogan

Jay Cooke

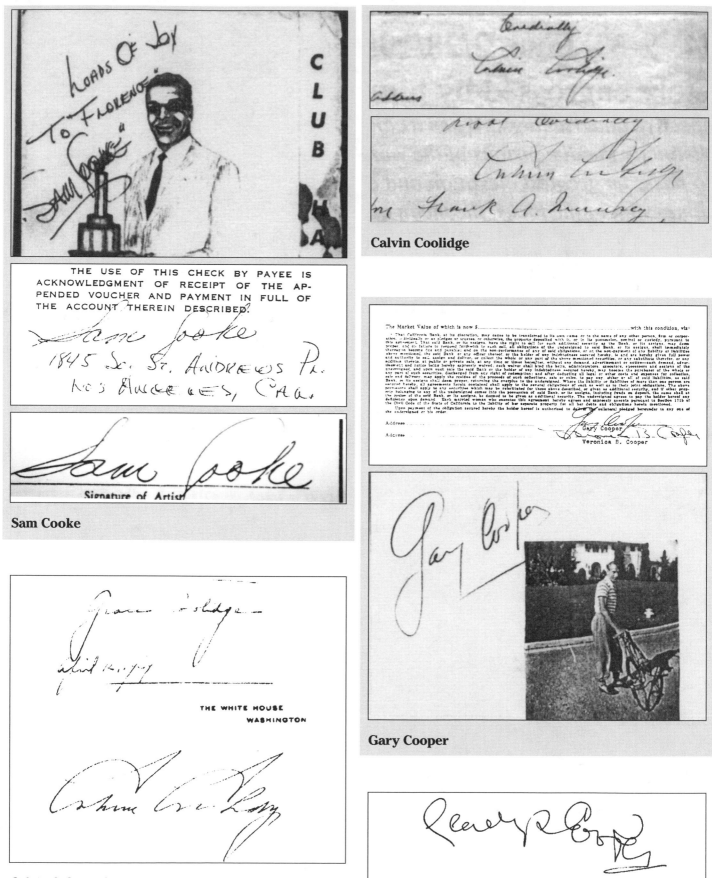

Sam Cooke

Calvin Coolidge

Gary Cooper

Calvin & Grace Coolidge

Gladys Cooper

Jackie Cooper

Ellen Corby

James Fenimore Cooper

Chick Corea

J. Fred Coots

Lord Edward H. Cornbury

John S. Copley

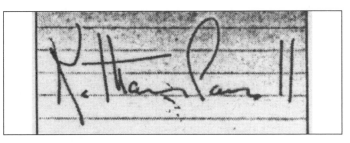

Katherine Cornell

Aaron Copeland

James Corbett

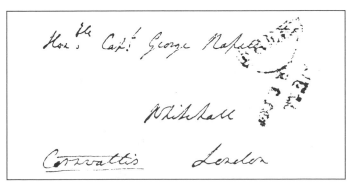

Charles Lord Cornwallis

Cornwallis

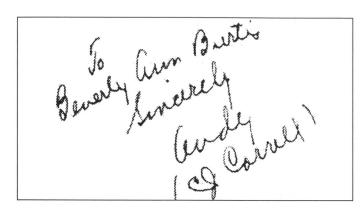

Charles J. Correll

Hernando Cortes

Ricardo Cortez

Lou Costello

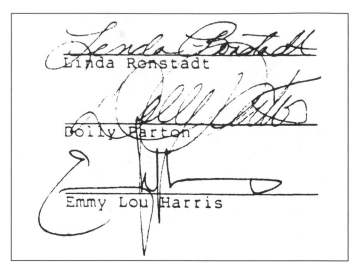

Country Singers - Linda Ronstadt, Emmy Lou Harris &
Dolly Parton

Jacques Cousteau

Noel Coward

Jane Cowl

Archibald Cox

Bob Crane

Frank Craven

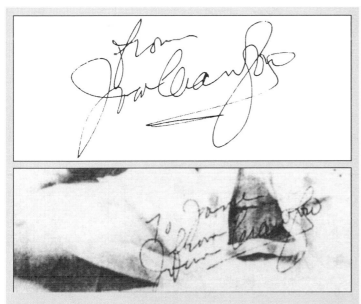

Joan Crawford

Johnny Crawford

Francis Crick

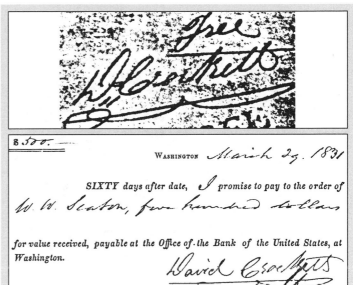

David Crockett

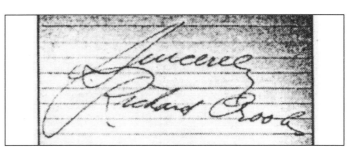

Walter Cronkite

Richard Crooks

Bing Crosby

Crosby, Stills and Nash

Laura Hope Crews

E.E. Cummings

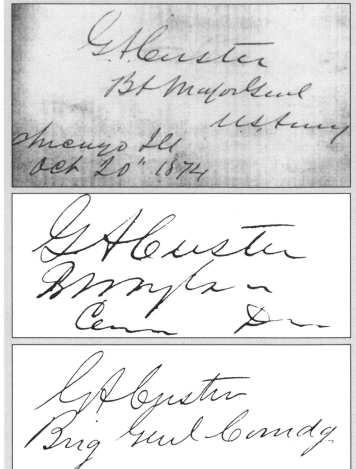

George A. Custer

Eugene D'Albert

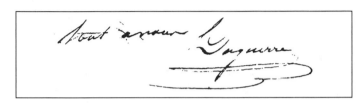

Louis J. Daguerre

Dalai Lama

Richard J. Daley

Salvador Dali

George M. Dallas

Emmitt Dalton

Lili Damita

Daniel of St. Thomas

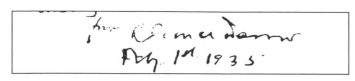

Bobbie Darrin

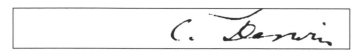

Charles Darrow

Charles Darwin

Jane Darwell

Marion Davies

William Davies

Bette Davis

David Davis

Jefferson Davis

Jim Davis

Owen Davis

Moshe Dayan

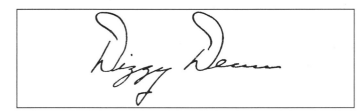

Dizzy Dean

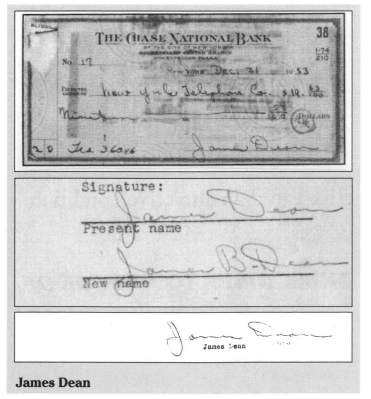

James Dean

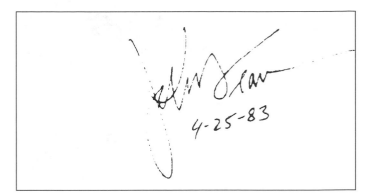

John Dean

Mountain Man Dean

Eugene V. Debs

Edgar Degas

Manuel De Falla

Claude Debussy

Charles DeGaulle

Frederick Delius

Cecil B. DeMille

Olivia DeHavilland

Jack Dempsey

Marquis de Lafayette

Jack Dempsey

Sandy Dennis

Jean DeReszke

Gen. Jacob Devers

Admiral George Dewey

John Dewey

Charles Dickens

John Dickerson

Babe Didrikson

Marlena Dietrich

Dudley Digges

John Dillinger

Joe DiMaggio

Vincent D'Indy

Celine Dion

Disney Illustrators, Frank Thomas, Ollie Johnston

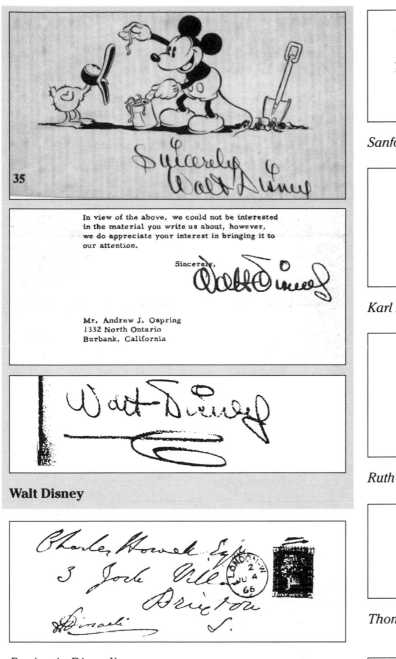

Walt Disney

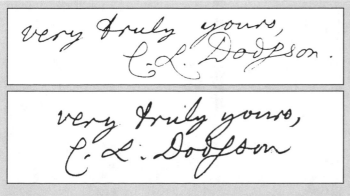

Benjamin Disraeli

Charles L. Dodson (Lewis Carroll)

Sanford B. Dole

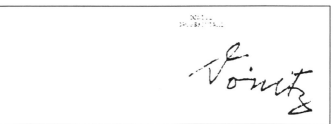

Karl Donitz

Ruth Donnelly

Thomas Dooley

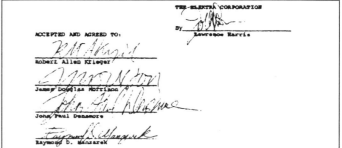

The Doors

Tommy and Jimmy Dorsey

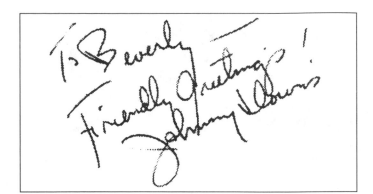

Johnny Downs

Desmond T. Doss

Desmond Doss

Arthur Conan Doyle

Arthur Conan Doyle

Respectfully
Fred. Douglass

Fred. Douglass

Frederick Douglass

Theodore Dreiser

Theodore Dreiser

Melvyn Douglas

Melvyn Douglas

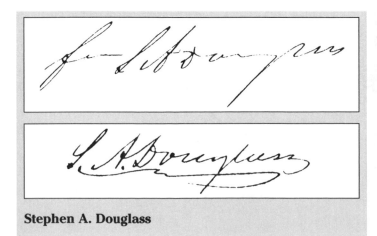

Stephen A. Douglass

Charlie Duke

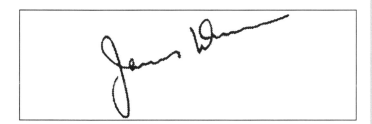

Alexander Dumas

Irene Dunne

James Dunne

Deanna Durbin

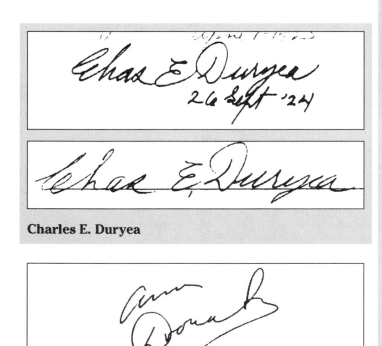

Charles E. Duryea

Ann Dvorak

Antonin Dvorak

Bob Dylan

E

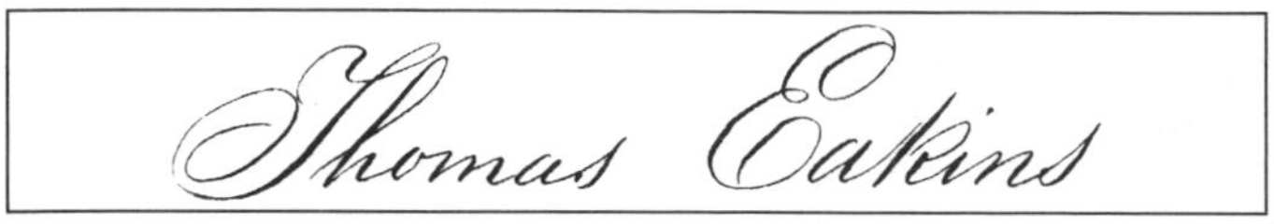

Thomas Eakins

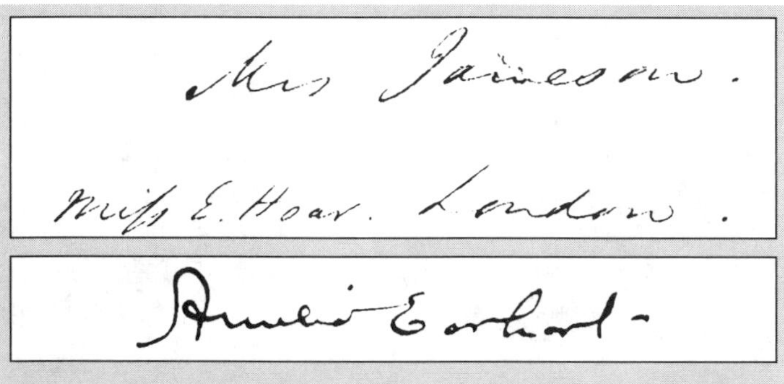

Amelia Earhart

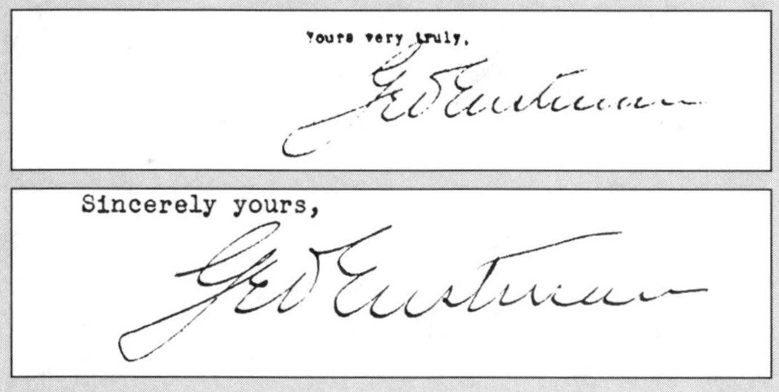

George Eastman

Hugo Eckener

Nelson Eddy

Thomas Edison

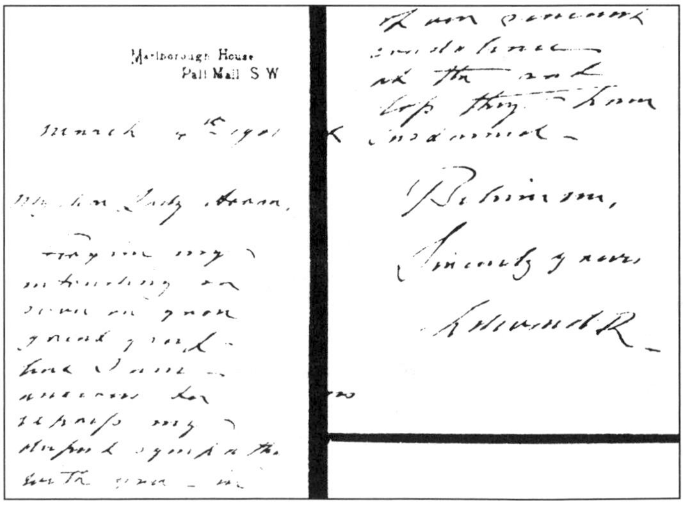

Edward VII

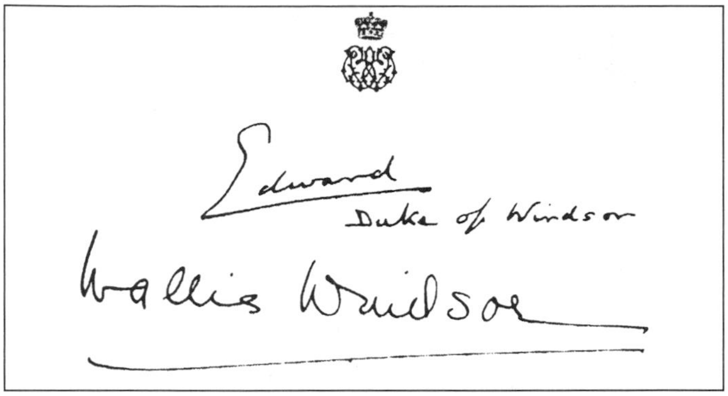

Edward VIII, Wallis Simpson

Cliff Edwards

Gustav Eiffel

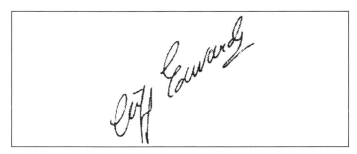

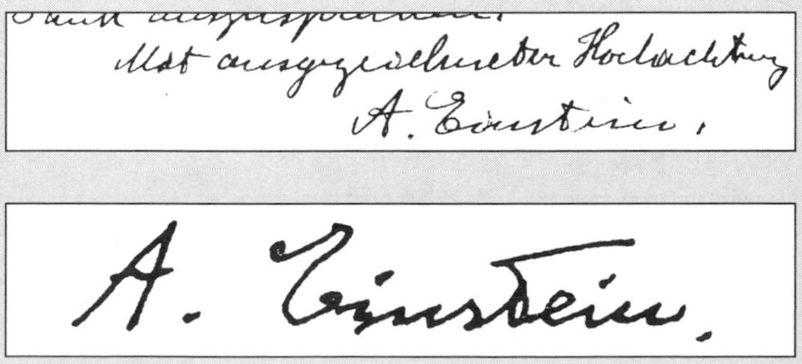

Albert Einstein

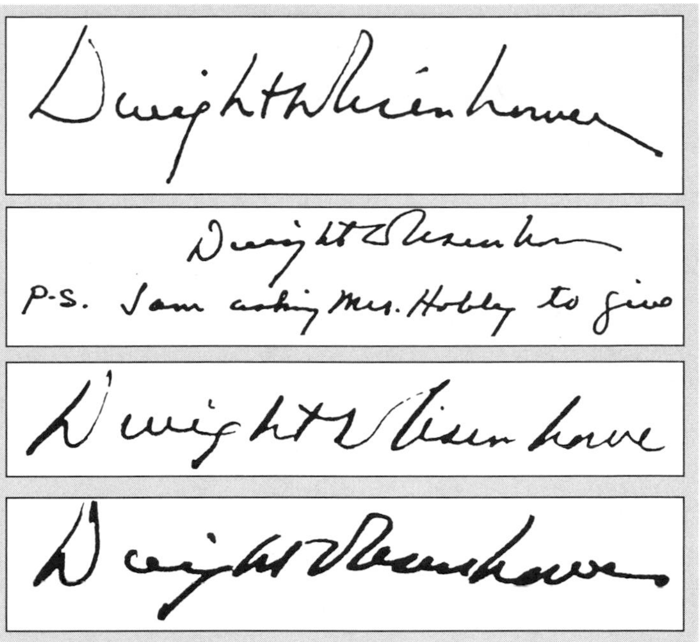

Dwight D. Eisenhower

Elizabeth I, Queen of England

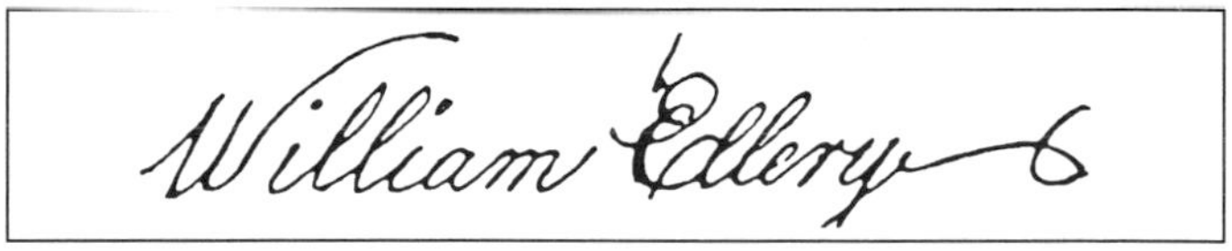

William Ellery

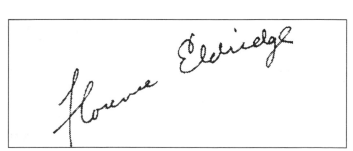

Florence Eldridge

Duke Ellington

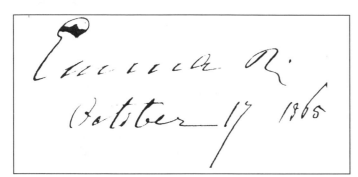

Emma, Queen of Hawaii

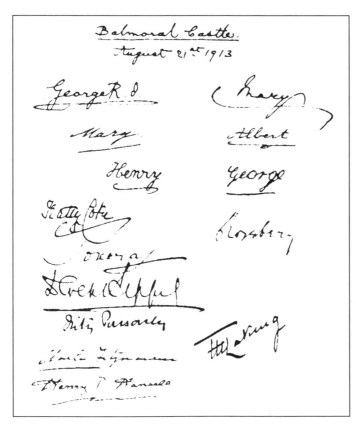

English Royalty - King George V, Queen Mary, King George VI (Albert), Prince George, Prince Henry, Princess Mary

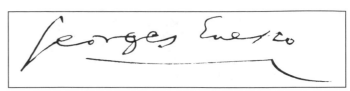

Georges Enesco

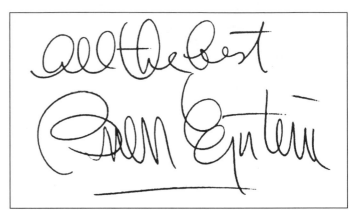

Brian Epstein

Leon Errol

Levi Eshkol

Madge Evans

Edward Everett

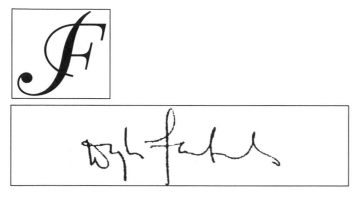

Douglas Fairbanks

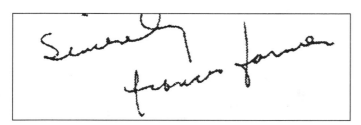

Frances Farmer

David G. Farragut

Glenda Farrell

Gabriel Faure

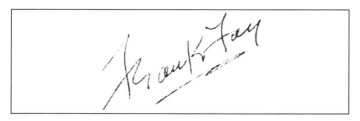

Frank Fay

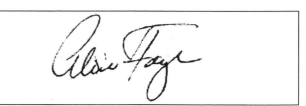

Alice Faye

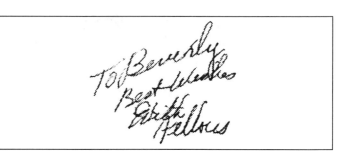

Edith Fellows

Ferdinand II, King of Spain

Enzo Ferrari

Jimmie Fidler

Cyrus Field

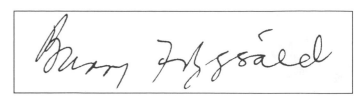

W.C. Fields

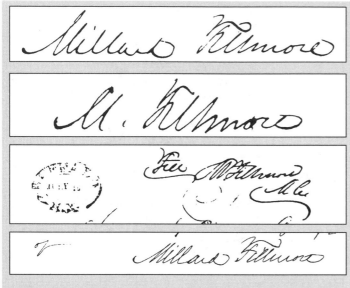

Millard Fillmore

Barry Fitzgerald

Ella Fitzgerald

Larry Fine

F. Scott Fitzgerald

Ham Fisher

James Montgomery Flagg

Alexander Fleming

William Floyd

Eric Fleming

Errol Flynn

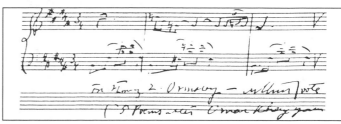

Henry Fonda

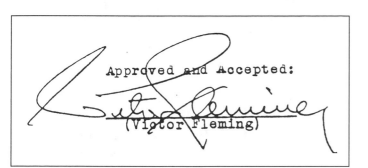

Victor Fleming

Arthur Foote

Dick Foran

Ralph Forbes

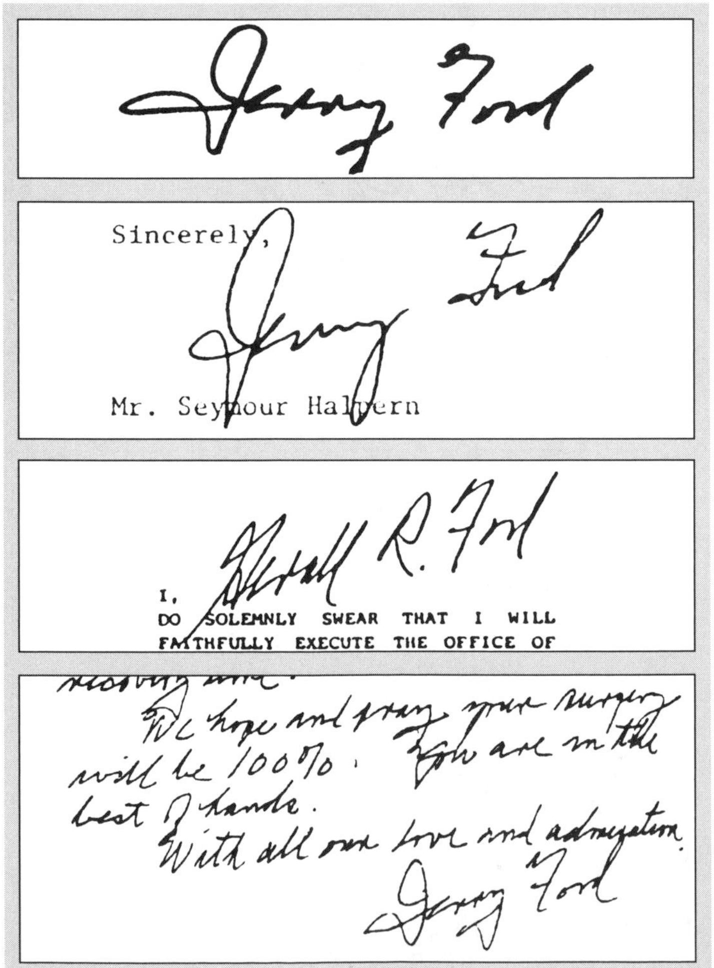

Jerry Ford

Sincerely,

Jerry Ford

Mr. Seymour Halpern

Gerald R. Ford

I,
DO SOLEMNLY SWEAR THAT I WILL
FAITHFULLY EXECUTE THE OFFICE OF

We hope and pray your surgery
will be 100%. You are in the
best of hands.
With all our love and admiration.
Jerry Ford

Gerald Ford

Henry Ford

Wallace Ford

Norman Foster

Preston Foster

Jimmy Foxx

Otto Frank

Benjamin Franklin

William Frawley

Pauline Frederick

John C. Fremont

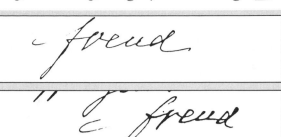

Sigmund Freud

Daniel Frohman

Robert Frost

Alfred C. Fuller

Melville W. Fuller

Robert Fulton

Harry Furness

G

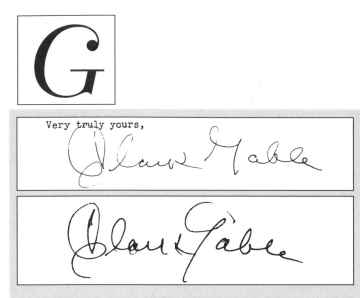

Clark Gable

Thomas Gage

William M. Gaines, Agent

William M. Gaines

Amelita Galli-Curce

Joseph Galloway

Mohandas K. Gandhi

Youre very truly

Greta Garbo

James A. Garfield

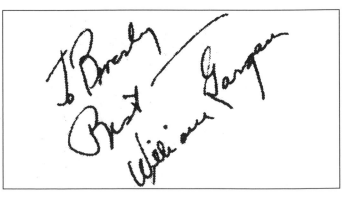

William Gargan

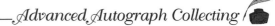

William Lloyd Garrison

R. Gatling

G. Garibaldi

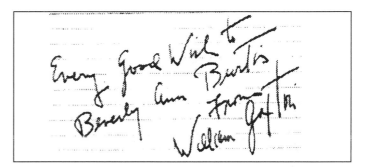

William Gaxton

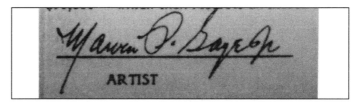

ARTIST

Marvin Gaye

ACCEPTED AND AGREED TO:

Judy Garland

GHS:mg
11/20/61   -2-

Judy Garland

Janet Gaynor

Pat Garrett

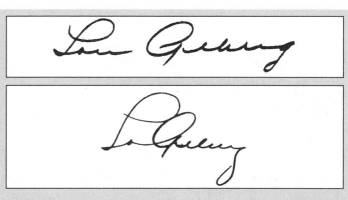

Lou Gehrig

Charlie Gehringer

Geroge V

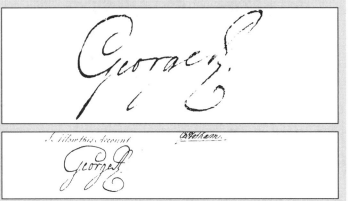

King George III

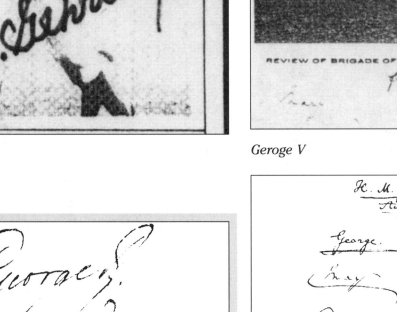

King George V< Queen Mary, Arthur

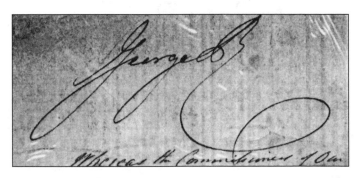

George IV

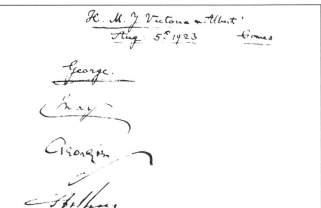

George VI and Elizabeth

George VI

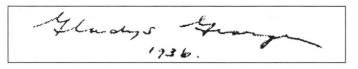

Gladys George

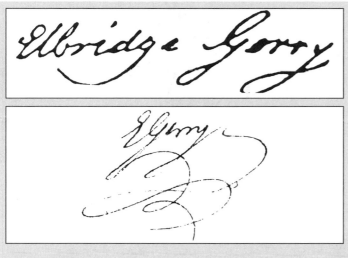

Albridge Gerry

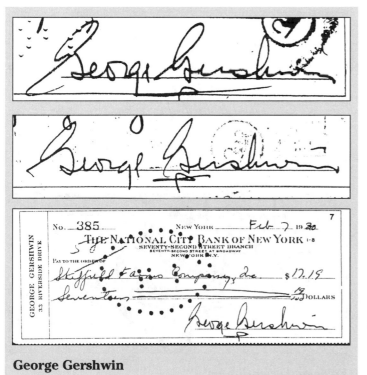

George Gershwin

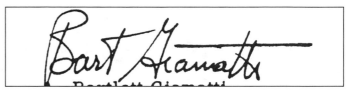

Ira Gershwin

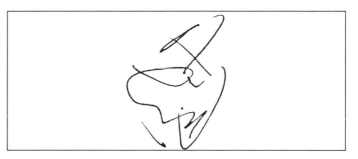

A. Bartlett Giamatti

Andy Gibb

Floyd Gibbons

Hoot Gibson

Sir John Gielgud

James Gleason

John Glenn

Robert Goddard

Joseph Goebbels

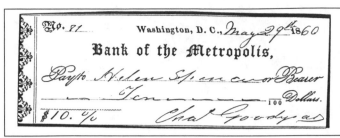

Charles Goodyear

Herman Goering

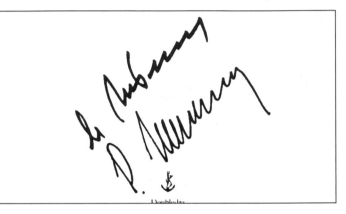

Mikhail Gorbachev

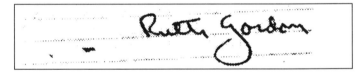

Ruth Gordon

Golfers - Irwin, Littler, Palmer & Watson

Igor Gorin

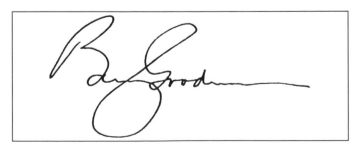

Benny Goodman

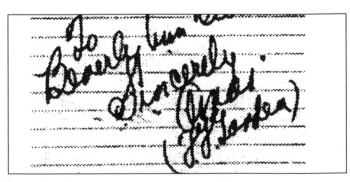

Freeman Fisher Gosden

Chester Gould

Betty Grable

Cary Grant

Edmund Goulding

Julia Dent Grant

Charles Gounod

Ulysses S. Grant

Ulysses S. Grant

Elisha Gray

Gilda Gray

Glenn Gray

Horace Greeley

Mitzi Green

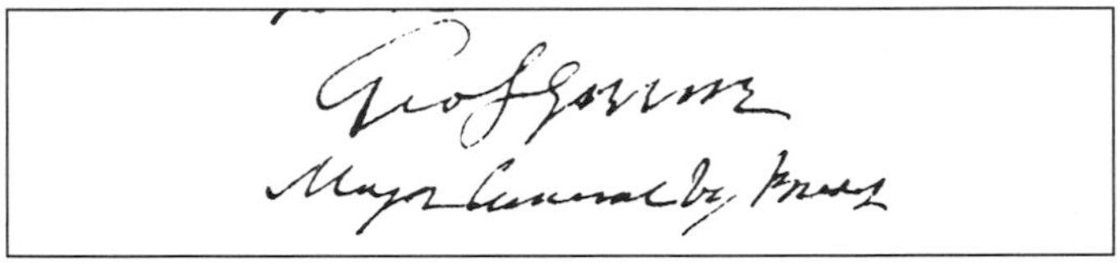

George Greene

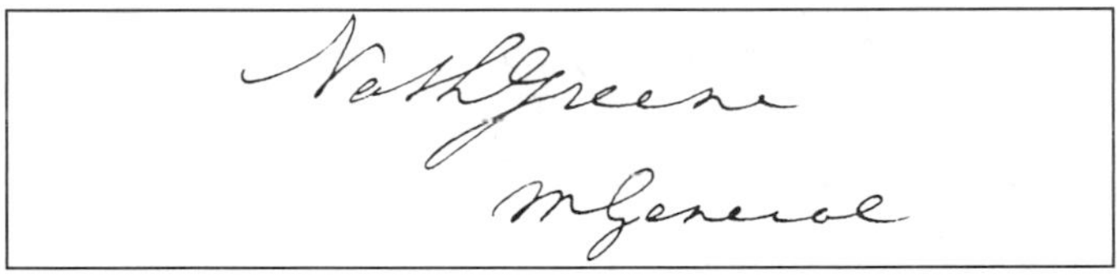

Nathaniel Greene

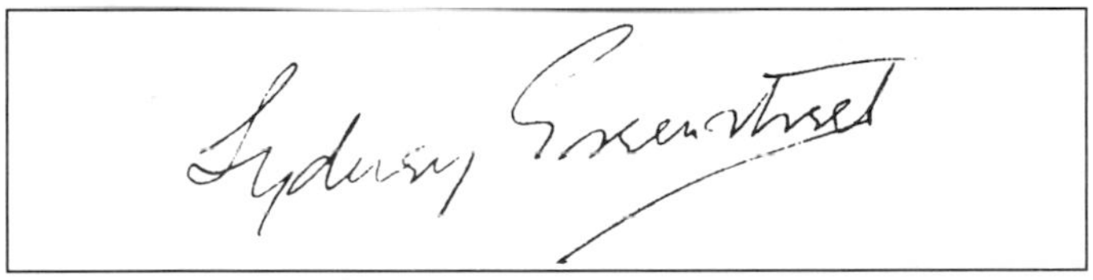

Sydney Greenstreet

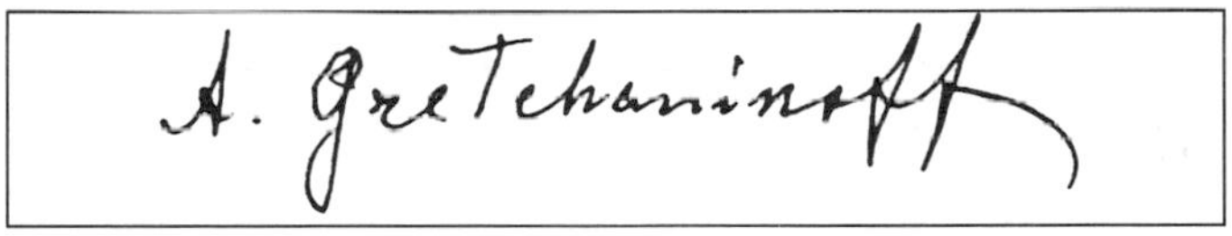

Alexander Gretchaninoff

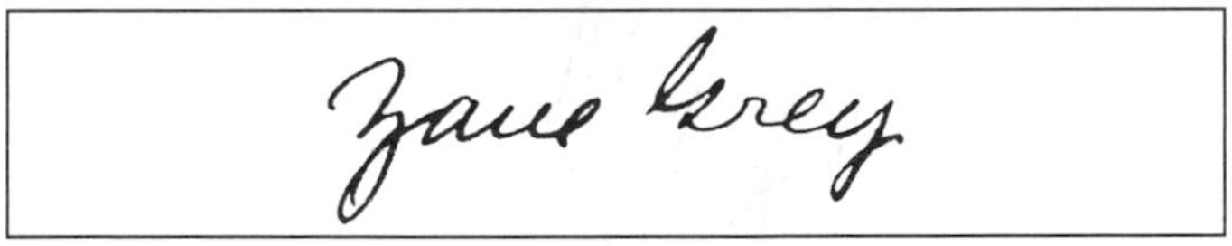

Zane Grey

Edvard Grieg

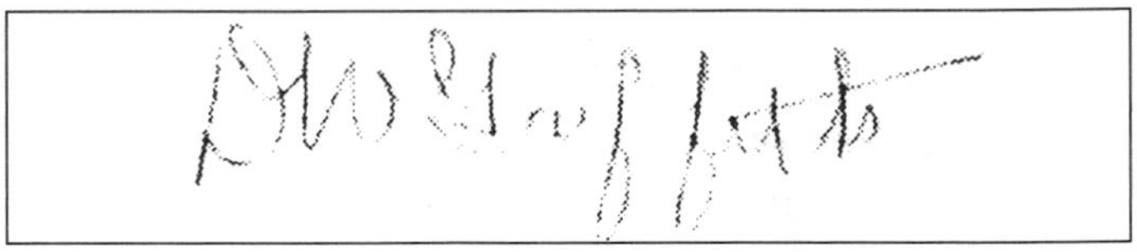

D.W. Griffith

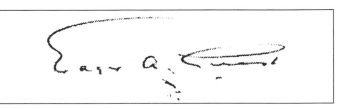

Gus Grissom and John Young

Edgar A. Guest

Charles Guiteau

Woody Guthrie

Arnold Guyot

Button Gwinnett

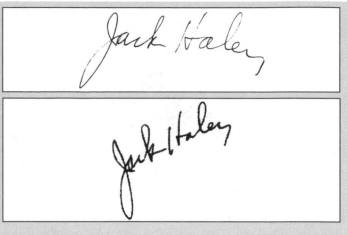

Jack Haley

Timoteo Haalilio

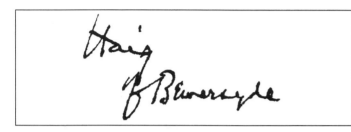

Douglas Haig

William N. Hailmann

William N. Hailmann

Nathan Hale

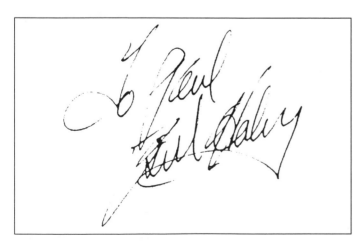

Bill Haley

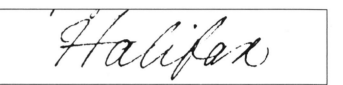

Second Earl of Halifax

Lyman Hall

William F. Halsey

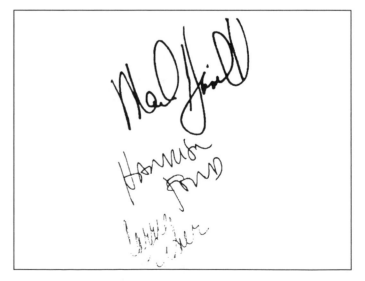

Mark Hamill, Carrie Fisher and Harrison Ford

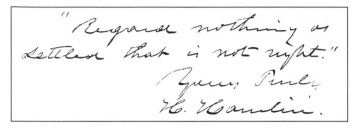

Hannibal Hamlin

John Hancock

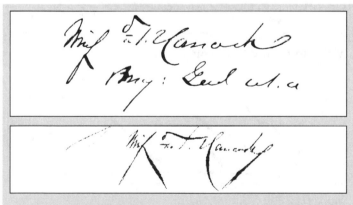

Winfield S. Hancock

Bill Hanna

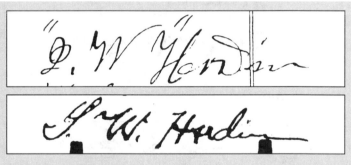

E.Y. Harburg

John Wesley Hardin

Edw: Hand

Edward Hand

Ann Harding

Florence K. Harding

Warren G. Harding

Sir Cedric Webster Hardwicke

George Harrison

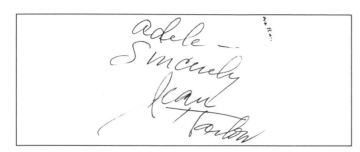

Jean Harlow

Heinrich Harrer

Frank Harris

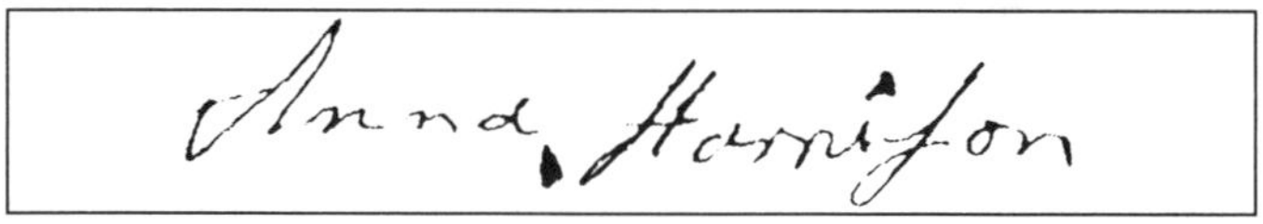

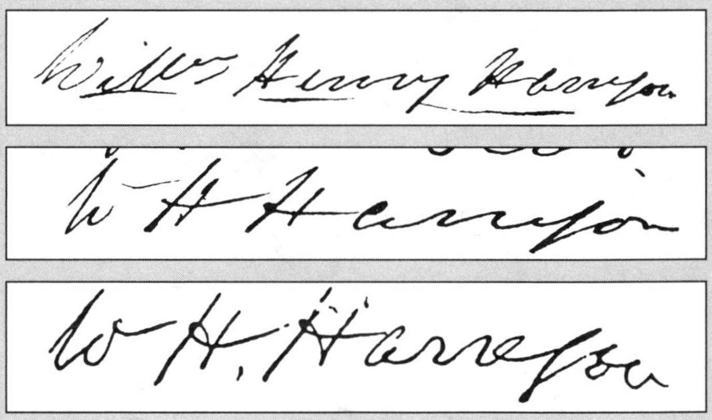

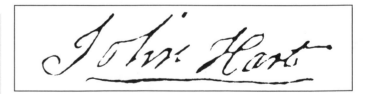

William Henry Harrison

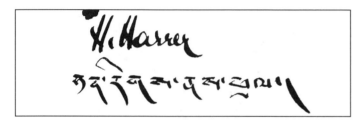

Anna Harrison

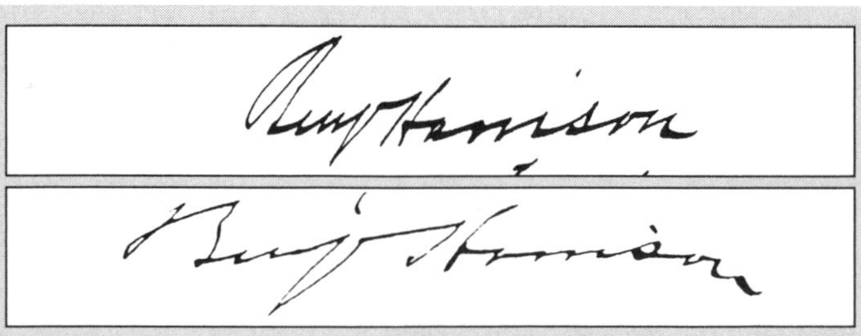

Benjamin Harrison

John Hart

Benjamin Harrison

William S. Hart

Erich Hartmann

Julie Haydon

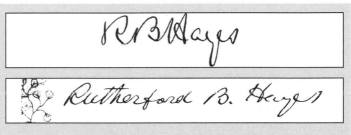

Helen Hayes

Nathaniel Hawthorne

Rutherford B. Hayes

Thomas Hayward

(F) Joseph Hayden

Dear Sir:

    I sincerely appreciate the interest and friendliness which prompt your letter, and I shall be happy to hear further from you at any time. Such advice or assistance as you care to give will always be welcomed by me.   I hope to have the pleasure of meeting you personally at some time.

             Yours sincerely,

Faithfully yours,

William Randolph Hearst

William Heath

Horace Heidt

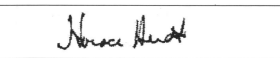

Jascha Heifitz

Heinrich Heine

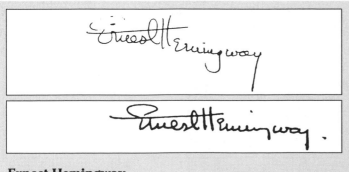

Sonja Henie

John Held Jr.

Ernest Hemingway

Fletcher Henderson

Jimi Hendrix

Charlotte Henry

O. Henry

Ernest Hemingway

Patrick Henry

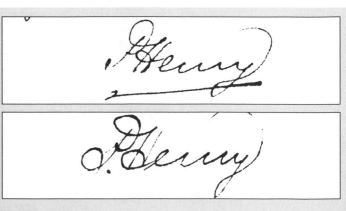

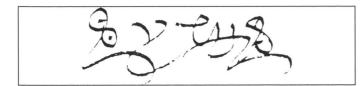

Henry IV, King of Castile

Henry VII, King of England

Audrey Hepburn

Jim Henson

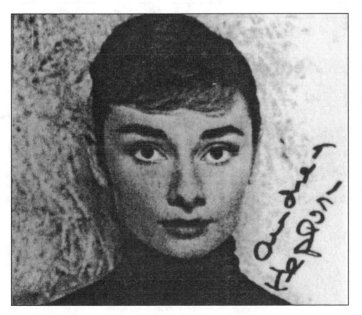

Audrey Hepburn

Katharine Hepburn

Emperor Hirohito

Katherine Hepburn

Hugh Herbert

Alfred Hitchcock

Victor Herbert

Jean Hersholt

Joseph Hewes

Adolf Hitler

Heinrich Himmler

Adolf Hitler with Wernher von Blomberg

James Hoban

Valerie Hobson

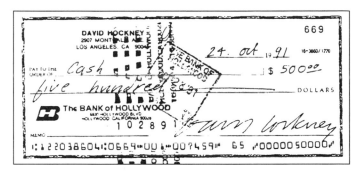

David Hockney

James R. Hoffa

Dustin Hoffman

Billie Holiday

Judy Holliday

Buddy Holly and the Crickets

Oliver Wendell Holmes, Jr.

Oliver Wendell Holmes (Sr)

Oliver Wendell Holmes (Sr.)

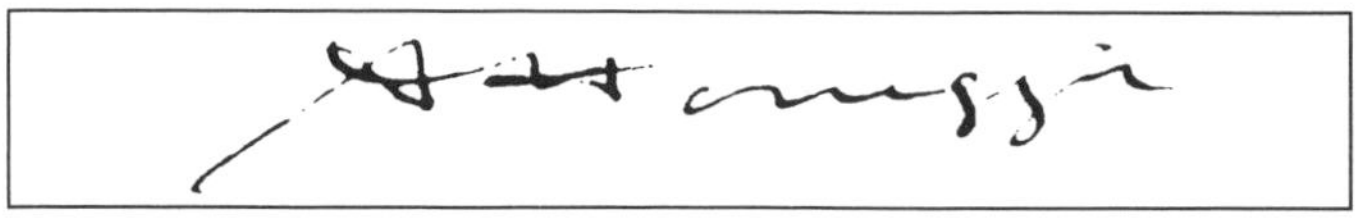

Arthur Honegger

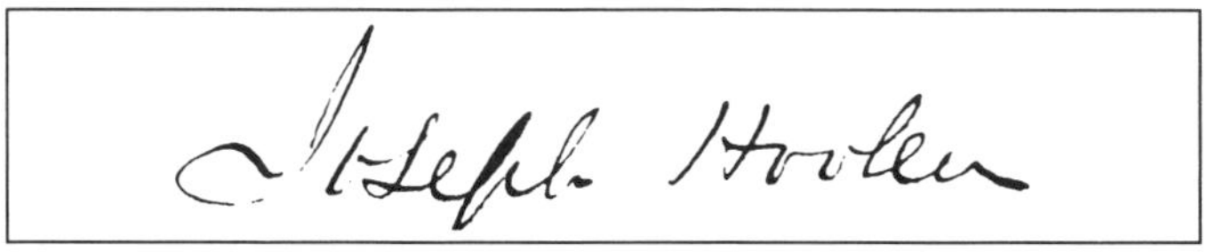

Joseph Hooker

William Hooper

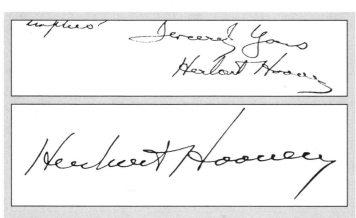

Herbert Hoover

J. Edgar Hoover

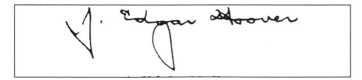

Lou Henry Hoover

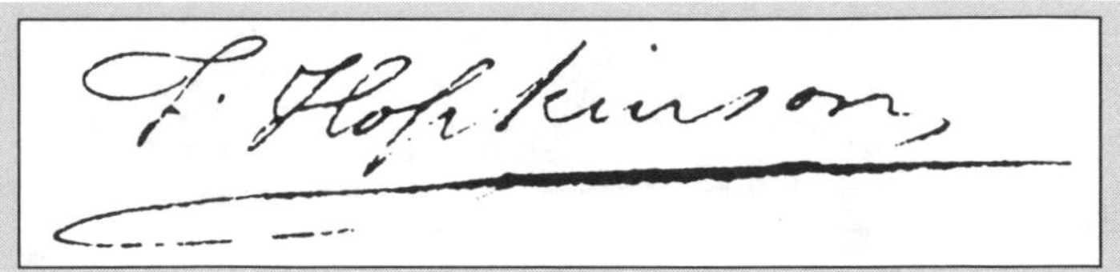

Francis Hopkinson

DeWolf Hopper

Vladimir Horowitz

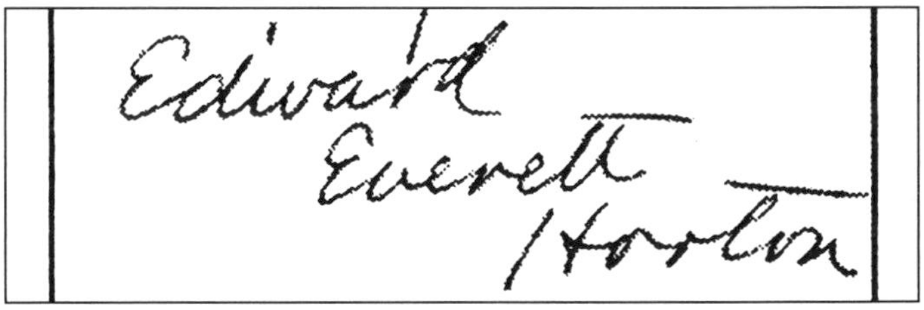

Edward Everett Horton

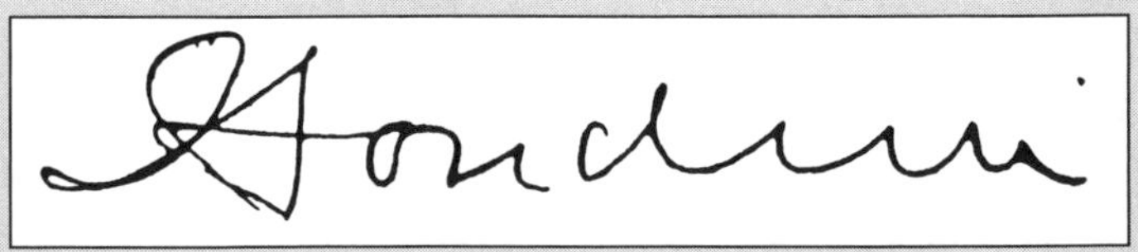

Harry Houdini

Harry Houdini

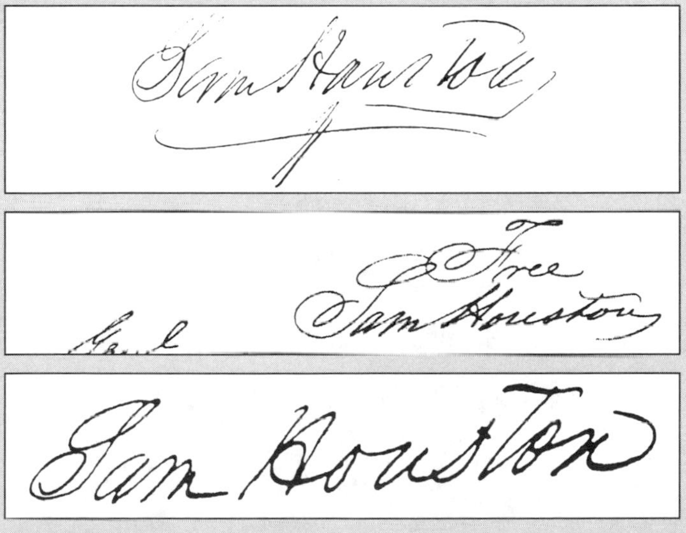

Sam Houston

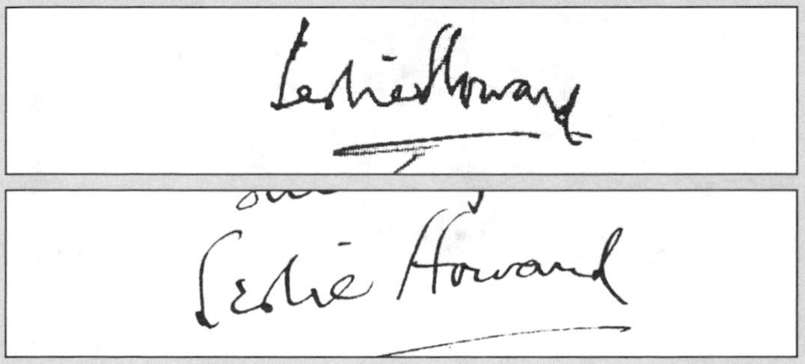

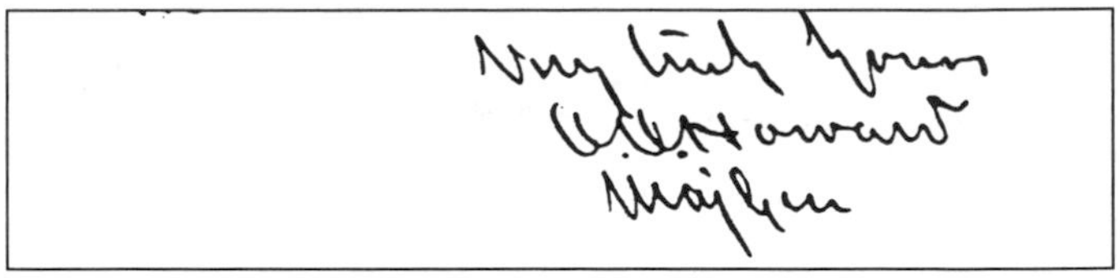

Oliver Howard

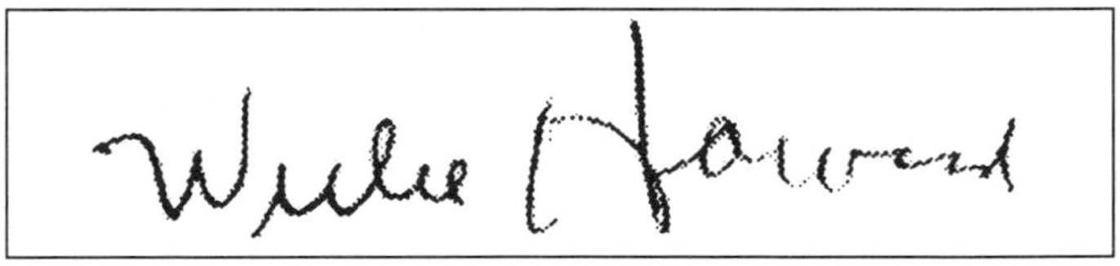

Willie Howard

Edwin Hubbell

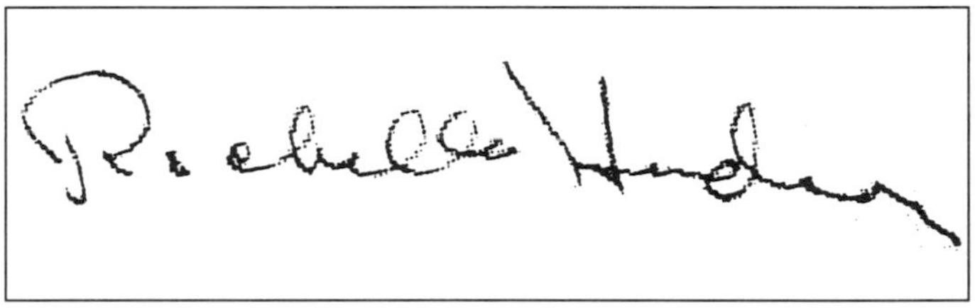

Rochelle Hudson

Charles Evans Hughes

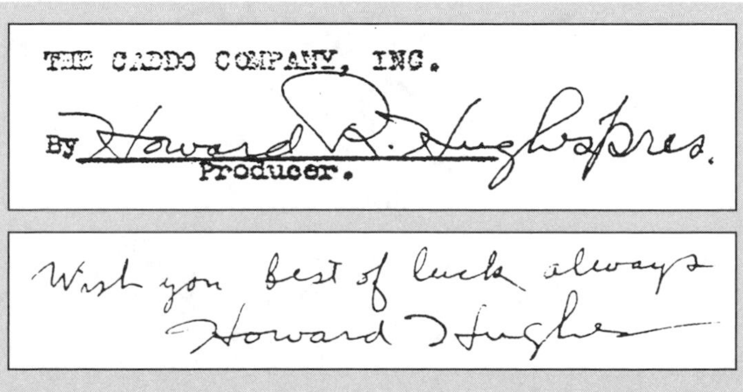

Leslie Howard

THE CADDO COMPANY, INC.

By Howard R. Hughes Pres.
Producer.

Wish you best of luck always
Howard Hughes

Howard Hughes

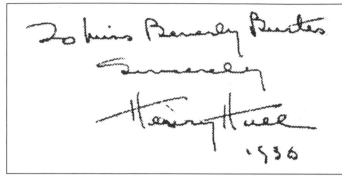

Henry Hull

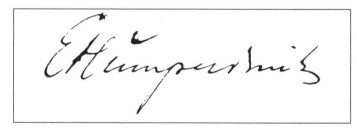

Warren Hull

Engelbert Humperdink

Ian Hunter

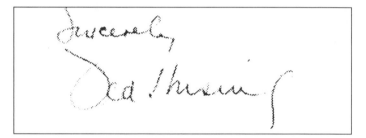

Collis Huntington

Samuel Huntington

Ted Husing

Hussein

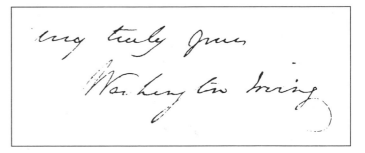

Washington Irving

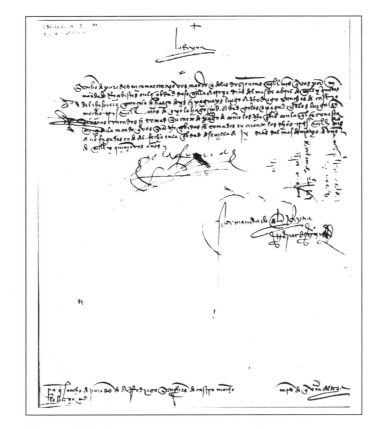

Henrik Ibsen

Queen Isabella

J

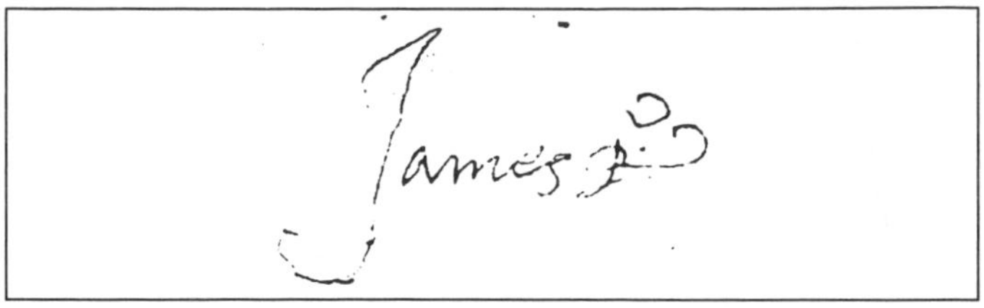

James I, King of England

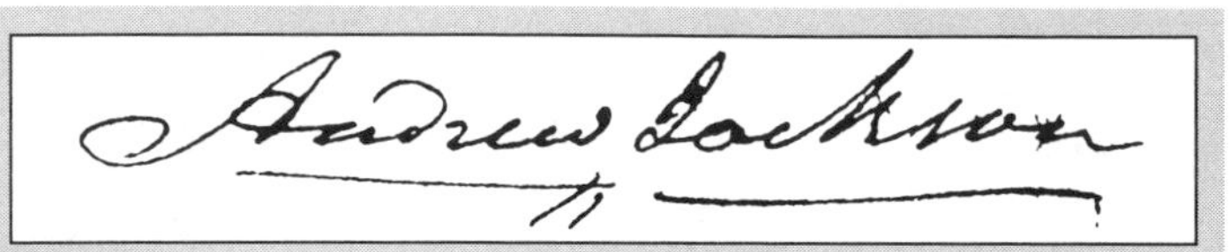

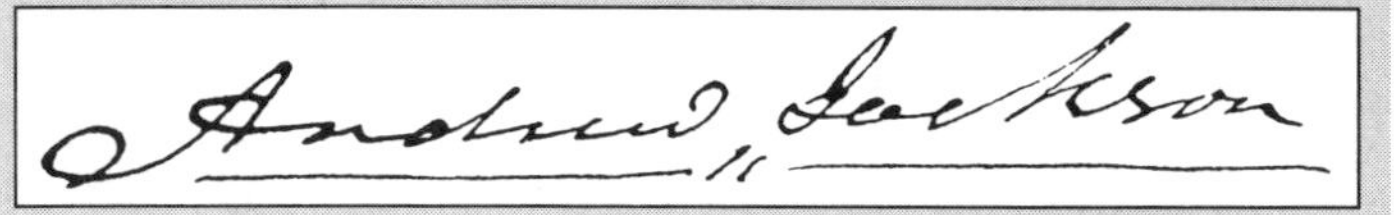

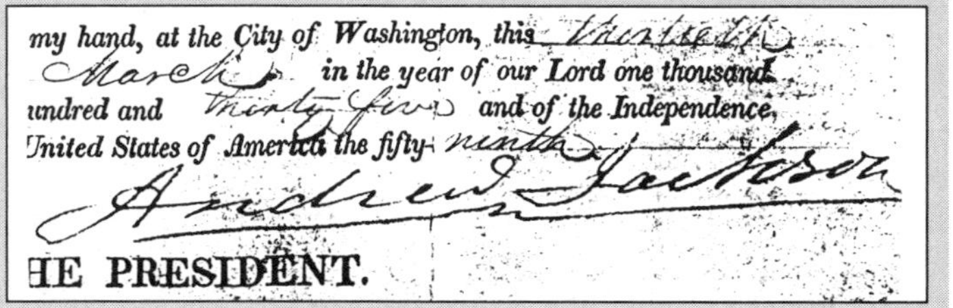
my hand, at the City of Washington, this thirtieth March in the year of our Lord one thousand undred and thirty five and of the Independence United States of America the fifty-ninth

Andrew Jackson

HE PRESIDENT.

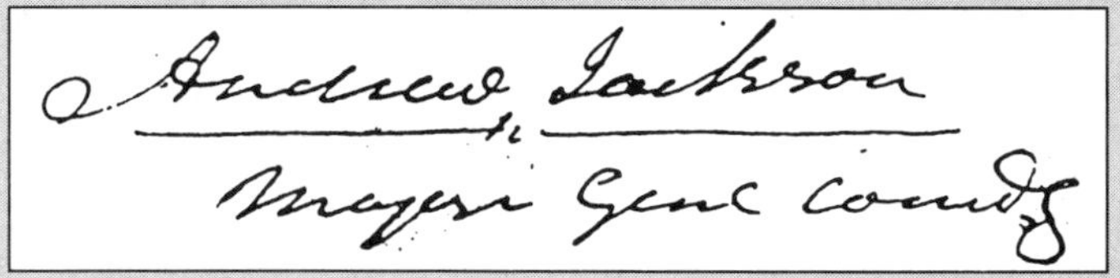

Andrew Jackson

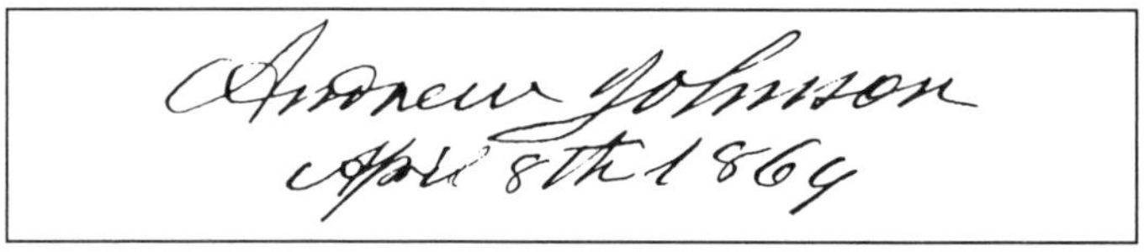

Andrew Johnson

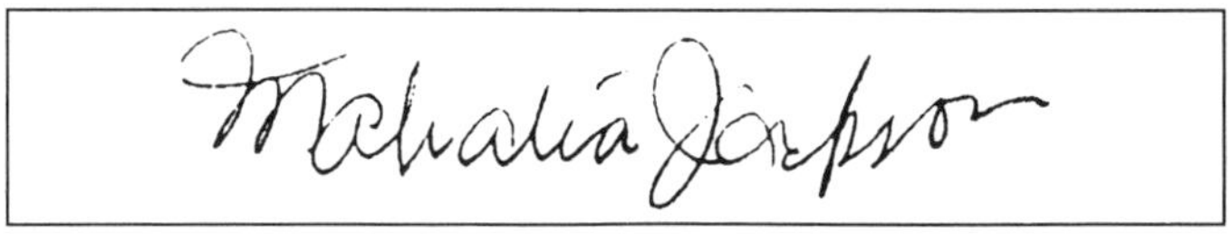

Mahalia Jackson

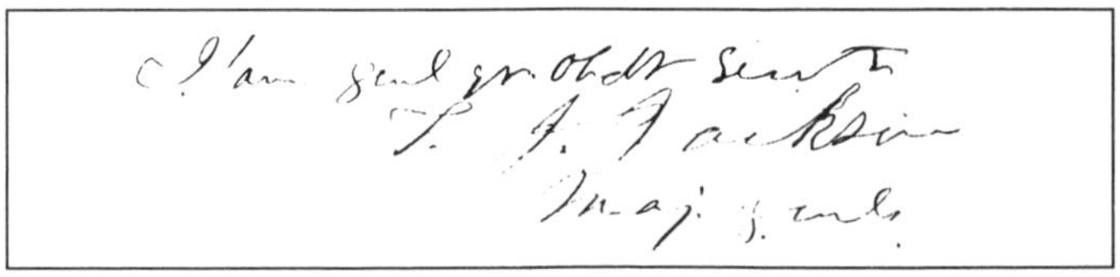

Thomas J. Jackson

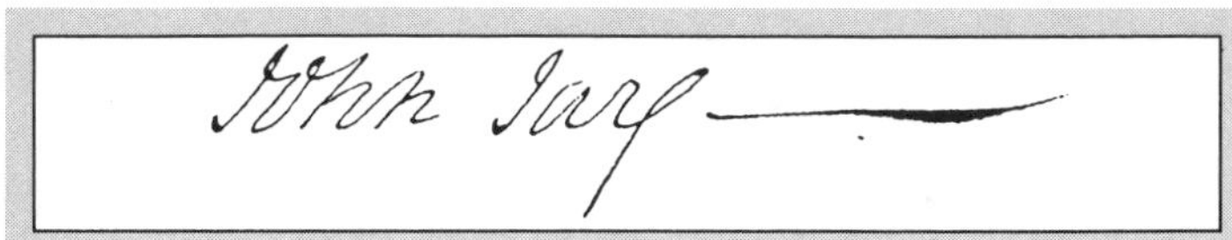

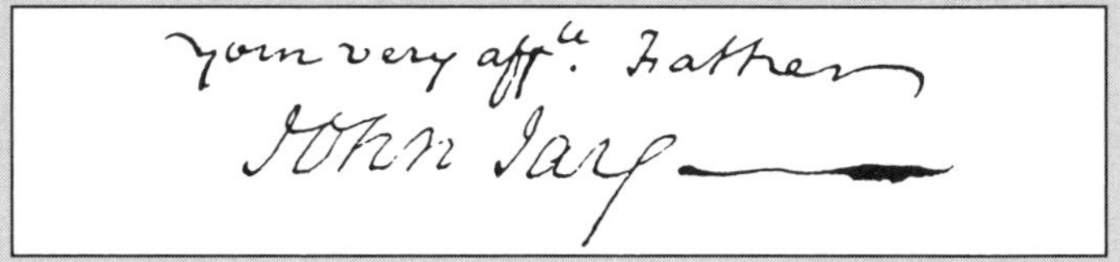

John Jay

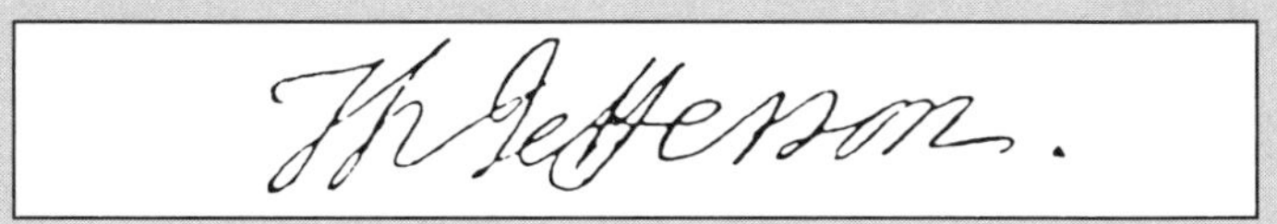

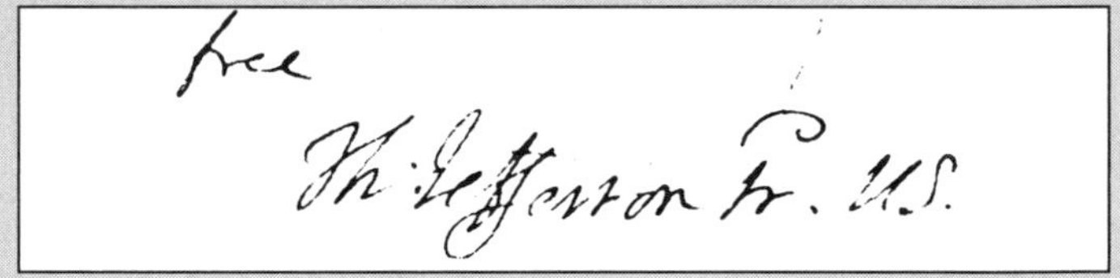

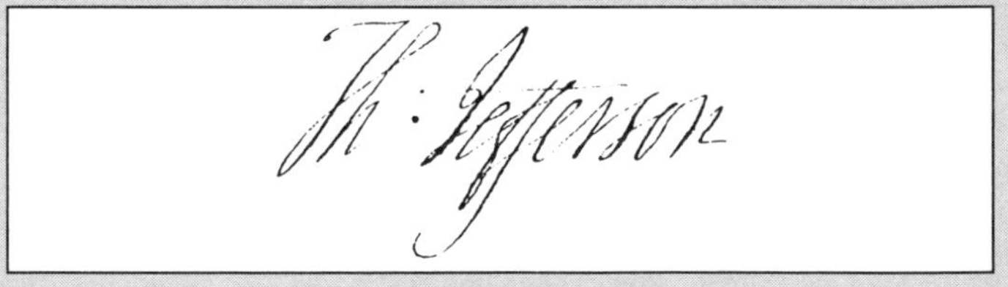

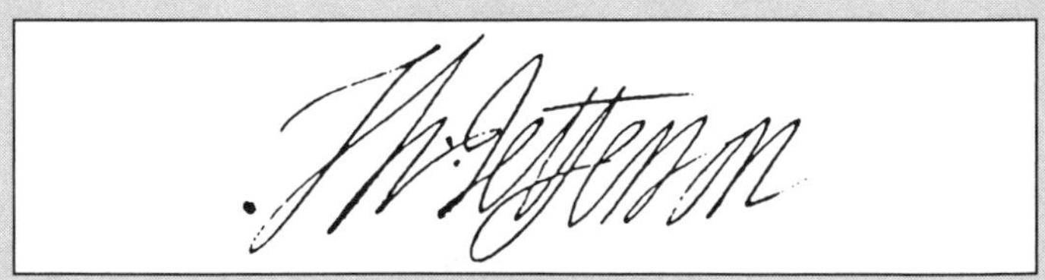

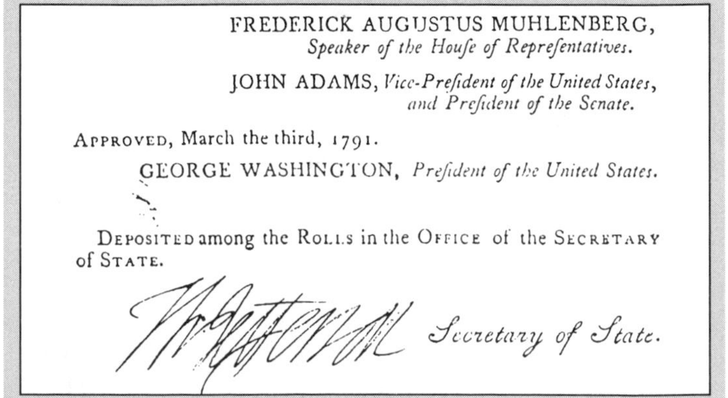
FREDERICK AUGUSTUS MUHLENBERG, *Speaker of the Houſe of Repreſentatives.*

JOHN ADAMS, *Vice-Preſident of the United States, and Preſident of the Senate.*

APPROVED, March the third, 1791.

GEORGE WASHINGTON, *Preſident of the United States.*

DEPOSITED among the ROLLS in the OFFICE of the SECRETARY of STATE.

Th: Jefferson *Secretary of State.*

Thomas Jefferson

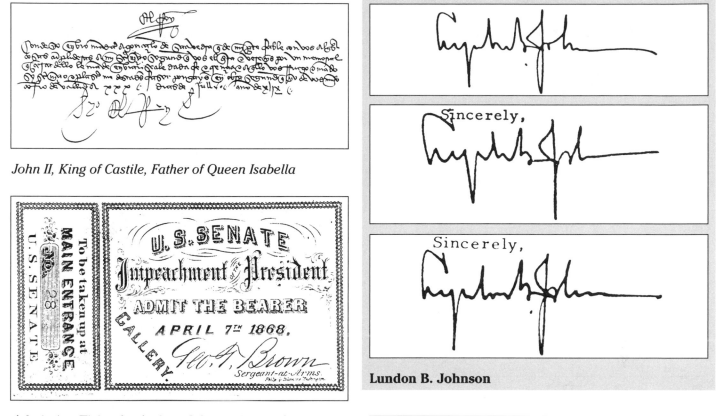

John II, King of Castile, Father of Queen Isabella

Admission Ticket for Andrew Johnson impeachment

Lundon B. Johnson

Richard Johnson

Andrew Johnson

Bradley T. Johnson

Walter Johnson

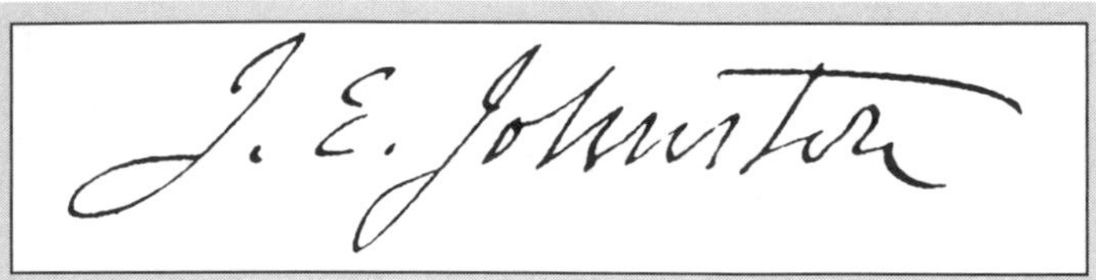

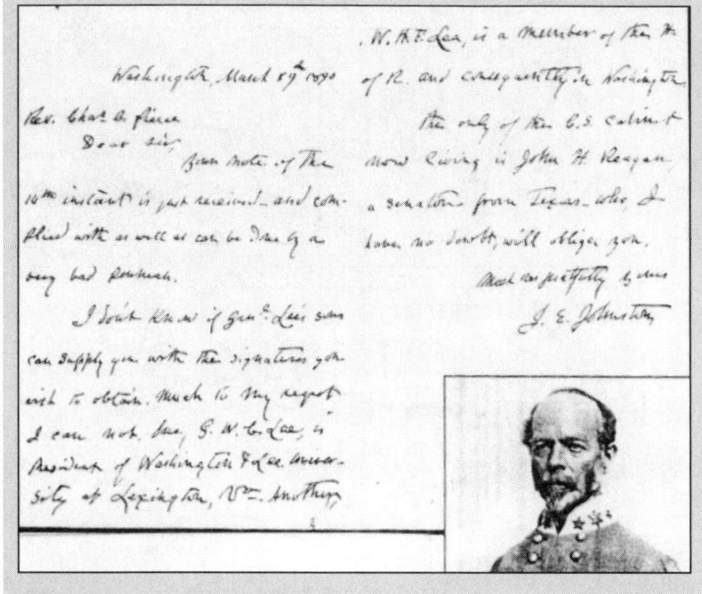

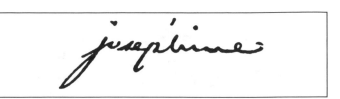

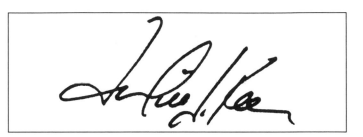

Washington, March 29th 1890

Rev. Chas. A. Pierce

Dear sir,

Your note of the 16th instant is just received - and complied with as well as can be done by a very bad penman.

I don't know if Gen'l Lee's sons can supply you with the signatures you wish to obtain. Much to my regret I can not. Gen. G. W. C. Lee, is President of Washington & Lee University at Lexington, Va. Another W. H. F. Lee, is a member of the H. of R. and consequently in Washington.

The only of the C.S. Cabinet now living is John H. Reagan, a senator from Texas - who, I have no doubt, will oblige you.

Most respectfully yours

J. E. Johnston

Joseph E. Johnston

Al Jolson

LOVE

Janis Joplin

Josephine

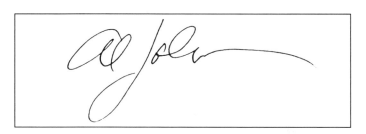

Jackie Joyner-Kersee

Dr. C. G. Jung

Küsnacht-Zürich
Seestrasse 228

den 31.Januar, 19333

Herrn N.Chiaromonte,
Via Po,33,
Roma (34).

Sehr geehrter Herr,

Empfangen Sie meinen besten Dank für die freundliche Zusendung Ihres Artikels in der "Stampa". Ich bin gerne bereit, Ihnen meine neueren Publikationen zukommen zu lassen, wenn Sie mir angeben, welche meiner früheren Bücher Ihnen schon bekannt sind.

Darf ich Sie bei dieser Gelegenheit auf einen kleinen Irrtum aufmerksam machen, der Ihnen unterlaufen ist. Der Autor der Complextheorie im strengen Sinne ist nicht Freud, sondern ich selber. Sie finden die Belege dazu in "Diagnostische Associationsstudien," Bd.II.1904. Und in meinem Buche"Über die Psychologie der Dementia praecox."

Mit vorzüglicher Hochachtung

C.G. Jung.

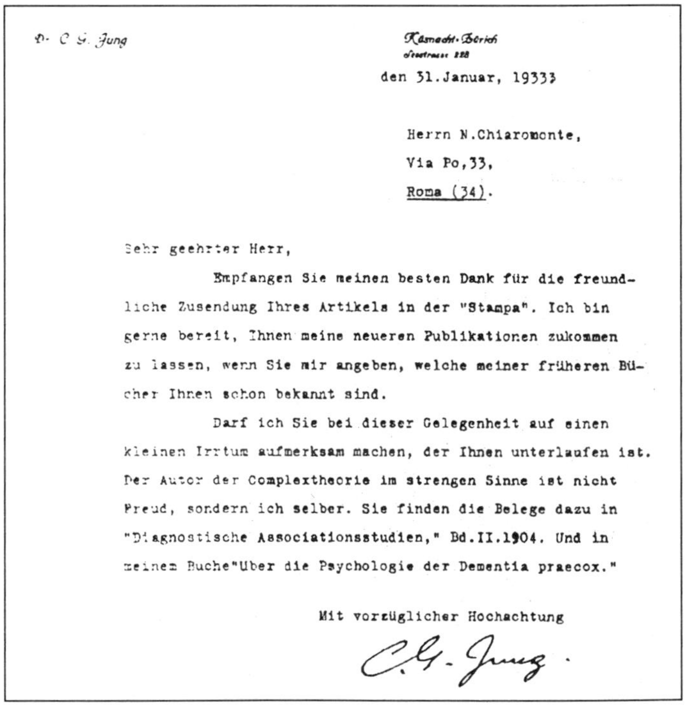

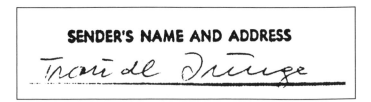

Carl Jung

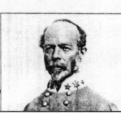

SENDER'S NAME AND ADDRESS

Gertrude Junge

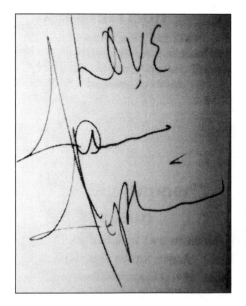

K

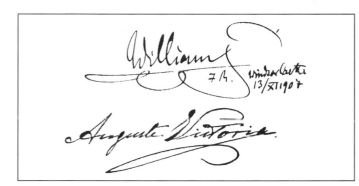

Dimitri Kabalevsky

King Kalakaua

Kaiser Wilhelm II and wife, Augusta Victoria

King Kamehameha

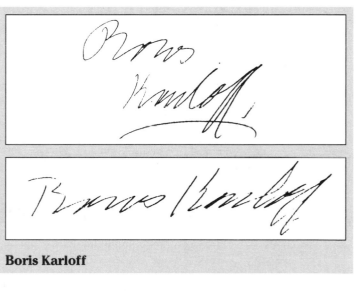

Boris Karloff

Chaing Kai-Shek

With all good wishes
Helen Keller
Christmas 1929

Helen Keller

Helen Keller

Grace Kelly

Eddie Kendricks

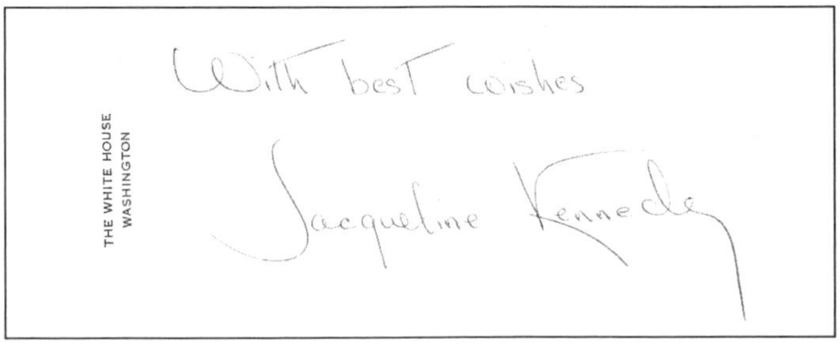

Jacqueline Kennedy

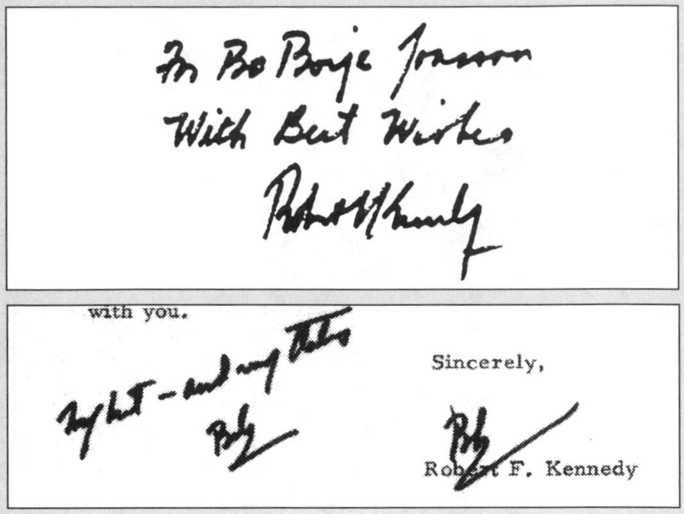

Robert F. Kennedy

Ken Kesey

Hank Ketchum

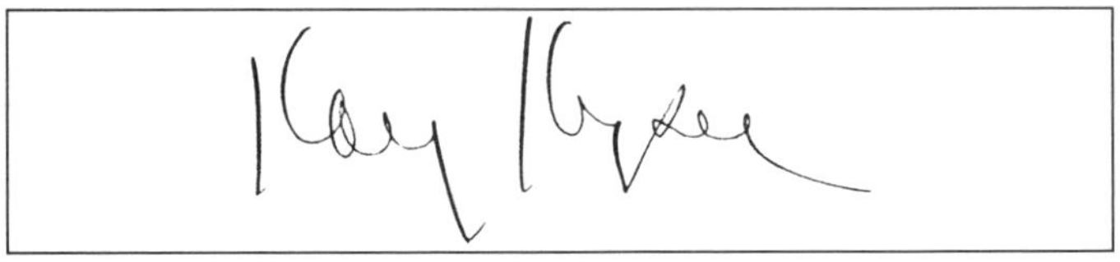

Kay Kyser

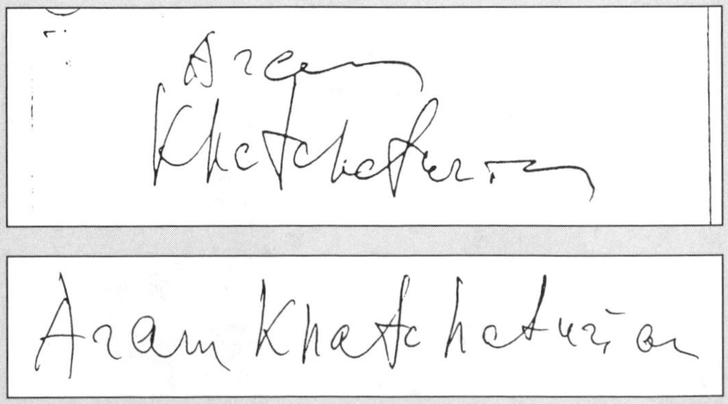

Aram Khatchaturian

John F. Kennedy

THE WHITE HOUSE
WASHINGTON

September 7, 1961

Dear Mr. Maxon:

Miss Kay Halle turned over to me a few days ago two albums
filled with letters from the artists and writers who were invited to the Inauguration ceremonies. Mrs. Kennedy and I
have had extraordinary pleasure in going through these volumes. We are grateful for the letters, and we shall treasure
them for the rest of our lives.

I am hopeful that this collaboration between government and
the arts will continue and prosper. Mrs. Kennedy and I would
be particularly interested in any suggestions you may have in
the future about the possible contributions the national government might make to the arts in America.

My wife joins me in extending best thanks and regards.

Sincerely,

Mr. John Maxon
Director
Art Institute of Chicago
Lake Shore Drive
Chicago, Illinois

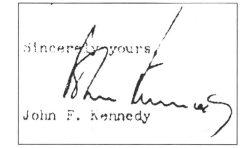

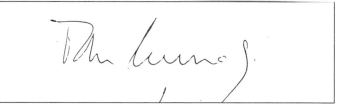

Jack Kilby

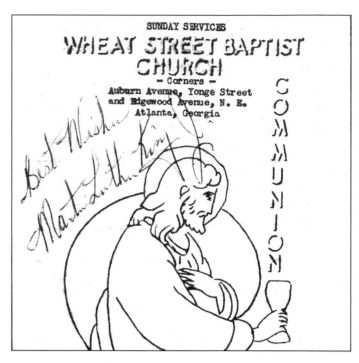

Martin Luther King, Jr.

Ward Kimball

Ben E. King

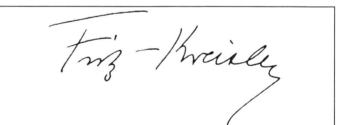

Rudyard Kipling

Fritz Kreisler

Martin Luther King, Jr.

Saburo Kurusu

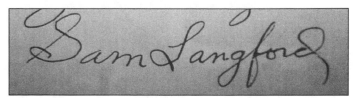

Sam Langford

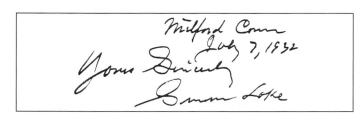

Bert Lahr

Jack LaRue

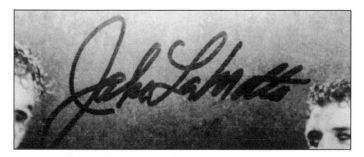

Simon Lake

Benjamin Latrobe

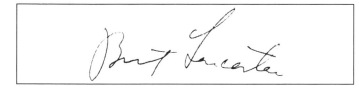

Stan Laurel

Jake LaMotta

Burt Lancaster

Stan Laurel and Oliver Hardy

Carole Landis

Tony Lazzari

Fitzhugh Lee

Francis Lightfoot Lee

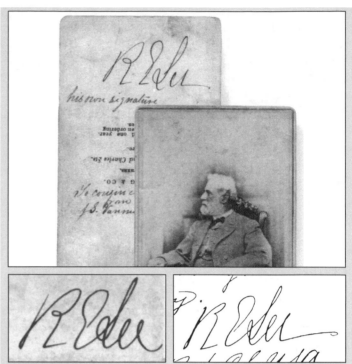

Robert E. Lee

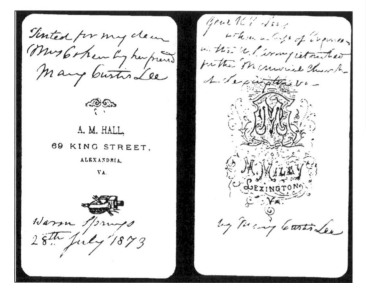

Mary Custis Lee

Richard Henry Lee

Franz Lehar

Robert E. Lee

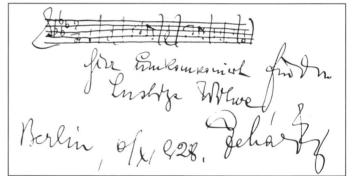

Vivien Leigh

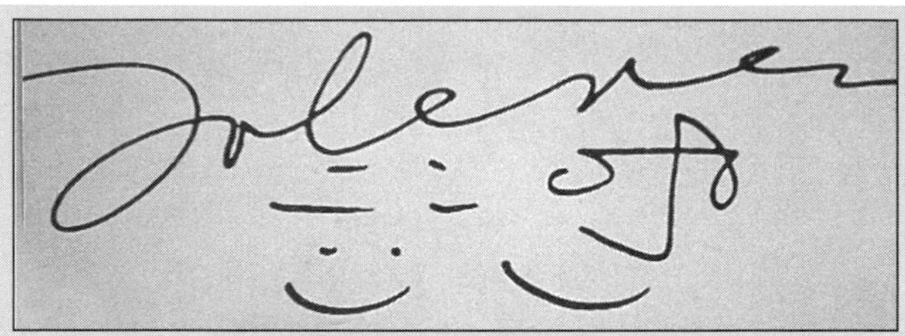

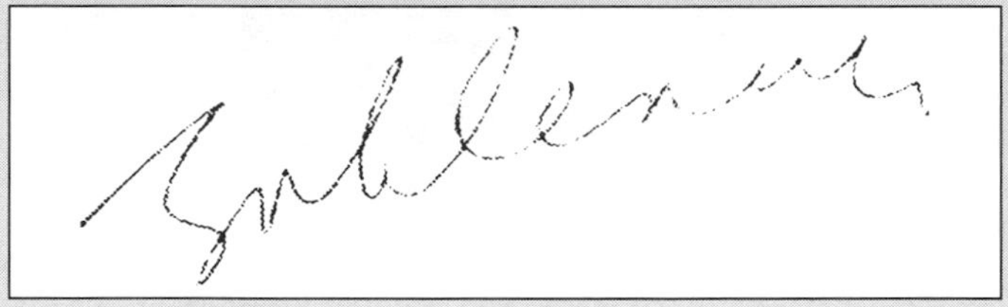

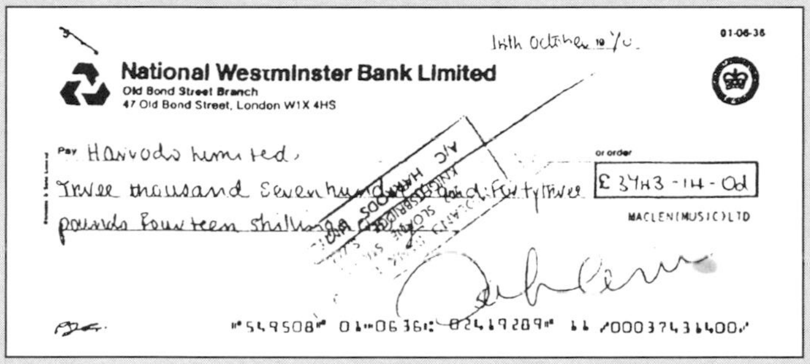

John Lennon

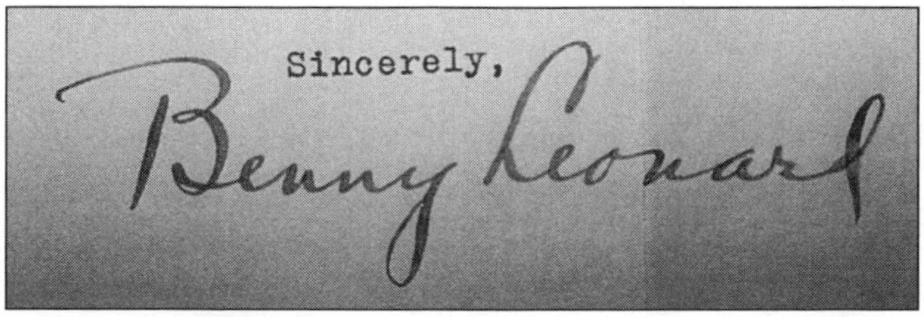

Benny Leonard

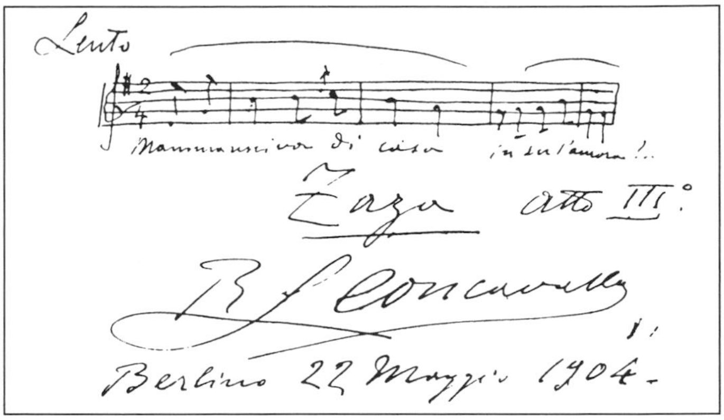

Ruggiero Leoncavallo

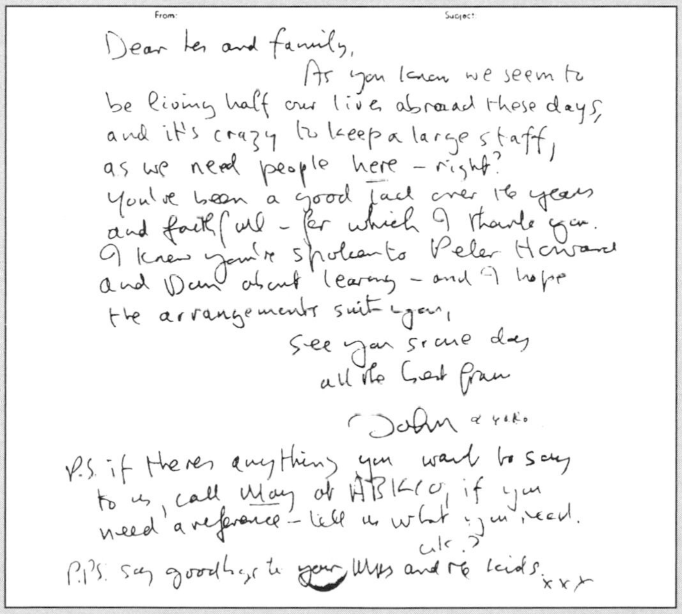

Mervin LeRoy

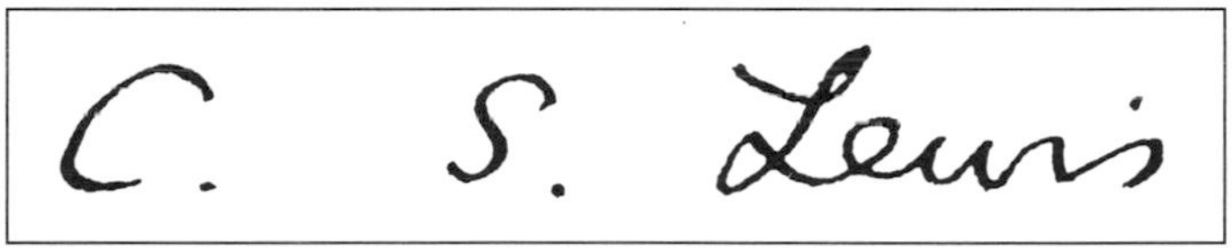

C. S. Lewis

C.S. Lewis

Francis Lewis

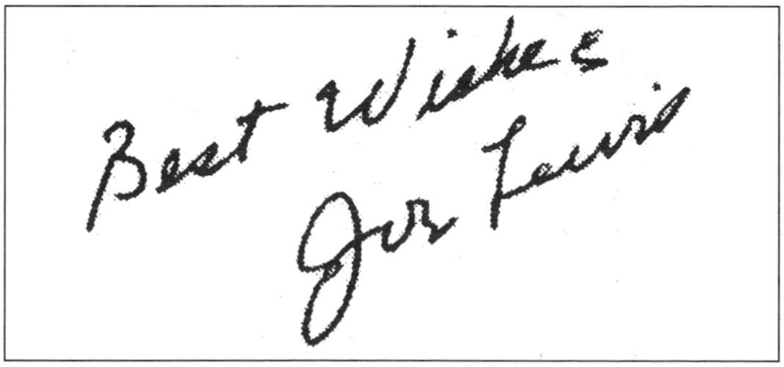

Joe Lewis

Meriweather Lewis

David Livingstone

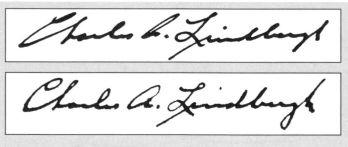

Eli Lilly

Robert Livingston

Mary Todd Lincoln

John A. Logan

Chalres A. Lindburgh

Carole Lombard

Lord Joseph Lister

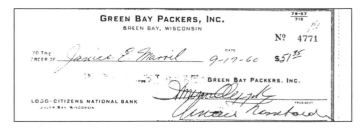

Franz Liszt

Franz Liszt

Vince Lombardi

Abraham Lincoln

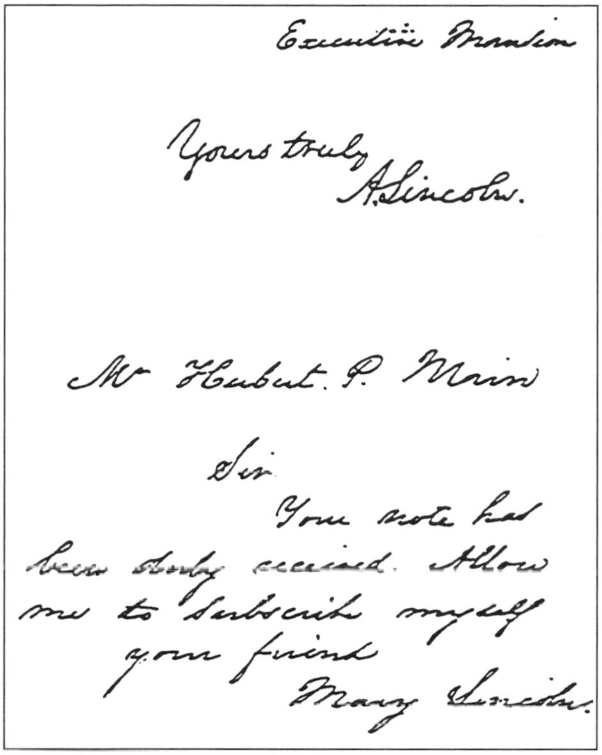
Executive Mansion

Yours truly
A. Lincoln.

Mr Hubert P. Main

Sir
You note has
been duly received. Allow
me to subscribe myself
your friend
Mary Lincoln.

Abraham & Mary Lincoln

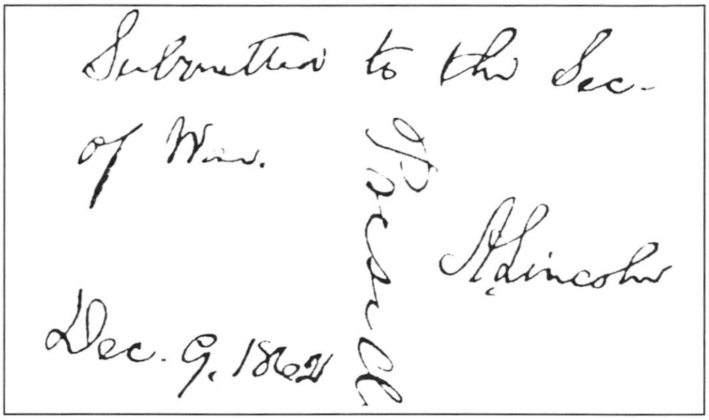
Submitted to the Sec-
of War.
A. Lincoln
Dec. 9, 1862

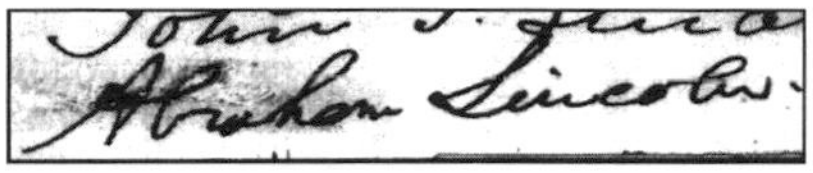
Abraham Lincoln.

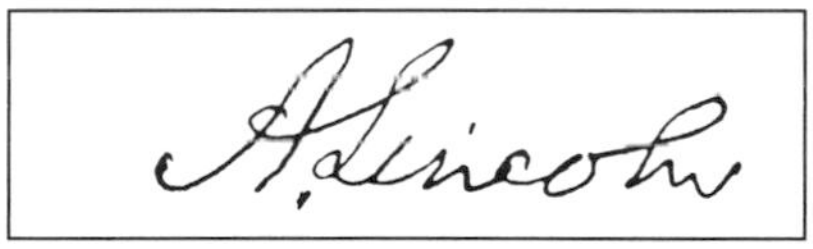
A. Lincoln

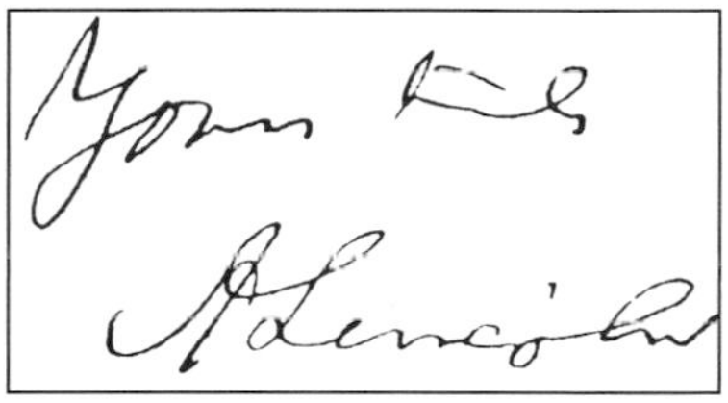
Yours truly
A. Lincoln

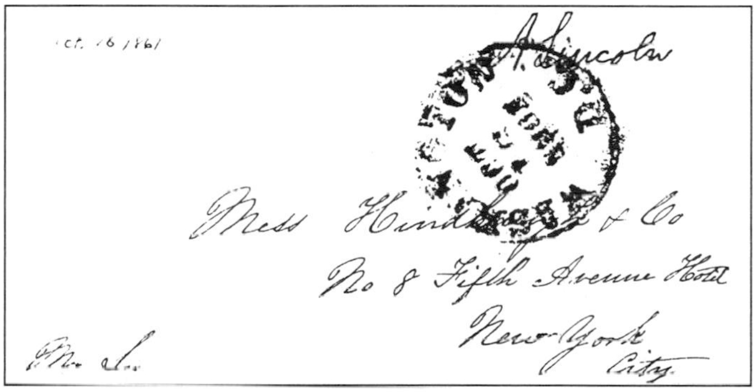
A. Lincoln
Mess Hendricks & Co
No 8 Fifth Avenue Hotel
New-York
City.

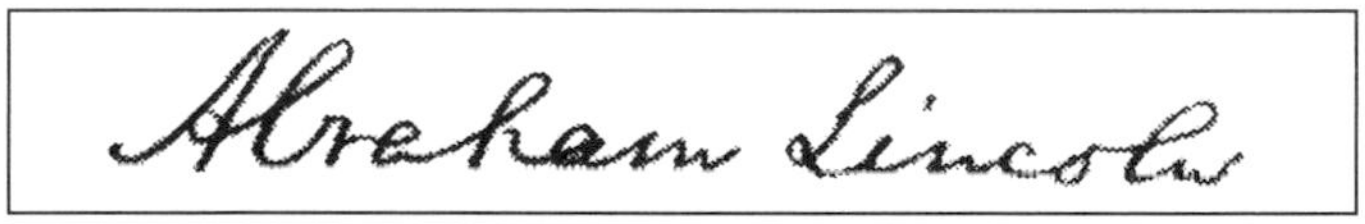
Abraham Lincoln

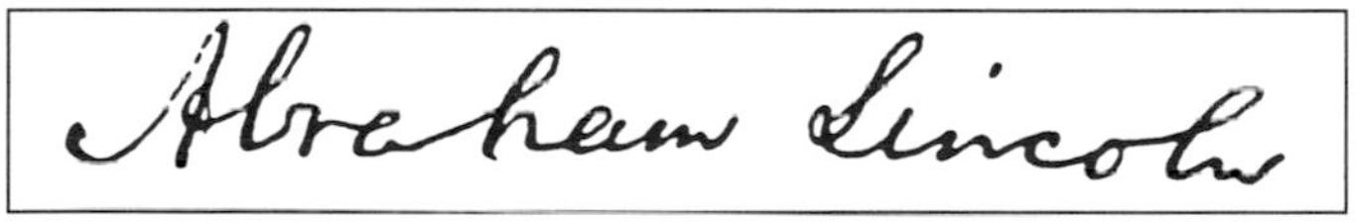
Abraham Lincoln

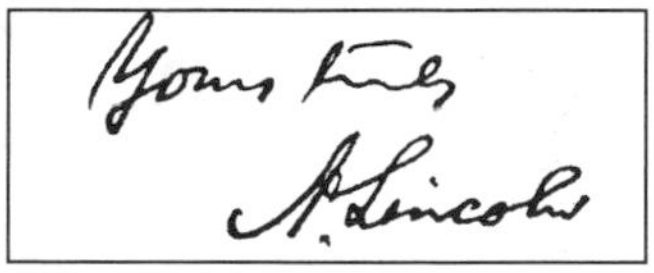
Yours truly
A. Lincoln

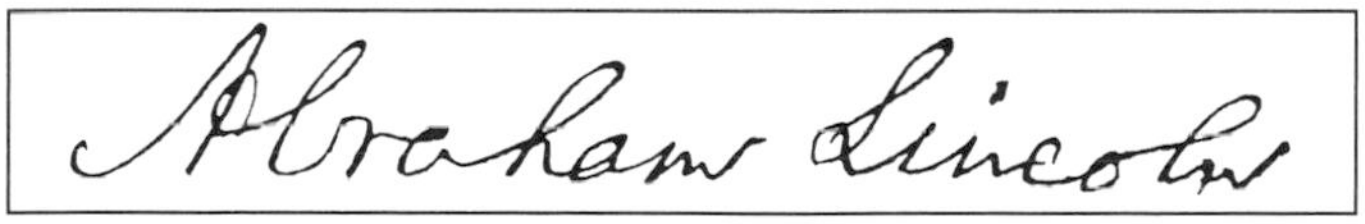
Abraham Lincoln

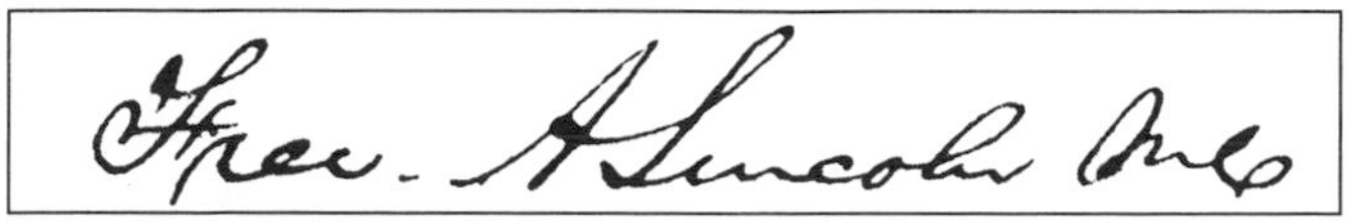
Free. A. Lincoln Mrs

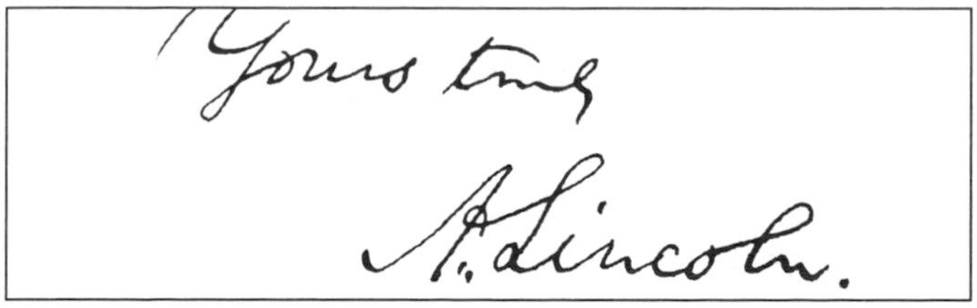
Yours truly
A. Lincoln.

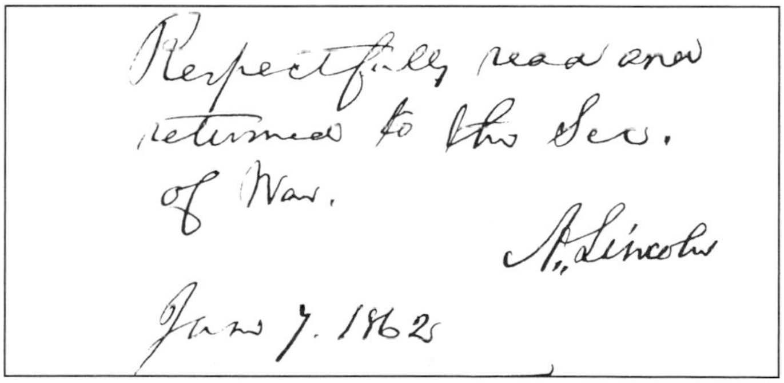
Respectfully read and
returned to the Sec.
of War.
A. Lincoln
Jan 7. 1862

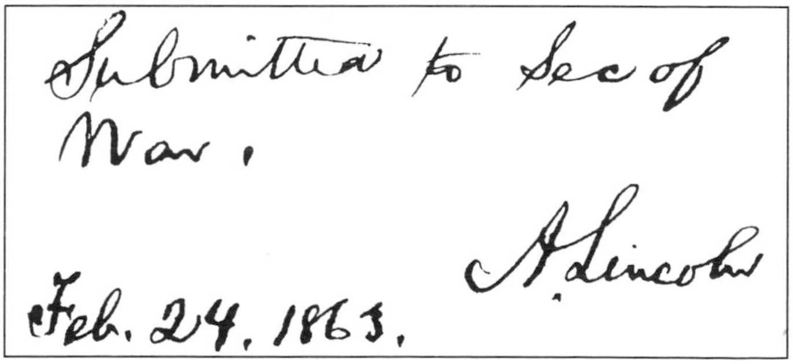
Submitted to Sec of
War.
A. Lincoln
Feb. 24. 1863.

"The stonewall," saith he, "doth fall aside;
Down must the stately columns fall;
Glass is all earthly Luck and Pride,
In fragments shall fall this earthly ball
One day, like the Luck of Edenhall!"

Henry W. Longfellow.

Henry W. Longfellow

Antonio Lopez de Santa Anna

Louis XI, King of France

Louis XIV, King of France

James Longstreet

Louis XV, Kong of France

Louis XV, King of France

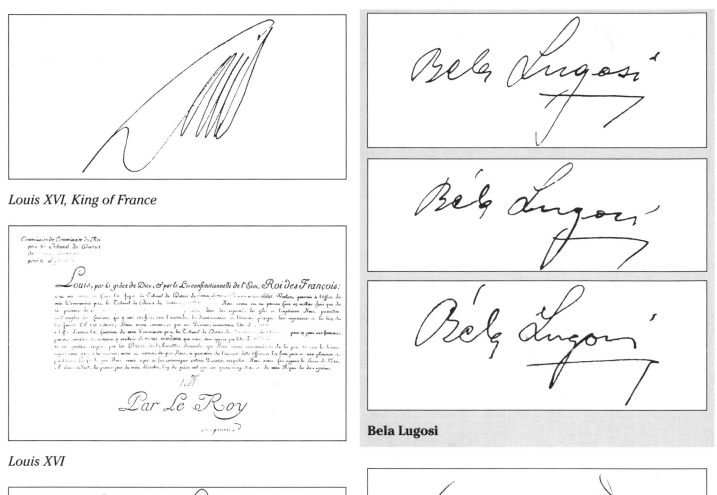

Louis XVI, King of France

Louis XVI

James Lovell

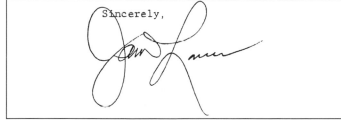

Henry R. Luce

Bela Lugosi

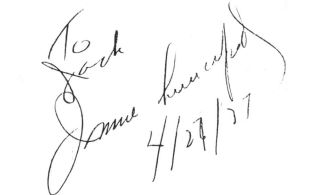

Jimmie Lunceford

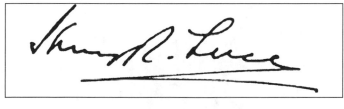

Thomas Lynch, Jr.

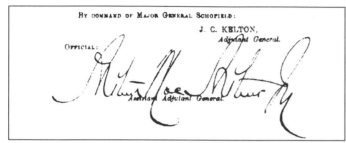

M

By command of Major General Schofield:

J. C. KELTON,
Adjutant General.

Official:

Assistant Adjutant General.

Arthur MacArthur

Douglas MacArthur

Connie Mack

Glad to —

Connie Mack

Dolly P. Madison

Free D.P. Madison

James Madison

James Madison   By the President,

Jas Monroe   Secretary of State.

James Madison

By the President

Jas Monroe   Secretary of

James Madison and James Monroe

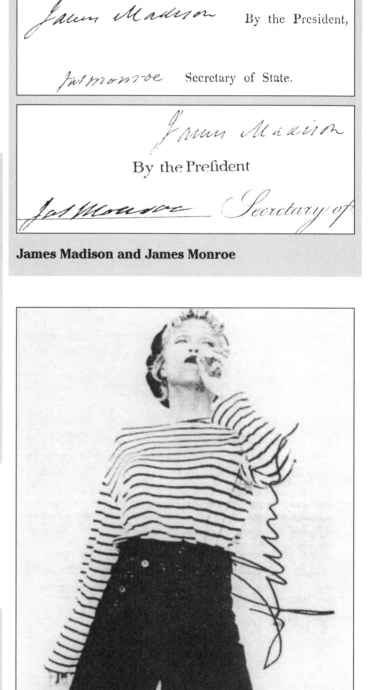

Madonna

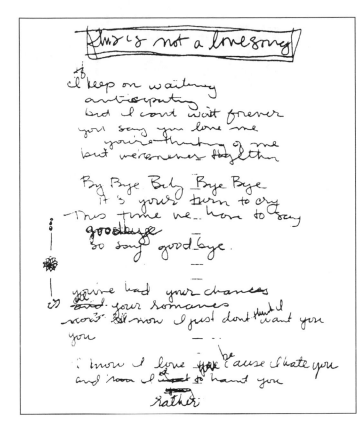

Madonna, lyrics

Best Wishes.

Maurice Maeterlinck

Gustav Mahler

Gustav Mahler

the Church of England, the Rabbinical Council of Jerusalem. The Messenger of God Elijah Muhammad is interpreting for the Lost-Found Black Nation of Islam here in the wilderness of North America. He is teaching here in North America the most powerful spiritual message on the earth today. The history of religions has seen new prophets emerge in every age of terrible crisis. A new prophet has come and changed the course of his nation.

Malcolm X

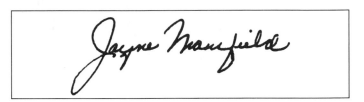

Edourd Manet

Jayne Mansfield

Jayne Mansfield

Gentlemen:

The bearer of this letter, Mr. Norman Landon, is a personal friend of mine and Rocky Marciano's. We believe strongly that he has something to offer.

As a special favor to us, would you kindly place him in the right hands.

Our good friend, Mr. Tony Plate says a nice hello.

Kindest Personal regards,

Mike Richel and Rocky Marciano

Rocky Marciano

Percy Chubb.   Aug 6. 23.
G Marconi

Guglielmo Marconi

Margot

F. Marion

F. Marion

Roger Maris

The Marx Brothers

GENERAL GEORGE C. MARSHALL

George C. Marshall

Mary II, Queen of England

Thurgood Marshall

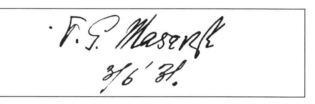

Thomas G. Masaryk

Dean Martin

Pietro Mascagni

John Masefield

Zeppo Marx

Jules Massenet

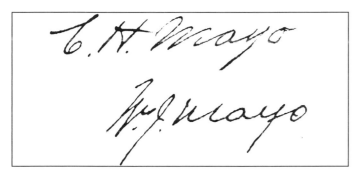

Henry Matisse

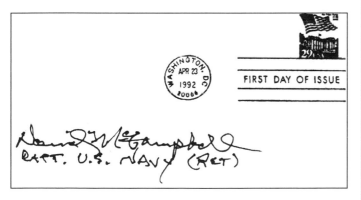

William Somerset Maughm

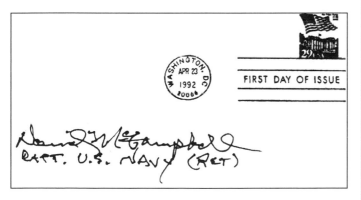

Charles and William Mayo

David McCampbell

Paul McCartney

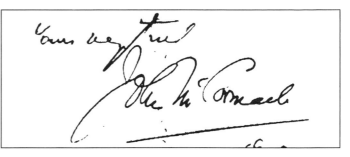

George B. McClellan

John McCormack

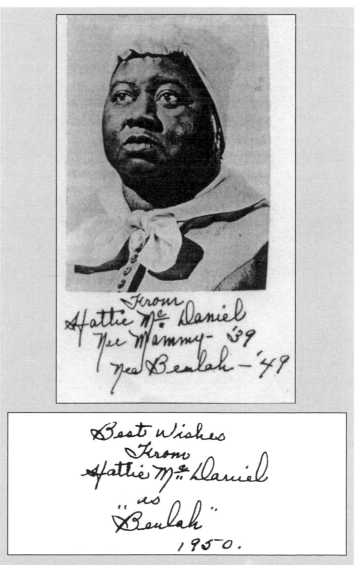

Hattie McDaniel

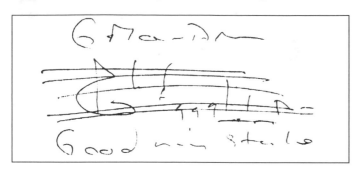

Galt McDermont

Thomas McKean

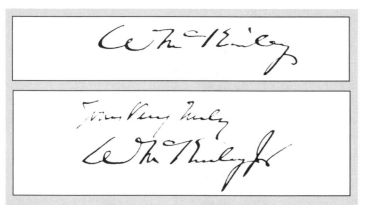

William McKinley

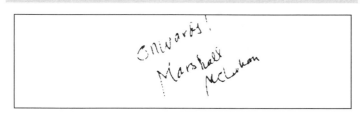

Marshall McLuhan

George McManus

George Meade

Felix Mendelssohn

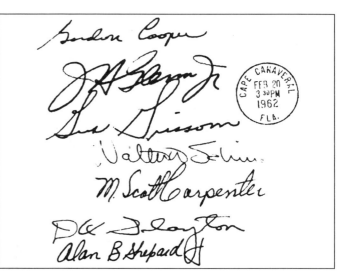

Mercury Astronauts

Willy Messerschmitt

Giacomo Meyerbeer

Arthur Middleton

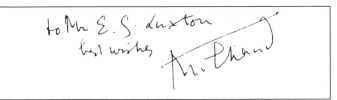

Darius Milhaud

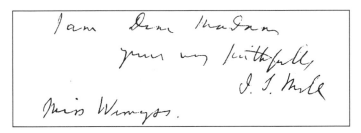

John S. Mill

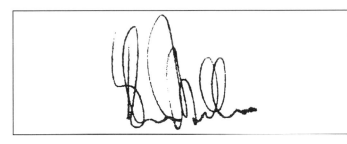

Glenn Miller

Henry Miller

Francis D. Millet

Bill Millman

Margaret Mitchell

William "Billy" Mitchell

Claude Monet

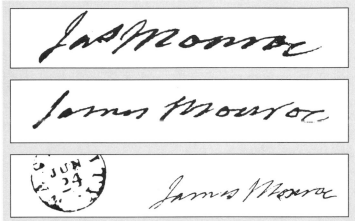

James Monroe

Marilyn Monroe

Bernard L. Montgomery

Paul Morphy

The Cast of Monty Python

Jim Morrison

Demi Moore

Bruce Morrow

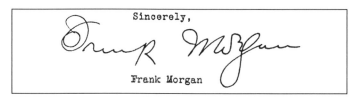

Frank Morgan

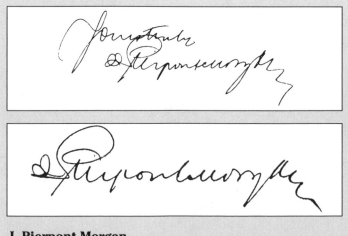

J. Pierpont Morgan

Lewis Morse

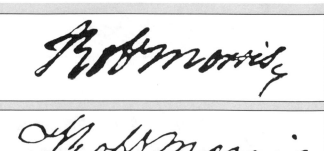

Robert Morse

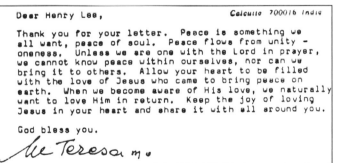

Samuel F.B. Morse

John Morton

John Morton

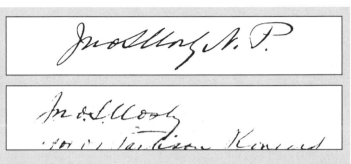

John S. Mosby

Dear Henry Lee,

Thank you for your letter. Peace is something we all want, peace of soul. Peace flows from unity - oneness. Unless we are one with the Lord in prayer, we cannot know peace within ourselves, nor can we bring it to others. Allow your heart to be filled with the love of Jesus who came to bring peace on earth. When we become aware of His love, we naturally want to love Him in return. Keep the joy of loving Jesus in your heart and share it with all around you.

God bless you.

Mother Teresa

Mother Teresa

Louis Mountbatten of Burma

Wolfgang Amadeus Mozart, manuscript

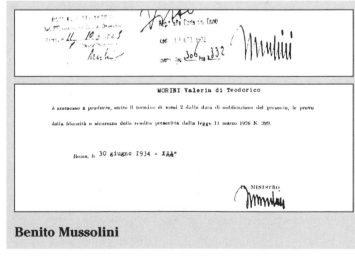

Elijah Muhammed

Turk Murphy

Edward R. Murrow

Clarence Muse

Benito Mussolini

Eadweard Muybridge

Napolean I

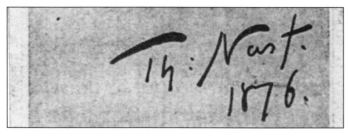

Thomas Nast

In the debate in the C. Globe, you
will see that the great Statesman
and true patriot, Hon. Thadeus
Stevens said. " The propositions
fall far short of my wishes, but
they fulfill my hopes." &c.
I am very busy in my judicial duties,
or would write you more fully.
                                    S. N.

Stephen Neal

Jawaharlal Nehru

Evelyn Nesbit

Paul Newman

Isaac Newton

Thomas Newton, Jr.

Nicholas and Alexandra

Nicholas II, Last Czar of Russia

John G. Nicolay

Chester W. Nimitz

Kichisaburo Nomura

Richard Nixon

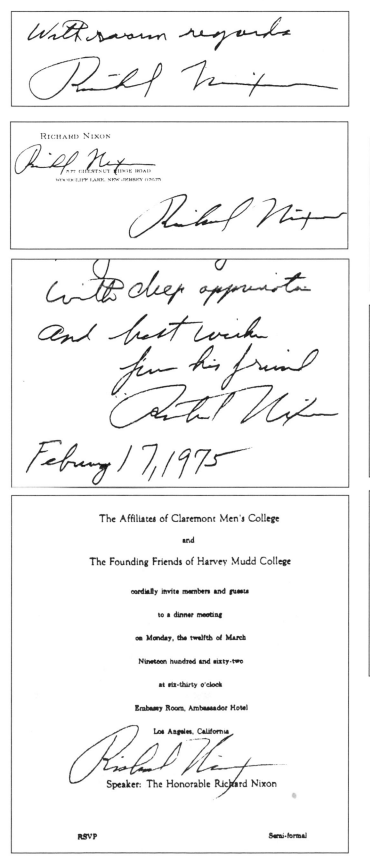

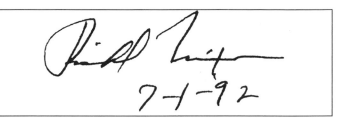

O

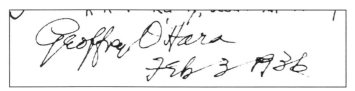

Annie Oakley

Geoffrey O'Hara

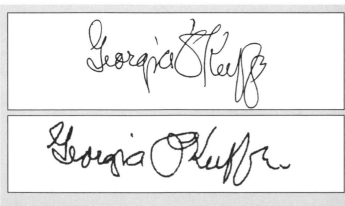

David Oistrakn

Georgia O'Keeffe

Warner Oland

Carl Orff

William Osler

Lee Harvey Oswald

Chief Owanneco

Jesse Owens

Isaac Parker, US Judge

Jack Paar

William Paca

Charlie Parker

Ignace J. Paderewski

Nicolo Paganini

Satchel Paige

Robert T. Paine

Boris Pasternak

Philippe Patain

Floyd Patterson

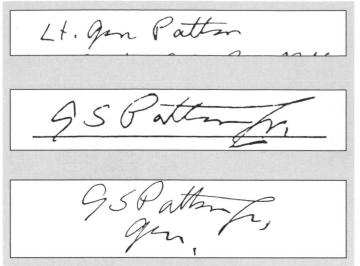

George S. Patton, Jr.

Charles W. Peale

Rembradnt Peale

John Penn

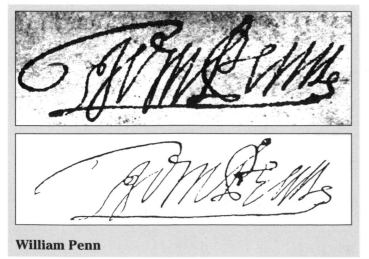

William Penn

John Pershing

Philippe II, King of Spain

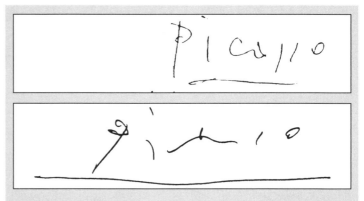

Pablo Picasso

Timothy Pickering

Mary Pickford

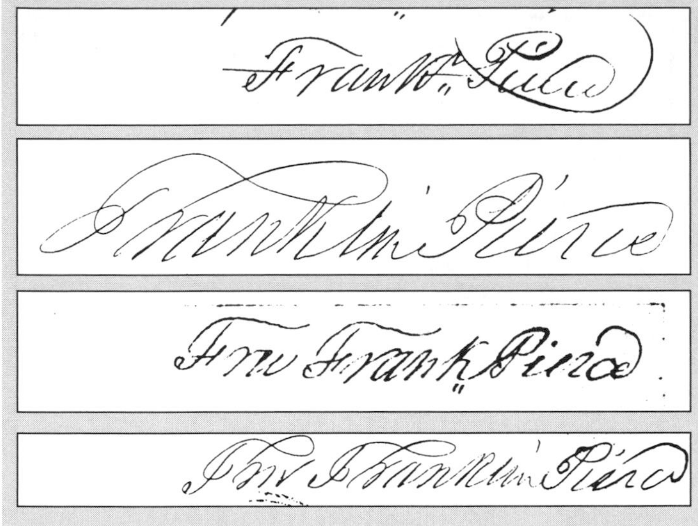

Franklin Pierce

J.K. Polk

Alan Pinkerton

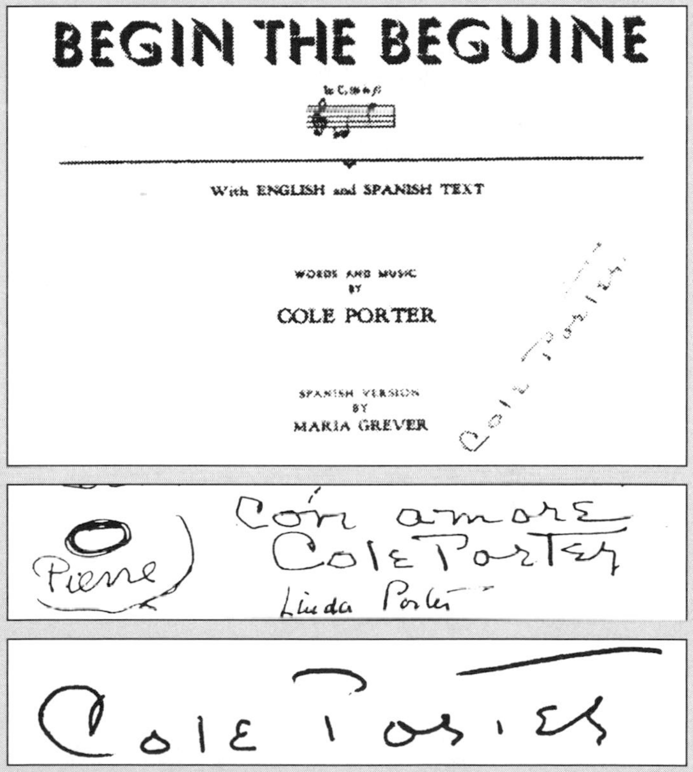

BEGIN THE BEGUINE

With ENGLISH and SPANISH TEXT

WORDS AND MUSIC
BY
COLE PORTER

SPANISH VERSION
BY
MARIA GREVER

Cole Porter

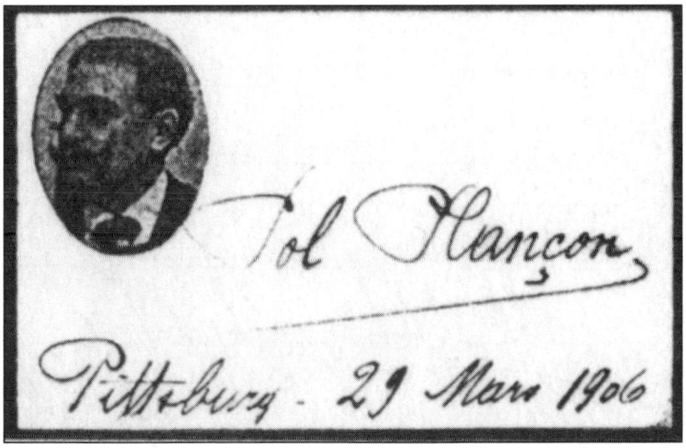

Pol Plancon

Joel R. Poinsett

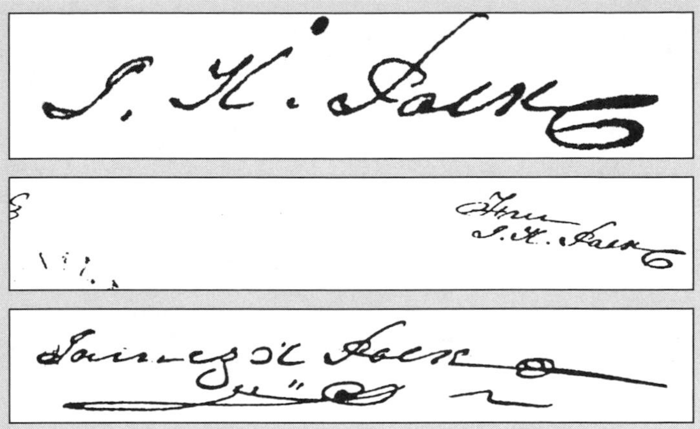

William S. Porter

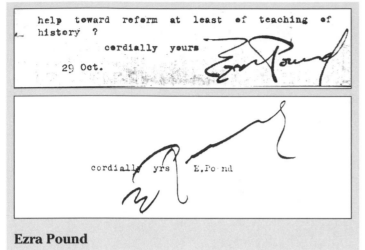

help toward reform at least of teaching of
history ?
cordially yours
29 Oct.

cordially yrs   E.Pound

Ezra Pound

Gen. Colin Powell

To Mrs Seguneller
by her old friend
Boston March 7/1890.   Louis Prang

Louis Prang

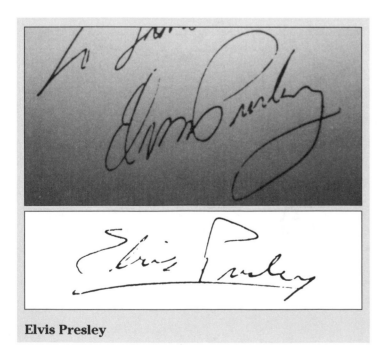

Elvis Presley

VINCENT L. PRICE, Jr.
315 SO. BEVERLY DR., NO. 500   553-0310
BEVERLY HILLS, CALIF. 90212
553
Oct 10 th 19 75   90-1010 / 1223
PAY TO THE ORDER OF   Jody Vierra $10 00
Ten   no/100   DOLLARS
SECURITY PACIFIC NATIONAL BANK
Beverly Hills Office
469 North Canon Dr., Beverly Hills, Calif. 90210
MEMO   birthday
⑆1223⑆1010⑈0553⑈ 136⑈ 116756⑈   ⑆000000 1000⑆

Vincent Price

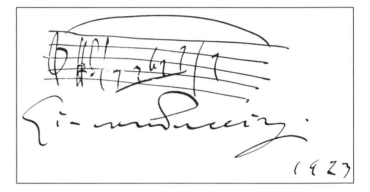

Serge Prokofieff

(1923)

Giacomo Puccini

Joseph Pulitzer

Israel Putnam

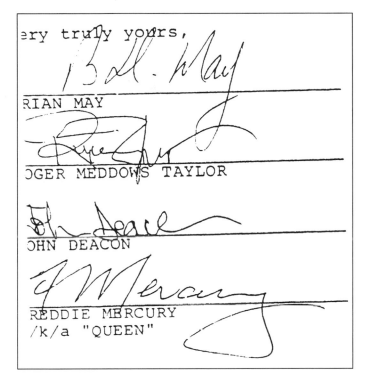

Queen - Brian May, Freddie Mercury, Roger Taylor, John Deacon

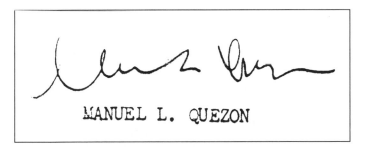

Manuel Quezon

Sergei Rachmaninoff

Ayn Rand

Maurice Ravel

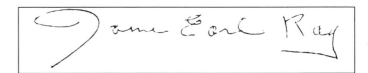

Jeanette Rankin

James Earl Ray

Basil Rathbone

George Read

Nancy and Ronald Reagan

Ronald Reagan

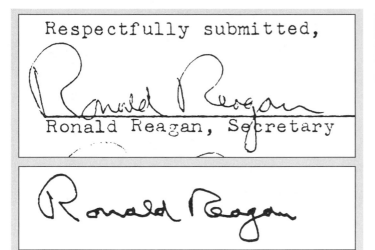

Ronald Reagan

Don Redman

Pierre J. Redoute

George Reeves

Eric M. Remarque

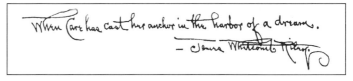

Cecil J. Rhodes

H. Brinley Richards

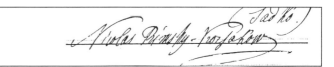

James W. Riley

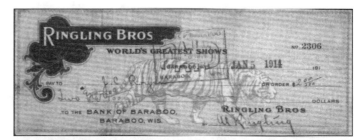

Nikolai Rimski-Korsakov

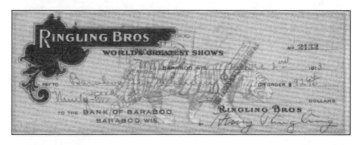

A. Ringling

Henry Ringling

John Ringling

John D. Rockefeller

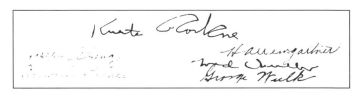

Robert Ripley

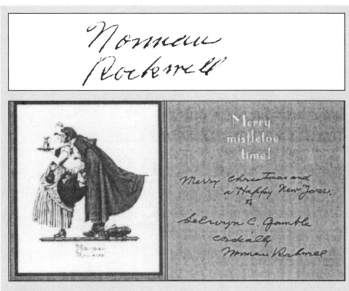

David Rittenhouse

Knute Rockne

Norman Rockwell

Bill Robinson

Edward G. Robinson

Gene Roddenberry

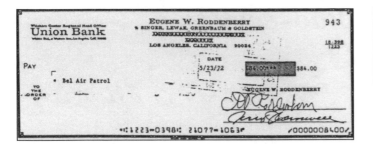

Gene Roddenberry

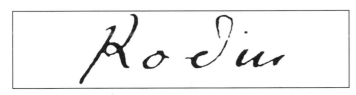

Jimmy Rodgers

Auguste Rodin

Cesar Rodney

Will Rogers

Ginger Rogers

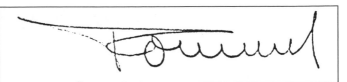

Irwin Rommel

Eleanor Roosevelt

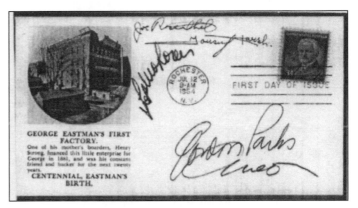

Joe Rosenthal, Yousef Karsh, Gordon Parks, Richard Avedon

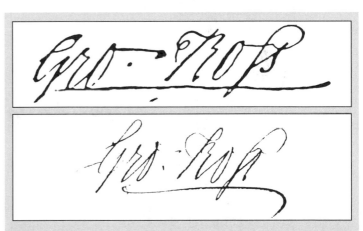

George Ross

John Ross

Franklin D. Roosevelt

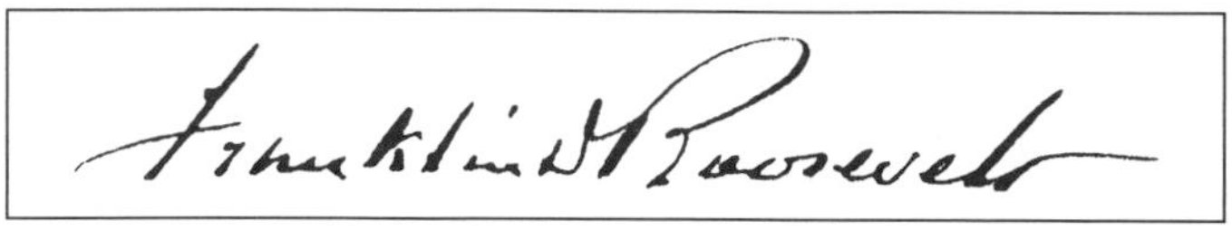

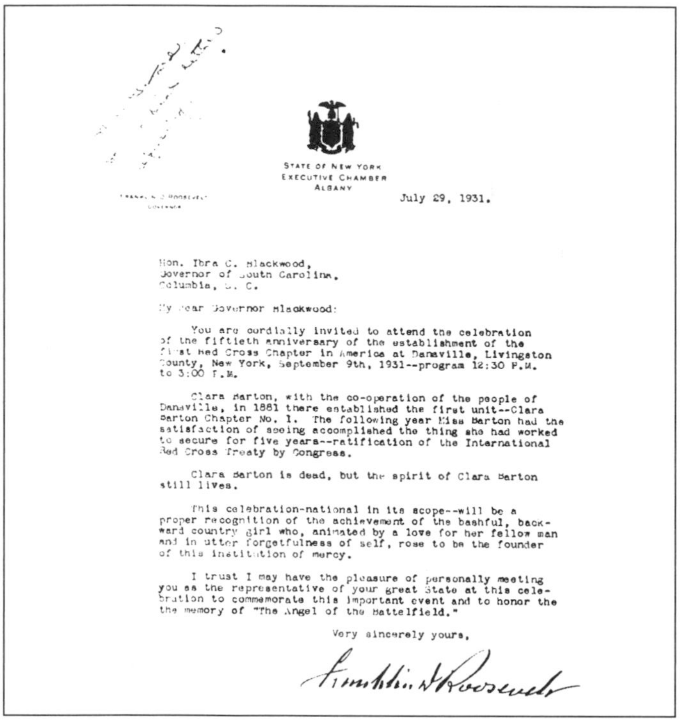

[Six signature samples of Franklin D. Roosevelt, including a typed letter.]

The letter reads:

STATE OF NEW YORK
EXECUTIVE CHAMBER
ALBANY

July 29, 1931.

Hon. Ibra C. Blackwood,
Governor of South Carolina,
Columbia, S. C.

My Dear Governor Blackwood:

You are cordially invited to attend the celebration of the fiftieth anniversary of the establishment of the first Red Cross Chapter in America at Dansville, Livingston County, New York, September 9th, 1931—program 12:30 P.M. to 3:00 P.M.

Clara Barton, with the co-operation of the people of Dansville, in 1881 there established the first unit—Clara Barton Chapter No. 1. The following year Miss Barton had the satisfaction of seeing accomplished the thing she had worked to secure for five years—ratification of the International Red Cross Treaty by Congress.

Clara Barton is dead, but the spirit of Clara Barton still lives.

This celebration-national in its scope—will be a proper recognition of the achievement of the bashful, backward country girl who, animated by a love for her fellow man and in utter forgetfulness of self, rose to be the founder of this institution of mercy.

I trust I may have the pleasure of personally meeting you as the representative of your great State at this celebration to commemorate this important event and to honor the the memory of "The Angel of the Battlefield."

Very sincerely yours,

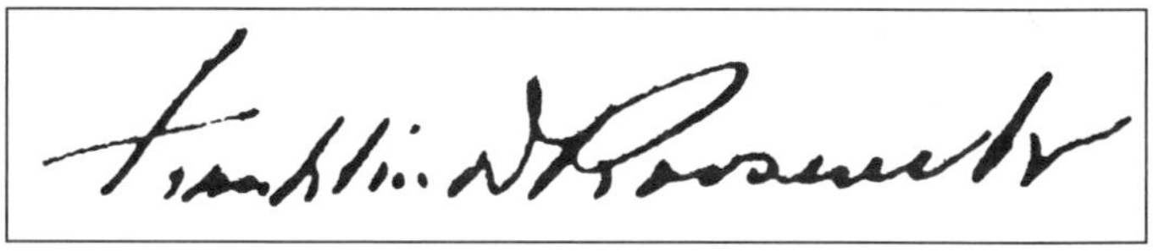

Theodore Roosevelt

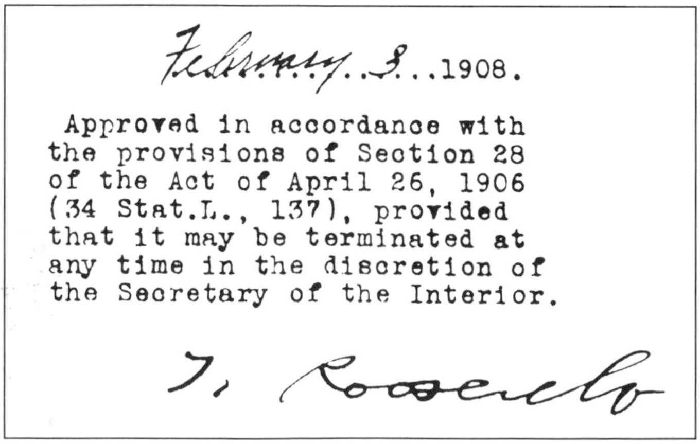

February 3...1908.

Approved in accordance with the provisions of Section 28 of the Act of April 26, 1906 (34 Stat.L., 137), provided that it may be terminated at any time in the discretion of the Secretary of the Interior.

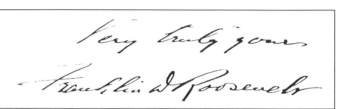

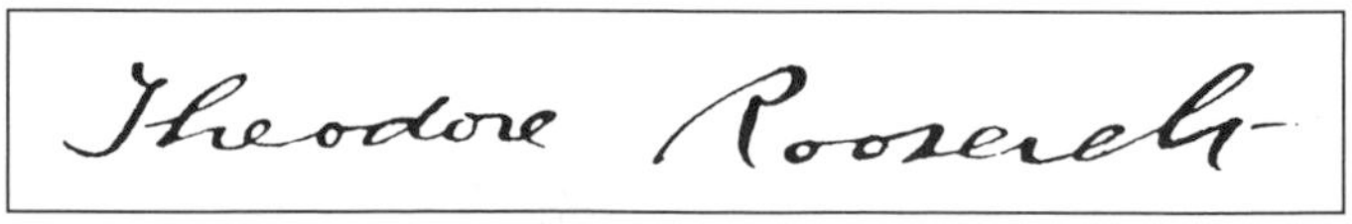

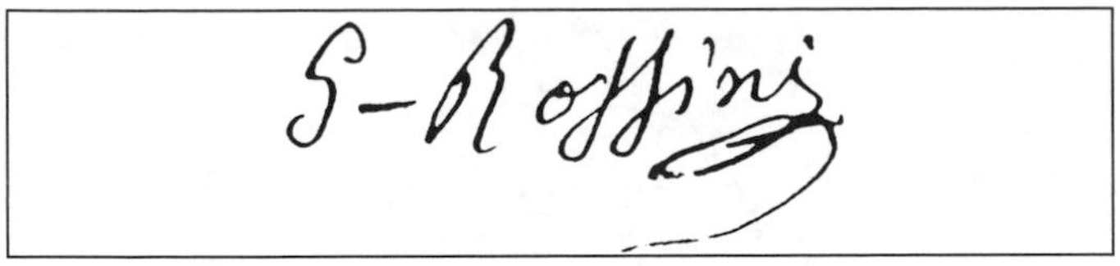

Gioacchino Rossini

Anton Rubinstein

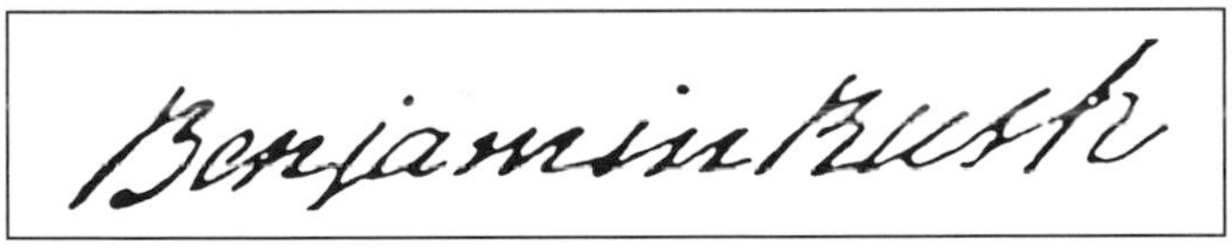

Benjamin Rush

Babe Ruth

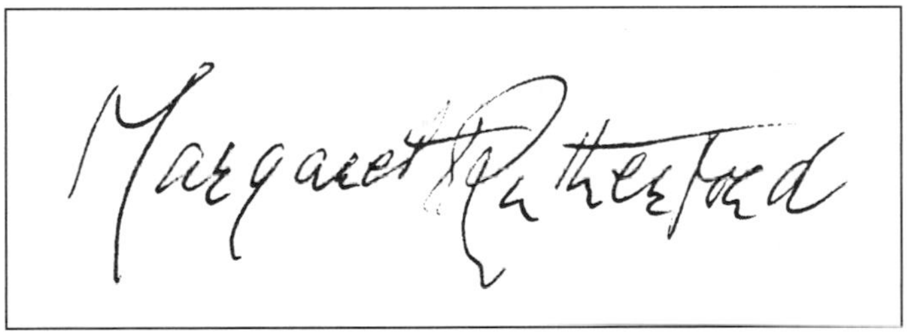

Margaret Rutherford

Edward Rutledge

Anwar Sadat

Santa Anna

J.D. Salinger

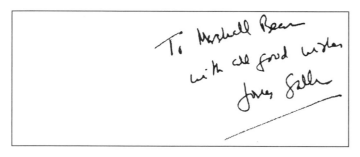

Jonas Salk

Carl Sandburg

Margaret Sanger

Dorothy Sayers

Frank Baker & Ray Schalk

Emilie Schindler

Max Schmeling

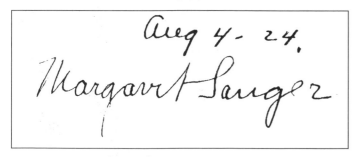

Arnold Schonberg

Charles Schulz

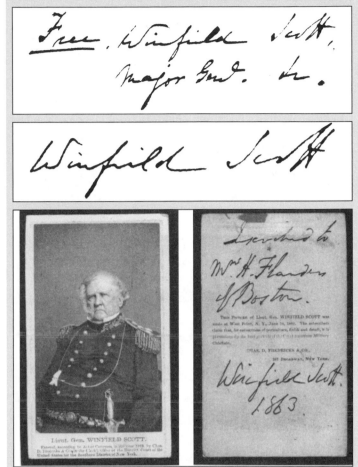

Winfield Scott

Brisquier avec mes bonnes pensées
albert Schweitzer

Albert Schweitzer

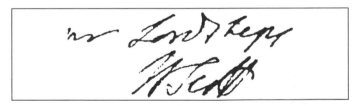

Sir Walter Scott

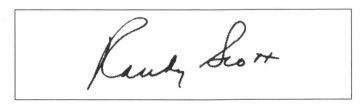

Randolph Scott

Glenn T. Seaborg

Gen. John Sedgwick

Segar

Mac Sennett

Rod Serling

Dr. Seuss

William H. Seward

George Bernard Shaw

Alan Shepard

Philip H. Sheridan

Roger Sherman

William T. Sherman

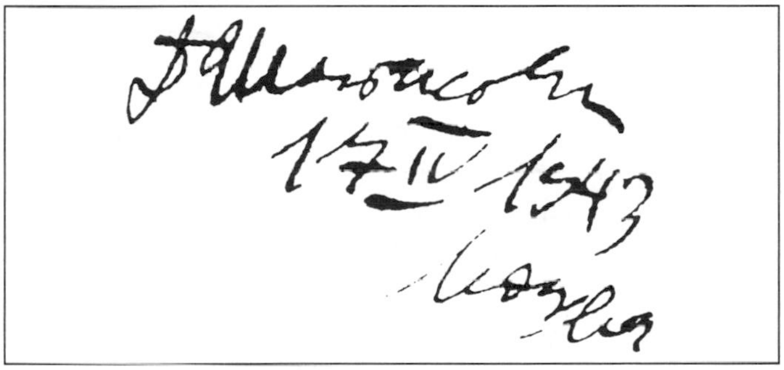

Simitri Shostakovich

Jean Sibelius

Al Simmons

Paul Simon and Art Garfunkel

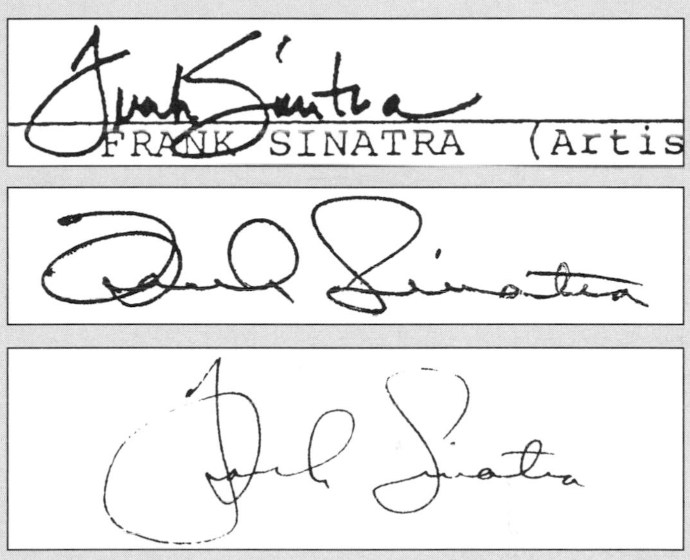

Frank Sinatra

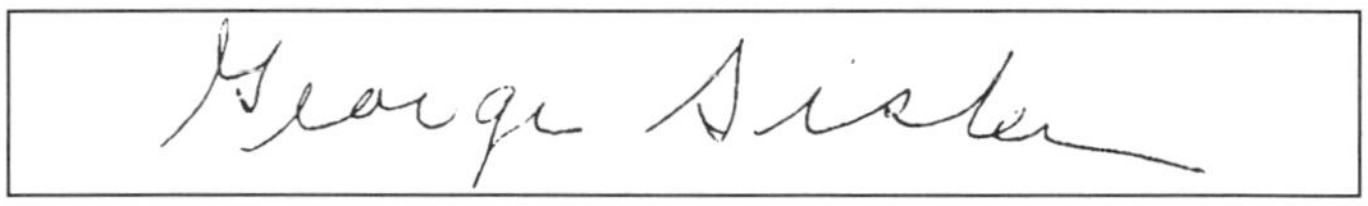

George Sisler

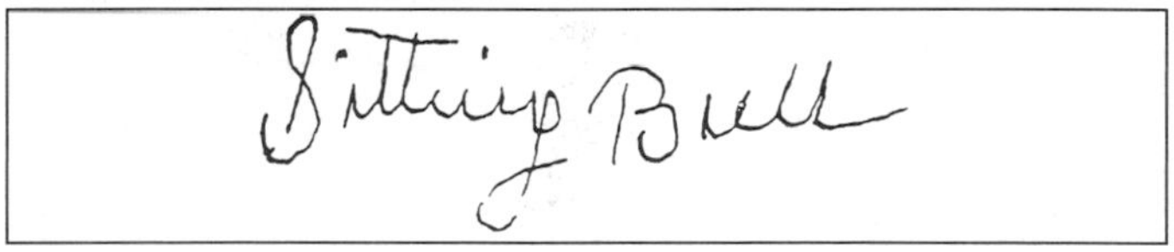

Sitting Bull

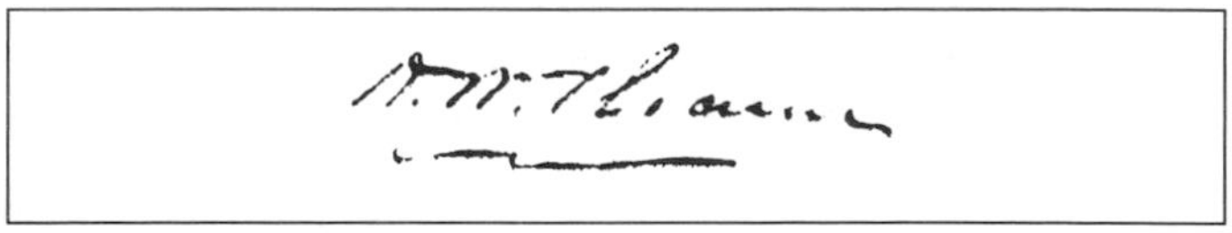

Henry W. Slocum

James Smith

Samuel F. Smith

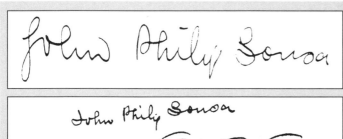

Otto Soglow

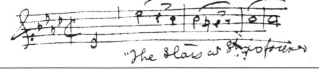

John Philip Sousa

Diana Spencer

Diana Spencer

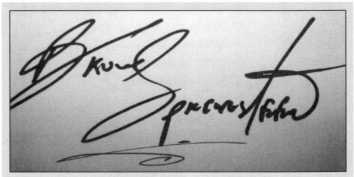

Michael Spinks

Bruce Springsteen

Henry Stanley

E.C. Stanton

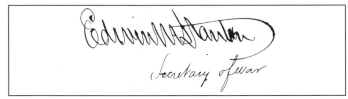

Edwin Stanton

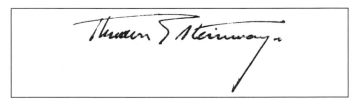

Gertrude Stein

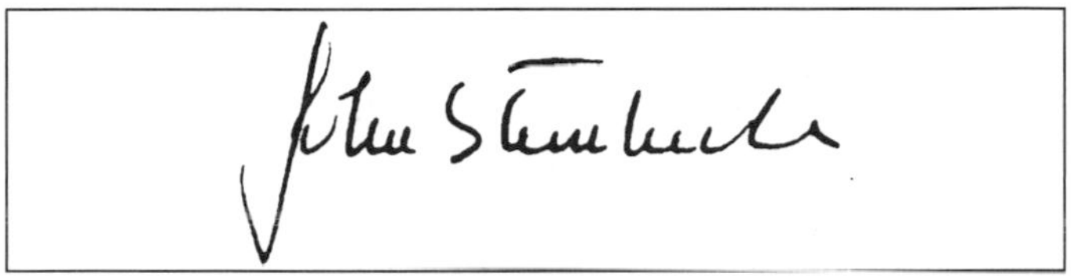

John Steinbeck

Theodore Steinway

George Stephenson, inventor

Thaddeus Stevens

Wallace Stevens

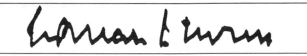

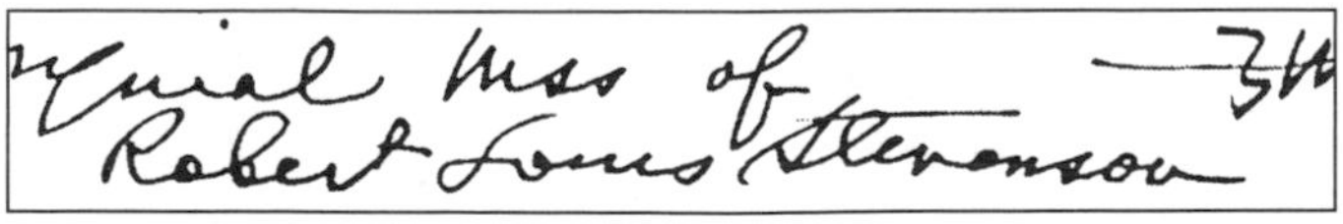

Robert Louis Stevenson

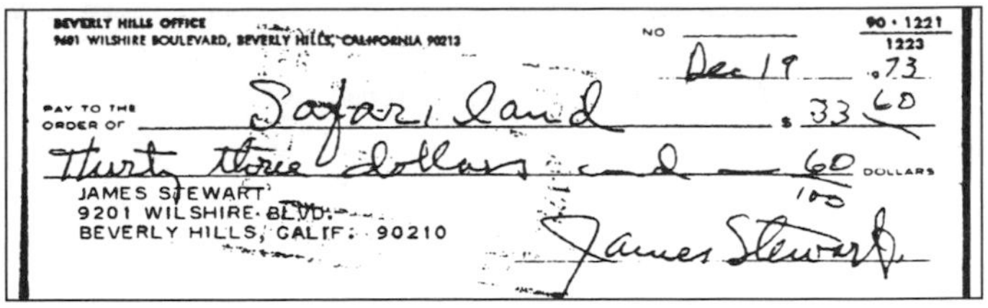

Jimmy Stewart

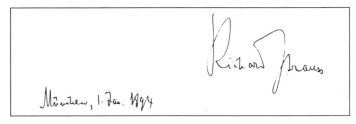

Richard Stockton

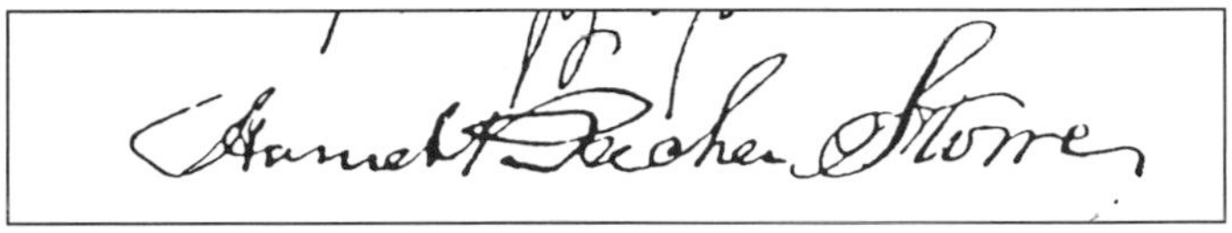

Harriet Beecher Stowe

München, 1. Jan. 1894

Richard Strauss

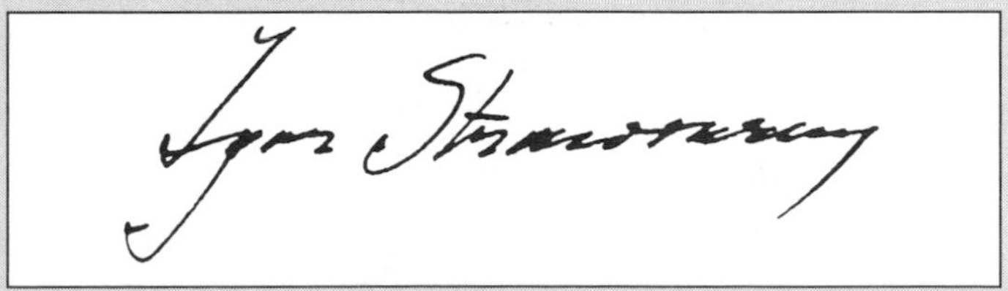

Igor Stravinsky

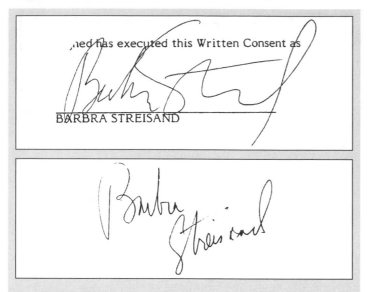

BARBRA STREISAND

Barbra Streisand

James E.B. Stuart

Peter Stuyvesant

Arthur S. Sullivan

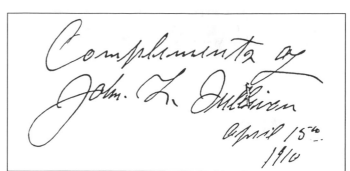

John L. Sullivan

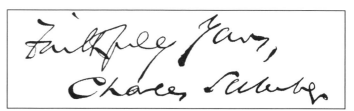

Charles Sumner

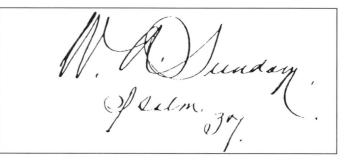

William Sunday

Sir Ernest D. Swinton

T

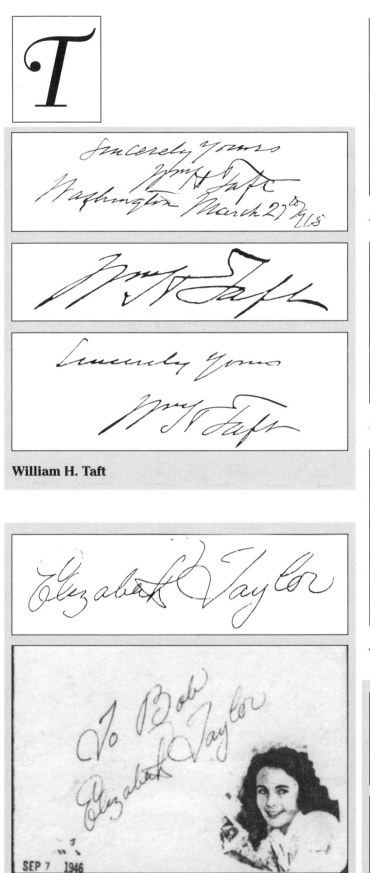

William H. Taft

Elizabeth Taylor

Elizabeth Taylor

Elizabeth Taylor-Burton

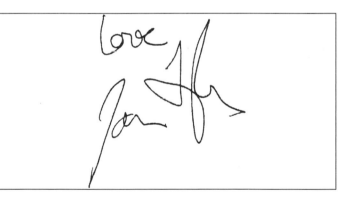

James Taylor

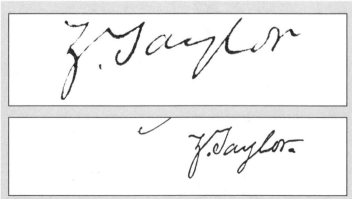

Zachary Taylor

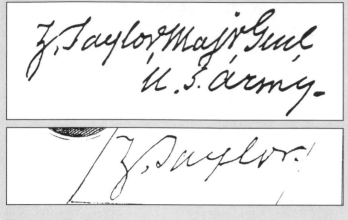

Zachary Taylor

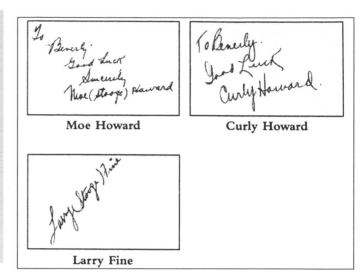

Moe Howard   **Curly Howard**

Larry Fine

The Three Stooges

Peter I. Tchiakovsky

Dr. Max Theiler.

Max Theiler

Shirley Temple

George H. Thomas

Matthew Thornton

Lord Alfred Tennyson

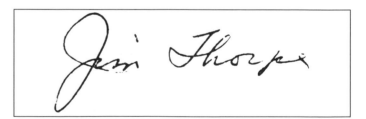

Jim Thorpe

Terry-Thomas

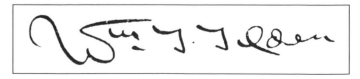

William Tilden

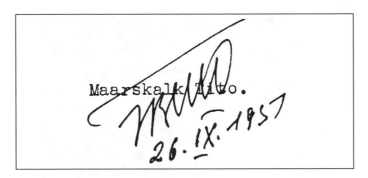

Josip Tito

Thelma Todd

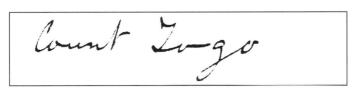

Togo

Leo Tolstoy

Arturo Toscanini

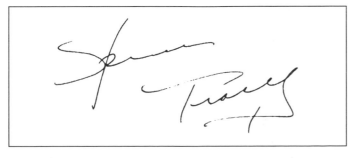

Spencer Tracy

Sir Frederick Treves

Isaac Trimble

L. Trotsky

Harry S. Truman

Harry S. Truman

John Trumbull

Donald Trump

Two Guns White Calf

Mark Twain

John Tyler

Maurice de Vlaminck

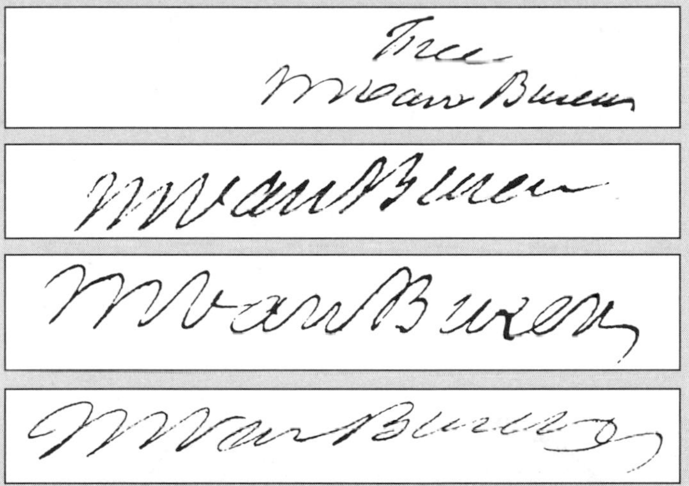

Martin Van Buren

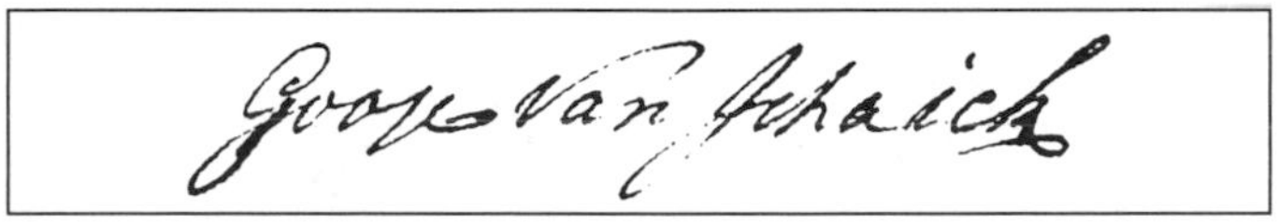

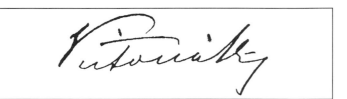

Goose Van Schaick

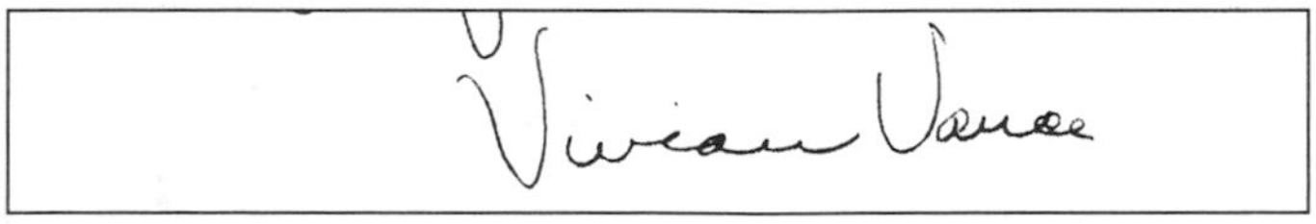

Vivian Vance

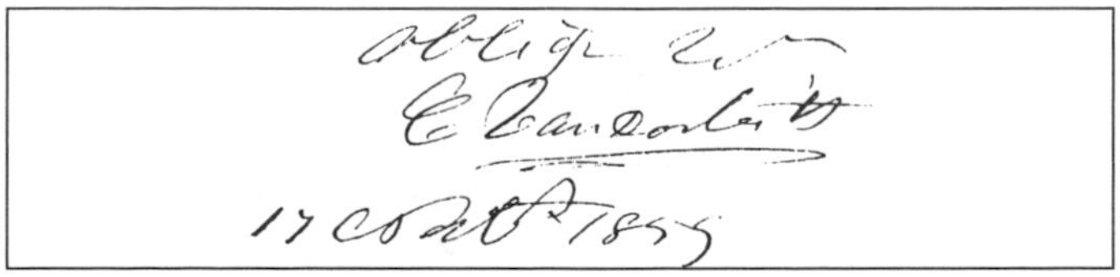

Cornelius Vanderbilt

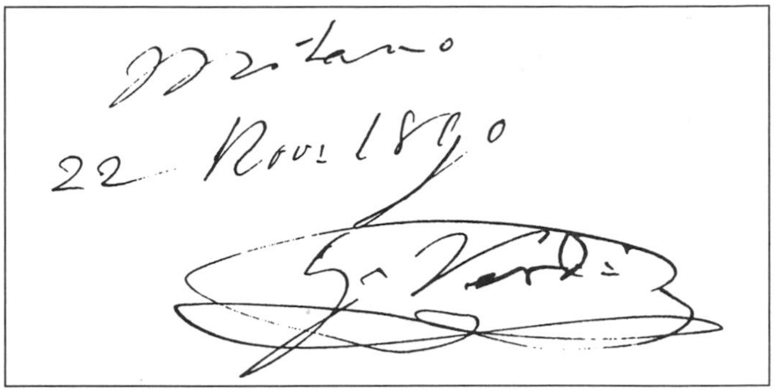

Guiseppe Verdi

Queen Victoria

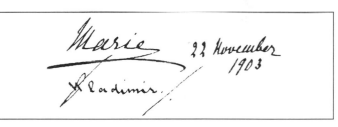

Grand Duke and Duchess Vladimire and Marie

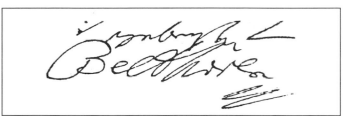

Ludwig von Beethoven

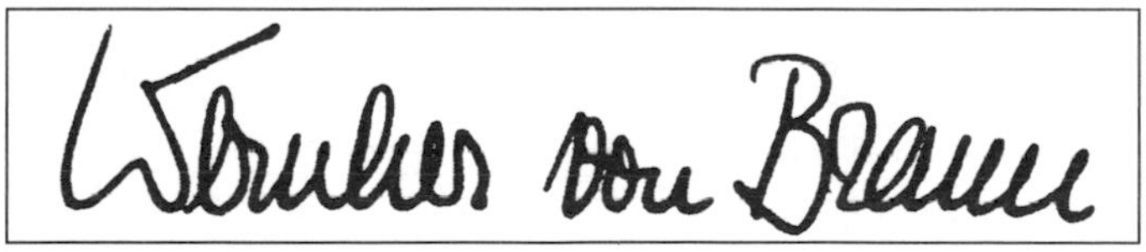

Werhner von Braun

Carl Maria von Weber

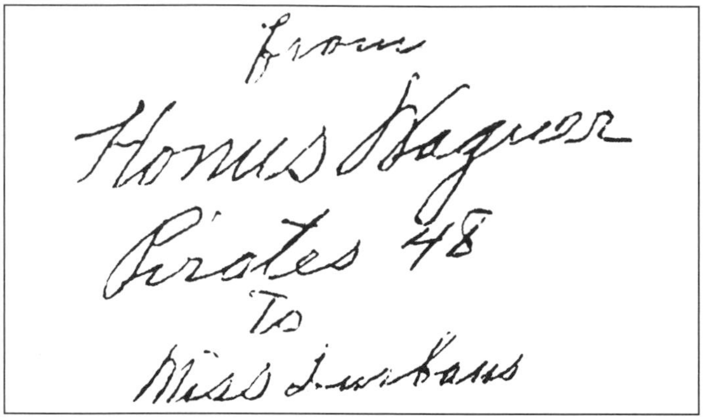

Honus Wagner

Richard Wagner

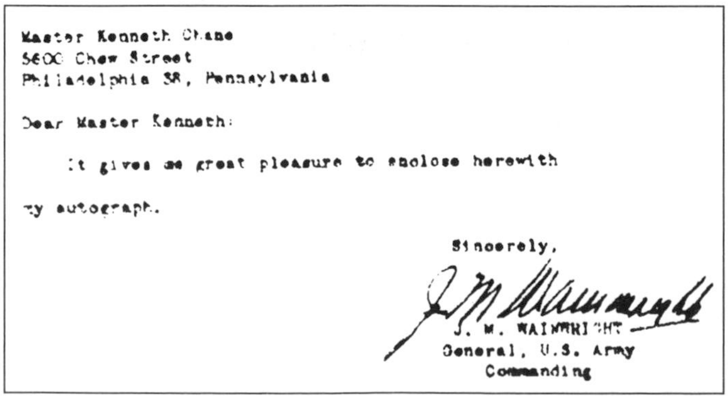

Master Kenneth Chane
5600 Chew Street
Philadelphia 38, Pennsylvania

Dear Master Kenneth:

It gives me great pleasure to enclose herewith

my autograph.

Sincerely,

J. M. WAINWRIGHT
General, U.S. Army
Commanding

Jonathan M. Wainwright

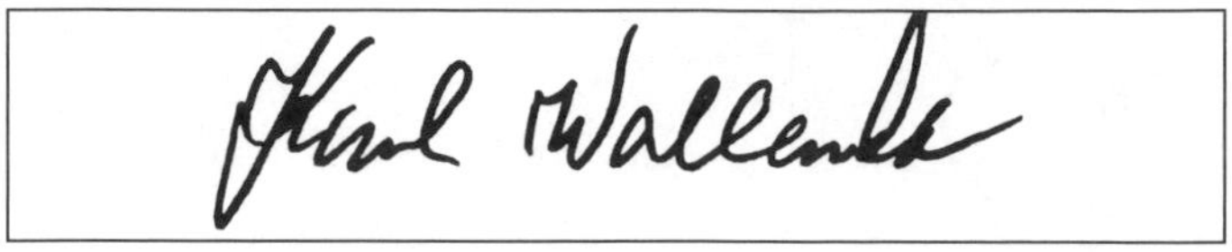

Carl Walenda

Lew Wallace

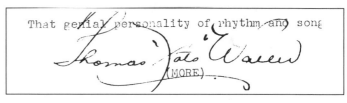

That genial personality of rhythm and song

(MORE).

Fats Waller

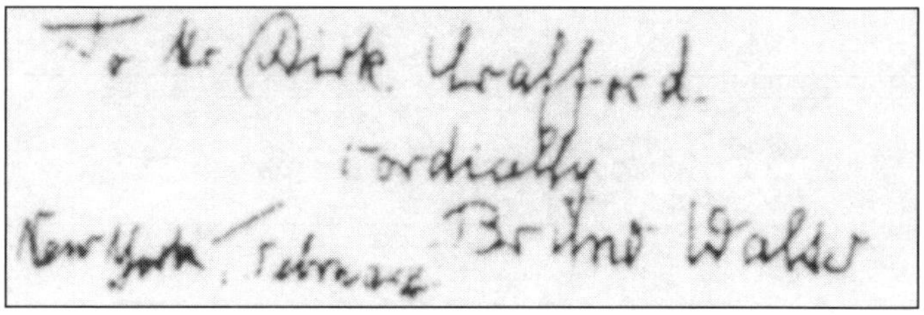

Walter Bruno

George Walton

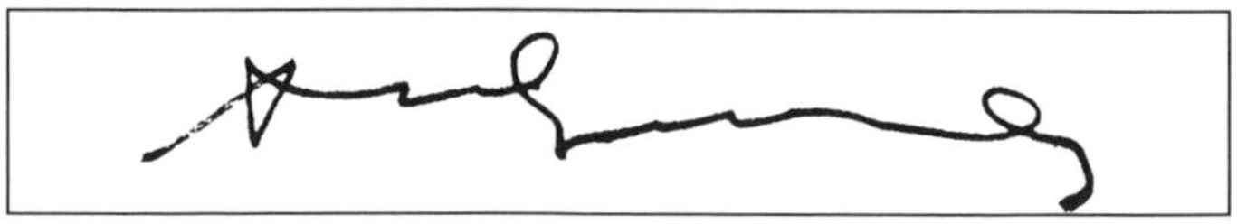

Andy Warhol

Glenn "Pop" Warner

Booker T. Washington

George Washington & Thomas Jefferson

George Washington (1752 - 2 signatures)

George Washington

Anthony Wayne

John Wayne

Chaim Weizmann

Gideon Welles

Orson Welles

The Duke of Wellington

Chick Webb

Benjamin West

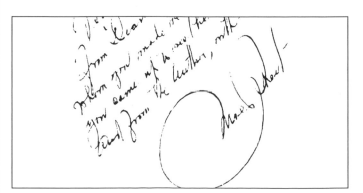

Daniel Webster

Mae West

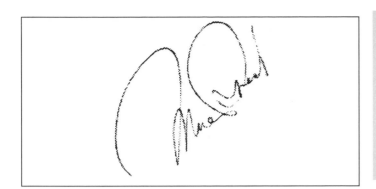

Mae West

Walt Whitman

George Westinghouse

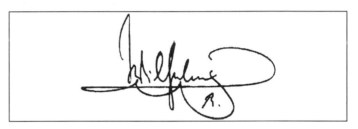

John G. Whittier

Joseph Wheeler

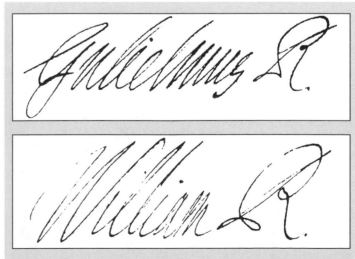

Wilhelm II

William Whipple

Jess Willard

James M. Whistler

Ed White

William III, King of England

Hank Williams

Sir George Williams

Ted Williams

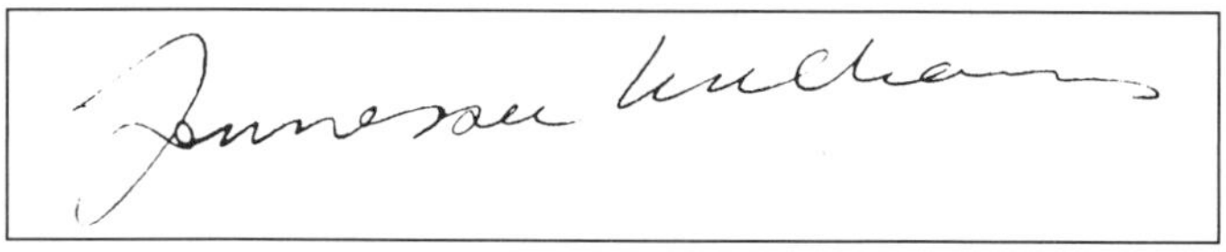

Tennessee Williams

William Williams

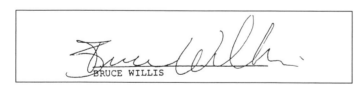

Bruce Willis

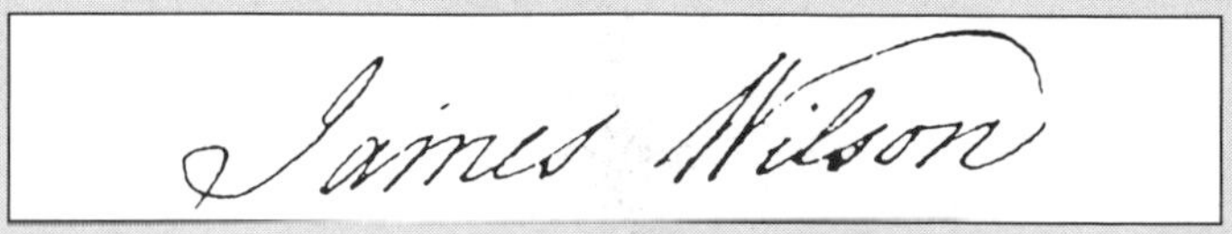

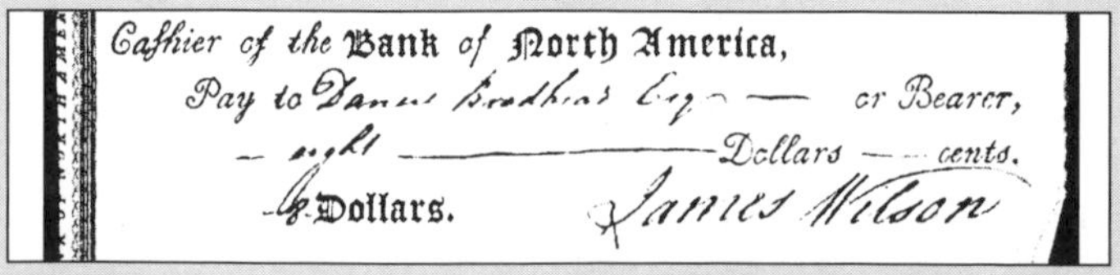

James Wilson

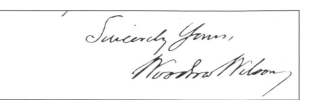

Woodrow Wilson

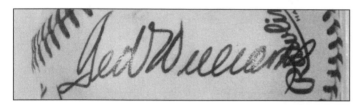

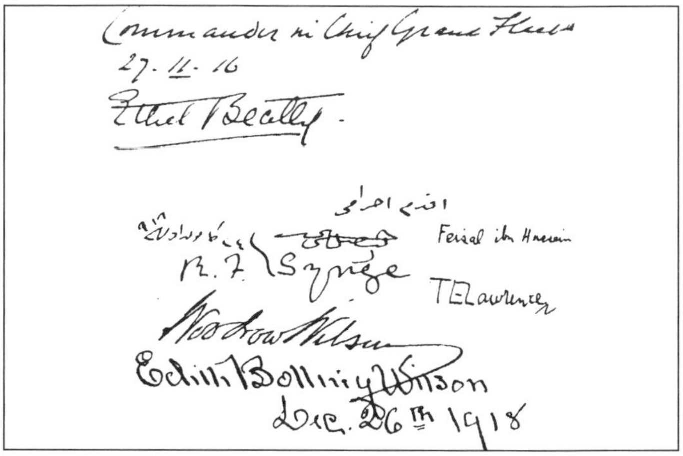

Woodrow Wilson, Edith Bolling Wilson, T.E. Lawrence and Prince Feisal ibn Hussein

John Winthrop

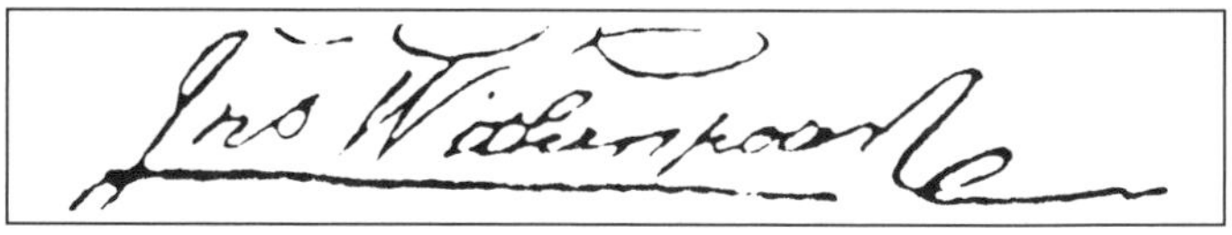

John Witherspoon

Oliver Wolcott

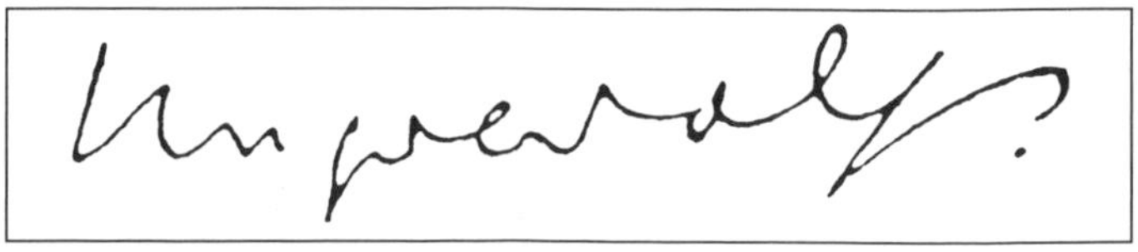

Hugo Wolf

Virginia Wolf

Thomas Wolfe

Natalie Wood

John Worden

Henry Clay Work

Steve Wozniak

Frank Lloyd Wright

Orville Wright

Wilbur Wright

Jamie Wyeth

George Wythe

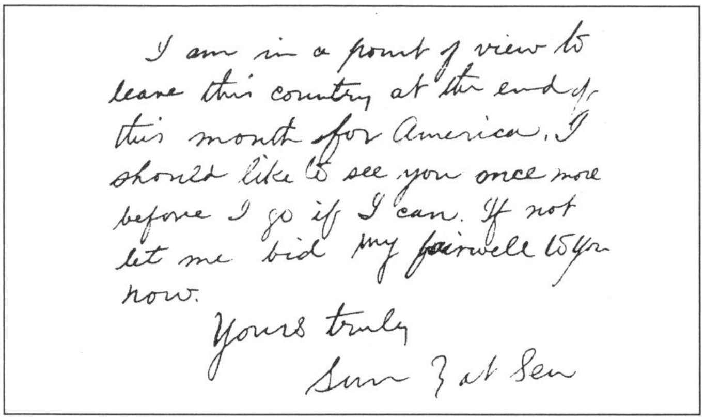

I am in a point of view to leave this country at the end of this month for America. I should like to see you once more before I go if I can. If not let me bid my farewell to you now.

Yours truly
Sun Yat Sen

Sun Yat-Sen

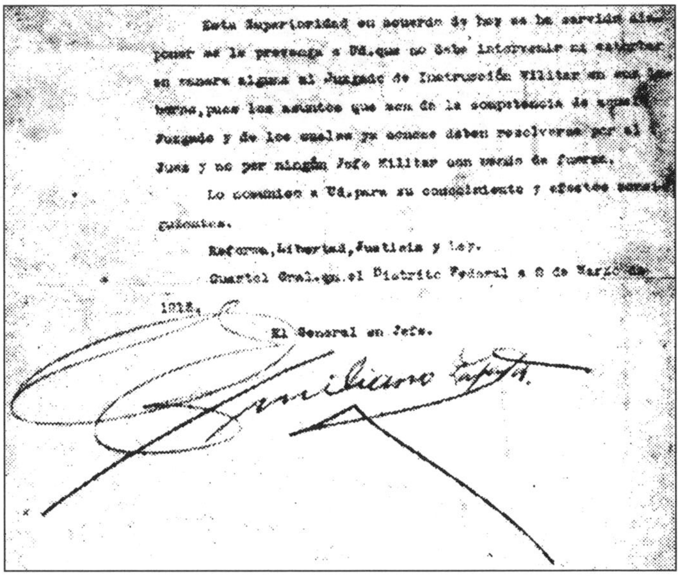

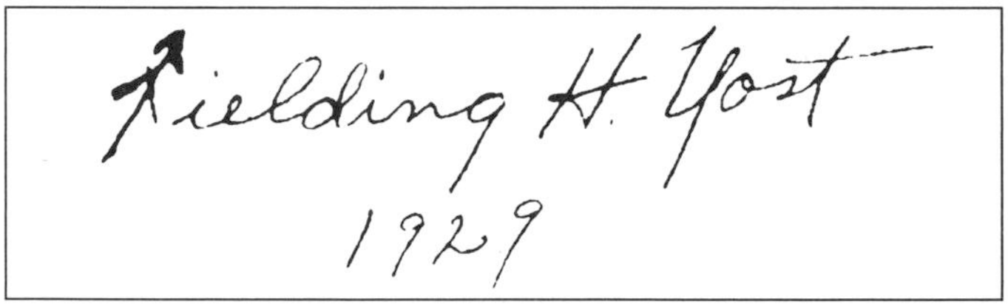

Fielding H. Yost
1929

Fielding Yost

Brigham Young

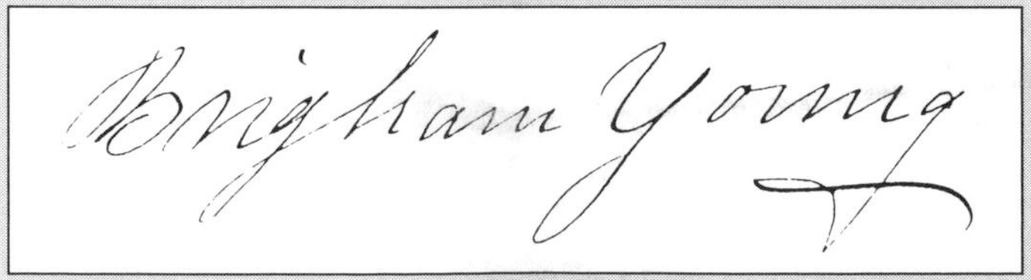

Brigham Young

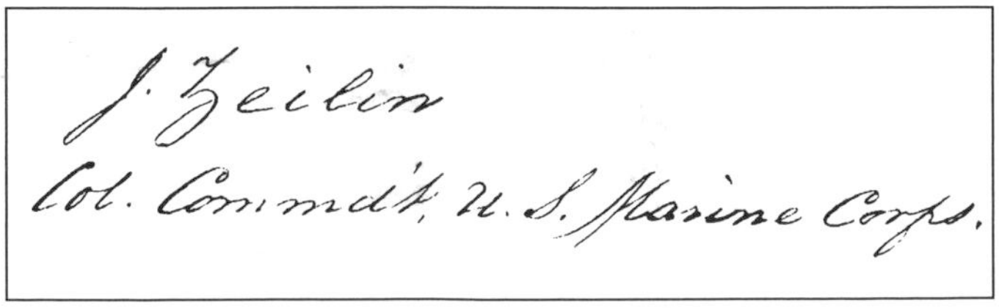

Brigham Young

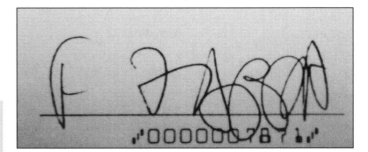

Emiliano Zapata

Frank Zappa

J. Zeilin
Col. Commdt. U.S. Marine Corps.

Gen. Jacob Zeilin